GLOBAL STUDIES

AFRICA

STAFF

GLOBAL STUDIES

AFRICA

Dr. Jane Martin, Contributing Editor
Boston University

The Dushkin Publishing Group, Inc., Sluice Dock, Guilford, Connecticut 06437

Africa

BOOKS IN THE GLOBAL STUDIES SERIES

- ● Africa
- ● China
- ● Latin America
- ● The Soviet Union and Eastern Europe
- The Middle East and the Islamic World
- India and South Asia
- Western Europe
- Japan and the Pacific Rim
- Southeast Asia

● Available Now

COVER PHOTO

Jill Harmsworth
Oxfam America
115 Broadway
Boston, MA 02116

First Edition

Manufactured by George Banta Company, Menasha, Wisconsin 54952

Library of Congress Catalog Card Number 84-072941

ISBN: 0-87967-493-8

Africa

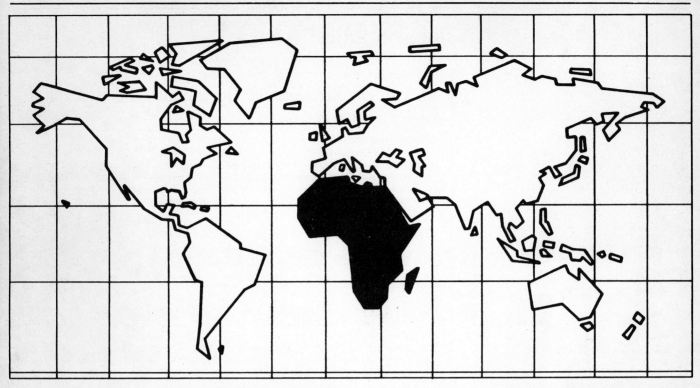

CONTRIBUTING EDITOR
Dr. Jane Martin

The contributing editor for AFRICA was the acting director of the Outreach Program at the African Studies Center, Boston University. Dr. Martin has taught at the University of Calabar, in Calabar, Nigeria, as well as the University of Liberia in Monrovia, Liberia.
She is currently Executive Director of the United States Educational and Cultural Foundation, Monrovia, Liberia.

CONTRIBUTORS TO THIS VOLUME

Selected regional essays and country reports were written by

William Freund, research associate
African Studies Center, Boston University

Bennet Fuller, Ph.D. candidate
Boston University

G. Michael LaRue, Ph.D. candidate
Boston University

F. Jeffress Ramsay, Ph.D. candidate
Boston University

Statistical summaries were developed by

Michael DiBlasi, Ph.D. candidate
African Studies Center, Boston University

SERIES CONSULTANT

H. Thomas Collins
Washington, D.C.

ADVISORY BOARD

Dan Connell
Research fellow, Boston University
Grassroots International
P.O. Box 312
Cambridge, MA 02139

Louise Crane
African Studies Center
University of Illinois

Lisa Anderson
Department of Middle Eastern Studies
Harvard University

D. Elwood Dunn
Department of Political Science
University of the South

Leon Spencer
Historical Collections
Taladaga College
Taladaga, AL

Contents

Global Studies: Africa

Africa   Page 1

North Africa   Page 19

West Africa   Page 27

Central Africa   Page 89

East Africa   Page 125

Southern Africa   Page 179

Introduction

THE GLOBAL AGE

As we approach the end of the twentieth century, it is clear that the future we face will be considerably more international in nature than ever believed possible in the past. Each day of our lives, print and broadcast journalists make us aware that our world is becoming increasingly smaller and substantially more interdependent.

The energy crisis, world food shortages, nuclear proliferation, and the regional conflicts in Central America, the Middle East, and other areas that threaten to involve us all make it clear that the distinctions between domestic and foreign problems are all too often artificial—that many seemingly domestic problems no longer stop at national boundaries. As Rene Dubos, the 1969 Pulitzer Prize recipient stated: ". . . [I]t becomes obvious that each (of us) has two countries, (our) own and planet earth." As global interdependence has become a reality, it has become vital for the citizens of this world to develop literacy in global matters.

THE GLOBAL STUDIES SERIES

It is the aim of this Global Studies series to help readers acquire a basic knowledge and understanding of the regions and countries in the world. Each volume provides a foundation of information—geographic, cultural, economic, political, historical, artistic, and religious—which will allow readers to better understand the current and future problems within these countries and regions and to comprehend how events there might affect their own well-being. In short, these volumes attempt to provide the background information necessary to respond to the realities of our Global Age.

Contributing Editors

Each of the volumes in the Global Studies series has been crafted under the careful direction of a contributing editor—an expert in the area under study. Each teaches and conducts research and has travelled extensively through the countries they are writing about.

The contributing editor for each volume has written the umbrella essay introducing the area. In this Africa volume, the contributing editor has written many of the regional essays and country reports. In addition, she has overseen the gathering of statistical information for each country being studied and reviewed country reports prepared by other contributors. The contributing editor is also instrumental in the final selection of the world press articles that accompany the regional sections.

Contents and Features

The Global Studies volumes are organized to provide concise information and current world press articles on the regions and countries within those areas under study.

Area and Regional Essays

Global Studies: Africa covers North Africa, Central Africa, West Africa, East Africa, and Southern Africa. Each of these regions is discussed in a regional essay focusing on the geographical, cultural, socio-political and economic aspects of the countries and people of that area. The purpose of the regional essays is to provide the reader with an effective sense of the diversity of the area as well as an understanding of its common cultural and historical backgrounds. Accompanying each of the regional narratives is a full page map showing the political boundaries of the countries within the region. In addition to these regional essays, the editor has also provided a narrative essay on the African continent as a whole. This area essay examines a number of broad themes in an attempt to define what constitutes "Africa." The introductory area essay is followed by a current chronology of events that have taken place within the regions and countries of Africa during 1983.

Special Note on the Regions of Africa

The countries of Africa do not fall into clear-cut regions. Many of the political divisions that exist today are the product of Africa's colonial heritage, and often they do not reflect cultural, religious, or historical connections. This has created tensions within nations, and it makes abstract divisions somewhat arbitrary. Nations that share geographical aspects with one group of countries may share a cultural history with a different group. The regional essays give rationales for the way countries have been grouped in this volume. Readers may encounter different arrangements in other sources. The regional essays should be read carefully to understand why the editor chose the divisions made here.

North Africa

North Africa is a "special case" in relation to the rest of the African continent. Culturally, geo-politically, and economically, the Moslem countries of North Africa are often major players on the Middle Eastern stage, as well as on the African scene. For this reason, we have included a regional essay for North Africa in this volume, but the individual country reports and the world press articles for that region appear as part of the expanded coverage of North Africa in *The Middle East and Islamic World* volume of the Global Studies series.

Country Reports

Concise reports on each of the regions with the exception of North Africa follow the regional essays. These reports are the heart of each Global Studies volume. *Global Studies: Africa* contains 48 *country reports* ranging in length from two to five pages.

The country reports are comprised of five standard elements. Each report contains a small, non-detailed map visually positioning the country amongst its neighboring states; a detailed summary of statistical information; a current essay providing important historical, geographical, political, cultural, and economic information; an historical timeline offering a convenient visual survey of a few key historical events; and four graphic indicators, with summary statements about the country in terms of *development, freedom, health/welfare,* and *achievements,* at the end of each report.

A Note on the Statistical Summaries

The statistical information provided for each country has been drawn from a wide range of sources. The most frequently referenced are listed on Page 240. Every effort has been made to provide the most current and accurate information available. However, occasionally the information cited by these sources differs significantly; and all too often, the most current information available for some countries is quite dated. Aside from these discrepancies, the statistical summary for each country is generally quite complete and reasonably current. Care should be taken, however, in using these statistics (or, for that matter, any published statistics) in making hard comparisons among countries.

World Press Articles

Within each Global Studies volume are reprinted a large number of articles carefully selected by our editorial staff and the contributing editor from a cross-section of international periodicals and newspapers. The articles have been chosen

(Oxfam photo)

We must understand the hopes, problems, and cultures of the people of other nations in order to understand our own future.

for currency, interest, and the differing perspective that they give to a particular region. There are world press articles for each region, with the exception of North Africa. Each of these article sections is preceded by a *Topic Guide.* The purpose of this guide is to indicate the main theme(s) of the articles that appear in that section. Readers wishing to focus on a particular aspect of life or culture may refer to the Topic Guide to find the articles that deal with that subject.

Spelling

In many instances articles from foreign sources may use forms of spelling that are different from our own. Many Third World publications reflect the European usage. In order to retain the flavor of the articles and to make the point that our system is not the only one, spellings have not been altered to conform with our system.

Glossary, Bibliography, Index

At the back of each Global Studies volume, the reader will find a *Glossary of Terms and Abbreviations,* which provides a quick reference to the specialized vocabulary of the area under study and to the standard abbreviations (UN, WHO, GATT, etc.) used throughout the volume, particularly in the country statistical summaries.

Following the glossary is a *Bibliography,* which contains specific references for most of the literary works mentioned in the body of the text. The bibliography is organized into general reference volumes, national and regional histories, novels in translation, current events publications, and periodicals which provide regular coverage on Africa.

The *index* at the end of the volume is an accurate reference to the contents of the volume. Readers seeking specific information and citations should consult this standard index.

Currency and Usefulness

This first edition of *Global Studies: Africa,* like other Global Studies volumes, is intended to provide the most current and useful information available necessary to understanding the events that are shaping the cultures of Africa today.

We plan to issue this volume on a regular basis. The statistics will be up-dated, essays rewritten, country reports revised, and articles completely replaced as new and current information becomes available. In order to accomplish this task we will turn to our contributing editors, our advisory boards and—hopefully—to you, the users of this volume. Your comments are more than welcome. If you have an idea you think will make the volume more useful, an article or bit of information that will make it more current, or a general comment on its organization, content, or features that you would like to share with us, please send it in for serious consideration for the next edition.

U.S.

CANADA

NORTH AMERICA

UNITED STATES

MEXICO

CARIBBEAN

EUROPE

CENTRAL AMERICA

SOUTH AMERICA

N

W   E

S

This map of the world highlights the nations of Africa that are discussed in this volume. Regional essays and country reports are written from a cultural perspective in order to give a frame of reference to the current events in that region. All of the essays are designed to present the most current and useful information available today. Other volumes in the Global Studies series will cover different areas of the globe and examine the current state of affairs of the countries within those regions.

Africa

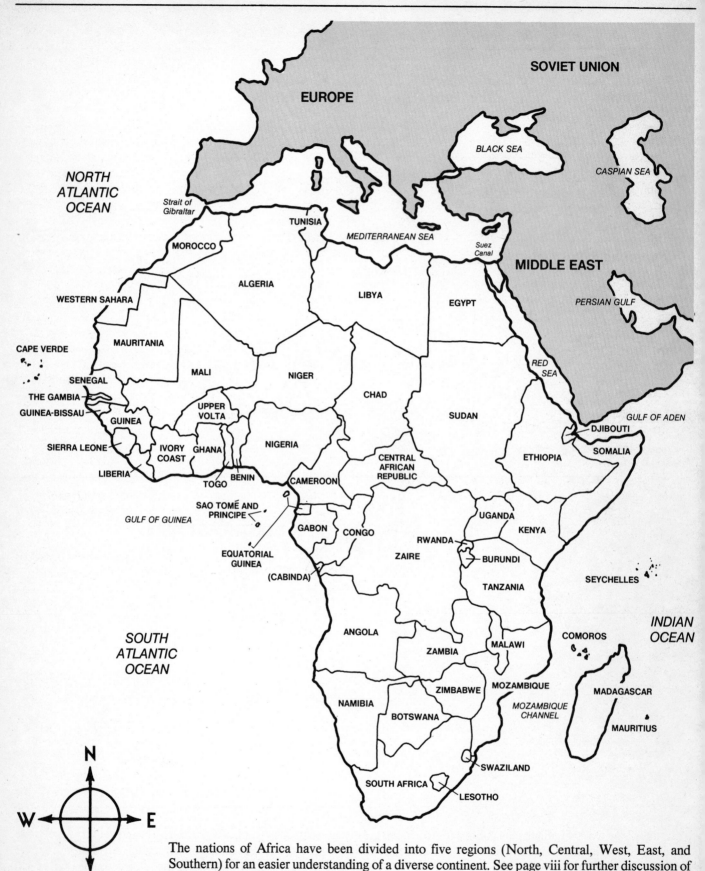

The nations of Africa have been divided into five regions (North, Central, West, East, and Southern) for an easier understanding of a diverse continent. See page viii for further discussion of regions within Africa.

Africa: The Struggle for Development

"This is Africa's 'age of glamour,' " Africans observed in 1960. The times were electric, as governments changed hands and country after country moved to independent nationhood. Leaders were acclaimed, new goals were proposed, and hopes were high. In the United States and other Western countries, some of the myths about Africa were being questioned.

Today, more than twenty years after "the age of glamour," conditions in Africa are sobering rather than euphoric, and development seems a desperate struggle rather than an exhilarating challenge. Africa is described in the media as "a continent in crisis," "a region in turmoil," "on a precipice," and "suffering"—phrases that sound like those of the nineteenth century explorers and missionaries.

Foreign governments have often become involved in African civil conflicts; the aid that is offered imposes restraints while relieving distress. Observers wonder whether a new imperialism, a new "scramble for Africa," is in the making. Old images of "the dark continent" resurface.

Africa's circumstances today are indeed difficult. Yet, there are reasons for hope. The last twenty years have brought progress as well as problems. Africans have remained in control of their own futures. The following review of the African heritage and of the achievements since independence, as well as Africa's current difficulties and their origins, will give a more balanced picture of Africa in the 1980s.

TRADITION AND CHANGE

The nearly 500 million contemporary Africans maintain extraordinarily diverse ways of life. Over a thousand languages and a variety of households, kinship systems, religious beliefs, and art styles—to mention only a few of the cultural areas—enrich the continent.

These ways of life have been changing over time. As cities have grown and people have moved back and forth between village and town, new social groups, new institutions, new occupations, new religions, and new schools make their mark in the countryside as well as in the urban centers. All Africans—the elite and the working class—have taken on new practices and interests, yet have maintained African traditions. Thus, whether they are professional civil servants, day laborers, or students, urban dwellers (whose numbers have increased drastically in recent decades) may still have their roots in the countryside. African institutions, African values, and African histories underlie their new life-styles.

The memories of ancient kingdoms are the sources of pride and community to peoples throughout Africa. The Mali Kingdom of the western Sudan, the Fulani Empire of northern Nigeria, the great Zimbabwe, and the kingdoms around the Great Lakes in Uganda are all remembered. In a continent where the majority of peoples are still farmers, land remains "the mother that never dies." It is valued for its fruits and because it is the place to which the ancestors came and where they are buried.

The art of personal relationships continues to be the most important art in Africa. Typically, people live in large families. Children are "precious like coral," and large families are still desired for social as well as economic reasons. Elders are an important part of a household; nursing homes and retirement communities do not exist. People are not supposed to be loners. "I am because we are" remains a valued precept—although the "we" may refer to an exclusive ethnic community even in this age of nation states. Obligations to the extended family often take precedence over other loyalties.

Religious forces continue to make their presence felt. A family is built on a good relationship with the ancestors. Traditional cults remain important. Well-educated professionals, migrant workers, and market women as well as country people still visit professional diviners who will explain an illness or suggest remedies for barrenness or bad fortune. Islam may accommodate traditional ways. People may also join new religious movements and churches, such as the Brotherhood of the Cross and Star in Nigeria or the Church of Simon Kimbangu in Zaire, that link Christian and traditional beliefs and practices as well as completely new

(World Bank photo by Pamela Johnson)

This is an electrical transformer at the Volta Aluminum Company Tema, Ghana. Modern technology and new sources of power are among the factors spurring economic development.

ideas and rituals. Like other new institutions in the cities, the churches provide new social networks. Old art forms reflect changes—an airplane is featured on a Nigerian *gelede* mask; the Apollo mission inspires an Upper Voltan form; or a Ndebele dance wand is a beaded electric pole.

THE TROUBLED PRESENT

Some of the crises in Africa today may threaten even the deepest traditions. The facts are grim: In material terms, Africans are poorer today than they were at independence, and it is predicted that poverty will increase in the future. Widespread famine exists in twenty-two of the fifty African nations. Drought conditions have led to abnormal food shortages in countries of every region; West, Central, East, and Southern. The Food and Agricultural Organization (FAO) of the United Nations estimates that seventy percent of the African people do not have enough to eat. While cereal production declines, the population rises. Diseases that were once conquered reappear: Rinderpest has been discovered

among cattle, and cholera has been found among populations where it has not been seen for a long time. Wood, the average person's source of energy, grows scarce.

Conflicts—including the destabilizing activities of South Africa in Namibia, Angola, and Mozambique; the civil wars in the Horn; and the past crises in Uganda, Zaire, and Burundi—as well as other disasters, have caused many people to flee their homes. At least three million refugees are registered with the United Nations Commissioner on Refugee Relief (UNHCR), but it is believed that a more accurate estimate of the number of people who have sought refuge and food in countries other than their own is five to seven million.

Almost all African governments are in debt (as is the United States). The entire debt of African countries is about $60 billion—a modest amount when compared to that of Latin America. However, the debt is rising very swiftly. The industrial output of African countries is lower than that of other nations of the world. While the majority of Africans are engaged in food production, not enough food is produced in most countries to feed the citizens. The foreign exchange

(Photo courtesy of African Studies Center, Boston University)

Good health is a national goal in Africa, and a sign of national development. Immunizations against cholera, tetanus and other diseases have cut the number of deaths.

needed to import food and machinery is very limited. The overall growth rate of African economies is only 2.9 percent and is expected to decline even further.

In order to get money to meet debts and to pay running expenses, African governments must accept the terms of world lending agencies such as the World Bank and the International Monetary Fund (IMF). Often these terms include austerity measures, the abandonment of price controls, and the freezing of wages—measures that can open the way to social distress and political upheaval in urban centers. Some African countries such as Tanzania have been forced to compromise socialist ideologies in order to meet the terms.

THE EVOLUTION OF AFRICA'S ECONOMIES

Africa has seldom been rich—although it has vast potential resources, and some rulers and classes have been very wealthy. In early centuries, the slave trade as well as other internal factors limited African material expansion. During the colonial period, Africa became increasingly involved in the world economy. Policies and practices developed that still exist today and are of mixed benefit to African peoples.

In the seventy or so years of British, French, Portuguese, German, Spanish, and Italian rule in Africa, the nations' economies were shaped to the advantage of the colonizers. Cash crops such as cocoa, coffee, and rubber began to be grown for the European market. Often, large numbers of African farmers benefited from these crops, but the cash crop economy also involved large foreign-run plantations. It also encouraged the trends toward use of migrant labor and the decline in food production. Many peoples became dependent for their livelihood upon the forces of the world market, which, like the weather, were beyond their immediate control.

Mining also increased during colonial times—again for the benefit of the colonial rulers. The ores were extracted from African soil by European companies. African labor was employed, but the machinery came from abroad. The copper and gold—and later, the iron ore, uranium, and oil—were shipped overseas to be processed and marketed in the Western economies. Upon independence, African governments received a varying percentage of the take through taxation and consortium agreements. But mining remained an "enclave" industry, sometimes described as a "state within a state" because such industries were run by outsiders who established Western-style communities, used imported machinery and technicians, and exported the product to industrial countries.

The inflationary conditions in other parts of the world have had adverse affects on Africa. Today the raw materials that Africans produce receive low prices on the world market, while the manufactured goods that African countries import are expensive. Local African industries lack spare parts and machinery; cash crop farmers cannot afford to transport crops to market for such low prices. The whole economy slows down. Thus, Africa—because of the policies of former

(Peace Corps photo)

Partnerships between the nations of Africa and the countries of Europe and North America may encourage Africa's development. Here a Sierra Leonean road is built with Peace Corps help.

colonial powers and present independent governments—is tied into the world economy in ways that do not always serve it.

THE PROBLEMS OF GOVERNMENT

Outside forces are not the only or even the major cause of Africa's present crises. The governments face major tasks of maintaining national unity with very diverse and sometimes divided citizenries. These problems have historical roots; they spring from the artificial nature of the states, the Western forms of their governments, and the development of class interests within the population.

Although the states of Africa may overlay and overlap historic kingdoms, they are new formations. Their boundaries were fashioned during the late nineteenth century, when colonial powers competed and (sometimes literally) raced to claim the lands. Ethnic groups were divided by arbitrary lines drawn on the African map at conferences in Europe during the 1890s and early 1900s. In the years of colonial rule, administrative systems, economic and educational structures, as well as road and rail lines linked areas that had not necessarily been joined before. Leaders of African independence movements worked within the colonial boundaries. Even when they joined together in the Organization of African Unity (OAU), member states agreed to recognize the sovereignty of these new nations, while espousing and working toward African unity.

...ment systems of the individual states also have
...s in the colonial past. To citizens of the Western
...here, these governments may seem familiar: There
a... parliaments, parties, presidents, ministers, elections, and
courts. Often these systems were inherited institutions,
created by colonial governors and practiced by African
nationalists before independence.

The forms of government have not necessarily fitted well
with the African foundations on which they have been built,
and many institutions have changed in the years since the
early 1960s. Almost all new governments had to unite
peoples of many ethnic groups, whose competitions and
claims could disrupt a new nation. The Biafran Civil War in
Nigeria and the Shaba (Katanga) secessionist movements in
Zaire have illustrated the explosive power of these internal
conflicts. The development of one-party states was one
solution to the disruptions resulting from ethnic politics.
Since 1965, in a large number of nations, frequent military
coups have brought new forces—and sometimes new forms—
to prominence.

Some of the strong personalities who led countries to
independence remain in power. Houphouet-Boigny of Ivory
Coast, Julius Nyerere of Tanzania, and Hastings Banda of
Malawi have gradually shaped the forms of the governments
they lead. Leaders such as Mobutu Sese Seko of Zaire, who
came to power in 1965, have eroded Western-oriented
institutions. Personalities and the ideologies centered around
them have become the bases of government. Western-
educated elites have often controlled governments to their
own advantage, and accusations of corruption and mismanagement abound.

Socialist regimes were established in many African states.
Though leaders often professed a Marxist orientation, they
were more concerned with building an African socialist
government. It was felt that a special African socialism could
be built on the communal and cooperative traditions characteristic of many African societies. In countries such as
Angola, Mozambique, and Guinea-Bissau, the present governments were first established in the liberated zones during
the struggles for independence and were differently based
than those handed over by the more benign colonial regimes
of Ghana or Senegal. Socialist governments have not been
free from personality cults, nor from corruption and oppressive measures. So too, governments that practice forms of
capitalism have also developed public corporations and
plans similar to those of Marxist governments for their
economic development. In recent years, more and more
governments—partly in line with IMF and World Bank
requirements, but also because of the inefficiency and losses
of their public corporations—have reformed their *parastatals*
(as the public corporations are called) and have encouraged
private enterprise.

African governments seem shaky and appear to be in
transition, whether they are socialist or capitalist in their
orientation. States discard old ways; some coup leaders seek
more than the rewards of power and look for better methods
of relating to their citizens and improving their life. Some
administrations are paying more attention to village cooperatives and local associations, recognizing their needs and their
potential for development. Agriculture (the livelihood of the
majority of the people), rather than industry, is increasingly
stressed. As governments develop closer ties with the
traditional forms of decision making in African societies,
African states may be greatly strengthened.

CAUSES FOR OPTIMISM

Although problems facing African countries have grown
since independence, so too have their achievements. The
number of persons who can read and write traditional
languages as well as English and French has increased
drastically—the result of universal primary education
schemes and important adult literacy campaigns. People can
peruse newspapers, follow instructions for fertilizers, and
read the labels on medicine bottles. Professionals who can
deal with modern technology, plan electrification schemes,
organize large office staffs, and develop medical facilities, for
example, are more available because of the large number of
African universities that have been developed in the last
twenty years. Health care has grown, and Western-educated
doctors and nurses as well as traditional midwives have
increased the ranks of those in the medical services. Infant
care has especially improved; the infant mortality figures
have declined, and Africans today can expect to live several
years longer than they could in 1960.

(FAO photo by W. Wisse)

Literacy has risen dramatically in many African nations as a result of
universal primary education and adult literacy campaigns often in
African languages.

Especially important is the increasing attention that African governments and intra-African agencies are giving to women. The pivotal role of women in agriculture is being recognized, and their work is being supported. Prenatal and hospital care for mothers and their babies has increased; conditions for women workers in factories have been highlighted; new cooperatives for women's activities have been developed; and ministries dealing with women's issues have been established. Women have been included in cabinets of government and on local village councils.

The advances that have been made in Africa are important ones, but they could be undercut if declining economic conditions continue. Africans need outside aid to maintain these gains and to move further toward a better life for ordinary people. Yet, as the African proverb observes, "someone else's legs will do you no good in traveling." Self-reliance and the African way is the key to development, no matter what help others offer.

The Organization of African Unity has been so split by ideological and leadership disputes in recent years that—while much has been done to fulfill the primary aim of liberation for Africans under colonial or South African rule—little has been done to promote higher standards of living, longer life, and better education. The effort of African countries to develop regional economic groups and to increase their power and their economic progress through cooperation is a hopeful development. The South African Development Coordination Conference (SADCC) and the Economic Community of West African States (ECOWAS) are two regional organizations within which African nations are developing practical programs so they can move ahead together. The Lagos Plan of Action adopted by African heads of state in April 1980 provides target goals and steps by which continent-wide aims might be reached.

CONCLUSION

Africa, as the individual country reports will reveal, is a continent of many and varied resources. There are rich minerals and a vast agricultural potential. The people—the youth who make up over half of the population, and the elders who have often maintained the traditions—are sources of African strength. The continent's history provides lessons for planning the future. The rest of the world can also benefit from the resources and learn from the activities and history of Africa.

(Oxfam photo)

"There is no wealth where there are no children" is an African saying.

Current Chronology of Events

JANUARY 1983

Libya: Saudi Arabia restores diplomatic relations with Libya after more than two years of tension.

Nigeria: Thousands of illegal aliens attempt to leave the country following the deadline imposed by the Nigerian government.

South Africa: The "Coloured" Labor Party gives support to a constitutional plan to give a limited role to South Africans of mixed and Indian descent.

Tanzania: Loyal forces thwart a coup attempt against President Julius Nyerere.

Upper Volta: The military government of Upper Volta appoints Captain Thomas Sankara to be prime minister.

Zaire: Chinese Premier Zhao Ziyang cancels Zaire's $100 million debt during a state visit.

Zimbabwe: Prime Minister Robert Mugabe holds talks with Joshua Nkomo aimed at ending violence in Matabeleland Province.

FEBRUARY 1983

Ghana: Security forces foil a third coup attempt against the government of Jerry Rawlings.

Kenya: The Kenyan government grants amnesty to more than 400 prisoners who were convicted of staging an abortive coup against President Daniel arap Moi.

Libya: Libyan forces are withdrawn from the borders with Egypt, Sudan, and Chad following the dispatch of United States AWACS radar planes to Egypt and the arrival of the aircraft carrier *Nimitz* off the coast of Libya.

Morocco: King Hassan II of Morocco and Algerian President Chadli Benjedid meet for the first time in seven years.

Senegal: President Abdou Diouf of Senegal wins national election with eighty-three percent of the vote.

Uganda: The Ugandan government gives owners of property expropriated by Idi Amin three months to present their claim for compensation.

MARCH 1983

Ghana: Ghana reopens borders with Upper Volta, Togo, and Ivory Coast that were closed to prevent smuggling.

Somalia: President Mohammed Siad Barre of Somalia bans the importation and cultivation of *Khat,* a narcotic.

Zimbabwe: Joshua Nkomo, Zimbabwe opposition leader, crosses border with Botswana following accusations of anti-government activities.

APRIL 1983

Algeria: The border between Morocco and Algeria is reopened after a seven-year dispute over the Western Sahara.

Nigeria: Nigerian and Chadian forces clash near Lake Chad.

Somalia: The armed forces are placed on full alert in Somalia in fear of an invasion from Ethiopia.

South Africa: Orlando Christina, Mozambique National Resistance leader, is shot to death in Pretoria.

Tanzania: President Julius Nyerere frees twelve hundred prisoners in celebration of the nineteenth anniversary of the union between Tanganyika and Zanzibar.

MAY 1983

Egypt: Idris I, King of Libya, dies at age ninety-three. He lived in exile in Egypt after being deposed by Colonel Muammar Qadhdhafi.

Kenya: President Daniel arap Moi calls elections two years early.

Mozambique: South African Air Force planes stage a retaliatory raid on suspected ANC positions in Maputo.

Nigeria: Nigerian and Chadian forces end border clashes.

South Africa: The African National Congress takes responsibility for a car bomb that is detonated in South Africa.

Tanzania: SADCC leaders meet in Tanzania to discuss the drought that has devastated the region.

Upper Volta: Security forces detain the prime minister, Captain Thomas Sankara, after he verbally attacks Western countries that provide aid.

Zaire: President Mobutu announces a general amnesty for those convicted of threatening state security.

JUNE 1983

Chad: Chadian President Hissein Habré announces general amnesty on the first anniversary of the capture of the capital by his Forces of the North (FAN).

Ghana: Security forces put down another coup attempt.

South Africa: For the first time in the more than one hundred years, a black mining trade union is recognized and negotiates a wage agreement for its members. Three members of the African National Congress are executed for their involvement in attacks on police stations in South Africa.

Tanzania: Tanzania grants citizenship to an additional one thousand refugees from Rwanda, bringing the total to forty thousand since 1977. Tanzania devalues its currency by twenty percent against the dollar.

JULY 1983

Chad: President Habré appeals to France for aid as fighting erupts in northern Chad against forces loyal to the former president, Goukouni Oueddi.

Ivory Coast: Israeli Foreign Minister (now Prime Minister) Yitzhak Shamir holds talks in Switzerland with President Houphouet-Boigny of Ivory Coast.

Seychelles: President Albert F. Rene pardons six European mercenaries for their part in the coup attempt in 1981.

Zimbabwe: Six members of the Southern Africa Development Coordination Conference (SADCC) announce that foreign reporters who are based in South Africa will not be permitted to work in those countries.

AUGUST 1983

Angola: UNITA rebels briefly hold the town of Cangumba in eastern Angola during an offensive supported by South Africa.

Cameroon: President Paul Biya announces that his forces have foiled a coup attempt in Cameroon.

Chad: Forces loyal to former President Goukouni Oueddi capture the town of Faya Largeau in northern Chad.

Equatorial Guinea: The first parliamentary elections in ten years are held.

Kenya: Daniel arap Moi is elected unopposed as President of Kenya.

Liberia: Diplomatic ties with Israel are restored.

Nigeria: Second general election since the 1979 Constitution took effect is held. President Shehu Shagari is elected by a wide margin.

Upper Volta: Captain Thomas Sankara takes control in a coup that leaves ten dead.

SEPTEMBER 1983

Ethiopia: The summit talks being held by the Organization of African Unity collapse after two sessions when the Moroccan representatives refuse to sit with the representatives of the Polisario movement.

Ghana: Former President Hilla Limann and former Vice-President de Graft Johnson are freed from detention.

Mauritius: The government of Mauritius declares itself to be a republic within the Commonwealth.

Somalia: Megistu Haile Mariam declares amnesty for twelve hundred Ethiopian prisoners.

Zaire: The government devalues its currency, the Zaire, by nearly eighty percent against the dollar.

OCTOBER 1983

Gabon: Burundi, Cameroon, Central African Republic, Chad, Congo, Equatorial Guinea, Gabon, Rwanda, Sao Tome and Principe, and Zaire form the Economic Community of Central African States.

Ghana: The government devalues its currency, the Cedi, nearly ten-fold against the American dollar.

Ivory Coast: Ivorian President Houphouet-Boigny returns after five months abroad.

Mali: Nation rejoins the West African Monetary Union (UMOA) after twenty years.

Mozambique: South African forces again attack ANC positions in Maputo.

Niger: Troops loyal to President Seyni Kountche suppress a coup attempt while he is abroad.

Sudan: President Hosni Mubarak of Egypt holds talks with officials in Sudan regarding demands of Moslem fundamentalists in both countries.

Zambia: Kenneth Kaunda is re-elected as President of Zambia with no opposition.

Zimbabwe: Former Prime Minister, Bishop Abel Muzorewa, is arrested in Zimbabwe for alleged subversive activities.

NOVEMBER 1983

Central African Republic: Television reports announce the second coup attempt this year.

Liberia: Coup attempt led by Brigadier Thomas Quiwonkpa is thwarted.

South Africa: White voters in South Africa approve the prime minister's proposal to create a three chamber parliament, with chambers for Coloureds and Indians.

Sudan: Eleven foreign workers are kidnapped in Sudan by anti-government guerrillas. They are later freed by the army.

Tanzania: Tanzania reopens its borders with Uganda following meetings to distribute the assets and debts of the former East African Community.

Zaire: The Inga-Shaba power line is officially switched on to link the copper-rich Shaba region with the Inga Dam.

DECEMBER 1983

Angola: Units of the South Africa Defense Forces advance further into Angola from positions they have held for weeks.

Central African Republic: Former Emperor Bokassa seeks asylum in France.

Nigeria: President Shehu Shagari is deposed by the military in a bloodless coup.

South Africa: The government offers a thirty-day extendable cease-fire, to apply to its forces in Angola beginning January 31.

Article 1

Africa News, January 30, 1984

WHAT COMMODITIES CAN BUY

This table shows the changes in the purchasing power of commodities exported by African countries. Purchasing power is measured in 1) how much oil one ton of each commodity can buy; 2) the capital in U.S. $ for which one ton can cover debt service payments at prevailing rates; and 3) the capital in Deutschmarks for which one ton can cover debt service payments at prevailing rates. The last two measures reflect a country's capacity to raise hard currency necessary for most imports of industrial goods, food and raw materials.

In 1975, for example, one ton of copper could pay for 115.40 barrels of oil, or pay the annual interest on a loan of $17,800, or pay the annual interest on a loan of DM67,039. By October 1983 one ton of copper could cover 49.94 barrels of oil, or interest on $15,102 or interest on DM63,792.

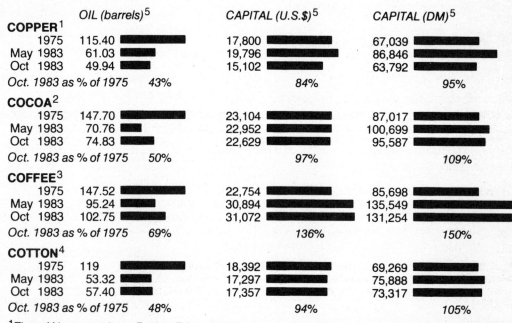

	OIL (barrels)[5]		CAPITAL (U.S.$)[5]		CAPITAL (DM)[5]	
COPPER[1]						
1975	115.40		17,800		67,039	
May 1983	61.03		19,796		86,846	
Oct 1983	49.94		15,102		63,792	
Oct. 1983 as % of 1975	*43%*		*84%*		*95%*	
COCOA[2]						
1975	147.70		23,104		87,017	
May 1983	70.76		22,952		100,699	
Oct 1983	74.83		22,629		95,587	
Oct. 1983 as % of 1975	*50%*		*97%*		*109%*	
COFFEE[3]						
1975	147.52		22,754		85,698	
May 1983	95.24		30,894		135,549	
Oct 1983	102.75		31,072		131,254	
Oct. 1983 as % of 1975	*69%*		*136%*		*150%*	
COTTON[4]						
1975	119		18,392		69,269	
May 1983	53.32		17,297		75,888	
Oct 1983	57.40		17,357		73,317	
Oct. 1983 as % of 1975	*48%*		*94%*		*105%*	

[1] Three African countries — Zambia, Zaire, and Botswana — are significantly dependent on exports of **copper.**

[2] Seven African countries — Benin, Cameroon, Equatorial Guinea, Ghana, Ivory Coast, Sao Tome and Principe, and Togo — are significantly dependent on exports of **cocoa.**

[3] Thirteen African countries — Angola, Burundi, Cameroon, Central African Republic, Ethiopia, Ivory Coast, Kenya, Madagascar, Rwanda, Sierra Leone, Tanzania, Uganda and Zaire — are significantly dependent on exports of **coffee.**

[4] Seven African countries — Benin, Chad, Egypt, Mali, Sudan, Tanzania and Upper Volta — are significantly dependent on exports of **cotton.**

[5] Eight African countries — Algeria, Angola, Congo, Egypt, Gabon, Libya, Nigeria and Tunisia — export **oil.** Only Libya and South Africa have sufficient surplus **capital** to grant loans and invest in other countries.

Data: *South* magazine, London / Chart by Africa News

Article 2

Africa News, March 5, 1984

'Dark Continent' Image Revived

[AN] There are indications that a late-twentieth-century version of the "dark continent" myth is in the making. Essays and novels of V.S. Naipul and his brother Shiva, the acclaimed fiction of such authors as John Updike and Philip Caputo, and recent coverage by prominent journalists share a perception of Africa as a continent of failed experiments and hopeless problems, brought on by its own unreadiness to rule itself.

Cover stories appearing the same week in *Time* magazine and *The New Republic* illustrate the trend. Both take the debate about underdevelopment and its causes—an issue that has generated thousands of books and articles and been the topic of hundreds of studies—and reduce it to a popularized tale of corruption, incompetence and tribalism.

"Only quite recently," writes Geoffrey Wheatcroft in *The New Republic* (Jan. 9 and 16) "has it become possible to talk openly of the failure of independent Africa. The old excuses—of European indifference or 'neo-colonialism'—are less frequently trotted out. It is even possible to discuss in respectable, liberal publications, as it was not a few years back, whether this failure might not say something about Africa itself."

And *Time* (Jan. 16) approvingly quotes a similar sentiment of British journalist Xan Smiley writing last year in the *Atlantic:* "The years of [African] freedom have mounted up, mocking the plausibility of the excuses for failure. Africa is back where it was 50 years ago."

That Africa is in desperate circumstances is undeniable. Indeed, there are ways in which the continent is in *worse* shape than half a century ago, when countries now facing famine were feeding themselves.

Furthermore, while social conditions deteriorated, some poor countries became so dependent on loans that their indebtedness rivaled—or even surpassed—their Gross National Products. By 1974, Somalia's ratio of debt to GNP was 127.5%, Botswana's 94.2%, and Zaire's, 72.5%. Of 29 nations whose ratio exceeded 30%, 18 were in Africa.

The litany of woes could continue indefinitely without generating controversy. It is in the complex search for causes that disagreements arise.

Wheatcroft and the *Time* writers pay passing homage to the bitter legacy of colonialism, and its drawing of illogical geopolitical boundaries that ignored ethnic, linguistic, religious and cultural differences. But they fix real responsibility for Africa's plight on itself, particularly on leaders they see as immature, corrupt, power hungry, tribalist and—worst of all—socialist.

"Europe has indeed imposed a succession of alien concepts on Africa, which never asked for them," opines Wheatcroft: "mercantile trade, Christianity, liberalism, democracy, and, as a final bad joke, revolutionary Marxist socialism. Some African rulers lucubrate about socialism as though it has relevance to their countries. But it is an utterly European concept."

Historical accuracy is often stretched to re-inforce the point. "One of the best examples that experiments in Marxist socialism have largely been unsuccessful," says *Time*, "is resource-rich Ghana, where the four-year-old government of Flight Lieut. Jerry Rawlings, 36, now faces an economy teetering on the brink of economic collapse."

Like similar statements about Angola and Mozambique, such reporting brushes aside the fact that in all three cases, left-leaning governments inherited from Western-oriented rulers economies that were already in shambles.

Tanzania is the most often-cited example of socialism's god-that-failed. David Lamb, former Africa correspondent for the *Los Angeles Times,* writes that Tanzanian President Julius Nyerere's experiment with socialism "has been one of the great failures in independent Africa, and one that should be a lesson for other countries."

"What Nyerere overlooked," says Lamb in his 1982 book *The Africans*, "was that people in Africa do not have to work to feed themselves, and in that setting socialism was a bad alternative. The rich soil and tropical climate provide ample food for subsistence. Take away the monetary rewards for increased production and people are perfectly content to live as they always have, growing just enough food for themselves and their families."

If that seems a breath-taking misstatement at a time when mass starvation threatens over two dozen African nations, including Tanzania, dissenters from the prevailing view argue that it is no less naive than blaming Africans for their own ills.

While Africa's current crises are often perceived as relatively recent, a betrayal of the bright promise of independence, there are development theorists who have chronicled—even predicted—what socialist thinker Michael Harrington calls "an important and dramatic phenomenon of the post-World War II years: the flow of money from the poor to the rich."

Even in showcase countries like Kenya, which is still held up, despite some recent tarnishing, as representing successful development on the Western free-enterprise model, there has long been trouble beneath the calm facade. A decade ago, development workers like Dutch agricultural specialist C.R. Ter Kuile were pointing out that the income of Kenya's rural poor—85% of the population—was declining.

The Development of Underdevelopment

The premise that underdevelopment is a process, a result of existing structural relations between rich and poor, is common among

Third World economists and politicians, socialists and non-socialists alike.

Elsewhere in this issue, Paul Fauvet of the Mozambique News Agency portrays the economy of Mozambique as vulnerable to its structural dependence on South Africa. His thesis parallels the argument that poor countries, in general, are at the mercy of decisions taken by wealthy nations to benefit themselves.

Also in this week's issue is a review of a book by Guy Gran, assistant professor of African and Development Studies at American University's School of International Service. His *Development by People* stakes out a position that sounds heretical in the limited context of the usual debate about foreign aid. It is, however, one often encountered among development workers in the field.

"Analyzing the IMF [International Monetary Fund] in theoretical terms," he writes, "means departing from the vast establishment literature generated by IMF economists and their academic and journalistic supporters and striking out directly against more than a generation of some of the most sophisticated intellectual mystification of modern times."

Gran, who is regarded as an expert on Zaire, uses it to illustrate the functioning of aid projects:

"Coming to power with Western assistance in the mid-1960s, President Mobutu [Sese Seko] inherited a potentially rich country. With the guidance of European mining interests, the World Bank, and the IMF, Mobutu proceeded to lock Zaire into an export-led growth model."

Gran asserts that "a misshapen triple alliance" of Western governments, private interests and the Zaire elite collaborates to fend off the bankruptcy that always appears inevitable. The result: "Mobutu profits by every delay. Private banks maintain their global credibility. Belgium still gets its copper and the U.S. its cobalt. The Zairian people still starve."

American University economics professor Howard Wachtel says such dependency relationships were in place prior to decolonization and were strengthened in the immediate postcolonial years.

His 1977 study of multinational banks in the Third World, published by the Transnational Institute, traces current lending practices to an Eisenhower administration policy of encouraging private, rather than public, financing of development programs.

Wachtel says the success of that drive is partly responsible for the threat of default facing so many poor countries. Private loans, he notes, are for a shorter period of time at higher interest rates and carry stiffer terms, thus measurably increasing the Third World's debt burden.

Delivering water in Ghana's capital, Accra: After defying efforts of several administrations, Ghana economy is finally showing signs of recovery.
United Nations

Like those they critique, the "structuralists" are a diverse lot, encompassing differing opinions on development issues. The view they share can be crudely summarized as a rejection of the hypothesis that aid, in isolation from changes in power relationships, can halt any nation's slide into increasing poverty.

Michael Harrington, for example, refutes arguments that the poor can help themselves by increasing their productivity. He cites World Bank statistics showing some of the poorest countries producing more efficiently than advanced nations. Since two-thirds of Third World exports are made in conditions of high productivity, while wages are but a fraction of those in the developed countries, the difference in product value over cost represents a subsidy of wealthy countries by poor ones.

Nor, Harrington claims, is the problem simply that poor countries rely on commodity exports while their richer neighbors are industrialized. Hong Kong, he notes, is more industrialized than the U.S., but still poor.

Rather, he argues, the U.S. benefits from

producing grains or cotton, because its economy is an integrated whole, and because it can dictate terms in the international market. Egypt's production of cotton, by contrast, fits into a pattern developed in colonial times. Like with other less developed nations, its economy is incoherent, with external links stronger than relations of various sectors within the country itself.

Also common to the structuralists is the antipathy to "export-led" economies that rely excessively on producing for export earnings. Food policy authors Francis Moore Lappe and Joseph Collins argue that prior to European intervention, Africans practiced diversified agriculture. "But colonial rule simplified this diversified production to single cash crops—often to the exclusion of staple foods—and in the process sowed the seeds of famine."

Critics of Western develpment criteria object to celebrating GNP growth in such countries as the Ivory Coast. Tanzania, they say, for all its problems and failures, has taught an astonishing 90% of its people to read and given nearly every Tanzanian access to clean water and health care. If the price was potholes in the streets of Dar es Salaam—as *Time* laments—the diversion of resources to rural areas was a conscious one.

Interesting also is Tanzania's tentative exploration of organic farming—a first attempt to move agriculture away from a heavy reliance on expensive chemicals and machinery. If successful, the program will mean a break with techniques promoted in the Third World by both East and West.

Development questions are more complicated than whether wealthy nations should give more foreign aid or less. But that choice is particularly stark at a time when an unprecedented drought in Africa has raised the spectre of hundreds of thousands—if not millions—of starvation deaths.

Over the long term, though, the development debate hinges less on immediate practical problems than on world views.

Proponents of a new international economic order are alarmed at the resurgence of viewing Africa as a victim of its own primitivism. Wheatcroft, for example, judges the former colonies of French West Africa as "successful"—and attributes this to the fact that their economies are still largely run by French expatriates.

But he defends himself against the charge of racism he seems to anticipate. "Certainly 'racism' in the sense of contempt for other peoples and cultures is odious," he concedes, "but it is not more silly and damaging than to lie about other peoples and cultures."

To those whose perception of Africa is "too gloomy," Wheatcroft offers this comfort: "De Tocqueville once pointed out to a racist friend who sneered at primitive peoples that the people of Britain were once the most barbarous and primitive in Europe and two thousand years later they were running the world. . . . Who knows? Africa may yet have something to teach us all."

Wheatcroft does not acknowledge that his comfort is a small one to Africans living in this century or the next. By contrast, the structuralists believe change is possible, a mater of human choices. Despite all their warnings of impending disaster, they emerge as the true optimists.

Article 3

Charting a New Course

THE GUARDIAN

A scenario for improvement

RENÉ DUMONT

René Dumont is a French agronomist. This report, extracted from "Stranglehold on Africa" (André Deutsch, London), written with Marie-France Mottin, is adapted from the liberal "Guardian" of London.

There is a scenario for Africa that we must envision. It may be hedged with difficulties, and it is likely to come up against various obstacles, both natural and official, but we must adopt it if we do not want to see Africa strangled.

The first task is to slow the spread of shantytowns by making village life more attractive and more interesting, and by restoring the powers of decision that the bureaucrats have, in many cases, stolen from the peasants. Obviously, absolute priority will have to be given to the villages.

Community groups could organize the equipment of their districts with essential sèrvices (water and drainage, roads, schools, and hospitals). After that it would be possible to upgrade the productive activities already being carried out, such as crafts that utilize the refuse produced by urban living (wood and metal) to make functional objects that would be produced and sold cheaply.

If they have no security of tenure, inhabitants of the shantytowns will have no incentive to improve their environment. They must be helped to use the most suitable technology and must be given technical advice, grants, and loans for the necessary amenities. Until now both advice and loans have too often been restricted to friends of those in power.

An important step will be to allocate local expenditure on a fairer basis. The people must be helped to improve output and to market their produce. For instance, they must be allowed to supply government markets without excess red tape.

When President Julius K. Nyerere of Tanzania spoke at the international conference on agrarian reform and rural development, he stressed that even the best-intentioned governments, including his own, tended to talk about rural development as if ordinary people had no ideas of their own. He claimed that political power automatically goes to the "haves," whereas both political and economic power ought to be in the hands of the people at the village, regional, and national level.

He said it was essential to insure that surpluses produced in rural areas remain there, so that the rural economy could be diversified by means of alternative sources of production and labor. Nyerere is undoubtedly a man of goodwill, but his own bureaucracy still forces Tanzanian peasants to grow a high proportion of export crops, even in places where they are by no means certain to do well.

You cannot give economic and political power to the peasants if they are not ready to accept it — if they have not organized themselves into groups to be reckoned with. Resistance movements opposed to the authorities are reported in various places. In 1968 some Senegalese started what was cautiously referred to as "peasant unrest." They succeeded in obtaining better conditions for themselves merely by reducing their crop acreage until prices went up.

The peasants' first priority is to have enough to eat, so they must concentrate on food crops. And, as in the days before the colonial era, they must build up reserves for their families, possibly in communal granaries rather than in cooperatives run by the authorities for their own benefit. They must once again set up economic, social, and political groups run by themselves and capable of providing effective and nonviolent opposition to the authorities exploiting them.

The authorities are not going to give up their prerogatives and privileges without a fight, especially when they know that they can expect support from the dominant developed powers. This underlines the fact that the decisive responsibility lies with us, with our privileges and our squandering of resources, which are destroying our small planet while we look on unconcerned.

Europe cannot manage without Africa and the Third World, because they supply it with cheap energy plus cheap metals, timber, and produce. It is, therefore, in Europe's interest that Africa survives.

In the long term it would run counter to our interests to have Africa strangled and the Third World destroyed, since this would result in the breakup of the Western economic system. Nor will the socialists in the West be in a position to function effectively until they show genuine concern for the Third World. They will then try to set up an international economic system whose first move will be to lessen inequities — rather than talk all the time about increasing our standard of living.

Priority must also be given to cutting back the squandering of the world's scarce resources. This means a series of austerity measures, initially for the rich but also for the majority of people in North America, Europe, Australia, and Japan — and later even for the Socialist bloc. Such a policy could well accord with a life that is more interesting and more convivial because it is less selfish.

Article 4

WEST AFRICA May 1983

OAU AT TWENTY

Descent into immobility

'The OAU is now no more than a token pan-continental ritual' writes Professor S. K. B. Asante, Head of the Department of Political Science, University of Ghana, Legon.

ON MAY 25 this year, the Organisation of African Unity, the world's largest continental organisation and the first tangible fruit of the dream of Pan-African unity, celebrates its 20th anniversary. The member states of the Organisation may not, however, be inclined to readily reaffirm their faith in the OAU Charter as has usually been the case on this auspicious African Liberation Day. For the OAU is no longer held in such high esteem by the African Heads of State as it was during the first decade of its existence. The Organisation would seem to have registered all its positive accomplishments by the end of its first decade. For example, the OAU was able, at least, to take a firm stand for a solution that preserved the integrity of Nigeria during the Civil War. This made it impossible for any big power to side effectively with Biafra. It was during this period also that OAU sometimes provided a basis for the peaceful settlement of disputes, particularly border conflicts, among its members. The relative successes constituted an example of effective action taken by an international organisation to safeguard regional peace and security.

Now, however, the OAU has become increasingly a laughing-stock, a butt for cheap ridicule and indeed, Africa's first instalment of Utopia. The "spirit of Addis Ababa", which had been the source of OAU's strength and vitality in the past, would seem to have evaporated into thin air. And the Organisation has continued to exhibit signs of decline in the face of challenges confronting it. Many African leaders do not really regard the OAU as a serious forum any more; it is, rather, a place to display their might by disrupting conferences with frequent and meaningless walkouts. The recent Tripoli (1 and 2) fiasco could as well mark the beginning of the Organisation's long-predicted demise. Briefly stated, then, the OAU is now no more than a token pan-continental ritual.

Perhaps the most crucial political challenge which has confronted the OAU in the last ten years is the dominant question of foreign intervention. Since the ignominous Angolan civil war, Africa has lurched from crisis to crisis and the continent has gradually become the focus of global politics. Foreign intervention, military and otherwise, has become an increasingly important factor in political developments in Africa. All the major Powers, as well as some of the smaller ones, have been drawn more deeply into the affairs of the continent. Perhaps at no time in the continent's history since the end of the 19th-century has Africa been embroiled in military confrontations on a scale comparable to the period immediately following the Angolan civil war. And, as has been in the past, the extra dimension has always been the ease with which foreign powers have taken Africa to be their Armageddon. Thus the 1884 Berlin Conference is being re-enacted in a 20th-century setting, in Zaire, Chad, Western Sahara, the Ogaden and Eritrea.

On the other hand, the OAU is firmly opposed to any external interference in the continent's internal conflicts. This commitment under the Charter was reinforced at the 1965 Accra summit where members agreed not to tolerate subversive activity directed from outside Africa against any member state. As if this was not enough, they were unequivocal in their determination 'to oppose collectively and firmly by any means at the disposal of Africa every form of subversion conceived, organised or financed by foreign powers against Africa, the OAU, or against its members individually! But despite this clear-cut policy statement on the issue of external military intervention, the OAU has not had much success in preventing "foreign meddling".

The OAU has been meeting this challenge of foreign intervention with a divided mind, and with no apparent result. Despite the attendance at Libreville July 1977 OAU summit of as many as 23 Heads of State and Government, the meeting showed few signs of "African Unity". No real effort was made to implement the Organisation's policy of resisting foreign intervention in essentially African disputes.

But it was at the subsequent summit at Khartoum in July 1978 that the African leaders, for the first time, seriously faced up to the challenge of foreign intervention in their affairs. The summit showed that the continent's leaders were no longer as confident of their ability to stop all foreign meddling in their affairs as they had been

in the 1960s; nor was there any longer even consensus about whether or not all forms of external intervention were undesirable. The main disagreements at Khartoum were over which of the foreign powers were responsible for the threats to the continent's stability.

The best the OAU could offer at Khartoum was to reach a disturbing compromise on this crucial issue of foreign military intervention: the right of African states to appeal for help to countries of their choice. This in effect was an "unofficial" OAU invitation to foreign powers to intervene in the affairs of the continent. Thus those that the founding fathers of the OAU in 1963 sought to exclude from shaping Africa's destiny are now being invited to come back to Africa to exploit Africa's political divisions and economic weakness to their own advantage.

Even in its role as peacemaker in Africa, the OAU has witnessed in recent years a serious decline. It had very little to do with ending the civil war in Angola, which was terminated not by negotiation but by the forces of external intervention. For example, in 1976 at the OAU summit at Port Louis the display of disputes between OAU members and the vigour with which the disputing parties fought each other completely over-shadowed the crucial problems which faced the organisation — the then unresolved issue of minority rule in Rhodesia, South Africa and Namibia. Morocco and Mauritania threatened to terminate their membership if the OAU continued to support Polisario; Uganda accused Kenya of complicity in the Israeli raid on Uganda's Entebbe airport; Ethiopia sought a firm stand by the OAU on what its delegation described as "expansionist plans of Somalia on the territory of the Afars and Issas"; President Numieiri of Sudan accused Libya of plotting a coup d'etat in Sudan to overthrow him.

More disturbing is the fact that the OAU has not been in a position to prevent any of the disputes breaking out into war. This has been clearly shown by the outbreak of hostilities between Ethiopia and Sudan along their borders in April 1977. Although both countries filed their complaints with the OAU the only thing the organisation could do was to register them. Even less was done about the conflict in the Zaire province of Shaba, despite the direct involvement of outside powers. And in recent years, the vexed issues of Chad and Western Sahara have effectively exposed the virtual impotence of the OAU, and the future of the Organisation is being seriously threatened following the failure of the two Tripoli attempts (August and November 1982) to hold the 19th summit.

What, then, has gone wrong? Is it the

fault of the OAU Charter? Have the African states really exhausted the untried resources and potentialities of the Charter? to what really can we attribute the present impotence of the OAU? Can it be justifiably attributed to the present type of political leadership in Africa?

The OAU Charter may not be perfect. But it is not the Charter that obstructs the way to peace and the course towards African unity. The Charter sets forth a few basic principles but leaves to the member states the responsibility of finding suitable means of carrying out those principles. The Charter is not a self-operating mechanism. Its operation depends not so much on the words of the Charter as on the way member states exercise their rights and meet their responsibilities. Some means are specified in the Charter, but these are not necessarily exclusive. Within widest limits other means are not prohibited.

To a great extent, therefore, it is not the inadequacy or limitations of the OAU Charter which have caused the present political paralysis. The principles and objectives enshrined in the Charter still hold good. It is a matter of the spirit that needs to be changed — the attitudes of the member states towards the Organisation.

For in the case of international organisation in particular, what politicians have put together, politicians can rip asunder. The constraints on the activities of the OAU in recent years reflect the preferences — and fears — of the heads of state who collectively determine what the Organisation should not do, or try to do. The positive accomplishments registered by the OAU in the past have resulted primarily from the collective determination by the heads of state to resolve African issues in African ways. A constant leitmotif in both debates and activities is minimisation of extra-African impact on the continent.

This type of collective will or collective determination would seem to have eluded the OAU in recent years. For the Organisation has since the February 1976 extraordinary summit on the Angolan war split right in the centre. Following the division at that summit, two strands of opinion have begun to coagulate into two openly opposed blocs, arbitrarily described as "progressive" and "moderate". This division of the OAU has in recent months been intensified by Gaddafi's Libya. For, on the issue of admission of Chad to the last November Tripoli OAU Ministerial meeting, for example, the Libyans claimed the support of what they termed "radical" countries in their bid to seat the Goukhouni delegation, as opposed to that of Hissen Habré which was supported by the "moderates". Furthermore at the previous OAU attempted summit in Tripoli in

August 1982, President Gaddafi actually mooted the idea of forming an alternative grouping of "radical states". While this division can not be neatly characterised in ideological terms, it is evidently clear that it is reminiscent of what was prevailing in the early years of the OAU when the Organisation comprised the radical Casablanca and moderate Brazzaville and Monrovia groups. It is these two opposing groups which seems to have resurrected. Thus today, as one scholar has recently commented, there is very little that one can lump together and call a common African position: there are two OAUs.

This division — and indeed the whole question about the current OAU's low profile in African affairs — seems to have been brought about by the type of political leadership emerging on the African scene. The "old boy" atmosphere of the first years of the OAU Assembly has diminished, of course, with the expansion of the membership and the passing from the scene of many of the founding fathers of African nationalism. In the earlier years, peer pressure could effect extraordinary reconciliations among those who shared a common history in the forging of nations out of European colonies. The statistics alone suggest that personal ties may be weakening as a cement for OAU actions. Of the 32 Heads of State and Government who were signatories to the OAU's Charter in May 1963, only four — Guinea, Ivory Coast, Tanzania and Tunisia remain in office*. Most of them had been casualties of the spate of the coups d'etat that began with the overthrow of Togo's Sylvanus Olympio in January 1963.

Hence, today, many political leaders gained power through coups d'etat, reflecting the military's emergence as the key political actor in contemporary Africa. Thus at an historical moment when Africa is confronted with pressing problems, the OAU has, either by fate or design, handed over the stewardship of African affairs to leaders who either cannot marshall the support of all OAU member states or are least interested in affairs outside their respective countries. For while the military backgrounds of more than half of Africa's current presidents could provide a set of shared experiences and assumptions facilitating co-operation, the prime concern of most governments dominated by members of the military appears often to be the resolution of the domestic grievances that brought them to power rather than the kinds of foreign policy issues to which their civilian predecessors gave attention. Closely related to this is the attempt on the part of the military to perpetuate their misrule or phoney regimes by purchasing most expensive and highly sophisticated arms to both protect themselves and suppress the civilian population who daily cry in vain for the basic necessities of life.

To such leaders, the current Southern African imbroglio, the inter-state conflicts in other parts of the continent, the grave economic problems, and even foreign intervention appear to be of secondary consideration. Attendance at OAU summits at which such issues are discussed means little to them, despite their rhetoric to the contrary. They are intensely pre-occupied with safeguarding their position against possible coups in their absence.

The trend towards military regimes in Africa — headed mostly by "low-cost-dictators" — has no doubt affected the quality and direction of continental international relations. Coups d'etat have upset not only inter-state relationships but also co-operative regional linkages and have often led to unstable governments for whom, as indicated above, foreign policy and the need to strengthen the OAU is subordinate to the need for political survival. Thus at 20, the OAU has come of age, the age of reason. But its respectable passage into manhood is being recklessly thwarted by the increasing incidence of military interventions, coups, counter coups, threat of coups and a new type of leadership which are diminishing commitment to pan-African goals.

Perhaps the time has come, therefore, to give the OAU "teeth" and to make it a positive instrument that can shape the destinies of the African peoples. The Organisation must be equipped in terms of mechanisms and organs to have a body which will have the power to react to conflict situations before they get out of hand. There is the need, also, to strengthen the powers of the Secretary-General; to completely overhaul the internal structure of the OAU Secretariat; and also to establish a supreme organ of the OAU to deal with the economic problems of Africa. Such reforms are necessary to enable the organisation to develop a greater capacity to enforce its authority over its member states in defence of its charter and to meet squarely the challenges of the 1980s.

*King Hassan of Morocco was absent from the summit and did not sign the charter until September 1963.

Article 5

UNESCO Courier, April 1984

The hunger belt

IN the 1970s, sub-Saharan Africa had the highest rate of population growth of any area in the world; furthermore, the rate of increase is still accelerating, whereas in all other developing regions it is tending to slow down. Food production, on the other hand, is increasing more slowly than in other tropical and sub-tropical areas.

As a result, Africa is the only region that is currently losing the race to keep food production ahead of population. The figures clearly bring out the drop in *per capita* production, but they also show that the results achieved during the 1970s were inadequate only in relation to the growing numbers of people to be fed. In terms of total production, the increase was greater than in the developed countries.

The attention of the international community is being increasingly directed

Photo © Oswald Iten, Switzerland

Centuries of grinding sorghum have left their moulds in the rocks of Lafon, southern Sudan. The Sudan is one of the few countries of sub-Saharan Africa which have kept food production ahead of population growth in recent years.

toward the "African food problem". In fact, a series of separate problems, rather than a single pattern of difficulties, underlies the disappointing performance of agriculture in tropical Africa. The situation varies widely by crop, by country and by agro-ecological zone.

In the production of staple food crops, the record since 1969-71 contains more failures than successes. Four of the largest producers of millet south of the Sahara saw their output drop in absolute terms, as did

five of the largest sorghum producers, four of the largest rice producers and six of the largest maize producers. In relatively few cases did production growth exceed the increase in population. Only in cassava was there no decline in production, although only four of the large producers managed to keep output ahead of population during the 1970s.

In some cases, declining production can be attributed to war or political instability. But many other factors have also been at work: the inherent difficulties of farming on fragile soils subjected to violent but irregular rainfall; lack of economic incentives; the migration of rural people (especially the young) to the cities.

Of forty-one sub-Saharan countries with a significant agricultural sector, only five (Cameroon, Central African Republic, the Ivory Coast, Rwanda and the Sudan) have kept food production consistently ahead of population growth in recent years. At the other end of the scale, countries in which food production per person dropped by more than 20 per cent between the start of the 1970s and 1982 include Angola, Gambia, Ghana, Mauritania, Mozambique, Senegal and Somalia.

The African food-deficit countries have made up their shortfalls by imports, particularly of cereals, and among cereals mainly of wheat. Urban and to a lesser extent rural populations have developed a taste for bread made from wheat flour, which offers considerable advantages over traditional foods in terms of convenience, and also has higher prestige. Yet wheat cannot be grown in the temperature regimes prevailing in most of Africa outside the eastern highlands. An escape from this "wheat trap" is being sought through technology for the processing of local crops, including cassava and traditional cereals. It is hoped that wheat flour can be at least partially substituted by local products in ways that will prove acceptable to townspeople. Rice, on the other hand, is well suited to tropical environments; however, production has been rising more slowly than demand, and imports have been soaring.

Cereal imports into sub-Saharan Africa are still below the average for developing countries in *per capita* terms. But they have been growing fast, doubling every seven years approximately. And they are already large in relation to the ability of low-income countries to finance food imports. In 1981, the region imported over 12 million tons of cereals, at a cost of about $2.5 billion. This absorbed over 27 per cent of the total receipts of all sub-Saharan developing countries from the export of agricultural, forestry and fishery products—the main source of foreign exchange apart from oil and mineral exports. Imports provided more than a fifth of total cereal supplies.

If the food situation in sub-Saharan Africa was difficult in 1982, it begins to look really alarming when recent trends are projected into the future. World Bank projections show the population of the developing countries south of the Sahara as quadrupling between 1980 and 2020. By the latter year, the population of Nigeria could be about 340 million, Zaire some 95 million and Kenya approximately 80 million. On the basis of food production trends in the 1970s, sub-Saharan Africa would be able to feed from domestic sources little more than half of its population. The food deficit in the year 2020 would correspond to the entire present-day agricultural production of India.

Even over the shorter term the picture looks grim. Few countries can continue to cover mounting food deficits with corresponding increases in cereal imports. Indeed, the general economic situation is forcing countries to cut back on food imports, rather than step them up. Food supplies per person will inevitably fall if deficits cannot be made up by imports or by food aid. Nutrition levels are, therefore, likely to come under increasing pressure, and the danger of worsening malnutrition on a wide scale should by no means be underestimated.

Nevertheless, there are certain plus-factors which can justify a measure of optimism. Foremost among these are the underestimated versatility and skills of the African farmer. His readiness to innovate is clear from the fact that many of the food and export crops most widely grown have been introduced from outside Africa in modern times. Furthermore, traditional cropping systems are frequently elaborate and—within their limits—efficient. The difficulty is that they were developed over many generations to feed an approximately stable population, and do not lend themselves to sustained increases in productivity. Indeed, no fully satisfactory approach has yet been found for continuous and intensive cropping under the agro-ecological conditions that prevail in much (though not all) of tropical Africa. There is a technological gap, particularly with regard to soil management and labour productivity, which must be filled before the African farmer can cope with the food needs of the continent.

Technology, however, is not all. Agriculture can prosper only in a favourable policy environment. At the time of their independence, many African countries appear to have seriously underestimated both the importance and the difficulties of the agricultural sector. As a result, domestic food production has seldom been given the priority it needed.

In a broader context, a bias against agriculture generally, and food production in particular, has become built into the socio-economic structure of many African States, and affects such fundamental issues as exchange-rate and taxation policies, relative price levels, and priorities for the development of infrastructure. It is reflected also in the relatively low prestige attached to work in the farm sector. If food production is to find a new vitality, many countries will have to alter profoundly the attitude toward agriculture held not only by planners and politicians but also by the population as a whole.

The international community, for its part, must find new ways of helping Africa to help itself. Investment and technical assistance are vitally needed, but a multiplicity of small projects, each with its own administrative requirements, can place disproportionate demands upon government services which are desperately short of trained people. Ways must be found of helping governments to redress the balance of economic power in favour of food producers, without precipitating a revolution in the cities. And it must be recognized that, if the African food crisis has been developing for twenty years, it may well take just as long to resolve.

The gravity of the situation has been fully recognized within Africa, for instance in the Lagos Plan of Action adopted in April 1980 by the members of the Organization of African Unity. A framework for action within Africa and by the international community is contained in FAO's Regional Food Plan for Africa. Many studies have been made by other organizations, notably the World Bank, and there is no shortage of analysis and prescription. However, there is as yet no clear evidence that the tide has started to turn. Africa south of the Sahara remains the world's principal food-problem area.

Article 6

afrique

The Fruits of Independence

Burgeoning urbanization, lagging industrialization

SOPHIE BESSIS

Sophie Bessis writes for the liberal newsmagazine "Jeune Afrique" of Paris, from which this is excerpted.

Africa has a propensity for agriculture; most of its population lives off the soil. Has it made the most of this? Grain production on the continent grew from 44 million tons in the late 1950s to 66 million tons at the start of the 1980s. Production of roots and tubers — the basic food source for central Africa —

grew from 63 to 85 million tons in twenty years. But the increase has been insufficient, because while food production has risen 1.8 per cent per year, the population has grown by 2.6 per cent.

Africa has long been an exporter of agricultural products, but growth in exports of its important crops such as coffee, cocoa, oilseeds, and cotton has been unspectacular. Peanut production shrank in 1960-80, and production of coffee and cocoa has stagnated.

The continent's crop-producing areas have shifted over the past quarter-century. In Nigeria, Ghana, and Zaire agricultural output has tumbled, while the Ivory Coast and Cameroon are filling the gap. Overall, Africa holds virtually the same position in worldwide agricultural production that it held twenty years ago. As a result, the agricultural trade balance has worsened as food imports have increased to feed the growing population. Those imports now weigh heavily on fragile economies.

In Africa's nonagricultural sector, the past twenty-five years have seen the rise of cities and factories and the birth of an industrial society that has changed, to some degree, the profiles of many cities. The seaport town of Gabès in southern Tunisia, for example, once a charming oasis depicted in picture postcards, is now smoke-enveloped and polluted — as are Casablanca and many other ports. In Tunis and Nairobi countless male and female workers line up at factory gates. Former members of Africa's traditional peasantry, they now belong to the world of salaried workers.

Africa's industrial development, however, has not compensated for the stagnation of agriculture. Manufacturing activities for both domestic and export markets still account for only a small portion of economic activity. In 1980 Africa's share of industrial exports by Third World nations did not exceed 5 per cent.

Most African countries in which the industrial sector is responsible for more than 30 per cent of the gross national product have mineral resources that undergo processing before they are exported — Guinea with its bauxite; uranium-rich Niger; Mauritania and Liberia with their iron ore; Zambia with its copper; and oil-and gas-exporting Algeria. Egypt and Tunisia, which are relatively poor in raw materials except for modest quantities of oil, have industrial sectors that furnish more than a third of the GNP, thanks to light industry.

Africa's transportation facilities are growing but, as in the past, they are intended to carry the continent's riches to foreign lands. This is the case with such major post-independence developments as the Tanzam and Zouerate railways. Despite some gains, the under-equipment of this sector is striking. Of the continent's 57,000 miles of track 13,800 miles are in South Africa. As for roads, only the Maghreb is adequate.

Few African countries extract the maximum wealth from their natural resources. Only 6 per cent of the continent's tobacco is made into tobacco products in Africa. More than 75 per cent of Africa's lumber leaves the continent as rough timber. And 98 per cent of the phosphate undergoes no transformation before being sent to enrich the countries of the North — who are also major agricultural exporters and supply Africa with the food it cannot produce. Had its industrial development been aimed at satisfying domestic demand and at domestic processing of raw materials, Africa might have escaped some of its balance-of-trade problems.

Under-industrialization has not prevented Africa from attempting to imitate Northern lifestyles. Hundreds of thousands of country dwellers leave their villages and head for cities — and their implicit promise of employment. Urbanization has been swift — as if Africa, with a later start than Asia or Latin America, is trying doggedly to catch up. The urban population outnumbers rural dwellers in Tunisia; in Algeria, Morocco, and Egypt it represents more than 40 per cent of the population. These countries are among the continent's least industrialized areas.

An African country's rate of urbanization has little to do with the structure of its economy. Almost half the population of the Central African Republic and the Congo, and one third of the population of Zaire and Somalia, live in cities where nothing has been planned to accommodate them. In some countries an estimated 50 per cent of adult city dwellers are unemployed.

The city is replacing the countryside as Africa's prime dwelling area — but industry still lags behind agriculture. This is one of the major challenges the continent must face. The mass migration is due partly to population growth but also to frustration. The city represents the hope of a better life than the hinterland offered.

One of the major consequences of recent economic change in Africa has been heightened socioeconomic differences. From Tunis to Abidjan, from Douala to Nairobi the emergence of a privileged class is obvious. The distribution of wealth is among the world's most inequitable.

On the global chessboard, Africa still has not moved the power relationships in its favor. Its negotiating strength remains modest despite its size, population, and potential wealth. While its living standard has improved slightly since the 1960s, it has not registered the leap forward that might have been possible if Africans were the masters of their fate.

North Africa

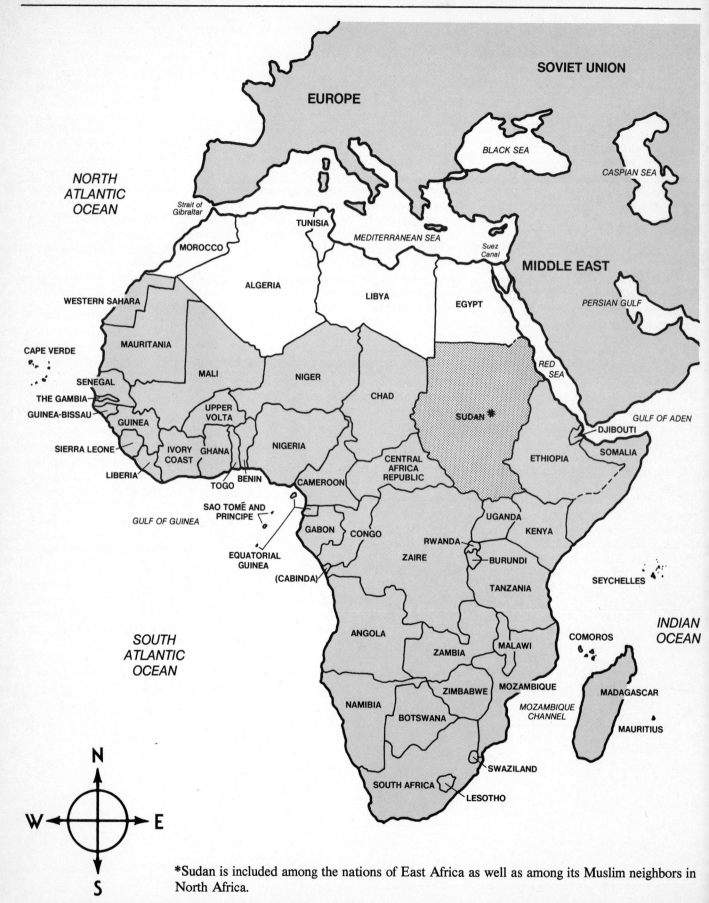

SOVIET UNION

EUROPE

BLACK SEA

CASPIAN SEA

NORTH
ATLANTIC
OCEAN

Strait of
Gibraltar

TUNISIA

MEDITERRANEAN SEA

Suez
Canal

MIDDLE EAST

MOROCCO

ALGERIA

LIBYA

EGYPT

PERSIAN GULF

WESTERN SAHARA

CAPE VERDE

MAURITANIA

RED
SEA

MALI

NIGER

SENEGAL

THE GAMBIA

GUINEA-BISSAU

GUINEA

UPPER
VOLTA

CHAD

SUDAN *

GULF OF ADEN

DJIBOUTI

SIERRA LEONE

IVORY
COAST

GHANA

NIGERIA

CENTRAL
AFRICA
REPUBLIC

ETHIOPIA

SOMALIA

LIBERIA

TOGO

BENIN

CAMEROON

SAO TOMÉ AND
PRINCIPE

GULF OF GUINEA

GABON

CONGO

UGANDA

KENYA

RWANDA

EQUATORIAL
GUINEA

ZAIRE

BURUNDI

SEYCHELLES

(CABINDA)

TANZANIA

SOUTH
ATLANTIC
OCEAN

INDIAN
OCEAN

ANGOLA

COMOROS

ZAMBIA

MALAWI

MOZAMBIQUE

ZIMBABWE

MADAGASCAR

NAMIBIA

BOTSWANA

MOZAMBIQUE
CHANNEL

MAURITIUS

SWAZILAND

SOUTH AFRICA

LESOTHO

N

W   E

S

*Sudan is included among the nations of East Africa as well as among its Muslim neighbors in
North Africa.

North Africa: Changing Islamic Cultures

Standing at the geographical and cultural crossroads between Europe, Asia, and the rest of the African continent, the northern edge of the African continent has long been both a link and a barrier to Africa's relations with the rest of the world. Historically, the region was an early source of African products to Western civilizations. "Moroccan" leather from West African artisans was brought to the Mediterranean coast by northern traders, as was gold, salt, and slaves. The region has also been known as the home of the mysterious Moors, such as Shakespeare's Othello, and the romantic, if terrifying, Barbary pirates. Their northern neighbors brought European and Asian goods to the sub-Saharan Africans and, perhaps more importantly, introduced them to one of the world's great universalist religions: Islam.

North Africa's role as an African crossroads declined with the European development of trans-oceanic navigation (and, eventually, of air transport), which fostered direct contact between Europe, Asia, and Africa. However, the countries of North Africa have continued to play an important part in the continent's history and development in recent centuries. Early supporters of African independence movements, they now participate actively in the affairs of the continent as full—indeed founding—members of the Organization of African Unity (OAU).

The countries of Northern Africa—Morocco, Algeria, Tunisia, Libya, and Egypt—differ a great deal from one another, but they share a heritage of common geography and culture, which distinguish them still more from the rest of Africa. To understand the culture and politics of northern Africa and its role in the rest of the continent, one must examine the geography of the region, which has provided the environment for social life as various as pastoral nomadism, peasant agriculture, merchant trade, and flourishing cities; the cultural and political heritage of Muslim and Middle Eastern as well as European influences; the diversity of contemporary political institutions within the region and the efforts at regional integration; and, finally, the role of North Africa in African organizations designed to give the continent a greater voice in world affairs.

GEOGRAPHY AND POPULATION

Except for Tunisia, which is relatively small, the countries of northern Africa are sprawling nations. Algeria, Libya, and Egypt are among the biggest countries on the continent in terms of square kilometers, and Morocco is not far behind. Their size can be misleading, however, for much of the land is empty and barren desert. The populations range from

(World Bank photo)

Regional cohesiveness is frustrated by the vast expanses of barren land.

Egypt's high of forty-one million to Libya's low of 2.5 million; Morocco and Algeria both have somewhat more than eighteen million people, and Tunisia is home to 5.6 million. The people hug the coastlines and riverbanks, in search of the precious and scarce resource that can make the land productive: water. The great Nile River courses through the Egyptian desert, creating a narrow green ribbon of agricultural productivity unrivaled in Africa. Ninety-five percent of Egypt's population lives within twelve miles of the river's banks. Ninety percent of the people of Algeria, Tunisia, and Libya live in the northern third of their countries, and they depend on the moderating influences of the Mediterranean sea coasts and low coastal mountain ranges to provide rainfall where there are no navigable rivers. Morocco, with both Atlantic and Mediterranean coastlines and with somewhat higher mountains, enjoys a more even distribution of its population, but here as well it is determined by the availability of water.

Not only has the temperate, if often too dry, climate of North Africa influenced where people live, it has also encouraged great diversity in local economies and life-styles. There is intensive agriculture along the coasts and rivers, and Morocco and Tunisia are well-known for their tree and vine crops—notably citrus fruits, olives, and wine grapes. Egypt's Nile Valley is intensively irrigated, and now produces world-famous, high quality cotton, as well as locally consumed foodstuffs. In the oases that dot the Sahara desert across the southern regions of these countries, date palms are irrigated, and their sweet fruit is harvested annually. Throughout the steppe lands, between the fertile coasts and the desert, nomads follow flocks of sheep and goats or herds of cattle and camels in search of pasture. Now very small in numbers, the nomads nonetheless enjoy a tradition of prestige as providers of meats, milk, and leathers. It was the nomads' knowledge of the landscape that permitted development of the extensive overland trans-Saharan trade. As paved roads and airports have replaced the caravan routes, long-distance nomadism has declined. But the traditions that it bred, including loyalty to family and love of independence, are still important to the cultural heritage of Northern Africa.

Urban life has also been a characteristic element of the North African economy and culture. Supported by trade and by local industries—especially by those involved in textiles, such as carpets, and metal-working—great cities have flourished. Cities such as Marrakesh, Fez, Rabat, Algiers, Tunis, Kairouan, and Tripoli as well as Cairo have been the administrative centers of great medieval empires. Those located by the sea have provided harbors for sea-faring merchants. In the modern era, these cities have been transformed into bustling industrial centers, ports, and political capitals.

Geography—or, more precisely, geology—has recently played an important role in providing resources for the national economies of Northern Africa. Although agriculture continues to provide employment in Algeria and Libya for as

(United Nations photo by Y. Nagata)

Oil and gas discoveries in North Africa have produced wide-ranging economic effects.

much as a third of the labor force, discoveries of oil and natural gas in the 1950s dramatically altered the nations' economic structures. The small Libyan population saw its per capita income jump between 1960 and 1980 from $50 to almost $10 thousand, transforming it from among the poorest to among the richest countries in the world. Algeria's larger population has also benefited from discoveries of oil, although less dramatically, and Tunisia and Egypt each have small oil industries that provide valuable domestic energy and foreign exchange. Morocco, while it has no oil, has profited from its control of much of the world's phosphate production, earning needed income for its development efforts.

CULTURAL AND POLITICAL HERITAGES

The vast majority of the inhabitants of Northern Africa are Arabic-speaking Muslims. Islam and Arabic entered the region between the sixth and eleventh centuries. By the time of the Crusades in the eastern Mediterranean, the society of Northern Africa was thoroughly incorporated into the Muslim world. Except for Egypt, where about ten percent of the population is Christian (principally followers of the Egyptian Coptic Church), there is virtually no Christianity among North Africans. Important Jewish communities existed in all of the North African countries, although the numbers have dwindled in the aftermath of the establishment of Israel in 1948. There are now very small Jewish communities in Morocco, Tunisia, and Egypt.

With Islam came Arabic, the language of the Arabian Peninsula and of the Qur'an. The local languages of North Africa—known collectively as Berber (from which the term "Barbary" was derived)—were almost completely supplanted in Egypt and Libya. Berber-speakers, often considered the indigenous inhabitants—in contrast to the Arabs who settled in North Africa in the wake of the expansion of the Muslim Empires—remain a significant proportion of the population of Tunisia, Algeria, and Morocco. As much as a third of the

(United Nations photo by M. Tzovaras)
Anwar El-Sadat altered the balance of regional politics by moving Egypt closer diplomatically to the United States.

Moroccans speak Berber as their first language. The mixture of Arabs and Berbers and their common adherence to Islam have left them virtually indistinguishable ethnically, although disputes have developed in Morocco and Algeria over the advisability of teaching Berber as a national language in schools. The linguistic issue has been complicated in Northern Africa, as well as for many of its sub-Saharan neighbors, by the legacy of European rule and the introduction of European languages—particularly French—as the language of technology and administration.

At the beginning of the nineteenth century, all of the countries of North Africa except Morocco were formally provinces of the Ottoman Empire, which was based in present day Turkey and included much of the contemporary Middle East. Morocco was an independent state and, indeed, one of the first to recognize the independence of the United States from England after the American Revolution. Throughout the nineteenth century, European expansion encroached on the independence of the Ottoman Empire; like their sub-Saharan African counterparts, all the states of North Africa eventually fell under European rule. Algeria was occupied by France in 1830, and France eventually ruled Tunisia (1881). Both France and Spain ruled Morocco (1912). Great Britain occupied Egypt in 1882, and Italy claimed Libya in 1911.

The different traditions of these European colonial rulers, while not weakening the underlying cultural unity of these predominantly Muslim and Arab states, did influence their political and social character, creating great diversity. Algeria, which was incorporated into France as a province for 130 years, did not win its independence until 1962, after a protracted and violent revolution. Morocco, by contrast, was accorded independence from France in 1956 after only forty-four years of French administration, during which the local monarchy continued to reign. Tunisia's three-quarters of a century of French rule also ended in 1956, as a strong nationalist party took the reins of power. Egypt, formally independent from Britain in 1936, was reoccupied during World War II and did not win genuine political independence until 1952, when Gamal Abdul Nasser came to power and overthrew the British-supported monarchy. Libya, which had fiercely resisted Italian rule, particularly during the Fascist era, became a ward of the United Nations after Italy lost its colonies in World War II. The nation was granted independence by the new world body in 1951 under a monarch whose religious followers had led much of the early resistance.

POLITICAL INSTITUTIONS AND REGIONAL POLITICS

Egypt

Egypt took a position on the world stage soon after Nasser came to power. One of the major figures in the Non-Aligned Movement, Nasser gave voice to the aspirations of millions

Population pressures continue to mount in Egypt, straining available resources and shaping domestic policies.

in the Arab world and Africa, championing nationalist movements throughout the region. Faced with the problems of a burgeoning population at home and his nation's limited natural resources, Nassar refused to let Egypt become dependent upon a single foreign power, declaring the country non-aligned. He adopted a policy of developmental socialism at home. Because of mounting debts, which were spurred by enormous military spending, and increasing economic problems, many people had already begun to reassess Egypt's activist foreign policy by the time Nasser died in 1970. His successor, Anwar El-Sadat, reopened Egypt to foreign investment in hopes of attracting much needed capital and technology. Eventually Sadat drew Egypt closer to the United States by signing the peace treaty that ended nearly thirty years of war with Israel in 1979. Sadat's abandonment of socialism made him a target of domestic discontent, however, and in 1981 he was assassinated. Sadat was succeeded by his vice-president, military officer Hosni Mubarak.

Libya

For years Libya was ruled by a pious autocratic king whose domestic legitimacy was always in question. The nation was heavily influenced by the foreign oil companies that discovered and produced the country's only substantial resource until 1969. In that year, Colonel Muammar Qadhdhafi overthrew the monarchy. Believed to be about twenty-seven at the time of the coup, Qadhdhafi was an ardent admirer of Nasser; he saw Libya as heir to Egypt's activist non-aligned foreign policy. He spent billions of dollars in ambitious, if poorly planned, domestic development—successfully ensuring universal health care, housing, and education by the end of the 1970s. He also spent billions more on military equipment and support of what he deemed nationalist movements throughout the world. Considered a maverick, he quarreled with many of the leaders of Africa and the Arab world, but his commitment to equitable distribution of the oil income lessened opposition at home.

Tunisia

Tunisia, with the fewest natural resources of the Northern African countries, is believed to have enjoyed the most stable and successful post-independence development experience of the region. Ruled by Habib Bourguiba—leader of the nationalist party known as the neo-Destour, which led the country to independence—Tunisia retained close economic and political ties with Europe. Bourguiba's government was a model of pragmatic approaches to both economic growth and foreign policy; it developed the nation's lovely Mediterranean coast as a vacation spot for European tourists and emphasized education and the private sector's contribution to development. In the early 1980s, after twenty-five years of single-party rule, many Tunisians were growing uneasy with the aging leader's continued refusal to recognize opposition political parties and open the system to electoral competition.

Algeria

Algeria, wracked by the long and destructive revolution which preceded independence in 1962, was ruled by a coalition of military and civilian leaders who had made their names as revolutionary partisans during the war. (Algeria became a republic with the creation of a constitution in 1976.) Although these leaders differed over what policies and programs to emphasize, they nonetheless agreed on the need for a foreign policy of non-alignment and for rapid industrialization at home—policies that came to be known in Algeria as "Islamic socialism." The country's substantial oil and gas revenues were invested in large-scale industrial projects. But by the end of the 1970s, the government noticed serious declines in agricultural productivity and major growth in urban unemployment, a situation that had sent hundreds of thousands of workers to France in search of jobs, and the leaders were taking steps to rectify these problems. The Algerian leadership, although it enforced a policy of domestic austerity, enjoyed a reputation both at home and abroad of commitment to equity and development.

Morocco

In the early 1980s, Morocco was ruled by King Hassan II, who came to power in 1962 when his highly respected father, Mohamed V, died. The political parties that had developed during the struggle against French rule continued to contest elections. However, Hassan rarely permitted them genuine influence in policy making, preferring to reserve the role for himself and his advisers. As in Tunisia, agricultural development was based on technological innovations rather than on land reform. The latter, while it would have raised productivity, might have angered the propertied supporters of the king. Much of the country's economic development was left to the private sector. High birth rates and unem-

(United Nations photo)

Morocco's King Hassan is a pivotal element in any North African regional planning.

ployment led many Moroccans to join the Algerians (and Tunisians) seeking employment in Europe.

During the 1950s and 1960s, regional integration was widely discussed in Northern Africa. Egypt was a leader of the pan-Arab movement and briefly joined Syria in a union from 1958 to 1961. The three former French colonies—Morocco, Algeria, and Tunisia, sometimes known as the Maghrib (Arabic for land of the setting sun)—considered proposals for economic integration, which might eventually lead to political unity. Libya, whose monarch at that time was faced with the more pressing problem of unifying his own regionally-divided countrymen, would pick up the theme of integration in the 1970s, when Qadhdhafi called for Arab and Islamic unions. By the early 1980s, none of these efforts had borne fruit. Indeed, many of the governments in the region had serious disputes with each other. Qadhdhafi had been accused of subverting the governments of all his neighbors; Algeria and Morocco were locked in disagreement over the disposition of the Western Sahara; and each country had, at one point or another, closed its borders to the nationals of its neighbors. The idea of regional cooperation, nonetheless, retained much of its original attractiveness, reflecting as it did the common cultural and social foundations of the region.

NORTHERN AFRICA AND THE REST
OF THE CONTINENT

Northern Africa's relations with the rest of the continent have reflected both its cultural and geographical roots in Africa, and the national interests and aspirations of each country. Both as members of the Organization of African Unity and as active supporters of anti-colonial movements, the North African countries have had strong diplomatic and political ties with the rest of Africa. They are, however, also deeply involved in regional affairs outside Africa—particularly those of the Arab and Islamic world—and there have been tensions because of these various commitments during the post-independence period. Requests by the northern nations that African countries break diplomatic relations with Israel were met promptly after the oil price rises of the early 1970s; many African countries hoped in return for Arab development aid. Although such aid was eventually offered (mostly from the Gulf countries, not the North African oil producers), it was less generous than expected and came only after some other conditions had been met. Many sub-Saharan African leaders were disappointed.

The dispute over the Western Sahara, formerly a colony of Spain and now claimed by Morocco (a claim opposed by a local political movement known as Polisario, which has counted among its supporters both Libya and Algeria), has badly divided the OAU. Indeed, after Qadhdhafi's intervention in Chad and widespread allegations of Libyan inter-ference in the internal affairs of a number of other African countries, many nations supported Morocco's proposal to refuse to seat Qadhdhafi as the chairman of the OAU in 1983, despite his earlier selection for the post. Thus, the North African influence in continental affairs has not been without its problems. Nonetheless, North African participation has been mutually beneficial. The Moroccan-Algerian border dispute was successfully resolved through OAU mediation in 1974, and the organization continues to play an important role in airing and resolving disputes as well as in presenting the African perspective on world affairs.

During August of 1984, a dramatic realignment occurred in the region. King Hassan of Morocco signed a unification agreement with Libya's Colonel Quadhdafi. The agreement created a union between the two countries, which are separated physically by Algeria and Tunisia. The Libyan leader has attempted to form unions with other North African nations, including Sudan and Egypt. Although this newest treaty may not last any longer than the earlier attempts, the terms of this union, which calls for mutual defense in the event of attack, have caused great concern among the nations of the region.

It remains unclear what the implications of this union will be, if it should succeed. The treaty was negotiated in secret, and the nature of the agreement is not known. It is possible that Quadhdafi offered to end his support for the Polisario movement in return for greater international respectability and influence. Clearly, events in North Africa will continue to unfold in unexpected ways.

(World Bank photo by Ray Witlin)

Geography has produced unique advantages and problems for North African nations.

Petroleum has assumed a critical position in the economies of North Africa.

West Africa

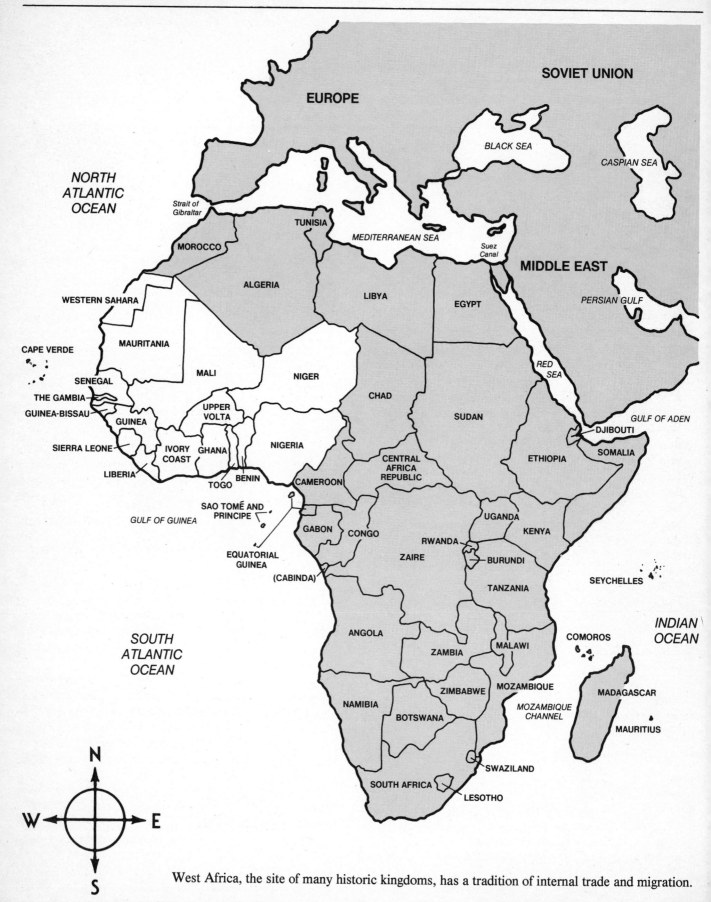

NORTH ATLANTIC OCEAN

EUROPE

SOVIET UNION

BLACK SEA

CASPIAN SEA

Strait of Gibraltar

TUNISIA

MEDITERRANEAN SEA

Suez Canal

MIDDLE EAST

MOROCCO

ALGERIA

LIBYA

EGYPT

PERSIAN GULF

WESTERN SAHARA

MAURITANIA

CAPE VERDE

MALI

NIGER

CHAD

SUDAN

RED SEA

GULF OF ADEN

DJIBOUTI

SENEGAL

THE GAMBIA

GUINEA-BISSAU

GUINEA

UPPER VOLTA

SIERRA LEONE

IVORY COAST

GHANA

NIGERIA

CENTRAL AFRICA REPUBLIC

ETHIOPIA

SOMALIA

LIBERIA

TOGO

BENIN

CAMEROON

SAO TOMÉ AND PRINCIPE

GULF OF GUINEA

GABON

CONGO

UGANDA

KENYA

EQUATORIAL GUINEA

(CABINDA)

ZAIRE

RWANDA

BURUNDI

TANZANIA

SEYCHELLES

SOUTH ATLANTIC OCEAN

ANGOLA

ZAMBIA

MALAWI

COMOROS

INDIAN OCEAN

ZIMBABWE

MOZAMBIQUE

MOZAMBIQUE CHANNEL

MADAGASCAR

NAMIBIA

BOTSWANA

MAURITIUS

SWAZILAND

SOUTH AFRICA

LESOTHO

N
W   E
S

West Africa, the site of many historic kingdoms, has a tradition of internal trade and migration.

West Africa: Building on Traditional Links

Anyone looking at a map of Africa will identify West Africa as the great bulge on the western coast of the continent. It is a region bound by the Sahara Desert to the north, the Atlantic Ocean to the south and west, and in part by the Cameroonian Mountains and the highlands to the east. Every boundary has, at one time or another, been a bridge to the rest of the world.

Within this area live over 150 million people, one-half of the population of Tropical Africa, in an area five-sixths the size of the United States. At first glance, the great variety of the region is more striking than any of its unifying features. It contains the extremes of desert and rain forest. The people who live there are predominantly agriculturalists; yet every type of occupation can be found—from herders to factory workers. Hundreds of different languages are spoken: Some are as different as English is from Arabic or Japanese. The cultural traditions and the societies that practice them are myriad.

Yet the more one examines West Africa, the more one is impressed with the developments that give the region a certain coherence and unity and that cross the boundaries of the sixteen states within the region. These states were the artificial creations of the competing colonial powers of Britain, France, and Portugal when Africa was partitioned by the imperialists at the end of the last century.

Some of the common characteristics and cross-cutting features of the area known as West Africa include: the vegetation belts that stretch across the region from west to east, creating somewhat similar environments in all the states; the common history and characteristics that distinguish many of the peoples of the West African region—especially the influence of the great kingdoms of the savanna and forest regions, the early development of urban centers, and the linking patterns of trade; the movement of peoples throughout the regions, providing a kind of social "glue"; and the efforts being made by West African governments to work for integration in the region primarily through economic organizations.

WEST AFRICAN VEGETATION AND CLIMATE ZONES

Travelling north from the coast in Nigeria, Ghana, or Ivory Coast, one first encounters tropical rain forests, then moves into woodland savanna areas, and later crosses more open and drier plains. In Mali, Niger, and other countries to the north, the trip would take one from savanna into the Sahel areas close to the desert, and finally into the desert itself. These vegetation zones stretching across West Africa are bands across the land, "citizens" of many countries.

The peoples of the countries share the benefits and the problems of these similar environments. Cocoa, coffee, yams, and cassava are among the cash and food crops planted in the cleared forest and woodland zones in Liberia or Nigeria, for instance. Groundnuts, sorghum, and millet

(United Nations photo)

Weaving long narrow strips of cloth is men's work throughout West Africa. The cloth is highly valued for blankets and chiefly robes.

are harvested in the savannas of Senegal, Gambia, Mali, and northern Nigeria. Niger herdsmen who cannot go too far south with their cattle because of the presence of the tsetse fly in the forest (and the accompanying danger of diseases that kill cattle) can more easily cross the borders into the savannas of Mali or Nigeria.

People in each country in the West African regions have felt the effect of the droughts of recent years, and population pressures on the lands have contributed to changing conditions. The border lands between savanna and desert, known as the Sahel, have deteriorated, leading to large-scale migrations. The woodland savannas farther south have given way to grasslands as more forests are cut to grow food and cash crops. The widespread brush fires in Ghana, Ivory Coast, Togo and Benin in 1983 may cause the forests to become savannas and the savannas to become deserts. The Harmattan, the dry wind that blows from the Sahara in January and February, now reaches to many parts of the coast. The dust and haze have become a sign of the new year—and of agricultural problems throughout West Africa.

The rivers of West Africa, including the Senegal, the Gambia, the Niger, and their tributaries, have become more and more important—not only because they are used for travel and trade but because of the water that they provide. Countries have united to harness the waters for irrigation and for hydroelectric power through joint organizations. Eight countries—Cape Verde, Gambia, Upper Volta, Mali, Senegal, Niger, Chad (in Central Africa), and Mauritania—have united in the Committee for Struggle Against Drought in the Sahel (CILSS) to counter the effects of the drought.

THE LINKS OF HISTORY AND TRADE

The peoples of West Africa have never been members of one political unit, and their diversity is far more noticeable than the features that they share. Yet some of the ancient kingdoms that overarched different regions are still remembered, providing bases for present and future cooperation. The Mali Empire of the thirteenth to fifteenth centuries, the Songhai Empire of the sixteenth century, and the

Northern Nigerian Fulani Empire of the nineteenth century were widely known and influential. They represent only a few, if the largest, of the expanding state systems and kingdoms that overlapped the savanna zones in earlier centuries. The kingdoms of the southern forests, such as the Asante Confederation of Ghana, the Dahomey kingdom, and the Yoruba states, were smaller than the Sudanese kingdoms to the north. Although later in origin and quite different in character from the Sudanese systems, the forest kingdoms were well known and influential throughout the regions where they developed.

One of the distinctive features of these kingdoms and of the history of the region was the presence of cities and traditional systems of trade. The remains of Kumbi Saleh, the capital of ancient Ghana, have been uncovered in Mauritania. Other cities which pre-date any Western influence include: present-day Timbuctu and Gao in Mali, Ougadougou in Upper Volta, as well as Ibadan and Benin and Kumasi in the forest zones nearer the coast. Traditional systems of trade linked many of these cities, and trade routes criss-crossed the area.

(IFC/World Bank photo by Ray Witkin)

A worker cuts cloth at a textile mill in Ivory Coast. The patterns are similar to traditional patterns. Most of the cloth will be exported.

Gold, kola, leather goods, and cloth were carried from the south to the north. Salt and other goods were transported to the south. The population density of some of the West African regions and the early agricultural surpluses of the predominantly agricultural areas may have encouraged the trade. These traditional marketing activities have long contributed to the vitality of the region's towns. Traditional trading, land-holding, and social systems in West Africa did change over time, but they were not radically disrupted by intruding groups of European settlers as were Southern and East Africa, where white settlers radically altered the pattern of development.

The trading cities of the savannas became the links to North Africa and were especially influenced by Islam, which early gained a following among the ruling groups of the savanna and later spread through trade and holy wars. The more southern areas were also influenced by the religion, and today there are many converts to Islam in the south. However, these southern areas were much more strongly influenced by other factors including: the mixed heritage of a disastrous slave trade; another faith (Christianity); and direct contacts with European explorers, officials, and others. New cities such as Dakar, Freetown, and Lagos developed rapidly in the southern areas because of the increased activities on the shorelines of the colonial powers. Today the impact from the north and south on West Africa is still evident. For example, in the north, Libya has offered military and other assistance to governments and their opponents, and the Western trading system has pulled cash crops and minerals to the south and out through the Atlantic ports.

THE MOVEMENT OF PEOPLES IN THE WEST AFRICAN REGION

Today, as in the past, one characteristic of the West African region has been the never-ending migration of people. Although Africa is often viewed as a continent of stable isolated groups, it is subject to constant ebbs and flows. Herders have moved east and west across the savanna zones and south into the forests; traders and laborers have moved north and south. Professionals have moved to new coastal centers or to interior towns in other countries to service bureaucracies and schools.

Some peoples of West Africa have been especially mobile, including the Malinke, Fulani, Hausa, and Mossi. In the past, the Malinke journeyed from Mali, the center of Malinke habitation, to the coastal areas in Senegal and Gambia. Over time, Malinke traders called *Dyoula* made their way to Upper Volta, establishing towns such as Bobo Dioulasso and Ougadougou, and took up residence in the interior towns of Sierra Leone and Liberia, where they are known as *Mandingoes.* And they are still on the move.

The Fulani have developed their own patterns of transition and seasonal movement, and herders have also developed patterns of seasonal movement. They herd their cattle south across the savanna areas in the dry season, move them north in the rainy season and then return to where they started. Town-oriented groups of Fulani historically made journeys west to east, introducing people to Islam and Islamic learning as well as to the possibilities of trade. Today, Fulani have moved south in large numbers as a result of the deterioration of their grazing lands. Although the residents of Monrovia, Abidjan, or Lagos may be startled to see Fulani herdsmen with their canes and hide bags on the city streets, the Fulani's presence there is not surprising, in light of their past ventures.

The Hausa, the traders of northern Nigeria and Niger, are also found throughout many areas of West Africa. They are known less for their large numbers than for their distinctive dress and dominant trading activities. Their presence is so widespread that Hausa has been suggested as a possible future common language for West Africa. Mossi migrations from Upper Volta are regular and extensive. The Mossi and other Upper Volta laborers as well as laborers from Niger and Mali have gone regularly to Ivory Coast and Ghana, for instance, establishing an interdependence between these northern and southern regions.

(Oxfam America photo)

Women often control the trade of West African markets and acquire independent incomes from their activity.

These migrations have been duplicated by the movements of other groups in West Africa. The drastic expulsion of aliens by the Nigerian government in February 1983 was startling to the outside world in part because few realized that so many Ghanians, Nigeriens, Togolese, Benineans, and Cameroonians had recently taken up residence in Nigeria. Such immigration is not new, even though in this case it was stimulated by Nigeria's oil boom. Peoples along the West African coast such as the Yoruba, the Ewe, and the Vai, who are divided by the boundaries that colonialism arbitrarily imposed, have silently defied such boundaries and maintained close links with their own peoples. Other migrations have roots in the past: Sierra Leoneans worked all along the coast as craftsmen; Dahomeyans became the assistants of French administrators in other parts of French West Africa; and Yorubans traded in markets in a number of cities.

(Malcolm Harper, Oxfam)

The Balafon, a distinctive zylophone with gourd resonators, is popular throughout West Africa, and probably spread with the movement of peoples.

THE PROGRESS OF WEST AFRICAN INTEGRATION

The governments of the countries in the West African region have recognized the weaknesses inherent in the proliferation of states. Most agree that the peoples of the region would benefit from political cooperation and economic integration. Yet there are many obstacles blocking the efforts at regional development. National identity is valued as much today as it was in the days when Nkrumah, the charismatic Ghanaian leader, spoke of African unity and met with reluctance from other states. The more developed states, such as Nigeria and Ivory Coast, are not willing to share their wealth with smaller countries, which feel threatened by Nigerian and Ivorian strengths.

The political and economic systems in West Africa include the military regime of Nigeria, the one party state of Togo, the multi-party government of Senegal, and the many states such as Liberia and Niger which are moving toward varied democratic constitutional systems. Constructing any type of umbrella organization that can encompass these diverse systems still challenges the most skilled political tactician. Because the countries were under the rule of different colonial powers, French, English, and Portuguese all serve as official languages in different nations, and a variety of administrative traditions still hang on. Moreover, during colonial times, independent infrastructures were developed in each country, and these continue to orient economic activities toward the coast rather than encouraging links between the West African countries.

Multinational Organizations

Despite these problems, multinational organizations have developed in West Africa, stimulated both by the common problems that the countries face and by the obvious benefits of cooperation. There are only a few political confederations, such as Senegal and Gambia (Senegambia) and the new Mali Guinea Union, although there are many other organizations with limited and specific goals. The river basin commissions that have been created to manage the area's river systems may prove to be building blocks for broader developments. Of these, the Organization for the Development of the Senegal River (OMVS) has shown the most practical progress. Five groundnut-producing countries work together in the Groundnut Council; seven countries of the Volta River Basin cooperate with the World Health Organization and other programs to eradicate river blindness; and the West African Examinations Council standardizes secondary school examinations in several countries.

The most important and encompassing organization in the region is the Economic Organization of West African States (ECOWAS), which includes all states except the Western Sahara. Established in 1975 by the Treaty of Lagos, ECOWAS aims to promote trade, cooperation, and self-reliance. The progress of the organization thus far has been limited. Its major accomplishment, say some people, is that it exists and is recognized.

In light of recent events, this is indeed a major accomplishment. The first provision of ECOWAS to be put into effect allows for the free movement of citizens between countries without visas for ninety days. The expulsion of the two million ECOWAS citizens from Nigeria seemed to proclaim the failure of this regulation. Yet there has been little overt animosity between the governments, and the issue was not raised publicly at an ECOWAS meeting in May 1983. This may be because Nigeria gave a million dollar fund to ECOWAS to aid countries settling the evicted citizens. Also, countries recognized that their citizens had failed to register after ninety days, and the nations themselves had expelled such citizens in the past.

ECOWAS can recount some achievements. A survey of the economies of the countries has been carried out under the direction of the Nigerian Institute of Social and Economic Research. Several joint ventures have been developed; steps toward tariff reduction are being taken; and the competition between ECOWAS and CEAO (Economic Community of West Africa) the economic organization of French-speaking states, has been solved by limiting CEAO. It is hoped that the ECOWAS organization can become more effective at a grass roots level, eventually developing an African solution to regional development. The cross-cutting geographic zones, the overlinking histories, and the long tradition of African migrations provide a base on which practical moves for unity such as ECOWAS can be built.

(FAO photo by F. Mattioli)

The nations of West Africa seek unity and cooperation in solving regional problems.

Benin

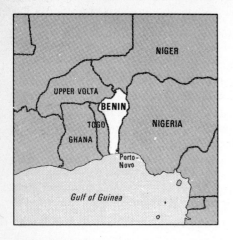

GEOGRAPHY

Area in Square Kilometers (Miles):
112,620 (43,483)
Land Usage: 80% arable; 19% forests
and game reserves; 1% nonarable
Capital (Population): Proto-Novo
(official: 144,000—1981); Cotonou (de
facto: 383,250—1981)
Climate: tropical

PEOPLE

Population
Total: 3,618,000 (1982 est.)
Per Square Kilometer (Mile): 32 (75)
Annual Growth Rate: 2.5%
Rural/Urban Population Ratio: 86/14

Health
Life Expectancy at Birth: 50 years
Infant Death Rate (Ratio): 154/1,000
Average Caloric Intake: 100% of FAO
minimum
Physicians Available: 1/17,050
Access to Safe Water: 20%

Languages
Official: French
Other Language Groups Represented:
Fon, Yoruba, Adja, Bariba, others

Religion(s)
80% traditional indigenous; 12%
Muslim; 8% Christian

Education
Adult Literacy Rate: 43% males; 17%
females
School Attendance: primary: 88%
boys, 42% girls; secondary: 27% boys,
14% girls

THE DAHOMEY KINGDOM

The Dahomey Kingdom, established in the early eighteenth century by the Fon people, was a highly organized state. The kings had a standing army, which included women; a centralized administration, whose officers kept census and tax records and organized the slave and, later, the oil trade; and a sophisticated artistic tradition. Benin, like Togo, has important links with Brazil, which date back to the time of the Dahomeyan Kingdom. Present Beninean families—such as the da Souzas, the da Silvas, and the Rodriguez—are descendants of Brazilians who settled on the coast in the mid-nineteenth century. Some were descended from former slaves, who may have been taken from Dahomey long before. They became the first teachers in Western-oriented public schools and continued in higher education themselves. In Brazil, Yoruba religious cults, which developed from those of the Yoruba in Benin and Nigeria, have become increasingly popular in recent years.

COMMUNICATION

Telephones: 16,000
Radios: 250,000
Televisions: 7,000
Newspapers: 1 daily; total circulation
1,100

TRANSPORTATION

Highways—Kilometers (Miles): 3,303
(2,052)
Railroads—Kilometers (Miles): 579
(360)
One international airport

GOVERNMENT

Type: one-party state, under military
rule since October 26, 1972
Constitution: 1979
Former Colonial Status: French
Independence Date: August 1, 1960
Head of State: General Mathieu
Kérékou (president)
Branches: National Revolutionary
Assembly; National Executive
Council; Central Committee of Party
Legal System: based on French civil
law and customary law
Political Parties: People's Revolu-
tionary Party of Benin
Suffrage: universal for adults

MILITARY

Number of Armed Forces: 4,160 (est.)
Armed Forces/Population: 1/909
Nuclear Weapons Status: none

ECONOMY

Currency ($ US Equivalent): 440 CFA
francs = $1
GDP: $830,000,000
Per Capita Income/GNP: $310
Workforce: 70% agriculture; 2% in-
dustry; 28% service
Inflation Rate: 9.1% (1970-1980)
Natural Resources: none known in
commercial quantities
Agriculture: palm products; cotton;
corn; yams; cassava; cocoa; coffee;
groundnuts
Industry: shoes; beer; textiles; cement
Energy Production: 19,500 kw
capacity
Energy Consumption Per Capita: 2
kwh

FOREIGN TRADE

Exports: agricultural products
Imports: consumer goods; cement;
lumber; fuels; foodstuffs; machinery;
transport equipment
Major Trading Partners: France; EEC
countries
Foreign Debt: $719,000,000
*Selected Membership in International
Organizations:* UN; OAU; West
African Monetary Union; Economic
Community of West African States

| Kingdom of Dahomey established **1625** | The French conquer the Dahomey Kingdom and declare a French protectorate **1892** | Dahomey becomes independent **1960** | General Mathieu Kerekou comes to power in sixth attempted military coup since independence **1972** | Name of Dahomey changed to Benin **1975** | Attempted coup involves exiles, mercenaries, and implicates Gabon, Morocco, and France **1977** | Nine million dollar loan agreement for rural development project signed with International Fund for Agricultural Development **1982** |

●IIII●IIIIIIIIIIIII●IIIIIIIIIIIIIIIIIIII●IIIIIIIIIIIIIIIIIIIIIIII●IIIIIIIIIIIIIIIIIIIIIIIII●IIIIIIIIIIIIIIIIIIIIIII●IIIIIIIIIIIIIIIIIIIIII●IIIIII●IIIII●● 1983

| March: Benin seeks loans to finance $1.8 billion development plan for 1983-1987 | October: Benin plays an active role in annual meeting of French-speaking African countries | April 1984: Pope John Paul II names Bernardin Cardinal Gantin of Benin to head powerful Congregation of Bishops |

BENIN

"I want the young people to stay and not to slip away to Nigeria," M. Armand, the district chief of Za-kpota in southern Benin, told a visitor. As a result, Armand has encouraged his people to build a cultural center with a dance hall and a cinema. Such attractions may offer short-term appeal, but it is doubtful that they will keep Benin citizens at home. Some will go to the larger cities; others will travel to Nigeria, Niger, or Togo.

COUNTRY OF MIGRANTS

For decades, emigration has been a way of life for many Benineans. Young men were educated in schools established by the French who ruled Dahomey (as Benin was called until 1975). The Benineans worked in the administration throughout French West Africa. After 1960, each independent country of French-speaking Africa developed its independent civil service, and Benin citizens lost their jobs. They returned home, where the competition for upper-level jobs intensified. This competition heightened the rivalry of different groups and regions in the political system.

Benin citizens continue to migrate today. Professionals may go to teach or practice in other West African countries. Other citizens go to Nigeria carrying goods to sell—especially food crops, which are in great demand across the border. The movement from Benin to Nigeria is a natural one, for Yoruba peoples in both countries are linked by strong family and cultural ties.

The area of transport and trade is one of the most vital sectors of the Beninean economy, and many people find legal as well as illegal employment in carrying goods. This is partly due to Benin's special geographical characteristics. The state is long and thin, encompassing several ecological zones and reaching back to the landlocked countries. Traditionally, it provided good routes to the coast because the savanna reaches the coast and there is little rain forest to impede travel. The roads are comparatively well developed, and the railroad carries goods from the port at Cotonou to northern areas of the country. An extension of the railroad is planned to reach Niamey, capital of Niger.

LIMITED DEVELOPMENT

While many citizens seek a living in other countries or through illicit trading across Benin's borders, there has been little development of the productive capacities of the country. Benin remains among the least-developed countries of the world. Production of cash crops such as palm oil, cocoa, coffee, and groundnuts has declined because of the declining official prices of such products. Some farmers are selling their cash crops on the black market, smuggling them across the borders. But a more promising development is the switch to yams, cassava, and other food crops. These crops are in demand in other regions of Benin, but they are actually sold in Nigeria where the price is right. There are very few industries, but sugar, cement, and palm oil factories are proposed, and a joint Libyan-Benin Company, *Belimines,* has been established for mineral development.

Some attribute the lack of the Benineans' progress to the government under which they live. For a dozen years after independence, there was little stability of government. In 1972 General Kerekou came to power and has maintained control of the country ever since. A 1977 coup attempt which involved European mercenaries and implicated Morocco and Gabon, provoked a long-lasting fear of opposition and criticism. However, the government seems less dictatorial and arbitrary than some would imply. The leaders declare themselves to be Marxist-Leninists. This orientation has resulted in a one-party state (the People's Revolutionary Party of Benin); the nationalization of industries, banks, and insurance companies; the nationalization of schools; and a special court system. (Other developments such as the encouragement of private investment, are not in line with the proposed Marxist-Leninism.)

Although the regime is still controlled by the military, a Constitution was developed in 1979; civilians now occupy the major offices. Recently, ties with France have been reinstituted. Local enterprise is encouraged by the government. Local committees and rural youth clubs are encouraged to be self-reliant and to take up self-help projects such as the sinking of wells and the construction of public buildings, such as the cultural center and cinema, which may encourage the youth of Za-kpota to stay at home.

DEVELOPMENT

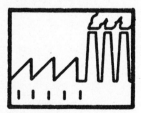

Palm oil plantations were established in Benin in the mid-nineteenth century by Africans. They have continued to be African-owned and capitalist-oriented in a society that is proclaimed socialist. Today, there are some thirty million trees, and palm oil products are a major export used for cooking, lighting, soap, margarine, and lubricants.

FREEDOM

The People's Revolutionary Party of Benin does not allow for much internal competition. Party and government control are more noticeable than in some other African countries with one-party states. The media is also controlled. There are perhaps 200 political prisoners.

HEALTH/WELFARE

One-third of the national budget of Benin goes to education, and the number of students receiving primary education has risen to fifty percent of the school-age population. College graduates have served as temporary teachers through the National Service System, but more teachers and higher salaries are needed.

ACHIEVEMENTS

Fon appliqued cloths have been described as "one of the gayest and liveliest of the contemporary African art forms." Formerly, these cloths were made and used by the Dahomeyan kings. Now they are sold to tourists, but they still portray the motifs and symbols of past rulers and the society they ruled.

Cape Verde

GEOGRAPHY

Area in Square Kilometers (Miles):
4,033 (1,557)
Capital (Population): Praia (21,494—
1970)
Climate: temperate

PEOPLE

Population
Total: 335,000 (1982 est.)
Per Square Kilometer (Mile): 83 (215)
Annual Growth Rate: 1.7%
Rural/Urban Population Ratio: 75/25

Health
Life Expectancy at Birth: 62 years
Infant Death Rate (Ratio): 82/1,000
Average Caloric Intake: 133% of FAO
minimum
Physicians Available (Ratio): 1/5,510

Languages
Krioulu, Portuguese, others

Religion(s)
65 Catholic; 35% indigenous traditional beliefs

Education
Adult Literacy Rate: 54% males; 34%
females

COMMUNICATION

Telephones: 2,000
Radios: 41,000
Newspapers: 7 weeklies

CAPE VERDEANS IN AMERICA

Large scale immigration of Cape Verdeans to the United States began in the nineteenth century. Today the Cape Verdean-American community is larger than that of Cape Verde itself and is concentrated in southern New England. Most early immigrants arrived in this region aboard whaling and packet ships. Racial prejudice has from the beginning served as a barrier to the economic and social advancement of Cape Verdeans. The community has, on the whole, prospered and is presently better educated than the national norm. The 1980 census was the first to try to count Cape Verdeans as a separate ethnic group.

TRANSPORTATION

Highways—Kilometers (Miles): 1,300
(808)
Railroads—Kilometers (Miles): none
One international airport

GOVERNMENT

Type: republic
Constitution: 1980
Former Colonial Status: Portuguese
Independence Date: July 1975
Head of State: Aristides Maria Pereira
(president); General Pedro Verona
Rodrigues Pires (prime minister)
Branches: president; cabinet; National
Popular Assembly; National Council of
Justice
Legal System: being formulated
Political Parties: African Party for the
Independence of Cape Verde
Suffrage: universal over age 15

MILITARY

Number of Armed Forces: 3,000-4,000
Armed Forces/Population: 1/98
*Military Expenditures (% of Central
Government Expenditures):*
$15,000,000 (5%)
Nuclear Weapons Status: none
Current Hostilities: none

ECONOMY

Currency ($ US Equivalent): 80
escudos = $1
GDP: $40,700,000
Per Capita Income/GNP: $350
Workforce: 57% agriculture; 14%
industry; 29% service
Inflation Rate: 12% (1982)
Natural Resources: fish; agricultural
land; salt deposits
Agriculture: corn; beans; manioc; sweet
potatoes; bananas
Industry: fishing; flour mills; salt
Energy Production: 6,000 kw capacity
Energy Consumption Per Capita: 27
kwh

FOREIGN TRADE

Exports: fish; bananas; salt; flour
Imports: petroleum products; corn; rice;
machinery; textiles
Major Trading Partners: Portugal;
UK; Japan; West Africa
Foreign Debt:
*Selected Membership in International
Organizations:* UN; OAU; Non-
Aligned Movement; ECOWAS

Cape Verdean settlement begins **1462**

Slavery abolished **1869**

Thousands of Cape Verdeans die of starvation during World War II **1940s**

PAIGC founded **1956**

Warfare begins in Guinea-Bissau **1963**

Amilcar Cabral assassinated **1973**

Coup in Lisbon initiates Portuguese de-colonization process **1974**

Independence **1975**

Hurricane devastates the islands **1982**

1983

March: Negotiations between Angola and South Africa take place on islands

September: President visits the UN and United States

THE REPUBLIC OF CAPE VERDE

The Republic of Cape Verde is an archipelago located about 400 miles west of the Senegalese' Cape Verde or "Green Cape," after which it is named. Unfortunately, green is a color that today is all too rarely seen by the islands' citizens, who for the last sixteen years have suffered from drought. As a result, the young republic—independent since 1975—has had to rely on foreign aid and remittances from Cape Verdeans living abroad for its survival. Despite this desperate situation, most Cape Verdeans are proud to finally be their own masters after nearly 500 years of Portuguese colonial rule.

Most Cape Verdeans are the descendants of Portuguese colonists (who were often convicts) and African slaves. Both groups began to settle on the islands during the mid-fifteenth century, and their early interaction led to the development of the Cape Verdean Kriolu language. This language today serves as a common language not only in Cape Verde but Guinea-Bissau as well. Under Portuguese rule, Cape Verdeans were generally treated as second-class citizens, although a few rose to positions of prominence. Economic stagnation exacerbated by cycles of severe drought drove many islanders to emigrate elsewhere in Africa, Western Europe, and the Americas. The largest of these overseas Cape Verdean communities today can be found in the United States.

LIBERATION STRUGGLE

In 1956 the African Party for the Independence of Guinea-Bissau and Cape Verde (PAIGC) was formed under the dynamic leadership of Amilcar Cabral, who was assassinated in 1973. Between 1963 and 1974, PAIGC organized a successful liberation struggle against the Portuguese in Guinea-Bissau, which was ultimately instrumental in bringing about the independence of both territories. For a period in the late 1970s Cape Verde and Guinea-Bissau were ruled separately by a united PAIGC, but after a 1980 coup in Guinea-Bissau, the party divided along national lines. In 1981, the Cape Verdean PAIGC formally renounced its Guinea links and became the PAICV.

The greatest challenge for the PAIGC/CV since independence has been coping with the effects of the drought. Lack of rainfall in the past has occasionally resulted in the deaths of up to fifty percent of the islands' population. Although the availability of international food aid—which presently accounts for about ninety percent of the caloric consumption—has warded off famine in recent years, malnutrition remains a serious problem. The government has undertaken a number of initiatives in order to strengthen local food production as well as to create employment opportunities for the nearly eighty percent of the workforce that is agrarian. These steps include drilling for underground water, terracing,

and irrigation. In addition, a water desalinization plant is being built with United States assistance. However, President Aristides Pereira, who is also chairman of the International Committee to Combat Drought in the Sahel, has frankly admitted that the islands are likely to remain dependent on imported food for the forseeable future.

LITTLE INDUSTRY

Although a few factories have been built recently, there is, at present, still very little industry and virtually no known exploitable mineral reserves on the islands. Exports pay for only five percent of the nation's imports. Trade deficits are partially offset, however, by the external earnings of the local service sector—most particularly the international airport on Sal island, which conducts lucrative business with South African Airways. Cape Verde's overall economic picture is likely to remain bleak for quite some time, however.

DEVELOPMENT

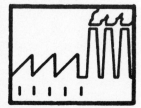

Since independence, the greatest progress has taken place in social services, particularly education. In 1980, ninety-five percent of primary school age children attended school.

FREEDOM

Dissent is limited, but tolerated, in Cape Verde's one-party system. Government decision-makers are answerable to elected bodies.

HEALTH/WELFARE

Greater access to health facilities has resulted in a sharp drop in infant mortality and a rise in life expectancy. Clinics have begun to encourage family planning.

ACHIEVEMENTS

Cape Verdean culture is renown for its artistic creativity, particularly in music and poetry. Popular Cape Verdean music groups, such as Balinundo, have begun to enjoy an increasing international audience.

The Gambia

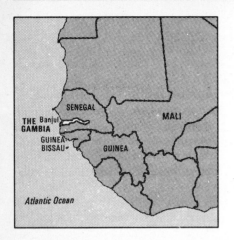

GEOGRAPHY

Area in Square Kilometers (Miles): 10,367 (4,003)
Land Usage: 25% savanna; 16% swamps; 4% forest parks; 55% upland arable areas, built-up areas, and other
Capital (Population): Banjul (49,181—1980)
Climate: subtropical

PEOPLE

Population
Total: 635,000 (1982 est.)
Per Square Kilometer (Mile): 56 (158)
Annual Growth Rate: 2.8%
Rural/Urban Population Ratio: 81/19

Health
Life Expectancy at Birth: 36 years
Infant Death Rate (Ratio): 198/1,000
Average Caloric Intake: 97% of FAO minimum
Physicians Available (Ratio): 1/11,470

Languages
Mandinka; Wolof; Fula; Sarakole; Diula; English; others
Official: English

Religion(s)
85% Muslim; 14% Christian; 1% traditional indigenous

Education
Adult Literacy Rate: 29% males; 12% females
School Attendance: primary: 67% boys, 37% girls; secondary: 19% boys, 8% girls

COMMUNICATION

Telephones: 3,500
Radios: 75,000
Newspapers: 6 dailies; total circulation 28,000

TRANSPORTATION

Highways—Kilometers (Miles): 3,083 (1,915)
Railroads—Kilometers (Miles): none
One international airport

GOVERNMENT

Type: republic
Constitution: April 24, 1970
Former Colonial Status: British
Independence Date: February 18, 1965
Head of State: Sir Alhaji Dawda Kairaba Jawara (president)
Branches: president and Cabinet; House of Representatives; independent judiciary
Legal System: based on English Common Law and customary law
Political Parties: People's Progressive Party; United Party; National Convention Party
Suffrage: universal for adults

MILITARY

Military Expenditures (% of Central Government Expenditures): 6.2%
Nuclear Weapons Status: none
Current Hostilities: internal conflicts; coup attempt in 1981

ECONOMY

Currency ($ US Equivalent): 4 dalasis = $1
GDP: $200,000,000
Per Capita Income/GNP: $360
Workforce: 79% agriculture; 9% industry; 12% service
Inflation Rate: 9% (1981)
Natural Resources: fish
Agriculture: peanuts; rice; millet; sorghum; fish; palm kernels; livestock
Industry: peanut products; brewery; soft drinks; agricultural machinery assembly; wood and metal working; clothing; tourism
Energy Production: 10,000 kw capacity
Energy Consumption Per Capita: 57 kw

FOREIGN TRADE

Exports: peanuts; palm kernels; fish; hides; skins
Imports: textiles; foodstuffs; machinery; transportation equipment
Major Trading Partners: EEC countries
Foreign Debt: $213,600,000
Selected Membership in International Organizations: UN; OAU; African Development Bank; Economic Community of West African States

June: Gambia
and Nigeria sign
a cooperative
agreement and
establish a
joint commission,
especially
concerned with
trade

August: After
Amnesty Interna-
tional reports on
the use of leg
irons in Gambian
prisons, the
government
outlaws them

April 1984: Final
trial in connection
with the plot of
1981 results in
24 death sen-
tences, but
commutations
may occur

GAMBIA

"The Gambia is a banana in the teeth of Senegal," is an African saying, and some believe that Senegal is preparing to enjoy a good meal. An agreement establishing the confederation of Senegambia was signed in December 1981, and the new alliance was inaugurated February 1, 1982. A cabinet of five Senegalese and four Gambians has been instituted to administer the evolving confederation.

Senegalese and Gambians can benefit from such an arrangement. Mandinka, Wolof, and Fulani peoples make up a substantial percentage of both countries' populations, and these peoples commute regularly across the borders. They share Islamic beliefs and practices as well as economic patterns based on herding and agriculture, including the cultivation of groundnuts as a cash crop.

SENEGAMBIAN PROSPECTS

Yet the confederation has not been the result of popular feeling and the two countries have different colonial traditions and are divided in their orientations today. In the seventeenth and eighteenth centuries, British merchants on the Gambia River competed against the French in present-day Senegal. The rivalry continued when British and French government authorities took control of the areas. During the colonial period, the peoples were influenced by different types of administration and education, and they learned different European languages. In the 1870s, the two colonial powers discussed exchanges of territory that would have made Gambia a French territory, but no exchange occurred.

In the years before and after independence, the possibility of union was raised but never followed through.

The Gambians—whose state is one of the smallest in Africa—seem very resistant to the present confederation. There was no popular referendum on the union, and opposition members of Parliament walked out when the agreement was presented for a vote. It is not only that Gambians fear being swallowed up by Senegal, whose economic and monetary policies would not be to their advantage; many people also believe the movement toward union is designed to keep President Dawda Jawara in power in the Gambia. The first public announcement about the confederacy followed on the heels of a coup attempt against Jawara's government in July 1981, during which 400 to 500 persons were killed. A group of the Gambian Paramilitary Field Force attempted to set up a National Revolutionary Council and a socialist state in the capital, Banjul, during Jawara's absence in England. Jawara called on Senegal for help, and President Abdul Diouf sent troops. Military integration of the two forces was the first step toward eventual union, and Senegalese troops remain in the country.

Jawara has been able to maintain his position. Over one thousand people were jailed at the time of the coup, and trials have resulted in some executions. Other Gambians have gone into exile. In the elections of May 4 and 5, 1982, Jawara received seventy-two percent of the ballots cast. His opponent, Sheriff Dibba, who was in prison at the time and who is against the confederation, received one-fourth of the vote.

ECONOMIC DIFFICULTIES

Economic and social conditions are likely to cause Gambians to question their government even further. The 1982 harvest of groundnuts, Gambia's major cash crop, was triple that of 1981. But three consecutive earlier harvests had adverse effects on farmers, and the price for the present harvest is lower than it has ever been. The tourist trade from the United States and the Scandinavian countries has been a major source of foreign exchange for Gambia in recent years, but economic conditions in Europe and the coup in Gambia have cut the number of tourists by about forty percent. The continuing effects of the droughts have caused crowded grazing conditions as well as food scarcity and have increased the migration of young people to Banjul.

The government hopes to alleviate the economic problems facing Gambians by emphasizing rural development, encouraging rice and cotton production, and expanding tourist facilities. The development of a bridge and dam on the Gambia River and the irrigation programs planned through OMVG—the Gambia River Organization, consisting of Senegal, the Gambia, Mali, and Guinea—may make life better for Gambians and also reconcile them to a future within Senegambia.

DEVELOPMENT

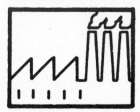

Groundnuts were Gambia's main economic support at the time of independence. The harvests have been reduced one-third during recent dry seasons. Now there are efforts to modernize the groundnut production and to develop alternate cash crops, such as cotton or rice.

FREEDOM

Gambia's record in human rights is strong, although restrictions, including a curfew, were instituted after the coup of July 1981. In order to insure fair trials for those accused of planning the coup, judges from neighboring countries were engaged.

HEALTH/WELFARE

The Community and Rural Development Training Center at Mansakonko provides a two-year course with field work for community development workers, who are then stationed in villages. The practical skills that they gain include forestry, brick making, and use of new stoves that can save the scarce wood of the Gambia.

ACHIEVEMENTS

Gambian *griots*—hereditary bards and musicians such as Banna and Dembo Kanute—have maintained a traditional art. Formerly, griots were attached to ruling families; now they perform over Radio Gambia and are popular throughout West Africa.

Ghana

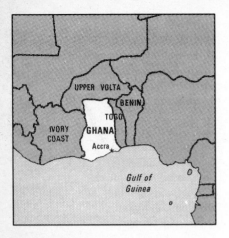

NKRUMAH

Kwame Nkrumah is a name that is remembered by peoples all over the world. Nkrumah developed ideas and institutions for peacefully but actively resisting British domination of Ghana, and he founded the Convention People's Party (CCP), which involved peoples of all walks of life in that struggle. Nkrumah believed that none of Africa was free until all of Africa was free. His efforts to develop a united Africa and his exploration of and warnings about neo-colonialism in Africa remain influential. Although his government was overthrown by a military coup, later regimes that criticized him nevertheless recognized his greatness and importance.

GEOGRAPHY

Area in Square Kilometers (Miles): 238,538 (92,100)
Land Usage: 19% agricultural; 60% forests and brush; 21% other
Capital (Population): Accra (564,194—1970)
Climate: tropical to semi-arid

PEOPLE

Population
Total: 12,244,000 (1982 est.)
Per Square Kilometer (Mile): 51 (133)
Annual Growth Rate: 3.1%
Rural/Urban Population Ratio: 64/36

Health
Life Expectancy at Birth: 55 years
Infant Death Rate (Ratio): 103/1,000
Average Caloric Intake: 85% of FAO minimum
Physicians Available (Ratio): 1/7,630
Access to Safe Water: 35%

Languages
Official: English
Others Spoken: Akan (including dialects, Fanti, Asante, Twi); Ewe; Ga; Hausa; English; others

Religion(s)
45% indigenous beliefs; 43% Christian; 12% Muslim

Education
Adult Literacy Rate: 43% males; 18% females
School Attendance: primary: 77% boys, 60% girls; secondary: 44% boys, 27% girls

COMMUNICATION

Telephones: 65,000
Radios: 2,000,000
Televisions: 70,000
Newspapers: 5 dailies; total circulation 345,000

TRANSPORTATION

Highways—Kilometers (Miles): 32,200 (20,009)
Railroads—Kilometers (Miles): 953 (592)
Two international airports

GOVERNMENT

Type: republic; governed by Provisional National Defense Council
Constitution: suspended in 1981
Former Colonial Status: British
Independence Date: March 6, 1957
Head of State: Flight Lieutenant Jerry Rawlings (chairman of PNDC)
Branches: executive authority vested in Provisional National Defense Council (PNDC)
Legal System: based on English Common Law and customary law
Political Parties: political parties banned after 1981 coup
Suffrage: universal over age 21

MILITARY

Number of Armed Forces: 15,300
Armed Forces/Population: 1/845
Nuclear Weapons Status: none
Current Hostilities: internal conflicts; coup attempts in 1982

ECONOMY

Currency ($ US Equivalent): 35 cedis = $1
GDP: $31,220,000,000
Per Capita Income/GNP: $360
Workforce: 53% agriculture; 20% industry; 27% services
Inflation Rate: 34.8% (1970-1980) 180% (1982)
Natural Resources: gold; diamonds; bauxite; manganese; fish; timber
Agriculture: cocoa; coconuts; coffee; subsistence crops; rubber
Industry: mining; lumber; light manufacturing; fishing; aluminum
Energy Production: 1,157,000 kw capacity
Energy Consumption Per Capita: 365 kwh

FOREIGN TRADE

Exports: cocoa beans; gold; timber; manganese ore; aluminum
Imports: petroleum; food; industrial raw materials; machinery; transportation equipment; alumina
Major Trading Partners: UK; Western Europe; West African countries
Foreign Debt: $1,309,700,000
Selected Membership in International Organizations: UN; OAU; Economic Community of West African States; British Commonwealth

Timeline

Portuguese fort built at Elmina **1482**	Establishment of Asante Confederation under Osei Tutu **1690s**	The "Bonds" of 1844 signed by British officials and Fante chiefs as equals **1844**	British finally conquer the Asante; a final step in British control of the region **1901**	Ghana is the first of the colonial territories in sub-Saharan Africa to become independent **1957**	Nkrumah is overthrown by a military coup **1966**	First coup of Flight Lieutenant Rawlings **1979**	Second coup by Rawlings; PNDC formed **1981**	Three justices, one retired military officer murdered; Ghana's borders closed by PNDC **1982**

1983

February: A million or more Ghanaians are expelled from Nigeria	January-February 1984: Plans for forthcoming elections to National Assembly are announced	June 1984: Borders with Ivory Coast and Togo are opened and curfew is lifted

GHANA
A PEOPLE'S REVOLUTION?

Not long after the December 31, 1981 coup that brought him to power in Ghana, for the second time in three years, Flight Lieutenant Jerry Rawlings said: "What we would like to do is to set up conditions to make sure that the people will not be taken for granted anymore." People must, he continued, "take their destiny into their own hands."

Right after the coup and the establishment of the Provisional National Defence Council (PNDC) of civilians and soldiers, People's Defense Committees, made up of ordinary citizens, began to operate throughout the country as watchdogs and overseers. Students marshalled forces in a volunteer emergency effort to move 100 thousand tons of cocoa down to the ports from interior farms. Later in 1982, People's Courts were formed, and laymen acted as judges. People indeed seemed to be taking their destiny into their own hands.

However the situation was not entirely positive. The new government moved slowly in dealing with the economic problems which brought the new leaders to power and the situation reached crisis proportions in early 1983. Food costs doubled and tripled. Ghana had almost no foreign exchange and the PNDC banned all imports, including the fertilizer needed to nourish the country's "Green Revolution." Nearly a million Ghanaians expelled from Nigeria strained the country's food resources and expanded the number of the unemployed.

The government acted slowly but planned carefully. A campaign to encourage agricultural production has led to increased cultivation. A three year economic program, including a devaluation of the cedi, encouragement of foreign investment and austerity measures is having results and has won praise from the World Bank and the IMF. Aid has been forthcoming from outside agencies.

GHANA'S STRENGTHS

Ghana has many strengths on which to build. The Ghanaians themselves, who number over twelve million persons, are the country's most important resource. They belong to nearly seventy-five different and varied ethnic groups.

The traditional leaders have maintained their positions and influence, if not their power, in Ghana today. They and the citizens around them are proud of the historically important state systems that they inherited, such as the Asante Confederation that was centered around the interior city of Kumasi. Modern Ghanaian governments cannot interfere with a chief's jurisdiction in traditional matters. As Rawlings himself has said, "The chief is the embodiment of his people."

PAST GOVERNMENT PATTERNS

Ghana became independent in 1957 and was a leader in the continental struggle for independence. People were optimistic about the country's future. Looking back it seems that Ghana has gone backward instead of forward.

Many explanations are given for this backward turn. There were no consistent government policies to meet the country's needs. During Nkrumah's time political controls increased the power of the government but did not lead to economic development or the fulfillment of socialist aims. Corruption increased. Mismanagement, limited technical resources and lack of skilled personnel were responsible for some failures. The decline in the price of Ghana's major export, cocoa, and the rise in the cost of imports contributed to worsening conditions.

In 1966 Nkrumah was overthrown by a group of military officers, and a National Liberation Council came into power. Other military groups have followed. In each case of takeover, the military leaders have maintained control until a Constitution and civilian rule could be established. In each case, the civilian regime has not fulfilled expectations and has been overtaken by military action. Rawlings first came to power in a coup of June 1979. Present government has superceded the civilian government that Rawlings' original regime had sponsored. Not everyone approves of Rawlings' leadership and there have been efforts by Ghanaian exiles to unseat him. The announcement of elections for a National Assembly indicate that a new civilian government may soon have the opportunity to prove itself.

DEVELOPMENT

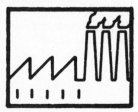

The Akosombo Dam, constructed on the Volta River in the early 1960s, was a great achievement of Nkrumah's government. Its electricity continues to benefit Ghanaian citizens, enterprises such as the VALCO alumina plant, and nearby countries to which it is sold. The lake formed behind the dam is one of the largest man-made lakes in the world.

FREEDOM

Curfews, closed borders, pressure on the press, and new courts that do not allow for appeal are measures that have been imposed by the present government. The strong tradition of respect for individual and community rights is evident in the protests raised against these restraints.

HEALTH/WELFARE

Ghanaians who were expelled from Nigeria in early 1983 brought home needed medicines, spare parts for cars, batteries for radios, and equipment—all of which have improved the people's welfare, if only temporarily. Permanent solutions to these problems are still needed.

ACHIEVEMENTS

Ghanaian arts are rooted in the past and are still lively today. In Asante areas, for instance, brass vessels, tiny gold weights, gold staffs, royal regalia, and brilliantly colored silk cloths are only a few examples of arts that are used in ordinary and ritual occasions and that are endowed with symbolic meanings.

Guinea

THE FOUTA DJALLON

The Fouta Djallon plateau of west central Guinea contains some of the largest bauxite deposits in the world, and the rivers that formed its valleys have great hydroelectric potential. Historically, the highlands have been a meeting ground for different trading systems from the north and south and the site of an important pre-colonial state. In the 1720s a reformist Islamic government was established in the area, the result of a *jihad* or religious war led by Fulani people. During the nineteenth century, this Muslim state was ruled by *almamis* (religious and political leaders) who represented two Fulani dynasties in an unusual arrangement whereby government offices alternated biannually.

GEOGRAPHY

Area in Square Kilometers (Miles): 246,048 (95,000)
Land Usage: 3% cultivated; 10% forests
Capital (Population): Conakry (525,671—1972)
Climate: tropical

PEOPLE

Population
Total: 5,285,000 (1982 est.)
Per Square Kilometer (Mile): 22 (56)
Annual Growth Rate: 2.6%
Rural/Urban Population Ratio: 81/19

Health
Life Expectancy at Birth: 44 years
Infant Death Rate (Ratio): 165/1,000
Average Caloric Intake: 78% of FAO minimum
Physicians Available (Ratio): 1/16,630
Access to Safe Water: 10%

Languages
Official: French
Others Spoken: Fula, Mandinka, Susu, French, others

Religion(s)
75% Muslim; 24% traditional indigenous beliefs; less than 1% Christian

Education
Adult Literacy Rate: 14% males; 4% females
School Attendance: primary: 44% boys, 22% girls; secondary: 23% boys, 9% girls

COMMUNICATION

Telephones: 10,000
Radios: 144,000
Televisions: 7,000
Newspapers: 1 daily; total circulation 20,000

TRANSPORTATION

Highways—Kilometers (Miles): 7,604 (4,725)
Railroads—Kilometers (Miles): 805 (500)
Two international airports

GOVERNMENT

Type: republic; military regime since April 1984
Constitution: November 12, 1958; suspended
Former Colonial Status: French
Independence Date: October 2, 1958
Head of State: Colonel Lansana Konté (president)
Branches: Military Committee for National Reconstruction
Legal System: based on French Civil Law and customary law
Political Parties: none
Suffrage: suspended

MILITARY

Number of Armed Forces: 9,900
Armed Forces/Population: 1/533
Nuclear Weapons Status: none
Current Hostilities: none

ECONOMY

Currency ($ US Equivalent): 24 sylis = $1
GDP: $1,750,000,000
Per Capita Income/GNP: $310
Workforce: 82% agriculture; 11% industry; 7% services
Inflation Rate: 4.4% (1970-1980); 25% (1981)
Natural Resources: bauxite; iron ore; diamonds; gold; water power
Agriculture: rice; cassava, millet; corn; coffee; bananas; palm products; pineapples
Industry: bauxite; alumina; light manufacturing and processing
Energy Production: 75,000 kw capacity
Energy Consumption Per Capita: 900 kwh

FOREIGN TRADE

Exports: bauxite; alumina; pineapples; bananas; palm kernels; coffee
Imports: petroleum; production materials; machinery; transportation equipment; foodstuffs
Major Trading Partners: Communist countries; Western Europe; United States
Foreign Debt: $1,620,900,000
Selected Membership in International Organizations: UN; OAU; African Development Bank; Economic Community of West African States

A major
Islamic kingdom
is established
in the Futa
Djalon
1700s

Samori Touré,
leader of a state
in the Guinea and
Ivory Coast
interior, defeated
by the French
1898

Guineans vote
"no" to continued
membership in
the French
Community;
independent
republic is
formed
1958

French President
Giscard d'Estaing
visits Conakry;
the beginning
of reconciliation
between France
and Guinea
1968

Touré is
unanimously
elected to
another 7-year
presidential
term; visits US
and Paris
1982

1983

March: Guinea
and Mali gov-
ernments sign an
agreement to
move toward full
integration

March 1984:
Sekou Touré
dies

April 1984: Army
officers take over
the government

GUINEA

Nineteen eighty-three marked the twenty-fifth anniversary of Guinea's independence from France, the colonial power that established dominance over the area and people in the late nineteenth century and determined their government for sixty years. In the referendum of September 28, 1958, Guineans voted to leave the community of self-governing West African states, which France had established. They were the only people in the community to opt for freedom. The French reacted harshly, withdrawing all aid, personnel, and equipment—even removing telephones and geranium plants. This event has had a major influence on the contemporary history of this formerly socialist one-party state. Guinea was isolated from Western countries, which did not come to its aid in this hour of need, and close ties were developed with countries of the Eastern bloc.

SEKOU TOURÉ AND HIS SUCCESSORS

Nineteen eighty-three also marked the end of an era with the sudden death of President Ahmed Sekou Touré in March 1984. It was Touré who urged people to vote for independence in 1958 and who had been reelected to the presidency in May 1982 by an overwhelming majority. Touré was descended from Samori Touré, the great revolutionary Malinke warrior who founded an extensive if short-lived Islamic state in West Africa in the late nineteenth century.

On April 3, a week after Touré's death, the army stepped in fearing a power struggle among his successors. The coup was accomplished without a shot and has been well received by Guineans. The powerful Democratic Party of Guinea has been disbanded, a new government formed under the leadership of Colonel Lansana Konté, and a ten point program for national recovery set forth, including the restoration of human rights and the renovation of the economy.

Over the years Sekou Touré had jailed all those whom he perceived as opponents to his rule and philosophy. Guinea exiles in France and other places as well as a 1982 Amnesty International Campaign had publicized human rights violations in Guinea. Sekou Touré's attitude that there were no political prisoners in Guinea only "traitors" may have been connected with a 1970 plot to overthrow his government which was timed to coincide with a Portuguese invasion of the capital city, Conakry. The new government has freed all political prisoners and Konté has declared that no members of the old government will be tried or executed for political crimes although they may be tried for economic crimes.

For twenty years Guinea maintained its socialist ideology despite the lack of progress in the economy. In the late 1970s, popular resistance included demonstrations by women's groups—usually Touré's strong supporters—over the scarcity of necessary commodities. Touré himself, in his last few years, began to modify socialist policies and seek new friends abroad. He encouraged private traders within the country. He sought ties with countries of the Arab world, stressing the unity that they shared in Islam. A renewed association with France

was highlighted by the visit of President Giscard d'Estaing to Guinea in 1978 and by the later contacts between Touré and his personal friend socialist President Francois Mitterand. In June 1982 Touré met with officials, businessmen and bankers during a visit to the United States.

The new government is dismantling the socialist economy, encouraging private enterprise, and seeking help from abroad. Public corporations have been disbanded and private traders further encouraged. The new regime met an empty treasury. Aid has already been contributed by outside countries such as Saudi Arabia, France, Morocco, and the Soviet Union.

Although the OAU meeting originally scheduled to be held in Conakry in November has been transferred to Addis Ababa, it seems certain that Guinea's long standing commitment to African unity will not change. Touré's recent efforts to improve relations with neighboring countries such as Mali, Sierra Leone, Liberia and Ivory Coast, also can be expected to continue.

The new government has maintained a low profile and indicates that it intends that its role will be a transitional one. The leaders have declared that they will stay in office until the evils of racism, regionalism, sectarianism and nepotism have been abolished.

DEVELOPMENT

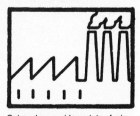

Guinea has a wide variety of minerals and mining has been described as the "linchpin" in its economy. Foreign capital investment has been encouraged for the exploitation of the 1.8 billion tons of iron ore found in the interior Nimba Mountain range. The mine is to open in 1983-1984 and will supplement the bauxite and alumina mines and plants that now provide ninety percent of Nimba's exports.

FREEDOM

A 1982 Amnesty International campaign focused on seventy-eight hundred disappeared political prisoners arrested during the 1970s. The new government has released all political prisoners, and has promised press freedom and formation of trade unions will be allowed.

HEALTH/WELFARE

Guineans have emphasized educational development. The new leaders are reorganizing the educational system, restoring French as only language of instruction, allowing private schools, securing school supplies, and seeking assistance for teacher training.

ACHIEVEMENTS

The sensitive and poetic writings of novelist Camara Laye (1924-1983) have introduced many African, European, and American readers to African ways of life and beliefs. The autobiographical *The Dark Child* illustrates the varied experiences faced by students in Africa in contemporary times.

Guinea-Bissau

GEOGRAPHY

Area in Square Kilometers (Miles):
26,400 (11,000)
Capital (Population): Bissau
(109,214—1979)
Climate: tropical

PEOPLE

Population

Total: 594,000 (1982 est.)
Per Square Kilometer (Mile): 16 (54)
Annual Growth Rate: 1.7%

Health

Life Expectancy at Birth: 41 years
Infant Death Rate (Ratio): 149/1,000
Average Caloric Intake: 74% of FAO
minimum

Languages

Official: Portuguese
Others Spoken: Krioulo; Fula;
Mandinka; Manjara; Balante;
Portuguese; others

Religion(s)

65% traditional indigenous beliefs;
32% Muslim; 3% Christian

Education

Adult Literacy Rate: 25% males; 13%
females
School Attendance: primary: 100%
boys, 61% girls; secondary: 33% boys,
7% girls

COMMUNICATION

Telephones: 3,000
Radios: 26,000
Newspapers: 1 daily; total circulation
6,000

AMILCAR CABRAL

Amilcar Cabral (1924-1973), born in Cape Verde and raised in Guinea-Bissau, was an idealist who developed plans for his country's liberation and an activist who worked to put these plans into action. He was a friend of Agostinho Neto of Angola, a founding member of Angola's present ruling party MPLA, and he worked in Angola. Cabral wanted and worked for an African system of government, a change in structures that would mean "a reorganization of the country on new lines." He believed that a revolution could not result from leadership alone; everyone must fight a mental battle and know their goals before taking arms. Cabral's work with peasants from 1952-1954, while carrying out an agricultural census, helped him to understand and reach rural peoples who were to be the crucial force in the development of Guinea-Bissau's independence from Portugal.

TRANSPORTATION

Highways—Kilometers (Miles): 3,218
(1,999)
Railroads—Kilometers (Miles): none
One international airport

GOVERNMENT

Type: republic; overseen by Revolutionary Council
Constitution: September 24, 1973;
abolished after 1980 coup
Former Colonial Status: Portuguese
Independence Date: September 24,
1973
Head of State: Brigadier General Joao
Bernardo Vieira (president and Revolutionary Council chairman)
Branches: president and Cabinet
overseen by Revolutionary Council
Legal System: based on Portuguese
Civil Law and customary law
Political Parties: African Party for the
Independence of Guinea Bissau and
Cape Verde (Paige)
Suffrage: universal over age 15

MILITARY

Number of Armed Forces: 6,250
Armed Forces/Population: 1/131
Nuclear Weapons Status: none
Current Hostilities: none

ECONOMY

Currency ($ US Equivalent): 82
Guinean pesos = $1
GDP: $200,000,000
Per Capita Income/GNP: $170
Workforce: 90% of economically active
population engaged in subsistence
agriculture
Inflation Rate: 50% (1981)
Natural Resources: bauxite; timber;
shrimp; fish
Agriculture: peanuts; rice; palm kernels
Industry: agricultural processing; hide
and skins; beer and soft drinks
Energy Production: 11,000 kw
capacity
Energy Consumption Per Capita: 1
kwh

FOREIGN TRADE

Exports: palm kernels; peanuts; timber;
hides and skins; shrimp; fish
Imports: manufactured goods; fuels;
rice and other food products
Major Trading Partners: Portugal;
Senegal; Cape Verde; Sweden; France
*Selected Membership in International
Organizations:* UN; OAU; Economic
Community of West African States

| First Portuguese ships arrive; claimed as Portuguese Guinea; slave trading develops 1446 | Portugal gains effective control over most of the region 1915 | The African Party for the Independence of Guinea-Bissau and Cape Verde (PAIGC) formed 1956 | Liberation struggle in Guinea-Bissau under the leadership of the PAIGC and Amilcar Cabral 1963-1973 | Amilcar Cabral is assassinated; PAIGC declares Guinea-Bissau independent 1973 | Revolution in Portugal leads to Portugal's recognition of Guinea-Bissau's independence and the end of war 1974 | Coup in Guinea-Bissau brings Vieira to power and leads to separation of Cape Verde and Guinea-Bissau 1980 | Guinea-Bissau and Cape Verde establish diplomatic relations 1982 |

●●● 1983

| August: Thirteen million dollar World Bank credit loan given for improving the port of Bissau | March-April 1984: Voters elect regional councils which then elect National Assembly members | May 1984: New Constitution is approved. Fifteen member Council of State elected |

GUINEA-BISSAU

Guinea-Bissau, a small country with an archipelago of islands, is wedged between Senegal and Guinea on the West Coast of Africa. It is best known for the liberation struggle waged by its people against the Portuguese colonial government in the years 1962-1974. This movement—similar to those in Angola and Mozambique but broader and deeper than those movements—was to become a model of resistance to colonialism that others around the world have followed.

Portuguese control of Guinea-Bissau reached back to the fifteenth century and was characterized first by the slave trade and later by policies of forced labor. Portugal claimed to offer equal rights to Africans who became assimilated to Western ways, but only .3% of the population could gain the education and other criteria necessary for "assimilado" status.

INDEPENDENCE MOVEMENT

In 1956 six such educated men, led by Amilcar Cabral, founded the African Party for the Independence of Guinea-Bissau and Cape Verde (PAIGC). The movement had many Cape Vedean leaders, but it developed its largest following and most numerous activities on the mainland. For several years, the PAIGC remained devoted to educating people and raising their consciousness rather than to fighting. By 1963, when armed resistance began, villagers were committed to its ideas and participated in its decision making. By the late 1960s, two-thirds of the territory of Guinea-Bissau was in the hands of the PAIGC.

The liberated communities, under the party's guidance, built new institutions—new administrations, people's stores, people's courts, and schools, as well as new opportunities for women and new fighting forces. A National Assembly was elected 1973. Portugal recognized this independence in 1974.

PROBLEMS OF INDEPENDENCE

Since 1974, the leaders of Guinea-Bissau have tried to confront the problems of independence while maintaining the goals of the revolutionary movement. Their efforts have had limited success. The developments of the liberated zones offered a foundation on which to build, but the new government inherited a very limited national economy, which had remained undeveloped during centuries of Portuguese domination and which was damaged during the liberation war. The predominantly agricultural population lost harvests during droughts in 1977 and 1980, and there were massive imports of rice.

There is little manufacturing, and although explorations have revealed major sources of oil, bauxite, and phosphates, these minerals have not yet been exploited. The lack of roads and rails and a limited communications network challenged the PAIGC forces during the liberation struggle, and visitors were impressed with the way members of the PAIGC confronted these difficulties and went on to victory. Now the limited infrastructure must be built up, and funds are needed to finance the road to Gambia and the new port at Bissau.

Initially, the democratic grass roots system of government found in the liberated zones was the base for the new government institutions. Elections for a National Assembly were carried out in 1976. Recent difficulties have increased the authoritarian nature of the government, and the former revolutionary zest is missing.

MILITARY COUP AND A NEW CONSTITUTION

Amilcar Cabral, the charismatic leader of the PAIGC, was assassinated in 1973 and his brother, Luis Cabral, who became president of the new state, was overthrown in a military coup in November 1980. João Vieira, military commander during the liberation war and later prime minister, took over and ruled without elected bodies. Relations between Cape Verde and Guinea-Bissau worsened during this time, and Cape Verde finally left the union.

Elections took place in early 1984 and a new National Assembly is presided over by Carmen Periera, a well known woman leader. A new constitution has been approved and President Vieira was unanimously elected Chairman of the Council of State.

"No fist is big enough to hide the sky" is a peasant saying in Guinea-Bissau; Amilcar Cabral sometimes quoted this adage to remind people that setbacks were only temporary. Today, as contemporary problems obscure the achievements of the past and goals remain unfulfilled, the saying still applies.

DEVELOPMENT

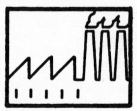

Two joint venture fishing companies, the Soviet-Guinean Estrela do Mar and the Franco-Guinean SEMPESCA, have exploited Guinea-Bissau's rich fishing reserves, and local fishermen are being supported by international funding. Fishing is a top priority, but production and consumption is still far behind that of other West African countries.

FREEDOM

PAIGC leadership, now in the hands of General Vieira, president of the Council of State, controls all organizations as well as the government. PAIGC nominated one-third of the candidates for recent elections to regional councils.

HEALTH/WELFARE

The development of schools and new texts was emphasized during the liberation struggle, but the illiteracy rate is high despite the campaigns of that period. A program of educational reform, which will provide six years of primary education and three years of secondary school, is being developed. Ninety-six percent of primary school age children are said to be enrolled.

ACHIEVEMENTS

A major agricultural-industrial complex at Cumeré was completed in 1981 through the support of Saudi Arabia, Italy, and the Islamic Development Bank. Groundnuts and cereals produced by farmers or rural development projects will be processed by Cumeré.

Ivory Coast

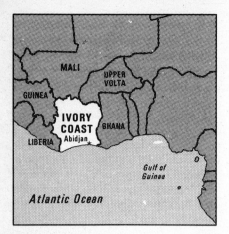

GEOGRAPHY

Area in Square Kilometers (Miles):
323,750 (124,503)
Land Usage: 40% forests and
woodland; 8% cultivated; 52% grazing,
fallow, and waste
Capital (Population): Abidjan
(900,000—1976)
Climate: tropical

PEOPLE

Population
Total: 8,568,000 (1982 est.)
Per Square Kilometer (Mile): 27 (69)
Annual Growth Rate: 3.4%
Rural/Urban Population Ratio: 60/40

Health
Life Expectancy at Birth: 46 years
Infant Death Rate (Ratio): 127/1,000
Average Caloric Intake: 112% of FAO
minimum
Physicians Available (Ratio):
1/21,040 (1975)
Access to Safe Water: 19%

Languages
Official: French
Others Spoken: Dioula; Agni; Baoulé;
Kru; Senufo; Mandinka; French; others

Religion(s)
66% indigenous beliefs; 22% Muslim;
12% Christian

Education
Adult Literacy Rate: 45% males; 24%
females
School Attendance: primary: 92%
boys, 60% girls; secondary: 25% boys;
9% girls

THE HARRIST CHURCH

The Harrist Church of the Ivory Coast is one of the four national religions recognized by the Ivory Coast government, along with Protestantism, Catholicism, and Islam. The church developed from the encounter of Ivorians with the Liberian prophet, William Wade Harris, who walked along the Ivorian coast in 1913 garbed in white, carrying a cross, and baptising from a gourd bowl. Thousands heard him and were converted to the Christian faith. Some joined the Methodist Church. Many others—responding creatively to the Christian message that Harris carried—founded a new church that adheres to Christian beliefs while addressing the special concerns of African members. The church incorporates age-grade patterns found in traditional societies; its music is based on African music; local languages are used, and witchcraft is condemned.

COMMUNICATION

Telephones: 78,400
Radios: 1,050,000
Televisions: 330,000
Newspapers: 1 daily; total circulation
53,000

TRANSPORTATION

Highways—Kilometers (Miles):
45,600 (28,336)
Railroads—Kilometers (Miles): 657
(408)
Two international airports

GOVERNMENT

Type: republic; one-party presidential
regime
Constitution: 1960
Former Colonial Status: French
Independence Date: August 7, 1960
Head of State: Felix Houphouet-
Boigny (president)
Branches: president; unicameral
legislature; separate judiciary
Legal System: based on French Civil
Law and customary law
Political Parties: Democratic Party of
the Ivory Coast
Suffrage: universal over age 21

MILITARY

Number of Armed Forces: 6,550
Armed Forces/Population: 1/1,308
Nuclear Weapons Status: none
Current Hostilities: none

ECONOMY

Currency ($ US Equivalent): 440 CFA
francs = $1
GDP: $7,560,000,000
Per Capita Income/GNP: $950
Workforce: 79% agriculture; 4%
industry; 17% services
Inflation Rate: 13.2% (1970-1980);
9.6% (1981)
Natural Resources: agricultural lands;
timber
Agriculture: coffee; cocoa; bananas;
pineapples; palm oil; corn; millet;
cotton; rubber
Industry: food and lumber processing;
oil refining; textiles; soap; auto
assembly
Energy Production: 721,500 kw
capacity
Energy Consumption Per Capita: 210
kwh

FOREIGN TRADE

Exports: cocoa; coffee; tropical woods;
cotton; bananas; pineapples; palm oil
Imports: manufactured goods; con-
sumer goods; raw materials; fuels
Major Trading Partners: France; other
EEC countries; United States
Foreign Debt: $5,790,000,000
*Selected Membership in International
Organizations:* UN; OAU; African
Development Bank; Economic Com-
munity of West African States; Non-
Aligned Movement

IVORY COAST

The Ivory Coast, say the forecasters, has a great economic future. It is already one of the most productive countries in West Africa. In the decade from 1960-1970, Ivory Coast had one of the highest growth rates in sub-Saharan Africa. Statistics indicate that Ivorians have a longer, healthier life than the residents of many other countries of the region. The average per capita income is $1,250—compared to that of about $200 for its interior neighbors, Mali and Upper Volta. Yet, Ivory Coast is a country of great diversity, and it has a capitalist economy; its prosperity is not shared equally by its people. Moreover, recent conditions have led to a slowdown in economic progress.

PROSPERITY FOR WHOM?

The large European (primarily French) ex-patriate community is fifty thousand strong. Many are "quasi-permanent" residents, managing plantations on which they have long leases. They are also advisors to the ministers and manage almost every sector of the economy. Their salaries are well above the average figure.

The Ivorian planter class is extremely large. These farmers grow cocoa, coffee, and sometimes bananas and pineapples as well as other cash crops for export. Ivory Coast is the world's largest producer of cocoa and the third largest producer of coffee. Coffee is one of the principal sources of income for the two and a half million Ivorians who grow and provide services for the industry. Some of the Ivorian farmers are wealthy. Yet cash crops like coffee and cocoa have received low prices on the world market in recent years. Moreover, the *caisse de stabilization,* or marketing board, through which farmers must sell their harvest pays lower prices for these crops than farmers might receive on their own. Now the government is encouraging farmers to replace cocoa with food crops such as yams, corn, and plantain—for which there is a broad West African as well as Ivorian market.

Ivorian planters often hire low-paid laborers who come from other West African countries. The average per capita income does not necessarily apply to them. There are two million ex-patriate laborers in Ivory Coast, employed in many sectors of the economy. Their employment is not a new phenomenon but goes back to colonial times. Upper Volta, where many laborers come from, was actually a part of the Ivory Coast at one time. Other areas were also associated with Ivory Coast because the French colonialists established an administration over all of their West African territories. The countries from which the

(United Nations photo)

The prosperity of the Ivorian economy is not shared equally by all the people.

laborers come need the foreign exchange that is gained from the wages that laborers send home. A good road system and the Ivorian railroad, which extends as far as Ougadougou in Upper Volta, helps migrant workers and Ivorians to travel to Abidjan and other cities, as well as to the cash crop areas.

Other factors may determine how much an Ivorian benefits from the country's development. Residents of Abidjan, the capital, and its environs near the coast receive more services than the citizens of interior areas. The professionals in the cities make better salaries than laborers on farms or in small industries. Yet inflation, now reaching twenty percent, and the world recession have made daily life difficult for the middle class as well as for peasants and workers. In April 1983, teachers went on strike to protest the discontinuance of their housing subsidies. The government refused to yield and banned the teacher's union; the teachers went back to work. The ban has been lifted but the causes of discontent remain, for no teacher can afford the high rents in the cities. Moreover, the teachers deeply resent the fact that the other civil servants, ministers, and French *cooperants* (helpers on the Peace Corps model) have not had their subsidies cut back, and they demand a more even "distribution of sacrifices."

Conditions are likely to become more difficult for Ivorians before they become better. State industries have been making low profits, and they are now being cut back if they are in debt. Serious brush fires, mismanagement in the timber industry, and the clearing of forests for cash crop planta-tions have all endangered one of the rich natural resources of the country. Plans for expansion of oil production have not been implemented because the billions of dollars needed for investment have not been raised. Ivory Coast has heavy debts to international banks, has been forced to borrow to pay interest on these debts, and has recently had to request rescheduling of some debts. Since 1980 the situation has led to austerity mea-sures that affect all citizens.

POLITICAL STABILITY

The government of the Ivory Coast has changed little in the years since indepen-dence in 1960. Felix Houphouet-Boigny, now seventy-seven, was the leader of the independence struggle and the founder of the *Parti Democratique de la Côte d'Ivoire* (Democratic Party of the Ivory Coast, or PDCI), the only legal party in Ivory Coast

today. Houphouet-Boigny has developed a system of councils, committees, and ad-visors through which he governs. He is a consummate politician, who has portrayed himself as the nation's grandfather and the citizens as his brothers, sons, and grand-children. He has prevented ethnic tension by incorporating representatives of several ethnic groups in his cabinet. He has brought dissenters over to his side by persuasive discussion (and perhaps through using fi-nancial incentives as well). It is a matter of concern to many Ivorians that Houphouet-Boigny has kept such a tight hold on power and has not indicated a successor.

Houphouet-Boigny's skills have not been able to prevent current disturbances. Stu-dents, as well as teachers, have demon-strated against the government. In February 1982, students demonstrated over the can-cellation of a lecture to be given at the university by one of the president's critics, as well as over larger issues of political freedom and the slowness of Ivorianization. Then, as in the later teachers' strike, the government responded quickly, broke the strike, and banned political activity at the university. The problem was not solved.

The president has blamed these conflicts on outside agitators and Communists. He has also taken a conservative line in foreign policy, which is hostile to Libya and recep-tive both to Israel and to dialogue with South Africa. France remains one of Ivory Coast's best friends, providing aid, giving military assistance, and encouraging French investment in the country.

TRADITIONAL STRENGTHS

A teacher in a school in Bouake, a worker

in a service industry in Abidjan, and a laborer on a cocoa farm in the south are examples of the many Ivorians who have left their homes but who keep attachments to rural communities and go back at holi-days. There are many different peoples living in the Ivory Coast with different traditions, histories, and languages. Eastern Ivorians, such as the Baoule who came from Ghana in the nineteenth century led by a woman, Awuta Poku, share traditions with many Ghanaian peoples; Ivorians from the west were once part of a confeder-ation with peoples of eastern Libera; Man-dinka traders from the north settled at Kong in northern Ivory Coast and developed an Islamic trading state in the mid-eighteenth century.

Many of these people have become well known in other parts of the world because of the tourist ventures encouraged by the Ivorian government. Moreover, the wood carvings of the Senufo, Dan, and Baoule are admired by outsiders who have never met the people for whom the art has social and religious importance. The Dan mask is not only beautiful; it also is worn by an official in the society, representing holy authority, and reminds the townspeople that laws are not personal but are backed by special power.

DEVELOPMENT

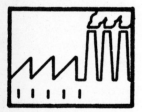

It has been said that Ivory Coast is a "power hungry" country. The Soubre dam, now being developed on the Sassandra River, is the sixth and largest hydroelectric project in Ivory Coast. It will serve the eastern area of the country. Another dam is already planned on the Cavalla River between Ivory Coast and Liberia.

FREEDOM

Houphouet-Boigny keeps a tight control over political processes. Until recently, the PDCI has given little choice to voters. In 1980 elec-tions were made more open and competitive at all levels, and this has led to changes of leadership locally as well as nationally.

HEALTH/WELFARE

Education absorbs about forty percent of the Ivorian budget, and interesting experiments in televi-sion courses have been tried out for over a decade in the Ivory Coast.

ACHIEVEMENTS

Ivory Coast textiles are varied and prized. Block printing and tie dye-ing produce brilliant designs; woven cloths made strip by strip and sewn together include the white "Korhogo" tapestries covered with Ivorian figures, birds, and symbols drawn in black. Manu-factured cloths often copy hand-made prints.

Liberia

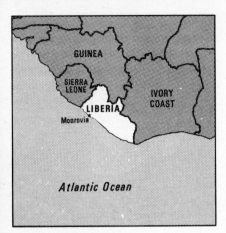

GEOGRAPHY

Area in Square Kilometers (Miles):
111,370 (43,000)
Land Usage: 20% arable; 30% tropical
rain forests and swamps; 40% forests;
10% unclassified
Capital (Population): Monrovia
(306,000)
Climate: tropical

PEOPLE

Population
Total: 2,113,000 (1982 est.)
Per Square Kilometer (Mile): 19 (49)
Annual Growth Rate: 4.5%
Rural/Urban Population Ratio: 67/33

Health
Life Expectancy at Birth: 53 years
Infant Death Rate (Ratio): 154/1,000
Average Caloric Intake: 114% of FAO
minimum
Physicians Available (Ratio): 1/9,610
Access to Safe Water: 20%

Languages
Official: English
Others Spoken: Kpelle; Bassa; Dan;
Vai; Loma; Kru; Grebo; Mano; Gola

Religion(s)
75% traditional indigenous beliefs;
15% Muslim; 10% Christian

Education
Adult Literacy Rate: 30% males; 12%
females
School Attendance: primary: 82%
boys, 50% girls; secondary: 29% boys,
11% girls

THE PORO SOCIETY

The Poro Society is a secret society to which all men belong in the
interior and western areas of Liberia as well as in parts of Guinea and
Sierra Leone. The society has political as well as religious and
educational responsibilities. Poro elders run traditional schools every seven
years, oversee chiefs, and act as a kind of Supreme Court—promoting
the laws of the community and meting out punishments. Special masks
and dress used by the leaders supposedly endow them with spiritual
power. In the past, the Liberian government tried to limit the society
without success. Poro is now respected by the government and has been
enlisted in support of government tasks. Many persons who have
Western education will also join Poro. Otherwise, despite important
positions, they may be considered "small boys" by traditional leaders.

COMMUNICATION

Telephones: 7,700
Radios: 350,000
Televisions: 22,000
Newspapers: 3 dailies; total circulation
11,000

TRANSPORTATION

Highways—Kilometers (Miles): 8,524
(5,296)
Railroads—Kilometers (Miles): 499
(310)
One international airport

GOVERNMENT

Type: interim government
Constitution: July 26, 1847; new
constitution will go into effect in 1986
Former Colonial Status: American
Colonization Society 1822-1847
Independence Date: July 26, 1847
Head of State: Samuel Kanyon Doe,
interim President
Branches: Interim National Assembly;
judicial: People's Supreme Tribunal
and lower courts
Political Parties: resumed July, 1984
Suffrage: universal over age 18

MILITARY

*Military Expenditures (% of Central
Government Expenditures):* 13.9%
Nuclear Weapons Status: none
Current Hostilities: none

ECONOMY

Currency ($ US Equivalent): Liberia
uses US currency
GDP: $950,000,000
Per Capita Income/GNP: $490
Workforce: 70% agriculture; 14%
industry; 16% services
Inflation Rate: 9.6% (1970-1980);
16% (1982)
Natural Resources: iron ore; rubber;
timber; diamonds
Agriculture: rubber; rice; palm oil;
cassava; coffee; cocoa; sugar
Industry: iron and diamond mining;
rubber processing; food processing;
lumber milling
Energy Production: 355,000 kw
capacity
Energy Consumption Per Capita: 534
kwh

FOREIGN TRADE

Exports: iron ore; rubber; timber;
diamonds
Imports: machinery; petroleum
products; transportation; equipment;
foodstuffs
Major Trading Partners: United
States; West Germany; Italy; Belgium
Foreign Debt: $764,500,000
*Selected Membership in International
Organizations:* UN; OAU; Economic
Community of West African States

LIBERIA

"Cassava can only grow in the shade of its own leaves." The military coup that occurred in Liberia in April 1980 is like the cassava that grows there. Just as the cassava's roots and branches cannot exist apart, so the origins of the coup lie deep in the society that the coup affects, and recent changes—even when dramatic—live in the shade of traditional life.

THE COUP AND ITS ORIGINS

In August 1980, Master Sargent Samuel Kanyon Doe and a group of seventeen non-commissioned officers and enlisted men entered the Executive Mansion and assassinated President William R. Tolbert, Jr. A ruling body, the Peoples' Redemption Council (PRC), was formed of civilian and military ministers. It was a revolutionary change.

For nearly a century and a half, the independent country of Liberia had been governed by an elite primarily descended from one group of Liberia's inhabitants. The New World Immigrants are descendants of black Americans and West Indians who returned to Africa under the auspices of the American Colonization Society. They made up a small percentage, perhaps five percent, of the Liberian population.

Most Liberians are descendants of peoples who came to Liberia from the interior several centuries ago. There are about sixteen different ethnic groups in Liberia, speaking languages as different as English is from Russian, and following different ways of life. Traditional village democracies and loose confederations resisted the dominance of the state, but Liberia won the struggles, often with the support of the United States Navy.

Gradually, people from groups such as the Vai, the Kru, and the Kpelle gained important positions in the state by accepting the standards and practices of the elite. Yet, Western education, Christian affiliation, and use of English helped a person to rise to power only if he or she accepted the status quo and developed a personal client relationship with an important Liberian. On the other hand, important chiefs could gain advantages from such relationships without taking on Western ways.

In the mid-twentieth century the system began to change as new forces such as the Firestone rubber plantations (established in 1927), the new iron ore mines, and urbanization occurred. President Tubman (1944-1971) proclaimed a Unification Policy and an Open Door Policy to encourage national integration and outside private investors. The conditions of investment benefitted outsiders, and most of the profits left the country. The wealth that remained went into the hands of the old

(FAO photo by G. Tortoli)

Changes in the political system of Liberia has had little impact on some of the traditional methods of subsistence.

elite. Tubman's government controlled the change, and the "powers that be" were not weakened.

In the decade after Tubman's death, during William Tolbert's administration, Liberians became more conscious both of the inequities of society and the ineffectiveness of government as well as the possibilities for change. The increasing number of professionals and students educated in Liberia or abroad refused to join the ranks of the regime. New groups such as MOJA (Movement for African Justice) and PAL (the Progressive Alliance of Liberia) criticized the government and organized for elections.

Meanwhile, economic conditions worsened. Four percent of the population controlled sixty percent of the wealth, while ordinary people lived a modest—indeed, a spare—existence. The well-to-do secured large farms in the interior and many people moved to Monrovia in a search for jobs. Inflation affected everyone. In a country where "if you haven't eaten rice you haven't eaten," it was not surprising that the government decision to increase the price of rice by fifty percent led to riots in April 1979. Forty to 140 persons were killed, and hundreds were injured when police fired into the demonstrating crowds. Chaos and

rioting resulted, and the government appealed to Guinea for troops. The feeling that the old regime must, and could, be changed grew during the following months. When the coup occurred just a year later, it had widespread support.

MAJOR CHANGES

Liberian history books talk of the revolution of 1871, when one settler government lost power to another. Nothing else changed. The 1980 coup seems different. Many of the new military leaders have become rich, causing many Liberians to comment: "Same taxi different driver." But this "car" may be a new model—even though, perhaps, a paste job. The soldiers who came to power were primarily people of northeastern Liberia, representative of traditional groups.

The new government has ended some formerly dominant institutions. The True Whig Party, through which the elite kept their political dominance, no longer exists. The formerly powerful Masons no longer meet. Government institutions such as the House and Senate do not operate. The hated hut tax was abolished, although it has since been reinstituted. There have been changes in the judicial system and efforts to develop peoples' courts. Offices have changed hands, and, although the old ad-

| The Vai moves onto the Liberian coast from the interior **1500s** | First Afro-American settlers arrive from the United States **1822** | First coup changes one Americo-Liberian government for another **1871** | League of Nations investigates forced labor charges **1931** | President Tubman comes to office **1944** | President Tolbert becomes president **1972** | The first riots in contemporary Liberian history occur when the price of rice is raised **1979** | Assassination of Tolbert; military coup brings Master Sargeant Samuel Doe to power **1980** | New regime raises rice prices **1981** | Doe visits the US; austerity measures announced **1982** |

•• 1983

ministrative system has persisted in the countryside, this may soon change.

The PRC intends to turn the government over to civilians in 1986. A new Constitution has been developed with input from citizens throughout the country, and it has been approved in a countrywide referendum. The new Constitution, like the old, is based on the United States model and has been carefully designed to put curbs on power without drastically changing the former economic system. The four year ban on political activity was lifted in July, but a long period lies ahead before the elections in October and November of 1985. Earlier postponements in the schedule and some government authoritarianism led to fears that the military will not return to the barracks. During the interim period, Doe will preside over an interim national assembly.

THE PERSISTENT PATTERNS

"No condition is permanent" is a common African exhortation, but in present day Liberia in a time of change, one is reminded that some things always seem to remain the same. The majority of Liberia's people continue to live in the countryside in small towns where electricity, health care, and good water are scarce or non-existent and where traditional "slash and burn" agriculture continues to produce the food crops. Many farmers grow a little coffee, cocoa, or rubber. The citizens of these towns travel widely, often stopping in Monrovia to visit relatives; to sell cane juice, kola, or cloth; to look for health care or schooling; or to seek wage employment or rice. People move in and out of the country's

many environments. Traditional organizations still exist in the rural areas yet have taken on new aspects. Now *kuus* (traditional work groups) may have constitutions, rule books, and fines.

Monrovia, the capital, remains a microcosm of Liberia—just as Liberia is a microcosm of Africa. Off the main street are found the many different sections of town where Bassa, Vai, or Glebo people live. Even the fence of a traditional Sande women's bush school can be seen in the heart of a Monrovia suburb. Ethnic associations give members of these communities support and pleasure.

Western ways are still valued. Christian ministers still have clout when they talk; the three-piece suit is as acceptable as the country cloth robe; and everyone has a briefcase. The interlinking of immigrant and indigenous families continues. Thirteen former government leaders lost their lives in a terrible public execution at the time of the coup, and houses and farms of leading government officials were stripped. But the former elite, as a group, were not destroyed or forced out of the country, and many former True Whig party members hold positions in the new government. Sometimes patron and client may have changed places, but personal relationships remain the gateway to securing a government position. The tradition of a lively press, reaching back to the 1830s, continues, although recent curbs and detentions have caused much concern.

So, too, continues the association that Liberia has had with the United States for over a century and a half. United States aid has increased from $5 million in 1979 to

November: Coup plot by former army commander Quiwonkpa is alleged

March 1984: Doe orders confiscated property returned to owners

July 1984: Constitution approved by referendum; PRC dissolved; New interim National Assembly formed; Ban on political activities lifted

$70 million in 1982. The military connections, the Voice of America installations, and the independent United States Christian missions remain. Doe—after some exploration of more radical friendships with Libya, Ethiopia, and Korea—has returned to Liberia's "special friend," the United States. Diplomatic relations with Israel have been established.

Financial problems also remain. When the military came to power, they claimed to have inherited an empty treasury and many debts—several resulting from the vast expenses of the OAU meetings in Liberia in 1979. The rise in the cost of oil, the decline in world prices for rubber and iron ore, and the closing of the sugar plant as well as one of Firestone's plantations are not the result of the coup, but they may determine the future of the government. The implementation of the Constitution is being done step by step, in line with limited finances. Two years ago, Doe's government had to take the dangerous step of raising the price of rice, and last year civil servants waited several months for their pay checks. It is not surprising that cassava, the hungry season crop, is grown in Monrovia yards; cassava can stay in the ground two years. Urban and country dwellers like to be in sight of its leaves.

DEVELOPMENT

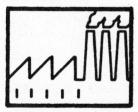

Liberia is the third largest exporter of iron ore in the world, and iron ore has been the main source of government revenue—superceding rubber—since the 1960s. The first iron ore mine at Bomi Hills has mined out the profitable ore, and its decline is an ominous illustration of the limited value of mineral exploitation.

FREEDOM

Presently no political activity is allowed, and students who agitated in 1981 were given the death sentence but were later freed by Doe. There are no political prisoners in Liberia, and an amnesty has been extended to exiles whose confiscated property will be returned to them.

HEALTH/WELFARE

Among the important educational institutions in Liberia are the University of Liberia, which began as Liberia College in 1862; Cuttington College, which is one of the only private higher educational institutions in Africa and is funded by the Protestant Episcopal Church and the government; and a series of self-help schools, which were built by townspeople in the western interior.

ACHIEVEMENTS

Through a shrewd policy of diplomacy, Liberia managed to maintain its independence when Britain and France conquered neighboring areas during the late nineteenth century. It espoused African causes during the colonial period; for instance, Liberia brought the case of Namibia to the World Court in the 1950s.

Mali

GEOGRAPHY

Area in Square Kilometers (Miles):
1,240,142 (478,819)
Land Usage: 25% arable; 75% desert,
pasture or forests
Capital (Population): Bamako
(419,239—1976)
Climate: tropical; arid

PEOPLE

Population
Total: 7,342,000 (1982 est.)
Per Square Kilometer (Mile): 6 (15)
Annual Growth Rate: 2.8%
Rural/Urban Population Ratio: 80/20
Age: 44% below 15 years

Health
Life Expectancy at Birth: 49 years
Infant Death Rate (Ratio): 154/1,000
Average Caloric Intake: 83% of FAO
minimum
Physicians Available (Ratio):
1/22,130
Access to Safe Water: 9%

Languages
Official: French
Others Spoken: Bambara; Mandurka;
Voltaie; Tamacheg (Tuareg);Dogon;
Fula; Songhai; French

Religion(s)
70% Muslim; 29% indigenous; 1%
Christian

Education
Adult Literacy Rate: 13% males; 7%
females
School Attendance: primary: 35%
boys, 20% girls; secondary: 13% boys,
5% girls

COMMUNICATION

Telephones: 7,800
Radios: 115,000
Television: begun in 1983
Newspapers: 1 daily; total circulation
4,100

TRANSPORTATION

Highways—Kilometers (Miles):
15,700 (9,756)
Railroads—Kilometers (Miles): 642
(400)
Three international airports

GOVERNMENT

Type: republic; military regime in power
since 1968; returned to civil rule in 1979
Constitution: June 2, 1974
Former Colonial Status: French
Independence Date: June 20, 1960
Head of State: General Moussa Traoré
(president)
Branches: Council of Ministers;
National Assembly; Supreme Court
Legal System: based on French Civil
Law and customary law
Political Parties: Democratic Union of
Malian People
Suffrage: universal over age 21

MILITARY

Number of Armed Forces: 4,950
Armed Forces/Population: 1/1,1431
Nuclear Weapons Status: none
Current Hostilities: none

TIMBUCTU

Timbuctu is not a mythical city but a contemporary town that is older
than any town in the United States. Located at the edge of the desert, on
the bend of the Niger River, Timbuctu was a major center of trade for
much of its history. As early as 1000 A.D., merchants from North Africa
brought copper, salt, swords, and beads to Timbuctu. Gold and slaves
were taken north across the trans-Saharan trade routes. Timbuctu was a
major stop on the route of Muslim pilgrims making the pilgrimage from
West Africa to Mecca. Schools of Islamic learning developed; chron-
icles and religious works were published in Arabic by Timbuctu's
scholars. The town is still made of mud bricks, and some of the buildings
have been repaired regularly, repeating the centuries-old forms. The
present inhabitants of Timbuctu come from many different backgrounds,
as they did in the past. Now, however, the town is smaller and less
important than it was in 1500.

ECONOMY

Currency ($ US Equivalent): 880 Mali
francs = $1
GDP: $1,030,000,000
Per Capita Income/GNP: $180
Workforce: 73% agriculture; 12%
industry; 15% services
Inflation Rate: 10.1% (1970-1980);
18% (1982)
Natural Resources: bauxite; iron ore;
manganese; lithium; phosphate; kaolin;
salt; limestone; gold
Agriculture: millet; sorghum; corn; rice;
sugar; cotton; peanuts; livestock;
groundnut
Industry: food processing; textiles;
cigarettes; fishing
Energy Production: 50,000 kw
capacity
Energy Consumption Per Capita: 17
kwh

FOREIGN TRADE

Exports: meat; livestock; cotton;
peanuts; fish; tannery products
Imports: food; machinery; vehicles;
petroleum products; chemicals and
pharmaceuticals; textiles
Major Trading Partners: France; West
Germany; United Kingdom; Ivory
Coast; People's Republic of China;
Senegal; United States; Cuba; USSR
Foreign Debt: $830,000,000
*Selected Membership in International
Organizations:* UN; OAU; West
African Economic Community; Asso-
ciate Member, European Economic
Community (EEC); African Develop-
ment Bank

| The Mali Empire extends over much of the upper regions of West Africa 1250-1400s | Songhai Empire controls the region late 1400s-late 1500s | French establish control over Mali 1890 | Mali gains independence as part of Mali Confederation; Senegal secedes from confederation months later 1960 | Military coup brings Lieutenant General Moussa Traore and Military Committee for National Liberation to power 1968 | Democratic Union of the Malian People (UDPM) is the single ruling party; Traore is Secretary General 1979 | School strikes and demonstrations; teachers and students detained 1979-1980 | Mali again denied admission to Monetary Union of West Africa (UMOA) because of Upper Volta veto 1982 |

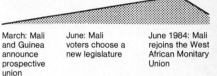

| March: Mali and Guinea announce prospective union | June: Mali voters choose a new legislature | June 1984: Mali rejoins the West African Monitary Union |

MALI

The epic of Sundiata Keita, the thirteenth century founder of the great Mali Empire, is well known among the peoples of Mali and the other countries that once shared in the empire. *Griots,* or traditional bards, sing of Sundiata's deeds at special gatherings and on radio programs. The story of this Malinke hero is a source of unity and pride for Mali's people.

A HERITAGE OF CONFEDERATION

Although Sundiata was a conqueror, the kingdom he founded was based on a confederation of rulers who accepted his leadership. In modern times, Mali has worked for cooperation or closer union with the other countries of the area who also share in the heritage of the Mali Empire. Under the French, in the period from the 1890s to 1960, Mali (then called the French Sudan) was part of the territory called French West Africa and was linked to Dakar. When the territories became independent within the French Community, Senegal and Mali formed the Mali Confederation. This union lasted only a few months. Mali and Senegal broke their political ties, but today they cooperate in the Organization for the Development of the Senegal River (OMVS) and other organizations, as well as in planning the exploitation of their joint iron ore resources.

Meanwhile, Mali has stengthened its ties with nearby Guinea. In March 1983, the two countries signed an agreement to unify their countries and established a permanent organization to harmonize policies and structures. Mali's President Moussa Traoré has said that this is the integration of "two lungs in the same body." President Sekou Touré of Guinea spoke of "the reconstitution on the basis of an egalitarian and democratic state, of the ancient Mali Empire," a political entity that will embrace all the states in the region.

ENVIRONMENTAL CHALLENGES

Despite their rich heritage, the people of Mali are very poor. There are few rich resources and those which exist such as the manganese and iron ore have not yet been exploited. The land on which people make their living are semi-arid, made drier by years of drought. The Niger River is the life-line of the Fulani pastoralists who depend on the water for their herds; Malinke and Bamana farmers also use it for their fields. In earlier centuries, the country sustained great trading cities such as Timbuctu and Djenne, whose merchants travelled the trans-Saharan trade routes and established other trading communities to the south and east. Today the most important city in Mali is Bamako, located where the river meets the railroad that links landlocked Mali to the Atlantic coast.

Successive governments have sought to better the conditions of the people. The first president, Modibo Keita, from the clan of Sundiata, established radical socialist policies and practices, but efforts to "go it alone" outside the French Franc Zone were not very successful. General (now President) Traoré led a coup against Keita in 1968 and has gradually modified, though not eliminated, Keita's policies. Recent agreements with the IMF have ended some government monopolies, but it is not cer-tain whether their functions can be carried out by private bodies. The reentry of Mali into the Monetary Union of West Africa should limit smuggling and encourage the economy. The increased cotton harvest may boost exports and add to foreign exchange. However, because of the costs of imported food and fertilizers and because a huge proportion of the budget goes toward civil servant salaries (seventy to eighty percent), there is little money to spend on development.

TRADITIONAL VALUES

Christianity has gained a small following in Mali, but most Malians are followers of Islam and of traditional religions. Some peoples, such as the Dogon of the Bandiagara Cliffs, have little interest in Islam and maintain the rituals that grow from their complex cosmological beliefs. Other groups, such as the Bamana, have increasingly accepted Islam while still practicing traditional ceremonies and belonging to secret associations. Even the Malinke, who are most likely to identify themselves as Muslims, continue to hold the religious beliefs of their non-Muslim ancestors. Sundiata himself, according to an ancient epic, did likewise. He was a Muslim king, but he was also a great magician who drew on sources of spiritual power from his own society and culture.

DEVELOPMENT

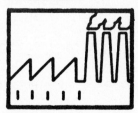

Water has always been one of Mali's major needs. It is estimated that only nine percent of the people, mostly in the urban areas, have access to pure water. A special cotton growing project, *Mali-Sud,* has encouraged village associations to purchase pumps as well as other items collectively.

FREEDOM

Party and state elections in 1981-1982 offered voters choices among party candidates. Teachers and students who were arrested for their part in strikes and demonstrations in 1979-1980 were all released in 1981, and only a few political prisoners are still confined.

HEALTH/WELFARE

Thirty percent of Mali's budget is devoted to education. A special literacy program in Mali teaches rural people how to read and write and helps them with the practical problems of daily life by using booklets that concern fertilizers, measles, and measuring fields.

ACHIEVEMENTS

The sculptured wooden masks made and used by the Bamana, Dogon, and Malinke people of Mali, which have become popular outside the country, play important social and sacred roles in Malian societies. Some masks are used in dances at initiation ceremonies, others at harvests, and still others at funerals.

Mauritania

GEOGRAPHY

Area in Square Kilometers (Miles):
1,030,700 (397,955)
Land Usage: 90% desert; 10% pasture;
less than 1% arable
Capital (Population): Nouakchott
(140,000—1979)
Climate: semi-arid; arid

PEOPLE

Population

Total: 1,730,000 (1982 est.)
Per Square Kilometer (Mile): 2 (4.3)
Annual Growth Rate: 2.9%
Rural/Urban Population Ratio: 20/80
Age: 42% below 15 years

Health

Life Expectancy at Birth: 44 years
Infant Death Rate (Ratio): 143/1,000
Average Caloric Intake: 94% of FAO
minimum
Physicians Available (Ratio):
1/14,350

Languages

Official: Arabic; French
Others Spoken: Hasanya Arabic;
Bambara; Fula; Sarakole; Wolof;
Berber languages

Religion(s)

Muslim

Education

Adult Literacy Rate: 17%
School Attendance: primary: 43%
boys, 23% girls; secondary: 16% boys,
4% girls
Teacher/Student Ratio: 1/151

WHO ARE THE MOORS?

The term "Moors" has been popularly used through history to refer to Muslims speaking Arabic and Berber, who lived in North Africa and across the Sahara. However, it is more accurate to refer to them by the names of the groups of which they are members. In Mauritania, Moors are peoples such as the Tuareg and the Sanhaja Berbers. They are probably descendants of the Almoravids who spread Islam through the Western Sahara during their conquests in the eleventh century. Traditionally nomadic, they maintain complex social systems. Aristocrats, including religious leaders and former warriors, are the "bones" (*adma*) of the society. Commoners are the "flesh" (*ahma*). Other groups in society are more subservient. Today, the life of these peoples is changing as—willingly or unwillingly—they move to cities and take up a settled life-style.

COMMUNICATION

Telephones: 5,000
Radios: 160,000
Newspapers: 1 daily; total circulation
3,800

TRANSPORTATION

Highways—Kilometers (Miles): 8,900
(5,530)
Railroads—Kilometers (Miles): 650
(404)
Two international airports

GOVERNMENT

Type: military republic
Constitution: military constitution—
1980
Former Colonial Status: French
Independence Date: November 28,
1960
Head of State: Lieutenant Colonel
Mohammed Khouna Ould Haidalla
Branches: executive (president);
legislative (Military Committee for
National Recovery); judicial (Supreme
Court)
Legal System: based on French and
Islamic law
Political Parties: none
Suffrage: universal for adults

MILITARY

Number of Armed Forces: 8,970
(backed by 200 French)
Armed Forces/Population: 1/175
Nuclear Weapons Status: none
Current Hostilities: conflicts with
Morocco over control of Western
Sahara in 1981; coup attempt in 1981
and 1982

ECONOMY

Currency ($ US Equivalent): 5
ouguiyas = $1
GDP: $640,000,000
Per Capita Income/GNP: $470
Workforce: 69% agriculture; 8%
industry; 23% services
Inflation Rate: 9.6% (1970-1982)
Natural Resources: iron ore; gypsum;
fish
Agriculture: livestock; millet; maize;
wheat; dates; rice
Industry: iron ore mining; fish
processing
Energy Production: 70,000 kw
capacity
Energy Consumption Per Capita: 69
kwh

FOREIGN TRADE

Exports: iron ore; fish
Imports: foodstuffs; petroleum; capital
goods
Major Trading Partners: France;
Spain; Italy; Japan; West Germany;
United Kingdom; Senegal
Foreign Debt: $1,524,400,000
*Selected Membership in International
Organizations:* UN; OAU; Arab
League; Economic Community of
West African States; African
Development Bank; Associate
Member, European Economic
Community (EEC)

The Almoravids
spread Islam in
the Western
Sahara areas
through conquest
1035-1055

Mauritanian area
becomes French
colony
1920

Mauritania
becomes inde-
pendent under
President Moktar
Ould Daddah
1960

A military coup
brings Khouma
Ould Haidalla
and the Military
Committee for
National Salva-
tion to power
1978

The Algiers
Agreement:
Mauritanian
makes peace with
Polisario and
abandons claims
to Western
Sahara
1979

Crop failure
leads to appeal
for international
aid
1982

▮▮▮●▮▮▮▮▮▮▮▮▮▮▮▮▮▮▮▮▮▮▮▮▮●▮▮▮▮▮▮▮▮▮▮▮●▮▮▮▮●▮▮▮▮▮▮▮▮▮▮●▮▮▮▮▮▮▮▮▮▮●▮▮▮▮▮▮▮▮▮▮▮▮●▮ 1983

January: Attack
on LeGuera
military base by
suspected
Moroccan forces

September:
South Korean-
Mauritanian
agreement allows
Korean fishing
in Mauritanian
waters

March 1984:
Mauritania
recognizes the
Polisario State in
Western Sahara
(SADR) as a
sovereign nation

REPUBLIC OF MAURITANIA

". . . as long as the wind continues to kick up sand, it is practically impossible to see in what direction you are advancing." This comment by a Mauritanian represents the attitude of many Mauritanians. Natural and human forces have led to revolutionary changes in the lives of the people, and the wind still blows.

FROM NOMADIC TO CITY LIVING

The country, most of which is desert, grows ever drier as unpredictable droughts continue. Grass cover has disappeared; the vast herds of cattle, camels, sheep, and goats are threatened; and sand has drifted over homes and highways. In the south, the arable land for growing grains and rice has been greatly reduced, and in 1982 a plague of grasshoppers destroyed fifteen percent of the already-diminished harvest. Ninety percent of Mauritania's food is now imported.

In the face of such natural disasters, people have moved. In 1962 only eight percent of the citizens lived in the country's few cities and towns. Now nearly twenty-five percent of the population are urban dwellers. The pastoralists come from a nomadic world where Arab culture and aristocratic Moorish-Berber values have been maintained. They have moved to places such as the capital, Nouakchott, and pitched tents in shantytowns on the outskirts of town. Often they have sold their camels and cattle to traders and bureaucrats. Many have gone south to settle in Mali.

LIMITED OPPORTUNITIES

As the cities have grown, poverty has become more obvious. People seek new ways to make a living away from the land but there are few jobs. About thirty thousand Mauritanians are employed; most work in the Tazadit iron ore mine in the northern desert. Although this mine will soon be depleted, a nearby iron ore complex will be operating by 1984. Iron ore provides seventy to eighty-five percent of the exports and foreign exchange of the country and gives Mauritania a figure for average per capita income which understates the basic needs of the people.

DIVISION AND UNITY

The government of Mohammed Khouna Ould Haidalla and the Military Committee for National Salvation came to power in a military coup of 1978. Steps toward constitutional rule were halted after a coup attempt in 1981, and new forms of political and social organization have been discussed but not implemented. Like its neighbor Chad, Mauritania is a nation of many different peoples, and there are some long existent hostilities between northerners and southerners. The Arab-oriented northerners claim to be in the majority, but ethnic black southerners contest that claim, and the census figures of 1977 have never been revealed. Southerners have objected to the exclusive use of Arabic in schools. In an attempt to "paper over the cracks in national unity," the government stresses the unity of Islam. The Sharia, or Islamic law, has been made an alternative to the regular legal system. However, a common faith has not always been able to harmonize some of the differences between the ethnic groups, and sometimes the differences have grown more obvious as peoples have lived closer together in the cities.

THE STRUGGLE IN WESTERN SAHARA

Fighting in the Western Sahara, on Mauritania's northern border, has made life uncertain for Mauritanian citizens and has eaten into the state's limited finances. Mauritania claimed portions of the Western Sahara in the 1970s and its army expanded tenfold, to seventeen thousand men, during this time. (The number of troops has since declined.) In 1979 the government renounced sovereignty over any part of the region and recognized the Polisario Front, the liberation movement of the Western Sahara.

The war of Polisario with Morocco continues. Now Morocco accuses Mauritania of allowing Polisario bases on its soil. Mauritania's relationship with Morocco, the freedom fighters, and other African states with an interest in the Western Sahara controversy, continues to kick up controversy for Mauritanians.

DEVELOPMENT

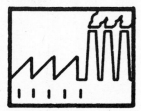

Mauritania is a member of the Organization for the Development of the Senegal River (OMVS) along with Senegal and Mali. The Manantali and Diama Dams being built on the river will increase the land available for farming by preventing the inland flow of salt water and irrigating forty thousand hectares in the three countries.

FREEDOM

In July 1980, the traditional forms of servitude were abolished by the Mauritanian government. Persons who formerly served aristocratic Berber nomads are now seeking land ownership and equal rights. The fulfillment of these claims will make drastic changes in the structure of society.

HEALTH/WELFARE

Former nomads now living in Rosso have built an innovative housing development in cooperation with the Association for the Development of Traditional African Urbanism and Architecture (ADAUA). Women, who head the majority of the households, took the initiative in the work.

ACHIEVEMENTS

There is a current project to restore ancient Mauritanian cities, such as Chinguette, which are located on traditional routes from North Africa to the Sudan. These centers of trade and Islamic learning were points of origin for the pilgrimage to Mecca and were well known in the Middle East.

Niger

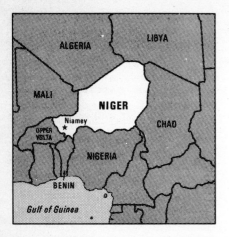

MATERNAL LANGUAGE SCHOOLS

In Niger, more and more primary school pupils are attending classes conducted in their native languages. These "maternal language schools," as they are called, have been developed over a number of years through careful planning and experimentation and are based on the idea that the mastery of basic concepts is most successfully achieved in one's native language. In addition, these schools work to foster and reinforce values of the community through a curriculum that reflects the cultural heritage of the pupils. Niger's maternal language schools are dedicated to providing students with strong foundations in reading, writing, and arithmetic as well as to the formation of individuals with a strong sense of their own cultural identity.

GEOGRAPHY

Area in Square Kilometers (Miles): 1,267,000 (489,191)
Land Usage: 17% arable; 3% cultivated; 50% grazing; 30% arid
Capital (Population): Niamey (225,314—1977)
Climate: arid; semi-arid

PEOPLE

Population
Total: 5,646,000 (1982 est.)
Per Square Kilometer (Mile): 4 (11.5)
Annual Growth Rate: 3%
Rural/Urban Population Ratio: 87/13
Age: 46% below 15 years

Health
Life Expectancy at Birth: 52 years
Infant Death Rate (Ratio): 143/1,000
Average Caloric Intake: 91% of FAO minimum
Physicians Available (Ratio): 2/38,790
Access to Safe Water: 27%

Languages
Official: French
Others Spoken: Hausa; Zarma/Songhai; Kanuri; Fula; Tamacheg (Tuareg); others

Religion(s)
80% Muslim; 20% indigenous beliefs

Education
Adult Literacy Rate: 14% males; 8% females
School Attendance: primary: 30% boys, 16% girls; secondary: 5% boys, 2% girls
Teacher/Student Ratio: 1/420

COMMUNICATION

Telephones: 8,500
Radios: 260,000
Televisions: 5,000
Newspapers: 1 daily; total circulation 3,000

TRANSPORTATION

Highways—Kilometers (Miles): 8,220 (5,107)
Railroads—Kilometers (Miles): none
Two international airports

GOVERNMENT

Type: republic; military regime in power since April 1974
Constitution: November 8, 1960 (suspended in 1974)
Former Colonial Status: French
Independence Date: August 3, 1960
Head of State: Brigadier General Seyni Kountché (president of Supreme Military Council)
Branches: executive (president and head of Supreme Military Council); legislative (suspended until 1986); judicial (four high judicial bodies)
Legal System: based on French Civil Law and customary law (suspended until 1986)
Political Parties: political parties banned
Suffrage: suspended until 1986

MILITARY

Number of Armed Forces: 2,220
Armed Forces/Population: 1/2,651
Military Expenditures (% of Central Government Expenditures): 3.9%
Nuclear Weapons Status: none
Current Hostilities: none

ECONOMY

Currency ($ US Equivalent): 440 CFA francs = $1
GDP: $1,560,000,000
Per Capita Income/GNP: $310
Workforce: 91% agriculture; 3% industry; 6% services
Inflation Rate: 12.2% (1970-1980)
Natural Resources: uranium; coal; iron; tin; phosphates
Agriculture: millet; sorghum; peanuts; beans; cotton
Industry: textiles; cement; agricultural products; construction
Energy Production: 32,800 kw capacity
Energy Consumption Per Capita: 14 kwh

FOREIGN TRADE

Exports: mining products; uranium; coal
Imports: fuels; machinery; transport equipment; foodstuffs; consumer goods
Major Trading Partners: France; EEC countries; Nigeria
Foreign Debt: $915,300,000
Selected Membership in International Organizations: UN; OAU; Economic Community of West African States; African Development Bank; Non-Aligned Movement

Mali Empire includes territories and peoples of present Niger areas **1200s-1400s**	Hausa states develop in the south of present Niger **1400s**	The area is influenced by the Fulani Empire centered at Sokoto, now in Nigeria **1800s**	France consolidates rule over Niger **1906**	Niger becomes independent **1960**	A military coup brings Colonel Seyni Kountché and a Supreme Military Council to power **1974**	Niger is one of the temporary members of the United Nations Security Council **1980-1981**	Plans for a "Development Society" are set forth **1982**

1983

July: Elections by consensus voting for 150 member National Council

October: Coup attempt is defeated

April 1984: President Kountché pardons prisoners including former President Hamani Diori

NIGER

"Before we cultivated much much larger areas and sometimes got nothing. Now, with the project, even on smaller plots we can produce enough millet," said Hassan Moussa, a Hausa farmer who participates in one of the programs of the Maradi Rural Development Project in Niger. The project is introducing new agricultural techniques and fertilizers, pesticides and seeds to over sixty-five thousand Nigerien farmers to help them expand and improve their harvests.

THE HERITAGE OF THE DROUGHT

Nigerien farmers need this help badly. The droughts of the late 1960s and early 1970s had a catastrophic effect, disrupting the delicate balance of desert and savanna in this very poor country, which is three times the size of California and located deep in the interior of West Africa. Only five percent of the land has been farmed; while another fifty percent can be used for grazing. Herders have also suffered during the droughts, losing sixty percent of their cattle. However, those losses have now been partly recovered.

The recovery in food production in recent years has been promising. Yet optimism must be tempered with caution. Projects like the one in which Hassan Moussa is involved are of limited value because the costs of bureaucracy and accompanying expenses have been great. Individual farmers could never afford these irrigation resources without outside assistance. The project manager himself has admitted that farmers would be better served by simple wells or other, more modest and integrated aids.

NIGER'S RESOURCES

Projects such as the one described above are funded by Niger as well as by outside agencies. This has been possible because Niger's deserts contain uranium ore. Two mines are now in operation, and 4,350 tons were produced in 1981—making Niger the fifth largest producer of uranium in the world. Thirteen other deposits are being investigated. Mining provides ninety percent of Niger's foreign exchange and has enriched the country. Yet, such developments have limited value. All the materials for uranium exploitation come from abroad, and the ore itself is exported and may someday be mined out. The mining communities are places where no one really belongs nor intends to stay. Niger is able to show a budget surplus, but the decline in uranium demand and prices since 1980 shows the dangers of depending on this one resource.

A NEW POLITICAL ORGANIZATION

It has been said that the development made possible through uranium exploitation may have diverted popular attention from the limits on political activity in Niger. A constitutional government under President Hamani Diori existed from 1960, the year of independence, to 1974 when Lieutenant Colonel (now General) Seyni Kountche, a leader described as austere and upright, took power in a bloodless coup. A military government has existed until recently. The government proposes that a Constitution be developed in the near future. There are no military representatives in the present cabinet and national development councils are being planned at all levels. The "Development Society" will be based on village youth and cooperative organizations as well as traditional values.

The French influence has remained important to Niger. There is a French military garrison as well as continued military assistance. During a visit to Niger in May 1983, President François Mitterrand declared that France would defend its allies against foreign intervention. His comment referred to Libya, which has disputed its border with Niger and is suspected of having backed an assassination attempt against Kountche in April 1983 and the military coup foiled in October of the same year. The fear of Libya has encouraged Niger's reliance on France and made the government more restrictive at home. As the funds for development projects such as the one in which Hassan Moussa participates dry up, the government may rely further on France and require more from Niger's people.

DEVELOPMENT

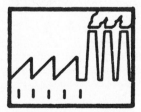

Village cooperatives, especially marketing cooperatives, pre-date independence and have grown in size and importance in recent years. They have successfully competed with the private well-to-do traders for control of the grain market.

FREEDOM

Although political parties remain suspended, the planned Development Society is to open up opportunities for political activity to Nigerien citizens. President Kountche has encouraged women's rights and freed some of his opponents, including former President Diori.

HEALTH/WELFARE

A national conference on educational reform in Zinder early in 1982 stimulated a program to use Nigerien languages in primary education and integrated the adult literacy program into the whole rural development efforts. The National Training Center for Literacy Agents is crucial to literacy efforts.

ACHIEVEMENTS

The government has made efforts to maintain harmony and unity among the six different ethnic groups in Niger and to avoid ethnic tensions by equally distributing economic benefits. President Kountche has visited the different regions regularly.

Nigeria

GEOGRAPHY

Area in Square Kilometers (Miles): 923,768 (356,669)
Land Usage: 24% arable (13% cultivated); 35% forests; 41% desert, waste, urban, or other
Capital (Population): Lagos (2,700,000)
Climate: tropical to arid

PEOPLE

Population

Total: 82,392,000 (1982 est.)
Per Square Kilometer (Mile): 89 (231)
Annual Growth Rate: 3.3%
Rural/Urban Population Ratio: 80/20
Age: 45% below 15 years

Health

Life Expectancy at Birth: 48 years
Infant Death Rate (Ratio): 135/1,000
Average Caloric Intake: 91% of FAO minimum
Physicians Available (Ratio): 1/12,550

Languages

Official: English
Others Spoken: Hausa; Yoruba; Ibo; others (250 languages are recognized by the Nigerian government)

Religion(s)

47% Muslim; 34% Christian; 19% indigenous beliefs

Education

Adult Literacy Rate: 46% males; 23% females
School Attendance: primary: 94% boys, 70% girls; secondary: 39% boys, 26% girls
Teacher/Student Ratio: 1/140

NIGERIA

Over the past thirty years, Nigeria has produced a significant number of major literary figures. Among the most interesting are Chinua Achebe, author of many novels including *Things Fall Apart,* Buchi Emecheta, who interprets Nigerian history and society from a woman's perspective; Christopher Okigbo, a lyric poet who died fighting for Biafra; and Felix Iyayi, who dramatizes social concerns and the lot of the poor. Perhaps the most multi-faceted is Wole Soyinka. Soyinka has written one major novel, *The Interpreters,* many distinguished plays (including a Pidgin version of the *Three Penny Opera* set in the streets of a Nigerian city), an extensive amount of poetry and, most recently, a memoir of his childhood as the school headmaster's son in the Yoruba town of Abeokuta.

COMMUNICATION

Telephones: 250,000
Radios: 5,800,000,000
Televisions: 480,000
Newspapers: 15 dailies; total circulation 319,000

TRANSPORTATION

Highways—Kilometers (Miles): 107,990 (67,104)
Railroads—Kilometers (Miles): 3,505 (2,178)
Four international airports

GOVERNMENT

Type: military government
Constitution: abolished in 1983
Former Colonial Status: British
Independence Date: October 1, 1960
Head of State: Major General Muhammed Buhari
Branches: Supreme Military Council; National Council of State (military governors appointed by federal ministers); Federal Executive Council
Legal System: based on English Common Law, indigenous law, and Islamic law
Political Parties: banned
Suffrage: none at present

MILITARY

Number of Armed Forces: 156,000
Armed Forces/Population: 1/528
Nuclear Weapons Status: none
Current Hostilities: none

ECONOMY

Currency ($ US Equivalent): .77 nairas = $1
GDP: $71,720,000,000
Per Capita Income/GNP: $860
Workforce: 54% agriculture; 19% industry; 27% services
Inflation Rate: 18.2% (1970-1980)
Natural Resources: oil; minerals; timber
Agriculture: peanuts; cotton; cocoa; rubber; yams; cassava; sorghum; palm; kernels; millet; corn; rice; livestock
Industry: mining: crude oil, natural gas, coal, tin, columbities; processing: oil palm, cotton, rubber, petroleum; manufacturing: textiles, cement, building products, chemicals; beer brewing
Energy Production: 1,823,000 kw capacity
Energy Consumption Per Capita: 66 kwh

FOREIGN TRADE

Exports: oil; cocoa; palm; products; rubber; timber; tin
Imports: machinery and transportation equipment; manufactured goods; chemicals
Major Trading Partners: UK; EEC countries; United States
Foreign Debt: $11,753,900,000
Selected Membership in International Organizations: UN; OAU; African Development Bank; Economic Community of West African States; OPEC; Commonwealth of Nations; Non-Aligned Movement

NIGERIA

Nigeria is a land of extremes that, for many, has typified both the hopes and frustrations of contemporary Africa. It is Africa's most populous country; at least two West Africans in three live there. No less than 65,304,818 voters took part in the recent elections. No accurate census has been taken in Nigeria since independence, but it is estimated that there are now eighty million or more Nigerians. Thanks to its oil fields, Nigeria is also the wealthiest African nation, with the largest Gross National Product—exceeding even South Africa. Yet its twenty-three years of independence have already witnessed a bloody civil war, terrible inter-ethnic violence, more than a decade of military rule, restoration of Western-style representative politics, and—finally, following a military coup in December 1983—the return to a military government again.

The river Niger, which flows to the sea through a great delta in Nigeria, links savanna and forest. For centuries, it was the route through which population groups and cultures interrelated. Nigeria is re-markable for its great cultural and historic variety. Archaeologists have revealed an artistic heritage that includes the ivory and bronze work of fifteenth-century Benin, the thousand-year-old sculpted heads associated with Ife, and the terra cotta figurines that are associated with the Nok culture and can be dated back to the time of Christ.

Nigerians speak more than 300 languages. Pidgin English, which is based on African grammar, is widely used in the towns. Roughly two-thirds of the Nigerians speak the three major languages: Hausa, Yoruba, or Ibo. During the colonial era, these three cultures became the basis of "tribes," the leaders of which clashed politically from their separate regional bases.

Before the colonial conquest, Nigerians established powerful states such as the Sokoto caliphate (which helped to Islamize much of the country), Oyo, and Benin. Meanwhile, thousands of smaller independent villages and family commonwealths held sway elsewhere. Pre-colonial Nigerians produced a wide range of craft goods, including leather, glass, and metalware; they grew such agricultural surplus products as cotton and indigo. The southern part of the country was a major source of slaves, particularly those destined for the United States, during the Atlantic slave trade era.

BRITISH RULE

The British, who conquered most of the country in the late nineteenth and early twentieth centuries, ruled Nigeria through a federal structure. The predominately Muslim north became something of a world unto itself because it was governed under "indirect rule." As in the southern Sudan, the British virtually excluded Christian missionaries from much of the "Holy North."

Through the relatively brief colonial era, Nigerians were able to show a dynamism unusual in Africa. The old ruling classes, especially in the North, remained very important. Commercial networks, while subordinated to British business, expanded and intensified to the benefit of African traders. In the south, Christianity and Western education spread rapidly. The Yoruba cultivated cocoa on a scale rivaling Ghana; the Ibo, who lacked an equivalent lucrative crop, spread throughout the fed-

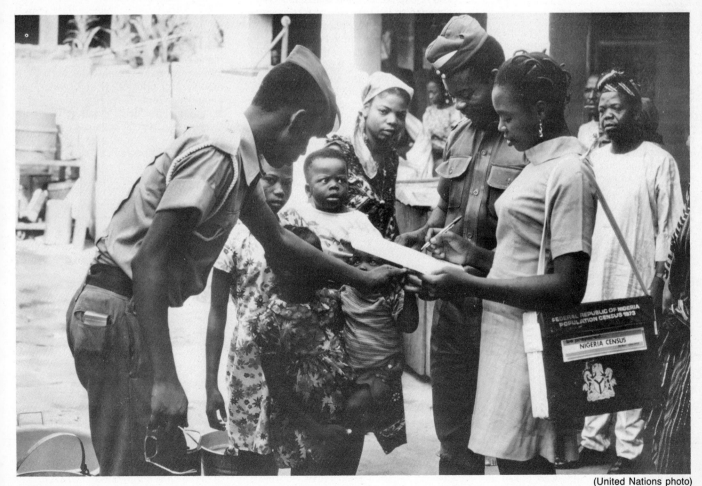

(United Nations photo)

Nigeria has the largest population of any African state but the controversial nature of the 1963 and 1973 censuses have caused governments to postpone the process.

eration in their roles as artisans, wage workers, and traders.

REGIONAL CONFLICTS

Following independence in 1960, Nigerian politics deteriorated into intensive conflict between the different regions, each of which threatened to secede at one time or another. Civilian government collapsed and two massacres led to the flight of Ibo from the north in 1966. The east then broke away and proclaimed itself to be the republic of Biafra. It took three hard years of war to reunite the country. Even before the war had begun, the military had determined to break up the regions into smaller states that would not be able to counterpose themselves against one another.

NATIONAL OUTLOOK

Not surprisingly, until recently most literature on Nigerian politics focused on the problem of national unity and contended that ethnic tensions were Nigeria's main problem. This ethnically-based conflict is now waning. For all its failings, the military government of Yakubu Gowon (1966-1975) succeeded in healing the worst wounds of the murderous ethnic politics of the First Republic through the policy of national reconciliation and the creation of new states. The oil boom helped this effort by concentrating vast resources in the hands of the federal government in Lagos. Today, the Nigerian political elite, which once thought almost exclusively in terms of "tribe," religion, or region, is increasingly national in outlook.

In 1979, thirteen years of military rule (never once producing a one-man dictatorship) ended. A new Constitution was implemented, which abandoned the British parliamentary model and instead followed the complex balance-of-powers system of the United States. There was a bicameral legislature, and to be elected, the president had to receive one-fourth of the vote in two-thirds of the states (now numbering nineteen).

FORMER POLITICAL PARTIES

Five political parties ran in 1979. All promised social welfare for the masses, coupled with support for Nigerian businessmen, and a nominal international stance of non-alignment. Radicals, who talked in terms of class conflict, were found in several parties, especially in the PRP (People's Redemption Party), which initially took the governorship in two northern states.

The most successful party in 1979 was the NPN (National Party of Nigeria), whose candidate, Shehu Shagari, won the presidency. Shagari, like a number of his principal rivals, was a survivor of First Republic politics, but the old regional/ethnic base (in the case of Shagari, that of the old north) was strengthened by new alignments that criss-crossed the country. Most observers classified the NPN as the most right-wing of the parties, with virtually no radical members. It emphasized policies that were consistent with previous Nigerian administrations in order to assist in the development of a strong and affluent native class of capitalists. "Indigenization" laws attempted to limit the role of foreigners in many sectors of the economy.

New national elections took place in August and September 1983. The NPN consolidated its national position, winning 264 of 450 seats in the House, fifty-five of eighty-five Senate seats, and thirteen of the nineteen state governorships. Shagari received just over twelve million of 25.5 million votes in the six-man presidential contest. However, the newly elected government did not survive long. On December 31, 1983, there was a military coup, led by Major General Muhammed Buhari, former petroleum commissioner in the military government of General Gowon. The 1979 Constitution was suspended; Shagari and others were arrested; and a federal military government (similar to that of General Obasanjo) was established. The change was welcomed by many.

FORMER REPUBLIC OF PRIVILEGED

Superficially, the political picture seemed very bright in the early 1980s. A commitment to national unity was well-established and effective. Two elections had successfully taken place and, given the scale of the country and the intensity of political rivalries, incidents of violence and overt corruption were relatively minor. Due process of law, judicial independence, and press freedom—never eliminated under military rule—were extended and were well-entrenched.

Many Nigerian intellectuals, however, were beginning to write about the new republic as "the republic of the privileged and rich," in which the poor masses held little stake. The whole electoral system, while balancing the interests of the power elites in different sections of the country, did not empower ordinary people. Moreover, economic circumstances were creating burdens almost too difficult for ordinary people to bear. The outlook was far different from that of the 1970s.

OIL BOOM

The 1970s were a period of very rapid social and economic change in the country. The recovery of oil production after the civil war and the subsequent hike in prices attracted Western business to the country on a large scale and made a few Nigerians very rich. At first, as a result of this wealth, there was a rapid expansion of social services. Universal primary education was introduced, and the number of universities grew from five in 1970 to twenty-one planned facilities in 1983. A great deal of money was spent on importing such commodities as automobiles, motorcycles, and phonograph equipment for private consumption. This fueled inflation, which ultimately undercut the economics of internal production.

The NPN government, however, promised to create many new states and was constructing, at vast expense, a new federal capitol at Abuja in the center of the country. Such forms of expenditure seemed prestigious and provided many opportunities for Nigerian businessmen and politicians, but they extended non-productive sectors of the economy while intensifying import dependence.

AGRICULTURE

Nigerian agriculture, unable to afford the higher wages spawned by inflation, entered a period of crisis, and the rapidly growing cities now import foreign food products to feed the urban populations. Lagos now contains more than one million inhabitants, as do Ibadan, Kano, Kaduna, and Port Harcourt. In 1983 Nigeria will import an estimated 630 thousand tons of rice and well over one million tons of wheat. The non-petroleum exports that were once so important have either entirely disappeared (as is the case with peanuts, once the staple of the colonial north) or declined drastically (as have cocoa, tin, rubber, and palm oil). While at first glance gross indicators

Nigeria becomes
independent as
a unified federal
state
1960

Military seizure
of power; pro-
clamation of
Biafra and the
civil war
1966-1970

Oil price hike
inaugurates the
oil boom
1973

Elections restore
civilian
government
1979

●1983

December:
Military coup led
by Muhammed
Buhari ends the
second republic

January 1984:
Special military
tribunals are
formed to take
up cases of 400
Nigerians ac-
cused of eco-
nomic crimes

April 1984: Four
former governors
sentenced to
22 years each

appear to report impressive industrial growth in Nigeria, most of the new industry depends heavily on foreign inputs and is geard toward direct consumption, rather than the production of machines or spare parts. Thus, in 1983, the largest single industrial sector was still beer brewing. Selective import bans merely serve to feed the immense smuggling business.

ADJUSTMENTS NECESSARY

The "golden years" of the middle and late 1970s were also banner years for inappropriate expenditure, corruption, and waste. At the time, given the scale of revenues coming in, it looked as if these were manageable problems. However, with world trade recession and the end of the expansion in oil revenues, it became apparent that Nigeria would be forced to make some painful and unprecedented adjustments. By April 1982, Nigerian imports amounted to double the value of the country's exports each month. In 1983 the Gross National Product fell by 4.4%. Debt repayment has become a substantial factor in the federal budget.

The entire social and political system owed its stability to the effective distribution of the oil wealth to many groups of Nigerians. However, Nigeria's new wealthy class was increasingly resented by the masses. Signs of restiveness were apparent. At the end of 1980, an Islamic movement condemning corruption, wealth, and private property defied authorities in the northern metropolis of Kano. The army was called in and

ultimately killed nearly four thousand poor Hausa-speaking peasant migrants. Attempts by the regime to control organized labor through reorganizing the union movement into one legal centralized federation met with unofficial strikes (including a general strike in 1981) and "illicit" breakaways.

One way to answer these problems was to get rid of foreigners. All foreigners who lacked appropriate documentation were expelled from Nigeria. As a result, more than one million West Africans, particularly Ghanaians, were forced out of Nigeria on short notice, despite the nominal freedom of movement across national boundaries that was guaranteed by the Economic Community of West African States (ECOWAS) treaty. Although there was considerable international outcry, the expulsions were popular with many Nigerians who hoped to regain the profits from the vanishing oil boom.

The main aim of the new military government has been to solve some of the economic problems of the nation. They have sought to apprehend and try those earlier political leaders whose economic crimes reached vast proportions. The discovery of private caches of millions of naira caused public outrage and added to the treasury. There have been some efforts to repatriate politicians who fled, although Nigeria's role in the attempted abduction of Umar Dikko, a former minister now residing in England, is not clear. Five special military tribunals have been trying the four hundred detainees.

FOREIGN POLICY

The oil boom encouraged Nigerian regimes of the 1970s to take an aggressive foreign policy stance supporting a radical nationalist view of the continent of Africa. In 1976 Murtala Muhammad, whose brief administration ended with his assassination in a Lago traffic jam, was quick to recognize the MPLA as the sole government of Angola, a decision which remains a source of pride to Nigerian nationalists. Nigeria took a lead in supporting the new Mugabe government in Zimbabwe in 1980 and was a founding member of ECOWAS due to its interest in promoting West African unity. It is also a member of the Organization of Petroleum Exporting Countries (OPEC).

The present military government has honored its commitments to other nations and maintained its relations with other states, as well as regional and international organizations. Yet, it seems likely that domestic concerns will continue to take priority. As Major General Buhari said in his New Year's Eve address: "This generation of Nigerians and indeed future generations have no other country than Nigeria. We shall remain here and salvage it together."

DEVELOPMENT

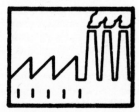

The Nigerian government recognizes the importance of creating an industrial base in the country. In the past two years, steel mills intended to feed Nigerian industry have begun production in Warri and Ajaokuta.

FREEDOM

When six senior journalists were arrested for sedition as a result of sensational allegations about presidential corruption in August 1981, the charges against them were thrown out of court by the judiciary. Several journalists have been detained without charges or trial by the present government.

HEALTH/WELFARE

Plans are afoot for four new diagnostic hospitals, and open-heart surgery is possible in sophisticated urban facilities. At the same time, health care for the poor is often appalling, with rural infant mortality rates of 150 per 1,000 and up.

ACHIEVEMENTS

While the big British publishing houses have tended to dominate the Nigerian book industry, in the last few years innovative and committed Nigerian presses such as Ikenga, Spectrum, and Fourth Dimension have emerged. Tama Press is devoted to publishing children's books.

Senegal

GEOGRAPHY

Area in Square Kilometers (Miles):
196,840 (76,000)
Land Usage: 13% forests; 40%
agricultural; 47% built-up areas,
waste, or other
Capital (Population): Dakar
(800,000—1976)
Climate: tropical

PEOPLE

Population
Total: 5,968,000 (1982 est.)
Per Square Kilometer (Mile): 30 (79)
Annual Growth Rate: 2.6%
Rural/Urban Population Ratio: 66/34

Health
Life Expectancy at Birth: 44 years
Infant Death Rate (Ratio): 147/1,000
Average Caloric Intake: 100% of
FAO minimum
Physicians Available (Ratio):
1/13,800
Access to Safe Water: 37%

Languages
Official: French
Other Spoken: Wolot; Fula; Dyola;
Mandinka; Sarakole; Serer

Religion(s)
75% Muslim; 5% Christian; 20%
indigenous

Education
Adult Literacy Rate: 31% males;
14% females
School Attendance: primary: 58%
boys, 38% girls; secondary: 16%
boys, 8% girls
Teacher/Student Ratio: 1/196

COMMUNICATION

Telephones: 45,000
Radios: 355,000
Televisions: 4,500
Newspapers: 1 daily; total circulation
25,000

LEOPOLD SEDAR SENGHOR

Leopold Senghor, the President of Senegal from 1960 to 1980, has distinguished himself in political and literary fields and in both arenas he has linked his inheritance from Senegal and his legacy from France. Raised in Senegal, he received his university education at the Sorbonne in Paris. In the late 1940s, he became a leading proponent of "negritude," a movement for African pride and identity among French-speaking Africans and West Indians. He helped to found the journal *Présence Africaine* in 1947 and the publishing company of the same name. In the late 1940s, he also helped to found the Senegalese Democratic Party, a mass organization that worked for independence. He served as a representative of Senegal to the French Parliament, and he was elected President of Senegal when the country became free from France. Senghor formulated and publicized ideas about African socialism. Throughout his life he created poetry that has reflected African traditions as well as other personal experiences. This year, in recognition of his literary achievements, Senghor was elected one of the forty members of the prestigious Academy in France.

TRANSPORTATION

Highways—Kilometers (Miles):
13,898 (8,635)
Railroads—Kilometers (Miles): 1,033
(641)
Four international airports

GOVERNMENT

Type: republic
Constitution: March 3, 1963
Former Colonial Status: French
Independence Date: April 4, 1960
Head of State: Abdou Diouf
(president)
Branches: executive (president;
prime minister); legislative (National
Assembly); judicial (Supreme Court)
Legal System: based on French Civil
Law
Political Parties: fourteen political
parties, including: Socialist Party;
Democratic Party; African In-
dependence Party; Republican Move-
ment; National Democratic Alliance
Suffrage: universal for adults

MILITARY

Number of Armed Forces: 9,560
Armed Forces/Population: 1/626
*Military Expenditures (% of Central
Government Expenditures):* 7.4%
Nuclear Weapons Status: none
Current Hostilities: none

ECONOMY

Currency ($ US Equivalent): 440
CFA francs = $1
GDP: $2,510,000,000
Per Capita Income/GNP: $490
Workforce: 76% agriculture; 10% in-
dustry; 14% services
Inflation Rate: 7.6% (1970-1980); 12/
(1982)
Natural Resources: fish; phosphates
Agriculture: millet; sorghum;
manioc; rice; cotton; groundnuts
Industry: fishing; agricultural product
processing; light manufacturing;
mining
Energy Production: 310,850 kw
capacity
Energy Consumption Per Capita: 92
kwh

FOREIGN TRADE

Exports: peanuts; peanut products;
phosphate rock; canned fish
Imports: food; consumer goods;
machinery; tansport equipment
Major Trading Partners: France;
EEC countries; United States; Japan
Foreign Debt: $1,771,300,000
*Selected Membership in International
Organizations:* UN; OAU; Economic
Community of West Africa;
Economic Community of West
African States

| French occupy present day St. Louis and, later, the Island of Goree **1659** | The Jolof Kingdom controls much of the region **1700s** | All Africans in 4 towns of the coast vote for representative to the French parliament **1848** | Interior areas added to the French colonial territory **1889** | Senegal becomes independent as part of the Mali Confederation; shortly after breaks from confederation **1960** | Senghor hands over power to Diouf **1980** | The political system is opened to an unlimited number of parties **1981** | Senegambian Confederation inaugurated; revolt in the southern Casamance area; debt rescheduled **1982** |

●II■■■■■■■■■■■●II■■■■■■■■■■■●II■■■■■■■●II■■■■■■●II■■■■■■●II■■■■■■II●II■■■■■■■II●II■■■■■■II●II■■■●1983

| February: Diouf receives 84% of vote in national elections | January 1984: Diouf is unanimously reelected Secretary General of the ruling Socialist Party | February 1984: Senegal expells Iranians for disseminating Islamic fundamentalist propaganda in the Muslim community |

SENEGAL

Ibrahima Dieng is an ordinary citizen of Senegal—a Muslim, who lives with his two wives in a traditional compound in the capital city, Dakar. When Dieng receives a money order from his nephew in Paris, he cannot cash it because he lacks the connections and skills to overcome the bureaucratic obstacles that stand in his way. The lawyer he enlists to help him steals the money. "In a country like ours only the scoundrels live well," says Dieng.

The story is fictional, the plot of an amusing and thought-provoking film, *Mandabi*, by the Senegalese filmmaker Ousmane Sembene. Yet, it illustrates a reality: the uneasy meeting of traditional African customs, Islamic practices, and Western influences in an important African city and, to a certain extent, in the interior beyond Dakar.

THE IMPACT OF ISLAM

The majority of Senegalese are Muslims like Ibrahima Dieng. The religion was introduced into the region as early as the eleventh century and spread through trade, holy men, and the practices of some theocratic Islamic states in the region during the seventeenth, eighteenth, and nineteenth centuries.

Most Muslims are associated with one of the Brotherhoods or "ways" of Islam, similar to Western Protestant denominations or Catholic orders. The leaders of the Brotherhoods, often called *marabouts*, have been identified as "spokesmen for the rural areas" as well as "spiritual directors." Abdou Diouf, the present president of Senegal, had the support of the marabouts

in his recent campaign for the presidency and won the election in February 1983.

The Brotherhoods have also been important economically. Members of the Mouride Brotherhood, who number about 700 thousand, grow groundnuts on the dry, flat Senegalese plains. This cash crop, the primary export of Senegal's predominantly agricultural economy, has made members of the Brotherhood prosperous.

THE INFLUENCE OF FRANCE

While Islamic influences have come into Senegal from the north and east, Western ways were introduced from the coast. French merchants developed bases for slave and gum trades and claimed the territory as French. Many Senegalese along the coast have had French connections for generations. People from the coastal towns acquired French citizenship after the revolutions in France in the late eighteenth and early nineteenth centuries, and they voted for representatives to the French Parliament.

The French language is the common language of the country, and the educational system maintains a French character. Many Senegalese, like Dieng's nephew, go to France, either to attend school or (more often) to work as ill-paid laborers. The French maintain a military force near Dakar, and are major investors in the Senegalese economy. The Constitution and government of Senegal are modeled after Western forms. The bureaucracy that plagued Dieng has its roots in the old colonial system. Diouf, successor of the renowned first President Leopold Senghor, has liberalized the government, welcomed the participation of all political parties, changed his cabinet to

make government more efficient and responsive, and fought corruption. Soon it may become easier for Dieng to cash his check.

THE STATE OF THE ECONOMY

Only twenty-five percent of the Senegalese citizens live in the cities; most are rural dwellers. The West African drought has made life more difficult for Senegalese farmers and herders. Groundnuts have been affected by "aflatoxin" mold as well as by a lack of water, and consequently groundnut exports have declined. The decline of prices on the world market affects the growers in the countryside. The government has become increasingly indebted to outside financial institutions in order to maintain development programs.

The Senegambian Confederation—inaugurated February 1, 1982—has long been sought by Senegal. It will increase communication between the south and the north of the country, now divided by the Gambia. It will allow Senegal to better control dissidents in the southern area of the Casamane, and it will make the Gambian River a more usable riverway. Whether the confederation or other plans of the government will bring about "an authentic African solution to the problems of Senegal" remains to be seen.

DEVELOPMENT

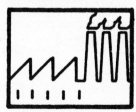

Diouf's administration is developing a water-supply program for the entire country. Many of the projects involve cooperation with Senegal's neighbors. The new dams planned for the Senegal and Gambian rivers will provide irrigation for agricultural projects.

FREEDOM

There are presently fourteen political parties in Senegal, seven of which claim to be Marxist-Leninist. Four call themselves socialist. While encouraging this diversity, the president urges that politicians "look for what unites us." There are three newspapers in Senegal, which express a wide variety of viewpoints.

HEALTH/WELFARE

The dams planned for the Senegal River will displace over a million people who have traditionally farmed in the area, end the yearly flood on which traditional agriculture depends, and introduce high-priced irrigation facilities. Thus, development may not benefit ordinary people.

ACHIEVEMENTS

Drastic reforms are expected in Senegal's educational system. A general conference on education in 1980 recommended that indigenous languages be used in the schools and that university students be directed into the types of training the nation needs.

Sierra Leone

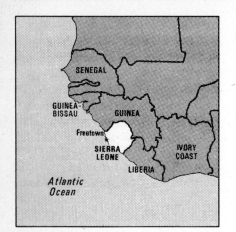

APPROPRIATE TECHNOLOGIES

The need for technologies that are modest, inexpensive, and relevant to people's ways of living is a constant theme of those concerned with Africa's development. Kupelian Brothers at the Raymond Garage in Sierra Leone repair old vehicles and also manufacture and market appropriate technologies. Their products include trailers for bulk transport, mobile grain silos, rice threshers and driers, and palm kernel breakers. Their inventions can make life easier for ordinary farmers, and Kupelian Brothers is planning mobile workshops to help farmers in the interior use the equipment efficiently.

GEOGRAPHY

Area in Square Kilometers (Miles): 72,325 (27,952)
Land Usage: 65% arable, (6% cultivated); 27% pasture; 4% swampland; 4% forests
Capital (Population): Freetown (214,000—1974)
Climate: tropical

PEOPLE

Population
Total: 3,672,000 (1982 est.)
Per Square Kilometer (Mile): 51 (131)
Annual Growth Rate: 2.7%
Rural/Urban Population Ratio: 78/22
Age: 43% below 15 years

Health
Life Expectancy at Birth: 48 years
Infant Death Rate (Ratio): 208/1,000
Average Caloric Intake: 85% of FAO minimum
Physicians Available (Ratio): 1/18,280

Languages
Official: English
Others Spoken: Krio; Temne; Mende; Vai; Kru; Fula; Mandinka; others

Religion(s)
70% indigenous; 25% Muslim; 5% Christian

Education
Adult Literacy Rate: 10% males; 4% females
School Attendance: primary: 41% boys, 29% girls; secondary: 16% boys, 7% girls
Teacher/Student Ratio: 1/118

COMMUNICATION

Telephones: 16,000
Radios: 350,000
Televisions: 20,000
Newspapers: 1 daily; total circulation 12,000

TRANSPORTATION

Highways—Kilometers (Miles): 7,460 (4,635)
Railroads—Kilometers (Miles): 84 (54)
One international airport

GOVERNMENT

Type: republic
Constitution: April 19, 1971
Former Colonial Status: British
Independence Date: April 27, 1961
Head of State: Siaka P. Stevens (president)
Branches: executive (president); legislative (House of Representatives); judicial (Court of Appeals, lesser courts)
Legal System: based on English law and customary laws
Political Parties: All People's Congress
Suffrage: universal over age 21

MILITARY

Number of Armed Forces: 2,680
Armed Forces/Population: 1/1,319
Military Expenditures (% of Central Government Expenditures): $11,300,000 (7.4%—1979)
Nuclear Weapons Status: none
Current Hostilities: none

ECONOMY

Currency ($ US Equivalent): 2.5 leones = $1
GDP: $1,130,000,000
Per Capita Income/GNP: $390
Workforce: 65% agriculture; 19% industry; 16% services
Inflation Rate: 11.6% (1970-1980); 30% (1982)
Natural Resources: diamonds; bauxite; rutile; chromite; iron ore
Agriculture: coffee; cocoa; ginger; rice; piassava
Industry: diamond, bauxite, and rutile mining; beverages; cigarettes; construction goods; tourism
Energy Production: 95,000 kw capacity
Energy Consumption Per Capita: 62 kwh

FOREIGN TRADE

Exports: mining products; agricultural products
Imports: food; beverages; tobacco; crude materials; chemicals; machinery
Major Trading Partners: United States; UK; Netherlands; China; Japan
Foreign Debt: $437,000,000
Selected Membership in International Organizations: UN; OAU; Commonwealth of Nations; Economic Community of West African States; African Development Bank

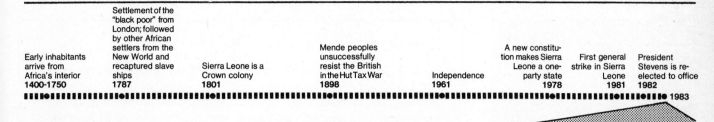

| Early inhabitants arrive from Africa's interior **1400-1750** | Settlement of the "black poor" from London; followed by other African settlers from the New World and recaptured slave ships **1787** | Sierra Leone is a Crown colony **1801** | Mende peoples unsuccessfully resist the British in the Hut Tax War **1898** | Independence **1961** | A new constitution makes Sierra Leone a one-party state **1978** | First general strike in Sierra Leone **1981** | President Stevens is re-elected to office **1982** |

SIERRA LEONE

"The train for Bo ei no wan gree for go," is the first line in a well known children's song in Sierra Leone. Although Westerners may not be able to decipher all the words, Sierra Leoneans hear the Krio lyric and know that the train "for Bo does not agree to go." Krio is a language widely spoken in Sierra Leone, especially near the coast. It has an African syntax and incorporates words from many different languages. It symbolizes the distinctive blend of cultures that one can find in this small country.

A DISTINCTIVE POPULATION

Many Sierra Leoneans are of ethnic groups such as the Temne or Mende that migrated to the region from areas farther in the interior several centuries ago. Some came from down the coast, like the Kru. Other residents arrived from overseas. "The Black Poor," a group of about four hundred, arrived in Sierra Leone from England in 1787; freed slaves from Nova Scotia and Jamaica soon joined them. About forty thousand recaptured Africans who were released from slave ships captured on the West African coast were settled in Freetown and the surrounding areas in the first half of the nineteenth century. The British became the governors of the colony and encouraged mission efforts, including the establishment of mission villages and schools such as the University of Fourah Bay.

The descendants of the settlers blended African and British ways and were called Creoles because of their mixed heritage. They travelled and lived in other places along the West African coast. Some found their original homes in Nigeria, from where they had been taken as slaves, and went back. When the British gained control over the interior, Creole people sometimes served as their administrators. Creoles in the interior were attacked during the Hut Tax Rebellion of 1898, and fear of Creole domination existed among traditional leaders through the twentieth century.

In the 1950s, as more and more people were given the vote, interior peoples—rather than Creoles—dominated the political system. The Sierra Leone People's Party (SLPP), under Sir Milton Margai, became powerful through the support of the traditional chiefs and remained the leading party when Sierra Leone gained independence in 1961. After 1967 the All People's Congress (APC), representing a broader spectrum of the population, won control. Siaka Stevens, the leader of the APC has been President of Sierra Leone for fourteen years and was reelected to the presidency in 1982. The APC became the only recognized party in 1978.

POLITICAL AND ECONOMIC COMPETITION

Although competition between ethnic groups is minor, there are other sources of controversy and conflict in Sierra Leone. In the recent elections, many seats were contested, and violence led some people in the interior to flee to Liberia. In the summer of 1981, a general strike—the first ever—occurred as a result of increased inflation, low wages, and worsening working conditions. Most people in Sierra Leone are

August: Government negotiations with Minerals International raises government share of joint diamond mining venture to 60%

January 1984: All People's Congress meets; Student demonstrations at the time lead to closing of Fourah Bay

May 1984: Cabinet shakeup occurs

farmers, but the laboring class is 125 thousand strong and well organized. Although the strike was settled and strikers were absolved by the APC after an investigation, tensions remain. As difficult economic conditions continue, there is more struggle over the national wealth.

That wealth is small. Sierra Leone is a poor country and was recently added to the list of Least Developed Countries by the United Nations. Its resources are limited. Deposits of diamonds, once central to the economy and the basis for the prosperity of the 1950s, will soon be depleted.

The rural population suffers the most. Falling prices for cocoa and coffee have cut into the income of farmers. Those who grow rice cannot compete with the imported rice, which the government subsidizes. The government's financial problems mean that development programs have been cut back. Already health care in the countryside is poor; educational facilities have become more limited; and clean water and electricity are scarce. Meanwhile the old train to Bo and beyond "no wan gree for go." It has been completely dismantled, and now people and goods do not find it easy to reach the facilities (and the problems) that Freetown, Sierra Leone's capital city of 300 thousand, has to offer.

DEVELOPMENT

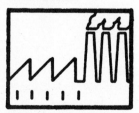

Sierra Leone's diamond rush occurred in the early 1950s, and ordinary people as well as the fifty-one percent government-owned National Diamond Mining Company sieved the sands of river beds looking for the precious stones. Smuggling cut into government customs receipts. Now, as shallow beds give out, production will depend on deep mining and heavy machinery.

FREEDOM

Human rights are guaranteed in the Sierra Leone Constitution, and there have not been major violations. One hundred and eighty persons, including eighty trade union leaders, were arrested after a general strike in 1982; they were later released. A high registration fee for new newspapers has restrained the press.

HEALTH/WELFARE

Medical care now reaches only thirty percent of the people, and the infant mortality rate is one of the highest in the world. Worker grievances have included hospital conditions. The new Department of Community Health at the University of Sierra Leone and the new Paramedical School will train medical assistants and medics in preventive medicine for rural areas.

ACHIEVEMENTS

The Sande Society, a women's organization that trains Mende young women for adult responsibilities and regulates women's behavior, has contributed positively to life in Sierra Leone. Beautifully carved wooden helmet masks are worn by women leaders in the society's rituals. Ninety-five percent of Mende women of all classes and education join the society.

Togo

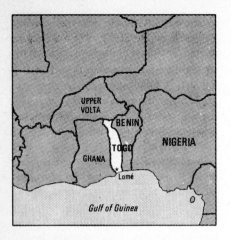

GEOGRAPHY

Area in Square Kilometers (Miles): 56,600 (21,853)
Land Usage: approximately 50% arable; less than 15% cultivated
Capital (Population): Lomé (229,400—1977)
Climate: tropical

PEOPLE

Population
Total: 2,747,000 (1982 est.)
Per Square Kilometer (Mile): 48/125
Annual Growth Rate: 3%
Rural/Urban Population Ratio: 80/20
Age: 46% below 15 years

Health
Life Expectancy at Birth: 48 years
Infant Death Rate (Ratio): 109/1,000
Average Caloric Intake: 92% of FAO minimum
Physicians Available (Ratio): 1/18,160
Access to Safe Water: 16%

Languages
Official: French
Other Spoken: Ewe; Mina; Dagomba; Kabye; others

Religion(s)
60% indigenous beliefs; 20% Christian; 20% Muslim

Education
Adult Literacy Rate: 27% males; 7% females
School Attendance: primary: 100% boys, 87% girls; secondary: 46% boys, 18% girls
Teacher/Student Ratio: 1/103

COMMUNICATION

Telephones: 13,000
Radios: 570,000
Televisions: 10,000
Newspapers: 1 daily; total circulation 7,000

TRANSPORTATION

Highways—Kilometers (Miles): 7,000 (4,350)
Railroads—Kilometers (Miles): 442 (274)
Two international airports

GOVERNMENT

Type: republic; under military rule since 1967
Constitution: 1979
Former Colonial Status: German; French
Independence Date: April 27, 1960
Head of State: General Gnassingbé Eyadema (president)
Branches: military government with civilian-dominated Cabinet; National Assembly; separate judiciary
Legal System: based on French Civil Law and customary laws
Political Parties: Togolese People's Union
Suffrage: universal for adults

MILITARY

Number of Armed Forces: 3,600
Armed Forces/Population: 1/773
Military Expenditures (% of Central Government Expenditures): $27,800,000 (8.5%—1979)
Nuclear Weapons Status: none
Current Hostilities: none

ECONOMY

Currency ($ US Equivalent): 440 CFA francs = $1
GDP: $800,000,000
Per Capita Income/GNP: $340
Workforce: 67% agriculture; 15% industry; 18% services
Inflation Rate: 9.8% (1970-1980)
Natural Resources: phosphates; limestone
Agriculture: yams; manioc; millet; sorghum; cocoa; coffee; rice
Industry: phosphates; textiles; agricultural products; tourism
Energy Production: 75,000 kw capacity
Energy Consumption Per Capita: 71 kwh

FOREIGN TRADE

Exports: phosphates; cocoa; coffee
Imports: consumer goods; fuels; machinery; foodstuffs
Major Trading Partners: France; UK; West Germany; Netherlands; People's Republic of China
Foreign Debt:$907,000,000
Selected Membership in International Organizations: UN; OAU; Economic Community of West African States

	Togo is mandated to Britain and France by the League of Nations following Germany's defeat in World War I	UN plebicites result in the independence of French Togo and incorporation of British Togo into Ghana		Murder of President Sylvanus Olympio; new civilian government organized after coup	Coup of Colonel Etienne Eyadema, now President Gnassingbe Eyadema	*Rassemblement du Peuple Togolais* (RPT) becomes the only legal party in Togo	A new Constitution comes into effect	Ghana closes its borders with Togo
Germany occupies Togo **1884**	**1919**	**1956-1957**	Independence is achieved **1960**	**1963**	**1967**	**1969**	**1980**	**1982**

1983

January: Assassination attempt against President Eyadema discovered	July: One-hundredth anniversary of German-Togo relations planned	October: President (General) Eyadema visits the US and talks with government and business leaders

TOGO

The problem of developing national unity in a country where people speak many different languages and have very different life-styles can be found in many African nations, including Togo. There are over forty ethnic groups in this long narrow country, which is about the size of West Virginia. A government commission of 1968 declared that unity was very difficult to achieve because the northern and southern groups differed so much economically, socially, and culturally.

NATIONAL UNITY ENCOURAGED

Togo, like other African states, was an artificial creation of the colonial powers. There are some age-old links between the regions. The cattle trade has operated in the north and south for generations. However, there was no unifying African kingdom. Now Togolese are all part of one nation, and the government of President (and General) Gnassingbé Eyadema is making efforts to encourage national unity. Following the example of Mobutu of Zaire, Eyadema has encouraged the use of indigenous names and of national languages in the schools, and he has proposed "an authentic model of national development," which would respect the culture of the country.

Eyadema is the focus of a personality cult. The Rassemblement du Peuple Togolais (Rally of the Togolese People or RPT), formed in 1969, is the only recognized party. All regional groups are represented in the party, which is about one million strong.

EWES SEEK REUNIFICATION

These efforts have limits, and ethnic problems remain. The Ewe people, one of the largest and most powerful groups, have a high proportion of educated persons and have monopolized many of the varied positions in the government and the economy. This has created some animosity. Ewe people live in Ghana as well as in southern Togo. They are very conscious of the fact that Ewe were all part of one German colony before World War I. With the defeat of the Germans in 1917, the territory was divided between the British and the French. Gradually, different languages and different administrative systems, as well as other colonial traditions, developed. When territory-wide votes were held in the mid-1950s, Ewe in the French zones decided to join Togo, while those in the British governed area chose to become part of the new Ghana. Now many Ewe people would like to reunite. The continued movement for unification is not favored by either government.

Other forms of conflict exist. Some people oppose President Eyadema because of his part in the murder of Sylvanus Olympio, the first president of Togo in 1963, and his illegal rise to power through the coup of 1967, which overthrew a constitutional government. The sons of Olympio maintain a government in exile, and there have been plots against the government—the most recent in January 1983.

ECONOMIC PROBLEMS

There are also economic problems that can disrupt the state. Togo is poor, with few resources. The government is concentrating on diversifying the economy, creating small- and medium-sized industries, and encouraging rural agriculture. The falling prices for Togo's major export, phosphates, has led to cutbacks in development programs. Cocoa production, which first began on African plantations established before 1914, is declining because of the continuing low prices for this product. Instead of working at home, Togolese are migrating to Ghana and other countries where they can make better money. Many northerners worked in Ghana in colonial times and continue that tradition. The government has made some efforts to control private trade.

Eyadema has worked for peace among the many peoples of Togo; he has also mediated many difficulties among African states, including the border conflicts between Upper Volta and Mali, and Nigeria and Cameroon. He helped to bring Houphouet-Boigny of the Ivory Coast and Sekou Touré of Guinea together. Togo was one of the first countries to join the Economic Community of West African States (ECOWAS), and Eyadema has a strong commitment to the success of this regional organization.

DEVELOPMENT

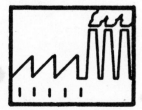

Phosphate mining has been the major source of exports and of development funds. The mines were nationalized in 1974. However, the fluctuating and unpredictable price of phosphates on the world market have made it an unreliable source of prosperity. A phosphoric acid plant is part of the 1982-1985 national plan.

FREEDOM

Some human rights are limited or unprotected by law in Togo, but this government ratified the African Charter on Human Rights, sponsored a conference on human rights practices in Africa in October 1982, and holds few political prisoners. New legal codes are expected to enhance the rights of women.

HEALTH/WELFARE

Togo has twenty-one hospitals and nearly 300 dispensaries and clinics; medical care is subsidized. However, doctors and nurses are in short supply, and only one doctor is available for every 17,900 persons.

ACHIEVEMENTS

Eyedema has acted as a mediator in several African disputes. In an interview with Anthony Hughes in *Africa Report* 1982, he noted the Togolese belief that no development can take place unless there is peace. Therefore, he contends Africans must preserve the continent from conflict "that might detract us from the economic struggle we are waging for the good of our people."

Upper Volta (Bourkina Fasso)

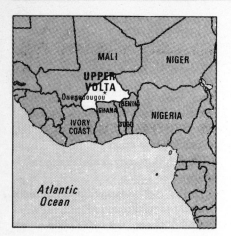

DEFENSE COMMITTEES

The new Revolutionary Defense Committees, in which both women and men play important roles, have been described as Sankara's "most important innovation." Designed to give more people a share in politics, they will carry on the work of local government, formerly in the hands of traditional chiefs. The committees are also mandated to mobilize the population for development work in agriculture and construction, for instance. A new constitution has been set forth to govern the work of the committees. Some union members have expressed concern about the committees, fearing that they are intended to replace the union organizations.

GEOGRAPHY

Area in Square Kilometers (Miles): 274,500 (106,000)
Land Usage: 50% pasture; 21% fallow; 10% cultivated; 9% forests and scrub; 10% waste and other
Capital (Population): Ougadougou (236,000—1980)
Climate: tropical and arid

PEOPLE

Population
Total: 6,360,000 (1982 est.)
Per Square Kilometer (Mile): 23 (60)
Annual Growth Rate: 1.7%
Rural/Urban Population Ratio: 90/10
Age: 43% below 15 years

Health
Life Expectancy at Birth: 44 years
Infant Death Rate (Ratio): 211/1,000
Average Caloric Intake: 95% of FAO minimum
Physicians Available (Ratio): 1/48,510
Access to Safe Water: 10%

Languages
Official: French
Other Spoken: Mossi; Senuto; Fula; Bobo; Senufo; Mande; Gurunsi; Lobi; others

Religion(s)
75% indigenous beliefs; 20% Muslim; 5% Christian

Education
Adult Literacy Rate: 18% males; 5% females
School Attendance: primary: 26% boys, 15% girls; secondary: 4% boys, 2% girls
Teacher/Student Ratio: 1/534

COMMUNICATION

Telephones: 8,600
Radios: 118,000
Televisions: 10,000
Newspapers: 1 daily; total circulation 1,500

TRANSPORTATION

Highways—Kilometers (Miles): 8,316 (5,167)
Railroads—Kilometers (Miles): 1,173 (728)
Two international airports

GOVERNMENT

Type: republic; under control of Military Council
Constitution: suspended after 1980 coup
Former Colonial Status: French
Independence Date: August 5, 1960
Head of State: Captain Thomas Sankara (president)
Branches: president; Military Committee of Reform for National Progress; Supreme Court
Legal System: based on French law and customary law
Political Parties: banned after 1980 coup
Suffrage: universal for adults

MILITARY

Number of Armed Forces: 3,775
Armed Forces/Population: 1/1,825
Military Expenditures (% of Central Government Expenditures): $33,000,000 (1980)
Nuclear Weapons Status: none
Current Hostilities: coup on August 5, 1983 removed former President Saye Zerbo from power

ECONOMY

Currency ($ US Equivalent): 440 CFA francs = $1
GDP: $1,000,000,000
Per Capita Income/GNP: $210
Workforce: 82% agriculture; 13% industry; 5% services
Inflation Rate: 10.1% (1970-1982)
Natural Resources: manganese; limestone; marble; gold; uranium; bauxite; copper
Agriculture: millet; sorghum; corn; rice; livestock; peanuts; shea nuts; sugar cane; cotton; sesame
Industry: agricultural processing; brewing; light industry
Energy Production: 30,000 kw capacity
Energy Consumption Per Capita: 13 kwh

FOREIGN TRADE

Exports: livestock; peanuts; shea nut products; cotton; sesame
Imports: textiles; food and other consumer goods; transport equipment; machinery; fuels
Major Trading Partners: France; other EEC countries; Ivory Coast; Ghana
Foreign Debt: $474,000,000
Selected Membership in International Organizations: UN; OAU; West African Economic Community; Economic Community of West African States

1983

BOURKINA FASSO (UPPER VOLTA)

"Speed it up PM" *(Accelerez la Vitesse)* read one of the banners displayed at a rally in Ougadougou, the capital of the state formerly called Upper Volta (now named Bourkina Fasso), on April 16, 1983.

The slogan illustrated the popular feeling that the government of Jean-Baptiste Ouedraogo had neither established a course for national regeneration nor begun to implement it. Prime Minister Thomas Sankara, to whom the opening statement was directed, is now head of state, having taken power August 5, 1983 in a military coup. The government of Upper Volta has changed several times since independence in 1960, and the military and civilian regimes have not been able to cope fully with the challenges of meeting the peoples' needs. It is still uncertain whether Sankara can "speed it up."

DEBILITATING DROUGHTS

There is far to go. Upper Volta, one of the poorest countries in the world, has been held back by successive droughts during the past decade and a half. In the countryside, traditional patterns of life have been disrupted by years of drought. Some farmers' needs have been served by the 100 aid missions that came to Upper Volta within the course of a year, and the five-year UN World Food Program that in October 1981 began to distribute thirty-five thousand tons of food to people in development work. Most important has been the work of farmers themselves and their families, working through the traditional cooperatives, or *naam,* to make the best use of new pumps, grinding mills, hoes, and medical supplies through community action.

Most Upper Voltans are agriculturalists and herders, but many are wage workers, members of a strong trade union movement and residents of the cities of Bobo-Dioulasso and Ougadougou, both with populations over 150 thousand. Many Voltaics combine farming and wage labor. At least a million persons work as migrant laborers in other parts of West Africa, a pattern that dates back to the early twentieth century. Approximately 700 thousand of these workers migrate to the Ivory Coast. Returning workers, a large number of them Mossi, infuse the country with a working class and cosmopolitan perspective.

UNIONS FORCE CHANGES

Trade union leaders representing these workers have been instrumental in forcing changes in government. They have spoken out vigorously against government efforts to ban strikes and restrain unions and have demanded that something be done to change the declining standards of living.

Since coming to office, Sankara has had some clashes with the unions, especially the teachers' union. Some suggest that the government-instituted Revolutionary Committees are designed to replace the unions, which are not easy to control.

Sankara has maintained the radical policies and the anti-imperialism that got him into trouble with the former regime. At the same time, he has recognized the importance of good relations with France and with the Ivory Coast. France is Upper Volta's major trading partner, a source of corporate investment and financial aid. French investment in the development of the 13.3 million ton manganese mine and the railroad now being built from

Ougadougou may contribute to economic growth in Upper Volta.

IVORY COAST TIES

Upper Volta has many ties with the Ivory Coast. Ten percent of the country's foreign earnings come from the wages that migrants to the Ivory Coast bring back. Ivory Coast is the main customer for Voltaic exports and Voltaic oil comes from the Abidjan refinery. Abidjan is the state's port, and the Ivorian railroad a vital line of transport. It is not surprising that Houphouet-Boigny, President of Ivory Coast, has been described as the "godfather of Voltaic political life." Hence, it is in the country's best interest to "consolidate the traditional friendship and cooperation" be tween the two nations, as Sankara declared in a message to Houphouet-Boigny. Yet, relationships between Sankara's government and the Ivory Coast have been strained and Sankara has accused the Ivory Coast of harboring rebels from Bourkina Fasso.

The new head of state in Bourkina Fasso has a reputation for staying in touch with the people. As prime minister, Sankara instituted direct contact with citizens through regional visits, direct dial radio programs, and rallies featuring questions and answers that emphasize the importance of the active participation of citizens in the development of their own communities may bode well for the future of Bourkina Fasso.

DEVELOPMENT

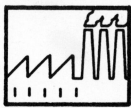

The traditional association of young people, the *naam,* has been the basis of new education about agricultural techniques and new crops that can stimulate production. One problem during the drought has been the need to assure that available foods are priced low enough for ordinary people and yet are not brought up by rich merchants.

FREEDOM

There is a strong tradition of respect for individual rights in Upper Volta. In general, despite the several recent military coups and the house arrests for former leaders, people have been able to organize meetings and to speak out critically. Political activities are restricted, and the policies of the new regime may differ from those of earlier governments.

HEALTH/WELFARE

Upper Volta has an integrated, country-wide health plan, which includes health education, improvement of water supplies, and immunization. All citizens are now being vaccinated against measles, polio, whooping cough, tetanus, and tuberculosis as part of that immunization program.

ACHIEVEMENTS

The eighth Pan-African Film Festival was held in Ougadougou in February 1983. This bi-annual festival has contributed significantly to the development of the film industry in Africa. Upper Volta has nationalized its movie houses, and the government has encouraged the showing of films by African filmmakers.

Western Sahara

GEOGRAPHY

Area in Square Kilometers (Miles):
266,770 (102,703)
Land Usage: mostly desert
Capital (Population): El Ayoun
(20,010—1974)
Climate: temperate coast; semi-arid
to arid inland

PEOPLE

Population
Total: 142,000 (1982 est.)
Per Square Kilometer (Mile): 1 (14)
Annual Growth Rate: 2.8%

Languages
Official: Arabic
Other Spoken: Spanish; Berber
languages

Religion(s)
Muslim

Education
Adult Literacy Rate: 20%

COMMUNICATION

Telephones: 1,000
Radios: 30,000
Televisions: 2,500

THE REGUIBAT

The *Reguibat* is the largest group or *qabila* in Saharawi. Like the other peoples of the country its members claim descent from a holy father of Islam. This group, often known as "people of the gun," were once warriors but now have a settled life-style. Like other Saharawi people, they speak Arabic and are of mixed Arab, Berber, and black African descent. The Reguibat people make up fifty-two percent of the population of Saharawi and live in Mauritania, Mali, and Morocco as well as in Saharawi. They are a majority within *Polisario.* However, as someone has said, Polisario is made up of many different ethnic groups, but they are all one people. In this way, the liberation struggle has forged the nation.

TRANSPORTATION

Highways—Kilometers (Miles): 6,100
(3,660)
Railroads—Kilometers (Miles): none
Two international airports

GOVERNMENT

Type: legal status of territory and
question of sovereignty unresolved;
Morocco now controls the major
northwestern area
Constitution: no independent
constitution
Former Colonial Status: Spanish
Independence Date: none
Suffrage: adult males

MILITARY

Nuclear Weapons Status: none
Current Hostilities: conflict between
Polisario Liberation Movement and
Morocco for administrative control
of the territory

ECONOMY

Currency ($ US Equivalent): Moroccan currency
Workforce: 50% pastoralism and
agriculture; 50% other
Natural Resources: phosphate; iron
ore; fish
Agriculture: camels; sheep; goats
Industry: phosphate and iron mining;
fishing; handicrafts
Energy Production: 56,000 kw
capacity
Energy Consumption Per Capita: 772
kwh

FOREIGN TRADE

Exports: phosphates
Imports: fuel; foodstuffs
Major Trading Partners: Spain;
Spanish possessions; Morocco

Sahrawi fight
against Spanish
colonialists
1934

Polisario move-
ment fights
against the
Spanish
1973-1974

SADR formed
1976

Mauritania
signs the Algiers
Agreement,
recognizes
Polisario and
withdraws from
the Western
Sahara
1979

Seating of SADR
delegation at OAU
results in walkout
of pro-Moroccan
delegations;
phosphate mine
reopens
1982

1983

September:
OAU talks on
Western Sahara
collapse

January-March
1984: Morocco's
defensive wall
around Western
Sahara industrial
and mining zone
is enlarged

February 1984:
Mauritania
recognizes
SADR as a
sovereign state

WESTERN SAHARA: THE SAHARAWI ARAB DEMOCRATIC REPUBLIC

"The baptism of a child before its conception," is how Sekou Touré of Guinea described the admission of the Saharawi Arab Democratic Republic (SADR) to the Organization of African Unity before a referendum had been carried out among the people. A majority of the states in the OAU have recognized SADR as the fifty-first member of the organization, but its existence as a sovereign state is still a matter of dispute.

DOES SADR EXIST?

Does SADR exist? A strong case can be made in its favor.

The country is situated on the Atlantic edge of the Sahara Desert. Spain claimed this desert land, and it was administered as a Spanish colony from the 1930s to 1975. In 1975-1976 Spain determined to withdraw from the territory. Despite the former moves that had been made toward self-government in the region, Spain secretly negotiated to give the area to Morocco and Mauritania.

The peoples of Western Sahara did not agree with this new colonialism. The liberation movement, the Polisario Front, which had fought against the Spanish from 1973 to 1975, continued to struggle against the Moroccans and Mauritanians. In 1979 Mauritania signed an agreement with Polisario and withdrew from Western Sahara. Morocco still claims the territory and is at war with the Polisario.

Today a majority of this arid land is controlled by the Polisario Front, which formed SADR in 1976. The only areas that Morocco controls are two important coastal enclaves. The main enclave, called "the useful triangle," is located in the extreme northwest of the country and contains the major settlements, including El Ayoun, and the valuable phosphate mines, which were reopened in July 1982 after six years of inactivity. This enclave is protected by a wall of sand, which is presently being extended, nearly doubling the territory behind which the Moroccans have established minefields, sensors, artillery, and troops. Between forty thousand and seventy-five thousand soldiers are estimated to be stationed in this tiny area. Meanwhile, Polisario forces number between three thousand and five thousand persons. However, unlike the Moroccans, the Polisario are Saharawi who know the desert intimately. They have fought a guerrilla war in which they have suffered few casualties. The war now appears to be at a stalemate.

PLANS FOR A REFERENDUM

Everyone has agreed that the Saharawi have a right to take part in a referendum to determine their future. According to the 1974 Spanish census, there are seventy-four thousand people in Western Sahara—over half of whom live in the area now occupied by Morocco. Traditional citizens are "sons of the clouds," nomadic people who seek water and food for their herds, but the people of the settlements have often developed a different life-style. There are also Western Saharans living in refugee camps in Algeria. It will be difficult to organize a referendum.

However, the greatest obstacle to discovering the people's view is the attitude of Morocco's King Hassan. Hassan has declared that Morocco will not give up its "amputated Saharan provinces," especially not to SADR, which Hassan views as an ally of Algeria. Division over the issue caused the breakdown in the OAU summit in 1982. Another crisis in June 1983 was avoided when Muhammed Abdelaziz, Secretary General of the Polisario Front, and other members of SADR's delegation to the OAU voluntarily withdrew from the summit meeting "in the interests of African unity." An OAU peace plan adopted at this time proposed direct negotiations between Polisario and Morocco, leading to a referendum on self-determination by December 1983. No referendum took place because Morocco would not talk directly to SADR representatives, whom Hassan considers to be the puppets of Algeria. A confrontation between Morocco and SADR at the November 1984 OAU meetings seems likely.

DEVELOPMENT

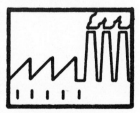

Phosphate deposits were discovered in 1943. There are reserves of 1.7 billion tons. Polisario has attacked the Fosbucraa conveyer belt used for transmission of the ore, but the operations continue. Western Sahara is the sixth major phosphate exporter in the world, with the returns going to Morocco.

FREEDOM

The United States has played a role in obstructing the freedom of SADR by tripling military aid to Morocco, and failing to challenge Morocco for use of United States military personnel in its war in the Western Sahara.

HEALTH/WELFARE

There is little evidence of increased health and well-being for Saharawi peoples in the midst of the liberation war.

ACHIEVEMENTS

Traditionally, Saharawi peoples had no central government administration. Decisions have been made at local levels by assemblies of free men. Polisario has been a focus for unity. The 600 representatives at the fifth Congress in October 1983 elected a president, a nine-member executive council and a twenty-one-member politboro.

Topic Guide to Articles: West Africa

TOPIC AREA	TREATED AS AN ISSUE IN	TOPIC AREA	TREATED AS AN ISSUE IN
Confederation	8. Shaky Start for Senegambia	**Medicine**	4. Herbs in Pharmacy
Culture	3. Upper Volta: Women on the March	**Natural Resources**	2. Unable to See the Trees for the Wood
Democracy	1. Nigeria: Why the Soldiers Ousted Shagari		4. Herbs in Pharmacy
	7. Guinea Coup Leaders Pledge 'Genuine Democracy' for Poor but Mineral-Rich Nation		5. Sahel Herders Excel
			6. Cape Verde: Drought as a Way of Life
	10. We Talk to Jerry Rawlings		8. Shaky Start for Senegambia
Economy	2. Unable to See the Trees for the Wood	**Political Development**	1. Nigeria: Why the Soldiers Ousted Shagari
	6. Cape Verde: Drought as a Way of Life		3. Upper Volta: Women on the March
	8. Shaky Start for Senegambia		7. Guinea Leaders Pledge 'Genuine Democracy' for Poor but Mineral-Rich Nation
	9. Nigeria and Her Neighbours		8. Shaky Start for Senegambia
	10. We Talk to Jerry Rawlings		10. We Talk to Jerry Rawlings
Human Rights	1. Nigeria: Why the Soldiers Ousted Shagari	**Regional Concerns**	9. Nigeria and Her Neighbours
	3. Upper Volta: Women on the March	**Women**	3. Upper Volta: Women on the March
	7. Guinea Leaders Pledge 'Genuine Democracy' for Poor but Mineral-Rich Nation		
	10. We Talk to Jerry Rawlings		

AFRICA NEWS/January 9, 1984

Nigeria: Why The Soldiers Ousted Shagari

[AN] "The way things were going, any government would be more acceptable to the people than the Shagari government."

That is the way one prominent Nigerian businessman—and former senator—explained to the BBC last week what seems to be a mix of acquiescence and relief at the latest military takeover in Africa's most populous nation.

The Dec. 31 coup, accomplished with what one reporter described as "surgical precision," left astonishingly few casualties, as resistance was almost nil. The only reported death was that of Brigadier Ibrahim Bako, who was allegedly killed when leading a battallion of troops charged with the task of arresting the President Shehu Shagari in the new federal capital, Abuja.

Despite the efforts of his Presidential Guard, Shagari was taken prisoner and is now being held in Lagos, Nigeria's largest city and longtime capital. Dozens of government ministers and members of the legislature are also said to have been arrested last week, some of them taken from their homes by soldiers in the early hours of Dec. 31.

What punishment, if any, awaits them is not yet clear. The new regime, a Supreme Military Council (SMC) headed by Maj. Gen. Mohammed Buhari, characterized the former administration as "inept and corrupt," leaving Nigeria a "beggar nation."

In its initial broadcast Saturday, the new junta was represented by Brig. Saleh Abacha, who cited the nation's debts, the high cost of staple foods and the disintegration of health services as the justification for the coup.

"After due consultation over these deplorable conditions," Abacha said, "I and my colleagues in the armed forces have, in the discharge of our national role as promoters and protectors of national interests, decided to effect a change . . ."

Abacha announced that the constitution had been suspended and ordered all elected and appointed officials to report to police within seven days.

Maj. Gen. Buhari had his first encounter with civil servants on Jan. 1, a session in which he warned that "accountability" would be the watchword of his administration and that anyone caught abusing the powers of office would be locked up.

According to a report of the meeting on Lagos Radio, Buhari told the assembled permanent secretaries that he "would not condone the nonsenses of litigation in dealing with culprits."

Buhari, 41, was one of the young colonels who toppled head of state Gen. Gowon in 1975. He has served as head of the Nigerian National Petroleum Corporation and is regarded as a political conservative.

While businesses reopened throughout the country almost immediately after the coup, a curfew has remained in effect and the borders were still closed at press time.

Reaction to the coup in the Western press, characterized at first by laments over the passing of an "African democracy," softened somewhat Tuesday when Barclays Bank in London disclosed that Nigeria has paid some $50 million on a $1.6 billion note that had been rescheduled last year. Later, however, banking sources said the payment might have been authorized prior to the coup.

Nigeria's Western allies were also reassured by the apparent lack of an ideological bent to the new regime.

Within Nigeria itself, the press reported a number of demonstrations of support for the military take-over. Any potential for anti-coup protests, however, may have been neutralized by the military's threat of reprisals against those who disturbed the peace.

Editorially, several papers were approving of the putsch, according to early dispatches on the BBC. *The Punch* welcomed the change in government; *The Nigerian Statesman* described the coup as "inevitable;" and the *Daily Times* argued that the military is capable of "containing the situation."

President Shagari was toppled just two days after launching a new austerity budget that was designed to cope with the decline in oil revenues because of the world market glut in recent years. A shortage of foreign exchange last year had forced Shagari to enact emergency legislation requiring constraints on state spending—a move that was politically un-popular.

One of the new regime's first steps was to attempt to force food vendors to sell at controlled prices. This move was greeted enthusiastically by consumers, but traders in Ibadan, Nigeria's second largest city, reportedly closed their stalls rather than follow the pricing guidelines.

"My own measure of our economic development," Buhari said last week, "will be based on such indicators as the availability of the essentials of life such as drinking water, electricity, food, and other such basic commodities in our local markets, at prices within the reach of the lowest income earner in the country."

In defending the coup, Buhari charged that the politicians had been guilty of "shameless thuggery" in rigging last summer's elections. Speaking to foreign diplomats last Wednesday, the new leader charged that Nigeria's "Second Republic"—as the 1979 constitution came to be known—had not been a "real democracy."

"Nigeria," he said, "had been enslaved by a handful of people who had been sharing the wealth among themselves and who were determined to stay in office at any cost."

Ironically, the twin issues of corruption and accountability repeatedly mentioned by the new SMC had become a prime focus of President Shagari as he began his second term. In appointing a new Cabinet team, for example, Shagari dumped 80% of his old ministers in an effort to give the impression of a thorough housecleaning.

Shagari also created a new Ministry of National Guidance in order to achieve what he termed an "ethical reorientation" and "disciplined, honest" society. "I am dismayed to understand," he said recently, "that corruption, fraud and smuggling are not only being institutionalized but are fast becoming a business pursuit."

Some observers had taken Shagari's substantial victory in last year's election—his National party of Nigeria (NPN) won an effective two-thirds majority in both chambers of the legislature—as a sign that Nigeria had begun to transcend a politics based on regional protectionism and ethnic divisions. Other analysts charged that the recent election was a failure, with irregularities marring the results and spoiling faith in the system.

Fraud and improprieties probably do not explain Shagari's substantial election victory as much as the facts that his party's machinery was the most effective and that even many discontented voters cast ballots for Shagari, believing him to be the only candidate that could at least keep the peace.

In spite of massive NPN victories in Niger State, for example, violent anti-government protests have taken place there in recent months. And all the while Nigerian pundits have continued to suggest the possibility of another military take-over.

Writing about this situation in *West Africa* magazine prior to the coup, political analyst Lindsay Barrett concluded: "At this stage of the growth of a political machinery in Nigeria there are still too many people willing to talk and too few willing to vote for their convictions."

"Unless the parties can achieve a high level of service," Barrett continued, "it is unlikely that the system will be able to survive the strains of distrust and electoral apathy."

Article 2   **WEST AFRICA** June 1983

Unable to see the trees for the wood

The destruction of Ivory Coast's rainforest may ruin the country's economy as well as its ecological balance. Howard Schissel found that in the face of numerous vested interests, government attempts at reforestation seem merely nominal.

A SPECTRE is haunting the Ivory Coast. The spectre is the growing menace that in less than a generation its primary rain forest, once the densest in all West Africa, is likely to be but a memory of the past. The rapid, and often abusive, exploitation of the Ivory Coast's forestry resources — a key factor in the country's relative prosperity in the 1960s and 1970s — has meant that since independence the tropical woodland has shrunk from over 12 million hectares to less than four million. In spite of calls to halt this massacre and timid government conservation efforts, cutting continues at the alarming pace of some 400,000 hectares a year.

A report prepared in 1980 by a team of experts from Abidjan's Institute of Tropical Geography dramatically emphasised the Ivory Coast's dilemma: "In the face of different consumers of land, the total disappearance of the wooded area is expected by the end of the century." The decimation of this natural resource will have serious consequences for the Ivorian economy and an incalculable impact on the eco-system.

Firstly, the jobs of around 40,000 people employed in the forestry and wood processing industry will be put into jeopardy in the medium term. Further downstream, the activity of the Port of Abidjan, a third of whose business involves wood export, and the Port of San Pedro, near the frontier with Liberia, will be severely affected. Likewise, a third of the Ivory Coast's road transport is accounted for by forestry-related traffic. Secondly, wood exports chalk up foreign currency earnings in the neighbourhood of CFA 85,000m. a year. This source of revenue is liable to rapidly dry up for the hard-pressed Ivorian exchequer.

As the forest recedes, replaced by less fertile savannah bushland, the environmental balance is thrown into disarray. Without the protection of the vegetal cover of the forest, rain water either rapidly evaporates or runs off, provoking serious erosion. This phenomenon has resulted in a dangerous lowering of the water table, even in the southern coastal areas. Yet another negative effect is the diminishing of secondary rainfall further north in the Sahel region.

Ivorian government officials have stressed on numerous occasions that the preservation of the forests must become a national priority. Most development experts, however, are highly sceptical about the government's ability and will to save what still can be saved of the country's forest lands. Important economic and political interests are involved in forestry and their influence often outweighs abstract notions like "the national good".

The most immediate cause of the Ivory Coast's fading forests is the activity of forestry companies. In the search for high immediate profit, these firms tend to log only the most valuable species like Assamele, Sipo, Acajou and Makere, disregarding legislation establishing quotas of different varieties of trees to be harvested. Illegal cutting of protected species is rampant, as is logging in closed national forest areas. A commonly used ploy to get around restrictive legislation is to declare, with the complicity of customs officials, rare tropical hardwood varieties as more common ones.

A government decree some years back theoretically designed to husband forestry reserves by limiting new logging permits to Ivorian nationals has proved to be counterproductive. Ivorian businessmen and politicians often receive these coveted permits thanks to their influence in the state administration. Lacking in both the capital and expertise necessary to properly exploit their concessions, they tend to sub-let them to either French or Lebanese operators. They, in turn, have a unique objective: squeeze to the highest rate of return from their investment. They have little reason to respect government conservation rules for their approach is based solely on short-term profit.

Of course, the forestry companies are not the only villains in the piece. Their activities open up vast tracts of virgin forest land to speculative agriculture. Land-hungry small farmers swarm after the woodsmen and clear remaining vegetation to plant cash crops such as coffee, cocoa,

pineapples and bananas. Once soil fertility has been exhausted, farmers often move on to new patches of land leaving behind them unproductive bush.

This process makes the rural areas more vunerable to the spread of fires like those which ravaged the Ivory Coast earlier in the year (*West Africa*, April 4). In this case not only were thousands of hectares of forest cover reduced to ash, but also large plantations. Even the classified forest of Banco, just north of Abidjan, suffered from the bush fires.

The government's will to go beyond words to action in the preservation of its forest patrimony will be put to a severe test in years to come at the forest of Taï, one of the few remaining wooded areas still relatively intact. Located in the south-western part of the country, it has already started to feel the impact of illegal cutting. A new threat will be posed by the Soubré dam: the population displaced by the dam's flooding will naturally be attracted to the still fertile forest lands in the nearby park.

The forestry industry, in principle, is based on the exploitation of a renewable resource and therefore can be a valuable money-spinner for generations. It is essential, however, that reforestation keep apace with logging so that the long-term potential of the industry is maintained at a satisfactory level. The World Bank has financed a project to replant 25,000 hectares by the mid-1980s. The state reforestation agency, SODEFOR, has not succeeded in replanting more than 3,000 hectares a year. Given the extent of forest destruction, this reforestation programme can be labelled as symbolic.

Article 3

WEST AFRICA 7 November 1983

UPPER VOLTA

Women on the march

By our correspondent in Ouagadougou

ALL COMMENTATORS are agreed: the women's march on October 9 was one of the largest demonstrations Ouagadougou has ever seen. Thousands upon thousands of women walked, shuffled, ran and even danced past, chanting and singing the myriad revolutionary songs and slogans that have appeared over the last two months. The noise was deafening. They

were young and they were old; they were smart office ladies and they were poor old women wearing their best cloth for the occasion. Many carried signs and banners held high; many more had a baby strapped tightly to their back.

The march was led by the hundred or so female members of Ouagadougou's Com-

mittees for the Defence of the Revolution who are receiving a basic military training: all wore a plain olive green military uniform. The Minister of Social Affairs, Bernadette Pale, was amongst them, also in military uniform, as they marched from the newly renamed Place de la Revolution to the Presidential Palace, along the main road which has just been resurfaced with voluntary labour from the Defence Committees.

Part of Thomas Sankara's growing charisma has its roots in saying what everybody already knows but nobody else has dared to say publicly. He had not planned to address this rally, but after prolonged appeals from a crowd far larger than anybody had anticipated, he eventually came out and made an improvised speech which shocked many male listeners. It will also have given food for thought to many of the women on the rally who had undoubtedly come for a social gathering.

He began by saying that he would not keep the women long because he knew that their reactionary husbands were at home waiting for their supper, but went on to outline concrete ways in which women could liberate themselves in their daily lives. Women must demand a savings account for the household money, to ensure that it is not being spent in bars or on bargirls. "How many men must a woman sleep with just to get a job as a secretary?" This must stop: telephonists and typists must denounce their bosses when they are corrupt. Voltaic women would have a chance to meet their sisters from Angola, Mozambique, Cuba, Nicaragua, Libya and Algeria to share their revolutionary experiences, he said.

Watching the march go past, I asked a close colleague of President Sankara what the revolution was going to do for these Voltaic women in concrete terms. He replied: "What are Voltaic women going to do for the revolution in concrete terms?" The history of women's development projects in Upper Volta suggests that this is the right approach to take.

There have been numerous so-called women's projects in Upper Volta, most of them directed at village women. The general objectives of these projects have been clear enough: increased revenue, improved health and literacy. But their results have not often been encouraging.

The reasons for this lack of success are many, but the most important appears to be village women's lack of involvement in the projects' design and implementation. This is where the new Voltaic government needs to build on the enthusiasm for participation so clearly demonstrated on the march.

Health projects have often emphasised the importance of clean water to prevent hookworm. Women are responsible for the supply of domestic water and so the promotion of water filtering has been directed at them. But the filter is made up of layers of gravel which have to be washed frequently and thoroughly to be effective. The dry season, when water is in short supply and most in need of filtering, is the time when water can least be wasted on washing the filter. If village women had been associated in the design stage of this piece of "appropriate technology", they would quickly have pointed out the drawbacks. As it is the water filter has been a failure in many villages.

Similarly, literacy has been promoted as an important part of women's projects. But reading and writing are not necessarily a women's priority, especially if they do not appear to be directly related to their daily lives. Consequently, attendance at classes has been low, and many women have failed to complete the course. This is another example of project planners drawing up their own list of priorities rather than listening to the expressed needs of women.

President Sankara first raised the question of men's exploitation of women in his Dori speech on September 22. "To make a woman believe that she is inferior to a man is just another method of exploitation and domination. Thus women are considered as baby-making machines . . . women are a source of profit to exploitative men . . . a source of pleasure."

That speech can now be seen as a preliminary to the major analysis of political direction which was given on the radio on October 2, the night before President Sankara flew to the Vittel summit. The speech lasted for an hour and a half, and while the first half was devoted to an analysis of class struggle in Voltaic society, President Sankara went on to talk about the three sectors which will be affected by the Revolution: the army, the economy and women.

The "woman question" had hardly surfaced in Upper Volta before August 4, and it was unthinkable for it to be given such priority by a national politician. "The basis of women's domination by men is found in the system of society's political and social life. In changing the social order which oppresses women, the revolution is creating the conditions for her real emancipation . . . The revolution and women's liberation go together. And it is no act of charity or outbreak of humanism to talk about the emancipation of women. It is a basic necessity for the triumph of the revolution. Women carry the other half of the sky" . . . "Real emancipation of women will make them responsible, will link them to productive activities and to the different struggles which confront the people. Real emancipation of women will make men respect and esteem them. Emancipation is like freedom: it is not conceded, it is conquered. And it is for women themselves to put forward their claims and to organise to bring them about."

The increasing involvement of women in the Defence Committees shows how the National Council for the Revolution is extending its power base in Voltaic society. The Ministry of Social and Women's Affairs has been restructured to take account of this new involvement. The women's march on October 9 symbolised how successful the country's new rulers have been in activating women's desire to participate: they now need to learn from the often negative experience of women's projects, and in doing so help channel this new found self-consciousness of women as a political force for national development.

Article 4

WEST AFRICA July 1983

Herbs in pharmacy

African pharmacists are looking at ways of integrating modern medicine with traditional herbal remedies. Ben Ephson reports from a recent conference in Accra.

PHARMACISTS convened at the E. J. Roye Building in Monrovia, Liberia, on October 26, 1976, and on October 30, the delegates of the West African Sub-region unanimously approved the establishment of the West African Pharmaceutical Federation (WAPF).

The fourth general assembly of the WAPF was held at the Kwame Nkrumah Conference Centre in Accra from May 25-27, 1983, under the theme "Pharmacy practice by the year 2000". The theme was chosen against the background of WHO programme of "Health for All by the Year 2000", also known as primary health care.

The formal opening address was by the PNDC Secretary for Health, Dr. Charles Y. Buadu. He spoke on "The role of the pharmacist in primary health care".

Dr. Buadu said the most important challenge the pharmacist faced in the primary health care was the introduction of traditional medicine, and herbal medicine which will be functioning side by side with orthodox medicine. "As we are all aware, almost all the countries in our sub-region are in ever-increasing economic difficulties. Pharmacists can help our countries by abandoning our taste for nicely-packed factory-produced medicines and then take on the task of persuading the patients to do the same. As a pharmacist myself, I know that Mist. Mag. Trisilicate prepared in the dispensary could be just as effective as the product with 25 ingredients made in the most sophisticated modern factory owned by a research-based pharmaceutical company," he added.

The keynote address on the Assembly's theme was delivered by L. I. L. Ndika, Professor of Pharmacology at the University of Benin, in Nigeria. Born September 30, 1930, Professor Ndika has been lecturing graduate and post-graduate dental and medical students for the past 23 years. He established the pharmacology department for the University of Lagos in 1962 and in 1971, established the Faculty of Pharmacy of the University of Benin.

He then took an analytical look at present pharmacy practice in West Africa with emphasis on Nigeria. He said about 77 per cent of all registered pharmacists work in community, 15 per cent in hospital, 5 per cent in manufacturing and distributive pharmacies, 3 per cent in government, teaching and other pharmaceutical activities.

It thus came to light that an overwhelming number of our pharmacists are engaged in community pharmacy practice where their representative functions include filling prescriptions in a legal manner, checking the prescription, transferring the medication to an appropriate container, preparing and applying the label and determining the selling price.

On traditional medicine, Professor Ndika said: "Africa's major contribution to drug discovery and consequently to medicine generally will be found in her relentless study of the medical potentials of her rich fauna and flora. The concept of forging a working understanding between pharmaceutical research scientists and the African medicine men or herbalists must be practicalised. The African traditional physician is an embodiment of the priest, physician and pharmacist. He possesses a remarkable knowledge of a variety of biological drugs. We do recognise that these traditional healers possess enormous healing skills, we do recognise that in their private practice, they have legitimate and tangible claims to success; they service the health needs of a vast majority of our people and have fields of specialisation".

To Professor Ndika, the course of pharmacy practice in the year 2000 in West Africa will be dictated by forces which are extrinsic and intrinsic to pharmacy. He predicted that the profession will respond to modalities of practice and secondly, by a considerable increase in the number of its practitioners as well as by improved and more efficient methods of health services.

By the year 2000, Professor Ndika concluded "pharmaceutical research scientists would have responded to social calls and needs by establishing a good working relationship with our herbalists, and would show greater interest in research into our traditional pharmacy. Industrial pharmacy would have begun to emerge in greater numbers as a direct result of better-trained and qualified industrial pharmacists and expanded pharmaceutical research activities." The long round of applause amply demonstrated the effect the one-hour speech had on the 120 or so delegates.

Dr. Wilfred Opakunle, of the Department of Pharmaceutical Technology and Industrial Pharmacy at the College of Medicine of the University of Ibadan, Nigeria, dwelt on "Manufacturing practice by the year 2000". Dr. Opakunle reviewed the current set-up of the drug manufacturing industry in West Africa. He said there is the notion in the industry that it is more profitable to import finished pharmaceutical products than to manufacture them locally because prices of raw materials, machinery and spare parts are dictated from developed nations.

"Drug manufacturing practice by the year 2000 should have come to a stage in our sub-region where local environmental conditions would be reflected in locally-developed 'good manufacturing practice' guidelines, development and the overall management of men, materials and machines," Dr. Opakunle concluded.

A paper on "General practice pharmacy by the year 2000" was presented by Mr. Murtada Sesay, from Sierra Leone. "It is thought-provoking and perhaps unfortunate when one considers the fact that in many parts of the developing world traditional healers have played a role in both diagnosing and dispensing 'medical products' to our rural folks, no traditional material or methods have been considered and deemed suitable to be included in the essential drugs list," Mr. Sesay argued.

He also felt general practice pharmacy has widened the gap between the patient and pharmacist because of the rather prominent commercial element in every thread of our fabric. To him, the shop-keeping/trading image has held the pharmacist back from his rightful place as a full member of the health care team.

With military precision, Major Isaac Buabeng, of the Ghanaian Ministry of Defence, spoke on "The supply and control of pharmaceuticals by the year 2000" with the aid of cinema illustrations. He said that in Ghana, as in other West African countries, the supply and control of pharmaceuticals had been severely impaired during the last 12 years. The causes of perennial shortages of medical supplies, he noted, were the regular excuses of the non-availability of funds, delays in clearing pharmaceuticals from the ports, lack of appreciation to assess population growth, the procurement process and lack of control of drugs in public hospitals. To solve these problems, Major Buabeng advocated the establishment of a pharmaceutical buffer stock and the encouragement of local drug manufacturing.

Like all the speakers, he touched on herbal medicines: "We should undertake a systematic survey of classification and collection of our indigenous medicines, compile their local use and where possible, confirm their efficacy, screen interesting and effective ones for their basic pharmacological activities."

A communiqué issued at the end of the assembly accepted that a proposed school of pharmacy should be sited in Monrovia to cater for Sierra Leone, The Gambia and Liberia. It also approved the establishment of a West African post-graduate college of pharmacists in a country yet to be named.

On traditional medicine, the communiqué said: "The assembly recognises the important role which traditional medicines can play in health care delivery in the community, particularly during the present world-wide economic recession. The pharmacist is therefore called upon to direct his attention towards the preparation of the traditional medicines currently in use in the sub-region into appropriate dosage forms."

The assembly elected Ghana's Mr.

James Pearce-Biney as its new president for a two-year term, with Mr. M. C. Azuike, of Nigeria, as the new secretary-general.

I managed to squeeze an exclusive interview with the busy executive secretary, Dr. John Ocran, on problems confronting the WAPF. He said: "The WAPF faces manpower problems, Sierra Leone has 16 pharmacists, 500 in Ghana, three in The Gambia and about 2,400 in Nigeria. Plans to arrest this problem led to the establishment of the School of Pharmacy in Monrovia where the first intake is expected in March, 1984."

He added that the WAPF had been trying to get a regional drug policy, and that the quality control committee of the WAPF, under the chairmanship of Mr. James Binka, had an important role in ensuring that manufacturers do not dump low-quality drugs in the sub-region.

Dr. Ocran said medical staff have not shown any genuine interest in traditional medicine and the WAPF is compiling a list of various herbs to get pharmacists to prepare it into acceptable forms, like one

Traditional healers: sought out by modern pharmacists for their knowledge of ancient cures.

calabashful be made into a half-concentrated glassful.

The Fifth International Symposium on Medicinal Plants will be held at the University of Ile-Ife, Nigeria, from July 13-15, 1983.

The desire to resort to herbal medicine to cure certain ailments even has international appeal. The May 26, 1983, issue of London's *Daily Mail*, carried a news item "Herbal war on migraine". It said: "A herbal remedy for migraine could have the rare distinction of being accepted by conventional medicine, 2000 years after its discovery. The health department has approved a clinical trial on the leaves of fever-few, a variety of chrysanthemum. The tests follow claims by migraine sufferers that they get relief by eating its leaves. Pharmacologist, Dr. Stewart Johnson, found seven in ten users of the plant claimed it made attacks less frequent. A third said it stopped attacks. The plant's medicinal qualities have long been claimed. In 1772, a doctor wrote that 'in the worst headaches, this herb exceeds whatever else is known'."

Article 5

AFRICA NEWS/November 14, 1983

SAHEL HERDERS EXCEL

[AN] The semi-nomadic method that the people of the Sahel have evolved for grazing their livestock produces from two to six times as much protein per land area as the methods used in similar climates in the United States and Australia.

That conclusion is one of the findings in a multi-year Malian-Dutch research project reported in the Sept. 30 issue of *Science*. The Dutch authors of the study, H. Bremen and C.T. de Wit, also contradict other widely-held impressions of the region.

The general image of the Sahel put forth by the news media over the past several years is one of drought, overgrazing, desertification and starvation. As Bremen and de Wit note, "It is generally thought that (i) the productivity of Sahelian pastures is limited by rainfall; (ii) livestock herds in the Sahel are too large because the nomadic and semi-nomadic herdsmen consider them a status symbol. . . ." Their report is intended to correct these mistakes.

Stretching from Senegal and Mauritania in the west through Mali and Niger into Chad, the Sahel forms a semi-arid southern border to

the Sahara Desert. The average annual rainfall varies between 600 millimeters (24 inches) at the southern edge of the Sahel and only 100 millimeters (4 inches) at the north where it meets the desert (see map).

This scant moisture budget is further constrained by the fact that the rain falls in a brief period of two to four summer months when high temperatures increase the evaporation rate.

The research project (entitled "Primary Production Sahel") included multidisciplinary teams from agricultural institutes in Bamako, Mali, and Wageningen, The Netherlands. In one of several approaches to the research, one group studied a 1250-kilometer (775-mile) Sahara-to-savanna cross-section of the Sahel.

Soil studies showed that lack of water is not the worst problem for Sahelian agriculture. When researchers added an optimum amount of water, plant production doubled. On the other hand, when they used natural rainfall and added an optimum amount of nitrogen and phosphorus, the production quintupled.

In the careful language customary in such

reports, the authors "conclude therefore that low availability of nitrogen and phosphorus is a more serious problem than low rainfall." Only in the northern Sahel approaching the Sahara did they find water to be the limiting factor.

The amount of forage available for grazing in the Sahel varies with the rainfall. In the rainy season there is much more than in the dry portions of the year. Surprisingly, however, the quality of the pasturage varies inversely with the quantity. Consequently, the dry season forage is nutritionally superior.

The relative availability of water, nitrogen and phosphorus determine the digestibility and protein content of the plants. (Nitrogen, in particular, is a crucial element in proteins.) During the dry seasons, lack of water limits plant growth rates. But under these conditions, the high ratio of nitrogen to water produces plants with a high protein content (beginning at about 18% and declining to 12% at the end of the growing season).

In the rainy season, by contrast, the increased water availability means that nitrogen is in short supply. The result is a large quantity of plant production at low quality (protein content as low as 3%).

Livestock requires a protein content of 7% to maintain good condition. In order to grow and produce milk, the animals need higher quality. Furthermore, cattle cannot make up for poor forage by simply eating more, because their digestive processes slow down with lower quality feed.

These facts show why settlement schemes that depend solely upon irrigation are doomed. The herdspeople of the Sahel maintain their migratory methods of cattle production not from ignorant adherence to tradition but from ecological necessity.

At the beginning of the rainy season in July, they take their herds north to the good rangelands (nitrogen high relative to water). By October the dry season's lack of drinking water (not food) drives them south. On the poor protein grazing there (nitrogen low relative to water), the cattle barely maintain life.

In spite of this restriction to poor pastures for much of the year, the Sahelian herders

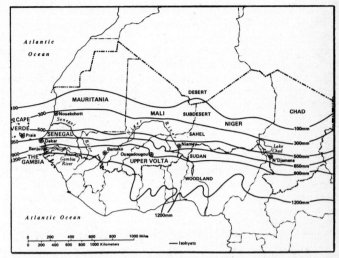

Map shows average annual rainfall (in millimeters) throughout the west African region. / *U.S. Agency for International Development*

produce two to six times as much animal protein per land area as do cattle producers in areas of comparable rainfall in the United States and Australia.

One drawback to the Sahelian system, however, is that herds, of necessity, become quite large. The Malian-Dutch study showed that the plant nitrogen available is most efficiently exploited by large herds that roam to find young plants, which are much higher in protein than older vegetation. The large herds also utilize plant nitrogen more thoroughly because less is lost to other nonproductive factors such as brush fire and the evaporation of moisture.

Sahelian cattle producers have one-tenth to one-thousandth as much land available to them as do ranchers in the United States and Australia. Yet for mere subsistence the Sahelian herder requires four or five animals per family member.

According to de Wit and Bremen, it is these factors, not a lack of rainfall or the irrational desire for large herds as a status symbol, that often leads herders to a grazing density "above the physical limits of the ecosystem."

Article 6

CAPE VERDE

Drought as a way of life

WEST AFRICA 6 February 1984

The West African community and international aid circles have become alerted to the drought throughout the region. But the people of Cape Verde have been living through water shortages since the early '70s. The economy is surviving on repatriated earnings from abroad, and the soil needs replenishment; from the gorges of Santo Antão to the desalination plant at Mindelo, the fight against the elements continues. Our Special Correspondent recently in Praia reports.

COWS have taken on goat-like characteristics in Cape Verde. They clamber on barren rocky slopes that descend to the sea, where townspeople tip garbage, and graze on brown paper and plastic bottles. The blades of grass they vainly seek are protected in mini-plantations behind stone walls, where the tireless struggle against 15 years of drought continues.

People remember the exact dates of rainfall for several years back. In 1983 it rained twice, and one of those days, which perhaps augurs well for the future, was September 12, birthdate of Amilcar Cabral, national hero, architect of the revolution, assassinated in Bissau in 1973.

The Cape Verde archipelago disappears off the edge of most maps of West Africa, but more often is missed out altogether. This horseshoe of 10 volcanic islands and eight islets lies 450 km west of the coast of Senegal, with a population of 300,000. A further million Cape Verdians live in economic exile, in the USA, Holland, Portugal, Italy and Senegal, and their remittances form an important source of foreign exchange.

The traditional *morna* ballads recall the bitter history of the islands — five centuries of Portuguese colonialism, an economy based on the slave trade, periodic famine brought on by droughts, emigration and struggle for survival.

Between 1748 and 1948, Cape Verde experienced 10 disastrous droughts, each one bringing the death from famine of between 10 per cent and 40 per cent of the entire population. The graph tracing the population growth of the islands over this period is a line of jagged peaks and depressions, as stark and inhospitable as any of the mountainous islands themselves. The drought of 1973, which devastated all the other countries of the Sahel from Senegal to Chad, drove a further 17 per cent of Cape Verdians abroad.

The lyrics of the *morna* are not out of date now: nostalgia and the separation of families remain the reality for most people, and about 6,000 more migrate annually. However, since the winning of independence (with Guinea Bissau) in 1975, a socialist oriented, but pragmatic political leadership has tried to motivate the population at home, through giving priority to the basic needs of the rural areas — health care, basic education, water.

President Aristides Pereira, veteran of the liberation struggle in Guinea Bissau, leads a government firmly committed to the equitable development of the country — which was totally abused and neglected by the Portuguese — through their policy of "popular participation". This means that the Cape Verdian population, suitably trained and organised, should be the principal creative and constructive force for national development. Mass organisations (youth, women, unions), plus housing and other community associations, the Ministry of Rural Development, and the party (the PAICV) have been attempting towards this ideal.

The first National Development Plan (1982-85), published in August 1983, apologises for the fact that its preparation was not made with "popular participation", because of the inherent deficiencies in the state's planning apparatus. It notes particularly the insufficient local planning organisations through which the popular voice could be channelled. Attempts to involve the population in development decision-making identified problems hampering such participation, namely the weakness of local organisations, lack of proper work programmes, inexperience of government cadres, and inadequate inter-island co-ordination.

Correcting deficiencies

The first Plan aims to correct these deficiencies, especially at the level of popular organisations, which should then form the necessary structures for the promotion of literacy teaching, agricultural training and credit, producer and consumer co-operatives, urbanism and sanitation, health education and so on. All these activities are going on already, but without the desired co-ordination and efficiency.

Many of the principles and guidelines of the Plan were inspired by the writings of Amilcar Cabral, whose picture (informal, smiling, in woolly hat and crooked spectacles) adorns the walls of all public places, alongside that of President Pereira. Cabral's words and slogans are painted on the walls of Praia, the capital (Santiago island), and Mindelo, the main commercial centre (São Vicente island). His words are visible from aircraft, as stones carefully arranged on vast bare mountain slopes; they preface books, magazines, local airline tickets, noticeboards . . . but manage, amazingly, not to become hollow clichés.

Cape Verde is nothing but stones and fish ("pedra e peixe") as the epithet goes. Fishing is, besides agriculture, the principal economic activity of the islands. Substantial support is being given to artisanal fisheries by the state; industrial fisheries, especially the export of lobster and tuna, bring in 36 per cent of all export earnings.

The island of Sal (meaning salt) is flat, and is the site of the international airport built by the Portuguese for strategic purposes, and largest industrial employer and earner of foreign exchange in Cape Verde. Many large airways use it as a refuelling and transit stop. When South Africa began to have problems about over-flying African countries, a bargain was struck with Cape Verde of benefit to both. The South Africans enlarged the airport and equipped it with modern radar and communications facilities. This displays the pragmatic political position the government is obliged to adopt in view of its impoverished economic base. In addition, salt is exported from Sal, constituting 5 per cent of export earnings.

For the rest, 95 per cent of all goods consumed in Cape Verde are imported, with Portugal remaining principal supplier. In view of this external dependence, the fight for an independent planned national economy, which the first Plan advocates, is a hard one. Cape Verde has been the destination of large amounts of food aid since 1976. This is sold, not distributed free, and the proceeds fund projects which aim to increase food production within the country through improved irrigation, conservation and reforestation. These projects are further supported by foreign aid and technical assistance, both governmental and non-governmental.

Lack of water and unemployment are the principal problems in Cape Verde. Massive labour-intensive work projects are being and have been carried out to exploit underground water resources and fight erosion. Barren mountainsides have been stone terraced by hand, as if a giant comb has scraped exactly parallel ridges into them. Mass campaigns have brought out whole organisations at once to plant three million trees between 1978-80. Planting at great altitude has enabled low cloud moisture to be captured and the cultivation of maize and beans (the local staple) possible. High up on Fogo island's volcanic crater, different shapes and textures of arid black cinders, rocks and sand abruptly give way to an Alpine valley in the clouds — coniferous trees, pink flowering oleander bushes, citrus and apple trees, carrots, even wild flowers.

Tailored dry stone walls and dykes are built as small catchments, together with reservoirs and irrigation works for increased agricultural production. Wind pumps are being tried out. Some extract literally only two or three drops of water at a time. A desalination plant is in operation at Mindelo.

Domestic water is piped to very few of the stone built cottages, some of which are perched precipitously on buffs overhanging dizzy valleys and gorges, especially on Santo Antão island. Such positioning of homes is a tradition from slave trade days, when slaves would be rounded up from the coastal settlements, but rarely from the unmapped wilderness of the "interior" as it is still called.

Forced labour built the first roads of hard hand-cut cobbled stone, and labour intensive roadbuilding continues, linking rural dwellers to the island "centres", and to roadside water points.

Water is supplied to public taps, usually housed in a small concrete building with iron bars on the gate — more like a prison cell than the fount of life. "Queues" of rusty tins, basins and buckets form well before the gate to the tap is opened — for two hours a day only.

This is the woman's social centre, but squabbling often comes to blows when it becomes clear that not everyone will be served in the two hours. An armed guard is often posted to these water points to break up fights and maintain order, particularly in the urban centres of Praia and Mindelo.

Men fill up tyre inner tubes with water to irrigate their plants, and transport them on donkey backs, like cargoes of shiny black seals, up the steep slopes. In the towns and villages, women and girls go around for days in hair curlers, perhaps a sign in this officially levelled society, that they are amongst the better off, not having to carry heavy tins of water on their heads!

The struggle for survival continues in Cape Verde as long as rain refuses to fall. The occasional hardy acacia tree, whose branches turn an angle of 90° from the top of the trunk through the constant battering of the trade winds; the four hour walk of a boy to market to sell the single large tuna fish he carries on his head; the cows eating dirty paper. All these glimpses symbolise a tough determination to keep going. While alarm bells are now ringing in international aid circles about "another drought in the Sahel like in 1973", Cape Verdians continue to muster forces to counter a drought situation they have known since 1968.

Article 7 THE CHRISTIAN SCIENCE MONITOR WEDNESDAY, APRIL 4, 1984

Guinea Coup Leaders Pledge 'Geuine Democracy' for Poor But Mineral-Rich Nation

Peter Blackburn
Special to The Christian Science Monitor

Abidjan, Ivory Coast

Guinea's new military rulers, who seized power early Tuesday morning, have freed political prisoners and promised the introduction of "genuine democracy" in the West African country.

The military's bloodless coup was launched one week after the death of President Ahmed Sékou Touré and shortly before Guinea's civilian political leaders were due to meet to discuss the selection of a successor.

In a statement broadcast on Radio Conakry, Guinea's new military rulers said they had acted to prevent the installation of another "personal dictatorship."

They also said they acted to forestall a potentially bitter succession struggle between rival factions within the ruling Democratic Party of Guinea.

The statement condemned the "bloody and pitiless dictatorship" of Sékou Touré, who ruled the country for 26 years after gaining independence from France in 1958.

The statement said that Sékou Touré's international success could not make up for his failures at home. (The President was one of the leaders of the struggle for African independence as well as a founder of the Organization of African Unity.) The fate of interim President and Prime

Béavogui: fate uncertain

Minister Lansana Béavogui, as well as other political leaders including members of the Touré family, is uncertain. Frequent political purges created a climate of terror and disrupted economic activity. Despite immense mineral wealth, Guinea is one of the world's poorest countries.

Basic services, such as electricity and water, are inadequate in the capital, Conakry, and almost nonexistent elsewhere.

The military condemned the "feudal power exercised by Sékou Touré's family, the dishonesty of his advisers, and the widespread corruption in government."

The military coup surprised many observers who believed Sékou Touré had purged the armed forces of any pretenders to power. These observers are also surprised at the apparent lack of resistance to the coup, but they await further signs that the military is firmly in control. Citizens apparently are calm, although the radio has reported scenes of popular rejoicing.

The coup leaders have not been identified, but observers say they are likely to be junior officers. Senior officers are political appointees and closely controlled.

The Guinean Army is Soviet-equipped and -trained and numbers some 10,000 men, according to the London-based International Institute for Strategic Studies. But it was distrusted and neglected by Sékou Touré, who had more confidence in a 9,000-man paramilitary force.

Apart from a promise to respect existing international commitments, military rulers have revealed little about their political leanings. But diplomatic observers believe they are nationalist- rather than Marxist-oriented. Guinea's Constitution has been suspended, and the ruling party dissolved. Its borders and airports, as well as telecommunication links, have been closed and a night curfew imposed.

Article 8

AFRICA NEWS/February 8, 1982

SHAKY START FOR SENEGAMBIA

[AN] *February 1 marked the formal beginning of the confederation linking the west African states of Senegal and Gambia. The new arrangement, which entails cooperation in a number of areas while preserving the independence of both states, was officially ratified by the two legislatures on December 29. But questions about its feasibility — and its legitimacy — remain.*

The mood in the Gambian capital of Banjul was not entirely festive last week, despite President Sir Dawda Jawara's efforts to put the best possible face on his new confederation, a scheme he says Gambians "have every possible reason" to embrace.

Critics of the Senegambia idea charge that Jawara is simply using the proposed union as a way of preserving his hold on power in the face of a turbulent domestic situation, and reminders of that turmoil were very much in evidence in the Gambian capital. A special court dealing with treason cases handed down six more death sentences February 2, while Senegalese troops with heavy weaponry patrolled the surrounding streets.

With last week's verdicts, a total of 12 persons have now been condemned to death for their part in last July's coup attempt against Jawara, while an estimated 900 more are in jail awaiting trial.

The Senegalese soldiers, who maintain a high profile in Banjul these days, first arrived in early August to squelch the plot against Jawara, an uprising fueled by a widespread mutiny in Gambia's 500-strong paramilitary Field Force. Some 400 to 500 persons are said to have died during the episode, including 33 Senegalese troops.

At the time of the failed coup, the intervention attracted only minor protest, particularly since Senegal acted at the behest of an elected government and was able to cite the terms of a 1967 mutual defense treaty as justification. In fact, Tanzania, Kenya and several other governments praised Senegalese President Abdou Diouf's swift decision to back up Jawara. But when, on August 18, Jawara and Diouf revealed plans for an immediate "military integration" and eventual confederation, many saw the move as premature and opportunistic.

Apologists for the Senegambia concept point out that it embodies principles already enshrined in the Organization of African Unity Charter and in the Economic Community of West African States (ECOWAS): African nations are committed to the idea that customs unions and other forms of practical cooperation will carry economic and political benefits and lessen dependence on the Western industrial powers. Proponents also argue that, given the geopolitical awkwardness of a sovereign Gambia within Senegal's borders (see map, p. 26), movement towards a union of some sort is virtually inevitable.

Historically, Gambia's British colonizers laid claim to this narrow enclave of what was then French West Africa on the theory that control of the Gambia River and its mouth would prove a great asset. Later, as African states approached independence, the United Nations consulted both Senegal and Gambia about going ahead with some form of political union, a negotiation that ultimately failed to bring agreement on an appropriate form of cooperation.

Though the two states have distinct colonial legacies regarding language and administration, there is a good deal of shared culture among people in the rural areas, where the

THE SHAPE OF THE CONFEDERATION

[AN] *It may be months before all the various treaties defining Senegambia are signed and sealed. From the initial accords, however, the following picture emerges:*

Senegal and Gambia will continue to function as independent governments but will contribute to a confederal army and be represented in a confederal structure with an executive and a parliament that will meet at least twice a year.

Senegal's head of state will be the president of the Senegambia Confederation and the Gambian head of state will be its vice president. Senegal will elect two-thirds of the parliament, the Gambia one-third. All actions at the confederal level, however, will require the Gambian leader's consent.

As first steps, the two governments have agreed to integrate their armies and harmonize foreign policies. A military reorganization is already under way, and foreign policies differ little.

More daunting will be the tasks of evolving an economic union. This involves ongoing steps to develop the Gambia River, the forging of a common policy on tariffs and eventual adoption of Senegal's CFA franc as the shared currency.

At present Gambia has considerably lower customs duties on imports than its neighbor. Consequently, Gambian traders do a lucrative business importing luxury items and smuggling them into Senegal to sell at inflated prices. Loss of this trade will hurt the Gambian economy.

The two governments have also spoken of creating a single organ to deal with the peanut industry that is the mainstay of both economies. A joint 'permanent secretariat' for cooperation established as far back as 1962, however, has done little to harmonize prices paid to the farmers.

cultivation of peanuts and subsistence farming are the mainstays. Roughly half of Senegal's citizenry and 30% of Gambia's population speaks Wolof. In addition, both countries are predominantly Muslim.

The River Gambia itself is of enormous importance to each nation and the governments are already pouring considerable resources into a joint Gambia River Development Organization, of which Guinea (Conakry) is also a member.

Despite the enthusiasm for such regional development schemes in many quarters, however, critics of Senegambia in its current political incarnation charge that the two governments involved lacked a legitimate popular mandate.

"A matter that involves a transfer of national sovereignty cannot be decided just like that between two heads of state," objects former Senegalese Prime Minister Mamadou Dia, who leads the opposition Democratic and Popular Movement. "The two peoples absolutely should have been consulted."

Fara Ndiaye, deputy chief of the Senegalese Democratic Party, agrees. "I think one should have taken the time to create a more favorable climate, for example by withdrawing Senegalese troops," Ndiaye told *West Africa* magazine. "What are they doing there now? Either Jawara is in control of his country and is welcome to his people, or he is not in control and is unpopular — and by that token, he does not have the right to decide the fate of his people."

By most accounts, the militants who led the coup against Jawara did not themselves have a large political base, but the very fact that one-half of the nation's security force joined the rebellion suggests, according to some observers, that Gambia's leadership is not as popular as its overriding parliamentary majority would indicate.

Radio Nigeria took this position in one of its political commentaries, saying: "Sir Jawara should summon the people of Gambia to the polls once again to ascertain that he still enjoys their absolute confidence."

Jawara and Diouf, of course, referred the issue to their parliaments. But there is a substantial body of opinion in both countries that questions the representatives of those bodies.

In Gambia, opposition legislators argued they had not been properly consulted on the confederation issue, and some stormed out before a vote was taken. Further clouding the situation in Banjul is the fact that a state of emergency remains in force, and this could obstruct the national elections that are scheduled for later this year.

Had a referendum been held on the confederation idea, some analysts believe it would have carried in Senegal and failed in Gambia.

Despite the political reservations of intellectuals in Dakar, the Senegalese see some obvious long-term advantages to a Senegambia. First, there is the matter of cross-border smuggling, which has worked to Gambia's benefit (see box). Secondly, Gambia presently separates Senegal's capital and heartland from the southern Casamance Province, a fertile region that has been a center for political opposition to the ruling Socialist Party. And, thirdly, Gambia's capital of Banjul is a good port which may provide a closer — therefore cheaper — alternative to Dakar for the export of products from the south.

Gambia's gains are harder to define, and according to British journalist Robin White, a veteran African specialist for the British Broadcasting Service (BBC) who recently visited Banjul, Gambians generally feel that none of this would be happening except for the bloody coup attempt last July.

"The vast majority of the Gambians I talked to were totally against it," says White. "The only ones who did like the idea of federation were mostly those who were in some way employed by the government."

Article 9

UEST AFRICA February 1983

Nigeria and her neighbours

Did Dr. Busia and his cabinet realise what would happen as a result of the government's order on November 19 that within two weeks aliens without residence permits should leave Ghana? Obviously not; a government which prides itself on its good relations with its neighbours, in contrast to those of Dr. Nkrumah, could not have wished to sour them. Why then did it embark on a venture which has not only affected its relations with half-a-dozen African countries, but throughout the world has damaged its reputation for humanity and competence?
Editorial in West Africa, *December 20, 1969*

IN NIGERIA at the moment, the expulsion of Nigerians from Ghana in deplorable circumstances in 1969-70 is often referred to as an illustration of how, though two wrongs do not make a right, Nigerians have been on the receiving end of expulsion measures. Not just from Ghana, but from Zaire, Congo, Gabon and Equatorial Guinea and elsewhere.

In 1969, Dr. Busia was only moving against those aliens who did not have residence permits, and was therefore acting within his rights, as head of a government, in what he considered to be his interests. It happened to be the large majority of non-Ghanaians, but it was legal. So, in Nigeria, the defence has been the legality of the situation. Any country, they say, has the right to take measures to enforce the law. This has been why any voices raised over the measure have tended to point to the unrealistic time limit for "illegals" to clear out of the country. This has been implicitly acknowledged in the extension of the time limit by one month for skilled workers, and the suggestion that in practice it may be extended for many others, too.

The short time limit and the hints of severe action also certainly helped to precipitate the rush of those that knew that they were in the country illegally (and maybe more) to try to get out. Lack of preparation and co-ordination with the countries concerned may also have helped create a certain panic atmosphere. Although Ghana eventually opened its border, the fact of this expulsion happening while the border was closed created an impression for illegal Ghanaians that they were somehow cornered. To those who argue that warning shots were necessary to enable the measure to be taken seriously, the tragic human problem created was certainly worsened. And Ghana was by no means the only country affected.

One question that may legitimately be asked is, if legality is the point at issue, how did so many enter Nigeria illegally in the first place? The answer is not hard to find, the conditions created by oil boom, just as the contraction of the economy following oil glut is a background factor in the growing hostility to the alien presence. Whether it will really bring economic benefits is an open question that can probably not be answered now. It is unlikely to harm Nigeria in the way that Dr. Busia's measure harmed Ghana's economy. Politically, the move seems to respond to the present mood in Nigeria, and should do the government good, since it is not immediately a party issue. But Dr. Azikiwe, who has some historic connections with Ghana, has criticised the measure.

The reaction from neighbouring African countries, as we pointed out last week, has been restrained, and the soft-pedalling has continued. The reasons for this may not just be understanding of Nigeria's difficulties, or a desire to remain on good terms with the most influential country in the sub-region. Every country in the area has a greater or lesser problem with immigrant population and might wish to reserve the right to take similar measures if, indeed, they have not already done so in the past. Expatriate Nigerians could be among those affected.

Another dimension has been added to the situation by the international reaction. Any mass movement of people, especially on this scale, is bound to create this kind of reaction, especially given the instant nature of modern media. But the initial human drama and anguish (what might be called the collapse of the "Agege" dream) and the humanitarian reaction which has been mobilised, has been overlaid by those seeking to score political points, either about the nature of the regimes in both Ghana and Nigeria, or about black Africa on a wider level. Various friends of Pretoria and enemies of Africa have rushed to present the situation as a kind of racism, and to grind various axes, so that genuine examination of the problem is submerged in a sea of anti-Nigerian propaganda. This is unfortunate, in that it is also likely to obscure rational discussion of ways in which any damage to regional spirit can be minimised.

To return to Dr. Busia, his measure probably tarnished his reputation in Africa irremediably. This need not happen with Nigeria if the right kind of measures are taken to mend fences and soothe wounds. It is important that Dr. Ouattara, the Executive Secretary of ECOWAS, has been seen to defend Nigeria's action in the ECOWAS context, since this is one area of vulnerability. He stressed once more that the quit order was in no way in conflict with the ECOWAS protocol on free movement of people.

What could also be said is that large numbers of Chadians and Cameroonians in Nigeria were also easily able to penetrate Nigeria's "porous borders" suggesting that even the influence of the 90-day visa on the influx may have been exaggerated. Would not the attraction of the oil boom have brought a huge influx anyway? What one hopes will be remembered, is that in spite of the post-1960 development of micro-nationalisms, the roots of economic unity in the region going back to pre-colonial times as outlined in a useful article in *West Africa* six years ago (February 7, 1977) are still valid, and an important part of those roots lay in the free movement of peoples, which created an economic interdependence.

Article 10   *New African,* August 1983

We Talk to Jerry Rawlings

Q. What has your Government achieved since coming to power? What has been learnt?
J.R. Our most important achievement is in the advance we have made towards the liberation of the minds of the people. People for decades have been treated as nobodies, have been contemptuously regarded by politicians as mere election-fodder, and have been led to regard themselves as impotent and dependent on the condescending benevolence of an elite minority. Many of them came to believe in this situation. Some still do. But we have broken the mould, and more and more workers, farmers and all the others who have carried this country on their backs are now able to question, to challenge and to act.

It is inevitable that in this process of rediscovering their initiative, some mistakes will be made. Revolution is a learning process. But the emergence of positive confidence can now be seen.

On the economic front, we have cleared up waste and corruption to an extent that has restored Ghana's financial credibility in international circles. It will take time before the benefits of this are felt by the people, but the scene has been set for our economic recovery. This will take longer than we had hoped, because of severe drought, bushfires, and the influx of over one million returnees from Nigeria. Nevertheless, we have created the conditions necessary for economic recovery to take place.

One thing we have learnt is not to underestimate the stubborn opposition of the minority whose privileges have been undermined by the revolution. We anticipated this, but the hypocritical rumours and open bribery become more desperate as they see their hopes of regaining control receding.

New African asked some particularly tough questions of Jerry Rawlings. Our aim was to probe the philosophy that lies at the basis for the new society that he is trying to create. His answers were clear, considered and thoughtful. Whether you agree with him or not, he has shed considerable new light on how he thinks in this major interview.

Q. A year after coming to power with popular support and high expectations, you had to face several attempted coups from within your own ranks. What went wrong?
J.R. Firstly, I would like to be clear about what you mean by "within your own ranks". If you mean the ranks of the revolution or the top levels of government, then there has been only one such attempt, which arose from differences of approach to the process of restructuring society. We do not believe that an impatient, dogmatic approach is the way to build lasting foundations for a new society. Unfortunately, some of our colleagues differed with this view.

Other attempts have made use of soldiers, but putting on a uniform does not automatically make anyone a committed revolutionary. The armed forces, like the rest of the people, include some individuals who can be subverted with money and promises, and can

therefore be used by those interests which are threatened by the events of 31st December 1981. This sort of action cannot be described as coming from within our ranks.

Q. There are continued reports of casual killings and the arbitrary exercise of power by leaders. Are they true? Is the military as a whole under control?
J.R. Again, I would question your use of words. What do you mean by "leaders"? In its context, it seems to mean the military. I should make it very clear that this is not a military government, nor is anyone a "leader" by virtue of a uniform. Leadership, whether civilian or military demands self discipline and high standards, and the ability to set an example to others.

There have been incidents where individuals in uniform have committed serious crimes. These are regarded and dealt with as crimes. What you describe as "casual killings" are,

I think, the products of the same vigorous rumour machine which seems capable of making even University students believe that the low level of the Volta Lake is due, not to drought, but to some secret pipeline which diverts the water to Libya! I hear that a rumour now in fashion says that bodies are daily dumped into the sea off Half Assini by helicopter. I also understand that I am supposed to spend my nights in a submerged submarine. All this would be humorous, if it were not such a sad commentary on the viciousness of one sector of our society and the gullibility of another.

Q. Do you find any sympathy for, or understanding of your intentions among Western governments? Do you find more or less understanding from other sources? Which other sources?

J.R. We have emphasised many times that Ghana is non-aligned and desires friendly relations with all countries which sympathise with our objective of building a society founded on social justice and broad participation by the people in their community, workplace and the nation.

We have met a great deal of goodwill and understanding from countries holding a wide range of political views. We have also received material help from a very wide spectrum of countries.

But it should be clearly understood that we are engaged in a process of evolving our own systems and structures. Whilst we can usefully adapt some of the ideas of other nations to our needs, this is a Ghanaian revolution. Interference in our affairs, or attempts to pressure our process into channels to suit certain vested interests abroad cannot enhance good relations.

Q. Are you happy with the terms offered by the International Monetary Fund for the provision of a standby financing facility?

J.R. To say that anyone is *happy* about the stringent austerity measures which are necessary to bring sanity into Ghana's economy would not be very realistic. The difficult time we will have to endure until these measures bear fruit is the price we have to pay for the many years of economic abuse, corruption and mismanagement.

But it is evident that in tightening up our economic management over the past one and a half years, we have been able to restore international confidence in Ghana's financial credibility.

The proposals which the PNDC Government submitted to the World Bank did not fit the orthodox pattern, but were argued and accepted on their merits. The system of graded bonuses on foreign exchange earnings and surcharges on imports should stimulate the export trade with less hardship than an orthodox devaluation would have imposed on the people.

Q. Have you seen any change in the attitudes of foreign banks since the agreement in principle with the IMF? What major new investments have you attracted in the last year?

J.R. There has certainly been a change in the attitude of foreign banks. Very soon after the budget statement was presented the Standard Chartered Bank of London agreed to a $100 million loan. This is a response to improved financial management and realistic policies, since no commercial bank is going to risk such a loan in the sort of economic muddle which prevailed in Ghana before 31st December, 1981.

Q. You have spoken of the need to "produce goods here which will remove the need to import". What goods? How?

J.R. We are not suggesting that Ghana can stand alone in total self-reliance, nor are we suggesting producing consumer junk which we do not need, such as cornflakes or skin-bleaching cream.

But there are many basic things which we can do for ourselves, instead of always looking towards imported goods. For example, we import tractors, but with a little ingenuity we can make the trailers instead of importing them.

And mentioning tractors, consider a developing country like Ghana with hundreds of types of tractors, possibly in the name of "healthy competition", and each one tying the owner to the importing of spare parts which fit only one type. Who could have permitted such an irrational inflow?

Too many of our existing industries consist of imported machines using imported raw materials. The only local input, apart from a minimum of labour, used in producing ideal milk is *water*! We must move away from this concept, and concentrate more on processing our own raw materials. In many cases, we can use simpler and more appropriate technologies in smaller scale industries, instead of continuing to be lured by huge, complex industrial plant and equipment which comes to a halt for lack of some delicate part.

Q. At a time when many African states are trying to cure inefficiency and corruption, by reducing state control of economic institutions, your economic recovery programme envisages a state monopoly of import and export trade and effective state control of banking and insurance. Why will you succeed where others have failed?

J.R. Firstly, I wonder how true your first statement is. How many African states *are* actually loosening control of economic institutions? And of these have *any* actually reduced corruption and inefficiency by such measures?

Secondly, the proof of our success must surely be in results. I have already mentioned the restoration of confidence in Ghana's

economic management, which indicates a measure of success already. And I do not think rigid control is the *only* way that we are tackling the problem. The principle of accountability depends on more than controls. It is a moral issue. Also when all the employees of an organisation begin to participate in taking decisions and gain a feeling of concern for its efficient functioning, they act as watchdogs to uncover corruption and inefficiency.

Q. Tribunals of laymen and leaders are handing down long jail terms for offences like price code violations which many observers judge to be necessary for daily survival. Are you happy with the tribunal's actions?

J.R. The tribunals and the Citizens Vetting Committees are dealing with a wide range of offences, ranging from treason to tax evasion. I think you will find that price control offences form a small proportion of the total number of cases dealt with.

Those people who do not like the idea of the tribunals, seeing them as a challenge to the ordinary courts (and they *are* a challenge to the delays, the ineffectiveness and the corruption which have diminished the people's confidence in the ordinary courts), often talk about the rule of law. And yet they resent the tribunals actually *enforcing* the laws, some of which have existed since long before PNDC days. Wealthy lawyers who have never paid income tax have little room to talk about the rule of law.

Are they the observers who say that it is necessary to break the law in order to survive? Are they condoning theft, tax evasion and other offences on grounds of necessity?

The ordinary man has always had to bear the brunt of law enforcement. What really upsets some observers now is that the tribunals catch, in their net, people who thought themselves immune to the laws they made and administered to others.

Q. In retrospect, has the influx of returnees been a stimulus or a setback for the country? How?

J.R. The returnees have obviously brought problems. They have compounded the immediate food shortage. So long as those in the urban areas are not productively employed, social problems will arise.

But they are, first and foremost, Ghanaians, and it is better to be at home with dignity and self-respect, even in times of hardship, than to sell their pride for material gains. Their return showed our ability to cope speedily and efficiently with the enormous trek to their hometowns. As a result, various countries are now prepared to give long-term help in resettling the returnees and creating conditions which will enable them to contribute to the development of Ghana.

Q. Most observers see Ghana as emerg-

ing from more than a year of self-imposed isolation. What principles will guide your foreign policy? How do you hope relations with America, in particular, will develop?
J.R. The only action which could reasonably be interpreted as isolationist is the closure of Ghana's borders. Even there, our motive is not to isolate this country, and a look at the facts will soon disprove the impression which casual observers seem to have.

We closed our borders in order to check the wholesale smuggling of goods into neighbouring countries. Before this was done, as much as 30 per cent and maybe more, of our exports such as cocoa and timber, and also large quantities of manufactured goods and petroleum products found their way illegally across the borders. This has now been curbed substantially. With new incentives to legal exporters, and more effective border patrols, it should be possible to ease the situation. Indeed, there are now three border points open into Upper Volta. Ghana has also opened border points with Togo and Ivory Coast and it is these countries which have not yet opened their side of the border.

I do not think that we have tried to isolate ourselves in any other way from other countries, although naturally we are most concerned with putting our own house in order. Regarding relations with the USA, we want friendly relations with all countries which recognise our right to find our own path towards a better life for Ghanaians.

Q. Do you think the expulsion helped create a greater Western awareness of Ghana's needs in general?
J.R. Certainly the exodus from Nigeria was a spectacular event which focussed attention on Ghana, and the more perceptive foreign media personnel who recorded this were also able to make their countries aware of the more general problems facing Ghana.

Q. Your political programme aims to create a society without corruption or privileged elite, but the placards at rallies show that the Revolution is still powered by Rawling's personality cult. How do you reconcile the contradiction?
J.R. My role as a leader is to help others to realise their capabilities as leaders. I do not agree that my position at the forefront of the struggle constitutes a personality cult, and I certainly do not give any encouragement to such a cult. But if I, or any other leader, were

to be completely self effacing, I could hardly be effective as a leader.

As for the supposed connection between leadership and corruption or privilege, I do not see it. Neither I nor my colleagues in the PNDC government expect to enjoy any special privileges beyond the bare means to do our work, and I have not heard of any allegations of corruption. So I really do not see any contradiction. The contradiction must be in the minds of those who equate leadership with privilege and corruption.

Q. You have said that you will not hand over power to civilian leaders "who do not represent the whole country". Will you be giving Ghanaians any opportunity to show—by referendum say—what they think?
J.R. We do not believe that the act of putting a piece of paper into a ballot box once every year or so is in itself a means by which Ghanaians can express their wishes in a meaningful way. It is an empty token of participation.

Now, as we sit here, Ghanaians have far more opportunity to take part in decision making. They can elect their executives and sub-committees in the People's Defence Committees at community and workplace levels, the levels which immediately affect their daily lives. The PDC structure is being gradually democratised, and will ultimately lead to a full People's Assembly and a governing council of their choice. Meanwhile they are learning how to use power, gradually realising the responsibilities which go with it, in situations where they have to face the reactions of their neighbours and workmates if they should misuse it. We also have a situation now where many opportunities exist for anyone, farmer, typist, nurse or factory worker, to express his or her views to members of the PNDC, the National Defence Committee, and PNDC Secretaries. Some of the bodies which have loudly complained about the lack of opportunity to express their views, bodies such as the professionals, some of the churches, and the student leaders, are always conspicuously absent when they are invited to seminars, forums and other assemblies convened for the exchange of opinions. Some of them have openly expressed their disgust at being expected to share what they regard as their unique fitness to make decisions for other people with the ordinary folk of this country.

Q. Why do you think your brand of popular Revolution has evolved only in Ghana?

J.R. Your question requires answering in two parts.

Firstly, why do revolutions occur at all?

Where there is real democracy (and by this I mean true participation and not just token gestures) you will not have revolution. Social changes which are needed will take place without disruption, because the system will yield to the legitimate needs of the people.

But it is a rule of human nature that where real democracy does not exist, revolution will occur. It may be suppressed, whether by the mental emasculation of the people or by intense repression, but it will ultimately erupt. We in Ghana are fortunate that it was a relatively mild eruption which could be steered quickly into positive channels.

The second part of the answer concerns the Ghanaian nature of the popular democratic Revolution here. The obvious answer is that this is Ghana. What sort of revolution should we have but a Ghanaian revolution, based on our history, our culture and our aspirations?

No nation has exactly the same combination of factors which has brought it to its present stage, and so if we are talking about forms of government within the broad framework of social justice, each one will have to evolve to fit the particular needs and situation of that nation.

It has been proved over and over again that trying to impose a system developed at another place and time, be it medieval Westminster, eighteenth century Washington or early twentieth century Moscow, does not work. We can borrow and modify ideas, but basically *Ghanaians* must decide what this nation's future should be and how we can all reach it. So if Ghana's brand of revolution is unique to Ghana, it is as it should be.

Q. What do you hope Ghana will be like in 10 years?
J.R. More important than what Ghana will be like in future is what Ghanaians will be like. If Ghanaians from all walks of life can recover their pride and self-respect, their creativeness and initiative—if they can shake off the apathy, jealousy and materialism which our history of colonialism and domination has imposed on the country—then the other things will follow.

If in 10 years time every Ghanaian can live decently in modest comfort, taking a full share of responsibility for the well-being of a nation and participating in the shaping of its destiny, then I hope that by then I can find time to live for 'myself'.

Central Africa

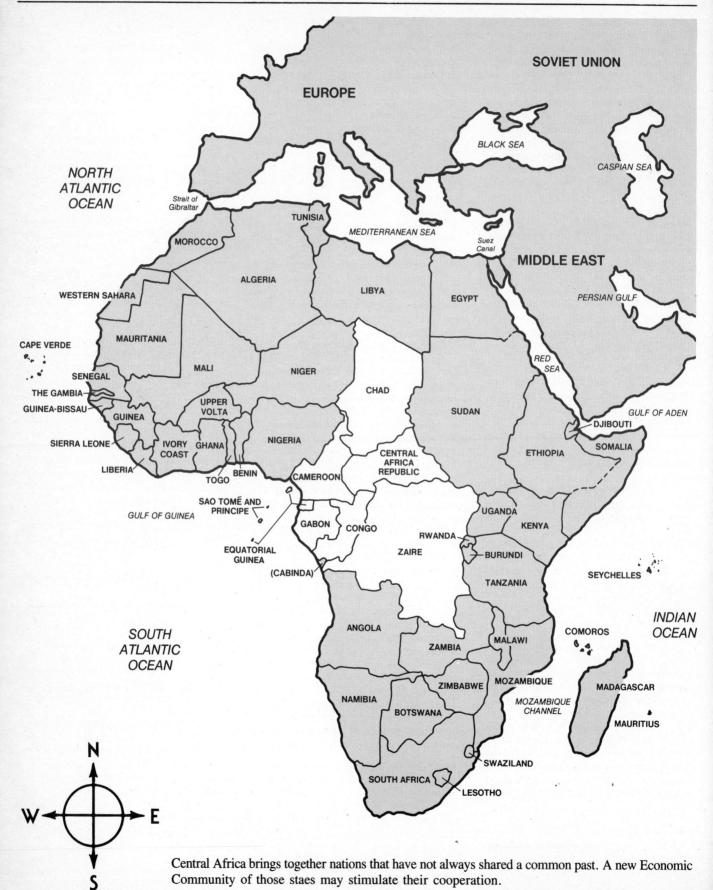

Central Africa brings together nations that have not always shared a common past. A new Economic Community of those staes may stimulate their cooperation.

Central Africa: Possibilities for Cooperation

The Central African region, as it is defined in this volume, brings together countries that have not always shared a common past, nor do they necessarily seem destined for a common future. Cameroon, Chad, Central African Republic, Congo, Gabon, Zaire, Equatorial Guinea (which includes the island of Fernando Po, now called Bioko), and the islands of Sao Tome and Principe have not historically been grouped together as one region. Indeed, users of this volume who are familiar with the continent will associate the label "Central Africa" with states such as Angola and Zambia as well as the states mentioned here. The peoples of southern Zaire have historic links with peoples of Angola and Zambia, but today these states seem more deeply involved with Southern African issues. Thus, there is an arbitrary and shifting nature of the "Central African" label.

THE DIVERSITY OF THE REGION

The countries of Central Africa incorporate a vast variety of peoples and cultures, resources, and environments, systems of government and national goals. Most of the modern nations overlay both societies that are village-based and localized and others that were once part of famous and extensive kingdoms. While Islam has had little influence in the region, except in Chad and the northern area of Cameroon, there is no unanimity of religious belief or practice; many Christian churches as well as traditional rituals and faiths are found throughout the area. Wooden sculptures are one of the great achievements of Central African societies. They are thought to have spiritual potential and are associated with beliefs in the ancestors or valued as prestige objects. However, the art forms are myriad and distinctive, and their diversity is more striking than the common features they possess.

Present-day governments range from the conservative regime of President Bongo of Gabon, the self-designated Marxist-Leninist government of the People's Republic of the Congo, the military regime of Kolingba (who replaced Emperor Bokassa's successor in Central Africa), and the "Mobutuism" practiced by Mobutu in Zaire. A long lasting civil war continues in Chad, and Central African states have taken opposing sides in that war.

Yet, there is much that the Central African states share. These include: some of the geographic features that characterize the area and influence the life of its peoples; the colonial backgrounds (primarily French and Belgian) that established political and economic patterns that have lasted until the present day; and the limited modern efforts to build a community of Central African states.

GEOGRAPHIC DISTINCTIVENESS

All the states of the Central African region except Chad encompass equatorial rain forests. Citizens who live in these regions must cope with a climate that is both hot and moist

(United Nations photo)

In Africa, cooperative workgroups often take on tasks that would be done by machinery in industrialized countries.

and must face the challenges of clearing and using the great equatorial forests. The problems of living in these heavily forested areas accounts in part for the very low population densities of the Central African states. The problems of creating roads and railroads impedes communication and development.

The peoples of the rain forest areas tend to cluster along river banks and rail lines. In modern times, because of the extensive development of minerals, many inhabitants have moved to the cities, accounting for a comparatively high urban population. The rivers are life-lines, perhaps more important than in other regions. The watershed in Cameroon between the Niger and Zaire Rivers provides a natural divide between the West and Central region. The Zaire is the largest of the rivers but the Oubangi, Chari and Ogooue, as well as other rivers, are also important for the communication and trading opportunities that they continue to offer. The rivers flow to the Atlantic and encourage the orientation of the Central African states toward the West.

Many of the countries of the region share similar sources of wealth, including the hydroelectric potential of the rivers and the rain forests. Every country except Chad and Sao Tome and Principe exports lumber. Other forest products such as rubber and palm oil have traditionally been widely marketed. Lumbering and clearing activities for agriculture have led to the disappearance of many of the rain forests in West and Central Africa, and there are now movements to halt this destruction.

As one might expect, Central Africa is one of the areas least affected by the conditions of drought that presently characterize much of Africa. Yet not all of these countries are drought-free. People in Chad and Central African Republic are presently suffering from food shortages. Savanna lands are found to the north and the south of the forests. Whereas rain forests have inhibited travel, the savannas have been transitional areas, great lanes of migration linking East and West Africa and providing opportunities for cattle herding as well as agriculture. Such regions characterize Chad, Central African Republic, northern Cameroon, and southern Zaire.

Beside the products of the forest, there are many other resources that the countries of the Central African region have in common. Especially important are the oil resources of Cameroon, Chad, Congo, and Gabon (although Chad does not exploit its petroleum reserves). Uranium, formerly exported by Zaire, is now mined in Gabon and the Central African Republic, and uranium deposits are found in Chad as well. Other mineral resources abound, and the problems of their exploitation as well as the demand for them among the developed nations of the world are issues of common concern in the region. Many of the states also grow coffee, cocoa, and cotton for export and are affected by the fluctuation of prices for these crops on the world market. The similarity of their environments and their products provide a foundation on which these states can build cooperative institutions and policies.

(Peace Corps photo)

The manufacture and sale of traditional handcrafts are important to many Central African economies. The Traditional Handicrafts Cooperative Society in Cameroon facilitates trade in these local items.

THE LINKS TO FRANCE

Many of the different ethnic groups in the region overlap national boundaries. The Fang are found in Gabon and Equatorial Guinea; the Bateke in Congo and Gabon; the Kongo in Zaire, Angola, and Congo. However, the widespread ethnic groupings seem less important for building regional unity than the European colonial systems that the countries inherited. Equatorial Guinea was controlled by the Spanish; Sao Tome and Principe by the Portuguese; Zaire by Belgium. The predominant power in the region was France. Central African Republic, Chad, Congo, and Gabon were all members of French Equatorial Africa. This administrative federation established by the French rulers, was to provide some links between the four territories.

The early economic impact of the colonialists was similar. All of the Central African states were affected by European companies, which were given concessions (often ninety-nine-year leases with economic and political rights) to exploit products of the forest zones such as ivory and rubber. At the beginning of the twentieth century, forty-one companies controlled seventy percent of the territory of present-day Congo, Gabon, and Central African Republic. Large plantations were developed to increase palm oil production, for example. Other companies exploited mineral resources. Individual production by Africans was encouraged. Pressure was used to force local inhabitants into service. Meanwhile, colonial companies encouraged production and trade but did little to encourage the growth of the infrastructure or to engage in development. Only in Zaire was industry more fully developed.

Neither the colonial policies of the Belgians and French nor the companies themselves offered many opportunities for Africans to gain training and education, and there was little

(WFP photo by F. Mattioli)

Women in Chad winnow sesame seed. Cash crops such as sesame seed and cotton can encourage the economy, but they also can divert labor from food production.

encouragement of independent entrepreneurs. Felix Eboué, the governor of French Equatorial Africa in the early 1940s, increased opportunities for the urban elite in Congo, Gabon, and Central African Republic. The Brazzaville Conference of 1944, recognizing the important role that the people of the French colonies had played in World War II, abolished forced labor and granted citizenship to all. Yet political progress toward self-government was limited in the Central African region. Only in Cameroon had political activity started early, and this was due to the fact that Cameroon was held by France as a trust territory of the UN. When the countries gained independence during the 1960s, there were few who could shoulder the bureaucratic and administrative tasks of the regimes that took power. This was especially true in Zaire. There were no people who could handle the economic institutions for the countries' benefit, and, in any case, the nations' economies remained (for the most part) securely in outside hands.

The Spanish of Equatorial Guinea and the Portuguese of Sao Tome and Principe also benefited from plantation agriculture while depending on forced labor. Here, too, political opportunities were limited. Neither country gained independence until the late 1960s and 1970s: Equatorial Guinea in 1968, and Sao Tome and Principe in 1975.

In the years since independence, most of the countries of Central Africa have been influenced, pressured, and supported by the former colonial powers, especially France. French firms in Congo, Central African Republic, and Gabon are exploiting new products as well as old resources. All are only slightly encumbered by the regulations of independent governments, and all are geared toward European markets and needs. Financial institutions are branches of French institutions, and all the countries are members of the Franc Zone. French ex-patriates serve in government as well as with companies, and French troops are stationed in the countries. France is not only the major trading partner of many of these states but contributes significantly to the budget. Zaire, although less influenced by the French, did call on French troops during civil disturbances in eastern Zaire in 1977 and hosted the annual meetings of French-speaking African nations in 1982. France played a role in the coup in Equatorial Guinea in 1979 and has increased its aid and investment to the present government there.

EFFORTS AT COOPERATION

Although many Africans in this region recognize that links among their countries would be beneficial, there have been fewer initiatives toward political unity or economic integration in this region—either at the time of independence or after that time—than in East, West, or Southern Africa. In the years before independence, Barthelemy Boganda of what is now the Central African Republic espoused and publicized the idea of a "United States of Latin Africa," which would include French and Portuguese territories as well as Zaire, but he was not supported by others in the region.

When France offered independence to the countries of French Equatorial Africa in 1960, a year after Boganda's death, the possibility of forming a federation was discussed, but Gabon, which was much wealthier than the other countries, declined to participate. Chad, Central African Republic, and Congo almost signed an agreement that would have created a federal legislature and executive branch governing all three countries, but there was concern over their separate diplomatic and UN status, and all of the countries became independent separately.

There have been some formal efforts at economic integration among the former French states. A Customs and Economic Union of the Central African states (UDEAC) was established in 1964, but membership did not remain stable. Chad and Central African Republic withdrew to join Zaire in an alternate organization. Later, the Central African Republic returned. The East and Central African states together planned an Economic Community in 1967, but this did not materialize.

Only recently have there been new and hopeful signs of

(World Bank/CIRC photo by Alain Prott)

Timber from the rain forests is one of the major resources of Central Africa but can only be exploited if good roads exist. This scene comes from Gabon.

progress toward economic cooperation. Urged on by the UN Economic Commission on Africa (ECA) and with the stimulus of the Lagos Plan of Action, signed in 1980, the Central African states met in 1982 to prepare for a new economic grouping. In October 1983, all of the Central African states, as well as Rwanda and Burundi in Eastern Africa, signed a treaty establishing the Economic Community of Central African States (ECCA) to promote economic and industrial cooperation. It is hoped that the union will stimulate industrial activity—already very promising—increase markets, and reduce the dependence on France and other countries for trade and capital.

Central African states, while sharing a difficult but rich environment, have suffered more than other regions in Africa from the neglect and exploitation or the European orientation of their former colonial powers. They have not found common ways to develop mineral and forest resources and to deal with outside companies. Little implementation has resulted from former unions. As the Swahili proverb goes: "The toughness of the hoe is tested in the garden." Hopefully, ECCA will lead to a Central African market and fulfill the need for a harmonization of trade and industrial policies. Eventually, it may become one of the building blocks of a continent-wide union.

(World Bank photo by Ivan Albert Andrews)

This palm oil processing mill was financed by the World Bank as part of a development project in Cameroon. It will help to meet rising domestic demand and will support efforts to stimulate the economy.

Cameroon

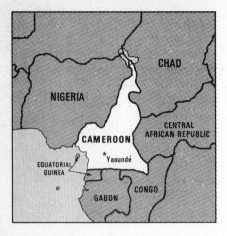

GEOGRAPHY

Area in Square Kilometers (Miles):
475,400 (183,568)
Land Usage: 4% cultivated; 18%
grazing; 13% fallow; 50% forests; 15%
other
Capital (Population): Yaoundé
(291,071—1976)
Climate: tropical to semi-arid

PEOPLE

Population
Total: 8,865,000 (1982 est.)
Per Square Kilometer (Mile): 19 (48)
Annual Growth Rate: 2.4%
Rural/Urban Population Ratio: 65/35

Health
Life Expectancy at Birth: 50 years
Infant Death Rate (Ratio): 109/1,000
Average Caloric Intake: 106% of FAO
minimum
Physicians Available (Ratio):
1/13,670
Access to Safe Water: 26%

Languages
Official: English; French
Others Spoken: Fula, Ewondo, Duala,
Bamilike, Bassa, Bali, English, French,
others

Religion(s)
50% traditional indigenous; 33%
Christian; 17% Muslim

Education
Adult Literacy Rate: 55% males; 25%
females
School Attendance: primary: 100%
boys, 97% girls; secondary: 25% boys,
13% girls

THE KORUP FOREST

"Do not call the forest that shelters you a jungle" is an African
proverb. The primary rain forests in Cameroon and other parts of
Central Africa are the homes of plants and animals that have developed
in this environment over thousands of years and that serve Cameroonians
and humanity. Korup is one Cameroon rain forest that is to be designated
a national park. A recent survey discovered over forty-two thousand
trees and climbers in Korup, including seventeen tree species never
described before. An international campaign has been launched to
preserve such rain forests, under the auspices of the World Wildlife
Fund (WWF) and the International Union for the Conservation of
Nature and Natural Resources (IUCN). Korup is the subject of a recent
film that is being shown to raise funds for its preservation and that of
other rain forests.

COMMUNICATION

Telephones: 26,000
Radios: 780,000
Newspapers: 3 dailies; total circulation
30,000

TRANSPORTATION

Highways—Kilometers (Miles):
32,226 (20,025)
Railroads—Kilometers (Miles): 1,173
(729)
Four international airports

GOVERNMENT

Type: unitary republic
Constitution: May 20, 1972
Former Colonial Status: German;
British and French
Independence Date: January 1, 1960
Head of State: Paul Biya (president)
Branches: executive (president);
legislative (National Assembly; judicial
(Supreme Court)
Legal System: based on French Civil
Law system
Political Parties: Cameroon National
Union
Suffrage: universal over age 21

MILITARY

Number of Armed Forces: 11,600
Armed Forces/Population: 1/780
*Military Expenditures (% of Central
Government Expenditures):*
$78,900,000 (7.4%)
Nuclear Weapons Status: none
Current Hostilities: none

ECONOMY

Currency ($ US Equivalent): 440 CFA
francs = $1
GDP: $7,370,000,000
Per Capita Income/GNP: $890
Workforce: 83% agriculture; 7%
industry; 10% services
Inflation Rate: 14.8% (1981)
Natural Resources: timber; oil; bauxite;
iron ore; rubber
Agriculture: coffee; cocoa; food crops;
cotton; bananas; peanuts; tobacco; tea
Industry: small manufacturing; con-
sumer goods; aluminum
Energy Production: 381,000 kw
capacity
Energy Consumption Per Capita: 160
kwh

FOREIGN TRADE

Exports: cocoa; coffee; timber;
aluminum; cotton; natural rubber;
bananas; peanuts; tobacco; tea
Imports: consumer goods; machinery;
transport equipment; petroleum
products; foodstuffs
Major Trading Partners: France; EEC
countries; United States
Foreign Debt: $2,584,000,000 (1980)
*Selected Membership in International
Organizations:* UN; OAU; African
Development Bank; Non-Aligned
Movement

| Establishment of a German Kamerun Protectorate 1884 | Partition of Cameroon; separate British and French mandates established under the League of Nations 1916 | UPC forms 1948 | UPC outlawed for launching revolts in the cities 1955 | Independent Cameroon Republic established, with Ahidjo as first president 1960 | Cameroon Federal Republic reunites the French Cameroon with the south British Cameroon after a UN supervised referendum 1961 | A new Constitution creates a unitary state 1972 | President Ahidjo resigns after 22 years in office; Paul Biya assumes the presidency 1982 |

1984

| January 1984: Biya is elected unopposed to the Presidency | April 1984: Attempted coup is put down | May 1984: Secret military tribunal questioned 1053 persons, sentenced 46 to death, jailed 185 and acquitted and freed the rest |

CAMEROON

Cameroon is frequently called the "hinge" of Africa. Its mountains divide the West African "peninsula" from the central lands, and it is thought that the Bantu-speaking peoples who now inhabit most of Central and Southern Africa originated from the area near the Nigerian and Cameroon border.

The colonial heritage has been diverse. The Germans were the first to claim the territory. After World War I, the area was divided between the British and the French. Now these areas have been united (except for the northwest region whose people joined Nigeria).

THE QUEST FOR UNITY

At the time of independence in 1960, the new government was a federation. President Ahmadou Ahidjo spearheaded a move toward a unified form of government. By 1966 regional parties were incorporated into a single party, the Cameroon National Union (CNU), and by 1971 a single trade union had absorbed other trade unions. In 1972 Ahidjo proposed the abolition of the federation, and a Constitution for a unified Cameroon was approved by an overwhelming vote. Such measures increased and extended the executive power and the possibilities of its use. Ahidjo exercised this power, creating what has been called a police state.

THE TRANSFER OF POWER

In November 1982, Ahidjo suddenly resigned after twenty-two years in office. In line with the constitutional amendment passed in 1979, Paul Biya, the prime minister, became the new president.

During his first year in office Biya made gradual changes. He took over the control of the Party from Ahidjo. He brought young technocrats into the ministries and he called for a more open and democratic society, proposing that the presidency, for instance, be opened to candidates from outside the party.

COUP ATTEMPT

The coup attempt of April 1984 appears to have changed Biya's approach. Some members of the Presidential Guard led the revolt and many suspect that they acted with the encouragement of Ahidjo who has been living in France. The revolt was put down but anywhere from 500 to 1,000 deaths occurred, mostly in the vicinity of the capital, Yaounde. More than 1,000 persons were arrested and have since been questioned and tried by a secret military tribunal.

Since April the government has tightened its control. The press is restricted. Drastic changes have occurred in the leadership of the party and it has been given a new role in mobilizing the people of the provinces. Ahidjo, a northerner, had sought regional and ethnic balance in his ministry and appointments. However, southerners now dominate in the government, perhaps because of continuing fears of Ahidjo's northern base, and Anglophone citizens of the west as well as northerners state their fears of the increasing centralization of the system.

CAMEROON'S RELATIONS WITH ITS NEIGHBORS AND OTHER COUNTRIES

Cameroon's relations with its neighbors have not always been easy. Smuggling between Nigeria and Cameroon during the past several years has led to border conflict. Tensions have also developed over disputed territorial waters thought to contain oil deposits.

There have also been conflicts in Gabon and Nigeria between ex-patriate Cameroonians and the nationals of those countries. One hundred and twenty thousand nationals returned to Cameroon when Nigeria expelled aliens from the country in February 1983.

RELATIONS WITH OTHER COUNTRIES

France remains the nation's most important partner. Cameroon purchases one-half of its imports from France and depends on the aid of French firms and French capital for its development.

Despite these strong ties with France, Cameroon has maintained independent foreign relations—including cooperation with countries of the Eastern bloc. A strong concern for the liberation of Southern Africa has led Cameroon to condemn some of the French policies.

DEVELOPMENT

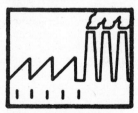

Cocoa and coffee comprise over fifty percent of Cameroon's exports. Unlike many other producing countries, Cameroon processes much coffee and cocoa that finds a market among chocolate and coffee lovers at home.

FREEDOM

Cameroon's lively independent regional press is now being restricted. The Cameroon Times, the oldest English language publication in Cameroon (founded 1960) has recently been closed and senior staff held. There is a new and controversial press law. Foreign publications are restricted.

HEALTH/WELFARE

Women are equal by law and are active in the Cameroon National Union (CNU) and in the state labor union. Social and educational programs have been developed for Cameroonian women.

ACHIEVEMENTS

The art of Cameroon societies is unusual and rich. Two interesting forms are the skin-covered helmet or top-of-head masks that are found only in this area of Africa, and highly decorated brass pipes made by the "lost wax process." Wax is formed around a mold in the shape desired, and another mold encloses it. When heated the wax is "lost" (runs out) and molten metal replaces it.

Central African Republic

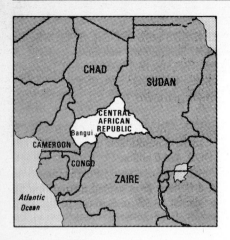

GEOGRAPHY

Area in Square Kilometers (Miles):
626,780 (242,000)
Land Usage: 10-15% cultivated; 5%
forests; 80-85% grazing, fallow, urban, and waste
Capital (Population): Bangui
(300,723—1975)
Climate: tropical to semi-arid

PEOPLE

Population
Total: 2,405,000 (1982 est.)
Per Square Kilometer (Mile): 4 (9.9)
Annual Growth Rate: 2.3%
Rural/Urban Population Ratio: 71/29

Health
Life Expectancy at Birth: 42 years
Infant Death Rate (Ratio): 149/1,000
Average Caloric Intake: 92% of
FAO minimum
Physicians Available (Ratio):
1/27,050
Access to Safe Water: 16%

Languages
Official: French
Others Spoken: Sangho; Banda; Baya
Mangia; M'Baka

Religion(s)
40% Protestant; 28% Catholic; 24%
traditional indigenous; 8% Muslim

Education
Adult Literacy Rate: 48% males;
20% females
School Attendance: primary: 74%
boys, 40% girls; secondary: 33%
boys, 13% girls

COMMUNICATION
Telephones: 6,000
Radios: 130,000
Televisions: 700
Newspapers: 1 daily; total circulation
700

BARTHELEMY BOGANDA

Barthelemy Boganda, the father of his country, wanted to see a vast
united central Africa. A contemporary of Leopold Senghor of Senegal,
Boganda, like Senghor, was influenced by his own culture and that of
France as well. Boganda was brought up in Catholic missions in Congo
Brazzaville and Yaounde. In 1946, he ran for the French National
Assembly and won. In 1949, he created MESAN, the Popular Movement
for the Social Evolution of Black Africa, and he sought to associate the
new organization with the traditional age grades in his country. Boganda
declared that "colonialism is slavery's eldest daughter," and he fought
for equal rights for all the people of Central Africa. He was especially
opposed to the division of the region into many states, and he spoke out
for a vast nation of former French, Belgian, and Portuguese territories in
the 1950s. He even wrote out a Central African constitution. Boganda
was considered an agitator by French residents in the area, and he
suffered imprisonment and condemnation during the independence
struggle. He never saw his country achieve independence, for he died in a
mysterious plane accident in 1959. Some of his followers still live. One
such follower is Abel Goumba.

TRANSPORTATION
Highways—Kilometers (Miles):
21,950 (13,639)
Railroads—Kilometers (Miles): none
One international airport

GOVERNMENT
Type: republic, under military rule
Constitution: 1959; suspended after
coup of 1981
Former Colonial Status: French
Independence Date: August 30, 1960
Head of State: General André-
Dieudonné Kolingba (Chief of State)
Branches: military committee;
judiciary; no legislature
Legal System: based on French law
Political Parties: banned in
September 1981
Suffrage: suspended

MILITARY
Number of Armed Forces: 1,860
Armed Forces/Population: 1/1,328
*Military Expenditures (% of Central
Government Expenditures):*
$13,500,000 (10.8%)
Nuclear Weapons Status: none
Current Hostilities: none

ECONOMY
Currency ($ US Equivalent): 440
CFA francs = $1
GDP: $660,000,000
Per Capita Income/GNP: $310
Workforce: 88% agriculture; 4% in-
dustry; 8% services
Inflation Rate: 9.7% (1980)
Natural Resources: diamonds;
uranium; timber
Agriculture: cotton; coffee; peanuts;
food crops; livestock
Industry: timber; textiles; soap;
cigarettes; processed food; diamond
mining
Energy Production: 44,000 kw
capacity
Energy Consumption Per Capita: 28
kwh

FOREIGN TRADE
Exports: cotton; coffee; diamonds;
timber
Imports: textiles; petroleum products;
machinery; electrical equipment;
chemicals; pharmaceuticals
Major Trading Partners: France;
Yugoslavia; Japan; United States
Foreign Debt: $251,000,000
*Selected Membership in International
Organizations:* UN; OAU; Economic
and Customs Union of Central
Africa (UDEAC); Associate
Member, European Communities
(EC); Non-Aligned Movement;
Economic Community of Central
African States (CEEAC)

Separate French administration of the Oubangui-Chari colony is established
1904

Gold and diamonds are discovered
1912-1913

Boganda sets up a movement for a social revolution (MESAN), which gains wide support
1949

Boganda dies; David Dacko, his successor, becomes president at the time of independence
1960

Jean-Bedel Bokassa takes power after first general strike
1966

Bokassa becomes emperor and is coronated in 1977
1976

Bokassa is involved in the massacre of students; Dacko returns as head of state
1979

Elections followed by violent opposition attacks against Dako; Andre Kolingba takes power in peaceful changeover
1981

Coup attempt by supporters of Ange Patasse is foiled; Abel Gouma is accused of plotting against the government
1982

1983

CENTRAL AFRICAN REPUBLIC

"We aim to make a nation out of a colonial territory and a united people out of all the ethnic groups" said David Dacko, the Central African Republic's first president, at a party congress in 1962. The goal has been a difficult one to achieve in this landlocked country with its predominantly rural population. The country's isolated geographic location and its history of conquest and destruction underlie today's problems. The continued influence of the French, the gap between the rich and the poor, and the conflicts among those at the top are among the factors that have shaped the country since independence.

FRENCH CONQUEST

In the late nineteenth and early twentieth centuries, the French conquered the region and claimed sovereignty over it. French pacification campaigns were destructive; even more destructive were the exploitations of the thirty-nine French concessionary companies that sought rubber and other raw materials—causing such havoc that many peoples, according to one historian, are yet to recover. The colony, which was called Oubangui-Chari, became part of French Equatorial Africa in 1910.

In 1960, after fifty years as part of the FEA, the country's population consisted of just over one million, five thousand administrative officials and agents, five thousand shop assistants, and thirty to forty thousand laborers employed on projects managed by Europeans, according to historian Pierre Kalck. The movement for independence was led by Barthelemy Boganda, a former priest who developed the Popular Movement for the Social Evolution of Black Africa (MESAN), which he hoped would build on the society's traditional age groups. The movement did gain popularity among the peasantry. Boganda recognized the weaknesses of the nation, the probability of continued French interests, and the need for regional unity. He sought a "United States of Latin Africa"—without success.

Boganda's mysterious death in an air crash just before independence put the mantle of the "father of the nation" on the shoulders of David Dacko. Despite Dacko's stated goal of building a nation, the difference between the life of city and country, as well as peasants and the elite continued to grow.

BOKASSA DECLARED EMPEROR

The country suffered greatly during the rule of Jean-Bedel Bokassa, who became head of state in the coup of 1966 and who made himself emperor in 1976 in a lavish ceremony. Bokassa declared that he would restore the imperial tradition to Africa, did away with democratic institutions, monopolized and dissipated the wealth of the country, and sparked international outcries after sanctioning the massacre of 100 young people jailed after a demonstration over school uniforms.

In September 1979, following this incident, former President Dacko, with French support, came back to power in a bloodless coup while Bokassa was out of the country. He was superceded by General Kolingba in 1981.

Politics both before and after Bokassa have reflected competition among politicians, several of whom have been especial-

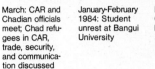

March: CAR and Chadian officials meet; Chad refugees in CAR, trade, security, and communication discussed

January-February 1984: Student unrest at Bangui University

March 1984: Cabinet shuffle by Kolingba

ly concerned about the gap between rich and poor. Abel Goumba, a leader of government opposition since 1960, once commented that, "A peasant's life is worth a month and a half of that of a member of Parliament." Opposition groups led by noted figures such as Abel Goumba and Ange Patasse continue to seek openings in the political system and have been repressed. Goumba is now under "house" arrest and Patasse has sought asylum in Togo.

FRENCH INFLUENCE PERVASIVE

Meanwhile, the French have continued to play an important role in the country. French troops have supplemented the national force since independence and presently number over one thousand, while the regular army is approximately two thousand strong. The French government donates the most aid and provides part of the yearly budget. Fifty percent of the exports of CAR go to France, and the French supply over half of the country's imports.

France has also influenced the course of recent political events. The French government contributed to the expenses of Bokassa's coronation, and—following the outcry and investigation of the murder of the young school students—French troops were involved in Bokassa's overthrow. The French have recently stated their support for Kolingba and his efforts to build up the economy.

DEVELOPMENT

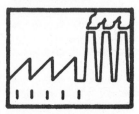

The Recovery Plan of 1980-1982 is especially directed at the development of agriculture and the infrastructure. Cotton production has declined, and many farmers have returned to subsistence farming. Food shortages in the capital, Bangui, in the last few years have contributed to some of the political disturbances.

FREEDOM

The military government of Andre Kolingba has declared that political activity will not be allowed until the groundwork for economic recovery and democratic practices have been laid. Many persons have challenged the regime and Amnesty International has claimed that 100 persons are now being detained for political offenses.

HEALTH/WELFARE

The literacy rate is very low in the Central African Republic, and teacher training is presently being emphasized, especially for primary school teachers.

ACHIEVEMENTS

Production of cotton, one of the country's most important exports, fell seriously in the 1970s, and the nation had one of the lowest yields per growing unit of all African producers. In 1983, the increases in cotton production have been encouraging.

Chad

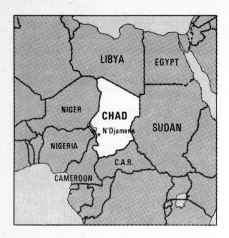

GEOGRAPHY

Area in Square Kilometers (Miles):
1,284,634 (496,000)
Land Usage: 17% arable; 35%
pasture; 2% forests and scrub; 46%
waste and other
Capital (Population): N'Djamena
(179,000—1972)
Climate: semi-arid to arid

PEOPLE

Population
Total: 4,643,000 (1982 est.)
Per Square Kilometer (Mile): 4 (9.4)
Annual Growth Rate: 2.0%
Rural/Urban Population Ratio: 82/18

Health
Life Expectancy at Birth: 43 years
Infant Death Rate (Ratio): 149/1,000
Average Caloric Intake: 72% of
FAO minimum
Physicians Available (Ratio):
1/47,530
Access to Safe Water: 26%

Languages
Official: French
Others Spoken: Chadian Arabic;
Fula; Hausa; Kotoko; Kanembou;
Sara Maba; others

Religion(s)
50% Muslim; 45% indigenous; 5%
Christian

Education
Adult Literacy Rate: 12% males; 1%
females
School Attendance: primary: 51%
boys, 19% girls; secondary: 6%
boys, 1% girls

COMMUNICATION

Telephones: 5,000
Radios: 110,000
Newspapers: 4 dailies; total circula-
tion 1,800

HISSENE HABRÉ

President Hissene Habré has lived an unusual life. Born into a simple
shepherd's family at Faya Largeau (the site of a struggle involving world
powers in 1983), he gained much of his education, including a doctorate
of law, in Paris. When he returned home, he fought against the
government of President Tombalbaye, which he had once supported.
Habré was and is a skillful military commander, known for his
ruthlessness as well as his nationalism. In the mid-1970s he was
responsible for holding two French scholars in captivity for two years in
the northern desert regions of Chad. Habré is now the head of Chad's
government, recognized by the French-speaking African nations and
officially invited to the meetings of the OAU. However, the civil war is
not over and the coming year will test Habré's political as well as his
military skills in dealing with northerners and southerners in Chad as
well as with other government leaders throughout Africa.

TRANSPORTATION

Highways—Kilometers (Miles):
27,505 (17,091)
Railroads—Kilometers (Miles): none
Two international airports

GOVERNMENT

Type: provisional military
Constitution: planned
Former Colonial Status: French
Independence Date: August 11, 1960
Head of State: Hissène Habré
(president)
Branches: following the national con-
sultative council of October 1983, a
representative government was
appointed
Legal System: based on French Civil
Law system and indigenous
customary law
Political Parties: Union for In-
dependence and Revolution
Suffrage: none at present

MILITARY

Number of Armed Forces: 3,200
Armed Forces/Population: 1/1,506
*Military Expenditures (% of Central
Government Expenditures):*
$22,200,000 (33%)
Nuclear Weapons Status: none
Foreign Aid: France is providing
military assistance to combat Libyan-
backed insurgents
Current Hostilities: civil war; former
recognized government now in op-
position to Habré is aided by Libyan
forces

ECONOMY

Currency ($ US Equivalent): 440
CFA francs = $1
GDP: $400,000,000
Per Capita Income/GNP: $80
Workforce: 85% agriculture; 7% in-
dustry; 8% services
Natural Resources: petroleum;
uranium; natron; kaolin
Agriculture: subsistence crops; cot-
ton; cattle; fish; sugar
Industry: livestock products; beer;
bicycle and radio assembly; textiles;
cigarettes
Energy Production: 38,000 kw
capacity
Energy Consumption Per Capita: 13
kwh

FOREIGN TRADE

Exports: cotton; livestock; animal
products
Imports: cement; petroleum;
foodstuffs; machinery; textiles; motor
vehicles
Major Trading Partners: France
Foreign Debt: $221,000,000
*Selected Membership in International
Organizations:* UN; OAU; African
Development Bank; Associate
Member, European Communities
(EC); Non-Aligned Movement;
Economic Community of Central
African States (CEEAC)

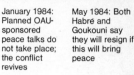

October: Revolt of private armies in the south threatens Habré's government; the Chad question dominates meetings of French-speaking African countries

January 1984: Planned OAU-sponsored peace talks do not take place; the conflict revives

May 1984: Both Habré and Goukouni say they will resign if this will bring peace

CHAD

The vast land of Chad in northern Africa's interior is one of the poorest countries in the world. Until recently it was unfamiliar to most of the world's citizens. However, Chad has made headlines around the world in 1983 as a result of the internationalization of the war in which Chadians have been engaged. The present government of Hissene Habré called for aid from outside forces during the battle at the oasis town of Faya Largeau against the Libyan-backed troops of Oueddei Goukouni and his supporters.

The United States, concerned about Libyan aggression and perhaps about the Middle Eastern sources of oil, sent military advisors and two AWACS radar planes to nearby Sudan in what *U.S. News & World Report* called "a high-technology version of gunboat diplomacy" in support of Habré. Habré's government also received air cover and troops from the French. Meanwhile, Habré also can rely on troops sent by President Mobutu of Zaire, who visited in person at the height of the struggle.

TWENTY-YEAR CIVIL WAR

This dramatic international encounter between Goukouni and Libya on one side, and Habré, the United States, and France on the other obscures the reality of the present situation in Chad. The military action is just the latest event in the civil war that began almost twenty years ago and that still continues today, despite short pauses. It started as a peasant uprising against the increased financial demands of the first independent government of President Tombalbaye. It continued as a National

Liberation Movement organized under FROLINAT (the National Liberation Front of Chad). During recent years, the number of groups involved in the fighting has grown. In 1982 at least eleven factions existed—each with its own base of support, its own army, and a determination not to compromise. N'Djamena, the capital, has changed hands regularly as a result of factional struggles. No leader seems able to develop a government in which all will participate or against which none will fight.

NORTH-SOUTH DIVISION

Behind this series of events lie long-standing differences between the northerners and southerners who became part of Chad as a result of the artificial boundaries established by the imperialists during their takeover of Africa in the late nineteenth and early twentieth centuries. Northerners, most of whom live in the grassland savanna belt of central Chad, engage in mixed farming and herding or are pastoralists, with an aristocratic heritage. They are followers of Islam who speak Arabic and value Arabic traditions. Even in the desert, they maintain a proud independence. The southerners, on the other hand, are agriculturalists. Over one-half million farmers are involved in growing cotton for export. Some southerners are urban dwellers who have been affected by French rule and Western education. Some are Christians, and some speak French. It was southerners who landed good government jobs during the years of French administration and who became leaders in government and the army when independence was achieved in 1960. Goukouni and Habré

represent northern areas and groups, and—no matter how accommodating each may be to southern interests—southerners remain suspicious of both of them.

Life for ordinary Chadians has never been easy; now it is further disrupted. During 1982, thousands of refugees moved in and out across Chad's borders. Crops have not been planted, herds have not been tended, schools have been closed for several years, and many people do not have enough to eat.

RELIEF FROM ABROAD

A UN/OAU-sponsored conference in Geneva in January 1983 brought together international relief organizations. Since that time, twenty thousand metric tons of emergency food aid has reached Chad from the UN and foreign governments such as the United States, France, and Saudi Arabia. Other private bodies have helped to establish programs for reconstruction. However, problems of food distribution connected with the present war have retarded these relief efforts. Moreover, such aid is only a stop-gap. The real development of Chad and a satisfying life for its people depend on a long-lasting peace, and that can only come about from within.

DEVELOPMENT

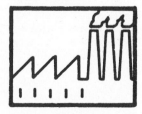

The cotton crop, one of the mainstays of the economy, has suffered during the war. The problems of the war have been compounded by the recurring droughts of the 1970s and 1980s. The 1983-1984 cotton harvest of 150,000 tons is double that of 1982—a significant recovery.

FREEDOM

The civil war has led to a breakdown in law and order. Not only are there battle casualties, but disappearances and arbitrary killings of civilians can be documented.

HEALTH/WELFARE

Malnourishment increases. The Medecins Sans Frontieres (composed of French, Belgium, and Swiss medical personnel) is commencing a $5 million project to build and reorganize Chad's health care system.

ACHIEVEMENTS

Achievements are difficult to ascertain in a time of such dislocation. There have been some signs of recovery during 1983-1984 in textile, sugar, and other enterprises, and state salaries are paid more regularly. Food production remains low.

Congo

GEOGRAPHY

Area in Square Kilometers (Miles):
349,650 (132,000)
Land Usage: 63% forests or
woodland; 33% arable or pasture
land; 4% urban or waste
Capital (Population): Brazzaville
(310,500—1978)
Climate: tropical

PEOPLE

Population
Total: 1,621,000 (1982 est.)
Per Square Kilometer (Mile): 5 (12)
Annual Growth Rate: 2.6%
Rural/Urban Population Ratio: 55/45

Health
Life Expectancy at Birth: 60 years
Infant Death Rate (Ratio): 129/1,000
Average Caloric Intake: 99% of
FAO minimum
Physicians Available (Ratio): 1/5,510
Access to Safe Water: 36%

Languages
Official: French
Others Spoken: Lingala; Kikongo;
Teke; Sangha; M'Bochi; others

Religion(s)
49% indigenous; 50% Christian; 1%
Muslim

Education
Adult Literacy Rate: 30% males; 3%
females
School Attendance: primary: 100%
boys, 100% girls; secondary: 100%
boys, 81% girls

RELIGIOUS LIFE

Many different religions have gained followings among peoples of the Congo in recent times. There is even a Tenrikyo Shinto center from Japan in the country. Most of the people claim affiliation with Christian faiths, and one-third are Roman Catholic. Swedish Evangelical missionaries came to the Congo in the early twentieth century, and the Salvation Army and the Jehovah's Witnesses gained followers in the pre-independence period. Many new religious movements developed after World War I, often centered around figures who were considered messiahs, such as Simon Kimbangu, who founded a Christian church that is now a member of the World Council of Churches, and Andre Matsoua, an early nationalist. Until the 1950s, the only secondary schools in the country were the two seminaries preparing priests for the Roman Catholic Church. The present government banned nearly thirty religious bodies in 1978 and has limited the legal groups to seven—none of which are allowed to teach religion to young people.

COMMUNICATION

Telephones: 13,900
Radios: 95,000
Televisions: 3,700
Newspapers: 3 dailies; total circulation 1,700

TRANSPORTATION

Highways—Kilometers (Miles): 8,246
(5,124)
Railroads—Kilometers (Miles): 800
(497)
Two international airports

GOVERNMENT

Type: republic; military regime
established September 1968
Constitution: 1979
Former Colonial Status: French
Independence Date: August 15, 1960
Head of State: Colonel Denis Sassou
Nguesso (president)
Branches: president; People's National Assembly; Council of
Ministers; judiciary
Legal System: based on French Civil
Law and indigenous customary law
Political Parties: Congolese
Workers' Party
Suffrage: universal over age 18

MILITARY

Number of Armed Forces: 13,225
Armed Forces/Population: 1/124
*Military Expenditures (% of Central
Government Expenditures):* 10.8%
Nuclear Weapons Status: none

ECONOMY

Currency ($ US Equivalent): 440
CFA francs = $1
GDP: $2,170,000,000
Per Capita Income/GNP: $1,180
Workforce: 34% agriculture; 26% industry; 40% services
Inflation Rate: 19.7% (1981)
Natural Resources: wood; potash;
petroleum; natural gas
Agriculture: cocoa; coffee; tobacco;
palm kernels; sugar cane; rice;
peanuts
Industry: processed agricultural and
forestry goods; cement; textiles
Energy Production: 116,000 kw
capacity
Energy Consumption Per Capita: 83
kwh

FOREIGN TRADE

Exports: oil; lumber; tobacco;
veneer; plywood
Imports: machinery; transportation
equipment; manufactured consumer
goods; iron; steel; foodstuffs;
petroleum products; sugar
Major Trading Partners: France;
other EEC countries
Foreign Debt: $1,573,000,000
*Selected Membership in International
Organizations:* UN; OAU; Central
African Customs and Economic
Union (UDEAC); Associate
Member, European Economic Community (EEC); Economic Community of Central African States
(CEEAC)

	Conference establishes French Union; Felix Eboue establishes positive policies for African advancement		A general strike brings the army and a more radical government (National Revolutionary Movement) to power	A new military government under Marien Ngouabi takes over; Congolese Workers' Party is formed			British trade mission identifies Congo's potential; Pointe Noire oil refinery officially opened
Middle Congo becomes part of French Equatorial Africa (FEA) **1910**	**1944**	Independence achieved, with Abbe Fulbert Youlou as first president **1960**	**1963**	**1968-1969**	Ngouabi is assassinated; Colonel Yhombi-Opango rules **1977**	**1982**	**1983**

August: Contract for construction of the northern highway has been signed with a Brazilian firm

January 1984: Congo loans 100 mil CFA to Ghana for drought relief

March 1984: Donors will fund construction of paper mill—the first plant to process timber resources locally—at Pointe Noire

CONGO

The People's Republic of the Congo is a country that is little known in the United States. North Americans are likely to confuse the awkwardly shaped former French colony with its southern neighbor, Zaire (once also called the Congo), or to be completely unaware of its existence. Its role in Africa deserves more recognition.

THE STRENGTHS OF THE PAST

The nation has an interesting past on which to build. Complex states such as the Kongo and Loango kingdoms were established over small chieftaincies in the region during the early centuries of this millenium. When the French claimed the area during the imperial competition of the late nineteenth century, they made Brazzaville, an interior town on the Congo River, the headquarters of French Equatorial Africa (which included Chad, Central African Republic, and Gabon as well as the Congo). As a result, the city expanded, and the area around the administrative center developed along with it. The Congo-Ocean Railroad was built from Brazzaville to Pointe Noire on the coast after World War I and was later extended north.

TODAY'S PROMISE

Today the Congo's circumstances seem more hopeful, and conditions for ordinary people are better than those in many other African states. As the economies of most African states decline, the Congo's economy, which depends to a large extent on oil revenues, continue to grow. Manufacturing,

including cement and textiles, has a longer history and is more fully developed than in most African countries. There is a large urban population (forty-five percent) and a large working class. The per capita income is estimated at anywhere from $667 to $1,000. Government statistics indicate that all primary school-age children are in school. The figures, however, are deceiving for there are deep inequities. Urban peoples of Brazzaville and Pointe Noire, for instance, benefit more than does the rural population, and figures of earnings and life expectancy are all higher for city dwellers.

POLITICAL INSTABILITIES

There are other problems that disturb the promising picture the economy and social indicators present. Politics in the republic since independence have been characterized by violent changes or attempted changes in leadership through coups, raids, and assassinations. Political figures have heightened tensions between ethnic groups, as each politician has used a base among one group as the lever for power in competitive situations.

ECONOMIC STRENGTHS AND WEAKNESSES

One of the country's great strengths is its location at a commercial crossroads. Its rails and rivers make it a center of trade for the Central African states. Its port, Pointe Noire, is the key to international trade for the region. Oil has become the Congo's most important resource—accounting for two-thirds of its revenues, and superceding

timber, which until 1973 had been the major export. French, Italian, and now United States companies are involved in oil exploitation.

The present decline in the price of oil is affecting Congo's prosperity and plans. The "hard core" of the present development plan will probably be maintained. This includes the realignment of the Congo-Ocean railroad, the construction of the northern highway, and projects in the rural areas that may cut down on the present high rate of urban migration and encourage the development of food crops, now imported from abroad.

The difficult contemporary circumstances are also altering socialist policies. Inefficient state companies have been brought under French-based management; state farms are giving way to peasant production; and an aggressive campaign is being developed to increase British as well as French investments and trade. One cannot tell if these policies will allow the growing expectations of the people of Congo to be realized.

DEVELOPMENT

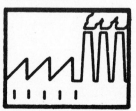

The Five Year Plan of 1982-1986 emphasizes the development of infrastructure. A recent credit of $17 million from the International Development Association will fund a project to improve transportation on the river that carries products from and to the Central African Republic as well as from Congo's interior forests.

FREEDOM

The Congo is a one-party state, and power is limited to the small membership of the Congolese Worker's Party (PCT). A series of regional and local congresses, as well as a National Assembly, have existed since 1972. Members of these organizations are elected from party-approved lists. They regularly debate public issues.

HEALTH/WELFARE

Formerly mission schools were important; now students aged six to sixteen must attend state schools. In the first decade after independence, the number of secondary students increased seven-fold, and a major adult literacy program was planned for the 1980s. The majority of students in higher education are studying in the USSR.

ACHIEVEMENTS

There are a number of Congolese poets and novelists, now in their forties and fifties, who combine their creative efforts with teaching and public service. The poet U'Tam'si is best known, but others include Maxine N'Debeka, satirist and army officer, and the poet Jean-Baptiste Tati.

Equatorial Guinea

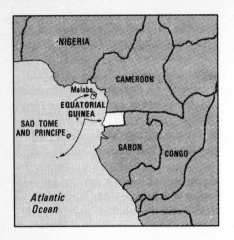

GEOGRAPHY

Area in Square Kilometers (Miles): 28,023 (10,820)
Land Usage: largely forests
Capital (Population): Malabo (37,237—1960)
Climate: equatorial

PEOPLE

Population
Total: 381,000 (1982 est.)
Per Square Kilometer (Mile): 14 (35)
Annual Growth Rate: 2.4%

Health
Life Expectancy at Birth: 46 years
Infant Death Rate (Ratio): 143/1,000

Languages
Official: Spanish
Others spoken: Fang; Benge; Combe; Bujeba; Balengue; Fernandino; Bubi

Religion(s)
60% Catholic; 40% Protestant; traditional indigenous beliefs

Education
Adult Literacy Rate: 38%
School Attendance: 80% boys, 67% girls; secondary: 50% boys, 28% girls

COMMUNICATION

Telephones: 2,000
Radios: 105,000
Televisions: 1,000
Newspapers: 2 dailies; total circulation 1,100

TRANSPORTATION

Highways—Kilometers (Miles): 2,760 (1,715)
Railroads—Kilometers (Miles): none
Two international airports

GOVERNMENT

Type: republic, governed by Supreme Military Council
Constitution: suspended
Former Colonial Status: Spanish
Independence Date: October 12, 1968
Head of State: Lieutenant Colonel Teodoro Obiang Ngeuma Mbasogo
Branches: executive and legislative powers held by Supreme Military Council; judicial process not clearly defined since 1979 coup
Legal System: in transition
Political Parties: political activities suspended
Suffrage: popular suffrage has been deferred

MILITARY

Military Expenditures (% of Central Government Expenditures): 21%
Nuclear Weapons Status: none
Current Hostilities: internal conflicts; coup attempts in 1981 and 1983

ECONOMY

Currency ($ US Equivalent): 322 Ekueles = $1
GDP: $100,000,000
Per Capita Income/GNP: $417
Workforce: majority of population engaged in subsistence agriculture
Natural Resources: wood
Agriculture: cocoa; coffee; timber; rice; yams; bananas
Industry: fishing; saw milling; palm oil processing
Energy Production: 7,000 kw capacity
Energy Consumption Per Capita: 99 kwh

FOREIGN TRADE

Exports: cocoa; wood; coffee; bananas; palm oil
Imports: foodstuffs; beverages; tobacco; textiles; machinery
Major Trading Partners: Spain
Foreign Debt: $98,500,000
Selected Membership in International Organizations: UN; OAU; Economic Community of Central African States (CEEAC)

Europeans explore modern Equatorial Guinea
1500s

The Dutch establish slave trading stations
1641

Spain claims area of Equatorial Guinea; process of establishing de facto control not completed until 1926
1778

The League of Nations investigates charges of slavery on Fernando Po
1930

The murder of nationalist leader Acacio Mane leads to the founding of political parties
1958

Local autonomy granted
1963

Independence; Marcias Nguema begins reign
1968

Coup ends the dictatorial regime of Macias Nguema
1979

The government claims that 95% of the voters back its new Constitution
1982

1983

June: Coup attempt foiled; leaders later executed

August: Obiang elected to seventh term as president; first parliamentary elections in ten years

October: Equatorial Guinea prepares to join the Central African Franc Zone and Central African Economic Community

EQUATORIAL GUINEA

In recent years Equatorial Guinea, a West African nation about the size of Maryland with a population of nearly one-third million, has been gradually recovering from the nightmare of its first decade of independence. Under the misrule of Macias Nguema (1968-1979), virtually all public and private enterprise had collapsed. During this period at least one-third of the nation's population went into exile, while an unknown (but certainly large) number of others were either murdered or allowed to die of disease and starvation. Many of those who remained were put to forced labor, and the rest were left to subsist off the land. This reign of terror and decay finally ended when Macias was overthrown in a coup, which installed his nephew and chief aide, Obiang Ngeuma, as the new ruler.

The modern decline of Equatorial Guinea contrasts sharply with the mood of optimism that characterized the country when it gained its independence from Spain in 1968. At that time, the new republic was buoyed by the prospects of a growing GDP, potential mineral riches, and exceptionally good soils. Although the major responsibility for the betrayal of Equatorial Guinea's promising potential must lie with Macias Nguema's dictatorial behavior, the historically uneven pattern of development among the nation's geographically diverse regions certainly contributed to its internal weakness. The republic is comprised of two small islands, Fernando Po (now known as Bioko) and Annonbon, and the relatively larger and more populous coastal enclave of Rio Muni. Before the two islands and the enclave were united during the nineteenth century as Spain's only colony in sub-Saharan Africa, all three areas were victimized by the slave trade. Under colonial rule, however, they suffered along separate paths.

CHARGES OF SLAVERY

Spain's major colonial concern was the prosperity of the large cocoa and coffee plantations that were established on the islands, particularly on Fernando Po. Because of local resistance, labor for these estates was imported from elsewhere in West Africa. Coercive recruitment and poor working conditions led to frequent charges of slavery. Although colonialism was accompanied by the emergence of a local educated elite on Fernando Po, about eighty percent of the island's population at independence was classified as "resident aliens." This category included about seven thousand Spanish settlers and nearly forty-five thousand laborers, mostly Nigerian. The common language of Fernando Po is Pidgin English, while that of Annobon is Ambu, a Portuguese Creole.

Despite early evidence of its potential riches, Rio Muni was largely neglected by the Spanish, who only occupied its interior in 1926. During the 1930s and 1940s, much of the enclave was under the political control of the *Elar-ayong,* a nationalist movement that sought to unite the Fang, Rio Muni's principal ethnic group, against both Spanish and French rule. The territory has remained one of the world's least-developed areas, with poor communications and few schools, hospitals, or other basic infrastructure.

Although no community was left unscarred by Macias Nguema's tyranny, the greatest disruption occurred on the islands. By 1976 the entire resident alien population had left, along with most surviving members of the educated class. Many of the plantations on Fernando Po were reportedly converted to marijuana cultivation. On Annobon, the government blocked all international efforts to stem a severe cholera epidemic in 1973. The near total depopulation of the island was completed in 1976 when all able-bodied men on Annobon, along with another twenty thousand from Rio Muni, were drafted for forced labor on Fernando Po. Annobon subsequently became a supply base for the Soviet navy.

CONTINUING OPPOSITION

Despite the dramatically improved economic and human rights situation inside the country, most of the exile groups that emerged under Macias have remained in opposition and denounced recent elections as fraudulent. Their hostile attitude is understandable given the fact that, like Obiang, most members of the new government had previously worked under Macias. Coup attempts in 1981 and 1983 were crushed with the support of the Moroccans.

DEVELOPMENT

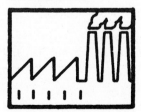

The cocoa, coffee, and plywood industries are reviving. Prospecting for a number of minerals is underway in Rio Muni.

FREEDOM

The new Constitution contains a Bill of Rights, which guarantees basic freedoms. While the human rights situation has improved over the last three years, there are still allegations of abuses.

HEALTH/WELFARE

At the time of Macias' overthrow, a handful of Chinese medics were the nation's sole health providers. Hospitals have since re-opened.

ACHIEVEMENTS

Primary education has rapidly revived and expanded since 1979, and now incorporates most of the school-age population. UNESCO is helping to train teachers.

Gabon

GEOGRAPHY

Area in Square Kilometers (Miles): 264,180 (102,317)
Land Usage: 75% forests; 15% savanna; 9% urban and waste land; less than 1% cultivated
Capital (Population): Libreville (100,000—1981)
Climate: tropical

PEOPLE

Population
Total: 563,000 (1982 est.)
Per Square Kilometer (Mile): 2 (5.5)
Annual Growth Rate: 1.1%
Rural/Urban Population Ratio: 63/37

Health
Life Expectancy at Birth: 49 years
Infant Death Rate (Ratio): 114/1,000
Average Caloric Intake: 102% of FAO minimum
Physicians Available (Ratio): 1/3,030

Languages
Official: French
Others Spoken: Fang; Eshira; Bopounou; Bateke; Okande; others

Religion(s)
55% to 75% Christian; less than 1% Muslim; remainder indigenous beliefs

Education
Adult Literacy Rate: 22% males; 5% females
School Attendance: primary: 100% boys, 100% girls; secondary: 100% boys, 76% girls

LAMBARENE

Lambarene, a town of about seven thousand on the Ogooue River, 175 miles in Gabon's interior, is the site of the mission hospital that Albert Schweitzer built and in which he practiced medicine. Schweitzer, born in Alsace-Lorraine, then a part of Germany, was a philosopher, theologian, organist, and specialist on Bach as well as a medical missionary. At the age of thirty-eight, he came to Lambarene where he lived and worked for fifty-two years. The hospital that he built was like an African village, consisting of many simple dwellings. It accommodated many patients and their relatives and operated without all the necessities of hospitals in Europe. In later times, innovative changes were not always accepted by the authoritarian Schweitzer or his staff. The work at Lambarene saved lives and cured thousands. Schweitzer was awarded the Nobel Peace Prize for his efforts for "the Brotherhood of Nations." Yet, he shared the distorted images of Africans so deeply engrained among Westerners, and he did not believe that Africans could advance in Western ways.

COMMUNICATION

Telephones: 11,600
Radios: 98,000
Televisions: 10,000
Newspapers: 1 daily; total circulation 600

TRANSPORTATION

Highways—Kilometers (Miles): 6,947 (4,316)
Railroads—Kilometers (Miles): 970 (602)
Three international airports

GOVERNMENT

Type: republic; one-party presidential regime since 1964
Constitution: February 21, 1961
Former Colonial Status: French
Independence Date: August 17, 1960
Head of State: El Hadj Omar Bongo (president)
Branches: president; unicameral National Assembly; independent judiciary
Legal System: based on French Civil Law and customary law
Political Parties: Gabonese Democratic Party
Suffrage: universal over age 18

MILITARY

Number of Armed Forces: 1,950
Armed Forces/Population: 1/1,338
Military Expenditures (% of Central Government Expenditures): 3.1%
Nuclear Weapons Status: none
Current Hostilities: none

ECONOMY

Currency ($ US Equivalent): 440 CFA francs = $1
GDP: $3,800,000
Per Capita Income/GNP: $4,000
Workforce: 77% agriculture; 11% industry; 12% service
Inflation Rate: 13% (1981)
Natural Resources: wood; petroleum; iron ore; manganese; uranium
Agriculture: cocoa; coffee; palm oil
Industry: petroleum; lumber; minerals
Energy Production: 175,400 kw capacity
Energy Consumption Per Capita: 369 kwh

FOREIGN TRADE

Exports: crude petroleum; wood and wood products; minerals; coffee; manganese; uranium
Imports: mining and road building machinery; electrical equipment; transport vehicles; foodstuffs; textiles
Major Trading Partners: France; United States; West Germany; Curacao
Foreign Debt: $1,089,000,000
Selected Membership in International Organizations: UN; OAU; Customs and Economic Union of Central Africa (UDEAC); Associate Member, European Communities (EC); Organization of Petroleum Exporting Countries (OPEC); Economic Community of Central African States (CEEAC)

Libreville
founded by
the French
as a settlement
for freed slaves
1849

Gabon becomes
a colony within
French Equa-
torial Africa
1910

The Free French
in Brazzaville
seize Gabon
from the pro-
Vichy govern-
ment
1940

Independence
is granted; Leon
M'ba is president
1960

Albert Bongo
becomes Gabon's
second president
after M'ba's death
1967

The Gabonese
Democratic
Party (PDG)
becomes the
only party of the
state
1968

Gabon gives
Angola funds for
the struggle
against South
Africa
1982

●1983

June: President
Bongo visits
President
Houphouet-
Boigny of the
Ivory Coast

December:
Government lifts
media ban on
France, resulting
from publication
of Pierre Pean's
Affaires Africaines,
which describes
Gabonese
scandals

GABON

"The small antelope is not the child of the elephant" is a proverb of the Fang people of Gabon. Often, the elephant symbolizes the European: powerful though slow. The antelope is clever, though small. The proverb reminds us that the Gabonese are not entirely dependent upon nor committed to the Western interests that predominate in Gabon today, as they did during colonial times.

In the countryside, traditional values, while changing, remain strong. The Fang peoples who migrated to Gabon in the late eighteenth and nineteenth centuries absorbed earlier populations. Village and lineage links form the basis of a single homogenous culture characteristic of much of Gabon. The values of this culture—the concern for wealth, the importance of land, and the significance of ancestors—are often symbolized by the sophisticated and unusual art forms such as the abstract figures that, like tombstones, guard ancestral remains and that have influenced many modern Western artists.

Meanwhile there is a strong urban and mining sector in Gabon. Libreville, Port Gentil, and Franceville/Moanda are the centers of modern mining developments. The major industry is oil. Oil fields began to be developed in 1957, and Gabon is now the second largest crude oil producer in sub-Saharan Africa. Gabon is also the world's largest exporter of manganese. Very rich uranium deposits are also being mined, and other untapped minerals include rich resources of iron ore.

FOREIGN DEVELOPERS

These ores are being mined by foreign corporations, which keep most of the profits from these operations. ELF-Gabon, a French owned corporation, and AMOCO, of Indiana in the United States, play major roles in the oil industry, and other corporations are involved in other ventures. The Gabonese government has a limited share in these industries: thirty percent in the oil companies, twelve percent in manganese, and twenty-five percent in the exploitation of uranium. Since 1974, there has been pressure on the firms to increase this share and to raise prices.

RELATIONS WITH FRANCE

France has a long history of relations with Gabon. The French established a colony of freed slaves in Libreville as early as 1849, and the French forces used Libreville as a base for the conquest of other parts of Central Africa. Gabon was part of France's colonial empire and, even after independence, France maintained a powerful role in the country. In 1964, four years after independence, President Leon M'Ba (whom the French had kept under house arrest in the colonial years) appealed to the French to restore him to power following a coup.

M'Ba and his chosen successor Albert Bernard (now Omar) Bongo have been able to maintain control of their government and of the only legal party, the Gabonese Democratic Party (GDP), with French support. The presidents have included representation from different ethnic groups in their Cabinets. Recent demonstrations for a multi-party system have been condemned for "resurrecting tribalism" and have resulted in arrests, trials, and long prison sentences.

UNEVEN DISTRIBUTION OF WEALTH

The exploitation of its rich resources has made Gabon appear to be a wealthy country, even though its percentage of the returns are small. Gabon's GNP (Gross National Product) of $3,100 is the highest in sub-Saharan Africa. However, people of the urban areas and a small elite have gained the most benefit from the sale of Gabon's mineral wealth. Large sums have been expended on symbols, such as the buildings erected for the 1977 OAU summit and the recently completed Presidential Palace. Ordinary people do benefit from the development of Gabonese transportation, including the as yet uncompleted Trans-Gabonese railroad, but the major customers of the railroad will be the mining companies, including potential investors in the iron ore that the railroad will transport.

FOREIGN POLICY

Meanwhile, Gabon has aroused the hostility of its African colleagues because of the conservative attitudes of its government, its receptivity toward trade with South Africa, and the strong evidence of its participation in a coup planned against Benin in 1977. Recent agreements with the socialist state of Angola may indicate a change in Gabon's foreign policy.

DEVELOPMENT	FREEDOM	HEALTH/WELFARE	ACHIEVEMENTS
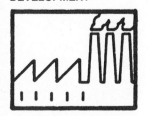			
Gabon's search for hydrocarbons and minerals has revealed vast and varied sources of wealth. Oil, uranium, manganese, and iron ore are already being exploited. Other deposits of these resources have been found and barytes (used in the oil industry), talc, lead, gold, and diamonds are also available.	Gabon is a one-party state. In 1982 university demonstrations for a multi-party system led to arrests including that of the university rector. Members of the opposition Movement for National Recovery (Morena) were tried in December 1982 for endangering the security of the state.	Education is compulsory for children ages six to sixteen and nearly all children are in school according to government figures. The building of rural schools is a high priority. The University of Libreville began in 1970.	Gabon has nearly achieved universal primary education and increased attention has been given to technical, secondary, and higher education. Some criticize the educational system because it is French-based in language and programs.

Sao Tome and Principe

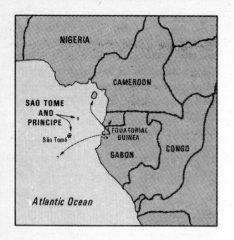

GEOGRAPHY

Area in Square Kilometers (Miles):
963 (372)
Capital (Population): Sao Tome
(5,714—1960)
Climate: tropical

PEOPLE

Population
Total: 86,000 (1982 est.)
Per Square Kilometer (Mile): 89
(232)
Annual Growth Rate: 1.1%

Health
Infant Death Rate (Ratio):
49.7/1,000
Average Caloric Intake: 78% of
FAO minimum

Languages
Official: Portuguese
Other Spoken: Creole; Krioulu

Religion(s)
80% Christian; 20% traditional
beliefs

Education
Adult Literacy Rate: 5-10%

COMMUNICATION

Telephones: 5,700
Radios: 24,000
Newspapers: 2 weeklies

THE PEOPLE OF THE ISLANDS

The present population of Sao Tome and Principe is mostly of mixed African and European descent. During the colonial period, the society was stratified along racial lines. At the top were the Europeans—mostly Portuguese. Just below them were the *mesticos* or *filhos da terra,* who were the mixed blood descendants of slaves. Descendants of slaves who arrived later were known as *forros.* Contract workers were labeled as *servicais,* while their children became known as *tongas.* Still another category was the *angolares,* who reportedly were the descendants of shipwrecked slaves. All of these colonial categories were used to divide and rule the local population and have begun to disappear as an important sociological factor on the islands.

TRANSPORTATION

Highways—Kilometers (Miles): 287
(178)
Railroads—Kilometers (Miles): none
One international airport

GOVERNMENT

Type: republic
Constitution: November 5, 1975
Former Colonial Status: Portuguese
Independence Date: July 12, 1975
Head of State: Manuel Pinto da
Costa (president)
Branches: president; Cabinet;
unicameral Popular Assembly;
Supreme Tribunal
Political Parties: Movement for the
Liberation of Sao Tome and Principe
Suffrage: universal over age 18

ECONOMY

Currency ($ US Equivalent): 36
Dobras = $1
GDP: $40,000,000
Per Capita Income/GNP: $370
Natural Resources: fish
Agriculture: cacao; coconut palms;
coffee; bananas; palm kernels
Industry: beer; soft drinks; palm oil;
copra; tourism; manufacturing;
construction
Energy Production: 3,000 kw
capacity
Energy Consumption Per Capita: 120
kwh

FOREIGN TRADE

Exports: cocoa; copra; palm kernels;
coffee
Imports: foodstuffs; textiles;
machinery
Major Trading Partners: Portugal;
Netherlands; United States; West
Germany
*Selected Membership in International
Organizations:* UN; OAU; Associate
Member, European Economic Com-
munity (EEC); Economic Communi-
ty of Central African States
(CEEAC)

Portuguese
settle Sao
Tome and Prin-
cipe
1500s

Slavery
abolished, but
forced labor
continues
1876

Portuguese
massacre
hundreds of
islanders
1953

Factions
within the
liberation
movement unite
to form the
MLSTP in Gabon
1972

Independence
1975

Pinto da Costa
deposes and
exiles Miguel
Trovoada, the
premier and
former number-
two man in the
MLSTP
1979

1983

February 1984:
Portuguese
foreign minister
visits islands
and announces
new aid
measures

March 1984:
Construction
begins on
new international
airport

SAO TOME AND PRINCIPE

On July 12, 1975, after a half millenium of Portuguese rule, the islands of Sao Tome and Principe took their place as one of Africa's smallest and poorest nations. Although the post-colonial years have been difficult, the approximately eighty-six thousand citizens of the new republic share little nostalgia for their colonial past. Before 1975, the islands' economic life centered around the interests of a few thousand white settlers—particularly, a handful of large plantation owners, who together controlled over eighty percent of the land. After independence, most of the whites fled, taking their skills and capital and leaving the economy in a state of disarray. Under government management, however, production on the plantations has been revived for the benefit of all segments of the society.

LONG HISTORY OF FORCED LABOR

The Portuguese began the first permanent settlement of Sao Tome and Principe at about the same time that Christopher Columbus was carrying out his explorations of the Americas. Through the intensive use of slave labor, the islands developed rapidly as one of the world's leading exporters of sugar. Only a small fraction of the profits from this boom, however, were consumed locally. High mortality rates, caused by brutal working conditions, led to an almost insatiable demand for more slaves. This appetite resulted in raids by local planters against various African coastal states, some of which were allies of the Portuguese crown. After the mid-sixteenth century profits from sugar declined (as rapidly as they had risen) due to competition from Brazil and the Caribbean, and a period of prolonged depression set in.

In the early nineteenth century, a second economic boom swept the islands when they became leading exporters of coffee and, more importantly, cocoa. Although Sao Tome and Principe's position in the world market has since declined, both cash crops have continued to be economic mainstays and in recent years have accounted for about ninety percent of the nation's export earnings. Although slavery was officially abolished during the nineteenth century, forced labor was maintained by the Portuguese into modern times. During the twentieth century involuntary contract workers, *servicais,* were imported to labor on the island's plantations. These workers usually died before long. Sporadic labor unrest and occasional incidents of international outrage did lead to some improvement in working conditions, but fundamental reforms came about only after independence had been achieved. An historical turning point for the islands was the Batepa Massacre in 1953, when several hundred African laborers were killed following local resistance to labor conditions.

POLITICS

Sao Tome and Principe is presently ruled as a one-party state by the Movement for the Liberation of Sao Tome and Principe (MLSTP), which had emerged in exile as the islands' anti-colonial movement. Although all political processes are carried out through the party, the party itself is answerable to internal elections, which incorporate all citizens. Power seems to have become increasingly concentrated, however, in the hands of Dr. Manuel Pinto da Costa, who has led both the party and the nation since independence.

ECONOMIC DEVELOPMENT

A top economic priority for the MLSTP leadership has been the encouragement of local food production. At present only about ten percent of the nation's food consumption is locally grown, a factor that has contributed to a large and growing balance-of-payments deficit.

Another priority area for development planners is fishing. In 1978 a 200 mile maritime zone was declared, but the local fleet is badly in need of improvement. Although some consider tourism to be a potential growth sector, the government has so far not favored its expansion. Manufacturing and construction make up about seven percent of GDP, and their short-term prospects appear to be limited. Given its smallness, the best hope for Sao Tome and Principe's future prosperity may lie in regional economic initiatives such as the newly constituted Economic Community of Central Africa of which the country is a member.

DEVELOPMENT

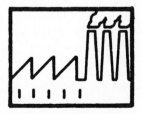

At present, the country lacks a deep water port. The government is hoping to find financial backing to build one.

FREEDOM

Individual freedoms are curbed, but there have been no reports of torture, disappearances, or state assassinations. A number of Pinto da Costa's political rivals have been exiled.

HEALTH/WELFARE

Health care is free but limited. The government has established pre- and post-natal care clinics as well as a malaria eradication program.

ACHIEVEMENTS

Sao Tome and Principe share in a rich Luso-African artistic tradition. The country is particularly renowned for poets such as Jose de Almeida and Francisco Tenriero, who were among the first to express the experiences and pride of Africans in the Portuguese language.

Zaire

GEOGRAPHY

Area in Square Kilometers (Miles):
2,300,000 (905,063)
Land Usage: 22% agricultural; 45%
forests; 33% other
Capital (Population): Kinshasa
(2,240,000—1975)
Climate: equatorial

PEOPLE

Population
Total: 27,100,000 (1982 est.)
Per Square Kilometer (Mile): 12 (30)
Annual Growth Rate: 3%
Rural/Urban Population Ratio: 64/36

Health
Life Expectancy at Birth: 50 years
Infant Death Rate (Ratio): 112/1,000
Average Caloric Intake: 94% of
FAO minimum
Physicians Available (Ratio):
1/14,780
Access to Safe Water: 16%

Languages
Official: French
Others Spoken: Swahili; Lingala;
Azande; Luba; Chokwe; Songye;
Kongo; Kuba; Lunda; Bemba; Alur;
and approximately 250 others

Religion(s)
50% Christian; 50% indigenous
beliefs

Education
Adult Literacy Rate: males 77%;
females 39%
School Attendance: 100% boys, 75%
girls; secondary: 33% boys, 13%
girls

COMMUNICATION
Telephones: 30,300
Radios: 200,000
Televisions: 9,000
Newspapers: 6 dailies; total circula-
tion 45,000

TRANSPORTATION
Highways—Kilometers (Miles):
20,683 (12,851)
Railroads—Kilometers (Miles): 5,254
(3,264)
Five international airports

GOVERNMENT
Type: republic; with strong presiden-
tial authority
Constitution: June 24, 1967
Former Colonial Status: Belgian
Independence Date: June 30, 1960
Head of State: Marshal Mobutu Sese
Seko (president)
Branches: president; National Ex-
ecutive Council; unicameral National
Assembly; Judicial Council
Political Parties: Popular Revolu-
tionary Movement (MPR)
Suffrage: universal over age 18

MILITARY
Number of Armed Forces: 22,100
Armed Forces/Population: 1/1,231
Nuclear Weapons Status: none
Foreign Aid: United States; Western
Europe
Current Hostilities: none

ZAIRE AND BELGIUM

Presently Belgium is a center of anti-Mobutu activity. In October
1982, Zairian political exiles in Brussels formed the Congolese Front for
the Restoration of Democracy (PCD) under the leadership of former
Prime Minister Nzuga Karl-I-Bond. Another, more moderate group, the
Union for Democratic and Social Progress, has been established by
Professor Dikonda. The level of feeling about Mobutu was evidently
responsible for the cancellation of his planned visit to Belgium in mid-
1982. Mobutu sees himself as "a victim of destabilization" and
condemns the campaign in Belgium as "interference." Some Zairians
contrast Belgium's attitude with that of the French government, which
refused to allow the Zaire opposition leader to hold a press conference in
Paris.

ECONOMY
Currency ($ US Equivalent): 37
zaires = $1
GDP: $5,380,000,000
Per Capita Income/GNP: $190
Workforce: 75% agriculture; 13% industry; 12% services
Inflation Rate: 32.2% (1970-1980);
50% (1982)
Natural Resources: copper; cobalt;
zinc; diamonds; manganese; tin;
gold; rare metals; bauxite; iron;
coal; hydroelectric potential; timber
Agriculture: coffee; palm oil; rubber;
tea; cotton; cocoa; manioc; bananas;
plantains; corn; rice; sugar
Industry: mining of minerals; consumer products; processed foods;
cement
Energy Production: 1,694,000 kw
capacity; 4,200,000,000 kwh
produced
Energy Consumption Per Capita: 143
kwh

FOREIGN TRADE
Exports: cobalt; copper; diamonds;
gold; coffee; manganese; wood
Imports: crude petroleum and
petroleum products; food; textiles;
heavy equipment
Major Trading Partners: Belgium;
Luxembourg; UK; United States;
France; West Germany
Foreign Debt: $4,682,000,000
*Selected Membership in International
Organizations:* UN; OAU; African
Development Bank; Non-Aligned
Movement; Economic Community of
Central African States (CEEAC)

ZAIRE

"Together, my brothers, we are going to start a new struggle which will lead our country to peace, prosperity and greatness.... [W]e are going to make the Congo the hub of all Africa."

So spoke Patrice Lumumba, the country's first prime minister, on June 30, 1960—the day when Zaire (then the Republic of the Congo) became an independent nation. Zaire had then, and still has, the potential to become the hub of all Africa, and yet the "peace, prosperity and greatness" of which Lumumba spoke are far from being achieved.

THE HUB OF AFRICA

In geographic terms, Zaire is certainly the hub of Africa. Located at Africa's "navel," it encompasses the entire Zaire River Basin and is a fourth the size of the United States. Although the tropical climate has impeded people's development of their environment, the country encompasses a great variety of land forms and has good agricultural possibilities. It contains a vast range of rich resources, some of which (such as copper) have been intensively exploited for several decades. The river itself is the potential source of thirteen percent of the world's hydroelectric power.

Zaire links Africa from west to east. The country faces the Atlantic, with a very narrow coast on that ocean. At the same time, peoples of the eastern Congo have been influenced by forces from the East African coast. In the mid-nineteenth century, Swahili, Nyamwezi, and other traders from Tanzania established control over areas in the present-day Shaba Province of eastern Zaire and traded for ivory and slaves. These events had deep cultural consequences. The Swahili language continues to be spoken in these regions, and Islam has also influenced peoples of the area.

THE PEOPLES AND THEIR HERITAGE

Zaire's nearly thirty million people are members of about 250 different ethnic groups, speak nearly 700 different languages and dialects, and have varied life-styles. Boundaries established in the late nineteenth century hemmed in portions of the Azande, the Kongo, the Chokwe, and the Songye peoples within present-day Zaire. However, these peoples maintain contacts with their kin, clan, and group members in other countries—again indicating Zaire's hub-like character.

Many important pre-colonial kingdoms were centered in Zaire, including the Luba, the Kuba, and the Lunda kingdoms—the latter of which in earlier centuries exploited the salt and copper of southeast Zaire, in the present Shaba Province. The elaborate political systems of these kingdoms are an important heritage of Zairian people. The artistic traditions are remarkable. Different art styles are connected with different political systems and religious associations; they range from the naturalistic to the abstract or cubist. These art forms had a deep influence on artists such as Picasso and Modigliani. Even such a seemingly minor craft as the making of raffia (fiber) mats involves rich decorative features. These artistic talents and traditions are also found in the neighboring countries where Zaire's peoples live.

A TROUBLED PAST

The European impact, like the Swahili and

(Photo by Joseph Cornet, Courtesy of the Peabody Museum, Harvard University)

The African cup that is used for drinking often satisfies the eye as well as sustaining the body. Ordinary and sacred wooden objects reveal the artistry of African sculptors. This cup reflects a part of the cultural heritage of Zaire.

Leopold sets up
the Congo Inde-
pendent State as
his private
kingdom
1879

The Congo
becomes a
Belgian
Colony
1909

The Congo gains
independence;
civil war begins;
UN Force is in-
volved; Lumumba
is murdered
1960

Arab influence from the east, was to have disruptive results for Zaire's peoples. The Congo Basin was explored and exploited by private individuals before it came under Belgian domination. King Leopold of Belgium, in his capacity as a private citizen, sponsored British adventurer H.M. Stanley's expeditions to explore the great river. In 1879 Leopold set up a so-called Congo Independent State over the whole region. This state was actually his private kingdom, and the companies and employees whom he admitted into the region took its ivory and sought the rubber that could be used by an industrializing Europe. Armed militias used force to collect quotas of rubber from the people, and the atrocities they committed gained worldwide attention. Finally, in 1908, the territories were transferred to Belgium. First a single person and then a tiny European country ruled over these vast African domains.

During the years of Belgian administration, control was more benign than during Leopold's regime. However, the colonial authorities did use armed forces for "pacification" campaigns, tax collection, and labor recruitment. New men were made chiefs and given power that they would not have had under the traditional systems. Concessionary companies used various means to recruit a steady labor force to work on plantations and in the mines. The most famous companies were Lever Brothers and the Union Minière, which exploited the minerals of Shaba Province.

The Belgian colonial regime encouraged the presence and work of Catholic missions in the Congo. Health facilities as well as a paternalistic system of education were developed. A strong elementary school system was part of the colonial program. However, since, in the Belgian view, the Congolese were "adult children" who could only carry out low-level jobs, the Belgians never instituted a major secondary school system, and there was no institution of higher learning. The small group of Western-educated Congolese, known as *évolués,* served the needs of an administration that never intended nor planned for Zaire's independence.

THE COMING
OF INDEPENDENCE

In the 1950s independence movements developed in the countries surrounding Congo and throughout the African continent. The Congolese—especially those in the towns—were affected by these forces of change. The Belgians themselves began to recognize the need to prepare for a different future. Small initiatives began to be allowed; nationalistic associations were first permitted in 1955. In the same year, a publication proposed independence in thirty years' time and sparked discussion. Some évolués as well as Belgians agreed with its proposals. Other Congolese, including the members of the Alliance of the Ba-Kongo (ABAKO), an ethnic association in Kinshasa, and the National Congolese Movement (MNC), led by Patrice Lumumba, reacted against it.

A serious clash at an ABAKO demonstration in 1959 resulted in fifty deaths and suddenly sparked the plans for immediate independence. A constitutional conference in January 1960 established a federal government system for the future independent state. There was, however, no real preparation for such a drastic political change. Belgian colonial civil servants expected that they would stay on to work with each new Congolese government minister or administrator. They were to be disappointed.

A DIFFICULT BEGINNING

The Democratic Republic of the Congo became independent on June 30, 1960 under the leadership of President Joseph Kasavubu and Prime Minister Patrice Lumumba. Before a week had passed, an army mutiny had stimulated widespread disorder. The majority of the extensive Belgian community fled the country. The wealthy Katanga Province (now Shaba) and South Kasai seceded. Lumumba called upon the United Nations for assistance, and troops came from a variety of countries to serve in the UN force. Later, as a result of a dispute between President Kasavubu and himself, Lumumba called for Soviet aid. The Congo could have become a cold war battlefield, but the army, under Joseph Desirè Mobutu, intervened, and the Soviets were expelled. By the end of the year, Lumumba had been assassinated under suspicious circumstances in which the United States CIA (Central Intelligence Agency) was implicated. Rebellion, supported by foreign mercenaries, continued through 1967, especially in Katanga Province, and reappeared in 1977.

MOBUTU'S GOVERNMENT

On November 24, 1965, the army Chief of Staff, Joseph Desirè Mobutu, led a coup that established a new government. He broke the deadlock between competing politicians and eliminated rebels in the Congo. Mobutu declared a five-year moratorium on party politics, which still continues today. In the last eighteen years, a one-party state has been developed, in which power has increasingly been centralized around the figure of Mobutu, "the Founding President." He runs the party, the Popular Revolutionary Movement (MPR), and the Central Committee (which has superceded the Political Bureau, the decision-making body of the party and government). Almost all the country's institutions come under the party's and Mobutu's jurisdiction.

Mobutuism is the ideology of the state, and "authenticity" (*authenticité*) is its slogan. This has meant the recovery of old symbols, the use of traditional rather than European names, and an emphasis on ancient rituals. Mobutu has changed his own name to Mobutu Sese Seko, and in 1971, the Congo became Zaire. The policy has been followed by many other African leaders, but it has not involved deep changes. To promote nationalism, Union Minière and other corporations have come under government control. In 1973-1974 plantations, commercial institutions, and other businesses were also taken over in a "radicalizing of the Zairian Revolution."

However, the expropriated industries and businesses have personally enriched a small elite, rather than benefiting the nation. Consequently, the economy has suffered; industries and businesses have been mismanaged or ravaged. Some individuals have become extraordinarily wealthy, while the population as a whole has suffered. Mobutu is said to be the wealthiest person in Africa, with a fortune estimated at $10 billion, most of it invested and spent outside of Africa.

Mobutu has allowed no opposition. Those who are critical of his government face imprisonment or, at the least, beating. Those who suggest that other political parties should be allowed can be jailed for sedition. Student demonstrations have twice

Joseph Desiré
Mobutu takes
command in a
bloodless coup
1965

The name of the
state is changed
to Zaire
1971

Mobutu normal-
izes relations
with Israel;
Senegal and
Saudi Arabia
sever ties
with Zaire
1982

●IIIIIIIIIIIIIIIIIIIIIIIIIIIIIIIIIIIIIIIIIII●IIIIIIIIIIIIIIIIIIIIIIIIIIIIIIIIIIIIIIIIIIIIIIIIIIIIII●IIACHIEVEMENTSIIIIIIIIII●●1983

resulted in the closure of the university and forced conscription into the army for students. Workers strikes are not allowed. Secessionist movements in Shaba Province in 1977 and 1978 were suppressed with Moroccan assistance. The Roman Catholic Church and the Kimbanguist Church of Jesus Christ Upon This Earth are the only institutions that have been able to speak out without fear of reprisal.

ECONOMIC DISASTER

Zaire's economic potential had been developed by and for the Belgians, but by 1960 that development had gone further than in many other African colonial territories. Zaire started its life as an independent nation with a good economic base. The chaos of the early 1960s brought such developments to a standstill, and little advancement has been made in Mobutu's time. Outside investment has been encouraged, but projects such as the Inga-Shaba hydroelectric dam have not been carefully planned. This project is now a burden rather than a benefit. World economic conditions, including the low prices of copper and other minerals on the world market, have contributed to Zaire's economic difficulties. However, "the corruption of the team in power" has been recognized as the main obstacle to economic progress.

An organized system of exploitation transfers wealth from peasants to officials to the elite. Ordinary people suffer. Real wages of urban workers in 1980 were only one-tenth of what they were in 1960; meanwhile, the cost of living has risen sharply. Rural conditions have deteriorated.

Although Zaire's agriculture has great economic potential, the returns from this sector continue to shrink. Zaire must now import food for its population. Rural people move to the city or, for lack of employment, move back to the country and take up subsistence agriculture, rather than cash crop farming, in order to insure their own survival. The deterioration of roads and bridges has led to the decline of all trade. The government has not implemented its plans for reform. Zaire has a debt greater than that of any African country. It has defaulted on its debt payments and rescheduled them four times since 1976.

UNITED STATES SUPPORT FOR MOBUTU

The Mobutu regime has been able to sidestep its financial crises and repress political opposition that could lead to its downfall because the United States government underwrites its survival. The United States has viewed Mobutu as the symbol of stability in Central Africa and as a firm opponent of the Soviet Union and communism. Mobutu has been a friend of the West since 1960. He supported the United States-backed National Front for the Liberation of Angola (FLNA) against the Marxist-oriented Popular Movement for the Liberation of Angola (MPLA) in the 1960s, and he has stood behind unpopular United States resolutions in the UN. Only recently, Zaire sent two thousand troops to Chad to support the United States-backed government of Hissené Habré. France, too, under President Mitterrand, has continued to recognize and support Zaire.

January 1984: Israeli President Chaim Herzog visits Zaire; Egyptian President Hosni Mubarak visits a few weeks later

March 1984: Exile opposition groups claim responsibility for explosions that damaged a national radio station and a post office in Kinshasa

July 1984: Mobutu is elected President of Zaire for a third 7-year term; all citizens above 19 years are required to vote

The United States has clear evidence of Mobutu's human rights violations and of the oppression and corruption that characterize the Zaire government. Defectors from the highest levels of government in Zaire have revealed many of the evils of the regime. Recent offers of amnesty to political prisoners by Mobutu may be a result of the urgings of the United States government to the head of state. The continued US support of Mobutu reflects the West's perception that there is no satisfactory alternative to his rule nor any successor who could replace Mobutu in this strategic area of Africa.

Mobutu has also allied himself with conservative forces in Africa. Moroccan troops came to his aid during the revolts in Shaba Province in 1977. He has maintained ties with South Africa, selling Zaire's diamonds through the DeBeers-owned Central Selling Organization, using South Africa's rails and ports, and importing almost half its food from the apartheid state. In 1982, Zaire was the first African country to renew diplomatic ties with Israel after the break following the takeover of the Sinai in 1973. Any claim that Zaire might have to be "the hub of Africa" is weakened by the positions that have been taken in African and world affairs today.

DEVELOPMENT

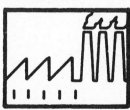

The Inga-Shaba power line, completed in 1982, is the largest of its kind in the world. It will be used for the increased production of copper and cobalt once prices for these items rise on the world market. Presently, the power line is not used enough to generate the revenues to repay the loans that financed it.

FREEDOM

Zaire has shown little respect for the human rights of individual citizens. In 1982 Professor Ernest Wamba-dia Wamba, a Zairian teaching in Tanzania, was arrested on a visit for smuggling "subversive literature into the country" and was not released for nearly a year. Thirteen parliamentarians were recently sentenced to fifteen years each for proposing an alternative political party.

HEALTH/WELFARE

In 1978 over five million students were registered for primary schools, and thirty-five thousand for college. However, the level of education is gradually declining. Textbooks are lacking, and teacher strikes are frequent. In one case, a strike was broken by deporting teachers to their home villages. The few innovative educational programs are outside the state system.

ACHIEVEMENTS

Kinshasa is a musical center, the home of creative popular styles of vocal music and new dance bands. "Souskous" is the newest style, and Pablo Lubadika of the group "Le Peuple" is one of the most popular singers. Rochereau and Franco are vocalists with long-standing reputations. Zaire music is popular and sets styles throughout Africa as well as in Europe and America.

Topic Guide to Articles: Central Africa

TOPIC AREA	TREATED AS AN ISSUE IN	TOPIC AREA	TREATED AS AN ISSUE IN
Colonial Influence	1. Central Africa Tries Again 2. The Member States	**International Relations**	1. Central Africa Tries Again 2. The Member States 4. The Chad Flashpoint 6. Mobutu Nets "Hundreds" of Opponents
Current Leaders	5. Cameroon Tense as Leader Shows He's More Radical Than Expected 6. Mobutu Nets "Hundreds" of Opponents 7. Central African Republic: Emperor Without a Country	**Natural Resources**	3. Congo's Economy: Low on Energy; Flush With Oil 8. Waters of Life
Economy	1. Central Africa Tries Again 2. The Member States 3. Congo's Economy: Low on Energy; Flush With Oil	**Regional Concerns**	1. Central Africa Tries Again 2. The Member States 4. The Chad Flashpoint
Environment	8. Waters of Life	**Trade**	1. Central Africa Tries Again 2. The Member States 3. Congo's Economy: Low on Energy; Flush With Oil

AFRICA NEWS/November 7, 1983

Central Africa Tries Again

[AN] Leaders of 10 central African nations with a total population of about 60 million, signed a treaty in the Gabonese capital, Libreville, on Oct. 18, to establish the Economic Community of Central African States (CEEAC).

The signatories are five former French colonies, Cameroon, Central African Republic, Chad, Congo and Gabon; three former Belgian territories, Burundi, Rwanda and Zaire; a former Spanish colony, Equatorial Guinea; and a former Portuguese colony, Sao Tome & Principe.

The five former French colonies have been working together in the Central African Customs and Economic Union (UDEAC), while the three former Belgian territories have been members of the Economic Community of the Great Lakes States (CEPGL).

A communique issued at the end of the Libreville meeting said nothing about the fate of these two older groupings. But the summit host, Gabon's President Omar Bongo, said the decision to establish the new sub-regional organization was in conformity with the 1980 Lagos Plan of Action.

The Lagos Plan was produced by the Organization of African Unity (OAU) at a special economic summit in the Nigerian capital. The meeting looked at ways to strengthen existing sub-regional cooperation and reaffirmed the OAU's commitment to the ambitious goals of setting up a continent-wide economic community and common market by the year 2000.

The initiative to group African countries into economically viable units originally came from the Economic Commission for Africa, a United Nations agency, in the late 1950s. Later, in 1976, the ECA published a document calling for the establishment of a "new international economic order" for Africa.

The OAU picked up the gauntlet that same year during a summit meeting in Kinshasa, where the organization issued its first call for the African community and common market. The following year African heads of state and government met in Libreville and endorsed the ECA "master plan."

The OAU also organized the Monrovia colloquium of 1979, at which economic experts discussed in detail development prospects for the continent through the year 2000. The Lagos OAU summit of 1980 then set out a schedule for realizing these goals.

According to the Lagos plan, during the 1980s new sub-regional groupings will be established and the old ones strengthened. During the next decade, efforts will be made to harmonize the policies of the communities and prepare them for the continent-wide merger or association by the turn of the century. (See also *AN*, March 28.)

With the exception of Equatorial Guinea and Sao Tome & Principe, the countries in the central African region conduct their business in French. In addition, five of the nations were once organized together in the colony of French Equatorial Africa, which remained an administrative entity from 1839 until the late 1950s.

For these states, the French even established a joint "grand conseil" in Brazzaville, Congo, where elected representatives from the five colonies discussed financial and community issues, in 1946.

Limited autonomy notwithstanding, the French maintained that the five territories were an integral part of France. But growing nationalism in the colonies challenged this notion throughout the 1950s.

In 1958 French President Charles de Gaulle ordered a referendum throughout French Equatorial Africa and French West Africa to determine whether the colonies wanted to federate with France, or accept independence "with all its consequences." Only Guinea, out of the eight French West African and five French Equatorial African colonies, opted for complete and immediate independence, which meant the withdrawal of all French aid and personnel.

Before the end of 1960, however, all the French colonies had become independent.

In 1961, Central African Republic, Chad, Congo and Gabon establishd the Union of Central African Republics. This grouping hardly got off the ground, and only three years later the four nations, together with Cameroon, established the Central African Customs and Economic Union (UDEAC).

Although the leaders of the 10 nations that met last month in Libreville said nothing about the fate of UDEAC and the CEPGL, it can be assumed that the two groupings have been effectively merged into the current union to avoid costly duplication of services.

Like the six-year-old Economic Community of West African States (ECOWAS), the new central African grouping aims to promote economic and industrial cooperation between the member nations. Other objectives include establishing joint development organizations, harmonizing monetary policies and coordinating economic and planning and transport policies.

Removing Trade Tariffs

ECOWAS links 16 former British, French and Portuguese colonies with a total population of about 160 million.

Angola, which was represented at the Gabon meeting by its foreign trade minister, Ismael Martins, did not sign the treaty, citing pressing security priorities. South Africa occupies parts of southern Angola, from which Pretoria-backed guerrillas of the National Union for the Total Independence of Angola (UNITA) carry out regular raids on Angolan installations.

However, Martins pledged Angola's total solidarity with the 10 nations, promising that his country will join the grouping at a convenient time, according to the Libreville radio, Africa Numero I.

Angola is a member of the nine-nation Southern African Development Coordination Conference (SADCC), which includes Botswana, Lesotho, Malawi, Mozambique, Swaziland, Tanzania, Zambia and Zimbabwe. Established in 1979, the SADCC has a total population of 65 million.

Angola is also a member of the six-nation "frontline group" with Tanzania, Botswana, Mozambique, Zambia and Zimbabwe. The group coordinates external aid and diplomatic moves to support liberation efforts in southern Africa.

According to a Luanda-based diplomat, it is unlikely that Angola will want to alienate itself from these two groupings by signing the central African treaty.

Meanwhile, the 16 ECOWAS states have drawn up a program to remove trade and movement barriers among member-states. ECOWAS has classified its members into three groups for this purpose.

Group I includes Cape Verde, Guinea-Bissau, Gambia, Mali, Mauritania, Niger and Upper Volta. These nations will progressively remove trade and movement restrictions and complete the process by the year 1990.

Group II includes Benin, Guinea, Liberia, Sierra Leone and Togo, and has until 1988 to establish free movement and free trade among its member-states.

Ghana, Ivory Coast, Nigeria and Senegal belong in the third group, and have until 1986 to reach the ultimate goal.

The grouping of these nations is based on the levels of industrial development, the importance of customs revenue in the national budget, and problems resulting from lack of accessibility pertaining particularly to island and land-locked countries.

As a result of the removal of trade tariffs, member states will face problems of balancing their national budgets. To help them, ECOWAS has established a special fund to compensate for the loss of revenue, according to the latest ECOWAS *Background Notes*, a new quarterly publication aimed at informing American business executives on the west African community.

The group plans to establish a common external tariff during the next 10 years. It is also considering establishing a West African Trade and Development Bank, according to the publication.

Background Notes is published in Washington, D.C., by Robert S. Smith, a former U.S. envoy to Ivory Coast, and former deputy assistant secretary of state for Africa, under an ECOWAS contract.

Article 2

AFRICA NEWS/November 7, 1983

THE MEMBER STATES

Burundi: Part of the German East Africa colony until 1923, when the League of Nations placed it under Belgian rule, it became independent in 1962. Mwami (King) Mwambutsa, who reigned from 1915, was ousted by his son, Prince Charles Ndizeye (later Mwami Ntare V), in 1966. His prime minister, Michel Micombero, ousted the

THE NEW COMMUNITY

Africa News

BASIC ECONOMIC INDICATORS

COUNTRY	Population (millions)	GNP Per Capita (US $)	Annual Growth Rate	Adult Literacy (%)	Life Expectancy (Years)	Average Rate of Inflation ('70-'81)
Chad	4.5	110	−2.2	15	43	7.4
Equatorial Guinea	0.8	180	3.7	—	48	—
Zaire	29.8	210	−0.1	55	50	35.3
Burundi	4.2	230	2.4	25	45	11.6
Rwanda	6.0	250	1.7	50	46	13.4
Central African Republic	2.4	320	0.4	33	43	12.6
Sao Tome & Principe	0.1	370	0.0	—	—	8.8
Cameroon	8.7	880	2.8	—	50	10.6
Congo	1.7	1,110	1.0	—	60	13.0
Gabon	0.6	3,740	6.3	—	48	10.6

Source: World Bank

young king later the same year and remained in power until 1976, when Jean-Baptiste Bagaza deposed him. Bagaza's coup came after a period of intense ethnic violence.

Cameroon: A German possession from 1884-1916, the League of Nations split it into two, French and British, colonies (1922-1960). The two reunited to form the Cameroon Republic on independence in 1960, under Ahmadou Ahidjo, who ruled until last year, when he handed over to Paul Biya. It produces about five million tons of oil per year.

Central African Republic: Achieved self-rule from France in 1958 under Barthelemy Boganda as prime minister. Boganda died a year later and was replaced by David Dacko, who became president on independence day in 1960. Dacko was ousted in 1965 by his cousin, Jean-Bedel Bokassa, who first declared himself life president in 1972, then emperor in 1976. In 1979, Dacko, with the help of the French, ousted Bokassa, who fled to Ivory Coast. In 1981, Dacko was overthrown by Gen. Andre Kolingba in a bloodless coup.

Chad: France gave it colonial status in 1916, after separating it from the old Oubangui-Chari, which became the Central African Republic of today. Self-rule was granted in 1959, under Francois (later Ngarta) Tombalbaye, who became president of the new republic in 1960. He died in a military coup in 1975. Chad has been in a state of civil war since then.

Congo: Gained self-rule from the French in 1958, under Abbe Fulbert Youlou, who became president in 1960. Youlou was ousted in 1963 after he tried to merge political parties. He was replaced by Alphonse Massamba-Debat, who was himself toppled in 1968 as he tried to control the sole party. Marien Ngouabi took over and established the Parti Congolais du Travail in 1969. He was assassinated in 1977 and Joachim Yhombi-Opango succeeded him.

Denis Sassou Ngueso replaced Yhombi-Opango in 1979.

Equatorial Guinea: The Portuguese occupied it in the late 15th century and later ceded it to Spain in 1778. In 1959 Spain granted all residents Spanish citizenship and declared the territory an integral part of Spain. Three blacks were elected in 1960 to sit in the Spanish *Cortes*. Limited autonomy was granted in 1963. After a heavy UN campaign, a new constitution was approved in 1968, and independence was declared the same year under President Francisco Macias Nguema Biyoyo. A new constitution was adopted in 1973, paving the way for Nguema to declare himself life president in 1975. Human rights violations led to the flight of more than 60% of the nation's population from the country until 1968, when Nguema's cousin, Teodoro Obiang Nguema, came to power in a bloody coup.

Gabon: Black Africa's richest nation, it produces more than three million tons of oil per year. When Gabon attained self-rule in 1958, Leon M'Ba became prime minister and later president. A military coup deposed M'Ba in 1964, but the French intervened and reinstated him. On M'Ba's death in 1967, Vice President Albert-Bernard (later Omar after his conversion to Islam) Bongo succeeded M'Ba as president and founded the Bloc Democratique Gabonais (BDG), the sole party.

Rwanda: Africa's most densely populated nation (230 persons per sq. k.m.), it was part of the German East Africa colony until 1923. The League of Nations placed it under Belgian care until independence day in 1962. The minority Tutsi ethnic group dominated the Hutus (90%) until a 1959 civil war. The monarchy was abolished in 1961. Gregoire Kayibanda, the first president, was deposed by Juvenal Habyarimana in 1973. Habyarimana established the

Mouvement Revolutionnaire National pour le Development (MNRD) in 1975. About 100,000 Rwandan refugees are settled in Tanzania.

Sao Tome & Principe: The smallest nation in Africa, it was declared independent from Portugal in 1975, under President Manuel Pinto da Costa. Several coup bids were foiled in 1977 and '78. These involved mercenaries that allegedly had Gabon's backing. The Movimento de Libertacao de Sao Tome & Principe (MLSTP) is the sole party.

Zaire: The largest country in the grouping, it was organized into a free state by the Belgian King Leopold II in the 1880s. It was declared a colony in 1908, and given independence in 1960, with Patrice Lumumba as prime min-

ister. Katanga Province then seceded with Moise Tshombe as leader, contributing to a national crisis. Lumumba was assassinated in 1960 in a power struggle between him and President Joseph Kasavubu. In the confusion, Joseph Desire (later Sese Seko) Mobutu (a U.S. favorite), seized power temporarily. The confusion was repeated in 1965, when Mobutu finally moved in permanently to stop a feud between Kasavubu and Tshombe. Mobutu named the country Zaire (from Congo) in 1971. In 1977 the Shaba region was invaded by opponents of the regime, and Mobutu beat the rebels with help from 1,500 Moroccan troops and Egyptian pilots, as well as French and U.S. assistance. The Mouvement Populaire de la Revolution (MPR) is the sole party.

Article 3

THE ECONOMIST JULY 2, 1983

Congo's economy

Low on energy, flush with oil

BRAZZAVILLE

By staying out of Opec and increasing exports of oil, the small equatorial African state of Congo has so far avoided the large international debts which have hammered many developing countries. But its weaknesses are familiar: poor management, a bloated public sector and price controls.

Oil, produced offshore in the Gulf of Guinea, has made Congo a lot less poor than some of its neighbours. Its economy grew by 11% in real terms in 1981 and 12% in 1982, according to the government, though the International Monetary Fund puts growth almost four points lower in each of those years. Congo ranks fourth among black African oil producers and per capita gross national product has shot up to around $1,000 a year.

Little else besides oil production is going well in Congo's economy. The country's population of 1.6m used to eke out a living by hunting and shipping goods from its landlocked northern neighbours to the rest of the world. Half of Congo is covered with tropical forest, a mere 1% is under cultivation and the bulk of the population lives in towns. The government's development spending is aimed at giving people something to live off when oil runs out.

"We've got the money all right", says a taxi driver, negotiating a pothole, "but what about the management?" Congo, once a French colony, was Africa's first self-styled Marxist state. Much of the

---

Euphoria

POINTE NOIRE

The best-run state company in Congo, L'Unité d'Afforestation Industrielle du Congo, is creating a thriving eucalyptus plantation out of the barren savannah surrounding the country's port of Pointe Noire. The firm is nominally under the ministry of water and forestry, but the management, headed by an enthusiastic director, Mr Yves Laplace, is largely French.

The company has put the humble technique of grafting plants to industrial use. Cuttings are taken, snipped into small pieces and then kept under a continuous drizzle for 25 days. Each piece then sprouts roots and can be planted.

By taking cuttings from large, fast-growing trees, the company has achieved record-breaking yields. When it started in 1965, it got 12 cubic metres of wood per hectare each year. By 1982, the yield was 40 cubic metres per hectare, twice the rate on most plantations elsewhere in the world. The trees grow about 20 feet a year and, when chopped down, will grow again from the roots. Mr Laplace reckons that when commercial logging begins in 1987, one tonne of eucalyptus logs can be grown for a quarter of what it costs elsewhere.

The plantation is designed to provide the raw material for a big pulp and paper mill the government wants to build at Pointe Noire for around $400m. Consultants said the project should be stopped but the government has ignored them and is now looking for foreign capital.

---

economy, with the notable exception of the oil industry, is run by the government. Last year, grossly overmanned state corporations lost $80m, and swallowed 16% of the government's budget.

Congo's president, Mr Denis Sassou Nguesso, wears a beautifully cut Cardin suit over a bulky bullet-proof vest. He says that his government "must be flexible". His ministers are keen to make

---

Congo's socialism sound businesslike. "If socialism can feed people, fine", says the agriculture minister, Mr Marius Mouambenga, who describes himself modestly as a cabbage farmer; "if not. . .", and he spreads his hands in a gesture of dismissal.

American and French management consultants called in recently by government advised it to let managers get on with their jobs without meddling ministers or political committees such as the Union of Congolese Socialist Youth, who have powers to intervene in the running of state-owned corporations. In May the government agreed to let some companies run their own affairs but it has not yet decided which ones.

All over Brazzaville, Congo's capital, are fading red and yellow bill boards with ponderous slogans such as: "The implementation of the five-year plan is the highest duty of all the people". Duty or no, the plan could soon run short of money. It assumes that oil revenues will finance two thirds of public spending between 1982 and 1985. Last year, it financed half.

Oil accounted for nearly 80% of export earnings last year, raising Congo's trade surplus from $16m in 1978 to $250m in

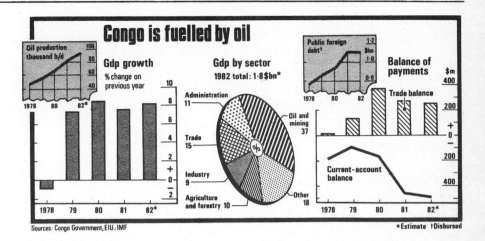

Congo is fuelled by oil

Oil production thousand b/d

Gdp growth
% change on previous year

Gdp by sector
1982 total: 1·8$bn*

Administration 11
Oil and mining 37
Trade 15
Industry 9
Agriculture and forestry 10
Other 18

Public foreign debt†

Balance of payments
$m
Trade balance
Current-account balance

Sources: Congo Government; EIU; IMF

*Estimate †Disbursed

1982. This year Congo is likely to have its first trade deficit since 1976; foreign exchange reserves have dwindled to the equivalent of one month's imports.

The Congolese admit that they will have to borrow more heavily from international banks to pay for their development plans. Bankers will probably oblige: servicing Congo's total external debt—$1.1 billion by early 1983—still absorbs only 15% of the country's foreign exchange earnings. The government be-

lieves it can afford to push that ratio up to 25% in the next two years. Because Congo is a member of Africa's franc zone, sharing with four other countries in the region the same central bank and currency, it is reckoned to be a good credit risk. The 10,000 Frenchmen now in Congo—double the number five years ago—also help to shore up confidence in the management of the economy.

Congo aims to raise its daily production of oil from 90,000 barrels to an average of 120,000 barrels this year. At this rate, the country's oil fields will begin to run dry in five years. The Emeraude oil field (see map), which holds two thirds of Congo's reserves of 840m tonnes, has yet to be exploited much because its oil is heavy ("like butter", says the energy minister). The French state-owned oil company Elf-Aquitaine, which has one of two 75%-owned foreign subsidiaries operating in Congo's oilfields (Agip of Italy owns the other one), says that oil must fetch $35 a barrel before extracting the country's heavy oil (by blasting down steam) becomes economic.

Roads to nowhere?

Oil accounts for over a third of Congo's gnp. It dwarfs other industries. Timber, Congo's second largest export, brings in only 5% of export earnings: the biggest forests are almost inaccessible.

Other cash crops are doing badly. Sugar plantations, for example, produced nearly 100,000 tonnes of raw sugar a year in 1967; by 1978, the bush had reclaimed most of them and output was down to 5,700 tonnes a year.

A Franco-Dutch consortium called in by the government has raised production to an annual rate of 30,000 tonnes, though the government's target was 53,000 tonnes for this year. But in mid-June, harvesting was a month behind

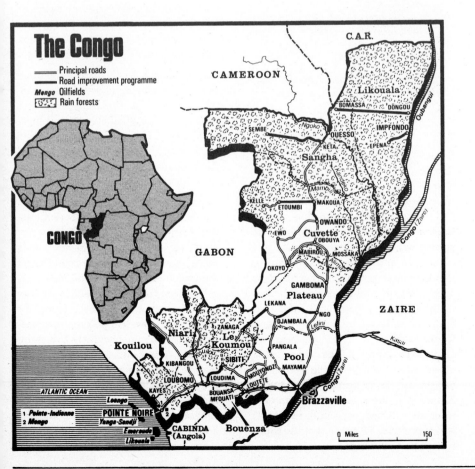

The Congo

Principal roads
Road improvement programme
Mengo Oilfields
Rain forests

CONGO

CAMEROON
C.A.R.
GABON
ZAIRE

Likouala
BOMASSA
DONGOU
SEMBE
Ngoko
OUESSO
IMPFONDO
KETA
EPENA
Sangha
KELLE
ETOUMBI
MAKOUA
OWANDO
EWO
Cuvette
OBOUYA
MABIROU
MOSSAKA
OKOYO
GAMBOMA
Plateau
LEKANA
NGO
DJAMBALA
Niari
ZANAGA
Le Koumou
PANGALA
Pool
SIBITI
MAYAMA
KIBANGOU
Kouilou
LOUDIMA
LOUBOMO
MOUYONDZI
LOUJETE
KAYES
BOUANSA
MFOUATI
Brazzaville
ATLANTIC OCEAN
Loango
1 Pointe-Indienne
2 Mengo
POINTE NOIRE
Yanga-Sandji
CABINDA
(Angola)
Bouenza
Emeraude
Likouala

0 Miles 150

schedule, some of the workers were going slow because they had not been paid for six weeks and the sugar mill was strewn with rusting spare parts.

With few promising industries to devel-op, no less than 40% of the government's spending under its five-year plan is going into roads, buildings and jetties on the country's vast network of rivers. The planners hope that these will open up the country's tropical forests. But, with price controls discouraging farmers from growing more crops, the new roads may equally encourage peasants to beat a quick retreat to the towns.

Article 4

World Press Review/September 1983

The Chad Flashpoint

Behind the rivalry for an obscure object of desire

FULVIO GRIMALDI
GEORGE HENDERSON

Fulvio Grimaldi and George Henderson write for the Arab-oriented monthly "The Middle East" of London, from which this report is excerpted.

The struggle for Chad is not a remote battle that can be ignored either by the big powers or by the African and Arab states in the region. On the face of it, this is puzzling. Chad, with an area twice that of Texas, has a mere four and a half million people. In 1981 the gross national product was $502 million. Often described as the poorest country in the world, how has Chad acquired such importance?

"Chad is the victim of outside aggression and bigger powers. It has every right to obtain all the necessary means of support to safeguard its independence," President Hissen Habré declared in July. As he spoke, the forces of his arch-rival, Goukouni Oueddei — who heads the Transitional Government of National Unity (Gunt) — were advancing from the north, with Libyan backing. France had already poured in military aid, and Zaire had sent troops to help Habré face this latest challenge.

Only a year before Habré, backed by Sudan, Egypt, and the U.S., had displaced Goukouni from power in a sim-

Habré—"victim of outside aggression."

Daniel Simon/Gamma-Liaison

ilar way, as part of the bizarre civil war that has ravaged Chad since the French granted independence in 1960. Internal differences now have become little more than a reflection of the various regional and international powers vying for influence there.

For each of the key actors — France, the two superpowers, Libya, Sudan, and Egypt — Chad has strategic value in the struggle for regional influence. For France, it has intrinsic value as a former colony. It is at the heart of French-speaking Africa and well placed as a base from which French interests can be protected. In addition, France still has considerable economic interests in Chad, especially in cotton, which provides 75 per cent of the country's export earnings.

France is not particular about what regime is in power. It has supported those as different as Ngarta Tombalbaye's, Gen. Félix Malloum's, Goukouni's, and now Habré's.

Chad is rich in many mineral resources, including uranium, wolfram, cassiterite (in the Aozou Strip), and gold. There may also be gold, uranium, iron, and bauxite in the Guera area.

This is without doubt one of the main motives for Libyan interest in the country, and for Col. Gaddafi's insistence that the Aozou Strip belongs to Libya, according to a 1935 French-Italian agreement. But Libya's actions are influenced also by ideology and its ambitions for regional influence.

Like France, Libya has shown a tendency to support whichever Chadian faction seems the strongest or, more particularly, whichever seems more amenable to Libyan retention of the Aozou Strip. Since 1980, however, it has been fairly consistent in its support of Goukouni against Habré, for Habré has now clearly come to represent Western — particularly U.S. — interests while Goukouni has tried to maintain an independent nationalist position. Inevitably, however, in Washington's eyes this stance along with Libyan support has identified Goukouni with the pro-Soviet line.

For the American administration

Chad, like most other states in the region, is viewed through the global perspective of the superpower struggle — and in the context of the Reagan team's almost obsessive hatred of Col. Gaddafi. U.S. anti-Libyan policies, including CIA backing for Habré's forces in 1982, were justified on the grounds that a number of Arab and African countries were complaining to the U.S. about Libyan interference.

No doubt the latent economic riches of Chad have not escaped notice by American policymakers, but it is the overall balance of power in the region that lies at the root of most of Washington's decisions. The Reagan admin-

istration painstakingly has developed a network of allies in Africa and the Middle East that will offer various facilities as the basis for a Red Sea and Mediterranean alliance to protect U.S. interests — in particular, the oil resources and markets of the Arab Gulf. Libya, more or less pushed into Moscow's arms by U.S. hostility, has always been the fly in the ointment.

For the moment, the Organization of African Unity is trying to prevent a widening of the conflict. It has called on the neighboring states, as well as Egypt and Zaire, to cooperate in efforts to find a peaceful solution "in order to stop inviting foreign intervention."

But both Egypt and Sudan have declared their support for Habré, regarding Libya as the real enemy.

So far only Zaire has succumbed to U.S. pressure and become directly involved, but it remains to be seen whether Egypt and Sudan will be able to resist if Washington urges them to act. As yet the Russians have shown little interest, except in expressing verbal support for Goukouni. If the conflict escalates, however, Moscow may well begin to view the matter differently and may act, through Libya, in giving more active support. The danger is that what started as a civil war may end in a much wider conflagration.

Article 5　　　　　　　　　　THE CHRISTIAN SCIENCE MONITOR　TUESDAY, MAY 1, 1984

Cameroon Tense as Leader Shows He's More Radical Than Expected

By Colin Legum
Special to The Christian Science Monitor

The prospering West African oil state of Cameroon has reached a dangerous crossroads only 18 months after its new President, Paul Biya, gained power.

ANALYSIS

An intense power struggle is raging. Its roots are found in religious and cultural differences, as well as in public reaction to radical policy shifts initiated by the new President, who many had not expected to be so forceful. The tensions stem from:

● Biya's accusation that his predecessor, Ahmadou Ahidjo — the man who brought Cameroon into independence in 1960 — and several other former officials plotted to assassinate him. Mr. Ahidjo and the others recently were tried and sentenced to death.

● An actual coup attempt early last month, apparently planned by the Republican Guard, the elite corps that pro-

CAMEROON

Biya squelched coup, tried ex-President

tects the presidential palace. The alleged coup leader was the guard's second in command. Biya put down the revolt, commanding the support of at least half of the 1,000-man guard.

• Conflict between the Muslim north of Cameroon and the mainly non-Muslim south. Biya is a Christian from the south, Ahidjo a Muslim from the north. Northerners, unhappy at seeing the presidency pass from their hands, became alarmed when Biya began trying to split the north into three parts and to consolidate his own power.

• A sense of discrimination alleged by the English-speaking minority in the western provinces, which abut on Nigeria, against the French-speaking majority.

It is the religious-regional conflict that is the major source of instability. But together, the factors are a dangerous mix—and a sad development for a country that was well on its way to becoming a major economic success story in Africa.

Cameroon was considered one of the safest countries in the continent for overseas investors, who were increasingly drawn to it for its oil-producing potential and its wise use of revenues in developing the agricultural sector. (Real growth has averaged a rare 6 percent a year at time when many African countries were registering zero growth rates.)

The immediate pretext for the coup attempt was that Biya, concerned about the preponderant influence of northerners in the Army, had decided to remove a number of senior Army officers whom he regarded as unreliable.

However, the putting down of the coup seems to be only the end of another chapter. The intense power struggle is still developing.

Before he assumed office, Biya was never regarded as strong presidential material. He was seen as a good compromise candidate to take over from Ahidjo, who resigned for health reasons. Ahidjo had brought Biya in as prime minister when the former British Trusteeship Territory, West Cameroon, became part of a unified country, whose official language is French.

Biya, however, did not see himself as the northerners saw him. Once he took office, he began to shuffle the government to strengthen his own hold on power.

In an attempt to reassure his fellow northerners, Ahidjo announced that he would not give up the influential post of chairman of the ruling party, the Union National Camerounais (UNC). In December 1982, he asked a close friend, Alhai Moussa Sarki Fadi Yaya, a wealthy northern businessman and politician, to reassure northern militants.

But instead of reassuring the northern militants, Yaya joined them and began to campaign against Biya. Ahidjo then asserted his role as party chairman of the ruling Union National Camerounais, trying to expel Yaya and several national assemblymen from the party.

From that point on, everything went wrong: Ahidjo lost some of his old influence in the north, and Biya became more determined than before to cut off the militants' challenge. In June 1983 he again reshuffled his Cabinet and dismissed four of Ahidjo's appointees.

Faced with a split in the ruling party, Ahidjo resigned as chairman in August and went to live in France. Soon afterward, Biya alleged that he had uncovered an assassination plot against him and accused his personal bodyguard and aide-de-camp, who were both arrested.

He then embarked on even more radical changes in the government and, more audaciously, proceeded to reform local government to allow for the northern province to be split into three parts.

He also changed the military command. Having displayed this amount of muscle, he summoned a special session of the ruling party and had himself elected as the new chairman of Ahidjo's place.

His next move was to call for early elections, and he secured a popular endorsement as President by the overwhelming margin of victory that is typical of election victories here.

In just over six months, the former President was condemned to death, and north-south tensions soared. A coup was not surprising.

From this position of apparent strength, he initiated more Cabinet changes, strengthening the number of his own appointees. He also expanded his patronage system.

Finally, in February 1984, he had two suspected assassins brought before a military tribunal, which also heard charges accusing the absent Ahidjo of involvement in the alleged plot. Although the prosecutor asked for a life sentence, all three were sentenced to death—Ahidjo in absentia.

Following this trial, Biya convened another military tribunal to try a former prime minister, a former defense minister, and the former head of the national gendarmerie—all of them powerful figures in the Ahidjo regime.

The three were found guilty in a trial that independent observers say was full of irregularities.

Bowing to French and international public opinion, Biya commuted all the death sentences to life imprisonment.

Thus, within a space of just over six months, the nation's politics had become polarized—with the former President and some of his leading lieutenants condemned to death for treason, and with tensions between the north and the south reaching dangerous levels. Under these circumstances, it was not surprising that northern elements in the Army planned a coup.

Multinational oil companies, who have wanted to expand exploration and development in Cameroon, now seem bound to lessen their activities until the country's future political shape becomes clearer.

Article 6

AFRICA NEWS/November 28, 1983

Mobutu Nets 'Hundreds' of Opponents

[AN] Several hundred opponents of Zaire's President Mobutu Sese Seko have been arrested this month, according to exiled Zairian politicians.

The largest crackdown apparently occurred on Nov. 13, when many members of the clandestine Union for Democratic and Social Progress (UDPS) and others were swooped in a surprise operation.

Gregoire Dikonda, a UDPS leader who fled Zaire 18 months ago, said in Brussels last week that the latest round-up suggests that Mobutu is fearful of the threat posed by his opponents and is less than serious about the amnesty he declared recently for political foes.

The opposition leader said the detainees have been sent into internal exile in various districts in Zaire.

In an interview earlier this month in Washington, D.C., Dikonda told *Africa News* that he was not surprised by the developments.

"More severe repression always follows Mobutu's every offer for amnesty," he said.

Dikonda was in the U.S. capital to take part in a two-day seminar sponsored by the Africa Committee of the National Council of Churches of Christ in the U.S.

The seminar, organized for Africa secretaries of various church denominations in the U.S. and Canada, was also attended by both supporters and opponents of the Zairian leader.

Zaire was chosen as a case study for the Nov. 2-4 symposium because the bilateral and multilateral attention given Zaire had portrayed it as an example of "the continuing impoverishment of the masses." The Zaire case also highlights "the gross inequities of a world market economy, which increase the powerlessness and victimization of states such as Zaire," according to John Pritchard, a former missionary to Zaire and currently on the staff of the Presbyterian Church (U.S.A.).

Pritchard said the damage inflicted by an unjust international economic system on poor nations, "increasingly provides the excuse for further victimization of their own citizens."

He said international capital, multinational corporations and international lending institutions "have played a significant role in defining Zaire's present situation."

Some opponents of Mobutu's regime supported the brief takeovers of Shaba Province mounted by the Congo National Liberation Front (FLNC) in 1977 and 1978. Here a solidarity demonstration in New York. / Africa News

Pritchard then asked: "Why do they find Zaire so attractive, so important? In light of Zaire's record of fiscal management, how can they continue to funnel money to the state and at whose ultimate expense is this being done? Have they considered the long term repercussions of the activities? Should we?"

Rep. Howard Wolpe (D-MI), who also spoke at the meeting, likened Zaire's Mobutu to Nicaragua's Somoza and Iran's former shah and said the U.S. leadership had seen them as allies against communism and had turned a blind eye on their violations of human rights at home.

Having stated his concern over Mobutu's suppression of dissent, Wolpe said "corruption has been legitimized from the top," and added: "Foreign aid has become subsidy for corruption."

He asked the U.S. government to deny Mobutu military and economic support to force him to make the necessary reforms. "Otherwise a repetition of the shah's Iran and Somoza's Nicaragua will be unavoidable," he said.

Jennifer Ward, a former chief of political affairs in the U.S. embassy in Kinshasa, the Zairian capital, said the U.S. supports Zaire for strategic reasons.

Beside providing the U.S. vital minerals for industry and security, Ward said, "Zaire and the U.S. have parallel views on South Africa and Israel."

Monique Garrity, a World Bank official specializing in African economies, said Zaire suffers from acute balance of payments deficit and a high inflation rate — "problems that are not of Zaire's own making."

She said Zaire had reacted to the economic boom of the 1970s by investing in heavy industrialization. Then, suddenly, commodity prices fell and confidence in Zaire suffered.

Today's copper prices are the "lowest in 20 years," Garrity said, and many of Zaire's heavy industries have become white elephants.

The World Bank has given Zaire $450 million in loans, while other bank affiliates have come up with $100 million to support a total of 18 projects.

Garrity said the World Bank is due to chair a meeting this month to determine Zaire's needs for the coming year.

A nine-man delegation from Zaire led by Itofo Bokeleale, president and general secretary of the Church of Christ in Zaire, also included Msgr. Nsolotshi, vicar general of the Lubumbashi Catholic diocese.

Bokeleale said Zaire has come a long way since the days when it was a personal property of the Belgian king, before it became a colony. Mobutu gave Zaire an orderly state, after years of anarchy, said Bokeleale.

Another critic of Mobutu, Nzongola-Ntajala of Howard University, criticized Mobutu for ruling the country "at the pleasure of foreign powers to the disadvantage of Zaire's own people."

Drawing attention to an article in the *Harvard International Review,* Nzongola-Ntajala said: "The embezzlement of public funds has been elevated into an administrative principle in Zaire. . . . Corruption begins at the top and pervades the entire structure of national, regional and local administration."

He warned: "As long as the U.S. and other Western powers continue to their access to mineral resources in Zaire to the survival of the Mobutu regime, no credible reforms will be made by a regime which is being helped to feel that it is indispensable."

Ntongola-Ntajala called for political rights for all Zairians. "The people who govern Zaire should not be chosen in Washington, Paris, Brussels, or any other world capital. They ought to be chosen by the people of Zaire, acting freely within a democratic political process."

Exiled Zairians claimed last week that the latest arrests were intended to coincide with a visit to Zaire by Chester Crocker, the U.S. assistant secretary of state for African affairs, so he would not meet opponents of the regime.

The detainees include 13 former members of parliament, who were previously jailed after they wrote to Mobutu critiquing his regime, according to exiled politicians. (See *AN,* Sept. 18.)

The former legislators were among 60 political critics, who were jailed last August after five of their number met with visiting U.S. members of Congress in Kinshasa, the capital.

Rep. Wolpe, one of the eight U.S. visitors, said the five Zairians were beaten by members of Mobutu's brigade before they were ushered to jail and beaten further.

The five were accused of attempting to form a political party rival to the ruling Popular Movement for the Revolutoin (MPR).

The U.S. lawmakers have lodged a strong protest with Mobutu, who has yet to respond, according to Wolpe.

Another exiled Zairian politician, former Foreign Minister Nguza Karl-I-Bond, has accused Mobutu of "state terrorism."

Both Nguza and Dikonda have appealed to human rights groups, including Amnesty International, to intervene with Mobutu on behalf of the detainees, many of whom have reportedly been sent into internal exile in Katanga, Kasai and Kivu provinces.

Article 7

AFRICA NEWS/December 12, 1983

CENTRAL AFRICAN REPUBLIC

EMPEROR WITHOUT A COUNTRY

[AN] Central African Republic's former self-styled emperor, Jean-Bedel Bokassa, and about 20 of his relatives, arrived in France last week after his host for four years, Ivory Coast's President Felix Houphouet-Boigny, booted him out of Abidjan and put him on a Paris-bound jet.

Bokassa's persistent craving for the office he lost in a 1979 coup reportedly led to his expulsion from Abidjan.

Houphouet-Boigny had reluctantly received Bokassa at the request of the French government after no country was willing to grant the former dictator asylum.

About two weeks ago Bokassa attempted to end his exile in Abidjan and return to Bangui, capital of the Central African Republic.

He had been living in exile in Ivory Coast since his overthrow in a French-backed coup which brought his nephew, David Dacko, back to powerForbidden by Ivorian President Houphouet-Boigny to travel without prior permission, Bokassa feigned illness to escape from his Abidjan residence.

Bokassa's exit turned out to be part of a scheme to return to Bangui. While the former emperor was leaving his house, a planeload of French journalists accompanied by Bokassa's French lawyer Roger Delbray and a handful of Bokassa's aides landed unscheduled in Abidjan, with the intention of spiriting the former leader away to his country.

The plot fell through when French intelligence services informed the Ivorian government of the arrival of the plane and the intended destination. Bokassa was later apprehended, and the plane was sent back to Paris. Bokassa followed.

In telephone interviews, Bokassa claimed that he was being held against his will and was unable to make a livelihood in Ivory Coast. He said he merely wanted to return to his birthplace, denying any intention to engage in politics. But he also maintained that the people of the Central African Republic were anxious for him to return.

On his arrival in Paris, Bokassa went straight to his house, west of the city. He was accompanied by 15 of his 54 children, the former empress, and several other women.

The house has been ringed by 200 French riot police, while French authorities consider their next move. Radio France reports the French prime minister as having said that the former emperor is not welcome to stay in France.

Senegal and Gabon have been mentioned as other possible homes for Bokassa, but observers say that Bokassa's thinly-veiled desire to return to power may induce potential host countries to shun him.

Bokassa's claim to French citizenship by virtue of the fact that he fought on the French side during the Second World War has been dismissed in Paris.

On his overthrow in 1979, Bokassa fled to Paris in a private jet. But French authorities turned him away and Ivory Coast received him.

France and Central African Republic have extradition treaties that could be evoked to send Bokassa back to Bangui to stand trial.

Just before his overthrow, Bokassa was the target of international protest for his dictatorial rule. He was also accused of having taken part personally in the killing of more than 100 schoolchildren who had protested the imposition of imperial uniforms.

The French government, which had been the nation's leading supporter, cut off aid at the height of Bokassa's rule. Bokassa hit back by revealing that the then-French President Valery Giscard d'Estaing had received a gift of diamonds from Bokassa. The revelation sparked off a national scandal in France, contributing to the defeat of Giscard in the 1981 elections.

Observers in Bangui said the Ivorian president had repeatedly warned Bokassa about the former emperor's declarations to the press regarding his intended return to office. Houphouet-Boigny reportedly reminded Bokassa that such statements violated the conditions for his asylum.

Bokassa is also reported to have made his intentions known to Central African Republic's new leader, Gen. Andre Kolingba.

Article 8   *Unesco Courier,* September 1983

Waters of life

by Henri Lopes

I have travelled so much that on occasion I have forgotten the map traced out by glow-worms, the village dance, and even the way of tightening the throat muscles to articulate, the men, the hand, the fire, the drop, the salt and that which burns, on the path from the thighs to the pectorals. But when, in some place or other on this earth, deprived of flamboyant trees and the odour of mangoes, my heart guided my footsteps aimlessly along beaches, questioning the fascinating mystery of the abyss, it was always to you that my thoughts returned.

For do not envy the ocean.

Do you know the River, just up-stream of M'Foa and Kinshasa? When the boat leaves the port and obliquely fends the *fantasia* of foam, its smoke still holds in long suspension the dream of the dreamer who follows it from the quays. It will have disappeared from view before it reaches Nsélé.

If you have never made the pilgrimage to Loango, do not hold out the begging bowl, go up to the plateau at the level of Malébo Pool.

You who hunt or fish by night, whatever your patience, whatever the art of

Photo Georg Gerster © Rapho, Paris

The Wagenia people, who live on the banks of the Congo near Boyoma Falls, are expert and daring fishermen. In the rapids they build ingenious wooden scaffolding structures from which are suspended manœuvrable, cone-shaped fish traps.

him who weaves your fish traps and nets, there's no point in trying, no trick will surprise the manatees the elders told us of when they taught us about life and about the country.

The river has been emptied. The caymans (or crocodiles, I have never really known which) have fled too. If you still insist on dreaming and on crossing a stretch or two of the spirit kingdom, then open *Ngando**, by the elder Lomani-Tchibamba, the first who wanted to set down the song of the mothers to their sons, the first to say:

"Beware! Don't go to the river. Go straight to school... We have enough water in our well; I will fill you the big pool and you can amuse yourself as you like... Beware, my child, not to the river."

He will also tell you about Ngando eating the child.

* *Literally* Crocodile.

He will tell you about Ngando the magnanimous returning his prey.

CONGO

- **Length: 4,370 km.**
- **Rises in the Shaba region of Zaire as the Lualaba River, but its remotest source lies between Lake Tanganyika and Lake Malawi, in Zambia, as the Chambesi river; empties into the Atlantic Ocean**
- **Mean discharge: 41,000 cubic metres per second**
- **Area of basin: 3,820,000 sq. km.**
- **Navigable up to Kisangani**
- **Also known as the Zaire, a corruption of the African word *nzadi* or *nzari* = river**

Ah! Do not say, with a sophisticated scholar's smile, that this is the world of tales, as beautiful as the unreason of styles, but a world which the present age has swept away. The outboard motor-boat fends the liquid and my heart breaks. Look at these men of water and nets on M'Bamou Island. And listen to them too. Above all listen to them when the tom-tom throbs to sing the bride and groom, to calm the river's pain, or simply to drive away the mosquitoes. Only yesterday a young man from the city came and, sneering, bathed there. All the arts of the swimming pool at his fingertips.

He went straight to the bottom.

Yes, right before our eyes. Thus lightning puts a stop to all who are oblivious of the oath to the spirits.

Why do you not learn the wisdom of silence and humility? By listening to the leaves of night, they could tell of the adventure that bends Congo.

As for those boats of yours...

Nodules of noise and grease...

The fish have lost their flesh. Nothing but bones, bones, bones!

Pass by, tenacious islets. No one will know the secret of the water hyacinths. Neither the source nor the sky. But where are the canoers with the athletes' voices and the ships with wheels, glow-worms of strange dreams which answered our boyish greetings with the lash of the insults of that time? Oh, you we wished to adore! Even my song of awakening goes astray, caught up in your gluey toils.

There must be a return to the water, to wet the feet there, for the washing of the hands, the face and the mouth. For gargling too, sometimes, so that you can cry until you can cry no more.

These waters gave life.

And like Nzambé, the Father, they took it away, in a sovereign game.

Always by surprise. Such is the rule, without explanation. Traveller deprived of muscled breasts, beware the eyes of our waters. Beware the beauty who glistens as she looks at a sky the colour of a rascally lover. In an overweening desire to caress her, a team of canoers smashes like an egg against the rock. They roll, rush and sink in the elements. The faithful women in mourning, on the banks of Kin and M'Foa, still hold their breath, seeking to decode in the howling of the tornado the songs of those who rush towards Djoué. Thus, like the hours, until the *matanga*** of joy.

You would need to go far, far across the seas, impossible now to say how far, beneath a like fiery sky, go to the Amazon, to find such speed, such surging. Power of light or of carcass, whatever you wish, what matter the geographer's figures. It can be sensed.

They came from the summit of the sea. They asked for your papers and we declared Nzadi, Nzadi the River, naturally.

Zaïre repeated their clumsy throats and they wrote it down on their sea-route.

But we do not give in, in spite of the seasons and the centuries. The brothers, over there, only remember two cradles: the other is Guinea. "Si no tienes de Con-

Photo Abbas © Gamma, Paris

Comparatively little of the vast hydroelectric potential of the Congo basin—estimated to be in the region of 130,000,000 kilowatts—has so far been harnessed. Above, the hydroelectric dam at Inga, about 40 kilometres upstream from Matadi, was completed in 1972 with an installed capacity of 300,000 kilowatts. The Inga dam represents only the first phase of a grandiose scheme which, if completed, would make this site the largest hydroelectric complex in the world, with a potential capacity of 30,000,000 kilowatts.

go, tienes de Carabali"*** chorus the Mambi neighbours.

Congo, then, baptismal fonts notwithstanding.

Diogo Cao died believing that you led to the kingdom of Prester John. We knew better, for once! This meander led only to the court of the Makoko, that one to the court of Mani Kongo.

Who has only one name, when all's said and done? There is the name given at birth. The name given at circumcision. That which is won in combat. That of the enemy. That of the time of the white beard.

And so it is with you: Oyez for Lukuga, oyez for Ruzizi, oyez for Luapulu, oyez for Luvua, oyez for Lualaba, oyez for the mystery of the heavenly host. And that's only part of the

magic. Lake Kivu and Lake Moéro too. Where does the lazy water end, the alphabet of your course? A weakling, at first you do not yet dare run. Who will recognize the tea-coloured youth who rushes headlong, horns foremost, towards Lukoléla, after his marriage with the river of the Sangos? Then, dignified and powerful, His Majesty pursues his course to the Djoué. And here is the inferno where the water can be heard seething, whirling in the dance of the demented, hurled in burning spray above the rocks, stirred up by an unmanageable fire down there beneath the crust. Paralysed and delighted, the indifferent traveller suddenly wants to question the heavens.

Then, Mai-Ndombé, San Antonio, the mouth and the horizon. Weary, your soul at peace, you will stretch yourself out for ever like a combatant, his task accomplished, in the salt of dissolution.

Congo.

___

** *A kind of funeral wake.*

*** *"If you're not Congo, you're Carabali"*

East Africa

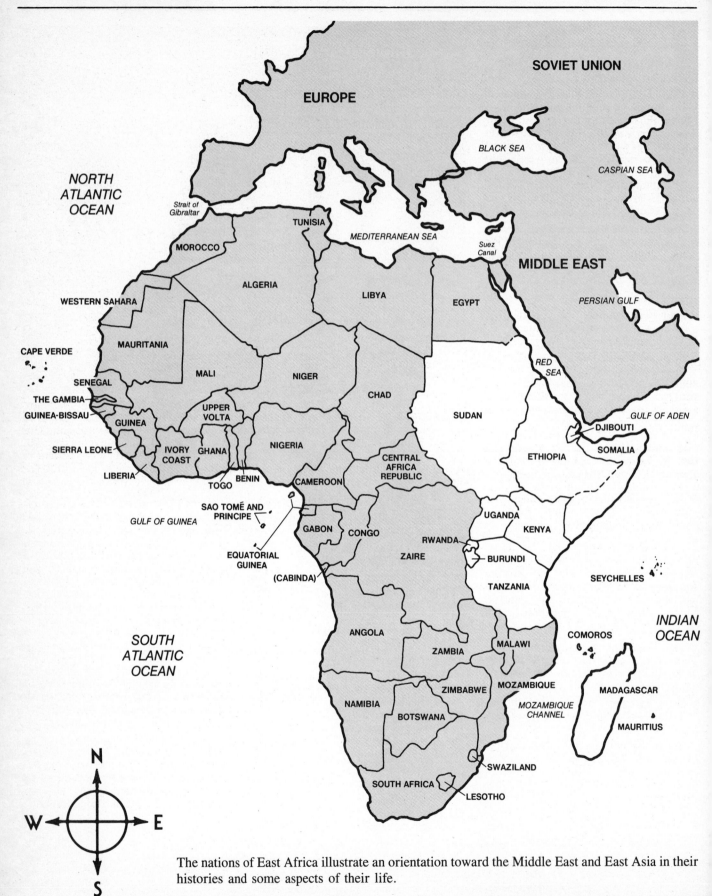

The nations of East Africa illustrate an orientation toward the Middle East and East Asia in their histories and some aspects of their life.

East Africa: A Mixed Inheritance

The vast East African region, ranging from the Sudan with its North African ties to Tanzania in the south, is an area of great diversity and complexity. Although the Indian Ocean islands have a distinctive civilization because of their Asian and Pacific ties, their interaction with the mainland give their inclusion here some validity. Ecological features such as the Great Rift Valley and the prevalence of savanna, cattle-herding life-styles, and historical Arab and Asian influences are aspects associated with the whole area.

CATTLE-HERDING SOCIETIES

A long-horned cattle seems an appropriate symbol for the East African region—more so, than the use of a similar symbol for the United States West. The increasing populations of the cities come from different backgrounds, but most rural inhabitants, who make up the majority of the populations from the Horn to Lake Malawi, value cattle for their social as well as their economic importance. The Nuer of the Sudan, the Somalis near the Red Sea (who, like many other peoples of the Horn, herd camels as well as cattle, goats, and sheep), and the Masai of Tanzania and Kenya are among the pastoral peoples whose herds are their livelihood and their companions. The Kikuyu and the Bugandans, whose communities are built on farming as well as herding, prize cattle. Even Malagasy devote over half of their lands to grazing, and their attitudes toward cattle are similar to those of mainland East Africans. The other Indian Ocean islands do not maintain cattle.

The land is well-suited for herding. In the rain forests of West and Central Africa, the presence of tsetse flies limits cattle holding. Tropical rain forests are almost nonexistent in East Africa; they are found only on the east coast of Madagascar and scattered on the East African rim of the Indian Ocean. Belts of tropical and temperate savannas have provided grazing lands for people and animals who have migrated north and south as well as east and west throughout history. Pastoralists predominate in the savanna zones of West Africa, as well as East Africa, and this region below the desert has historically been a trans-African highway.

People have been moving into and through the East African region throughout its history. The Great Rift Valleys, which continue from the Red Sea as far south as Malawi and Zambia, are characterized by mountains as well as valleys and feature the Great Lakes such as Lake Albert, Lake Tanganyika, and Lake Malawi. These natural barriers have limited movements on the west. According to linguistic and archaeological evidence as well as oral tradition, over the centuries, agricultural peoples speaking Bantu languages, iron workers, pottery makers, local traders, Nilotic speakers, warriors, and others have moved into the area and settled or moved beyond. Inhabitants of the region—then and now—have had to confront insufficient and unreliable rainfall. Drought and famine in the Horn and in areas of Kenya and

(World Bank photo by Kay Muldoon)

Lively and extensive trade and migration patterns have characterized East Africa throughout much of its history.

Tanzania have caused suffering and prompted refugee movements.

ISLAMIC INFLUENCE

Many of the areas of East Africa have been influenced and continue to be influenced by the Middle East, and to an extent by Asia. Even Christian Ethiopia and the inland states of Rwanda and Burundi were familiar with the followers of Islam and the Arab traders of the Swahili Coast or the Sudan. Somalia, Djibouti, and Sudan, which border the Red Sea and are in close range of the Arabic Peninsula, have been most influenced by the travelers who came across the straits. Mogadishu, the capital of Somalia, began as an Islamic trading post in the tenth century. The Islamic faith, its various sects or brotherhoods, the Koran, and the Sharia (the Islamic law code) have influenced the people and the governments in the Horn. Today, many Somalis and others migrate to the oil-rich states of Arabia to work.

Farther south, in the communities and cultures on the perimeters of the east coast, Arab newcomers and African people mixed as early as the ninth century, but especially during the 1200s to 1400s. The result of this intermingling is the culture and the language that we now call Swahili.

Much later, in the first half of the nineteenth century, the Sultan of Oman, Seyyid Said, transferred his capital to Zanzibar, thereby recognizing the important positions that Omani Arabs were holding in the East African lands. Arab traders settled in towns in the interior and developed contacts (not always as peacefully or as positively as residents would have liked), leading some interior peoples to accept Islam or, at the least, to take part in—and sometimes to take over—the trading systems that the Arabs operated.

The whole region from the Horn to Tanzania was affected by the slave trade through much of the nineteenth century. Slaves went from Uganda and the southern Sudan north to Egypt and the Middle East or from Ethiopia across the Red Sea. Many were taken to the coast by Arab, Swahili, or African traders to work on the plantations in Zanzibar or were shipped to the Persian Gulf or the Indian Ocean islands.

In the late nineteenth and early twentieth centuries, Indian laborers were brought in by the British to build the East African railroad. Indian traders already resided in Zanzibar; others now came and settled in Kenya and Tanzania, becoming shopkeepers and bankers in inland centers such as Kampala and Nairobi, as well as on the coast in Mombasa and Dar es Salaam or in smaller stops along the railroad.

The subregions of East Africa include the following: the countries of the Horn, Ethiopia, Somalia, and Djibouti as well as Sudan, farther north, which have a common identity not because of a common heritage or because of the compatibility of their governments (for, indeed, they are often hostile to each other) but because of the movements of peoples across borders in recent times; the East African states of Kenya, Tanzania, and Uganda, which have underlying cultural ties and a history of economic relations in which Rwanda and Burundi have shared; and the Indian Ocean islands of Madagascar, Comoros, Mauritius, and the Seychelles, which—despite the expanses of ocean that separate them—have cultural aspects and current interests in common.

ETHIOPIA, SUDAN, AND THE HORN

Traditionally, Ethiopia has had a distinct and isolated history, which has separated the nation from its neighbors. The early Christian Empire was centered in the dissected highlands of the interior, surrounded by peoples whom the nation was later to dominate. Only infrequently was it reached by outside envoys. In the latter part of the nineteenth century, Ethiopian rulers made major conquests over Somali and other peoples who today resist Ethiopian rule. Although Islam influenced some of the peoples, the empire was not as affected by Islamic forces as was the rest of the Horn.

(United Nations photo by Ray Witlin)

In the drought affected areas of East Africa, people must devote considerable time and energy to the search for water.

Great Power Interference

Yet peoples of Ethiopia, like the peoples of present-day Somali, Djibouti, and Sudan, were to be influenced by the great world powers who have historically been involved in the area because of its strategic location. In the nineteenth century, Britain and France became interested in the Horn because the Red Sea was the link between the home countries and the territories they had acquired in Asia. When the Suez Canal was completed in 1869, the importance of the region to these countries increased. In the 1880s, France and England both acquired ports on the Red Sea. The issue of who would control the Nile also absorbed the attention of France and England during the imperialist decades. In the 1890s, the French forces, led by Captain Marchand, literally raced from the present-day area of the People's Republic of the Congo to reach the upper Nile before the British. England won at the diplomat's table and claimed Sudan as a British territory.

The Italian interest in the Horn was first encouraged by the British to keep out the French. Italy's defeat by the Ethiopians at the battle of Adowa in 1896 did not deter its efforts to dominate the coastal areas, and parts of present-day Somalia soon fell into the hands of the very young Italian state. Later, Italy, under Mussolini, was to conquer and hold Ethiopia for the years between 1936 and 1941.

Today, great power competition for control of the Red Sea and the Gulf of Aden—the gateways to the Middle East—continues as the United States and the USSR vie for power. Events in Africa have led to shifts in the power plays. Before 1977, for instance, the United States was allied with Ethiopia—first, during the empire and then when the new socialist state of the Dergue took control. In 1977-1978, Ethiopia allied with the Soviet Union, receiving in return billions of dollars of military aid, on loan, for use in the civil war in the southern province of Ogaden where Somali peoples live, as well as for use in Eritrea. The United States soon established relations with President Siad Barre of Somalia, formerly the ally of the USSR, who agreed to terms whereby the US military would support the Somali regime. Cuban as well as Soviet presence in Ethiopia is now matched by United States access to port facilities in Somalia, and increased military aid to Sudan is seen as a "buffer to US interests in the Middle East."

The countries of the Horn, unlike the East African states farther south or the island states, have been alienated from each other and no regional community appears to have been contemplated. The introduction of world power conflicts in the region has only widened the distances between these countries. An African proverb seems relevant: "When two elephants fight, it is the ground that gets trampled."

Drought and Disorder

Meanwhile, the problems of drought and disorder have created population movements that affect all the countries. Today, the Horn is bound together—or torn apart—by its millions of refugees. The movements of peoples are so great that they are certain to unsettle traditional ways of life and bring about changes that go deep into the fabric of societies. Only half of the refugees of the Horn and Sudan (perhaps over a million) are directly supported by international relief agencies, indicating that their hosts—sometimes, but not always, of their own ethnic group—have taken them in temporarily or helped them to recreate their lives in a new society.

Ethiopians leave their homes for Somali, Djibouti, and

(WHO photo)

East African peoples, especially along the coast, blend heritages from Asia and the Middle East and Africa.

Sudan for relief from droughts, famines, and civil wars. Every countries harbors not only refugees but dissidents from neighboring lands or has a citizenry related to those who live in adjoining countries. Peoples such as the Affars, a minority in Djbouti, seek support from their kin in Ethiopia during their troubles. Somali liberation fighters who have left Somalia mobilize against Siad Barre's regime. Somali soldiers help other Somalis in the Ogaden as they fight against Ethiopia and claim their right to Somalian citizenship. The situation grows more complex. Cooperative effort is needed if the problems are to be solved.

EAST AFRICA

The peoples of Kenya, Tanzania, and Uganda, as well as Burundi and Rwanda, have some underlying connections from the past, despite the great variety of life-styles that characterize them today. Kingdoms around the Great Lakes in Uganda, Rwanda, and Burundi, though they have been overridden in modern times, are remembered. Myths about a heroic dynasty of rulers, the Chwezi, who supposedly ruled over an early Ugandan kingdom, are widespread. Archaeological evidence attests to their existence, probably in the sixteenth century. Peoples in western Kenya and Tanzania, who live under less centralized systems, have rituals similar to those of the Ugandan kingdoms. The Chwezi dynasty became associated with a spirit cult, which has been spread by mediums through many areas.

The Swahili culture and language of the coast, like the specialized kingship and social relationships of the Great Lakes area, was spread west and north—along with iron, salt, pottery, and grain—through regional trading networks as well as by warrior groups, changing as it developed new forms.

Rwanda and Burundi both became Belgian colonies in the late nineteenth century and were administered differently and have a different colonial heritage from Tanzania, Uganda, and Kenya. The latter three nations were taken over by the British in the late nineteenth century.

The British colonials first affected Kenya, which became distinguished by a large settler community. These settlers took over the land, had access to political power, and demanded exactions from the African populations, while whites in neighboring nations did not. Development was fostered there by a colonial government that expected whites to stay. As a result, Kenya had certain advantages at the time of independence which made integration with its poorer neighbors difficult.

Perhaps the most important British policies for the integration of the areas under British control were those connected with the East African Common Services Organization (comprised of Kenya, Tanzania, and Uganda), which was transformed into the East African Community (EAC) in 1967. The EAC collectively managed the railway system, a harbor scheme, an international airway, posts, and telecom-

(United Nations photo)

Major General Said Barre of Somalia has turned to the United States for economic and military aid.

munication facilities. It also maintained a common currency and a common market, a Development Bank, and other economic, cultural, and scientific services. Peoples moved freely across the borders of the three states in the Community. The links between the three countries were so important in the early 1960s that President Nyerere of Tanzania proposed that Tanzania wait to become independent until Kenya was given freedom, in hopes that the two countries would then join together.

This did not occur. Gradually the East African Community itself began to unravel, as conflicts over its operations grew. It fell apart in 1977. The countries disputed over the benefits of the association, which seemed to be garnered primarily by Kenya. The ideologies and personalities of Nyerere, Kenyatta, and Amin differed so much that there was little to encourage the three leaders to solve the problems of the Community. Relations between Kenya and Tanzania deteriorated so drastically that the border between them was closed when EAC ended.

In November 1983 Kenya, Tanzania, and Uganda agreed on the division of the assets of the old community and Kenya took on the largest losses. Tanzania and Kenya have opened their borders and it may be that they can start rebuilding their close relationship. The overthrow of Amin and the return of Obote, as well as the change in leadership in Kenya where

Daniel arap Moi presides, means that more compatible relationships are possible. Moreover the economic strains that all three countries face in their dealings with the world economy make the Community's importance clear.

A number of joint projects in East Africa may help set a mood or an example for a new community. Tanzania and Rwanda as well as Burundi and Uganda have reached agreement on a massive hydro-electric project on the Kagera River. Italy and Austria have offered funding for a rail link proposed by these members of the Kagera Basin Development Organizations. Several other projects are being undertaken to improve the lake traffic and the lake ports, which are especially important for Rwanda and Burundi.

These two states are also members of the Economic Community of Central African States (CEEAC), which links them with their western neighbor, Zaire. However, their economic ties with the East African states have led the UN Economic Commission on Africa as well as others to include them in the East African regional groupings. The Preferential Trade Area of nineteen East and Southern African nations, established in 1981 and still being signed (Tanzania has not yet signed), is one regional group that can increase the economic integration of the region.

Recently, there has been much talk of improving relations. "Think East Africa" the *Standard* of Kenya has written, commenting on the cultural links that existed in the area before colonialism. Salim Salim, Tanzania's Minister of Foreign Affairs, noted "You can choose a friend, but you cannot choose a brother... In this case Kenyans and Ugandans are our brothers."

On the other hand, the ideological differences that contributed to the split remain, and the economic worries all three countries share can lead just as easily to further barriers as to increased cooperation. For instance, Kenya has recently repatriated all Tanzanians and Ugandans until they get resident and work permits in Kenya. This may limit movement between the countries.

THE ISLANDS

The Seychelles, Mauritius, and the Comoros are like satellites surrounding Madagascar, but each island polity holds its own in this relationship. There is much which all four share. They have populations which derive from early East Asian contacts, either with India or Indonesia, and some have Arab and French as well as African ancestors. Madagascar and the Comoros have populations that originated in the Pacific Melanesian Islands as well as in Africa. The citizens of Mauritius and the Seychelles are European as well as African and Asian.

All four island groups have been influenced by France. Mauritius and the Seychelles were not permanently inhabited until the 1770s. French settlers came with African slaves and were later joined by Asians and other Africans. The British took control of these two island groups after the 1830s but a French-based Creole remains the major language today.

In 1978 the islands, along with Réunion, formed the Indian Ocean Commission. Originally a body with a socialist orientation, the Commission campaigned for independence for Réunion and the return of the island of Diego Garcia to Mauritius as well as the dismantling of the United States naval base located there. Now the aims of an alternate body made up of Madagascar, Mauritius, and Seychelles is to work for economic cooperation, police the fishing grounds, and encourage the search for oil and stimulate trade among the islands. President Albert René of the Seychelles recently appealed for cooperation among the islands for conservation of the environment.

(United Nations photo)

President Daniel arap Moi of Kenya, Kenyatta's successor, has moved to improve relations with neighboring nations.

Burundi

GEOGRAPHY

Area in Square Kilometers (Miles):
28,490 (10,747)
Land Usage: 37% arable; 23% pasture; 10% scrub and forests; 30% other
Capital (Population): Bujumbura (78,810—1970)
Climate: tropical to temperate

PEOPLE

Population

Total: 4,460,000 (1982 est.)
Per Square Kilometer (Mile): 160 (415)
Annual Growth Rate: 2.4%
Rural/Urban Population Ratio: 98/2

Health

Life Expectancy at Birth: 45 years
Infant Death Rate (Ratio): 122/1,000
Average Caloric Intake: 99% of FAO minimum
Physicians Available (Ratio): 1/45,020 (1975)

Languages

Official: Kirundi; French
Others Spoken: Swahili, others

Religion(s)

60% Christian; 38% traditional indigenous; 2% Muslim

Education

Adult Literacy Rate: 39% males; 16% females
School Attendance: primary: 40% boys, 25% girls; secondary: 4% boys, 2% girls

COMMUNICATION

Telephones: 6,000
Radios: 180,000
Newspapers: 1 daily; total circulation 300

A NEW CONSTITUTION

The government of Jean Baptiste Bagaza, which came to power in a bloodless coup in 1976, proposed a new Constitution for Burundi in 1981. This Constitution provides for the protection of basic civil rights, an elected National Assembly, and confirmation of the president for a five-year term. Suffrage is universal. Elections for the National Assembly were held for the first time in seventeen years on October 22, 1982. This followed the approval of the proposed Constitution by ninety-eight percent of the ninety-four percent of eligible voters who went to the polls. Election of the president is expected to take place early in 1984. These formal institutions will add a great deal of stability to a nation that has been shaken by rivalries and tensions between the ruling Tutsi minority and the Hutu majority.

TRANSPORTATION

Highways—Kilometers (Miles): 7,800 (4,846)
Railroads—Kilometers (Miles): none
One international airport

GOVERNMENT

Type: republic, presidential system
Constitution: November 18, 1981
Former Colonial Status: German; Belgian
Independence Date: July 1, 1962
Head of State: Jean-Baptiste Bagaza
Branches: executive (president, prime minister); National Assembly; Supreme Court
Legal System: based on German and Belgian Civil Codes and customary law
Political Parties: Union for National Progress
Suffrage: universal for adults

MILITARY

Number of Armed Forces: 7,500
Armed Forces/Population: 1/591
Military Expenditures (% of Central Government Expenditures): $35,500,000 (21.8%)
Nuclear Weapons Status: none
Current Hostilities: none

ECONOMY

Currency ($ US Equivalent): 100 Burundi francs = $1
GDP: $1,110,000
Per Capita Income/GNP: $280
Workforce: 84% agriculture; 5% industry; 11% service
Inflation Rate: 20% (1977-1980)
Natural Resources: nickel; uranium; cobalt; copper; platinum
Agriculture: coffee; tea; cotton; food crops
Industry: light consumer goods; beer brewing
Energy Production: 17,000 kw capacity; 35,000,000 kwh imported from Zaire
Energy Consumption Per Capita: .05 kwh

FOREIGN TRADE

Exports: tea; cotton; hides; skins
Imports: textiles; foodstuffs; transport equipment; petroleum products
Major Trading Partners: United States; EEC countries
Foreign Debt: $407,000,000
Selected Membership in International Organizations: UN; OAU; African Development Bank; Associate Member, European Communities (EC); Non-Aligned Movement; Economic Community of Central African States (CEEAC)

| Mwami Ntare Rugaamba expands the boundaries of the Nkoma kingdom **1795** | The area is mandated to Belgium by the League of Nations after the Germans lose World War I **1919** | Prince Louis Rwagasore leads nationalist movement and founds UPRONA **1958-1961** | Rwagasore is assassinated; independence is achieved **1961** | Failed coup results in purges of Hutu in government and army; Micombero seizes power **1965-1966** | Hutu uprising is followed by massacre of nearly 100,000 Hutu **1972** | Colonel Jean-Baptiste Bagaza comes to power in military coup **1976** | New Constitution is overwhelmingly approved by Burundi citizens over age 19 **1981** | Ninety-six percent of voters participate in elections for National Assembly; chose 52 deputies from 104 candidates **1982** |

1983

July: Former President M. Micombero dies of a heart attack

May 1984: Bi-annual Joint Committee on Franco-Burundi cooperation is held in Paris; French aid is increasing

BURUNDI

Burundi is a small, beautiful, and crowded country, where contemporary changes appear to have increased historical internal divisions. Those in power have been successful in maintaining traditional systems of status and obligation. Efforts to change historic practices and values have not only been ineffective, but, in the early 1970s, have led to the destruction of 100 thousand people and accompanying terror and flight.

ETHNIC GROUPS

Three distinctive groups of people live in Burundi: The Twa, the first inhabitants, are a pygmy people and make up less than one percent of the population. Most Burundi are Hutu (eighty-five percent), and they are usually farmers. The dominant group has been the cattle-holding Tutsi; members of Tutsi clans have been rulers and made up the aristocratic class in the society. The long-horned cattle of the Tutsi have prestige value as well as economic importance. The Hutu and the Tutsi differ in both their appearances and in some biological characteristics, but historians do not believe that the Tutsi first came as conquerors. It is possible that the two peoples lived in adjoining regions, gradually developing the relations that have become characteristic of the Hutu and the Tutsi in the nineteenth and twentieth centuries. Hutu became clients of Tutsi aristocrats, receiving cattle and protection in return for services.

The elaborate social and political system in Burundi was continued under the Germans, the first colonialists, and later by the Belgians to whom the region was mandated by the League of Nations after 1919.

NATIONALIST MOVEMENT

In the late 1950s, Prince Louis Rwagasore tried to unite all the Burundi people in a movement for nationalist goals, and he established the Union for National Progress (UPRONA) for this purpose. He was assassinated before independence, but the king remained a symbol of unity and established governing Cabinets, where Hutu and Tutsi were equally represented. This effort, never overly successful, was abandoned in the mid-1960s when Hutu leaders attempted a coup. Colonel Michel Micombero took over the government after abolishing the monarchy, and his "Government of Public Safety" purged Hutu members from the government and the army.

CHALLENGES TO A NEW GOVERNMENT

In 1972 a second Hutu uprising killed one thousand Tutsi and resulted in a government massacre of an estimated 100 thousand Hutu, who were chosen for death because their education and skills might lead to competition with the ruling clans. Another 100 thousand Hutu fled to Uganda, Rwanda, Zaire, and Tanzania; most still reside in these countries. The hatreds that resulted from this destruction have not died easily.

The present government of President (Colonel) Jean-Baptiste Bagaza seeks to heal past divisions, but the Five Year Plan (1978-1983), which emphasizes rural agricultural development, has not had positive results. Although the new Constitution allows citizens over nineteen years of age the right to elect deputies and a president for the first time in nineteen years, the control of UPRONA—the only legal party— by upper class elements is one of the factors that will limit Hutu (and Tutsi who are not of the favored clan) from gaining power.

LAND REFORMS

Burundi remains one of the poorest countries in the world, despite its rich volcanic soils and its dense population. Indeed, the region has the highest population density in Africa. Most Burundi are peasants who live on separate farms rather than in villages. Peasants have recently been released from certain taxes (enforced savings has been substituted) and from former services and obligations to landlords. However, patron-client relationships still exist, and the land reform program is being implemented very slowly. Increasing pressure on the land means that the farmers cannot grow enough for survival, let alone for sale, and efforts at "villagization" have not succeeded.

The sources of wealth are limited. There is no active development of mineral resources, although sources of nickel have been located and may be mined soon. There is little industry, and the coffee crop, which contributes seventy-five to ninety percent of export earnings, has declined.

DEVELOPMENT

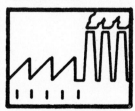

Increased transport facilities are crucial for Burundi's development. Road building within Burundi is actively pursued, and the Kigoma port on Lake Tanganyika is gradually being modernized. Plans to develop the East African rail network will especially aid Burundi and Rwanda.

FREEDOM

The government of Colonel Micombero, which was implicated in the genocide practiced against the Hutu people of Burundi, was overthrown in 1976. Lieutenant Colonel Bagaza's government is Tutsi with few Hutu representatives, and ethnic bitterness is an obstacle to equal rights for all.

HEALTH/WELFARE

The Roman Catholic and other church groups have played important roles in education and in social work. However, the Roman Catholics did not speak out at the time of the 1972-1973 killings. The government remains suspicious of church groups that allow the development of independent organizations outside of the UPRONA party.

ACHIEVEMENTS

Burundi's plans for future economic development show careful consideration of regional possibilities. Brarudi, the state beer industry, will expand to meet the needs of nearby markets in Zaire. Sugar, cheese, cooking oil, and soft drink factories are expected to benefit from the demands throughout the area.

Comoros

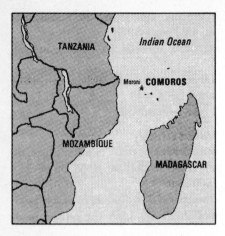

GEOGRAPHY

Area in Square Kilometers (Miles):
2,171 (838.2)
Land Usage: 16% forests; 7%
pasture; 48% arable; 29% other
Capital (Population): Moroni
(22,000)
Climate: tropical; marine

PEOPLE

Population
Total: 380,000 (1982 est.)
Per Square Kilometer (Mile): 175
(453)
Annual Growth Rate: 3.3%

Health
Life Expectancy at Birth: 47 years
Infant Death Rate (Ratio): 93/1,000
Average Caloric Intake: 102% of
FAO minimum

Languages
Official: Shaafi Islam (Swahili
dialect)
Others Spoken: French; Swahili;
English

Religion(s)
86% Shirazi Muslim; 14% Catholic

Education
Adult Literacy Rate: 66% male; 52%
female
School Attendance: primary: 100%
boys, 85% girls; secondary: 33%
boys, 17% girls

COMMUNICATION

Telephones: 2,000
Radios: 46,000

MAYOTTE

In 1974, when the other Comoran islands voted overwhelmingly for independence, Mayotte opted to remain French by a two-to-one margin. Since then, the French have continued to administer the island with the support of the local population—over ninety-five percent of whom have, in recent years, voted in favor of becoming an overseas department of France. Unlike the other islands, Mayotte is predominantly Christian. Historically, it has been greatly influenced by Malagasy and French culture. Comoran claims to the island are supported by the OAU, and in the United Nations only France voted against a resolution calling for their inclusion in the Comoros. Despite the location of its naval base on the island, the present socialist government in France is also eager to withdraw from Mayotte but is reluctant to do so against the wishes of Mayotte and domestic opinion.

TRANSPORTATION

Highways—Kilometers (Miles): 1,000
(621)
Railroads—Kilometers (Miles): none
One international airport

GOVERNMENT

Type: Islamic republic
Constitution: October 1, 1978
Former Colonial Status: French
Independence Date: July 6, 1975
Head of State: Ahmed Abdallah
(president)
Branches: president; Federal
Assembly
Legal System: based on Islamic law
Political Parties: Comoran Union for
Progress
Suffrage: universal for adults

MILITARY

Number of Armed Forces: 700-800
*Military Expenditures (% of Central
Government Expenditures):*
$2,900,000 (16%)
Nuclear Weapons Status: none
Current Hostilities: none

ECONOMY

Currency ($ US Equivalent): 440
CFA francs = $1
GDP: $78,800,000
Per Capita Income/GNP: $340
Natural Resources: agricultural lands
Agriculture: perfume essences;
copra; coconuts; cloves; vanilla; cin-
namon; yams; cloves; rice
Industry: perfume distillation;
tourism
Energy Production: 2,400 kw
capacity
Energy Consumption Per Capita: 11
kwh

FOREIGN TRADE

Exports: perfume essences; vanilla;
copra; cloves
Imports: rice; wheat flour; cotton
textiles; cement
Major Trading Partners: France;
United States; West Germany;
Madagascar; Kenya
Foreign Debt: $105,000,000
*Selected Membership in International
Organizations:* UN; OAU; African
Development Bank; Non-Aligned
Movement

Various groups settle in the islands, which become part of a Swahili trading network **1500s**	French rule over Mayotte is established **1843**	French protectorate over the remaining Comoro islands proclaimed **1886**	Islands are ruled as part of the French colony of Madagascar **1914-1946**	Independence is followed by a mercenary coup, which installs Ali Soilih **1975**	Ali Soilih is overthrown by mercenaries; Abdallah is restored **1978**	*Union Comorienne pour le Progress* is made the sole political party **1982**	**1983**

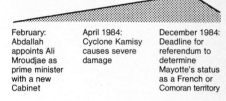

February: Abdallah appoints Ali Mroudjae as prime minister with a new Cabinet	April 1984: Cyclone Kamisy causes severe damage	December 1984: Deadline for referendum to determine Mayotte's status as a French or Comoran territory

REPUBLIC OF COMOROS

At the time of its unilateral declaration of independence from France in July of 1975, the Comoros was listed by the United Nations as one of the world's least developed nations. The years since have not been especially kind to the approximately one and one-quarter million Comorans; their lives have been made more difficult by natural disaster, eccentric leadership, and external intervention. Lately, however, Comorans have begun to make progress in meeting the challenges of their independence.

HISTORY AND POLITICS

The Comoros archipelago was populated by a number of Indian Ocean peoples, who—by the time of the arrival of the first Europeans during the early sixteenth century—had already combined to form the predominantly Muslim, Swahili-speaking society found on the islands today. In 1886 the French, who had already colonized the neighboring island of Mayotte, proclaimed a protectorate over the three main islands that presently constitute the Islamic Republic. Throughout the colonial period, the Comoros were especially valued by the French for strategic reasons. A local elite of large landholders prospered from the production of cash crops, while life for most Comorans remained one of extreme poverty.

A month after independence, the first Comoran government, led by the wealthy Ahmed Abdallah, was overthrown by mercenaries, who installed Ali Soilih in power. The new leader promised a socialist transformation of the nation and began to implement a program of land reform. This program was never completed, however, because Soilih rapidly lost support both at home and abroad. Under his leadership, gangs of undisciplined youths terrorized society, while the basic institutions and services of government all but disappeared. The situation was made even worse by a major volcanic eruption, which left twenty thousand people homeless, and by the arrival of sixteen thousand Comoran refugees after a massacre of Comorans in Madagascar.

In May 1978, another band of mercenaries—this time led by the notorious Bob Denard, whose exploits in Zaire during the 1960s had made his name infamous throughout Africa—overthrew Soilih and eventually restored Abdallah to power under the republic's first functioning Constitution. Because of the prominent role played by Denard and his followers, the new regime was isolated by other African governments during its first months in power. The removal of most of the mercenaries by the end of 1978 finally allowed the Comoros to become an active member of the international community. This, in turn, has allowed the government to attract much needed outside aid, principally from France, Saudi Arabia, and international donor agencies. In 1982 the country legally became a one-party state.

ECONOMY AND DEVELOPMENT

After experiencing a twenty-three percent decline during the two years of Ali Soilih's rule, the economy has begun to recover. Annual per capita income is still only about $350 and is, furthermore, quite unevenly distributed. Up to ninety percent of the population is supported by farming, which contributes forty percent of the national GDP. The Comoros is the world's leading exporter of *ylang-ylang,* an essence used to make perfume, and is the second leading producer of vanilla. Export earnings for both of these crops have not kept pace with rising import costs, particularly for petroleum and food. Rice is the island's staple, but only twenty percent of the country's consumption is produced locally. The government has tried to encourage agricultural diversification by promoting alternative crops, such as maize. A terrible setback was suffered in January 1983, when at least one-half of the nation's crops were destroyed by a cyclone.

What little industry exists on the island consists almost entirely of agricultural processing, including perfume distillation. Unfortunately, the waters around the islands are not well suited for commercial fishing. The one sector of the economy with the greatest potential for immediate growth is tourism, which, when compared with the neighboring Indian Ocean islands, is now miniscule. At present, the few hotels on the island are run by a French company.

DEVELOPMENT

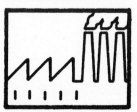

One of the important projects undertaken since independence has been the on-going expansion of the port at Mutsamudu, which will allow the country to dock large cargo ships for the first time.

FREEDOM

A degree of political dissent is tolerated, but instances of government repression are known to occur. In 1981 the government quietly acted on criticisms levelled at it by an Amnesty International Investigative mission that visited the islands.

HEALTH/WELFARE

The two hospitals and five clinics now operating are totally inadequate to meet the nation's needs. Life expectancy is only forty-seven years, and the infant mortality rate is among the world's highest.

ACHIEVEMENTS

The Comoros has been known as a center of the world's finest perfumes since very early in its history.

Djibouti

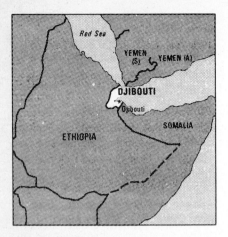

GEOGRAPHY

Area in Square Kilometers (Miles): 23,310 (9,000)
Land Usage: 89% desert wasteland; 10% permanent pasture; less than 1% cultivated
Capital (Population): Djibouti (102,000—1976)
Climate: arid to semiarid

PEOPLE

Population
Total: 332,000 (1982 est.)
Per Square Kilometer (Mile): 15 (37)
Annual Growth Rate: 6.4%

Languages
Official: French
Others Spoken: Somali; Afar; Arabic

Religion(s)
92% Muslim; 6% Christian; 2%other

Education
Adult Literacy Rate: 5%

COMMUNICATION

Telephones: 4,350
Radios: 17,000
Televisions: 5,200
Newspapers: 3 weeklies

TRANSPORTATION

Highways—Kilometers (Miles): 1,387 (862)
Railroads—Kilometers (Miles): 97 (60)
One international airport

GOVERNMENT

Type: republic
Constitution: partial constitution ratified in 1981
Former Colonial Status: French
Independence Date: June 27, 1977
Head of State: Hassan Gouled Aptidon (president)
Branches: president; prime minister; cabinet; Parliament
Legal System: based on French Civil Law, Islamic law and indigenous law
Political Parties: People's Progress Assembly
Suffrage: universal for adults

MILITARY

Number of Armed Forces: 2,400 (supported by 3,500 French)
Armed Forces/Population: 1/127
Military Expenditures (% of Central Government Expenditures): $2,900,000 (3.4%)
Nuclear Weapons Status: none
Foreign Aid: France
Current Hostilities: none

ECONOMY

Currency ($ US Equivalent): 150 Djibouti francs = $1
GDP: $264,700,000
Workforce: small number of semi-skilled laborers at port facility
Natural Resources: none
Agriculture: goats; sheep; camels; cattle; coffee
Industry: port and maritime support; construction
Energy Production: 55,000 kw capacity
Energy Consumption Per Capita: 770 kwh

FOREIGN TRADE

Exports: hides; cattle; coffee
Imports: textiles; consumer goods; foodstuffs
Major Trading Partners: France; Ethiopia; Japan
Foreign Debt: $31,500,000
Selected Membership in International Organizations: UN; OAU; Arab League; Non-Aligned Movement

France buys port of Obock 1862	France acquires port of Djibouti 1888	Addis Ababa-Djibouti railroad completed 1917	Djibouti votes to remain part of Overseas France 1958	Independence; Ogaden War 1977	Refugee problems mount 1980	Part of new Constitution issued 1981

● 1983

September: Repatriation of Ethiopian refugees from Djibouti begins	November: International donors meet to discuss five-year plan to aid Djibouti's development	March 1984: Mengistu Haile Mariam of Ethiopia visits Djibouti; President Aptidon offers Djibouti's services as regional mediator

DJIBOUTI

Tiny Djibouti, situated between Ethiopia and Somalia, guards the southern mouth of the Red Sea. Because the historic domains of the two main ethnic groups (the Somali-speaking Issas in the south and the Afars near Ethiopia and Eritrea) are cut by international boundaries, external conflicts often have internal ramifications.

Much of Djibouti's territory is a barren desert, with harsh volcanic outcroppings, shifting sands, high temperatures, and minimal rainfall. Despite this, humidity can be very high during the monsoon seasons in May and September. The country is roughly the size of the state of Massachusetts (23,310 square kilometers). Of the 323 thousand inhabitants, about one-third live in the capital and port of Djibouti.

HISTORY

Djibouti's modern history is closely linked with international competition over the Red Sea routes. France responded to Britain's earlier moves in Aden by first exploring and then negotiating to open up trade with the kingdom of Shoa in what is now Ethiopia. In 1862 France bought the port of Obock and its hinterland, later part of Djibouti.

With the opening of the Suez Canal in 1869, the Red Sea was the major route from Europe to India and the Far East. Italy began its expansion in Eritrea that same year. In the 1880s, France began developing Obock as a port, and in 1888 the French acquired the town of Djibouti, later the capital of French Somaliland. A treaty with the Emperor of Ethiopia permitted the construction of the Djibouti-Addis Ababa railroad, which ensured the prosperity of the port of Djibouti. Franco-Italian rivalries in the region were heightened by Italy's invasion of Ethiopia in 1935, and these hostilities continued throughout World War II.

Following World War II, Djibouti became an overseas territory of France, and all residents became French citizens. By 1960, other French colonies had gained independence. The Somali Republic had been created next door, and interest in independence grew in Djibouti. To counter the effects of Somali nationalism, the French favored the Afars in local politics and hired them for jobs in the civil service and the port. In 1967, an electrified barbed wire fence was built around the capital to prevent Issas from entering the town illegally.

After the 1967 Arab-Israeli war, the Suez Canal was closed until 1975, and Djibouti's port suffered. Supertankers, developed to lessen the high cost of transporting oil around Africa, were too large to use the Canal even when it reopened. This crisis made Djibouti rely on French economic aid. In 1974 Ethiopia's revolution and the Somali drought transformed the situation in Djibouti. Ethiopia's new government sought new outlets for its trade. The Somali drought forced ethnic Somali refugees into Djibouti, tipping the electoral and ethnic balance away from the Afars and toward independence from France.

On June 27, 1977, the Republic of Djibouti became independent. An ethnically balanced cabinet was formed with an Issa, Hassan Gouled Aptidon, as president, and an Afar, Ahmed Dini, as prime minister. Later in 1977, war broke out in Ogaden between Ethiopia and Somalia. Djibouti remained neutral, but ethnic tensions mounted as more Somali refugees arrived. In 1978 the Afars withdrew from the government. By 1981 the Eritrean and Ogaden conflicts had caused nearly fifty thousand refugees to flee to Djibouti, where many were settled in camps set up by the United Nations High Commission for Refugees (UNHCR).

ECONOMY

Djibouti is unable to feed its own people. The agricultural sector consists of little more than some small-scale market gardening and date cultivation. More than half of the population still are nomadic pastoralists, following their flocks of goats, sheep, camels, and cattle, and selling hides, skins, and live camels for export

Aside from the port, there is little industry in Djibouti. The port, unable to handle supertankers, now faces competition from Ethiopian and Arab ports.

Because of its strategic location, Djibouti has received foreign aid from many countries, including France, Saudi Arabia, Iraq, Libya, and Gulf states, and West Germany as well as from multi-lateral agencies. The continued French military presence has helped to support the economy and to prevent Djibouti from being swallowed up by either of its larger neighbors.

DEVELOPMENT

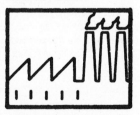

Construction of an international container terminal valued at $23 million was begun in 1981 and is scheduled to open in 1984. In June 1983, Djibouti's new radio transmitter was dedicated. Capable of transmitting up to a radius of fifteen hundred kilometers, the recently completed radio station was built with French and West German aid.

FREEDOM

Djibouti's first Constitution is still incomplete, although the first parts of it were introduced in 1981. For topics not yet covered by local laws, the courts draw on the Napoleonic code, a relic of the nation's French colonial past, or the Muslim *Sharia,* which is based on the Koran.

HEALTH/WELFARE

Life expectancy is only fifty years, caused partly by a high level of infant mortality. The government has responded to the lack of agricultural potential that lies at the base of the country's nutritional and health problems by encouraging Djiboutians to supplement their diets with fish caught locally.

ACHIEVEMENTS

In September 1983, repatriation of the Ethiopian refugees began when 170 Ethiopian nationals boarded trains in Djibouti for the trip home. They were resettled near their original homelands. Already over a thousand refugees had been repatriated by mid-November through the UNHCR program.

Ethiopia

GEOGRAPHY

Area in Square Kilometers (Miles):
1,178,450 (472,000)
Land Usage: 10% cultivated; 55%
pasture; 6% forests and woodland;
29% waste, urban, and other
Capital (Population): Addis Ababa
(1,408,086—1982)
Climate: temperate in highlands;
semi-arid to arid in lowlands

PEOPLE

Population
Total: 32,775,000 (1982 est.)
Per Square Kilometer (Mile): 27 (69)
Annual Growth Rate: 2.6%
Rural/Urban Population Ratio: 86/14

Health
Life Expectancy at Birth: 46 years
Infant Death Rate (Ratio): 147/1,000
Average Caloric Intake: 78% FAO
minimum
Physicians Available (Ratio):
1/58,490
Access to Safe Water: 6%

Languages
Official: Amharic
Others Spoken: Tigrinya; Oromo;
Somali; Arabic; Italian; English;
others

Religion(s)
35-40% Ethiopian Orthodox Christian; 40-45% Muslim; 15-25% traditional indigenous religions and others

Education
Adult Literacy Rate: 35%-40%
School Attendance: primary: 60%
boys, 33% girls; secondary: 16%
boys, 8% girls

ETHIOPIAN CHRISTIANITY

The Christian heritage of Ethiopia differs from Roman Catholicism and is related to that of Egypt and Syria. Like these churches, the Christian church in Ethiopia derives from beliefs that the Roman church considered heretical because its followers believed that Christ has one nature that is both human and divine, instead of two. It is often called *Mono*physite Christianity. The church has very distinctive rituals and a special priestly class. Ethiopian Christian crosses are beautifully carved or cast in metal and include neck crosses, which every Christian was expected to wear in earlier centuries. The church was closely allied with the royal family. In the eleventh century, the Emperor Lalibela sponsored the construction of stone churches, hewn from the living rock, which stand as a memorial to early Christian influence. The new government, after some efforts to erase religious practices, has developed a good relationship with the church.

COMMUNICATION

Telephones: 80,000
Radios: 260,000
Televisions: 31,000
Newspapers: 5 dailies; total circulation 52,000

TRANSPORTATION

Highways—Kilometers (Miles):
44,300 (27,528)
Railroads—Kilometers (Miles): 1,089
(677)
Four international airports

GOVERNMENT

Type: provisional military
government
Constitution: abolished in 1974
Former Colonial Status: none
Head of State: Mengistu Haile
Mariam (Chairman of Provisional
Military Administrative Council)
Branches: Provisional Military Administrative Council (Dergue);
judiciary
Legal System: based on Western
legal patterns
Political Parties: none
Suffrage: universal over age 21

MILITARY

Number of Armed Forces: 80,000
(including guerrilla groups); backed
by 11,000 Cuban forces
Armed Forces/Population: 1/382
Nuclear Weapons Status: none
Current Hostilities: internal conflicts
with various liberation groups in
several provinces; border disputes
with Somalia

ECONOMY

Currency ($ US Equivalent): 2 Ethiopian birrs =$1
GDP: $4,010,000,000
Per Capita Income/GNP: $140
Workforce: 80% agriculture; 7% industry; 13% services
Inflation Rate: 15% (1978-1981);
35% (1982)
Natural Resources: potash; salt;
gold; copper; platinum
Agriculture: cereals; coffee; pulses;
oil seeds; livestock
Industry: processed food; textiles; cement; building materials; hydroelectric power
Energy Production: 330,000 kw
capacity
Energy Consumption Per Capita: 25
kwh

FOREIGN TRADE

Exports: coffee; hides; skins
Imports: petroleum; machinery;
transport equipment
Major Trading Partners: Saudi
Arabia; Japan; Italy; West Germany;
Iran; UK; France; United States
Foreign Debt:$1,192,000,000
*Selected Membership in International
Organizations:* UN; OAU; African
Development Bank; Non-Aligned
Movement

ETHIOPIA

Ethiopia is a country with a long recorded history. Haile Selassie, the last emperor of Ethiopia, claimed he was descended from Solomon and the Queen of Sheba, and the history of the country has been traced from the Axum kingdom, founded in the first century A.D., to the military coup in 1974. This coup, which overthrew Haile Selassie, led to the demise of the ancient kingdom. Coup leaders later declared that the empire had become a socialist state. Many changes have taken place; yet old patterns persist.

THE COUP'S ORIGINS AND RESULTS

The past dominance of an Amhara ruling class in Ethiopia had developed through history and regional aristocracies were built on peasant bases. The modernization of the Ethiopian kingdom had begun as far back as the mid-nineteenth century by the Emperor Tewodros and was continued by Menelik II in the late nineteenth century. Haile Selassie gave Ethiopia the appearance of a constitutional state in the 1930s by establishing a constitution, promoting some social reforms, opening Western schools, and supporting new constructions in Addis Ababa, the capital city. In the 1950s and 1960s the regime began to be affected by new forces—such as the rise of nationalism throughout Africa, the impact of foreign capital, and the intrusion of military and economic advisors from the United States. Resistance to the emperor grew, especially in the university and among workers in Addis Ababa, teachers, and the military forces. Peoples such as the Tigre, the Somalis, the Oromo, and the already nationalistic Eritreans became more conscious of their different identities.

The coup itself was triggered by problems resulting from the sharp rise in food and oil prices and the terrible famine in Tigray and Wolo provinces in 1972-1973. It was said that 200 thousand persons died during this famine. Meanwhile, conditions in the drought regions contrasted sharply with the growing wealth of the emperor and the urban upper class. Strikes, military mutinies, and peasant revolts reached their height in February 1974. In September, a group of military officers deposed the emperor.

(United Nations photo by Y. Levy)

Most people in Ethiopia (86%) are engaged in agriculture and, to some extent, animal husbandry, but cities have long histories and are not just a twentieth century phenomenon.

A Provisional Military Administrative Council (PMAC), a group of over 120 military men known as the *Dergue* (Amharic for "committee") took command. By the end of 1974, the Dergue had moved from a philosophy of "Ethiopia First" to "Ethiopean Socialism." The Dergue took drastic measures. Companies and lands were nationalized. A national campaign for development sent students into the countryside to assist in land reforms, to teach literacy, and to encourage the formation of active peasant associations, which remain important today. Associations called *kebeles* were also formed among workers in the cities.

However, the Dergue did not implement the plans for reconstruction, nor did it put a new peoples' government into effect because it was unable to stabilize its own leadership nor to agree on the groups that should be supported. The intense political rivalries of 1974-1978 resulted in the execution of numerous individuals and the destruction of certain groups. Undetermined numbers of people lost their lives.

In 1978, Mengistu Haile Mariam came to power; he presently controls the government and presides over a forty-man Dergue. Mariam also leads a Commission for Organizing the Party of the Working People of Ethiopia (COPWE), which oversees government-sponsored national organizations. COPWE became a political party in September 1984. No plan has yet been established to diffuse power from the central committee.

THE PRESENT SITUATION

The development of a new socialist state has been delayed by present crises as well as by personal political rivalries. The main crisis is civil war. There are liberation movements among the Tigre, the Oromo, the Somalis, and the Eritreans. The Dergue's answer to their ethnic pride and their desire for self-determination has been military repression. The size of the Ethiopian army has been increased to almost 400 thousand soldiers, often through forced conscription. Recently the age of draftees was lowered to nineteen. The Dergue has sought arms from abroad. The arms build-up led to a secret arms agreement with the Soviet Union in December 1976, and a diplomatic realignment in 1977 whereby Ethiopia, once the ally of the United States, became closely attached to the Soviet Union. This move was to have many repercussions. The intensity of the war was increased, and the resistance of those in opposition grew—now fueled by the USSR arms the opposition captured from the Ethiopians.

The World Bank and the International Monetary Fund, Western-Oriented institutions, withheld loans to Ethiopia. Consequently, in the several years before 1981, Ethiopia received less aid than any of the UN-designated Least Developed Countries from these organizations. Ethiopia has been accused of using relief funds for the purchase of military equipment from the Soviet Union and of diverting Ethiopian

(UNICEF photo)

Ethiopia's government has limited financial resources and depends on help from international agencies to cope with problems resulting from the widespread drought.

| The Eritrean Liberation Struggle begins 1961 | Famines in Tigray and Wolo provinces result in up to 200,000 deaths 1972-1973 | Emperor Haile Selassie is overthrown; PMAC is established 1974 | Diplomatic realignment and new arms agreement with USSR 1977 | World Bank resumes lending operations to Ethiopia 1981 |

1984

January-March 1984: Eritrean struggle intensifies

January 1984: Eritrean Liberation Movements continue to discuss unification

September 1984: COPWE becomes a political party

grain harvests to the USSR in return for aid. (International investigators have since cleared Ethiopia of these charges.) Recently, Ethiopia has improved its relations with Western countries, and the international bodies as well as the United States seem receptive to these efforts to rebuild ties.

ECONOMIC PROBLEMS

There are still vast economic problems to be solved. Falling prices for coffee on the world market and the rising costs of imported goods have compounded the losses resulting from the civil wars. Land reforms have been a mixed blessing. Farmers now guard their harvests for themselves, while the populations of the cities remain unfed. The drought of the last four years has affected more people than that of 1972-1973. There are a dozen refugee camps in Ethiopia for victims of the drought, and it is estimated that 450 thousand persons need assistance. Thousands of refugees have moved across the borders of Ethiopia into neighboring Sudan and Somalia to escape the drought, the civil wars, and conscription into the army.

THE CONTINUITIES OF ETHIOPIAN HISTORY

Some of the features of the past continue to characterize, shape, and trouble the new Ethiopia. Perhaps most important is the heritage of ethnic diversity. The empire was a feudal kingdom, and ruling landed aristocrats in the local areas were local magnates rather than representatives of the central government. Local independence

was maintained. The geographic variety of Ethiopia, its dissected plateau and mountains, have helped to maintain the variety of languages and cultural traditions. But this geography has also worked against the consolidation and national integration of the different communities. Now the different groups have risen against the socialist state, which they proclaim is fascist. The Eritrean movement is one of the oldest and most vital of the liberation movements. Eritreans were supporting an independent state in 1945, when they became independent of Italy and were put under Ethiopian jurisdiction. The Eritrean Peoples' Liberation Front, the most active group, successfully resisted Ethiopian military campaigns in 1982 and 1983. They have organized a government and active, creative communities in the liberated areas.

The resistance of ethnic communities within Ethiopia to the new state is heightened by the failure of the leaders to give any power to these communities within the central government or to suggest plans of federation that might satisfy ethnic aspirations. The Amharic peoples have always been the dominant ruling people in the empire. Today Amharic people continue to be important. The ruling body of military officers is almost entirely Amharic. Again, the Dergue is following patterns of the past.

The continuity of modern Ethiopia is also seen in the present religious life. Tradition claims that Christianity, in its distinctive Ethiopian form, was first introduced into the country in the fourth century A.D. It became allied to the emperor and

the ruling class, and it developed distinctive national rituals, churches, and a special priestly class. Today, although the church is no longer a state church, and church lands have been nationalized, the membership of the church continues to grow. Islam, too, has a long heritage in Ethiopia, and there is no evidence that this faith has been attacked since the new government came to power.

CONCLUSION

A most important characteristic of Ethiopia is its leadership role in continental Africa. During the colonial period, Ethiopia was an example that inspired dominated peoples. The kingdom had defeated the Italians in 1896 and had maintained its independence, except for the period from 1936 to 1945 when Mussolini and Fascist Italy controlled the state. Ethiopia was a founding member of the United Nations and the home of the Organization of African Unity (OAU). Even today, the headquarters of the OAU remains in Addis Ababa. Ethiopia played a leading role in maintaining the organization in 1982-1983, when conflicts over the Western Sahara and Chad threatened the OAU's destruction.

DEVELOPMENT

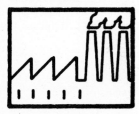

Land reforms under the Dergue have allowed peasants to control their own production, but the whole country does not benefit, and surpluses do not reach the cities.

FREEDOM

Thousands of political prisoners are still said to be held in Ethiopia, but human rights are more secure than in the terrible years from 1974-1978—especially 1977-1978 when arbitrary arrest, executions, and violence were widespread. In Eritrea, under Operation Red Star, the level of violence is still high.

HEALTH/WELFARE

The per capita income (approximately $140) is one of the lowest in the world, and sixty to sixty-five percent of the people are said to live below the poverty level. The deepest poverty is now in the urban areas.

ACHIEVEMENTS

Informal as well as formal education has been expanded in recent years. In 1979, an ambitious literacy campaign began, and at least ten million people in rural and urban areas have taken part. Fifteen languages are used. Ethiopia received a UNESCO award for its progress in literacy in 1982.

Kenya

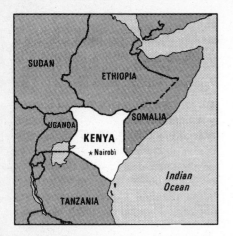

GEOGRAPHY

Area in Square Kilometers (Miles): 582,488 (224,900)
Land Usage: 21% forests and woodland; 13% arable; 66% grassland suitable for grazing
Capital (Population): Nairobi (959,000—1978)
Climate: tropical to arid

PEOPLE

Population
Total: 17,864,000 (1982 est.)
Per Square Kilometer (Mile): 31 (79)
Annual Growth Rate: 4.1%
Rural/Urban Population Ratio: 86/14

Health
Life Expectancy at Birth: 56 years
Infant Death Rate (Ratio): 87/1,000
Average Caloric Intake: 88% of FAO minimum
Physicians Available (Ratio): 1/10,500
Access to Safe Water: 17%

Languages
Official: English; Swahili
Others Spoken: Kikuyu; Dholuo; Kisii; Luhya; Maasai; Kalenjin; Nandi

Religion(s)
38% traditional indigenous beliefs; 37% Protestant; 22% Catholic; 3% Muslim

Education
Adult Literacy Rate: 60% males; 35% females
School Attendance: primary: 100% boys, 100% girls; secondary: 23% boys, 15% girls

CULTURE AND POLITICS

In the past as well as today, cultural activities in Kenya have been closely connected with politics, encouraging nationalism and revealing inequities. Events occurring at the Kamriitha Community Educational and Cultural Center illustrate this statement. The center was built by community efforts in Kamriithu, a Kenyan town of ten thousand. The villagers developed a program at the center and ran it. The literacy committee organized a literacy study course, and the community organized dramas that illustrated the people's experiences and ideas. Ngugi wa Thiong'o was commissioned to write the first play—about the townspeoples' own lives—and they discussed and criticized it as well as performed it in a theatre that the town had built. The production was highly successful but was banned because the authorities felt it encouraged class conflict. Ngugi was detained [he is now in exile]. Later the center was closed and the theatre destroyed.

COMMUNICATION

Telephones: 168,200
Radios: 570,000
Televisions: 70,000
Newspapers: 3 dailies; total circulation 156,000

TRANSPORTATION

Highways—Kilometers (Miles): 52,250 (32,468)
Railroads—Kilometers (Miles): 2,040 (1,267)
Two international airports

GOVERNMENT

Type: republic; one-party state
Constitution: 1963
Former Colonial Status: British
Independence Date: December 12, 1963
Head of State: Daniel arap Moi (president)
Branches: president; unicameral National Assembly; High Court
Legal System: based on British law and customary law
Political Parties: Kenya African National Union (only party by constitutional amendment)
Suffrage: universal over age 21

MILITARY

Number of Armed Forces: 14,750
Armed Forces/Population: 1/1,209
Military Expenditures (% of Central Government Expenditures): $168,600,000 (8%)
Nuclear Weapons Status: none
Current Hostilities: none

ECONOMY

Currency ($ US Equivalent): 12 Kenya shillings = $1
GDP: $5,340,000,000
Per Capita Income/GNP: $390
Workforce: 78% agriculture; 10% industry; 12% services
Inflation Rate: 12.2% (1981); 20% (1982)
Natural Resources: wildlife; land; soda ash; wattle
Agriculture: corn; wheat; rice; sugar cane; coffee; tea; sisal; pyrethrum; livestock
Industry: petroleum products; cement; beer; tourism
Energy Production: 481,000 kw capacity
Energy Consumption Per Capita: 90 kwh

FOREIGN TRADE

Exports: coffee; petroleum products; tea; hides and skins; meat and meat products; cement; pyrethrum; sisal; soda ash; wattle
Imports: crude petroleum; machinery and vehicles; iron; steel; paper products; pharmaceuticals; fertilizers; fabrics
Major Trading Partners: EEC countries; United States; Canada; Zambia; Iran; Japan; Australia; India; People's Republic of China
Foreign Debt: $3,404,100,000
Selected Membership in International Organizations: UN; OAU; Commonwealth of Nations; African Development Bank; Non-Aligned Movement

KENYA

Tom Mboya, Kenya's Minister of Economic Development and Planning in 1969, made these remarks in an article written for the *New York Times* a few months before his assassination:

We suffered during our struggle for independence, but in many ways it was a simpler period than today. The present period is less dramatic. Nationalist sentiment must remain powerful, but it can no longer be sustained by slogans and the excitement of independence. Rather, it must itself sustain the population during the long process of development. For development will not come immediately. It is a process that requires time, planning, sacrifice, and work.

Someone observing Kenya in 1983, fourteen years after Mboya's remarks, might agree with his sentiments. The quotation also raises questions about independence and development in Kenya today.

KENYA'S PAST

The African people who are now citizens of Kenya were members of small-scale local societies in pre-colonial times. The Maasai, then as now, were herders who exchanged cattle for the crops of farmers such as the Kikuyu and Kamba. Organized Swahili city states developed on the coast. In the nineteenth century, caravans of Swahili and Arab traders stimulated economic and political changes. However, the peoples who had the greatest impact on the Kenya farmers and herders were the European white settlers who came to Kenya as early as the first decade of the twentieth century.

By the 1930s, the area of the temperate highlands near Nairobi had become "white man's country." Over six million acres of land—much of it the land of the Maasai—had been taken from the original owners, and many Africans had been moved to reserves. Kikuyu laborers, often migrants from the reserves, now worked for the new owners—sometimes on lands that they had once farmed for themselves.

By the 1950s, African grievances had been heightened by increased settlement, growing African nationalism, and repression resulting from white fears. The movement called Mau Mau developed when a state of emergency was declared by the British colonial authorities. The resisters, unassisted by any outside aid, fought the regime for ten years. During this time, thirty-two whites lost their lives, and thirteen thousand Kikuyu were killed. Eighty thousand Africans were detained in detention camps by colonial authorities, and over a million persons were resettled in controlled villages.

When political activity was finally allowed in Kenya, the person who emerged as a leader was the already-popular Jomo Kenyatta, who had been detained during the emergency and accused—without evidence—of leading the Mau Mau movement. Kenyatta, a charismatic leader, became prime minister and later president when Kenya gained independence. He led the country from 1963 until his death in 1978.

During the early years of Kenyatta's leadership, the situation in Kenya looked promising. Kenyatta's government encouraged racial harmony, and the slogan *Harambee* ("Let Us Pull Together") was a call for people of all races to work together for Kenya's development. The political system seemed open, and there were (as there still are) regular elections. Land reforms provided plots to one and a half million farmers, who made a little money from the production of cash crops, such as coffee, which received good prices on the world market in these years. A policy of Africanization opened businesses to Kenya entrepreneurs. Many new enterprises were begun—often developed with foreign capital. Kenya was called "the showcase of capitalism" and was compared to the similarly prospering Ivory Coast in West Africa.

KENYA'S POLITICAL LIFE

According to the news reports and the general surveys of Kenya, "politics is king" in Kenya today. Daniel arap Moi, Kenyatta's successor, has sought to follow Kenyatta's policies and to use them in keeping his opponents and his followers in line. *Nyayoism* ("in the footsteps—of Kenyatta) and "peace, love and unity" are the slogans of Moi's government. In Kenya, the game of politics has many ambitious practitioners. Moi has sought to mediate as well as to lead these political forces. He has restrained some individuals. Oginga Odinga, Kenyatta's (and now Moi's) political opponent, was detained for criticizing Kenyatta, and Charles Njonjo, a minister and powerful member of government, has been suspended from office under suspicion of sedition.* In 1982, a constitutional amendment was passed making KANU (the Kenya African National Union) the only legal party—thus restraining opponents—such as Odinga—who were planning to develop a second party. Within the party, there has been much dissension. There have been cabinet reshufflings, and new posts have been created that allow for increased patronage.

*Njonjo's trial has not proved his treason. It *has* revealed his personal use of power and his popularity.—ed.

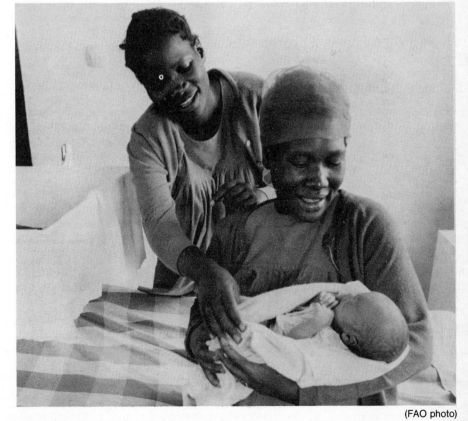

(FAO photo)

Kenya has made social and political progress, but a high birth rate threatens to reduce available resources.

		State of emergency declared by colonial government; "Mau Mau," a predominantly Kikuyu movement, resists colonial rule	Kenya gains independence under the leadership of Jomo Kenyatta	Tom Mboya, a leading trade unionist and government minister, is assassinated	Daniel arap Moi becomes president upon the death of Kenyatta	Assembly of Heads of State of OAU is held in Nairobi; Moi becomes OAU chairman for 1981-1982	A coup by members of the Kenya Air Force is put down
The British East African Protectorate is proclaimed 1895	British colonists began to settle in the Highlands area 1900-1910	1952	1963	1969	1978	1981	1982

●ⅡⅠⅠⅠⅠⅠⅠ●ⅠⅠⅠⅠ●ⅠⅠⅠ●ⅠⅠ●ⅠⅠⅠ●ⅠⅠⅠ●ⅠⅠ●ⅠⅠⅠ●ⅠⅠⅠ●ⅠⅠⅠⅠ●ⅠⅠⅠ●ⅠⅠ●ⅠⅠⅠ●Ⅰ●ⅠⅠⅠ●1983

In August 1982, a coup was attempted by members of the Kenya Air Force, against Moi's government. It did not succeed, but there was much violence in Nairobi. About 250 persons died, and approximately fifteen hundred persons were detained. The Air Force has since been disbanded. The university, whose students came out in support of the coup makers, was closed; it finally reopened in the summer of 1983.

The coup has had a damaging effect on Kenya's image as an orderly, prosperous, and democratic state. Although Moi and the government seem to have recovered, the repercussions of this event are still uncertain. In the spring of 1983, Moi spoke of traitors who threatened to overthrow the government with foreign aid and said that powerful politicians like Charles Njonjo were suspect. Moi surprised both friends and opponents when he called for elections in September 1983—a year earlier than expected. Nearly one thousand candidates vied for 158 parliamentary seats. Although some ministers lost their seats, and new persons took office, the elections did not result in a radical change in government.

EXAMINING THE SHOWCASE

Meanwhile, Kenya, like other African countries, has been adversely affected by the conditions of the world economy. Until the late 1970s, Kenya had one of the highest growth rates of the sub-Saharan African countries (over six percent during 1970-1978). Kenya is the most industrialized country of East Africa, and the cash crops that it exports are extensive and varied, thus buffering the nation's economy

from the uncertainties of the world market. Nevertheless, the present low return for its cash crops abroad is one reason for Kenya's worsening economic situation.

The elite must take some responsibility for the problems of the Kenyan economy. They have spent their efforts in politicking; often they have used their wealth, not for the advancement of production, but for the development of affluent life-styles. Rather than struggling *for* development they have struggled *over* what development there is. "Ten millionaires and ten million beggars," is how J.M. Kariuki, a reforming politician, described Kenya in the mid-1970s. The richest tenth of the population receive forty percent of the wealth, while the poorest quarter of the people receive only six percent. The middle class has benefitted from this unequal division of wealths and accusations of corruption abound. Ordinary Kenyans have called this "tribe" the *Wabenzi* because they are known for their Mercedes Benz cars. In order to prevent further inequities, there is now a requirement that land sales must go through official government channels.

The lack of enterprise on the part of this middle class has encouraged the foreign ownership of production. These foreign-owned industries and services are monopolies and are protected by the government; they send their surplus earnings back to their own countries. Many enterprises are from the United States. US corporations have played a large part in Kenya's development and are part of a consortium that is providing loans to help Kenya meet its debts in 1983.

September: Elections to Parliament are hotly disputed	February 1984: Ochuka and Okumu, two leaders of the 1982 coup are tried and sentenced to death, having been repatriated from Tanzania after their escape	May 1984: Final agreement ending the East African Community is signed at Arusha, Tanzania

The United States government has also taken a special strategic interest in Kenya. In February 1980, Kenya agreed to allow the United States to use the Nairobi Airport for its forces, and the port of Mombasa is a base for the US Navy. Israel, too, has close relations with Kenya.

CONCLUSION

Kenya celebrated the twentieth anniversary of independence in December 1983. The occasion has stimulated reflection about the years since independence. There have been many achievements—in education and in agriculture, for instance. The opening of the border with Tanzania, closed since 1977, has been an encouraging sign for the future. However, problems remain. The jobless in the cities are increasingly restive. Many of the gains of economic development are absorbed in the four percent rate of population growth—one of the highest in the world. Land reform has slowed down. The game of politics continues. Some people believe that the promises of independence have been fulfilled; others, including some of the old fighters of maumau, still await the results that they had hoped would result from that struggle.

DEVELOPMENT

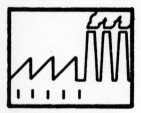

Kenya's game parks and safaris are well known in the Western world. Four hundred thousand to 500 thousand persons visit Kenya every year, and tourism is among the major sources of foreign exchange. It is a mixed blessing. The tourists who enrich the country use facilities and services geared to a wealthy enclave class, and promote a servant mentality.

FREEDOM

The coup of August 1982 against the government of Daniel arap Moi resulted in eleven death sentences and prison sentences up to twenty-five years for nearly one thousand persons. Seventy students and over 500 service men were recently freed. The Preservation of Public Security Act allows persons to be held for an indefinite period without trial.

HEALTH/WELFARE

Individual Kenyan communities have raised considerable amounts of money for self-help projects through *Harambee* events during which politicians compete in pledging large amounts for schools, clinics and other developments. This practice was banned during the electioneering process in 1983.

ACHIEVEMENTS

The Kenya Tea Development Authority (KIDA) is the world's largest exporter of black tea and oversees its production and processing in Kenya. In general, high standards, incentives, and growers' participation in KIDA have benefitted a million people of tea-growing households and many others.

Madagascar

GEOGRAPHY

Area in Square Kilometers (Miles): 592,800 (228,000)
Land Usage: 5% cultivated; 58% pasture land; 21% forests; 8% wasteland; 2% rivers and lakes; 6% other
Capital (Population): Tananarive (650,000)
Climate: tropical and moderate

PEOPLE

Population
Total: 9,233,000 (1982 est.)
Per Square Kilometer (Mile): 16 (40)
Annual Growth Rate: 2.7%
Rural/Urban Population Ratio: 82/18

Health
Life Expectancy at Birth: 48 years
Infant Death Rate (Ratio): 71/1,000
Average Caloric Intake: 111% of FAO minimum
Physicians Available (Ratio): 1/10,240
Access to Safe Water: 26%

Languages
Official: Malagasy
Others Spoken: French; others

Religion(s)
55% indigenous; 40% Christian; 5% Muslim

Education
Adult Literacy Rate: 41% males; 27% females
School Attendance: primary: 100% boys, 87% girls; secondary: 13% boys, 10% girls

COMMUNICATION

Telephones: 37,100
Radios: 1,800,000
Televisions: 60,000
Newspapers: 12 dailies; total circulation 53,000

TRANSPORTATION

Highways—Kilometers (Miles): 27,500 (17,087)
Railroads—Kilometers (Miles): 884 (549)
Three international airports

GOVERNMENT

Type: republic; authority in hands of Supreme Revolutionary Council
Constitution: December 21, 1975
Former Colonial Status: French
Independence Date: June 26, 1960
Head of State: Colonel Didier Ratsiraka (president)
Branches: president; Supreme Revolutionary Council; People's National Assembly; High Council of Institutions
Legal System: based on French Civil Law and customary law
Political Parties: Advance Guard of the Malagasy Revolution; Congress Party for Malagasy Independence; Movement for National Unity; Malagasy Christian Democratic Union; Militants for the Establishment of a Proletarian Regime; National Movement for Independence of Madagascar
Suffrage: universal over age 18

MILITARY

Number of Armed Forces: 19,550
Armed Forces/Population: 1/459
Military Expenditures (% of Central Government Expenditures): $114,400,000 (10.3%)
Nuclear Weapons Status: none
Current Hostilities: none

ECONOMY

Currency ($ US Equivalent): 390 Malagasy francs = $1
GDP: $2,900,000,000
Per Capita Income/GNP: $320
Workforce: 87% agriculture; 4% industry; 9% services
Inflation Rate: 15-30% (1980-1982)
Natural Resources: graphite; chrome; coal; bauxite; ilmenite; tar sands; semi-precious stones; timber; mica; nickel
Agriculture: rice; livestock; coffee; vanilla; sugar; cloves; cotton; sisal; peanuts; tobacco
Industry: processed food; textiles; mining; paper; refined petroleum; automobile assembly; construction; cement; farming
Energy Production: 100,000 kw capacity
Energy Consumption Per Capita: 47 kwh

FOREIGN TRADE

Exports: coffee; vanilla; sugar; cloves; livestock
Imports: consumer goods; foodstuffs; crude oil; fertilizers; metal products
Major Trading Partners: United States; France; EEC countries
Foreign Debt: $1,664,900,000
Selected Membership in International Organizations: UN; OAU; Non-Aligned Movement

Merina rulers gain sovereignty over other peoples of the island 1828	French complete the conquest of the island 1904	Revolt is suppressed by the French, with great loss of life 1947-1948	Independence from France is achieved without armed struggle; Philibert Tsiranana first president 1960	Coup leads to the fall of the First Malagasy Republic 1972	Didier Ratsiraka becomes president by military appointment 1975	Attempted coup is foiled; Indian Ocean Commission is established; Ratsiraka is reelected president 1982

1983

February: There is unrest in the university and in Tananarive

June: Malagasy will meet IMF requirements, including increase in producer prices, ceiling on salaries, and austerity measures

MADAGASCAR

Madagascar, like the other island polities of the western Indian Ocean, lies on Africa's periphery. To a large extent, the nation has had a separate history. Yet, in modern times Malagasy peoples have become conscious of the concerns that they share with the Africans on the continent, and Madagascar is a full member of the Organization of African Unity (OAU).

The island's isolation and its early settlement by peoples from the Pacific have given Madagascar a distinctive character. The present population, while small, is very varied. The Malayo-Polynesian peoples arrived in the early centuries A.D., and their descendants make up the majority of the eighteen different Malagasy ethnic groups of the island.

FRENCH COLONIALISM

France claimed the island as a colonial territory in 1896 and spread its administration and language. New ways were selectively added to traditional patterns and were widely adopted. There were about fifty thousand French residents by World War II. As opposition to colonialism developed during the mid-twentieth century, the French regime became more repressive. A revolt in 1947 was violently suppressed, resulting in somewhere between eleven thousand and eighty thousand deaths. Its memory is still fresh in the minds of the country's people.

INDEPENDENCE

Madagascar gained its independence in 1960 when all the member countries of the French Community became nations. The new government was led by Philibert Tsiranana and the Social Democratic Party (PSD). Its conservative stance soon led to discontent. There were uprisings among the peasants in southern Madagascar and disorder among the workers and students in the capital, Tananarive. In 1972, Tsiranana gave controlling power to the popular General Gabriel Ramanantsoa, and, after much political disturbance, the military put Didier Ratsiraka in the office of the president in 1975.

RADICAL CHANGES

Since 1972 the system of government and the orientation of the country have changed. Ratsinaka's Charter, "the little red book" described the regime's new socialist and non-aligned approach. It continued some of the policies instituted by General Ramanantsoa—including efforts to stimulate and re-create the traditional agricultural village communities called the *fokonolona,* approximately seventy thousand of which had been developed during General Ramanantsoa's administration.

In spite of its echoes of Marx and Mao, the Malagasy experiment is primarily an effort to revitalize the Malagasy society. Many associations (like parties) are included in the ruling coalition although all must be part of the National Front for the Defense of the Socialist Malagasy Revolution, an umbrella organization that encompasses all the nation's political parties.

THE PROBLEMS OF THE 1980s

Agriculture is a major Malagasy strength. Most of the people (over eighty percent) are rural, and a diverse group of crops are cultivated, including rice and yams. Important cash crops include vanilla (of which Madagascar provides half the world's supply) and cloves. Unfortunately, nature's disasters—such as cyclones—as well as the sluggish performance of the new peasant fokonolona have limited the economy, and the "Battle for Rice" has not been won.

"OPEN HORIZONS"

Since 1972 the government has tried to break and limit the ties with France, withdrawing from the Franc Zone and the French-oriented regional organization, OCAM. It has been renegotiating more advantageous terms with French companies and seeking support from other countries in both the East and West. Yet, France remains Madagascar's major trading partner.

Ratsiraka has also worked to make the Indian Ocean free of foreign naval bases, has refused to lease such bases to either France or the United States, and continues to press—without success—for the withdrawal of the United States at Diego Garcia. Thus, in foreign as in domestic policy the Malagasy Republic has since 1975, sought to develop a true independence—with mixed results.

DEVELOPMENT

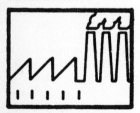

Madagascar has a fairly small population for its size. Only five percent of the land is used for agriculture, indicating the potential for agricultural expansion. However, government efforts to open new lands to production have not been successful, and the harvest has steadily declined. One estimate indicates that rice imports in 1983 will double the 200 thousand tons imported in 1982.

FREEDOM

The Advance Guard of the Malagasy Revolution (AREMA) is the militant, well-organized government party of right- and left-wingers. Six political associations beside AREMA make up the National Front for the Defense of the Socialist Malagasy Revolution (NFDR). The government is freely criticized in the press.

HEALTH/WELFARE

"Better health for everyone" is a national goal. Today, ten percent of the national budget goes to the health services. UN agencies are supporting government efforts. There are only 670 Malagasy physicians in the country; 450 others continue to practice in France.

ACHIEVEMENTS

A new wild life preserve will allow the unique animals of Madagascar to survive and develop. Sixty-six species of land animals are found nowhere else on earth, and include the aye-aye, a nocturnal lemur which has bat ears, beaver teeth, and an elongated clawed finger, all of which serve the aye-aye in finding food.

Mauritius

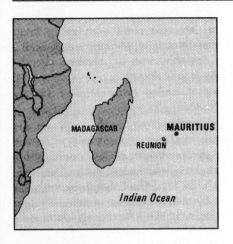

GEOGRAPHY

Area in Square Kilometers (Miles):
1,865 (720)
Land Usage: 50% agricultural; 39%
forests, woodlands, and mountains;
3% built-up areas; 5% water bodies;
3% wastelands and other
Capital (Population): Port Louis
(146,844—1981)
Climate: sub-tropical; marine

PEOPLE

Population
Total: 984,000 (1982 est.)
Per Square Kilometer (Mile): 481
(1,367)
Annual Growth Rate: 1.6%
Rural/Urban Population Ratio: 47/53

Health
Life Expectancy at Birth: 66 years
Infant Death Rate (Ratio):
32.9/1,000
Average Caloric Intake: 122% of
FAO minimum
Physicians Available (Ratio): 1/2,000

Languages
Official: English
Others Spoken: French; Creole; Hindi; Urdu

Religion(s)
32% Hindu; 16% Islamic; 30%
Roman Catholic and Protestant

Education
Adult Literacy Rate: 86% males;
72% females
School Attendance: primary: 100%
boys, 100% girls; secondary: 52%
boys, 49% girls
Teacher/Student Ratio: 1/42

DIEGO GARCIA

On the eve of the nation's independence, secret negotiations between British and Mauritian representatives resulted in Mauritius' sale of the small island of Diego Garcia and neighboring atolls to the British for the small sum of $7 million dollars. The inhabitants of Diego Garcia were completely ignored; moreover, they were subsequently moved to Mauritius in order to make room for a United States military base. The people of Mauritius, through their government, have demanded the island's return. Britain and the United States have offered more money to former inhabitants of the island and agreed to their eventual return in a unspecified, but distant, future. Mauritian claims enjoy widespread support from the international community, but the issue remains unresolved.

COMMUNICATION

Telephones: 36,400
Radios: 200,000
Televisions: 85,000
Newspapers: 8 dailies; total circulation 74,000

TRANSPORTATION

Highways—Kilometers (Miles): 1,786
(1,109)
Railroads—Kilometers (Miles): none
One international airport

GOVERNMENT

Type: independent state recognizing
British monarch as Chief of State
Constitution: 1968
Former Colonial Status: British,
French
Independence Date: March 12, 1968
Head of State: Aneerood Jugnauth
(prime minister)
Branches: prime minister and Council of Ministers; unicameral National
Assembly
Legal System: based on French and
English law
Political Parties: Mauritian Labor
Party; Mauritian Militant Movement;
Mauritian Socialist Party
Suffrage: universal over age 18

MILITARY

Number of Armed Forces: no standing defense force
Military Expenditures: $4,500,000
Nuclear Weapons Status: none
Foreign Aid: UK
Current Hostilities: none

ECONOMY

Currency ($ US Equivalent): 11
Mauritian rupees = $1
GDP: $890,000
Per Capita Income/GNP: $1,240
Workforce: 30% agricultural; 24%
industry; 20% government; 14%
unemployed; 12% other
Inflation Rate: 11.4% (1982)
Natural Resources: agricultural land
Agriculture: sugar; tea; tobacco
Industry: sugar production; consumer
goods; labor-intensive goods for export; tourism
Energy Production: 180,000 kw
capacity
Energy Consumption Per Capita: 385
kwh

FOREIGN TRADE

Exports: sugar; tea; molasses
Imports: foodstuffs; manufactured
goods
Major Trading Partners: United
Kingdom; United States; Canada;
South Africa; Australia
Foreign Debt:$486,900,000
*Selected Membership in International
Organizations:* UN; OAU; Associate
Member, European Economic Community (EEC); Non-Aligned
Movement

| Dutch claim, but abandon, Mauritius 1600s | French settlers and slaves arrive 1722 | Treaty of Paris formally cedes Mauritius to the British 1814 | Slavery abolished; South Asians arrive 1835 | Rioting on sugar estates shakes the political control of the Franco-Mauritian elite 1937 | Expanded franchise allows greater democracy 1948 | Independence 1968 | Labor unrest leads to detention of MMM leaders 1971 | Cyclone destroys homes, as well as much of the sugar crop 1979 | MMM-Socialist party coalition sweeps the elections 1982 |

| August: New Socialist government formed | January 1984: Mauritius expels all Libyan diplomats | Spring 1984: New splits in the labor party threaten the governing coalition |

MAURITIUS

Mauritius, "the sugary pearle of the Indian Ocean," was not permanently inhabited until 1722. Today nearly a million people of South Asian, Euro-African, Chinese, and other origins live on the island nation, which is about one-half the size of Rhode Island. The major force behind this growth has been the labor and capital needs of the local sugar industry, which has always been the dominant influence on the island's development. In recent years, ninety percent of the cultivated land has been planted with sugar. Sugar provides for nearly one-half of the nation's export earnings as well as about a third of its employment.

Although by regional standards most Mauritians enjoy a relatively good quality of life, dependency on sugar has had both social and economic costs. The price of imported food and other items as well as local wages have often risen faster than the international price of sugar, which has tended to fluctuate. In addition, major inequalities exist within the local sugar industry itself.

THE PEOPLE

The first sugar plantations were founded during the eighteenth century by French settlers, who used African slaves for labor. Approximately one-quarter of the Mauritian population is presently of mixed Euro-African (Creole) origin, while another two percent claims pure French descent. This latter group has traditionally formed the economic elite of the island. Today over fifty-five percent of the agricultural land is comprised of twenty-one large Franco-

Mauritian plantations, while the rest is divided between nearly twenty-eight thousand small land-holdings. French cultural influence also remains strong. Most of the newspapers on the island are in French. However, most Mauritians speak a local, French-influenced, Creole language.

In 1810 Mauritius was occupied by the British, who remained and ruled the island until 1968. When the British abolished slavery in 1835, landowners turned to large-scale use of indentured laborers from what was then British India to work on the plantations. Today nearly two-thirds of the population is of South Asian descent; over half are Hindu, and the rest Muslims. A number of Chinese also arrived during the nineteenth century.

POLITICS

Since 1886 Mauritius has maintained an uninterrupted record of parliamentary-style democracy, although the majority of the island population only achieved the right to vote after World War II. Ethnic divisions play an important political role, and this is often reflected in voting patterns. It is important to note, however, that ethnic constituency building has not led, in recent years, to ethnic polarization. Other factors—such as class and ideology—have been important in shaping the character of political allegiance. All post-independence governments have been formed by coalitions.

In June 1982, a coalition between the Marxist Mauritian Militant Movement (MMM) and the Socialist Party was elected by a landslide. Within months a split emerged between the two parties as well as

within the MMM itself. New elections were held in August 1983, and a coalition led by the Socialist Party, whose ranks had become enlarged by defections from the MMM, won. The present Socialist prime minister, Aneerood Jugnauth, was also the leader of the last government, but then he served as a member of the MMM. Mauritius will soon sever its remaining links with the British Crown and become a republic. The new president will be Seewoosagur Ramgoolam, who was prime minister between 1968 and 1982.

POPULATION AND DEVELOPMENT

A major challenge facing any Mauritian government is the rising number of unemployed. The elimination of malaria after World War II triggered a population explosion on the island. By the early 1970s the population growth rate had fallen substantially. The earlier baby boom has, nonetheless, put an increasing strain on the nation's job market. Despite the growth of light manufacturing, processing, and tourism, up to a third of the population—particularly the young—are without work. Underemployment is also a serious problem. Falling sugar prices and a major cyclone have recently aggravated Mauritius' problems.

DEVELOPMENT

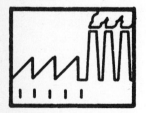

During the 1970s, a number of new industries were attracted to Mauritius by the establishment of Export Processing Zones (EPZ), within which investors enjoy significant tax advantages. Although a modest success, the EPZs have not ended Mauritius' dependence on sugar or solved the growing problem of unemployment.

FREEDOM

Political pluralism and human rights are respected on Mauritius. The nation has over thirty political parties, of which about a half-dozen are important at any given time.

HEALTH/WELFARE

Medical and most educational expenses are free. Food prices are heavily subsidized. Rising government deficits threaten future social spending.

ACHIEVEMENTS

Perhaps Mauritius' most important modern achievement has been its successful efforts to reduce its birth rate. This has been brought about by government-backed family planning as well as by increased economic opportunities for women.

Rwanda

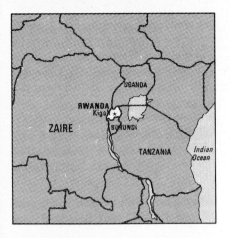

GEOGRAPHY

Area in Square Kilometers (Miles):
26,338 (10,169)
Land Usage: 33% cultivated; 33%
pastureland; 33% other
Capital (Population): Kigali
(117,749—1978)
Climate: temperate

PEOPLE

Population

Total: 5,109,000 (1982 est.)
Per Square Kilometer (Mile): 200
(511)
Annual Growth Rate: 3.2%
Rural/Urban Population Ratio: 96/4
Age: 44% below 15 years

Health

Life Expectancy at Birth: 46 years
Infant Death Rate (Ratio): 107/1,000
Average Caloric Intake: 94% of
FAO minimum
Physicians Available (Ratio):
1/31,510
Access to Safe Water: 35%

Languages

Official: French; Kinyarwanda
Others Spoken: Kiswahili

Religion(s)

54% Christian; 45% indigenous
beliefs; 1% Muslim

Education

Adult Literacy Rate: 62% males;
37% females
School Attendance: primary: 75%
boys, 69% girls; secondary: 3%
boys; 1% girls
Teacher/Student Ratio: 1/168

RWANDA'S HISTORIANS

A number of specialists were attached to the ruling dynasty of the traditional kingdom of Rwanda, including several categories of official historians. Each group was responsible for preserving particular materials. Some were genealogists who told the lists of kings and queens; some told *ibisigo*, dynastic poems that glorified the rulers; and others preserved secrets of the dynasty. This traditional knowledge was all passed down orally, since the language was not written. Particular families were responsible for passing this knowledge from one generation to another; it was memorized exactly. Such historical information is different from the written sources upon which Western historians have relied, but it is valid data that can be used in the reconstruction of Rwanda's past.

COMMUNICATION

Telephones: 4,600
Radios: 152,000
Newspapers: 1 daily; total circulation
5,400

TRANSPORTATION

Highways—Kilometers (Miles): 9,020
(5,605)
Railroads—Kilometers (Miles): none
One international airport

GOVERNMENT

Type: republic
Constitution: November 24, 1962
Former Colonial Status: German;
Belgian
Independence Date: July 1, 1962
Head of State: Major General
Juvenal Habyarimana (president)
Branches: president; cabinet;
legislative (National Development
Council); Supreme Court
Legal System: based on German and
Belgian Civil Law and customary
law
Political Parties: National Revolu-
tionary Movement for Development
(MRND)
Suffrage: universal for adults

MILITARY

Number of Armed Forces: 5,150
Armed Forces/Population: 1/1,090
*Military Expenditures (% of Central
Government Expenditures):*
$22,000,000 (14%)
Nuclear Weapons Status: none
Current Hostilities: none

ECONOMY

Currency ($ US Equivalent): 80
Rwanda francs = $1
GDP: $1,260,000,000
Per Capita Income/GNP: $260
Workforce: 91% agriculture; 2% in-
dustry; 7% services
Inflation Rate: 14.2% (1970-1980);
7.5% (1982)
Natural Resources: tungsten; tin
Agriculture: coffee; tea; pyrethrum;
beans; potatoes
Industry: food processing; mining;
light consumer goods
Energy Production: 38,000 kw
capacity
Energy Consumption Per Capita: 31
kwh

FOREIGN TRADE

Exports: coffee; tin; pyrethrum;
tungsten; tea; cassiterite
Imports: textiles; foodstuffs;
machinery; petroleum products
Major Trading Partners: United
States; Japan; EEC countries
Foreign Debt: $324,700,000
*Selected Membership in International
Organizations:* UN; OAU; Associate
Member, European Economic Com-
munity (EEC); African Development
Bank; Non-Aligned Movement

| Mwami Kigeri Rwabugiri expands and consolidates the kingdom **1860-1895** | Belgium rules Rwanda as a mandate of the League of Nations **1916** | Hutu rebellion **1959** | Rwanda becomes independent; Gregoire Kayibana is president, and Parmehutu becomes the majority party **1962** | Major General Juvenal Habyarimana seizes power **1973** | A new party, the National Revolutionary Movement for Development (MRND), is formed **1975** | A new Constitution is approved in a nation-wide referendum; Habyarimana is re-elected president **1978** | Unsuccessful coup attempt **1980** |

1983

March: Rwanda and Uganda dispute citizenship of thousands of refugees on both sides of the border

June: Habyarimana is elected for a third term as head of MNRD

December: Election for 50 members of Parliament and for president; Habyarimana is sole presidential candidate

RWANDA

In the beginning (according to a dynastic poem of Rwanda) the godlike ruler, Kigwa, fashioned a test by which to choose his successor. He gave each of his sons a bowl of milk to guard during the night. His son Gatwa drank the milk; Yahutu slept and spilled the milk. Only Gatutsi guarded it well. The myth reflects a reality that Rwandans (Banyarwanda as the inhabitants are sometimes called) adhered to throughout their history: The Twa, pygmy peoples, (one percent of the population) have been the outcasts; the Hutu (eighty-nine percent) have been the servants; and the Tutsi (ten percent) have been the aristocrats. Hutu and Tutsi were linked through personal "cattle contracts" by which Hutu received cattle and protection and Tutsi received services. There were many other ties between these groups, whose members are still evenly distributed throughout the country. All of the people were subjects of the *mwami,* or king, who was very powerful and who headed a royal family that had a special status in Rwanda.

RADICAL CHANGES

This society no longer exists in its historical form, and the changes have been revolutionary. During the early decades of the twentieth century, when first the Germans (and later the Belgians) ruled through few administrators, primarily using the existing political system, traditional caste distinctions and royal prerogatives were maintained. New ideas and practices were introduced through Catholic missions and schools and through the encouragement of growing cash crops, especially coffee. Even before the colonial era, discontent was evident, due to the pressure of people and herds on already crowded lands. As time went by, these problems increased.

The most radical developments occurred in the late 1950s and the early 1960s. Gradually, in the late 1950s, because of pressure from the UN, Belgium began to introduce political opportunities to the native Rwandans. In 1959, after the death of the *mwami,* oppression by the Tutsi who took power led to bloody Hutu uprisings against the Tutsi. In 1961 Hutu leaders and the Hutu majority party, *Parmehutu* (the Hutu Emancipation Movement), gained support, won victories at the polls, and became the governors of Rwanda. The aforementioned uprisings and later Tutsi attacks and Hutu reactions in 1963-1964 caused thousands of deaths and the flight of tens of thousands to neighboring countries.

HABYARIMANA TAKES POWER

Major General Juvenal Habyarimana, a Hutu from the north, took power in a coup in 1973 and initiated the National Revolutionary Movement for Development (MRND) to bring together the hostile elements in the country. Habyarimana has maintained tight control over Rwanda, although a few opportunities for popular initiative have been evident recently. Voters have been given choices of electoral candidates; union activity is to be allowed, and church publications are allowed to criticize the government.

Hostility between Hutu and Tutsi remains. In an effort to keep down friction, an informal quota system, which allocates jobs and educational opportunity according to the size of ethnic groups, has been established. Large numbers of Hutu and Tutsi left Rwanda during the upheavals of the late 1950s and 1960s and took up residence in nearby countries such as Burundi and Uganda. Formerly, people had moved back and forth among these countries, and up to 300 thousand Rwandans had worked as migrants on Ugandan coffee farms in earlier years. The extreme population pressure in Rwanda (one of Africa's most densely populated countries) has encouraged young people to migrate and has made the government reluctant to encourage those outside to return. Now, however, refugees and migrants in Uganda are being evicted. In the last few years, approximately forty-five thousand refugees have returned to Rwanda. In 1982, thousands were pushed from their homes in Uganda, supposedly because of involvement in property thefts. Many are now on the borders waiting for the two governments to decide their fate.

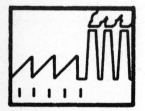

DEVELOPMENT

With the help of the European Economic Community (EEC), Rwanda is attempting to increase the variety of crops grown for export so it may become less dependent on coffee. Tea, tobacco, and pyrethrum are among the products whose growth is being encouraged.

FREEDOM

The 1982 elections to the National Development Council gave some indication of the state of Rwanda's political freedom. Electors were offered a choice of 128 candidates for sixty-four offices. Candidates had to be active members of MVND, with secondary school education and French training. The list of candidates was compiled by the provincial governors.

HEALTH/WELFARE

The government recognizes that the over 3.2 rate of population growth can eat up economic gains as well as increasing already severe pressures on land. A national population office was created in 1982, and resources committed to family planning have increased.

ACHIEVEMENTS

Abbé Alexis Kagame, a Rwandan Roman Catholic churchman and scholar, has written studies of traditional Rwanda poetry and has written poetry about many of the traditions and rituals. Some of his works have been composed in Kinyarwanda, the official language of Rwanda, and translated into French. He has gained an international reputation among scholars.

Seychelles

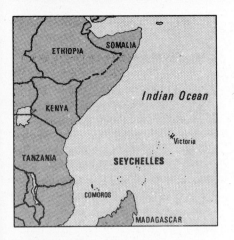

GEOGRAPHY

Area in Square Kilometers (Miles):
308 (119)
Land Usage: 54% arable; 17% wood
and forest land; 29% other
Capital (Population): Port Victoria
(23,012—1977)
Climate: subtropical; marine

PEOPLE

Population
Total: 64,000 (1982 est.)
Per Square Kilometer (Mile): 230
(537)
Annual Growth Rate: 1.2%

Health
Life Expectancy at Birth: 65 years
Infant Death Rate (Ratio):
26.6/1,000

Languages
Official: English; French
Others Spoken: Creole

Religion(s)
98% Christian; 2% other

Education
Adult Literacy Rate: 56% males;
60% females

COMMUNICATION

Telephones: 5,000
Radios: 26,000
Newspapers: 2 dailies; total circulation 3,500

THE NATIONAL YOUTH SERVICE

One of the most controversial programs of the new regime has been the National Youth Service (NYS), a work-study camp for the nation's sixteen and seventeen-year-olds, which will become mandatory in 1984. During the two year period of enrollment, contact between the students and the outside world is quite restricted. At the camp, practical training, politicization, and strict social discipline are combined in an above-the-board attempt by the state to mold a new Seychellois—one committed to egalitarian ideals and less inclined toward alcoholism and the procreation of "illegitimate" children (marriage is a minority institution on the isles). How effective the NYS will be in meeting its goals remains an open question. Initial introduction of the program provoked violent riots.

TRANSPORTATION

Highways—Kilometers (Miles): 196
(121)
Railroads—Kilometers (Miles): none
One international airport

GOVERNMENT

Type: republic
Constitution: March 26, 1979
Former Colonial Status: British
Independence Date: June 28, 1976
Head of State: France Albert René
(president)
Branches: president; Cabinet; National Assembly; Supreme Court
Legal System: based on English
Common Law; French Civil Law;
and customary law
Political Parties: Seychelles People's
Progressive Front
Suffrage: universal for adults

MILITARY

Number of Armed Forces: 3,250
Armed Forces/Population: 1/20
Nuclear Weapons Status: none
Foreign Aid: Tanzania; USSR; People's Republic of China
Current Hostilities: none

ECONOMY

Currency ($ US Equivalent): 6
Seychelles rupees = $1
GDP: $90,000,000
Per Capita Income/GNP: $1,330
Inflation Rate: 12% (1982)
Natural Resources: agricultural products; fish
Agriculture: vanilla; coconuts;
cinnamon
Industry: tourism; copra and vanilla
processing; coconut oil; construction
Energy Production: 16,000 kw
capacity
Energy Consumption Per Capita: 703
kwh

FOREIGN TRADE

Exports: cinnamon and coconut
products
Imports: food; tobacco; manufactured
goods; machinery; transport equipment; petroleum products; textiles
Major Trading Partners: India;
United States; UK; Kenya
Foreign Debt:$59,100,000
*Selected Membership in International
Organizations:* UN; OAU; African
Development Bank; Non-Aligned
Movement

| French settlement begins 1771 | British rule established 1814 | British end slavery 1830 | Seychelles is detached from Mauritius by British and made a Crown colony 1903 | Legislative Council with qualified suffrage introduced 1948 | Universal suffrage 1967 | Independence 1976 | Coup of René against Mancham 1977 | Mercenary coup attempt fails 1981 | Internal coup is quashed by pro-government force 1982 | 1983 |

REPUBLIC OF SEYCHELLES

The Republic of the Seychelles consists of a series of archipelagos off the coast of East Africa, with a total land area roughly equal to that of Martha's Vineyard, Massachusetts, and Nantucket, Rhode Island. Over the last decade, the lives of the Seychellois have been dramatically altered through rapid economic growth, political independence, and the establishment of a self-styled revolutionary socialist state. Behind this transformation has been the political rivalry of two very different, but equally controversial, leaders—James Mancham and Albert René—who together have guided the nation from an isolated colonial past into an uncertain future.

Although their existence was long known by Indian Ocean mariners, the Seychelles were not permanently inhabited until the arrival of French colonists and their slaves in 1771. A half century later, the British took over and controlled the territory until 1976.

ROOTS OF CONFLICT

Today's political struggle had its roots in 1963, when Mancham's Democratic Party and René's People's United Party were established. The former favored free enterprise and the retention of the British imperial connection, while the latter advocated an independent socialist state. Electoral victories in 1970 and 1974 allowed Mancham, as chief minister, to pursue his dream of turning the Seychelles into a "little Switzerland" through policies designed to attract outside investment. Mancham was notably successful in promoting tourism, which, following the opening of

an international airport in 1971, fueled an economic boom. Between 1970 and 1980, per capita income rose from nearly $150 to over $1,700. At the same time, however, Mancham gained a reputation in many quarters as a freewheeling jet-setter who was indifferent to government detail. Some people believed Mancham's approach offered capital from wealthy outsiders. His opponents, including the idealistic and outwardly austere René, saw Mancham's playboy life-style as a national embarrassment and contended that his administration was unconcerned with the impoverished majority of the population.

In 1974 Mancham, in an about face, joined René in advocating the island's independence. The following year the Democratic Party, despite its parliamentary majority, set up a coalition government with the People's United Party. At midnight on June 28-29, 1976, the Seychelles became independent, with Mancham as president and René as prime minister. From the beginning, this was a curious union, given the differences in personality and politics between the two.

COUP BY RENÉ

On June 5, 1977, when Mancham was out of the country, René, with Tanzanian assistance, staged his successful "coup of sixty rifles," thus turning a temporary separation into a permanent one. A period of rule by decree gave way in 1979, without the benefit of a referendum, to a new constitutional framework in which the People's Progressive Front, successor to the People's United Party, was recognized as the sole political voice.

| August: General elections, under single party Constitution, lead to new cabinet | January 1984: Franco-Seychelles talks lead to greater political and economic cooperation between the two countries | June 1984: President René is reelected, unopposed, to the presidency |

The first years of René's rule were characterized by continuing prosperity, coupled with an impressive expansion of social welfare programs. Nonetheless, enemies of the regime, both at home and abroad, have been active in plotting its overthrow. In November of 1981, a group of international mercenaries, who were believed to have had backing from Kenya and South Africa as well as exiled Seychellois, were forced to flee in a highjacked jet after a shootout with the new Seychelles' army. During the following spring, however, one-fifth of the army was itself detained without trial following another successful coup attempt.

CONCLUSION

The coup and various attempted counter-coups have contributed to a recent decline in tourism, which in turn has depressed the economy. Although the Seychelles government is seeking to restore and expand tourism, it is also eager to diversify the nation's economic base by investing heavily in agriculture and fishing. Given the country's legal jurisdiction over some 400 thousand square miles of excellent fishing waters, official attempts to build a modern seafood industry hold enormous potential, despite the problems of a shortage of skilled manpower and the threat of foreign poaching.

DEVELOPMENT

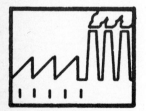

The government continues to pursue a flexible economic program designed to encourage healthy outside investment while promoting the growth of local government-owned companies. The environmental effects of development have become an important public issue.

FREEDOM

Since the 1977 coup, press censorship, mail openings, preventive detention, forced exile, and political indoctrination of the youth have become a part of life. There have been a few reported disappearances, but no confirmed cases of torture or officially sanctioned assassinations have been publicized.

HEALTH/WELFARE

Under the new government, a national health program has been established, and private practice has been abolished. Free lunch programs have raised nutritional levels among the young. Education is also free up to age 14.

ACHIEVEMENTS

Under its present government, Seychelles has become a world leader in wildlife preservation. An important aspect of the nation's conservation efforts has been the designation of Aldabra Island as an international wildlife refuge.

Somalia

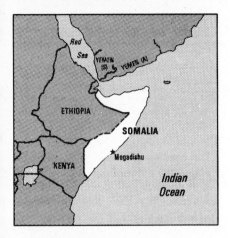

GEOGRAPHY

Area in Square Kilometers (Miles): 638,000 (246,331)
Land Usage: 13% arable; 32% grazing; 14% scrub and forests; 41% desert, urban, or other
Capital (Population): Mogadishu (400,000—1973 est.)
Climate: semi-arid; arid

PEOPLE

Population
Total: 5,116,000 (1982 est.)
Per Square Kilometer (Mile): 8 (21)
Annual Growth Rate: 7.2%
Rural/Urban Population Ratio: 70/30
Age: 45% below 15 years

Health
Life Expectancy at Birth: 39 years
Infant Death Rate (Ratio): 147/1,000
Average Caloric Intake: 100% FAO minimum
Physicians Available (Ratio): 1/14,920
Access to Safe Water: 33%

Languages
Official: Somali
Others Spoken: Arabic; Italian; English; others

Religion(s)
99% Muslim; 1% other

Education
Adult Literacy Rate: 60% (1978)
School Attendance: primary: 38% boys, 21% girls; secondary: 16% boys, 6% girls

COMMUNICATION

Telephones: 6,000
Radios: 120,000
Newspapers: 1 daily; total circulation 4,500

TRANSPORTATION

Highways—Kilometers (Miles): 15,215 (9,454)
Railroads—Kilometers (Miles): none
Six international airports

GOVERNMENT

Type: republic; under revolutionary military regime since 1969
Constitution: 1979
Former Colonial Status: Italian; British
Independence Date: July 1, 1960
Head of State: Major General Mohamed Siad Barre
Branches: executive authority exercised by the Supreme Revolutionary Council, headed by the president; National Assembly; Supreme Court
Political Parties: Somali Revolutionary Socialist Party

MILITARY

Number of Armed Forces: 62,550
Armed Forces/Population: 1/98
Military Expenditures: $95,000,000 (1979)
Nuclear Weapons Status: none
Current Hostilities: border disputes with Ethiopia; conflicts with Ethiopian-backed Somali rebels

ECONOMY

Currency ($ US Equivalent): 15 Somali shillings = $1
GDP: $411,000,000
Per Capita Income/GNP: $290
Workforce: 82% agriculture; 8% industry; 10% services
Inflation Rate: 12.4% (1970-1980); 40% (1982)
Natural Resources: uranium; timber; fish
Agriculture: livestock; bananas; sugar cane; cotton; cereals
Industry: sugar refining; tuna and beef canneries; textiles; iron rod plants; petroleum refining
Energy Production: 90,000 kw capacity
Energy Consumption Per Capita: 20 kwh

FOREIGN TRADE

Exports: livestock; hides; skins; bananas
Imports: textiles; cereals; transport equipment; machinery; construction materials; petroleum products
Major Trading Partners: Arab countries; Italy
Foreign Debt: $1,316,000,000
Selected Membership in International Organizations: UN; OAU; Arab League; African Development Bank; Non-Aligned Movement

SOMALI DEMOCRATIC REPUBLIC

"Abundance and scarcity are never far apart; the rich and poor frequent the same house."

(Quoted by I.M. Lewis in *The Somali Democracy.*)

This popular Somali proverb testifies to the delicate balance between subsistence and famine in a dry land where living is not easy. The majority of Somalian peoples (eighty percent) are pastoralists. The country, located on the horn of Africa, is best suited to a herding life. Ordinary people, knowledgeable about their environment, have adjusted their life to it. Agriculture is possible in the area between the Juba and Shebelle rivers and in a portion of the north. There, people raise crops as well as keeping animals. In the other areas, people move to secure good grazing for their herds of cattle, camels, sheep, and goats. Although cattle are valued more than other animals, owners vary the composition of their herds to accommodate the changing conditions of the land.

Such a life-style does not lend itself to city living. A half dozen families may live in encampments and move as circumstances dictate. However, despite such small community groups, all Somalis have clan relationships that extend over a large area. Moreover, Somalia is a country whose citizens, unlike those of most African countries, are all of one group and all speak Somali. Islam, the state religion, is also a binding feature, and Islamic culture and traditions as well as the faith are deep-rooted.

Somalia links Africa and Arabia, and Islam is one of the bridges. The nation's art and poetry also indicate shared influences. The art and poetry are sophisticated forms of expression, familiar to everyone. In their richness and elaborateness, they contrast with and complement the spare environment and simplicity of home, clothing, and utensils. The traditional values of Somali ways of life have been maintained as life changes.

Ecological changes and other influences, such as the policies of the present government, have affected Somali life and the Somali nation.

POLITICAL DEVELOPMENTS IN RECENT TIMES

Although Somalis traditionally have shared a common language and common

(United Nations photo)

Somalis who had lived under the different administrations of the British and Italians in two colonial territories were united when independent Somalia was formed in 1960.

life-styles, colonial policies divided the peoples. For about seventy-five years, the northern regions were governed by British authorities who used English and British forms of administration, while the southern and eastern portions of this boomerang-shaped country were subject to Italian rule, language, and other influences. The different institutions colonialism imposed have contributed to recent seccession movements in the north, as people have become dissatisfied with Somali government politics.

The Somalis became independent in 1960. In 1969, Siad Barre, the present president of Somalia, came to power through a military coup. He introduced radical changes in governing concepts and organization that, in the beginning, appeared innovative and significant. Under Barre's leadership, a scientific socialism was to be built on an African base and not in conflict with Islam. Efforts were made to develop local councils, to initiate committees at the workplace, and to increase participation in government. New civil and labor codes were written. A new political party, the

Somali Revolutionary Socialist Party (SRSP), was developed, and a Constitution was approved in a national referendum. The government program, including literacy education, was spread among the nomadic groups through a rural development campaign in 1974-1975. Roads were built in order to encourage movements between regions. The theme was: "Tribalism divides, Socialism unites." Tribalism in this case stood for the divisions of clans.

Gradually, the promise of Barre's early years in office has faded. Little is being done to follow through the developments of the early 1970s. Indeed Barre seems to be bypassing the institutions he had advocated. A national cult has grown up around the president, confirming other tendencies toward autocracy. The president has taken on emergency powers in recent times. He has relieved members of the governing council of their duties and has surrounded himself with clansmen and close kin and isolated himself from the broader public.

IRREDENTISM AND RESISTANCE

Barre has also isolated Somalia in Africa through the pursual of policies called irre-

Said Barre comes to power through an army coup; Supreme Revolutionary Council established
1969

Ogaden war in Ethiopia results in Somalia's defeat
1977-1978

State of emergency declared; pact signed with the US—a diplomatic realignment after Soviet ties dissolve
1980

100% devaluation of currency
1981

March: State of emergency is ended; Barre visits US

March-April: Two resistance movements unite in the Democratic Front for the Salvation of Somalia
1982

●1983

dentist that would unite all Somali peoples. Somalis live in Kenya and Ethiopia, and some ex-patriate Somalis want to join the Somali nation. Their aspirations have had some official support. Somalis in Kenya and Ethiopia initiated guerrilla warfare in an attempt to free themselves from these countries so they could join Somalia. The bad relations between Somalia and Kenya were eased in 1982 when Barre and President Moi of Kenya discussed the matter in person. The war in the Ogaden region of Ethiopia has been less easily solved. Somali aggression was bitterly resisted by Ethiopia (which was victorious against Somali in 1977) and has been condemned by all members of the OAU.

The policy of irredentism has had other repercussions. It has committed the Barre regime to a massive buildup of the army, which now numbers over sixty thousand, and to negotiations for arms from the great powers. In the early years of the Barre government, there were close ties between Somalia and the USSR. Then, in 1977, in a diplomatic revolution, the USSR became allied with Somalia's enemy, Ethiopia. As a result, Barre developed ties with the United States. Now United States Marines conduct military exercises in Somalia, and the United States uses air and naval facilities developed by the USSR at Berbera. Somalia is the third largest recipient of American aid in Africa.

In recent years, Somali resistance movements have developed outside the country. In the spring of 1982, the Democratic Front for the Salvation of Somalia, headquartered in Addis Ababa, and the London-based Somali National Movement agreed to unify their forces "against the fascist regime in Somalia" and proposed a future democratic program.

REFUGEES IN SOMALIA

Somali life has been disrupted by the droughts and their repercussions. Somali is a poor country materially, with a per capita income estimated by the UN of $197. The drought of 1974-1975 led to the development of refugee camps—140 thousand nomadic peoples were relocated to agricultural areas through the assistance of a Soviet airlift. There, people have had to plan their life anew. In 1979-1980 the drought affecting Ethiopia brought thousands of people into Somalia. Although there is now more rain, the refugee situation continues. At least 700 thousand persons reside in the thirty-four refugee camps of the National Refugee Commission, and relief agencies are anticipating and planning for a total of 900 thousand people. Thus, about one in every six or seven Somali residents is a refugee. Ninety-one percent of the refugees are women and children. Men leave the refugee camps to care for the herds that have not been decimated by the drought.

The situation has put pressure on Somalia's budget. But at the same time, the refugee situation has meant a massive injection of outside aid, constituting up to one-third of the GNP. New sources of livelihood are also needed for those who have lost their herds and left their homes. In a country with a seventeen hundred-mile coastline, fish are a potentially rich source of food, and fishing projects are presently a top priority.

February: Barre offers political amnesty to all political prisoners

November: US Marines conduct military exercises in Somali

January 1984: Ethiopian MIGS reportedly attacked Northwestern Somalia; Ebel Somali National Movement claims 1,500 Somali government soldiers defected in this month

A LIVELY INFORMAL ECONOMY

Most people, even the refugees, continue to hold to the traditional herding life. Efforts to increase livestock production seem to have had little success, but the exports of livestock—especially cattle—to the Middle East is massive and involves over 1.25 million animals yearly. Often the cattle are sold through private traders whose financial deals and supplies of imported items (through unofficial channels) may not benefit the government; they certainly aid large numbers of individuals. The increased migration of Somali workers to the Gulf States has been an alternative source of employment and sustenance. The workers bring back foreign exchange and goods.

All of these elements of present-day Somalian history—the policies of government (and the resistance to them), the moves for Somali unification throughout the region, the great changes wrought by the refugee movements, the influence of great power competition, and the economic benefits gained from informal relations with the Gulf and other states—may change the life of ordinary pastoral Somalis in contemporary times.

DEVELOPMENT

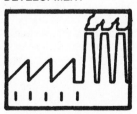

Labor migration to the Gulf States involves 100 thousand to 200 thousand Somalis whose yearly earnings may average $5,000. Some of the money is sent home to families. Wages are also used to purchase spare parts, cement, trucks, and other essentials. These items, formerly allowed into the country under a special arrangement, have been restricted since 1981.

FREEDOM

Freedoms are restricted in Somalia. The media are government-owned, and criticisms of the government are prohibited. Outside publications, such as *Newsweek* may be censored. Public rallies are usually government-organized, and the country's only labor union is government-controlled.

HEALTH/WELFARE

Oxfam America's solar pumps provide sixty to seventy percent of the water supply for refugees in the northwest area and are also used in traditional Islamic cooperatives, where they provide drinking water and irrigation for vegetable gardens.

ACHIEVEMENTS

The Somali language has effectively taken the place of the colonial languages (British and Italian) as the official language. A written version of Somali was developed in the 1970s, and mass literacy campaigns were waged during that decade by teachers and students who went out to teach nomadic citizens how to read and write. Sixty percent had passed the literacy test by 1977.

Sudan

GEOGRAPHY

Area in Square Kilometers (Miles): 2,505,813 (967,500)
Land Usage: 37% arable; 15% grazing; 33% desert, waste, and urban; 15% forests
Capital (Population): Khartoum (561,000—1980)
Climate: arid and semi-arid in north; tropical in south

PEOPLE

Population
Total: 19,451,000 (1982 est.)
Per Square Kilometer (Mile): 8 (20)
Annual Growth Rate: 3.1%
Rural/Urban Population Ratio: 75/25
Age: 39% below 15 years

Health
Life Expectancy at Birth: 46 years
Infant Death Rate (Ratio): 124/1,000
Average Caloric Intake: 101% of FAO minimum
Physicians Available (Ratio): 1/8,780
Access to Safe Water: 46%

Languages
Official: Arabic
Others Spoken: English; Nuer; Dinka; Shilluki; Masalatis; Fur; Nubians; others

Religion(s)
70% Muslim; 25% indigenous beliefs; 5% Christianity

Education
Adult Literacy Rate: 38% males; 14% females
School Attendance: primary: 61% boys, 43% girls; secondary: 20% boys, 16% girls
Teacher/Student Ratio: 1/55

COMMUNICATION

Telephones: 63,400
Radios: 1,330,000
Televisions: 105,000
Newspapers: 3 dailies; total circulation 180,000

TRANSPORTATION

Highways—Kilometers (Miles): 20,000 (12,428)
Railroads—Kilometers (Miles): 5,516 (3,427)
Five international airports

GOVERNMENT

Type: republic; under military control
Constitution: May 8, 1973
Former Colonial Status: British (jointly administered by Britain and Egypt)
Independence Date: January 1, 1956
Head of State: General Gaafar Muhammed Nimeiri (president and prime minister)
Branches: president and Cabinet; People's Assembly; Supreme Court
Legal System: based on English Common Law and Islamic law
Political Parties: Sudanese Socialist Union
Suffrage: universal for adults

MILITARY

Number of Armed Forces: 71,000
Armed Forces/Population: 1/279
Military Expenditures: $245,000,000 (1980)
Nuclear Weapons Status: none
Current Hostilities: internal regional conflicts; Anya Nya II movement; Sudan People's Liberation Movement (SPLM); Southern People's Liberation Army; tense relations with Libya

ECONOMY

Currency ($ US Equivalent): 1.1 Sudanese pounds = $1
GDP: $9,290,000,000
Per Capita Income/GNP: $440
Workforce: 72% agriculture; 10% industry; 18% services
Inflation Rate: 20-30% (1980-1982)
Natural Resources: iron ore; copper; chrome; other industrial metals
Agriculture: cotton; peanuts; sesame seeds; gum arabic; sorghum; wheat; sugar cane; livestock
Industry: cement; textiles; pharmaceuticals; shoes; food processing
Energy Production: 310,000 kw capacity
Energy Consumption Per Capita: 65 kwh

FOREIGN TRADE

Exports: cotton; peanuts; gum arabic; livestock
Imports: manufactured goods; machinery and transportation equipment; food; livestock
Major Trading Partners: European Community; People's Republic of China; United States; Japan; Egypt; India
Foreign Debt: $6,004,000,000
Selected Membership in International Organizations: UN; OAU; Arab League; African Development Bank; Non-Aligned Movement

| Egypt invades Northern Sudan 1820 | Mahdist Revolt begins 1881 | Anglo-Egyptian Condominium begins 1899 | Independence 1956 | Nimeiri comes to power 1969 | Hostilities end in Southern Sudan 1972 | 1983 |

September: Islamic law replaces former penal code

February 1984: Foreign oil and construction companies in the south are attacked by rebels

March 1984: Ethiopia withdraws from scheduled Sudan-Ethiopian talks, charging US-Sudan collusion against Ethiopia

REPUBLIC OF THE SUDAN

Sudan's vast size and strategic location have long provided the nation with unique opportunities and potential liabilities. Covering nearly one million square miles, the Sudan is the largest nation in Africa.

Of the eighteen million people of the Sudan, approximately two-thirds are Muslim; one-third are Christian or practice local religions. But this religious division between the largely Muslim north and the non-Muslim south belies the ethnic diversity within each of these regions.

Sudan is a single-party state, and the Sudanese Socialist Union (SSU) is the only legal party. The military, which brought the current regime to power in a coup of 1969, continues to play a vital role in Sudanese politics.

President Jaafar Nimeiri assumed power as chairman of the Revolutionary Command Council on May 25, 1969, and quickly moved to consolidate his power by eliminating challenges to his government from the Islamic right and the Communist left. By the fall of 1971, he was sufficiently confident of his position to hold a referendum on his presidency, in which he won 98.6 percent of the vote, and was sworn in for the first of his three six-year terms.

INTERNAL PROBLEMS

The ethnic and religious divisions between the largely Muslim north and the non-Muslim south have not yet been overcome. Tensions between north and south have their roots in the history of the Sudan. The first Muslim Arabs arrived in the Sudan in the seventh century, and the new religion was slowly adopted by the peoples of the northern Sudan, some of whom had previously been Christians. A trans-Saharan slave trade developed as early as the seventeenth century. Raids were made on the non-Muslim peoples to the south. This practice continued well into the nineteenth century, and it is one of the main reasons for the sensitive relationship between northern and southern Sudan today. Tensions between northerners and southerners have increased because of the neglect of development in the south and the replacement of Sudan's former penal code with the Islamic code, the Sharia, which has been arbitrarily applied. Fighting has occurred, and people fear that the civil war has been rekindled.

ECONOMIC PROSPECTS

Sudan is still one of the poorest nations in the world, with a per capita GNP of under $300. Development plans have been hindered by the inadequacy of Sudan's transportation infrastructure, by the lack of foreign exchange, and by rampant inflation. Over half a million refugees, who have fled to Sudan from neighboring countries, add a burden to the already weak economy, and they are a source of friction between Sudan and some of its neighbors.

Sudan has tremendous agriculture potential; however, it needs to find a means of developing that potential to get tangible results. Most development schemes for the Sudan attempt to capitalize on the country's greatest resource: the waters of the Nile.

Oil has been discovered in western and southern Sudan in quantities believed to be sufficient to meet the country's domestic needs. The oilfields are now being exploited by Chevron and Royal Dutch Shell Oil Companies. With the decision not to build a refinery in the south, the oil will be piped to the Red Sea. The operations and the development of the pipeline are now at a standstill because of attacks by rebel groups.

RELATIONS WITH OTHER COUNTRIES

Sudan's vital geopolitical position is due not only to its location on the Nile and its intermediary role between African and Arab nations but also because it has borders with eight countries: Egypt, Libya, Chad, Central African Republic, Zaire, Uganda, Kenya, and Ethiopia. Only the Red Sea lies between Sudan and Saudi Arabia.

Recently Sudan has been courted by both Egypt and Saudi Arabia. Egypt's President Hosni Mubarak and Sudan's Nimeiri signed a charter in October 1982 to integrate their countries' economic, military, social, and cultural policies. Saudi Arabia has supported the Sudan economically, in particular by subsidizing Sudan's petroleum purchases.

DEVELOPMENT

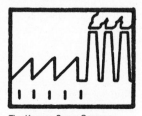

The Kenana Sugar Company, established in 1976, grows sugar cane, which is irrigated with Nile water and processed on the spot for domestic and foreign consumption. The company employs 12,700 people and runs one of the largest sugar refineries in the world.

FREEDOM

In September, 1983, President Nimeiri ordered that all thirteen thousand of Sudan's prison inmates be released and be given a small sum of money to ease their re-entry into normal life. Sudan has recently adopted Islamic law to replace the old civil penal code. Muslims and non-Muslims alike who are convicted of crimes will be subject to Islamic punishments.

HEALTH/WELFARE

Sudan's population is growing at a rate of 2.8 percent per year—one of the highest rates in the world. Infant mortality is 124 per one thousand. The Sudanese Family Planning Association has played a pioneering role in educating women to the dangers of repeated pregnancies. The association hopes the government will establish a family planning program and a national population policy.

ACHIEVEMENTS

Work has begun on a 900-mile-long double pipe line from the Bentiu oil fields to Port Sudan on the Red Sea. The estimated cost is 2.5 billion. The 260 mile Jonglei Canal, a joint project of Egypt and Sudan, is half finished. Both of these projects have been halted by Southern rebel activity.

Tanzania

GEOGRAPHY

Area in Square Kilometers (Miles): 939,652 (363,950)
Land Usage: 15% cultivated; 31% grassland; 48% bush, forests, and woodland; 6% inland water
Capital (Population): Dar es Salaam (757,346—1978)
Climate: tropical; arid; temperate

PEOPLE

Population
Total: 19,111,000 (1982 est.)
Per Square Kilometer (Mile): 20 (53)
Annual Growth Rate: 3.2%
Rural/Urban Population Ratio: 88/12
Age: 47% below 15 years

Health
Life Expectancy at Birth: 52 years
Infant Death Rate (Ratio): 103/1,000
Average Caloric Intake: 87% of FAO minimum
Physicians Available (Ratio): 1/17,550
Access to Safe Water: 39%

Languages
Official: Swahili
Others Spoken: Chagga; Gogo; Ha; Haya; Luo; Masai; Hindi; Arabic; others

Religion(s)
40% indigenous beliefs; 30% Christian; 30% Muslim

Education
Adult Literacy Rate: 78% males; 70% females
School Attendance: primary: 100% boys, 98% girls; secondary: 4% boys, 2% girls
Teacher/Student Ratio: 1/182

COMMUNICATION

Telephones: 88,700
Radios: 570,000
Televisions: 9,000
Newspapers: 2 dailies; total circulation 189,000

TRANSPORTATION

Highways—Kilometers (Miles): 34,227 (21,268)
Railroads—Kilometers (Miles): 3,555 (2,209)
Three international airports

GOVERNMENT

Type: republic
Constitution: 1965
Former Colonial Status: German and British
Independence Date: December 9, 1961
Head of State: Julius K. Nyerere (president)
Branches: president; unicameral National Assembly; High Court
Legal System: based on English Common Law, Islamic law, and customary law
Political Parties: Chama Cha Mapinduzi (Revolutionary Party)
Suffrage: universal over age 18

MILITARY

Number of Armed Forces: 44,850
Armed Forces/Population: 1/441
Military Expenditures (% of Central Government Expenditures): $179,000,000 (9%)
Nuclear Weapons Status: none
Current Hostilities: none; troops were withdrawn from Uganda in 1981

ECONOMY

Currency ($ US Equivalent): 10.5 Tanzanian shillings = $1
GDP: $4,600,000,000
Per Capita Income/GNP: $280
Workforce: 83% agriculture; 6% industry; 11% services
Inflation Rate: 11.9% (1970-1980); 30% (1982)
Natural Resources: hydroelectric potential; unexploited iron and coal; gem stones; gold; natural gas
Agriculture: cotton; coffee; sisal; tea; tobacco; wheat; cashews; livestock; cloves
Industry: agricultural processing; diamond mining; oil refining; shoes; cement; textiles; wood products
Energy Production: 275,000 kw capacity
Energy Consumption Per Capita: 51 kwh

FOREIGN TRADE

Exports: cotton; coffee; sisal; cashews; meat; diamonds; cloves; tobacco; tea
Imports: manufactured goods; machinery and transport equipment; cotton goods; crude oil; foodstuffs
Major Trading Partners: People's Republic of China; UK; Hong Kong; India; United States
Foreign Debt: $2,341,000,000
Selected Membership in International Organizations: UN; OAU; African Development Bank; Commonwealth of Nations; Non-Aligned Movement; Southern Africa Development Coordination Conference (SADCC)

TANZANIA

"The development of a country is brought about by people, not by money. Money, and the wealth it represents, is the result and not the basis of development. The four prerequisites of development are different. They are i. People; ii. Land; iii. Good Policies; iv. Good Leadership."

The Arusha Declaration, from which this quotation is taken, has been the cornerstone of Tanzanian socialism since 1967. Tanzania's leader, President Julius Nyerere, as well as this program for development have been widely admired. The aim of Tanzanian socialism has been to build on Tanzanian communal values and the people's self-reliance. The Arusha Declaration declared that Tanzanians should determine their own future. Loans, foreign aid, and outside investment could contribute—but could not be central—to development. It is the peoples' hard work, intelligence, and democratic cooperation that advance their development.

Over a decade and a half have passed since the Arusha Declaration was set forth. During those years, Tanzania has continued to strive toward the declaration's goals.

MEETING ARUSHA'S GOALS

In 1967 Tanzania, a country which had been independent for six years and which had joined with Zanzibar in 1964, was one of the poorest countries in the world. Today Tanzania is still a poor country. However, in the years since independence, the well-being of Tanzanians has increased, and the other goals of equality and democracy espoused in the Arusha Declaration have been realized to some extent. At the same time there have also been failures.

One of the major government efforts has been the creation of *ujamaa* villages. *Ujamaa* is the Swahili word for "family-hood," and the aim of the villages is to build on the traditional values of the Tanzanian family. Historically, rural peoples in Tanzania lived either as pastoralists in temporary settlements or as farmers in scattered individual households. In the late 1960s,

people were encouraged to move to the ujamaa villages and form new communities that would cooperate in production and be better served by government social agencies. Now there are over eight thousand ujamaa villages in Tanzania. However, the revolution in living patterns has not been easy to achieve, nor has it achieved all that was hoped for. Not everyone was willing to make the move. In the 1970s, the government began to use force, to achieve villagization. The process aroused resistance and dampened the ujamaa spirit.

Despite these problems, many of the goals of Arusha have been achieved. There has been increased participation by people in their governance and efforts to advance equality and to improve the public welfare. Village assemblies and councils, partly appointed and partly elected, have been established by law in all new villages. The Revolutionary Party of Tanzania—Chama Cha Mapinduzi (CCM)—formed by the union of the Tanganyika African National Union (TANU) and the Afro-Shirazi Party of Zanzibar, has encouraged internal criticism as well as competition for office. In 1980 over half of the eighty-four members of parliament seeking re-election were voted out of office. A new party constitution in 1982 provided for secret balloting for major offices. Government and party powers were separated, and efforts were made to avoid concentration of power at the top.

The government has sought to spread the benefits of development to the countryside as well as to the cities. Income distribution among civil servants has become more equitable than it was twenty years ago. Accumulation of capital is illegal, and hoarding and black market activities are recognized as "economic sabotage." Women's rights have been promoted. There have been special efforts to increase female enrollment in secondary schools, and the government has used its appointive powers to assure that twenty percent of the village council members are women.

Life is better in many ways for ordinary Tanzanians. Education and health care have improved and are more readily available. Life expectancy has risen from age thirty-five to age fifty. Nearly forty percent of all villages have access to clean water. Infant mortality rates are lower, and clinics are nearer.

Yet despite these improvements and the exertions made toward meeting socialist goals, other goals seem far away. Tanzania remains one of the twenty-five Least Developed Countries in the world, according to UN statistics. Social services are better than they were ten years ago, but people are poorer. Prospects look dim. The national wealth is more equally distributed but it is

(United Nations photo)

Equality and democracy have been increased in Tanzania since independence.

Sultan of Oman transfers capital to Zanzibar as Arab commercial activity increases **1820**	Germany declares a protectorate over the area **1885**	The Maji Maji rebellion unites many ethnic groups against German rule **1905-1906**	Tanganyika becomes a League of Nations mandate under Britain **1919**	Tanganyika becomes independent; Julius Nyerere is leader **1961**	Tanzania is formed of Tanganyika and Zanzibar **1964**	Arusha Declaration establishes a Tanzanian Socialist program for development **1967**	Tanzanian invasion force enters Uganda **1979**	

1984

January 1984: President Jumbe of Zanzibar resigns amid rising secessionist sentiment and criticism of his leadership of CCM	April 1984: Mwinyi is elected president of Zanzibar in Pemba election; Salim Ahmed Salim is appointed prime minister and viewed as a possible successor to Nyerere	June 1984: The Tanzanian shilling is devalued by 25%; budget of 1.5 billion is announced

no bigger. Moreover, self-reliance has not been achieved, and the advances that have been made have depended on foreign aid, of which Tanzania receives more than almost any other African country. Enthusiasm wanes, and Nyerere's leadership has been questioned.

THE ECONOMY'S DOWNWARD SPIRAL

Some blame Tanzania's circumstances on government inefficiency and mistakes in management, as well as on other domestic factors. Yet the economic problems facing Tanzania are similar to those facing other African countries. The conditions of world trade have deteriorated; cash crop exports have declined in price. In July 1981, for instance, coffee was getting only one-third of what it had been worth a year earlier. Meanwhile, imports such as oil, which absorbs fifty percent of the foreign exchange, and needed equipment are more expensive than they were in 1967. People may work hard, as Arusha exhorts; yet their increased production of crops may not give them as large a return as earlier, smaller harvests did.

Tanzania lacks the money to buy needed imports. Industries have slowed down to an estimated thirty percent of their capacity because they lack machinery, raw materials, or spare parts. Some have closed. The transportation system—so vital to the scattered Tanzanian population—has especially suffered. Cars wait for spare parts and seven out of ten bus trips reportedly end in breakdowns. Basic necessities, including food, are in short supply, and people in need

have turned to smuggling or the black market.

Agriculture is the basis of the economy, and yet, as has been noted, cash crops grown for export do not offer satisfactory sources of foreign exchange. Indeed, the government, concerned about the food crisis, has encouraged farmers to turn from cash crops to food production. Other options for exports do not seem viable. There are few mineral resources, although discoveries of natural gas reserves may someday bring in wealth. Industries neither satisfy consumer needs at home nor provide products to sell abroad.

The Tanzanian government has responded to the crisis by formulating a National Economic Survival Plan (NESP), and a reform program which has been developed with the help of outside experts, has been set in motion to increase the efficiency of the economy. Nyerere and other leaders have encouraged production for export. There have been crackdowns on economic exploiters; recognition of earlier mistakes and mismanagement; and efforts to revise programs that had been disbanded and replaced with large-scale, often unsuccessful, farming ventures have been revitalized.

Open discussion and a willingness to try new solutions has been accompanied by a determination to maintain Tanzania's socialist model. The nation's leaders estimate that $1 billion or $1.5 billion are needed to revitalize the economy. World financial institutions such as the World Bank and the International Monetary Fund can provide such aid, but they impose economic restraints that conflict with Tanzanian

socialism. Tanzania has met some of those conditions: devaluing the currency, reducing the government subsidy on maize, and lifting price controls on consumer goods. But leaders refuse to abolish all food subsidies or to encourage capitalist enterprises.

TIMES OF TRANSITION

Political controversy, opposition to the Nyerere government that has been in power for so many years, and the declining zest for pursuing former goals have all accompanied the increased economic hardship. Nyerere has confirmed that he will retire in 1985, but there have been some efforts to replace him before that time. In 1982, hijackers of a Tanzanian Airlines plane demanded his resignation, and an attempted coup in January 1983 involved both military and government officials.

These are changing times for Tanzania. Gains in health and education may be cut back with the decreases in funding. The economic and political system that has provided the framework for the activities of the past may be modified. It seems certain, however, that whatever happens, Nyerere's declaration of 1968 will continue to guide the country: "The policies of Tanzania are for Tanzanians to determine. To everyone else we say 'Hands off!'"

DEVELOPMENT

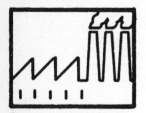

Over seventeen hundred health centers and dispensaries have been built in Tanzania since independence. A maternal and child health care program launched in 1974 and a school health program piloted in two regions in 1981 have improved health and educated Tanzanians, both professionally and on the lay level, in health care practices.

FREEDOM

On the celebration of the twenty-first anniversary of independence (December 1982), 3,640 prisoners were granted amnesty. In the midst of difficult times, government has continued to allow, and sometimes to encourage, criticism of its policies while clamping down on "economic sabotage."

HEALTH/WELFARE

Tanzania has made great advances in education and literacy. Universal Primary Literacy (UPE) was recently established and a national literacy campaign has been very successful. Two out of ten Tanzanians could read at the time of independence; now nine out of ten are literate, and the August 1983 adult education exam is expected to reveal that Tanzania is the most literate nation in Africa.

ACHIEVEMENTS

Tanzania has played a leading role in advancing all-African causes in African and international forums. President Nyerere and Tanzania have spearheaded efforts of the Frontline States in the liberation struggles of Southern Africa. Refugees have been welcomed in Tanzania and have been offered permanent homes.

Uganda

GEOGRAPHY

Area in Square Kilometers (Miles): 235,885 (91,076)
Land Usage: 45% forests, woodland, and grassland; 21% cultivated; 21% inland water; 13% national parks and game reserves
Capital (Population): Kampala (330,700—1969)
Climate: tropical; semi-arid

PEOPLE

Population
Total: 14,057,000 (1982 est.)
Per Square Kilometer (Mile): 60 (154)
Annual Growth Rate: 3.2%
Rural/Urban Population Ratio: 91/9
Age: 44% below 15 years

Health
Life Expectancy at Birth: 48 years
Infant Death Rate (Ratio): 97/1,000
Average Caloric Intake: 83% of FAO minimum
Physicians Available (Ratio): 1/26,810
Access to Safe Water: 35%

Languages
Official: English
Others Spoken: Swahili; Baganda; Iteso; Basoga; Banyankore; Acholi; Lugbara; Banyoro; others

Religion(s)
50% Christian; 10% Muslim; 40% traditional indigenous beliefs

Education
Adult Literacy Rate: 65% males; 40% females
School Attendance: primary: 62% boys, 46% girls; secondary: 7% boys, 3% girls
Teacher/Student Ratio: 1/35

COMMUNICATION

Telephones: 49,000
Radios: 300,000
Televisions: 76,000
Newspapers: 1 daily; total circulation 21,000

TRANSPORTATION

Highways—Kilometers (Miles): 6,763 (4,202)
Railroads—Kilometers (Miles): 1,216 (756)
One international airport

GOVERNMENT

Type: republic
Constitution: suspended
Former Colonial Status: British
Independence Date: October 9, 1962
Head of State: Milton Obote (president)
Branches: president; National Assembly; High Court
Legal System: based on English Common Law and customary law
Political Parties: Ugandan People's Congress; Democratic Party; Conservative Party
Suffrage: universal for adults

MILITARY

Number of Armed Forces: 7,500
Nuclear Weapons Status: none
Current Hostilities: internal conflicts with opposition guerrilla forces of the Uganda Patriotic Movement (UPM)

ECONOMY

Currency ($ US Equivalent): 230 Ugandan shillings = $1
GDP: $8,630,000,000
Per Capita Income/GNP: $230
Workforce: 83% agriculture; 6% industry; 11% services
Inflation Rate: 30.4% (1970-1980); 50% (1982)
Natural Resources: copper; miscellaneous minerals
Agriculture: coffee; tea; cotton
Industry: processed agricultural goods; copper; cement; shoes; fertilizer; steel; beverages
Energy Production: 228,500 kw capacity
Energy Consumption Per Capita: 61 kwh

FOREIGN TRADE

Exports: coffee; tea; cotton; copper
Imports: petroleum products; machinery; transportation equipment
Major Trading Partners: United States; France; West Germany; Japan; Italy; UK
Foreign Debt: $779,600,000
Selected Membership in International Organizations: UN; OAU; Commonwealth of Nations; African Development Bank; Non-Aligned Movement

| Establishment of the oldest Ugandan kingdom, Bunyoro, followed by the formation of Buganda and other kingdoms 1500 | Kabaka Mutesa I of Buganda welcomes British explorer, H.M. Stanley 1870s | British protectorate over Uganda is proclaimed 1893 | Agreement gives Buganda special status in the British protectorate 1900 | Kabaka of Buganda is exiled to the UK by the British for espousing Bugandan independence 1953 |

UGANDA

In early 1982, appeals went out from Uganda for six million hoes for Ugandan farmers to use to produce the crops on which the country depends. Hundreds of thousands of hoes came from all over the world, donated by the United Nations Development Program (UNDP), the European Economic Community (EEC), the United States, West Germany, China, and many other countries. The call illustrates the very basic needs that have been part of the negative heritage of General Idi Amin's regime. The fact that in 1983—even before the arrival of many of the hoes—Ugandans have been able to produce more than enough to feed themselves is testimony to the rich environment and potential of the country and its peoples. Uganda has made progress in other areas besides agriculture since the terrible years of General Amin; yet, in other ways, recovery has been difficult to achieve.

THE TRADITIONAL INHERITANCE

Uganda's lands are located in the area of the Great Lakes of East Africa and include the volcanic Ruwenzori Mountains. It has been said that in Uganda you can drop anything into the soil, and it will grow. The country's political heritage is also rich. Complex kingdoms such as Buganda, Bunyoro, Ankole, and Toro stretched back in history to the fifteenth and sixteenth centuries. These kingdoms were characterized by elaborate institutions and rituals; a variety of officials including oral historians; a ruling class that was often cattle-holding; and systems of client-patron relations. Early European visitors were impressed by the kingdoms and their seeming similarities to early European feudal monarchies. When the British took over the region, they maintained the Buganda kingdom and allowed the Buganda *Kabaka,* or ruler, and his chiefs to rule under British "protection."

During the colonial years, the Bagandans (citizens of Buganda), who today still maintain a feeling of pride in their own achievements and advancements, shaped political conditions to their best advantage—and to the disadvantage of neighboring kingdoms such as the Bunyoro. During the nineteenth century, many of the peoples of the region began questioning long-standing beliefs and values and therefore were receptive to the new Christian faith as well

(World Bank/Y. Nagata)

Uganda has maintained a steady performance in agriculture, but officials want to diversify away from coffee, the leading cash crop.

as to Islam, and to the educational opportunities that the mission schools offered. As a result, Ugandans, and especially Bagandans, learned many of the skills needed by the new state after independence. Unfortunately, Bagandans used their new skills to serve Buganda, rather than the larger Ugandan state. This threat of Bagandan dominance was to raise opposition and conflict.

In the 1950s, the Bugandan royal government, recognizing that Bagandans were a minority within the colonial state and fearing that Buganda's interests would suffer after independence, sought to secede from the proposed new nation. Although this did not happen, Buganda did manage to procure federal status (which gave Buganda a certain amount of independence) under the first Constitution, and a limited federal position was also granted to the other indigenous kingdoms.

In the years following independence, Milton Obote, prime minister and head of the majority Ugandan People's Congress (UPC)—and not a Bagandan—developed

a more unified government, though he had to use force against the Bagandans in order to do so. The move increased opposition to his rule inside and outside of his party. The socialist program that Obote developed also met resistance. In 1971, when Obote was out of the country, the armed forces under General Idi Amin, seized power.

THE DESTRUCTIVENESS OF AMIN'S RULE

Deaths, violations of basic human rights, threats to ordinary security, and the destruction of a promising economic base characterized Idi Amin's eight years in power. It is estimated that there were anywhere from fifty thousand to 300 thousand arbitrary killings. Many of those killed were well-known and respected leaders, such as the Anglican Archbishop of Uganda Janani Luwum, and the former Chief Justice and Prime Minister Benedicto Kiwanuka.

Other aspects of Amin's rule have shaped the present situation in Uganda. The assets of all Asian non-citizens were taken over, and forty thousand Asians fled the country. British firms were nationalized. The wealth that came into government hands as a result of these takeovers was used to reward the military and gain support for Amin's regime. Amin destroyed the old administrative system in Uganda and instituted ten provinces, each headed by a military governor who was literally a warlord. The army changed and grew as troops that were suspect were dropped and outsiders such as the Sudanese and Zairois were added. It became an army of occupation, twenty-five thousand strong, rather than a source of security.

"Development" had no place in Amin's Uganda. The economy was destroyed. Peasant farmers survived by abandoning cash crop production and turning to subsistence agriculture. By 1979 industries were producing at only fifteen percent of capacity, and the factories that manufactured equipment such as hoes had no steel. Outsiders—including the British, Israelis, the United States, Arab countries, Libya, and others—continued to trade with Amin's Uganda, providing materials to the elite who participated in his government. Amin's officials stole from the farmers, smuggled out cash crops through a highly organized network, received plunder, or—

| Buganda becomes independent **1962** | Milton Obote introduces a new unitary Constitution and forces Bugandan compliance **1966** | Major General Idi Amin seizes power while Obote is in Singapore **1971** | Amin invades Tanzania **1978** | Tanzania invades Uganda and overturns Amin's government **1979** | Obote's UPC wins in the first elections since 1962 **1980** | Tanzania withdraws its troops; Obote announces major economic changes recommended by IMF and receives loans **1981** | United Popular Front of anti-Obote groups is formed in London; 60,000 Rwandans in Uganda expelled **1982** |

1983

| February: Bill is passed allowing former Asian residents to reclaim seized properties | March: National resistance army claims to have sealed off main roads to Kampala | January 1984: Uganda aid donors meet in Paris and approve loans for 1984/85 |

like many others—fled to neighboring countries.

AMIN'S DEFEAT

Resistance movements existed within Amin's Uganda, but they were not successful. Individual critics were forcibly silenced. Striking workers, student protestors, and rebel ethnic groups directed their efforts against the regime. Assassination and coup attempts were frequent. None of these efforts led to the end of Amin's rule. It was Tanzanian troops that finally invaded Uganda and deposed Amin. The war began after Amin's troops attacked Tanzania, late in 1978. Ugandan exiles in Tanzania—including A. Milton Obote—took part in the war of liberation. In March of 1979, Tanzanian President Julius Nyerere said, "There are two wars going on in Uganda; one is that by Ugandans fighting to free themselves from a fascist dictator; the other by Tanzanians fighting to defend their national sovereignty."

The campaign was successful. A demoralized army was defeated, and Amin fled—first to Libya and then to Saudi Arabia. Yet, the challenge of national recovery may be greater than the challenge of Amin's defeat.

THE NEW GOVERNMENT

In March 1979, during the fighting, representatives of nineteen exile groups met at Moshi in Tanzania and formed the Uganda National Liberation Front. A provisional government grew from this organization with Ususf Lule, a Bugandan and former chancellor of the University of Makerere, as president. Objections to his authoritarianism led to his forced resignation, and his successor, Godfrey Binaisa, was soon removed in a dispute over presidential powers. A military commission took over and administered the elections earlier planned for December 1980. Milton Obote won these elections. However, his victory has not led to a peaceful and prosperous Uganda. Current political slogans emphasize reconciliation and reconstruction, but political and economic problems test the new government.

THE NEED FOR RECONCILIATION

Obote did not gain an overwhelming victory in the elections. The Democratic Party, led by the Bugandan Paul Ssemogerere, won two-thirds as many seats as Obote's Ugandan Peoples' Congress. Although Commonwealth observers were generally satisfied with the course of the elections, the losing parties claimed that the elections were rigged. The Democratic Party has been bitterly critical of the government's practices, charging that more Ugandans were killed in 1982 than in any year of Amin's rule. Three opposition legislators have been murdered since 1980. One opposition party went into exile and has formed a guerrilla resistance movement. Other resistance groups, such as the National Resistance Movement (NRM), have developed in the south as well as in the west Nile area, Amin's home area. These "bandits," as the government calls them, may have received assistance and weapons from outside countries such as Egypt and Libya as well as from civilians who, having lasted out Amin's forces, now suffer from the marauding practices of legitimate government forces. These new troops need to be retrained and returned to the barracks.

THE POSSIBILITIES OF RECONSTRUCTION

Economic problems, also great, seem somewhat easier to solve at the present time than do the problems of political and social unity. The debts, the low level of industrial and agricultural productivity, the lack of necessities, and the corruption accompanying scarcity demand attention. Obote has turned from socialist to capitalist solutions to the nation's economic problems. International Monetary Fund (IMF) negotiations have led to the devaluation of the currency and debt rescheduling. The debt has been reduced and the real Gross National Product has risen. Food production is back to normal, and the percentage of export crops, including the traditionally strong crops, cotton and coffee, is growing—although smuggling continues. Asian citizens have been invited to return home and have been assured that their properties will be returned. There are efforts to rebuild the great game parks and encourage tourism.

The picture in Uganda, therefore, is mixed and the country that had such promise at independence is recovering its lost prospects as it moves on.

DEVELOPMENT

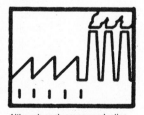

Although cash crops production has not risen since 1979, food production has improved in the last few years. In the drought-troubled year of 1983, Uganda exported its food surplus to its neighbors.

FREEDOM

Life is more secure for Ugandans than it was in the Amin years. However, anti-government troops as well as members of the present armed forces still threaten the lives and homes of Ugandans from time to time.

HEALTH/WELFARE

The two year recovery program announced in March 1982 is concentrating on projects such as the rehabilitation of hospitals.

ACHIEVEMENTS

The "two window system" of exchange in Uganda has stimulated the economy in the last few years while preventing "get rich quick" schemes. There are two rates of exchange for foreign currency. A lower fixed rate is for government, for repayment of loans and acquisition of essential imports. Another rate, about two or three times higher than the first window rate, is available.

Topic Guide to Articles: East Africa

TOPIC AREA	TREATED AS AN ISSUE IN	TOPIC AREA	TREATED AS AN ISSUE IN
Colonial Influence	1. Continuing Problems in Africa's Horn	**Natural Resources**	1. Continuing Problems in Africa's Horn
Current Leaders	4. Moi Emerges From Kenyatta's Shadow		2. Nation With the Fastest Growing Population Tries to Alter Parent Attitudes
	5. Nyerere on Refugees	**Political**	3. Kampala Tries to Rebuild—and Regain Its Dignity
Economy	1. Continuing Problems in Africa's Horn	**Development**	5. Moi Emerges from Kenyatta's Shadow
	3. Kampala Tries to Rebuild—and Regain Its Dignity		6. Kenya Savors a Sordid Saga
	8. Political Will and National Interests		7. Tanzania: Union at the Ballot Box
Human Rights	1. Continuing Problems in Africa's Horn		8. Political Will and National Interests
	3. Kampala Tries to Rebuild—and Regain Its Dignity	**Refugees**	1. Continuing Problems in Africa's Horn
	5. Nyerere on Refugees		5. Nyerere on Refugees

Article 1

CURRENT HISTORY, MARCH, 1983

Continuing Problems in Africa's Horn

BY W. A. E. SKURNIK
Professor of Political Science, University of Colorado

Walter Skurnik is a frequent contributor to journals on African affairs and is the author of "The Military in Dahomey," in Claude E. Welch, ed., *Soldier and State in Africa* (Evanston: Northwestern University Press, 1970), *Foreign Policy of Senegal* (Evanston: Northwestern University Press, 1972), and *International Relations: Sub Saharan Africa* (Detroit: Gale Research, 1977).

I N 1982, in the Horn of Africa, there were attempted coups d'état, civil wars, armed attacks across international political boundaries, millions of refugees, and not enough to eat.[1] Uneasy and suspicious, regional and neighboring states watched developments, finding it difficult enough to manage their own problems without worrying about Djibouti, Ethiopia and Somalia. And then there were the superpowers and their friends, looking after their own national interests—the Soviet Union comfortably ensconced in Ethiopia and the United States trying to stay out of Somalia's irredentist adventures.

Yet a chronicle of these events masks the tragedy afflicting the peoples of that area. Both Ethiopia and Somalia have hailed nationalism, trying at the same time to earn a living that is meager at best (both Ethiopia and Somalia are among the world's "least developed" states). In the Horn, many people paid taxes destined for remote governments; tens of thousands were inducted into the armed forces; many more thousands were victims of oppression; others fled to neighboring states or took up arms against the "new order." The three countries of the Horn host between 1.5 million and 2.5 million refugees—estimates vary— a number equivalent to one-fourth of their population.

Led by Mengistu Haile Mariam and his Supreme Council, Ethiopia is still reeling from the aftermath of the 1974 revolution. The military government is seek-

ing to demonstrate its legitimacy as the heir to a feudal empire, to overcome internal rebellion and threatened secession, to control Somali-dominated territory in the southeast, to bolster a disastrous economy, to minimize Soviet influence, and to prevent further political disaffection, particularly among the military. The regime is one of the continent's most brutal and repressive, singled out by organizations like Amnesty International as a major violator of human rights.

The Council was encouraged by the Soviet Union to create a political structure to control the country more effectively, which led to the Commission Organizing the Party of the Working People of Ethiopia (COPWE). Trade union and peasant organizations were placed under COPWE supervision in 1982, but its effectiveness remains to be demonstrated. Not all Ethiopians accept Mengistu's dependence on a foreign power, and his many failures are sharply resented. The possibility of a military coup cannot be discounted, particularly given Mengistu's viciousness in dealing with his opponents.

One of Ethiopia's major long-range problems is the dissatisfaction of important ethnic groups. By far the most serious of these centrifugal forces is Eritrea, which borders the Red Sea and provides Ethiopia with its only international port (a French-built railroad connects Addis Ababa with Djibouti, which explains Ethiopian interest in an enclave either independent and neutral or controlled from Addis). Although Eritrea is "part" of Ethiopia, the Italians (from about 1935) and the British (from 1941 to 1952) helped to weaken ties that were never strong. Italy began the modernization process, and the British later allowed local political activity and hence consciousness, so that Eritrea acquired a distinct identity and never accepted its formal annexation into a feudal Ethiopia in 1962. Nonetheless, Addis did not take the opposition seriously until Eritrean liberation movements became active and secured outside help. By the late 1960's, they had adopted guerrilla tactics; and after the 1974 revolution and the confusion at the center of Ethiopia's empire, they prepared for larger-scale battle. As a strong Emperor was succeeded by a weak and inexperienced group of military leaders, demands for Eritrean autonomy grew; following repression, they became demands for independence.

---

[1] Unless otherwise noted, quotations are taken from a variety of public materials, including Congressional hearings, the United States press, the *State Department Bulletin,* and *Africa Research Bulletin.* I am grateful to Bernd Schwieren for research assistance.

Tens of thousands of Ethiopian soldiers, many of them conscripts, have died in vain attempts to impose Ethiopian rule over Eritrea since 1974. Given substantial Soviet military aid and Cuban and East European advisers, it is remarkable that Ethiopia has not been able to control Eritrean freedom fighters—themselves at times fighting pitched battles against each other. Without foreign military clout, Addis would probably not have any soldiers in the region.

The other problem for Ethiopia's leaders is Somali irredentism, which concerns the Ogaden, a large chunk of imperial territory. British and Italian rule over Somalia and the British administration of part of Ethiopia—liberated from Italy by South African troops after World War II—effectively enlarged the area controlled by Ethiopia and inhabited mostly by Somalis. (The British proposed a new entity uniting all Somalis, but nothing came of it.) The Ethiopian-Somali conflict underlies much of the behavior of the two states toward nations outside the Horn, including the superpowers.

Ethiopian "control" over the Ogaden, although intermittent, goes back many centuries, and Ethiopia takes the uncompromising position that Somali irredentism is illegitimate and a threat to regional peace. The Ogaden Somalis would probably prefer to be left alone, occasionally fighting over grazing and water rights; they view political, national boundaries as alien, and about a million Somalis fled to Somalia after the 1978 Ethiopian military victory and occupation.

After Soviet weapons and Cuban troops helped defeat Somalia in the Ogaden several times, Ethiopia stationed permanent troops in the province and supported Somali liberation movements. Three Somali dissident groups—the Salvation Front, the Democratic Front for the Liberation of Somalia, and the small but ideologically oriented Workers party—merged in October, 1981, to form the Somali Democratic Salvation Front (SDSF). Colonel Abduhalli Yusuf Ahmed, one of many Somali opponents of the present government, is head of the SDSF, which is ethnically and regionally based (among the Issaq and in the Midjertein region) and thus has limited appeal in Somalia.

SDSF headquarters are in Addis, and the Ethiopian government allows it to operate a powerful radio transmitter, Radio Kulmis, from the outskirts of the Ethiopian capital. More to the point, Western intelligence and diplomatic sources believe that SDSF military units are being trained near Dire Dawa, some 100 miles from the Somali border; these units have conducted frequent raids into Somalia.

The Ethiopian economy is fragile; it depends largely on agriculture for home consumption and export earnings and is sensitive to domestic and external fluctuations. Annual per capita income is about $100, and available resources cannot foot the bills for modernization and development, petroleum imports, and a large military budget simultaneously. The trade deficit has grown substantially—from $210 million in 1978 to $400 million in 1982. Short-range problems include a shortage of food staples and inadequate distribution, and the ever flourishing black market. If political problems can be contained, long-range prospects for agricultural self-sufficiency are good. Meanwhile, foreign aid helps to keep the economy going.

The Mengistu regime has made some progress, although political and economic costs are high and the regime depends on extraordinary external military help. Ethiopia may well reduce Eritrean secessionist demands to a nuisance rather than a danger. To help bring about a change in government or in policy in Somalia would be a major triumph, but to employ explicit intervention might be a Pyrrhic victory.

SOMALIA

Political developments in Somalia were punctuated in 1982 by severe discontent in the north (particularly in the Hargeisa and Burao areas), apparently focused on the Midjurtein region and the Isaaq clan but with overtones of unrequited economic expectations and a feeling of isolation from the "national" center at the capital city of Mogadishu. Discontent also reflected the north's British and the south's Italian colonial experience. At the end of 1982, it was not clear whether northern frustrations were being ameliorated or whether General Siad Barre's chances for continued rule were improving significantly.

The critical question concerned the armed forces: as the only structure capable of maintaining relative political stability, could it be shielded from the centrifugal forces inherent in Somali society? The answer was not apparent, but there were signs that President Barre's rule was shaky.

In January, the government summarily executed several senior officers for alleged cooperation with the externally based Somali Salvation Front (SOSAF). Most of the Eighth Army, stationed in seven garrisons in the north, mutinied shortly thereafter, but the mutiny was crushed. Despite heavy official censorship, it was evident that the fighting was fierce; government pronouncements denied the existence of a mutiny and attributed the trouble to Moscow and Addis Ababa and to "an irresponsible Reuters correspondent in Nairobi." The Somali News Agency dismissed the episode, noting only that security forces were sent to "disperse people."

Barre subsequently restructured some of the formal elements of the political system and tried to return the ruling political party to center stage. In the spring, he lifted martial law imposed in October, 1980; he reappointed General Mohamed Ali Samatar as Defense Minister and shifted Cabinet members to give his close supporters greater responsibility. He sought—and received—American political support during a three-day official visit to the United States in March, 1982.

In Washington, Barre described Somali-American relations by suggesting that the "atmospherics are excellent" and managed to conceal his disappointment that he did not receive more tangible, immediate rewards—although he appreciated the symbolism of the visit to Mogadishu of the United States cruiser *John Hancock* to coincide with his return from the United States. The press reported an attempt to overthrow Barre in June, 1982, involving a number of Cabinet members including highly placed but disgruntled military leaders. The former Defense Minister, General Umar Hadji Masaleh, demoted to Health Minister following an attempted coup in April, was also involved in June.

The July, 1982, Ethiopian attack produced a rise in Somali nationalist sentiment, and was certainly not welcomed by the international community. Perhaps the SDSF, bolstered by Libyan funds, had persuaded Mengistu that disaffection in northern and central Somalia was ripe for a politically inspired military foray. At year's end, however, the evidence suggested that the attack was a mistake, although not all returns were in. The event reverberated beyond the Horn into southern Africa, the Middle East, and the United States. Kenyan President Daniel arap Moi, in his capacity as chairman of the OAU (Organization of African Unity), called on both countries to cease firing, thus explicitly blaming the Ethiopian government—with which Kenya has a defense agreement against Somalia—for violating Somalia's sovereignty and territory.

African reactions were of some significance and may help cool tempers. Despite the history of Somali incursions into Ethiopia, the Ethiopian attack could not be condoned. Djibouti, a small state squeezed between two larger neighbors, announced its continued neutrality and called for a cease-fire. Egypt and the Sudan strongly condemned Ethiopia, no doubt reflecting inter-Arab solidarity and a generally pro-Western orientation. An Arab summit meeting resolved to "help drive out the Ethiopian forces"; although it had no effect on the situation in the field, this action was interpreted as a Somali diplomatic victory. The Ethiopians had perhaps painted themselves into a corner.

President Barre subsequently asked the United States to make available some of the military equipment it had agreed to provide but had held since 1980. Washington's response was swift but limited. It airlifted the better part of $10-million worth of defensive equipment, mostly radar, anti-aircraft weapons, trans-portation and communications equipment and small arms. This was a symbolic gesture, in harmony with Africa's opposition to military solutions for border disputes.

SOMALIA'S ECONOMY

Somalia is one of the world's poorest countries with a per capita annual income below $200.00. The five year economic plan introduced by the government in January, 1982, regards the north and the south as distinct entities. In the south, major emphasis will be placed on harnessing the Juba River, flowing south from the Ethiopian highlands into the arid lowlands near the Kenya border. A $650-million dam for irrigation and electric power is under construction at Bardera. Trade with Kenya has been growing, and the government plans to introduce regular commercial shipping service between Mogadishu and Mombasa and to modernize the harbor, which is frequently clogged with traffic.

The government also hopes that the very large salt deposits about 120 kilometers north of Mogadishu will act as a development center. These deposits have not been worked since 1939 and need capital investment, and the vexing question of a market outlet has not yet been settled—Japan has indicated some interest. Some external assistance contributes to the development of the south, including French funds for a cement plant near the Juba dam, and a contribution by the Arab Fund for Social and Economic Development for completion of a road (a project that has run into cost overruns and other difficulties).

About three-fourths of the Somali people raise stock for a living and contribute about 80 percent of the country's foreign exchange earnings. Yet there are indications of some subsoil mineral deposits (Somalia sponsored a trade fair in Houston, Texas, in September, to tempt investors); because most of these are in the isolated north, their commercial exploitation could make an important contribution to the social, economic and political unity of the country. Oil exploration has not yet met with commercial success but is being continued. Significant deposits of natural gas were found about 40 miles north of Mogadishu, in addition to deposits of uranium, meerschaum, nickel, bauxite, iron ore, tin, and chromite.

Despite these possibilities, the official development plan for the north placed great emphasis on the growth of the fishing industry. From the point of view of domestic consumption, this is a difficult task, because most people prefer meat and milk products. But the prospects for exports seem reasonable. The present catch is negligible; the government plans to build ten fishing ports as initial infrastructure along the

4,000-kilometer coastline and estimates a potential catch of some 200,000 tons per year.

General Siad Barre is a survivor and a skillful politician. Yet the obstacles he faces are formidable. He has suffered repeated military defeats by Ethiopia; hence the image of a Greater Somalia has been shattered. Somalia sustained a national humiliation in the summer of 1982; there is disaffection in the north and possibly the central region. Barre has an increasingly narrowing power base and is currently unable to extract more than token support from the United States: thus he may well become the victim of a combination of domestic and external factors.

The Republic of Djibouti is a small former French territory which derives signal benefits from its strategic location; its economy is the most promising in the Horn in the short and medium term. The country is slightly larger than Massachusetts and has a population numbering about 350,000 (less than Alaska). The people are about equally divided among Issa of Somali origin and Afar, whose ties are with Ethiopia. Most Issa live in the country, whereas urban centers, chiefly the capital city of Djibouti, are dominated by Afar. Political leaders must maintain a reasonable ethnic balance and give the two groups the impression that their interests are served by remaining an independent political entity. A new legislature was elected in May, 1982; the ruling single party chose the candidates, and the results were seen as strengthening President Hassan Gouled Aptidon.

DJIBOUTI'S ECONOMY

Fortunately for Djibouti, its economic situation and immediate prospects are favorable. The 1981 national budget was balanced and supplemented by a good balance of payments. The country's location at the southern tip of the Red Sea lends itself to economic and strategic exploitation. The government helped create a climate favorable to private enterprise, and points out that the presence of several thousand French troops helps make the country the safest in the Horn.

Most of the people are pastoral nomads, difficult to integrate into or mobilize for national economic development objectives. The country's economic future lies less in agriculture than in strengthening its role as an entrepôt for regional trade.

Generous government policies attracted banking and contributed to making the national currency a safe and desirable medium of exchange. It may be traded freely for other currencies, and transactions can remain secret; Djibouti would like to become Africa's Switzerland. Banking serves mostly as a base for the short-term financing of trade for customers in Ethiopia, Somalia, and both South and North Yemen. Flex-

ible policies contrast sharply with the lumbering, nit-picking and morose bureaucracies of other states in the area.

Land prices in Djibouti have begun to climb in anticipation of an economic boom. The capital city's port, somewhat ineffectual because it is clogged on occasion, is being modernized and expanded; by the end of 1983, it should serve as the major container terminal and distribution center in the Horn and beyond. The international airport will also be expanded and modernized.

As a result of these policies, Djibouti attracts external investment and foreign aid. Yet it remains one of the world's poorest states. It has applied for United Nations recognition as a least developed state to qualify for more aid, and the government plans to undertake a population census to "prove" that its annual average per capita income is significantly lower than the United Nations estimate of $400.00.

INCREASING SOVIET INFLUENCE

The Horn's importance in international affairs derives chiefly from its geographic location at the juncture of black and Arab Africa, the southern end of the Red Sea, the western flank of the Indian Ocean, and its proximity to the Persian Gulf. The basis for its importance has hardly changed from the days of imperial "coaling stations"; since World War II, Britain and France have been supplanted by the United States and the Soviet Union. Today, Soviet interests and activities are increasing, whereas those of the United States are waning.

The Soviet Union has not been too successful in its adventures in the Horn. It helped create and then defeat a Somali military threat, as Moscow changed its definition of Soviet national interests. While Moscow was arming Somalia, it was also supporting Eritrean liberation movements and was thoroughly familiar with General Barre's commitment to a Greater Somalia. By switching its alliances from Somalia to Ethiopia, Moscow "traded up"; Ethiopia is the larger power and Soviet influence was increased accordingly. The abrupt Soviet switch in allies was not in harmony with Soviet ideological rationalizations about its obligations to support national liberation movements in the third world, particularly in view of the fact that the leaders of both the African states claimed to be Marxist. Today the Soviet Union is silent about self-determination in Eritrea and aspirations for a Greater Somalia, or refer to them as capitalist plots.

The Soviet image has been tarnished for other reasons. First, the Soviet Union's credibility as a reliable military ally was sharply questioned when Somalia was abandoned for a larger prize. Second, it remains to be seen if Soviet leaders are willing to use massive transfusions of military aid elsewhere in Africa; there are few Ogadens in Africa, and Eritrea is closer to Czechoslovakia than Afghanistan as an analogy. Third, Moscow's repeated efforts to restructure Ethiopian society reveal blatant insensitivity toward the third world (reminiscent of its attempt to unseat President Sékou Touré in Guinea in 1961) and have been met with polite but clear resistance by the proud Ethiopians.

Fourth, if the Soviet Union supports Ethiopian armed incursions into Somalia, it will lose goodwill, since its support would violate a basic rule of inter-African behavior. And if it tries and fails to dissuade Mengistu from such adventurism, the news of domestic African constraints on Soviet influence will travel far and fast.

SOVIET MOTIVES

It is tempting (and perhaps not too farfetched) to suggest that Soviet policy in the Horn is a building block for the Imperium Sovieticus, part of the overall political objective of expanding influence into the third world to align itself with the anti-colonial revolution and to weaken the influence of the dominant Western powers. Ethiopia has great strategic value in Africa and the Middle East, although it is more important for the Red Sea than the Persian Gulf. Given the magnitude of Moscow's investment, it would be difficult to dismiss it as "minor" or vaguely opportunistic. The Kremlin's decision to spend over $2 billion in military aid in Ethiopia in two years, far more than it spent on the entire continent since the inception of its aid program, is a matter of policy rather than caprice.[2]

Nor should one shrug off Soviet efforts, in a country where Moscow has no vital economic or military security interests, to maintain some 12,000 Cuban military advisers and over 1,000 Soviet and East European personnel, or the services of top Soviet generals planning and executing military operations or to favor Ethiopia with over half its needs for petroleum imports. Soviet access to air and naval facilities in Ethiopia could, of course, be used to "interdict" or deny Western access to the Persian Gulf; but from a strategic point of view, Ethiopia probably belongs to Moscow's version of a worst case scenario.

DECLINING AMERICAN INTERESTS

In September, 1982, United States Secretary of State George Shultz addressed the United Nations General Assembly to trace the outlines of United States foreign relations. There was a fleeting reference to Namibian independence; in another passage about foreign policy in general, he told the United Nations: "Don't expect too much." These examples illustrate a tacit United States agreement that Africa remains Europe's chief responsibility and that United States policy is supplementary unless its national interests are involved. Such a stance is unpalatable to many African and American observers, but nothing in recent developments in the Horn suggests that it has changed.

The pattern of United States policy in the Horn follows the general retrenchment inaugurated by the Nixon doctrine, which changed President John F. Kennedy's "we shall bear any burden" injunction to a "we shall bear only select burdens as required by our national interests" guideline. "Our interests," President Richard Nixon specified, "must shape our commitments, rather than the other way around." It is easy to forget that the United States was turning over the Kagnew facility to Ethiopia and had turned down the Emperor's request for more military aid long before the revolution. The presence of Soviet and Cuban forces in Ethiopia did not unduly alarm Washington; it was the Soviet invasion of Afghanistan in December, 1979, and Moscow's heavy subsidies to Iran's Tudeh party that raised the Horn's profile in American policy.

Washington's response was twofold. First, it increased aid to the Sudan and Kenya to try to contain Soviet influence. Second, it secured Somalia's agreement to allow it to use naval and air facilities in Berbera at the southern end of the Red Sea and at Mogadishu, which faces the Indian Ocean, both serving as a link to move conventional units like the Rapid Deployment Force into the Persian Gulf. Somalia is an emergency stepping stone between Egypt and Israel to Saudi Arabia and Oman. For all that, United States expenditures in the Horn indicate a low priority, the massive Soviet effort in Ethiopia notwithstanding.

Neither Presidents Jimmy Carter nor Ronald Reagan sent Somalia even part of the $40-million worth of defensive military equipment authorized by Congress until the Ethiopian incursion in the summer of 1982. United States interest in Somalia seems to be declining, partly because technology has decreased Somalia's usefulness, but also as a result of some second thoughts about continued access to petroleum.

In the Horn, in 1983, there is a fortunate coincidence between a growing American sensitivity to African problems and a decreasing emphasis on national security considerations in the area.

The violence and misery that shook the Horn in 1982 and in previous years were not inevitable. The decisions to allow or to prevent self-determination or autonomy for Eritrea and to follow pan-Somali dreams were made consciously by ruling elites. There are alternatives to violence in the Horn, and there are elites who favor peaceful settlement. The African ta-

[2]See Daniel S. Papp, "The Soviet Union and Cuba in Ethiopia," *Current History*, March, 1979.

boo against border changes without the consent of the parties involved, which is enshrined in the Charter of the OAU, is an exercise in relative efficiency rather than in justice.

Nonetheless, the Africans have locked themselves into that system, and African leaders will ultimately have to answer if their abstract principles are implemented without flexibility. In the case of the Horn, how many lives and refugees can be justified in the name of political frontiers that make little sense?

Article 2   *The Christian Science Monitor*, April 19, 1983

By R. Norman Matheny, staff photographer

Schoolchildren on tour in Nairobi: More than half Kenya's population is under age 15

Nation with the fastest growing population tries to alter parent attitudes

By Paul Van Slambrouck
Staff correspondent of The Christian Science Monitor
Kawangware, Kenya

Cecilia Njeri pauses from her laundry chores to pronounce that she is "happy her husband is not like other men."

What sets him apart? He has quietly agreed to his 25-year-old wife's wishes to have no more children. She is already the mother of four.

The story of the Njeris is both hopeful and worrisome. It offers one of the first glimmers that efforts to bring under control Kenya's exploding population, now growing at the fastest recorded rate in the world, are making headway.

This tentative sign of success is being supported by a new government family planning initiative that is considered by experts the most ambitious in the country's history.

Yet the fact that this young couple's acceptance of family planning stands out from the attitudes of most of their neighbors in this poor community on the outskirts of Nairobi is a matter of grave concern. It demonstrates that while population control efforts have done well in some developing countries, they continue to face an uphill slog in changing attitudes in sub-Saharan Africa.

Kenya was one of the first states in sub-Saharan Africa to formulate a population policy in 1967. But as in other African states, the political sensitivity of the issue of family planning made the Kenyan government extremely wary of putting into practice what was spelled out in official policy statements.

Government policy clearly recognizes that Kenya's 4 percent annual population growth is potentially disastrous. That high growth rate stems from extremely high fertility and success in reducing the country's mortality rate.

A 4 percent annual rate of growth means Kenya's current population of 18 million will more than double by the year 2000. Food requirements will be roughly double those of today, but the annual rate of increase in agricultural production is already falling. It means a near doubling of primary school enrollments, where capacity is already stretched and one-third of the teachers are unqualified. It means, in short, social demands the government cannot possibly meet.

Particularly worrisome is the already high dependency ratio. About 51 percent of Kenya's population is under the age of 15, meaning for every 100 adults, there are an equal number of children who need to be supported and educated.

Demographic experts point out that slowing Kenya's population expansion requires not only making contraceptives and family planning information available to a populace that is 80 percent rural, but also changing attitudes, which is perhaps more difficult.

"People here take having many children as a source of security," says Damaris Kinyua, a nurse at the family planning clinic here.

This community is full of migrants from rural areas who hope to find work in Nairobi. Most lead a hand-to-mouth existence and figure a large family increases the chances that at least one of their children will be successful enough to provide them some security in their old age.

In the rural areas the view that children are a means of wealth is even stronger, population experts say. They are seen as "labor units" to work the land. In one sense they are easier to care for than their urban counterparts, since most farmers are able to subsist on their small plots of land.

Other prevailing views that encourage large families (the average woman in Kenya has eight children) are that big families are a sign of high status and that contraceptives are bad for a woman's health and tend to encourage promiscuity.

At the Kabiro family planning clinic in Kawangware, nurse Kinyua says local people view family size as such a personal matter that she encourages family planning only as a means of "having children when you want them."

This clinic was started in 1980 by the Institute of Cultural Affairs, a nonprofit rural development organization. The men in the community are most resistant, Kinyua says. Many women come to the clinic surreptitiously, claiming health problems, so their husbands and men friends will not know the nature of their visit.

But nurse Kinyua says she can see attitudes changing and "slowly it is getting easier" to encourage family planning. The hard economic times in Kenya and the widespread unemployment in Kawangware are helping. "Right now they know there are no jobs and they can see how difficult it is to feed, clothe, and educate a large family."

The government's new push in family planning comes in the form of the National Council on Population and Development, which convened last November. Population experts look on the council as Kenya's the most serious and ambitious effort yet toward population control.

"The council's main function is to change people's attitudes towards having smaller families," says a council official who prefers not to be identified. "We are optimistic so long as we handle it properly. It is a very sensitive issue."

The council's program should take shape in the next few months. Generally it will coordinate efforts by a half dozen volunteer organizations as well as 12 government ministries. International donors have already pledged some $11.5 million for the program over the next three years.

The aim will be to promote family planning, primarily in the rural areas, with a particular effort made in converting men to the idea.

Article 3

THE CHRISTIAN SCIENCE MONITOR   **August 30, 1983**

Kampala tries to rebuild — and regain its dignity

By Louise Lief
Special to The Christian Science Monitor
Kampala, Uganda

Driving in from the airport at Entebbe toward Kampala, the visitor is struck by what a beautiful, verdant country Uganda is. Everything is green — the yellow-green of the banana trees that line the road, the blue-green of the grass, and the waxy green of the foliage.

The rich, red earth of Uganda is irrepressibly fertile. If you eat a mango and throw it on the ground, Ugandans say, two or three weeks later it will have sprouted, and in no time you will have a mango tree. "We just put it in the ground and it grows," says one woman.

It is therefore a shock in this soothing landscape with its temperate climate, gently rolling hills, and the lovely Lake Victoria teeming with fish, to enter Kampala.

First there are the roadblocks, which have been a fixture in Ugandan life for several years. There are several on the airport road, and on every road leading into or out of Kampala. There are also roadblocks on most of the major roads throughout the country.

Sometimes these roadblocks are marked by nothing more than a branch in the road or a tin can. But if a driver does not stop, soldiers armed with automatic rifles may shoot up the car.

Roadblocks are reportedly less dangerous these days than they were two or three years ago. At that time, travelers were terrorized by men dressed as soldiers who may have been government soldiers or bandits or guerrilla rebels or the Tanzanians who had been sent to "liberate" the country from the bloody rule of Idi Amin. Often the travelers were robbed, and sometimes they were shot.

Now, although Ugandans complain that the soldiers at the roadblocks still fleece them for cash, the situation seems much better. But on the road to Jinja, the country's industrial center, for example, one can still see long lines of Ugandans waiting patiently next to their buses or cars as they go through roadblock after roadblock.

Kampala was once the hub of East Africa and made Nairobi, where the center has now shifted, look like a provincial backwater. As is common here, Ugandans speak of the "good old days" before 1971 and Idi Amin, when Uganda was, in Winston Churchill's phrase, the "pearl of East Africa" and Kampala was its gay, glittering capital.

But now Kampala is a shadow of its former self. After the liberation war in 1979 and the looting that followed, its skyscrapers stand as empty hulks, the hotels are in shambles, and the lovely villas set in the hillsides are stripped down, even to the lightbulbs and doorknobs. The shops still operate behind heavy metal grates designed to discourage thieves. Many buildings are boarded up, so dilapidated they cannot be used. The roads are filled with potholes.

Ugandans are rebuilding their capital, but they have learned to scale down their expectations. Most are resigned to the fact that the "good old days" are gone for good, and they are trying to salvage and improve what they can on a much more modest scale.

For beginning with the Amin period, there was a slow, steady deterioration in every sector of the economy, in the conditions of the roads, the factories, and the public utilities. The country went from an 8 percent growth rate to bankruptcy.

What Amin began was finished in the liberation war, as both the liberating Ugandan and Tanzanian troops and Amin's retreating forces also "liberated" the cities' cars, stores' inventories, and the like.

The damage done to the country during that period was not only physical, but also moral and spiritual. Order broke down, and people lost the ability to work together toward community goals. Residents who have returned from exile at President Milton Obote's call to help rebuild the country note the sharp rise in the rate of theft and armed robbery since they left.

The Uganda Times, the country's official English-language newspaper, which appears sporadically, carried an ad recently by the city's water pumping station. It asked for reports on the whereabouts of an employee who had stolen eight of its motors.

A factory manager who returned from exile complained that it was hard to get his men to work well at the factory. They kept wanting to tend their own garden plots, he said. This was part of a trend begun during the Amin years, when people left the cities and the danger of Amin's security forces to return to the countryside and subsistence farming.

A foreign aid worker recounts that when building supplies were delivered to a village for rebuilding the roof of the school, villagers stole the material to reroof their own houses.

The phrase the Ugandans use now for the process they are working through is "moral rehabilitation," or the effort to restore a sense of dignity, of right and wrong, to a population that has lived too long with brutality, in fear and insecurity.

Even in this uncertain atmosphere, there are many Ugandans with the energy and desire to help rebuild their country.

The faculty at Makerere University and their 5,000 students are extremely motivated, in spite of shortages of books, paper, and pencils. An English literature class this reporter visited was lively. The students were articulate and

Amin: nation struggles to surmount his legacy   Camerapix

eager for intellectual contact and exchange with the outside world.

Women have become more vocal. There is a desperate shortage of skilled labor in the country (during Amin's time 65 percent of the technocrats fled or were killed). So many women have found new avenues open to them.

There is another reason for the new prominence of women: Most of the Ugandans killed during Amin's time were men. (According to some counts, 300,000 were killed under Amin's rule, with many more killed during the liberation war and the ensuing chaos.) Many widows are now the single heads of households.

The national theater, whose last director was killed by Amin, cannot afford to keep a resident company. But more than 132 amateur theater groups are registered there, and the theater is open year-round.

The roadside market stalls, which had closed, have reopened and the government has raised producer prices on such export crops as tobacco, tea, and cotton to stimulate production.

Although economic indicators have improved somewhat, there are still obstacles to the smooth recovery of Uganda. Fear and violence are two such obstacles. Recently, several members of the ruling Uganda People's Congress party were killed on one day in separate incidents on the outskirts of Kampala. Reports of killings in different areas of the country also inhibit the distribution and transport system.

The atmosphere of insecurity is amply demonstrated by Ugandans' worry about being out after dark. At 2 p.m. people start toward home to be there by nightfall. By 6 p.m. Kampala looks like a ghost town. The theater gives its performances at 10:30 a.m. and 2:00 p.m. to give people time to get home before sunset. One still hears sporadic gunfire at night.

The security situation is worsened by the country's economic predicament. During the Amin years, the Ugandan economy kept going by reverting almost entirely to the black market and barter system. The official economy became, in a sense, meaningless.

In an attempt to eliminate the black market, the Bank of Uganda has accepted the suggestion of the International Monetary Fund to "auction" off hard currency every Friday to the highest bidder.

Currency exchange is controlled according to two different rates — Window 1, a lower rate for development imports, and Window 2, a higher rate for other imports.

The IMF's cure is showing some success. It is narrowing the gap between the government exchange rate and the market rate of the currency. But it is also giving rise to some distortions.

The most serious consequence of this is that Ugandan salaries bear no relation to actual costs. The salary of a Ugandan soldier, for instance, is 1,000 Ugandan shillings a month, the equivalent of $4, enough to support him for three days. The salaries of civil servants are not much better.

So some soldiers continue to fleece travelers, and many workers hold two or three jobs. Others steal. Almost everyone grows his own food or has access to a family member with a farm.

A newspaper editor who wanted better coverage for his newspaper asked, "How can I press my reporters to work when I know they cannot even feed their families?"

Nevertheless, many Ugandans have returned from exile — despite salaries they cannot live on — in order to rebuild.

The discussions these days in Kampala and its environs seem to center on the limited alternatives the country faces at this point. Many have voiced unhappiness with the country's current leader, President Obote, but others argue that there is no other figure of sufficient stature in the country at this point to lead it back to health.

But many Ugandans are impatient for the recovery of their country, hoping to build new and better structures than the old ones that have broken down.

Article 4   THE CHRISTIAN SCIENCE MONITOR OCTOBER 18, 1983

Moi emerges from Kenyatta's shadow

Kenya's President shrewdly engineers himself into position of true power through election and juggling of his Cabinet; new appointments show he means to tackle economic problems head-on

By David Winder
Staff writer of The Christian Science Monitor

President Daniel arap Moi of Kenya, who speaks with a soft voice and rarely carries a big stick, is letting it be known he means business.

The boldness with which President Moi is moving on both political and economic fronts is producing new political realignments within Kenya, and a perception that the low-key President has finally emerged from under the shadow of the "Mzee" or "Wise Old Man" as the leonine and legendary former President, Jomo Kenyatta, was affectionately called.

Some Africa-watchers even go so far as to say that with his opposition in disarray — testimony to his political acumen—and his neighbors, Uganda and Tanzania, in deep economic trouble, President Moi is quietly emerging as the respected elder statesman of East Africa.

How much this image grows depends on two things:

● How well he addresses serious economic troubles in his own country, which has an unemployment rate of 30 percent and a $2.9 billion external debt.

● His political nimbleness in keeping his alliances alive with other minority tribal groups in the country.

President Moi, a member of the Tujen, a subgrouping within the minority Kalenjin tribe, was appointed vice-president to President Kenyatta, in Kikuyu, in order to maintain harmony in a multitribal society without taking anything away from the then dominant Kikuyu.

Africa-watchers see a logical sequence in Moi's efforts to take charge.

First, he maintained a low profile before shrewdly engineering himself into a position of political primacy by neutralizing tribal politics.

Second, he has exploited his political position by calling an election a year ahead of time and seeking a fresh mandate from voters to consolidate his position.

Third, having won overwhelming endorsement from the voters last month, he has been putting his troubled house in order.

The election swept out more than 40 percent of the sitting members of Parliament, including five Cabinet ministers not considered as close to President Moi as those who were retained. It also halved Kikuyu representation in the Cabinet.

At his inauguration, which formally installed him in office for a second five-year term, President Moi pledged the East African nation would honor all its foreign debt obligations and not borrow more than it could repay. Africa-watchers are keeping a sharp eye for signs of how he is going about ensuring that happens.

In a move that has been welcomed by foreign experts who feel Kenya's economic problems must be tackled first, Moi has appointed a Cabinet geared more to solving economic problems than to maintaining political alliances. The Cabinet has been streamlined, with the number of ministries reduced from 25 to 21. Some ministers from the previous Cabinet who were reelected have been dropped from the new Cabinet.

Underscoring the importance Moi places on the need to rescue the economy, he has fused the feuding Economic Planning and Financing ministries into a single unit.

The man who heads that department and who has in effect been put in the driver's seat of the economy is Prof. George Saitoti, a respected technocrat from Nairobi University. Significantly, Professor Saitoti was not an elected member of Parliament, but was nominated by the President.

A top African businessman, Kenneth Matibi, also has been nominated to the Cabinet.

"This doesn't look to me like a political fence-mending Cabinet," says Prof. Isebill V. Gruhn, a Kenya expert and visiting professor at the Harvard Center for International Affairs. Rather, she suggests, the inclusion of technocrats points to the seriousness of the country's economic situation and to Moi's determination to do something about it.

A Kikuyu Kenyan involved in Kenyan politics said she was unhappy with the outcome of the election, in which Kikuyus lost ground, although she conceded Moi was universally respected.

The decline in the political fortunes of the Kikuyus has prompted some speculation that elements of the old and once dominant KANU (Kenya African National Union) alliance consisting of the Kikuyu, Luo, and Kamba might be revived to wrest back the political initiative. Few African experts think the existing divisions make it a viable alternative.

The more likely scenario, they say, is that Moi has bought time — with the Kikuyu unlikely to rock the boat for fear any political instability would imperil their considerable economic interests.

Article 5   *Oxfam America News,* Fall 1983

Nyerere on Refugees

Ahmed Farah, Oxfam America Projects Officer for Southern and Eastern Africa, recently attended a conference in Tanzania with representatives of voluntary agencies and the Organization of African Unity to discuss refugee aid in Africa. Here are excerpts from the keynote speech by Tanzanian President Julius Nyerere, a speech as yet unreported in the U.S. media.

The number of refugees in Africa has increased from about 3.2 million in 1979 to about 5 million—and this terrible figure does not even include the forced internal migrations caused both by famines and by violence and civil war. Of course it is possible to take a lofty historical perspective and talk of the inevitable problems of creating nations with artificial boundaries. I could explain the social unrest created by poverty and disappointed hopes, especially when ambitious men or external forces seek to turn these problems to their own advantage. But today we are talking about PEOPLE; about five million suffering individuals and how you can most effectively help them.

I have spoken of the problem created for a host country by what is now called "spontaneous settlement" of refugees. It is argued that UNHCR (United Nations High Commission on Refugees) and the voluntary agencies should not help with the creation of new schools, dispensaries, etc. because this is "development" which should be dealt with by other UN agencies from the "country aid allocation." But if 10,000 or 100,000 refugees are spared the trauma of living in temporary camps because the local population helps them from a spirit of kinship, this is surely an advantage for both refugees and the aid agencies. It is, however, still a burden to the local government. To demand that other projects be dropped in favor of the in-comers is . . . likely to create the kind of hostility and mutual suspicion which causes refugee problems in the first place. Nor is it helpful to demand that if the UNHCR finances a school it must be used only by refugees; such an idea is contrary to the basic principle of helping refugees to reestablish their lives and their ability to look after themselves.

Sometimes refugees can return to their homes after a few weeks or months. More usually, it is years before they feel they can safely return; indeed, a large proportion will never go back home at all, and their children will have no known connections with the country from which their parents came.

In African terms, there is nothing strange about this. If one looks at what are called African tribal migrations over recent centuries, many of the movements would today be defined as "refugee problems." Minority groups, or dissident families, were fleeing from the dominant authorities and moved to what is now a different country. Very many African nations are made up of a lot of old waves of refugees. If we can create a nation out of all the different tribal groups which happened to have arrived in our countries before independence, it is surely not impossible to integrate into our developing societies the post-independence victims of oppression or hunger.

Once it is clear that the problem which caused people to flee is not a temporary one, then all the resettlement programs should be directed at the long-term integration of the new communities. This cannot be done by our nation states without assistance. But when we get help at what I understand you regard "Stage II" of a refugee problem—the first being emergency feeding and shelter—it should be of a kind which allows the growing community eventually to fit in with the local society and nation if this proves to be necessary.

In Tanzania we have seen that this can happen. Thirteen different settlements have been established in our country since the 1960's; all except the newest of these have now achieved full self-supporting status, or are well on the way to it. A large number have therefore been handed over by the UNHCR and the Voluntary Agencies to the (Tanzanian) District and Regional Administration and are treated like all other villages in our country. Further, tens of thousands of the earliest refugees have now applied for Tanzanian citizenship. Hundreds have already been granted citizenship, and we expect that almost all of them will receive it when their applications have been processed. It is our hope that all the long-term refugees will become Tanzanians. In the meantime, according to our law, all children born in this country can opt for Tanzanian citizenship when they reach adulthood.

I want to stress your responsibility, as agencies and as field workers, to encourage the integration of refugees into the host community. It is more difficult, especially in the early stages, to look after refugees as part of a total community than it is to look after them in isolated camps. There are clashes and misunderstandings and mutual fears which have to be dealt with; plans have to meet what appear to be local prejudices, or compromises reached between what appears to you as experts to be an ideal organization and what the local people think is appropriate.

But your aim is to help the refugees to recreate their lives; they can only do that as part of the society into which they have moved.

Article 6

N° 5 AfricAsia   May 1984

Kenya Savours a Sordid Saga

Ex-Minister Charles Njonjo seems determined to ensure that his own political downfall will bring others in its wake.

By Joyce Robinsons

When he was in the government, Charles Njonjo, the former Minister for Constitutional Affairs, used to inject a dose of excitement in an otherwise humdrum political climate, though rarely for positive reasons. Sometimes a report on the proceedings in Parliament would detail a heated exchange with one of the handful of courageous MPs who dared cross swords with him, such as Martin Shikuku (Butere) on Europeans and Asians, Onyango Midika (Nyando) on trade unions, or any of the so-called "seven sisters," most of whom he hounded to prison or exile before his resounding fall from power in June 1983.

After an eight-month absence from centre stage following his removal on accusations of being groomed by foreign powers to take over the presidency, Njonjo has been back in the limelight and in the local headlines over the last two months. The occasion has been his appearance before a commission of inquiry set up to investigate the allegations against him.

True, this is not a trial but an "inquiry." Nevertheless, the evidence of misuse of power does appear overwhelming. He did obtain foreign exchange irregulary, use the national carrier, Kenya Airways, as he pleased without paying his bills, go in and out of the country at will without heeding immigration regulations, travel to South Africa and have South Africans admitted into Kenya illegally, and help his friends import arms that were sometimes not accounted for. All these things and more seem to be amply documented by the prosecuting counsel. However, more astonishing than the revelations themselves is that he was able to do it all apparently with impunity. Thus the inescapable and troubling conclusion is that the head of state had, to all intents and purposes, given Njonjo free rein to do as he saw fit, to use, unimpeded, the machinery of state—the judiciary and the prisons, the central bank and the police, and even the army, for mention has been made of his hopping around in an army helicopter and boasting of the fact to emphasize his power.

Some witnesses, such as the MP for Bungoma South, Lawrence Sifuna and Francis Mutwol, former MP for Kericho East, have testified that he tried to constitute, through bribery, blackmail and coercion, a sufficient personal following in the National Assembly to pass a motion of no confidence in the president, and supposedly engineer his own election to the post. But then that would have been perfectly constitutional.

Accusations

Quite expectedly, the inquiry has produced a host of innuendos and accusations such as involvement in the 1982 attempted coup d'etat for which the alleged leader, Senior Private Hezekiah Ochuka, was extradited from Tanzania and sentenced to death on March 19. Njonjo has also been linked with the assassination of Tom Mboya in June 1969, then the most powerful minister in the government and secretary general of the ruling party, KANU. But these and many other insinuations have yet to be substantiated. What appears to be in no doubt, as the inquiry unfolds, is that Njonjo very often acted as a power unto himself, oblivious to the law, and even to the presidency. To that extent, the inquiry is gradually turning into a probe into the firmness of the president's grip on the helm of state, as much during Njonjo's heyday as today.

There seem to be clear indications that top civil servants. vice ministers and even ministers were appointed at Njonjo's behest. Thus, the impression that emerges is that President Moi had abdicated—willfully or by force of circumstances—some of his authority to his right-hand man.

With the constitution of a smaller government following the September 1983 elections, the general expectation was that the new team would be more coherent and controllable than the previous unwieldy and faction-ridden one that Njonjo had had a Machiavellian hand in setting up. It was also presumed that surrounded by people who were loyal to him, mainly without a power base of their own, the president would no longer demonstrate the kind of paranoiac fear of dissent that set rolling a mounting tide of harsh and often unconstitutional repression culminating in the 1982 wave of detentions of lecturers, students and members of parliament. Events increasingly show that hesitation and fear are still rife and the revelations of the inquiry have brought such impressions into ever sharper focus.

To mention just one ministry, that of Education and Technology—entrusted to the president's long-time friend, business associate, fellow tribesman and self-styled professor Jonathan Ng'eno—the old problem of hasty decisions of far-reaching import leading to embarrassing reversals is as evident as ever. Out of the blue in January came the announcement that the biggest and best equipped girls' secondary school in the country, Kenya High School in Nairobi, was being abolished to make way for a teachers' training college. This provoked such a clamour that the president had to intervene and cancel the move. Then came the decision that students who had finished their A-levels and gained admission to university for the 1984-85 academic year would be required to do national service as from February. Accordingly, advertisements summoning the 2,500 "conscripts" were inserted in newspapers. Then shortly before they were due to report, it seems to have dawned upon the authorities that they would need boarding facilities, equipment, personnel, etc., that did not exist. Hence a hurried broadcast putting off the call until March 1, and four days before this date, yet another radio announcement, this time for an indefinite postponement. Hardly a picture of proper management and cohesion.

What emerges from these observations on President Moi's uncertain hold on power is being confirmed with devastating force by the proceedings of the Njonjo inquiry. The weaknesses manifest now are the same ones that led to his giving Njonjo too long a rope. To that extent, the inquiry is turning out to be as much a trial of the presidency as of the alleged "traitor". Indeed, the studied flippancy and calm flamboyance of Njonjo's advocate, never missing an occasion to link accusations of abuse of power by his client to negligent forbearance if not tacit delegation of authority by the president, has succeeded in glamourizing Njonjo while casting aspersions on his accusers. Thus, if the trend to date is anything to go by, the sooner this inquiry is over, exciting though it may be, the better, before the president's credibility suffers irreversible and crippling damage.

Article 7

Nº 5 AFRICASIA MAY 1984

Tanzania: Union at the Ballot Box

The threats to Tanzania's unity have subsided with last month's elections in Zanzibar. The new president of the islands is committed to maintaining the union and getting a better deal for Zanzibar at the same time.

By Songe Mbele

Tanzania has celebrated its twenty years of existence as a united state with a presidential election on the island of Zanzibar to replace the previous president, Aboud Jumbe, who had resigned in January! For Zanzibaris, it is the first time they have had the opportunity directly to vote for their own president and, indeed, the poll was important for the whole of the United Republic, since the president of

1 See AFRICASIA, nº 4, April 1984.

Zanzibar is also the vice-president of Tanzania.

General elections were held on April 19, five days before the Union Day celebrations which commemorate the act of union between the former Tanganyika and Zanzibar. The Interim President of the island,

Ali Hassan Mwinyi, as expected, won more than the necessary 50 percent of all votes cast to become confirmed as the new president. Indeed, he was the only candidate for the job since the other contender, former diplomat and Minister Abdul Wakil, had withdrawn his candidacy even before the vote of the National Executive Committee of Tanzania's ruling Chama cha Mapinduzi (Revolutionary Party or CCM) in March. The NEC, as supreme organ of the party, elects candidates for the presidency both for the islands and the mainland.

Mwinyi, a former schoolmaster, diplomat and minister, had been elected Interim President of Zanzibar and Interim Chairman of the Zanzibar Revolutionary Council at an emergency session of the NEC held in Tanzania's new future capital, Dodoma, last January. The NEC was originally convened to discuss and forestall attempts by some Zanzibaris, including powerful figures in the former government of Aboud Jumbe, to have the islands secede from the Union.

It is against this background that Zanzibar's first presidential elections since the revolution twenty years ago assume great significance. The Union has survived a frightening crisis and, in the words of President Nyerere, come out stronger. The choice of Mwinyi is intended to ensure at the same time that while Zanzibar continues to retain its considerable autonomy, any future attempts at secession are not ignored or tolerated, as happened under Jumbe. Mwinyi is a great believer in, and advocate of, the Union and, unlike Jumbe who was not really very popular amongst his people, is acceptable both on the islands and on the mainland.

Most important, however, is the fact that the elections promise to usher in a new era in Zanzibar where people won't feel they have to look over their shoulders before expressing their views, and where the power of both the Revolutionary Council and the islands' security police will be drastically

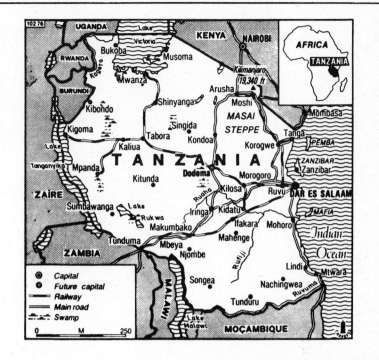

reduced. Mwinyi has already promised to proceed "without letup" on the road to democratization. He has also promised to strengthen the instruments for assuring personal security and freedom and to stamp out the abuse of power. Only when these rights are guaranteed, he believes, can people's energies be harnessed for the development of Zanzibar.

To achieve that will require a radical reorganization of the islands' political and administrative structure, which Mwinyi hasn't ruled out. With thousands of its better-educated citizens in exile, however, Zanzibar is suffering a serious shortage of trained personnel. Mwinyi is thus hoping that the new political climate will attract many of the exiles home. Already he has appealed to all of them to return, and in recent weeks Zanzibari diplomats and officials have been criss-crossing the Middle East, Europe and the Americas to appeal to Zanzibaris, most of whom fled the country during the iron rule of the islands' first President, Sheikh Karume, to go back.

Whether many of them will heed the call will undoubtedly depend on the degree of good faith with which they think the appeal is made and whether they really believe "a wind of change," as one Zanzibari described what was happening on the islands, is really blowing. There is every indication, however, that the new regime is earnest in wanting all Zanzibaris to take part in developing the islands. Winning the hearts of these people may be the first real battle Mwinyi will have to win as President before he can seriously think of taking on the ailing economy and the broader issues of democracy.

Article 8   **The Weekly Review, November 25, 1983**

Political Will and National Interests

THE accord reached in Arusha last week by the three East African presidents on the disbursement of the former East African Community's assets and liabilities was more the result of political will and consideration of the national interests of the countries concerned than anything else. This political will and consideration of national interests was reflected in the speedy manner in which the accord was reached, given the manner in which the community broke up and the complex process that was required to sort out and apportion its assets and liabilities.

When the community collapsed in 1977, each of the three member states grabbed whatever joint property was within its borders, or reach, in the case of movable assets. Fixed assets became "nationalised" by the countries in which they were based. Thus, for instance, Kenya retained the former East African Railways Corporation headquarters and the Railway Training School, which were both based in Nairobi; Uganda retained the Posts and Telecommunications headquarters in Kampala and the East African Flying School at Soroti, while Tanzania took over the former community headquarters in Arusha and the Harbours Corporation buildings in Dar es Salaam.

In movable assets, Kenya grabbed most of the planes belonging to the defunct East African Airways to form the virgin fleet for its newly-launched Kenya Airways. Kenya also retained most of the posts and external communications equipment besides such fixed assets as the Extelcoms headquarters and the Posts and Telecommunications Training School at Mbagathi. Tanzania, in turn, impounded several Kenya light aircraft and retained most of the Harbours Corporation equipment and a number of sea-going vessels. Of the 11,183 wagons and coaches owned by the East African Railways Corporation at the time of the collapse of the community, Kenya was left with 6,109, Tanzania took over 3,987 while Uganda ended up with only 1,087. In addition, there were thousands of other forms of assets of the former community that were tied up within the borders of one country or the other - vehicles, service equipment, stock and other machinery, building and construction materials worth millions of shillings, staff houses and other buildings, furniture, vital documents and stationery that would take millions to duplicate or purchase anew and monies in the accounts of the various EAC institutions. All these had to be accounted for before a formula for their redistribution could be worked out and agreed upon.

Then there were the debts owed to various local and international lending organisations by the individual institutions of the former community. These loans had been guaranteed by the governments of the three member countries and a system had to be worked out whereby the loans could be passed over to the newly-created

Moi, Nyerere and Obote: arduous task of sorting out

national institutions in the correct proportions.

Sensing the imminent collapse of the community late in 1976, the World Bank, which was the chief financier of most of the East African Community institutions, brought together the three governments and worked out a system for dividing the loans on an individual government basis under what was then called the Damry formula, so that when the East African Railways collapsed, the Kenya part of the liabilities to creditors in the defunct corporation was inherited by the newly-formed Kenya Railways. But the World Bank-initiated system did not take into account other unsecured unilateral creditors, forcing the liquadition of some of the East African corporations at the auctioneer's table, as happened with the former East African Airways early the following year. In this case, Kenya, which had taken over most of the assets of the former EAA, was left to settle with the two major creditors, British Aircraft Corporation (manufacturers of the Super VC-10 jets flown by EAA) and the American McDonnell Douglas (makers of the DC-9).

It was, however, in the establishment and valuation of how much of the former community's assets each country was holding, and how the assets were to be distributed, that the sorting out process hit the most snags. After months went by with each country, especially the main protagonists -

Kenya and Tanzania, accusing each other of holding this or that, the World Bank again brought the three governments together and got them to agree to the appointment of a mediator to work out the assets and liabilities and the method of their distribution under the auspices and financing of the bank. Dr. Victor Umbritch from Switzerland was appointed to the job in 1978, and the arduous task began.

First, an inventory of all the community's assets had to be taken and their geographical locations recorded and verified. Then they had to be valued before their redistribution could be agreed upon. Reports by valuers commissioned by Umbritch were often rejected by one or the other or a combination of two or all the member governments. If, for instance, the community headquarters in Arusha was valued at a certain figure, Kenya might object to the value, claiming that without the community the complex was mere buildings and therefore of much less value than when the community was functional and housed there. In other cases, some of the member governments would object that some of the assets identified for valuation did not belong to the defunct community but to national institutions or had always been the property of the individual country concerned. Scores of fact-finding meetings were held between experts - valuers, engineers, quantity surveyors, public accountants and economists, bankers - appointed by all four sides (the World Bank - with Umbritch in charge, Kenya, Uganda and Tanzania). These experts travelled thousands of miles within East Africa, verifying that the various assets actually existed and were indeed what they were reported to be. In the meantime, the value of some of the assets were constantly changing. Vehicles and rolling stock and other machinery were depreciating in value, and so were buildings; land value was going up.

Four years later, the parties seemed to have come to an agreement on the value of the assets of the former community, but the sore issue of how they were to be redistributed still had to be settled. Seven ministerial meetings were held between the three countries to sort out this matter over the years that followed. During these meetings, each of the three countries took a different stand. Uganda, which held only 12.7 per cent of the almost shs. 12,000 million worth of assets owned by the former community, used the inverse theory, arguing that Kenya and Tanzania (which held 52.1 and 35.2 of the total assets of the former community, respectively) had benefitted for all those years and therefore most of the assets should now go to Kampala. Tanzania rejected the Ugandan position, arguing that all the East African countries were sovereign states and the former community assets should be distributed equally among them since they were intended for common use. Kenya wanted the assets distributed on an equity basis according to each country's capital contribution. The other two countries rejected the contribution theory on the basis that most of the assets were not bought by the member states as such, having existed long before any of the three countries was independent. The Tanzania railway, for instance, was built by the Germans long before the present boundaries of mainland Tanzania were charted; similarly, the "Uganda Railway", which ran from Mombasa to Kasese in Uganda was constructed within the then British East Africa, long before Kenya

and Uganda existed as separate British territories with their distinct borders.

After more years of agonising, the ministerial committee finally agreed on a formula for redistribution of the assets based on what they called an element of "equality and geographical location". The formula encompassed a partial acceptance of the equity system suggested by Kenya and recommended by Umbitch, where Tanzania was to retain 32 per cent of the community's assets, Kenya to retain 42 per cent and Uganda 26 per cent. The "equality and geographical location" theory required that since Kenya and Tanzania held assets in excess of their equity shares in the community, they should compensate Uganda, which had a deficit, partly in cash and partly by handing over some of the former community's physical assets to Uganda. This was in recognition that most of the physical assets held by Kenya and Tanzania were required there as a matter of need. Uganda, while accepting this formula, wanted 80 per cent of the compensation in actual movable assets and the remaining 20 per cent in payment. Kenya, with the larger share of the compensation to make, did not see it that way and was pressing for the compensation to be half in capital assets and half in cash. Sources within the Kenya delegation said Kenya was also worried by Uganda's demand that the cash payments be in foreign exchange, preferably American dollars. Uganda and Tanzania also wanted interest rates paid on all the excess assets since the break-up of the community six years ago - a condition that would have cost Kenya a considerable amount.

The ministerial committee was stalemated at this point. Said one official, "the ministers had come as close as they would ever come. The rest was upon the three heads of state if the situation was to be saved." Only political goodwill and a new spirit of co-operation among the three leaders could save that situation. The goodwill had to be based on the advantages that their individual countries, and the

region in general, could derive if a speedy solution could be reached. National and regional interests combined had to over-ride the national pride and personal considerations that have characterised previous attempts to reach an agreement.

For the two main protagonists, Kenya and Tanzania, a speedy solution would pave the way to the re-opening of their common border, closed since 1977. The opening of the border meant new markets for Kenyan goods, while Tanzania would no longer have to foot large shipping bills for goods available in Kenya that were being obtained from countries farther afield at greater cost. The tourist industry in both countries could thrive again. There would be no more sanctuary for political and economic saboteurs escaping from either country, thereby enhancing the security of both neighbours and ensuring greater stability of both their political systems and the region generally. Most important, the accord would remove some of the serious hitches that stood in the way of the realisation of the Preferential Trade Agreement area for East and Central Africa.

With the necessary goodwill and the foregoing national considerations in mind, both Kenya and Tanzania prevailed upon Uganda to accept compensation based on half in capital assets and half in convertible cash, the provision of goods and services and the offsetting of existing bilateral claims and counter-claims to the tune of 191 million dollars. Interest on the payments will only be payable on future instalments but will not be retroactive from the time of the break-up of the community. Kenya and Tanzania, for their parts, also agreed on the immediate reopening of their common border, subject to normal immigration requirements.

One official at the Arusha meeting commented on the results of the meeting saying, "It was not to the total satisfaction of any one of the parties involved, but it was the most practical solution for all concerned."

Southern Africa

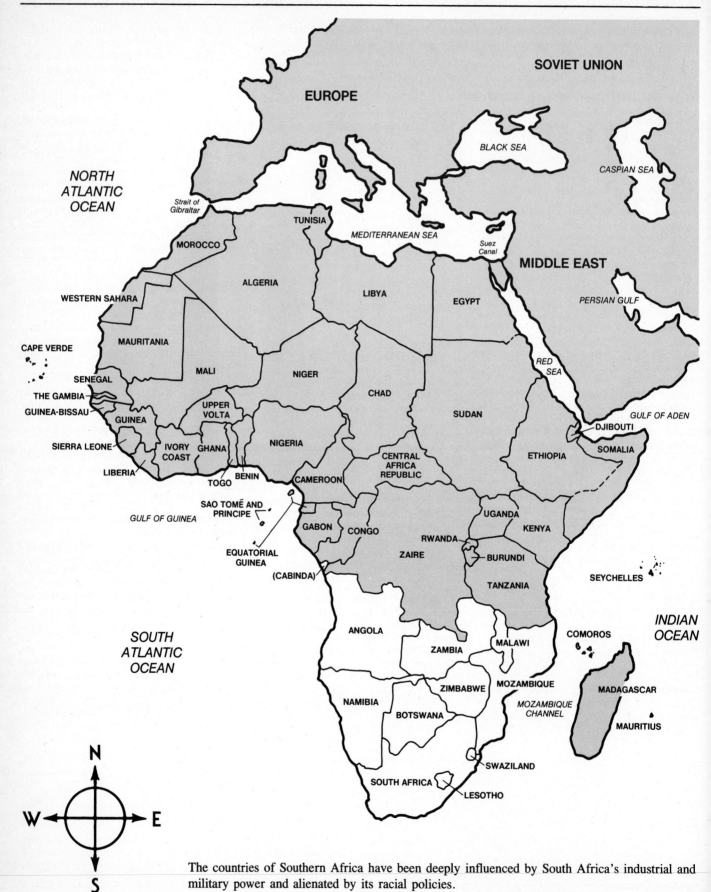

The countries of Southern Africa have been deeply influenced by South Africa's industrial and military power and alienated by its racial policies.

Southern Africa: Destabilization Obstructs True Independence

Southern Africa—which includes Angola, Zambia, Malawi, Mozambique, Zimbabwe, South Africa and its col-

ony Namibia, Lesotho, Botswana, and Swaziland—is a region of savannas and desert (the Namib), plateaus, and a Mediterranean climate that encourages comparisons between this area and North Africa. It is not so much the geographic features, however, as the peoples and their past interactions that give the region its identity. It is history that provides the keys for understanding the forces that both unite and divide Southern Africa.

The peoples of the region include the first inhabitants (hunters and gatherers such as the Khoisan-speaking bushmen who now live in the dry regions of Namibia and South Africa), the many different Bantu-speaking groups who came into the region in the first millenium A.D., and white settlers who arrived later. The continuing impact of the settlers and their communities has made much of Southern Africa what it is today.

WHITE MIGRATION INTO AREA

In the seventeenth century, whites from Holland settled at the Cape of Good Hope, and their population gradually expanded, moving into the interior and eastward along the coast. The British took over these settlements beginning in 1795, and English colonists began arriving in 1820. In the 1820s, Shaka, the Zulu leader, was engaged in nation building and conquest. His wars stimulated the movement of vast numbers of people from the eastern areas of present-day South Africa to the west and north. Many present-day residents of Mozambique, Malawi, Zimbabwe, even Tanzania are descended from the Africans who came north and settled during that time. The whole area still bears the marks of that revolution, called the *Mfecane*.

The conservative Dutch-descended Boers, or Afrikaners, ancestors of the white leaders in South Africa today, trekked inland in the 1830s to found Boer nations, which were free from British control. Later, when gold and diamonds were discovered, white miners and entrepreneurs traveled to the Transvaal, spreading out in the regions around Johannesburg and Pretoria and moving farther north. In 1890, a "column of pioneers" of Cecil Rhodes' British South Africa Company made their way to Zimbabwe. Others spread to Zambia. British traders and missionaries and other settlers came separately to the area that is now known as Malawi. The territories now known as Angola and Mozambique were also settled by white colonists from Portugal.

By 1900, all of these areas were under the colonial rule of either Britain or Portugal, while Germany controlled present-day Namibia. South Africa had the largest white population, and the Afrikaner and British settlers there had the longest heritage. Although defeated in a war with the British (1899-1902), these settlers were able to gain virtual independence in 1910. With their rich resources and outside aid as well as their own skills, they were able to industrialize and develop in ways that far surpassed the other colonies of

(United Nations photo by Alon Reininger)

Countries throughout Southern Africa are developing projects to employ laborers who otherwise migrate to South Africa, a pattern established in colonial times. This worker is building a highway in Lesotho.

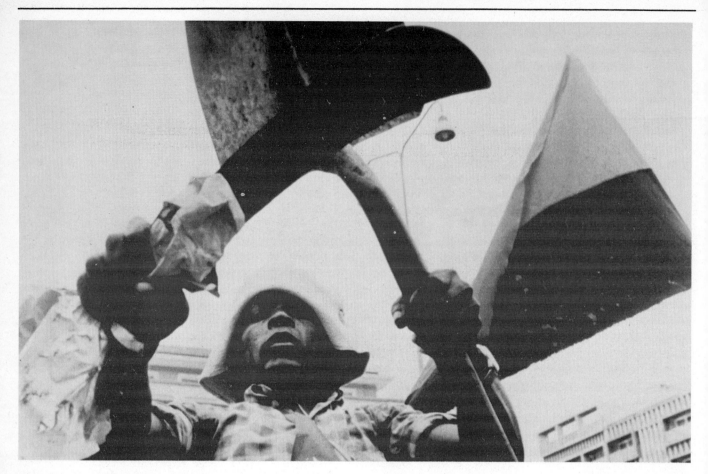

(United Nations photo)

Supporters of independence movements, such as this member of the MPLA in Angola, celebrated success in their struggle against colonial powers in the region.

the region. Their development depended on the black labor that they drew from throughout the area. Migrants came from Portuguese as well as British territories to serve the South African economy. Meanwhile, policies of land reservation, labor regulation, and discrimination could be found in varying degrees in all these territories. Portugal's white colonists claimed to follow policies different from the British—more readily accepting blacks as equals once they were "civilized"—but the results seemed the same: There was power for whites and little advance for the colonized peoples.

NATIONS BECOME INDEPENDENT

During the 1950s and 1960s all of the countries of Southern Africa were affected by the "winds of change" (as British Prime Minister Harold McMillan described the forces of flux in Africa in the 1960s), but the struggle for national independence was slow and hard. In the countries with small settler groups, however, the movements for independence had more chance for success. First Malawi and Zambia, then Lesotho, Swaziland, and Botswana, became recognized as independent nations. The area appeared to be polarized between liberated and unliberated

countries. In 1974, the Portuguese revolution and the liberation forces brought statehood to Mozambique and Angola. Finally, in 1980, Zimbabwe became free. South Africa stood alone, a white minority-ruled state with its unwilling satellite, Namibia, confronting independent black governments.

Now in 1983, the contrast between apartheid South Africa and the black states remains. Yet every part of the region is deeply influenced by South Africa. Neighboring countries hope to free themselves from its powerful presence. The attachments fashioned in the past are economic, as well as historical. Roads and rails lead to Johannesburg and Capetown, where ex-patriate workers have worked in the industries and mines for generations. The countries of the north use the infrastructure for their exports and import the South African-manufactured goods and food that the northern states do not produce.

The destabilizing policies practiced by South Africa have been even more disturbing than the north's economic dependency upon the state. The black independent states are hostile to South Africa's apartheid policies, and they have provided havens for South Africa's exiles who have built bases for liberation struggles in these countries. South

Africa's armed forces have attacked supposed bases and encouraged insurgency within the independent states. However, security agreements signed between South Africa and Mozambique and between South Africa and Angola in 1984, may alter relations between South Africa and its neighbors and limit South African support for dissident movements in those countries. Opposition to South Africa has stimulated movements for economic integration among the other countries. Nine countries, including Tanzania in East Africa, have joined together in the South African Development Coordination Conference (SADCC) to free themselves from dependence on South Africa and to cooperate on projects of economic development. Such cooperation is especially important for meeting the danger from another enemy—the drought that has been active everywhere in the area, including South Africa, in the last few years.

In this essay, we will look more closely at these features of the Southern African region: the threat of South Africa and its recent agreements with its neighbors, the historic economic dependence upon that country, the widespread impact of the drought, and the efforts to develop viable regional alternatives to dependence upon South Africa.

SOUTH AFRICA'S MILITARY POWER AND DESTABILIZING POLICIES

South Africa is a superpower, and its influence in the southern part of the continent reflects the vast difference in its development and that of its neighbors. South Africa's generals compare their country to the Soviet Union in Eastern Europe or Israel in the Middle East. Its militarization is recent but growing. Despite the United Nations arms embargo of South Africa, established in 1977, the country's military establishment has been able to secure both arms and sophisticated technology from the West to develop its own military industry. South Africa is almost self-sufficient in arms, with a vast and advanced arsenal of weapons and a possible nuclear capacity. The country has begun worldwide sale of its armaments. Military spending has tripled since 1976. The army numbers over fifty thousand, and the reserve consists of most white males below the ages of fifty-five, many of whom are on call against urban insurgents at home while the army itself fights the forces of the Southwest African People's Organization (SWAPO) in Namibia and Angola.

All the countries in Southern Africa share an unwilling acquaintance with South Africa's military strength and suffer from its impact. South Africa has directed military attacks against any country harboring South African exiles who support the African National Congress (ANC) or any other movement of resistance against South Africa. Angola, Lesotho, and Mozambique have been bombarded by South African planes.

South Africa has supported guerrilla movements within neighboring states. These movements have directed their attacks against the rail lines and oil depots so essential to the well-being of these developing economies. In Angola, South Africa's "overflights" have protected the National Union for the Total Independence of Angola (UNITA) in its attacks on railroads including the Benguela railroad, which is used by Zambia and Zimbabwe. In December 1982, the Mozambican National Resistance (MNR) in Mozambique attacked the port and oil depot at Maputo by sea in an exceedingly sophisticated operation, which created crises not only for Mozambique but also for the other landlocked countries of the region, especially Zimbabwe. The MNR also appears to have had South African aid in its destructive raids on Mozambican villages.

There are conflicts within Southern African countries, which South Africa can heighten. Some Zimbabweans have claimed that the dissident movements in Zimbabwe's Matabeleland in 1982 were encouraged by South Africa, and Lesotho authorities have accused South Africa of manipulating the anti-government movement: the Lesotho Liberation Army. There are other signs of South African adventurism. The assassinations of anti-apartheid foes, Joe Gqabi and Ruth First, appear to have been engineered by South Africa.

RECENT AGREEMENTS BETWEEN SOUTH AFRICA AND ITS NEIGHBORS

In past years, Prime Minister Pieter Botha has expressed South Africa's desire for making non-aggression pacts with neighboring states. The first of these agreements, only recently revealed, was signed between Swaziland and South Africa in 1982. In March 1984, South Africa and Mozambique signed a non-aggression pact: the Nkomati Accords. Mozambi-

(United Nations photo)

Followers of Steve Biko left South Africa after the Soweto riots and after his death. They added to the numbers and spirit of the South African Liberation Movement.

(United Nations photo by Jerry Frank)

South Africa's economic and military dominance overshadow the region's planning.

que has agreed to limit acts against South Africa by African National Congress representatives in Mozambique, and the South African government will withdraw support from the MNR fighters in Mozambique. A less formal agreement with Angola will limit Angolan aid to SWAPO forces from Namibia and South Africa's assistance to the anti-government UNITA movement in Angola.

The current economic problems of Southern Africa, the years of drought, the patterns of dependence on South Africa inherited from colonial times, and diplomatic intiatives on the part of the United States have been among the factors leading to the agreements. Whether the pacts will be successful in limiting the actions of the ANC in South Africa or of the MNR and UNITA in Mozambique and Angola is open to question. Although most ANC members have left Mozambique—which continues its moral and diplomatic support of the ANC—the organization has continued its acts of sabotage in South Africa from within. Meanwhile the MNR and UNITA continue their activities, perhaps from their own viable bases, perhaps with South African help.

Thus, the recent agreements may have less significance for keeping peace than was expected. On the other hand, the aid that South Africa has offered to Mozambique and other countries joining the "constellation" may strengthen ties that the black African states also wish to loosen.

FACTORS OF DEPENDENCE

Regional dependence on South Africa has forced many of its neighbors to take a cautious attitude toward South African political refugees, even though they may refuse South African pacts. Seventy-five percent of Southern Africa's rail lines are South African. Fifty percent of Zambia's traffic, as well as sixty to seventy percent of Zimbabwe's exports, move over these rails. Tanzanian and Zimbabwean troops now protect the pipelines and oil depots in Mozambique for these reasons. It is not surprising that Zimbabwe does not allow ANC bases to launch attacks on South Africa from within its boundaries.

The countries of the region also trade with South Africa, as do many other African countries farther north. Economically, South Africa is the most developed country on the continent, with manufactured goods and agricultural surpluses that Africa needs. Forty-six countries in Africa import South African goods and crops, and exports were $1.2 billion in the first ten months of 1980.

Lesotho and Botswana, which are surrounded by South Africa, and Swaziland, which borders South Africa on the east, are especially bound to South Africa, and all three belong to the South African Customs Union, through which they gain South African subsidies. They have also been the recipients of South Africa's expertise. South Africa is building a railroad in Botswana, and a water project in Lesotho is South African-financed. Both projects will benefit South Africa through the increased rail traffic to the country and through the water resources it will gain from the Orange River. These projects illustrate both the readiness of the apartheid state to invest its capital in nearby developing economies and the return that South Africa anticipates.

Migrant laborers who come to work in South Africa increase these interdependencies. Laborers from Mozambique, Lesotho, and Malawi migrated to the mines of South Africa as early as the 1890s; they were driven by colonial taxation policies or were recruited by employers and their agents. After independence, the pattern continued. In 1980, 140 thousand workers left Lesotho to work in South Africa; fifty-six thousand Mozambicans and forty thousand Zimbabweans were also employed there. This is not a tie that is easy to break. For instance, forty percent of Lesotho's national income depends on these wages from abroad. Northern governments unwillingly maintain the pattern because the foreign exchange that migrants provide buys needed imports—one of the most essential of which is food. Often, limited food production in the region has been connected with the fact that agricultural laborers had migrated to the mines. Lack of rainfall has historically been a problem in this region, and in the last few years, the problems of food supply have been greatly increased by one of the worst droughts to affect the region in recent times.

THE DROUGHT

The drought in Southern Africa has neither lasted as long nor been as widely publicized as the drought of West Africa or the Horn, yet it is no less destructive. Authorities note that the lack of rainfall is not an isolated phenomenon but part of a weather pattern or cycle that is likely to last well into the 1980s. Although some countries such as Zimbabwe, Mozambique, and Botswana as well as areas of South Africa have suffered more than others, the same features of the crisis are found everywhere: Water reserves have been depleted; cattle and game, historically a dominant characteristic of this region, are dying; and crop production has declined, often by a half or a third. Human lives are threatened as malnutrition spreads.

Rainfall has declined to forty percent of normal figures in Zimbabwe, and the evidences of such shortage is graphically illustrated in other areas, such as southern Mozambique, where all the dams have dried up and river beds are only sand. In Namibia and South Africa, periods of drought have been followed by heavy rains that have been destructive, rather than regenerating. The sheep industry in Namibia has collapsed; an estimated 500 thousand cattle are threatened in Zimbabwe—150 thousand in the South African homelands. Slaughter houses in South Africa cannot handle the demands of those who fear their cattle won't survive the dry spells;

(United Nations photo)

Although not as severe as the East African drought, conditions have worsened for many Southern Africans.

whereas in Swaziland, where herds are socially valued, people suffer the death of their cattle rather than sell them to the Meat Commission, which offers to buy them.

Maize and cereal production have suffered everywhere. Harvests are estimated to be one-third to one-fourth the size of former yields. In Mozambique, the MNR guerrilla movement has burned and looted food supplies and disrupted farming practices. Zimbabwe and South Africa, which have always had surpluses to sell to other countries of the region that are not self-sufficient, must now import food themselves. In South Africa, there are noticeable contrasts between white areas, where irrigation saves crops, and black homelands, which have no such facilities and depend on the "foreign aid" of the white government. The projects that South Africa has planned to secure further water resources may rob the rivers on which the Sotho and Zulu people depend.

The estimates of human suffering range in the millions. Two million could starve in Zimbabwe; four million are malnourished in Mozambique—one half million in Botswana. Typhoid and, perhaps, cholera threaten. Rinderpest, a cattle disease that had disappeared, has now reappeared, destroy-

ing herds. Other diseases are likely to appear as malnutrition increases. People are moving to the cities, and the potential for further social and political problems in the region increases. It is not a hopeful picture.

THE SOUTH AFRICAN DEVELOPMENT COORDINATION CONFERENCE

A recently established cooperative effort among Southern African states may help to coordinate food assistance as well as to loosen the ties with South Africa and lessen the threat from that country. Southern Africa's black states recognize that they can only break out of South Africa's "constellation" if they can find alternative sources of foreign exchange and other trading partners, increase their mutual infrastructure, and develop their energy resources. They are trying to cooperate on these tasks. The South African Development Coordination Conference (SADCC) was established by an agreement signed in April 1980 in Lusaka.

Several of the states, known as the Frontline States, have coordinated their foreign relations policies in the past and

(World Bank photo)

Regional planning, such as the building of the Kariba dam, is critical to the development of independent economies.

(United Nations photo)

South Africa's neighbors object to the apartheid policy, including the homeland's policy which excludes blacks from citizenship in South Africa proper.

played important roles in the liberation of Zimbabwe and the continuing effort to extract Namibia from South Africa's grasp. Recently, the states of Angola, Botswana, Mozambique, Zambia, and Zimbabwe as well as Tanzania have taken a step to control the world distribution of their news. They have "in principle" banned journalists who report to bureaus in South Africa. South Africa seldom permits journalists from Frontline States to report from within its boundaries, and the authorities in South Africa have passed laws to control outsiders reporting on events within and without of the country. The independent African states want to encourage international media organizations to establish full-time bureaus in their countries. Yet SADCC also seeks to avoid clashes with South Africa and SWAPO, and ANC observers were not invited to the SADCC meeting of early 1984.

SADCC members are doing more than just talking. They are working at practical tasks to exploit the vast potential of their countries, which combined contain sixty million people, one-fifth of Africa's hydroelectric potential, and sixty percent of the continent's coal. Each country has been assigned an arena for research and planning: Angola is responsible for energy; Mozambique for transport and communication; and Tanzania for industry. Already projects are being implemented. Of 119 projects of the Southern African Transport and Communication Commission (SATCC), five are completed, thirty-nine are being implemented, fifty-one are either ready or nearly ready for financing, and only twenty-four are in the early stages of preparation. A new railroad between Mozambique and Malawi has already been started as part of the commission's work.

The organization faces problems besides the threat of South Africa and the problems of drought. The world recession and the related problems of low export and high import prices affect all of the members. Moreover, the ideology of the states differ, ranging from the socialism of Tanzania, Mozambique, and Angola to the capitalist orientations of Zambia and Malawi. Malawi's diplomatic and other relations with South Africa have met with strong disapproval. Disagreements related to these differences may develop as SADCC advances, especially if outside capital and transnational corporations become involved. This is likely to happen, for financial assistance is needed and the organization is actively seeking donors. Yet, SADCC's economic needs and the importance of countering South Africa's power take precedence over these differences at present. SADCC countries are determined to prevent fissures and to avoid such dangers as an overloaded bureaucracy and substantial debts. Moreover, financial donors should be attracted by goals of SADCC, by the possibility of giving financial assistance multilaterally, and by the practical achievements which the conference has already recorded. Financial pledges of over $1 billion have already been made, and this backing may help to brighten the future of a region that has been faced with many difficult challenges.

Angola

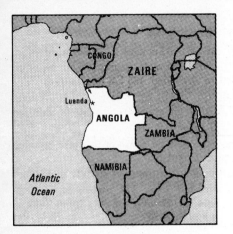

GEOGRAPHY

Area in Square Kilometers (Miles):
1,246,699 (481,351)
Land Usage: 1% cultivated; 44%
forests; 22% meadows and pastures;
33% other
Capital (Population): Luanda
(500,000—1970)
Climate: tropical and subtropical

PEOPLE

Population

Total: 7,452,000 (1982 est.)
Per Square Kilometer (Mile): 6 (15)
Annual Growth Rate: 2.5%
Rural/Urban Population Ratio: 79/21

Health

Life Expectancy at Birth: 41 years
Infant Death Rate (Ratio): 154/1,000
Average Caloric Intake: 83% of
FAO minimum
Physicians Available (Ratio): 1/9,130
(1970)

Languages

Official: Portuguese
Others Spoken: Ovimbundu; Kimbundu; Bakongo

Religion(s)

84% traditional indigenous; 12%
Roman Catholic; 4% Protestant

Education

Adult Literacy Rate: 36% male; 19%
female
School Attendance: primary: 78%
boys, 53% girls; secondary: 30%
boys, 22% girls

COMMUNICATION

Telephones: 10,000
Radios: 140,000
Televisions: 30,000
Newspapers: 5 dailies; total circula-
tion 120,000

CABINDA

The tiny enclave of Cabinda, administered by Portugal as a separate colony until 1950, has an eighty-mile coast north of the mouth of the Zaire (Congo) River. Separated from Angola by a twenty-five-mile strip of land, which allows the vast central African nation of Zaire to "breathe" on the Atlantic, it is the home of about eighty-five thousand people. Gulf Oil Corporation pumps 150 thousand barrels of oil each day from its offshore fields—and royalties are paid to the MPLA government in Luanda. In 1974, a group of politicians tried to declare Cabinda's independence. Although the attempt failed, there was some guerrilla activity, which has all but died out today. Some government and Cuban troops maintain watchful garrisons in the territory.

TRANSPORTATION

Highways—Kilometers (Miles):
73,828 (45,877)
Railroads—Kilometers (Miles): 3,189
(1,982)
Two international airports

GOVERNMENT

Type: people's republic; one-party
rule
Constitution: 1975
Former Colonial Status: Portuguese
Independence Date: November 11,
1975
Head of State: Jose Edouardo dos
Santos (president)
Branches: executive (president);
legislative (National Assembly plann-
ed); judicial
Legal System: changing to "socialist
model"
Political Parties: Popular Movement
for the Liberation of Angola-Labor
Party (MPLA - Labor Party)

MILITARY

Number of Armed Forces: 33,000
(backed by an estimated 19,000
Cubans and 2,500 East Germans)
Armed Forces/Population: 1/200
Nuclear Weapons Status: none
Foreign Aid: Cuba; USSR
Current Hostilities: internal conflicts
with UNITA groups; periodic attacks
from South African forces

ECONOMY

Currency ($ US Equivalent): 30
Kwanza = $1
GDP: $3,900,000
Per Capita Income/GNP: $591
Workforce: 59% agriculture; 16% in-
dustry; 25% service
Inflation Rate: 21% (1970-1980)
Natural Resources: oil; diamonds;
manganese; gold; uranium
Agriculture: coffee; sisal; corn; cot-
ton; sugar; manioc; tobacco;
bananas; plantains
Industry: oil; diamond mining; fish
processing; brewing; tobacco; sugar
processing; textiles; cement; food
processing; construction
Energy Production: 600,000 kw
capacity
Energy Consumption Per Capita: 206
kwh

FOREIGN TRADE

Exports: oil; coffee; diamonds; sisal;
fish; iron ore; timber; corn; cotton
Imports: capital equipment; wines;
bulk iron and ironwork; steel and
metals; vehicles and spare parts; tex-
tiles and clothing; medicines
Major Trading Partners: Cuba;
USSR; Portugal; United States
Foreign Debt:$2,262,000,000
*Selected Membership in International
Organizations:* UN; OAU; African
Development Bank; Non-Aligned
Movement; Southern African
Development Coordination Con-
ference (SADCC)

ANGOLA

Sheets of tin nailed to posts
driven in the ground
make up the house

Some rags complete
the intimate landscape

The sun slanting through cracks
welcomes the owner

This excerpt comes from a poem called *Western Civilization* by the late Agostinho Neto, who was a poet, physician, and liberation fighter and served as the first president of independent Angola. Angola has had a long history of contact with Western countries, but, as the excerpt indicates, such contrast has not bettered the life of its citizens.

The nation's beginnings were ominous. The Portuguese first made contact with peoples of the Kongo State in the northern area of present-day Angola in 1483. The Kongo rulers developed relations with the Portuguese government. Jesuit missionaries arrived; rulers were baptized; and schools were established. Even the art of the time reflected the Portuguese influence. However, Portuguese slave traders soon destroyed these promising beginnings, and the slave trade became the predominant institution connecting Angolans and Westerners during the sixteenth, seventeenth, and eighteenth centuries. Meanwhile, the Portuguese expanded among the kingdoms of the south.

Aside from the slave trade, the Portuguese presence had little impact in earlier times. Then, in the late nineteenth and early twentieth centuries, Portuguese penetration increased, and Portuguese settlement was encouraged. Three hundred thousand Portuguese settlers were living in Angola when the liberation war began. Coffee plantations and diamond mining in Angola had contributed to Portugal's development and had depended on the forced labor of Angolans. Although the Portuguese claimed that they encouraged Angolans to learn Portuguese and to practice Catholicism and Portuguese ways of life (thus becoming "assimilated" and equal to their colonizers), less than one percent of Angolans had achieved this status by the middle of the twentieth century.

Angola is potentially one of the richest countries of Africa, but both the heritage of colonialism and the circumstances since independence have prevented Angolans from fully developing their economic and their human potential. A heritage of war and world conditions have held back the nation.

A HERITAGE OF WAR

The liberation struggle against the Portuguese began with a powerful rebellion in 1961 and lasted for thirteen years. In many

(United Nations photo by J.P. Laffont)

The war for independence from Portugal led to the creation of a one-party socialist state.

ways, it was a constructive struggle. Members of the Popular Movement for the Liberation of Angola (MPLA) were deeply influenced by Marxist ideology and worked to develop new structures and new attitudes among the populations of liberated zones. Women as well as men took an active part in the war and the decision making. Although the MPLA military efforts did not reach the major population centers, by the 1970s, the MPLA had the support of most of the regions. However, there were divisions among the liberation fighters. The National Front for the Liberation of Angola (FLNA) and the National Union for the Total Independence of Angola (UNITA) were never reconciled to MPLA leadership.

When the popular revolution in Portugal in 1974 led to the decolonization of the country's overseas territories, Angola became independent under MPLA. Its leaders were immediately engaged in a new war involving South Africa. It was not until 1976 that the MPLA government could claim to have defeated the South African forces, and they were able to do so only with the assistance of Cuban forces, which have remained in the country since that time.

South African aggression did not end in 1976. Namibia, which borders Angola on the south, is illegally claimed by South Africa. Thirty-five thousand refugees from Namibia have settled in camps in southern

Angola and the South West African People's Organization (SWAPO) has established bases there.

Regularly every December, South African troops have stepped up their attacks on SWAPO bases. In early 1984, at the time of South Africa's Operation Askare, talks between Angola and South Africa in Lusaka led to an agreement for the withdrawal of South African troops and SWAPO and for the formation of a joint monitoring commission. However, by mid-1984, the disengagement had slowed down. South Africa claimed that SWAPO's fighters remained in Angola; Angola declared that South Africa's assistance to UNITA continued.

UNITA has been fighting against the MPLA government since 1975. Nearly destroyed in 1976, UNITA now controls a good one-third of the country, including some of the most fertile agricultural regions. UNITA seems to have support in the countryside and now appears to be carrying the war to the cities. Savimbi has gained international recognition through visits to the United States and Portugal, which put him in touch with important leaders. British, Czech, Phillipine, and other ex-patriates employed by the Angolan government have been taken hostage and released only after direct relations between UNITA and the foreign countries have taken place. Foreign journalists have been encouraged to visit and report on this "state within a state." Meanwhile, Savimbi has publicized his willingness to take part in a coalition government that would unify Angola.

GOVERNMENT SURVIVAL

The legitimate MPLA government is recognized by all countries in the world, with the exception of the United States. However, the government has spent most of its existence fighting for survival. The wars against South Africa and UNITA have eaten up sixty percent of the budget, and the problems of world recession as well as the destruction within the country have meant that the needs of the population are great and the means to satisfy those needs are small. The government has tried to restore the economy by depending upon elected committees of peasants and workers, but practical problems remain.

The major source of government revenues is oil. One hundred and sixty thousand barrels are pumped daily by various oil companies, including Gulf and Texaco. Fifty-one percent of the return goes to Angola, providing ninety percent of its export earnings. The government is concentrating on a major expansion of the oil industry. Production is expected to

| Kongo Kingdom develops **1400** | Kongo Kingdom contacted by Portuguese **1483** | Queen Nzinga defends the Mbundu kingdoms against the Portuguese **1640** | MPLA is founded in Luanda **1956** | National war of liberation begins **1961** | Portuguese grant independence to Angola **1975** | Angolan war against South Africa succeeds with Cuban help **1976** | President Agostinho Neto dies; Jose Eduardo dos Santos becomes president **1979** | Third annual South African incursion into Angola begins; President dos Santos assumes emergency powers **1982** |

1983

| December: South African troops move into Angola in Operation Askare | February 1984: Lusaka talks between Angolans and South Africans lead to formation of a joint monitoring commission of disengagement in southern Angola | July 1984: UNITA blows up a pipeline in Cabinda |

reach 500 thousand barrels by 1990. The government hopes to use the revenue from oil for arms to defeat South Africa and UNITA and for the development that will counteract UNITA's appeal.

Other sources of wealth appear less promising. All earnings are below pre-independence levels. Prices for diamonds, Angola's second major mineral enterprise, have declined, and production of coffee, the major cash crop, went from 225 thousand tons in 1974-1975 to twenty-six thousand in 1978-1979. Many coffee plantations remain untended. Industrial production has also dropped since independence, in part because of the emigration of Portuguese residents, many of whom had technical skills. Now only ten thousand Portuguese remain as Angolan citizens. Railroads, such as the independently-owned Benguela line, need new engines and are disrupted by UNITA attacks.

Even more serious is the decline in food production. The turmoil of recent years has displaced approximately a half a million people. Farmers have not been able to plant their crops, and harvests have declined. Not only has the government been forced to import ninety percent of its food, but it has had to spend needed foreign exchange to do so. In 1981 the United Nations Disaster Relief Organization estimated that one-half million people needed food and other assistance.

In December 1982 President Edouardo dos Santos was given emergency powers to deal with the current crisis. It is speculated that recent changes in the leadership of the government and the party will increase

government efficiency and accommodation with the West. In general, despite the exclusive attention given to the Cuban presence in the country, Angola has shown a non-aligned approach in its world trading relations and in its acceptance of advisors—depending on partners as varied as Brazil, Japan, Portugal, Russia, and Cuba. Eighty percent of its trade is with the West. Western bankers and businessmen have found that Angola is a reliable partner, who plays bills on time and honors contracts. The government has tried to avoid borrowing, and this has kept the country out of debt. However, Angola has not been able to avoid the repercussions of the recent world recession, and austerity measures are now being effected.

CONCLUSION

Angola's hardships will be lessened when the negotiations over Namibia are completed and that country moves to independence. As of mid-1984, the situation seemed unchanged, despite the agreement for withdrawals between Angola and South Africa. South Africa continues to maintain troops and administration in Namibia, and the withdrawal of SWAPO and South Africa from Angola seems an unlikely prospect.

One of the main disagreements of the two countries is the issue of the Cuban troops. The United States and South Africa have linked movement toward Namibian independence to the withdrawal of the approximately 20,000 - 25,000 Cuban troops from Angola. Angola and Cuba agree that

the troops should stay until South Africa withdraws from Namibia.

As UNITA has gained more influence and territory in Angola, the MPLA government has turned to its Cuban allies for aid against these so-called "bandits," whom the government suspects are still funded by South Africa. UNITA's base, developed over long years, is strong. In the future, the MPLA government may have to agree to a coalition government or continue to fight a civil war. Thus, the Cuban factor is likely to play a continuing and important role in Angola and in the negotiations about its future and the future of Namibia.

"No one/can stop the rain," wrote Neto in one of the poems he composed in jail in 1960. He was alluding to the inevitability of independence. Angolans and others still wait for "the winds of history" to bring forth an Angola that is truly free.

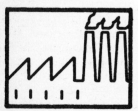

DEVELOPMENT

The Ulysses Motorcycle factory in Huambo, Central Angola, which is run in cooperation with Yamaha of Japan, is a promising—if small—example of development. Its bicycles and motorcycles are made by a predominantly female workforce, led by a woman factory director, and its products are desired and useful throughout Angola.

FREEDOM

The MPLA party organs direct activities in Angola, but there have been efforts to increase popular participation in recent years. Provincial assemblies were created in 1980, and elections for a national People's Assembly occurred in November 1980.

HEALTH/WELFARE

The insurgency movement, UNITA, claims to have two hundred health centers, and a network of hospitals exists. The health care that UNITA offers in areas of South Eastern Angola have brought it support.

ACHIEVEMENTS

Despite the present turmoil, Angola has been able to improve its educational system. Eighty-two percent of the primary school age population is enrolled in school, and the basic literacy programs have been expanded. Important educational programs exist at SWAPO refugee camps in the south.

Botswana

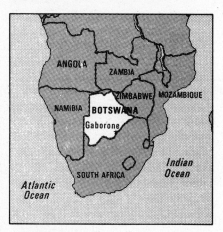

GEOGRAPHY

Area in Square Kilometers (Miles): 569,800 (220,000)
Land Usage: 6% arable; less than 1% under cultivation; 93% desert
Capital (Population): Gaborone (59,700—1981)
Climate: arid; semi-arid

PEOPLE

Population
Total: 859,000 (1982 est.)
Per Square Kilometer (Mile): 1.5 (3.9)
Annual Growth Rate: 3.3%
Rural/Urban Population Ratio: 80/20

Health
Life Expectancy at Birth: 51 years
Infant Death Rate (Ratio): 83/1,000
Average Caloric Intake: 90% of FAO minimum
Physicians Available (Ratio): 1/9,970

Languages
Official: Setswana; English
Others Spoken: Khoisan

Religion(s)
85% traditional indigenous; 15% Christian

Education
Adult Literacy Rate: 37% males; 44% females
School Attendance: primary: 94% boys, 100% girls; secondary: 21% boys, 25% girls

COMMUNICATION

Telephones: 11,700
Radios: 80,000
Newspapers: 1 daily; total circulation 17,000

TRANSPORTATION

Highways—Kilometers (Miles): 10,784 (6,701)
Railroads—Kilometers (Miles): 726 (451)
Three international airports

GOVERNMENT

Type: parliamentary republic
Constitution: 1966
Former Colonial Status: British
Independence Date: September 30, 1966
Head of State: Quett K.J. Masire (president)
Branches: president and cabinet; National Assembly; High Court
Legal System: based on Roman-Dutch law and local customary law
Political Parties: Botswana Democratic Party; Botswana National Front; Botswana People's Party; Botswana Independence Party
Suffrage: universal over 21 years

MILITARY

Number of Armed Forces: 3,260
Armed Forces/Population: 1/304
Military Expenditures (% of Central Government Expenditures): $28,700,000 (4.6%)
Nuclear Weapons Status: none
Current Hostilities: none

ECONOMY

Currency ($ US Equivalent): 1 pula = $1
GDP: $856,300,000
Per Capita Income/GNP: $900
Workforce: 78% agriculture; 8% industry; 14% service
Inflation Rate: 16.5% (1982)
Natural Resources: diamonds; copper; nickel; salt; soda ash; potash; coal
Agriculture: livestock; sorghum; corn; millet; cowpeas; beans
Industry: diamonds; copper; nickel; salt; soda ash; potash; frozen beef; tourism
Energy Production: 75,000 kw capacity
Energy Consumption Per Capita: 120 kwh

FOREIGN TRADE

Exports: diamonds; cattle; animal products; copper; nickel
Imports: foodstuffs; vehicles; textiles; petroleum products
Major Trading Partners: South Africa; UK
Foreign Debt: $310,000,000
Selected Membership in International Organizations: UN; OAU; Commonwealth of Nations; Non-Aligned Movement; African Development Bank; Southern Africa Development Coordination Conference (SADCC); Frontline States

Tswana establish
themselves in
Southern Africa
1400s

Invading groups
of Nguni and
Southern Sotho
threaten the
Tswana
1820s

Afrikaners begin
to encroach on
Tswana land
north of the
Orange River
1839

British establish
colonial rule over
Botswana
1885

Botswana gains
independence
1966

Seretse Khama,
the nation's first
president, dies
in office
1980

1983

February: Severe
drought causes
crop failure;
previous year's
austerity
measures relaxed

April: Refugees
from Western
Zimbabwe enter
the country

Spring 1984:
Diamond sales
up sharply
in 1983

REPUBLIC OF BOTSWANA

Botswana, an arid country about the size of Texas that has a population of just under a million, has been the Cinderella story of post-colonial Africa. The country emerged from eighty years of not-so-benign British colonial neglect in 1966 as a drought-stricken, underdeveloped backwater with a per capita income of only $69. In the seventeen years since this less-than-auspicious beginning, however, the nation's economy has grown at an annual rate averaging thirteen percent, one of the world's highest. Social services have gradually been expanded, and Botswana's success has gradually been translated into a better standard of living for the majority of its population. Yet the country also remains vulnerable to the uncertainties of international markets, the problems of weather, and the designs of its powerful neighbor: South Africa.

Most of Botswana's citizens are Tswana, a group that is also represented in the population of South Africa. A number of minority groups also exist, but there has been relatively little ethnic conflict during contemporary times. A notable characteristic of the Tswana is their historic preference for living in large settlements with populations of ten thousand or more. In the past, these communities centered around crops, cattle, and trade. A radical transformation took place in the late nineteenth century, when colonial taxes and economic decline stimulated the growth of migrant labor to the mines and industries of South Africa. In many regions, migrant earnings remain the major source of income.

DROUGHT DEVASTATING

The standard Tswana greeting, *"pula"* ("rain") reflects the traditional significance attached to water in a society prone to its periodic scarcity. The country is presently undergoing a severe drought, which—despite the availability of underground water supplies—has had a devastating effect on both crops and livestock. Small-scale agro-pastoralists have been particularly hard hit.

The cattle industry is an important part of the economy, dominating the agricultural sector. The Lobatse slaughterhouse, which opened in 1954, stimulated the growth of the cattle industry, and a second planned slaughterhouse will serve northern producers. An outbreak of foot and mouth disease in the late 1970s led to a marketing decline, and revived production may now be threatened by the drought.

Mining is the most important aspect of the economy. Since independence, the rapid expansion of local mining activity has fostered Botswana's recent internal growth. The dominance of South African capital in most new enterprises has caused concern, but the Botswanan government has a good record of maximizing Botswana's share of benefits. The Selebi-Pikwe nickel/copper mine is the nation's largest employer and accounts for roughly twenty-five percent of the country's export earnings. A fifty percent cutback in diamond purchases in 1981 created a balance of payments crisis that caused the government to adopt stringent austerity measures. The situation has since eased somewhat, and major expansions in diamond output are scheduled for the future.

Despite recent setbacks—as well as a concern by both individuals and the government over the social implications of a growing gap between the relatively well-off and the poor—Botswana's future prospects are considered relatively bright. Much optimism rests on the still considerable potential of the country, particularly in the north and west. A significant step forward could be the construction of the long-discussed trans-Kgalagadi railway to Namibia, a project that is jeopardized by South Africa's continued occupation of Namibia.

THE SOUTH AFRICA PROBLEM

South Africa remains a lingering problem. For many years, refugees from racist oppression have found a haven in Botswana. The on-going South African campaign of regional destabilization has caused fear in many quarters that Botswana could become a future military and/or economic target. Nevertheless, the nation has maintained its principled opposition to apartheid and has been active in promoting majority rule as a member of the Frontline States.

Since independence, Botswana has survived as one of the few multi-party democracies in Africa. The nation's record in human rights is spotless. Its liberal character and on-going concern for social justice have made Botswana a symbol of peace and progress for people of all races in Southern Africa.

DEVELOPMENT

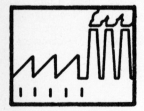

Progress is being made toward fulfilling the goals of the nation's third five-year plan, despite the recent economic slowdown. In 1981 Gaberone was chosen to house the secretariat of the new Southern African Development Coordinating Council (SADCC).

FREEDOM

Botswana's reputation for tolerating pluralism has recently been reinforced by the publication of two new privately-owned daily newspapers—*The Examiner* and *Botswana Guardian*. The government-owned *Botswana Daily News* continues to air criticisms by opposition groups.

HEALTH/WELFARE

Recent progress is said to have brought eighty-five to ninety percent of the country's population to within fifteen kilometers of a health care facility. Many Tswana students have been sent abroad for training as health professionals.

ACHIEVEMENTS

The Tswana are renown as innovators. In 1909 one of Africa's first indigenous government-owned corporations was founded in northern Botswana. More recently, researchers have succeeded in developing a light low-cost plow/planter/cultivator that could have a significant impact on peasant farming in Central and Southern Africa.

Lesotho

GEOGRAPHY

Area in Square Kilometers (Miles):
30,344 (11,716)
Land Usage: 15% arable; largely
mountainous
Capital (Population): Maseru
(45,000—1976)
Climate: temperate

PEOPLE

Population
Total: 1,409,000 (1982 est.)
Per Square Kilometer (Mile): 46
(120)
Annual Growth Rate: 2.5%
Rural/Urban Population Ratio: 88/12

Health
Life Expectancy at Birth: 52 years
Infant Death Rate (Ratio): 115/1,000
Average Caloric Intake: 107% of
FAO minimum
Physicians Available (Ratio):
1/18,640
Access to Safe Water: 17%

Languages
Official: English; Sesotho
Others Spoken: Xhosa; Zulu

Religion(s)
70% Christian; 30% traditional indigenous beliefs

Education
Adult Literacy Rate: 58% males;
82% females
School Attendance: primary: 84%
boys, 100% girls; secondary: 13%
boys, 20% girls

THE SESOTHO LANGUAGE

Since the mid-nineteenth century, Sesotho has been a leading literary language in Africa. Basotho writers have produced a wealth of prose, poetry, and nonfiction in their vernacular. The *Leselinyane La Lesotho,* first published in 1863, is sub-Saharan Africa's oldest continuous vernacular newspaper. Thomas Mofolo's play *Chaka* and Paulas Mopeli's novel *Blanket Boy* are among the many works which have been translated for international audiences. Sesotho also continues to be a major medium in music, journalism, and broadcasting. The South African government has promoted a separate Sesotho alphabet for use among Sotho peoples living in South Africa. This has created one more barrier for South Africans who have tried to encourage re-convergence among various regional dialects.

COMMUNICATION

Telephones: 4,500
Radios: 35,000
Newspapers: 3 dailies; total circula-
tion 1,300

TRANSPORTATION

Highways—Kilometers (Miles): 4,033
(2,506)
Railroads—Kilometers (Miles): 1.6
(.994)
One international airport

GOVERNMENT

Type: constitutional monarchy with
king as chief of state
Constitution: suspended in 1970
Former Colonial Status: British
Independence Date: October 4, 1966
Head of State: Moshoeshoe II (king)
Branches: prime minister and
Cabinet; Interim National Assembly;
High Court
Legal System: based on British law
and customary law
Political Parties: Basutoland National
Party; Basutoland Congress Party;
Marematlou Freedom Party; United
Democratic Party
Suffrage: universal over age 21

MILITARY

Number of Armed Forces: 1,500
Armed Forces/Population: 1/930
Nuclear Weapons Status: none
Current Hostilities: none

ECONOMY

Currency ($ US Equivalent): 1
Maluti = $1
GDP: $300,000,000
Per Capita Income/GNP: $510
Workforce: 87% agriculture; 4% in-
dustry; 9% services
Inflation Rate: 11.2% (1981)
Natural Resources: diamonds; water;
agricultural and grazing land
Agriculture: mohair; corn; wheat;
sorghum; peas; beans; potatoes;
asparagus; sheep; cattle
Industry: carpet; woolen apparel;
candlemaking; pottery; jewelry;
tapestry; tourism; mining
Energy Production: 35,000,000 kwh
imported from South Africa

FOREIGN TRADE

Exports: wool; mohair; cattle;
diamonds; agricultural goods
Imports: manufactured goods;
foodstuffs; machinery; transport
equipment
Major Trading Partners: South
Africa; Europe
Foreign Debt:$188,100,000
*Selected Membership in International
Organizations:* UN; OAU; Com-
monwealth of Nations; Southern
African Customs Union; Non-
Aligned Movement; Southern Africa
Development Coordination Con-
ference (SADCC)

Lesotho emerges
as a leading
state in
Southern Africa
1820s

Afrikaners annex
half of Lesotho
1866

The Sotho
successfully fight
to preserve
local autonomy
under the British
1870-1881

Independence
restored
1966

Elections and
Constitution
declared void
by Prime Minister
Leabua Jonathan
1970

Uprising against
the government
fails
1974

Lesotho Libera-
tion Army (LLA)
begins sabotage
campaign
1979

South Africa
raids Maseru
1982

1983

February: Oil
depot at Maseru
destroyed; LLA
claims respon-
sibility; university
closed following
unrest

May: Elections
under old Con-
stitution approved

Spring 1984:
Relations with
South Africa
appear to improve
with new nego-
tiations and a
lessening of LLA
activities; author-
ities detain
members of the
Lesotho Evan-
gelical Church

KINGDOM OF LESOTHO

The beauty of its snow-topped mountains has led visitors to proclaim Lesotho
the "Switzerland of Africa." Unlike its
European namesake, however, this small
independent enclave in the heart of South
Africa has recently enjoyed neither peace
nor prosperity. Listed by the United Nations as one of the world's Least Developed
Countries, each year the lack of opportunity at home causes half of Lesotho's
adult males to seek employment in South
Africa. Foreign aid and a share of customs
collected by South Africa are the next
largest sources of revenue. A small-scale
local insurgency campaign as well as escalating tensions with South Africa and its
homeland client states have lately added to
the burden of chronic underdevelopment. A
restoration of constitutional rule and elections have been promised in the coming
year (1984), which could prove to be an
especially significant time for Lesotho
citizens.

HOMOGENOUS NATION

Lesotho is one of the most ethnically
homogenous nations in Africa. Almost all
its citizens belong to the Sotho group. The
country's emergence and survival were
largely the product of the diplomatic and
military prowess of its nineteenth-century
chiefs, especially the greater founder Moshoeshoe. During the 1860s, warfare with
South African whites led to the loss of land
and people, as well as an acceptance of

British overrule. For nearly a century, the
British preserved the country but taxed the
inhabitants and generally neglected their
interests. Consequently, Lesotho remains
dependent on its neighbor, South Africa.
However, despite South African attempts
to incorporate the country politically as
well as economically, Lesotho's independence was restored by the British in 1966.

Lesotho's politicians were bitterly divided
at independence, and opposition leaders
boycotted the ceremony. In 1970, Prime
Minister Leobua Jonathan of the ruling
National Party nullified an election won by
the rival Congress Party and suspended the
Constitution. A multi-party Interim National Assembly was appointed in 1973,
but failed to bring about a reconciliation.
An apparent coup attempt was repressed in
1974. Since 1979 there has been an escalating campaign of violence within the
country, which has been carried out by the
Lesotho Liberation Army, an armed faction of the Congress Party. The government
maintains that this group is aided and
abetted by South Africa as part of that
country's regional destabilization efforts.

LIMITED COOPERATION WITH SOUTH AFRICA'S POWER

While consistent in its opposition to
apartheid, the government recognizes the
necessity for limited cooperation with South
Africa. Producers of wool (the nation's
largest export after labor) must rely on the
South African marketing boards. South

African interests are also heavily involved
in Lesotho's small tourist and diamond
industries. The Lesotho National Development Corporation actively seeks to
attract further South African investment.
The project that appears to have the greatest potential is a long-standing scheme to
exploit Lesotho's hydroelectric potential
for South African industry. At present,
negotiations on this project are stalled over
who would have ultimate control of the
facility.

South Africa has been less-than-subtle in
exerting pressure on Lesotho. When the
nation gave verbal support to the OAU call
for a boycott of South Africa (in 1974), oil
deliveries were cut back, and ten thousand
Sotho migrant workers were fired. In December 1982, the South African army
raided the capital city, Maseru, and murdered a number of Sotho as well as South
African refugees. Since then, there has
been a major slow-down of traffic and
reports of new armed incursions from the
South African side of the border.

DEVELOPMENT

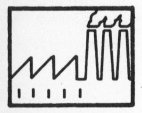

A major governmental priority is
the improvement of internal communications. Presently, many
communities are only accessible
via South Africa. An international
airport is also being built.

FREEDOM

Since the suspension of the Constitution, there have been allegations of human rights abuses,
many of which have involved the
nation's paramilitary Police Mobile
Unit. The government blames
South Africa and the Lesotho
Liberation Army for continued violence and has scheduled elections in 1984.

HEALTH/WELFARE

Much of the resident population
relies on subsistence agriculture.
Despite efforts to boost productivity, malnutrition is a serious
problem, which has been aggravated lately by drought.

ACHIEVEMENTS

Lesotho has long been known for
the high quality of its schools,
which for over a century and a half
have trained many of the leading
citizens of Southern Africa. The
national university at Roma was
established in 1945 and for a while
served as the main campus of the
University of Botswana, Lesotho,
and Swaziland until it resumed its
autonomous status in 1976.

Malawi

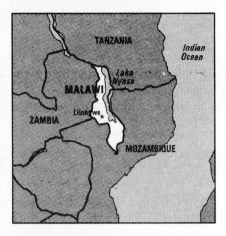

GEOGRAPHY

Area in Square Kilometers (Miles):
118,484 (45,747)
Land Usage: 31% arable; 25%
forests; 6% meadow and pasture;
38% other
Capital (Population): Lilongwe
(98,718—1977)
Climate: subtropical

PEOPLE

Population
Total: 6,267,000 (1982 est.)
Per Square Kilometer (Mile): 53
(137)
Annual Growth Rate: 2.6%
Rural/Urban Population Ratio: 90/10

Health
Life Expectancy at Birth: 56 years
Infant Death Rate (Ratio): 172/1,000
Average Caloric Intake: 97% FAO
minimum
Physicians Available (Ratio):
1/41,010
Access to Safe Water: 33%

Languages
Official: Chichewa; English
Others Spoken: Chewa; Nyanja;
Lomwe; Yao; Sena; Tumbuka

Religion(s)
indigenous; Christian; Muslim

Education
Adult Literacy Rate: 48% males;
25% females
School Attendance: primary: 70%
boys, 49% girls; secondary: 6%
boys, 2% girls

JOHN CHILEMBWE

In 1915, John Chilembwe of Nyasaland (now Malawi) "struck a blow" against British colonialism and died in the attempt. Chilembwe was a Christian minister who had studied in South Africa as well as in the United States. He had returned home to establish the Providence Industrial Mission and to build a great church. His feelings against the British settlers developed from the injustices he perceived: the European takeover of lands for plantations, the poor working conditions for laborers, the increased taxation, and, especially, the recruitment of Africans to fight and die in Europe's World War I. He rallied a few followers and planned an uprising, which led to the death of three settlers and the death or imprisonment of the Africans involved or suspected of involvement. Chilembwe appears to have planned his martyrdom. This uprising was the first effort in East Africa to resist colonialism and yet maintain many of the aspects of society that had developed from its influence.

COMMUNICATION

Telephones: 28,800
Radios: 275,000
Newspapers: 2 dailies; total circulation 31,000

TRANSPORTATION

Highways—Kilometers (Miles):
11,311 (7,028)
Railroads—Kilometers (Miles): 754
(470)
Two international airports

GOVERNMENT

Type: republic; one-party state
Constitution: July 6, 1966
Former Colonial Status: British
Independence Date: July 6, 1964
Head of State: H. Kamuzu Banda
(president-for-life)
Branches: president and Cabinet;
unicameral National Assembly; High
Court
Legal System: based on English
Common Law and customary law
Political Parties: Malawi Congress
Party
Suffrage: universal over age 21

MILITARY

Number of Armed Forces: 5,000
Armed Forces/Population: 1/1,282
Nuclear Weapons Status: none
Current Hostilities: none

ECONOMY

Currency ($ US Equivalent): 1
Malawi kwachas = $1
GDP: $1,320,000,000
Per Capita Income/GNP: $210
Workforce: 86% agriculture; 5% industry; 9% services
Inflation Rate: 9.8% (1970-1980);
14% (1982)
Natural Resources: limestone;
uranium potential
Agriculture: tobacco; tea; sugar;
corn; peanuts
Industry: food; beverages; tobacco;
textiles; footwear
Energy Production: 124,000 kw
capacity
Energy Consumption Per Capita: 55
kwh

FOREIGN TRADE

Exports: tobacco; tea; sugar; peanuts
Imports: machinery; transportation
equipment; manufactured goods; oil
Major Trading Partners: United
Kingdom; United States; South
Africa; Netherlands; West Germany;
Japan
Foreign Debt:$867,300,000
*Selected Membership in International
Organizations:* UN; OAU; Commonwealth of Nations; Associate
Member, European Communities
(EC); World Bank; African Development Bank; Non-Aligned Movement;
Southern African Development Coordination Conference (SADCC)

								Austerity budget bans new government development projects; creditors reschedule debts 1982
Malawi trading kingdoms develop 1500s	David Livingstone arrives along Lake Malawi; missionaries follow 1859	British protectorate of Nyasaland (present-day Malawi) is declared 1891	Reverend John Chilembwe and followers rise against settlers and are suppressed 1915	Nyasaland African Congress, first nationalist movement, is formed 1944	Independence under the leadership of Hastings Banda 1964	Diplomatic ties established with South Africa 1967	Dr. Hastings Kamuzu Banda becomes "life president" 1971		

● 1983

May: Traditional court sentences Orton and Vera Chirwa to death for treason	June: Malawians vote for a new legislature, which serves under President Banda

MALAWI

Malawi is a beautiful country, which is little known to outsiders because it rarely appears in the news. Foreign journalists are not often allowed in the country. What little we learn from the media comes from government sources or exiles in opposition. One must construct the reality from opposing images.

President-for-life Dr. Ngwazi Hastings Kamuzu Banda, now in his mid-eighties, has developed and maintained an unusually tight reign over the government and the nation. Cabinet reshufflings limit the development of possible power bases by rising politicians. Anyone—even Banda's close associates—who receives too much public praise or attention may be suspect, imprisoned, or prone to "accidents." No successor has been designated, and those suggested have reason to worry. Banda's "official hostess," Cecilia Kadzamira, and her uncle, John Tembo, are the only individuals known to have influence with the president, and Tembo has recently been replaced as Governor of the Central Bank.

DISSIDENT GROUPS

Dissident groups based outside the country began to be formed in 1964—the very year of independence—when six senior ministers were dismissed or resigned after protesting slow Africanization and accommodation to South Africa. Presently, there are three liberation groups outside Malawi: MAFREMO (the Malawi Freedom Movement), LESOMA (the Socialist League of Malawi), and the Congress for the Second Republic. Members of these opposition groups are in danger from Ban-

da's regime even when they are in other countries; Attati Mpakatiso, leader of LESOMA, was assassinated while in Harare, Zimbabwe. Orton and Vera Chirwa of MAFREMO—whose appeal against the death sentence has recently been denied—claim they were captured in Zambia.

The president, while ruthless, has been politically astute and seems to have the respect and support of ordinary citizens. There is no evidence of rebellions, strikes, or refugee movements to other countries. Government controls are evident. Migration to the cities is restricted. The government oversees popular groups.

RURAL LIFE IMPROVED

Life seems to have improved for the plain farmers who make up the majority of Malawi's inhabitants. They have been served by projects initiated and aided by government and by outside agencies. Self-reliance has been encouraged. The country is fortunate to have some of the most fertile soil of the region, and Malawians have not suffered from the droughts presently affecting other Southern African countries.

Yet the country remains very poor, and figures for health care, life expectancy, and infant mortality are low and have shown little improvement. While workers, such as those on the tea plantations, have complained about conditions without achieving any results, some citizens have benefitted more than others from the economy. The owners of tea, tobacco, and sugar estates, rather than ordinary farmers, have gained from the influx of aid into the country. Ministers of government and higher civil servants, as well as President Banda, accumulate wealth and land.

CONSERVATIVE COURSE

Banda has kept Malawi on a conservative course in its foreign relations policies. Early in his presidency, he established diplomatic relations with South Africa, and he has accepted loans and exchanged visits with South African leaders. In recent years, the country has developed better relations with its neighbors: Zambia, Tanzania, and Mozambique. It has become an active member of SADCC, working for the development of links between Southern African countries, without dependence on South Africa.

Despite what sources describe as cautious policies and good financial management, Malawi, like many other African nations, has suffered financially from the recent world recession as well as the problems accompanying the rising prices of oil and industrial goods and the declining prices of raw materials and cash crops. An austerity budget passed in March 1982 banned any new development plans, and official debts were rescheduled at a September 1982 meeting of Malawi with its creditors.

The government has always claimed that economic development can only be accomplished in an atmosphere of "peace and calm, law and order," but limits on freedom and social inequities may not be so acceptable in the future if people believe that their lives are getting worse instead of better.

DEVELOPMENT

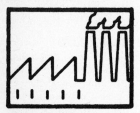

A National Rural Development Program (NRDP), begun in 1977, is Malawi's largest single project and will take twenty years to fulfill. Integrated health, administrative, and agricultural services are being developed in each of four target areas of the country.

FREEDOM

The climate of suspicion in Malawi resulting from President Banda's fear of opposition has led to arbitrary arrests and numerous detentions without charges. Orton Chirwa of the Malawi Freedom Movement was supposedly captured in Zambia, and he and his wife have recently been sentenced to death for treason in Malawi.

HEALTH/WELFARE

Educational opportunities have increased greatly in recent years and 800 thousand were attending schools in 1979. Secondary schools are limited to an elite group. The Kamuzu Academy, which opened in 1981, hires foreign teachers and trains students who will attend universities abroad.

ACHIEVEMENTS

Piped water is increasingly available to villagers in Malawi through their own efforts. Nearly three thousand kilometers of pipes have been laid from hills to plains, and four thousand standpipes have been installed at the cost of about $5 per person. Malawians are now working on a groundwater program that will supply thirty thousand more Malawians with clean water.

Mozambique

GEOGRAPHY

Area in Square Kilometers (Miles):
786,762 (303,769)
Land Usage: 30% arable; 56%
woodland and forests; 14% waste
and other
Capital (Population): Maputo
(850,000—1982)
Climate: tropical to subtropical

PEOPLE

Population
Total: 11,052,000 (1982 est.)
Per Square Kilometer (Mile): 14 (36)
Annual Growth Rate: 2.7%
Rural/Urban Population Ratio: 91/9
Age: 43% below 15 years

Health
Life Expectancy at Birth: 46 years
Infant Death Rate (Ratio): 115/1,000
Average Caloric Intake: 78% FAO
minimum
Physicians Available (Ratio):
1/39,110

Languages
Official: Portuguese
Others Spoken: Wayao; Tumbuka;
Batonga; Makua

Religion(s)
65% indigenous; 22% Christian;
11% Muslim; 2% other

Education
Adult Literacy Rate: 44% males;
23% females
School Attendance: primary: 100%
boys, 78% girls; secondary: 9%
boys, 4% girls
Teacher/Student Ratio: 1/272

COMMUNICATION
Telephones: 51,600
Radios: 255,000
Televisions: 1,500
Newspapers: 2 dailies; total circula-
tion 42,000

OPERATION PRODUCTION

Low stocks of food, high populations, unemployment in the cities, drought, and a scarcity of labor in the countryside are among the problems that are facing Mozambique presently. The government has attempted to solve these problems in many ways. Nearly fifty thousand "unproductive individuals" have been rounded up in cities such as Maputo and Biera and resettled in the northern areas, often on state cotton, tea, and sugar farms. People who commit economic crimes such as smuggling, hoarding, or black marketeering may be flogged—a colonial punishment that has now been reintroduced. Execution is one punishment for economic crimes. These policies reveal the urgency of the crisis Mozambique is facing. The economic disruption caused by a South African supported resistance movement may lessen as a result of a recent South Africa-Mozambique security pact.

TRANSPORTATION
Highways—Kilometers (Miles):
26,498 (16,465)
Railroads—Kilometers (Miles): 3,436
(2,135)
Three international airports

GOVERNMENT
Type: people's republic
Constitution: June 25, 1975
Former Colonial Status: Portuguese
Independence Date: June 25, 1975
Head of State: Samora Machel
(president)
Branches: executive (president, cen-
tral and executive committees of
FRELIMO, Cabinet); legislative
(none); judicial
Legal System: based on Portuguese
Civil Law and customary law
Political Parties: Mozambique
Liberation Front (FRELIMO)
Suffrage: not yet established

MILITARY
Number of Armed Forces: 26,700
(with advisors from Cuba, China,
USSR, and German Democratic
Republic)
Armed Forces/Population: 1/475
*Military Expenditures (% of Central
Government Expenditures):*
$157,800,000 (27.8%)
Nuclear Weapons Status: none
Foreign Aid: USSR; People's
Republic of China; Portugal
Current Hostilities: raids by South
African forces

ECONOMY
Currency ($ US Equivalent): 35
Meticals = $1
GDP: $2,800,000,000
Per Capita Income/GNP: $272
Workforce: 66% agriculture; 18% in-
dustry; 16% services
Inflation Rate: 11.2% (1970-1980)
Natural Resources: coal; iron ore;
tantalite; flourite; timber
Agriculture: cotton; tobacco;
cashews; sugar; tea; copra; sisal;
subsistence crops
Industry: processed foods; textiles;
beverages; refined oil; chemicals;
tobacco; cement; glass
Energy Production: 2,166,000 kw
capacity
Energy Consumption Per Capita:
1,080 kwh

FOREIGN TRADE
Exports: cashews; cotton; sugar;
copra; gasoline; tea; wood products
Imports: machinery; transportation
equipment; metal; petroleum pro-
ducts; cotton textiles
Major Trading Partners: Portugal;
South Africa; United Kingdom; West
Germany; USSR; People's Republic
of China; United States
Foreign Debt: $500,000,000
*Selected Membership in International
Organizations:* UN; OAU; Non-
Aligned Movement; Southern Africa
Development Coordination Con-
ference (SADCC)

MOZAMBIQUE

Ordinary life is difficult—even desperate—for many people in Mozambique today. Three years of extensive drought and other natural disasters has been compounded by war. Many people are hungry, must move to live, are separated from their loved ones, and barter because of lack of money. These circumstances interfere with the new society that Mozambique has been seeking to build since independence.

"Let us make the entire country into a school where everybody learns and everybody teaches." Independent, Mozambique has been a country where everyone is encouraged to contribute their ideas to the building of the nation. Dynamic democratic responsibility is actively practiced. Not only are leaders elected to their positions, but the people themselves participate in making decisions.

In a small and growing number of communal villages, citizens work together to develop productive communities. Worker councils are found in the factories; participatory committees exist in towns. Ordinary people with some training run the 300 people's courts, which make an "offensive for legality," especially in the rural areas. Civilian militias, which include women members, are active throughout the country. In the schools, students are involved in formal lessons, but they also decide among themselves how they will work collectively to solve some of the very real problems of the community. There is much social pressure, but there is also much enthusiasm throughout the society for learning and teaching.

Mozambique has a Marxist-Leninist Socialist Government, and the Mozambique Liberation Front (FRELIMO), which has about 100 thousand members, is the legal political party. The government controls the press, puts limits on the rights of assembly, and oversees all organizations. Yet, ordinary people play an important role in criticizing government policy and making suggestions for future development. In 1983, seventy-two percent of the party members of the Fourth Annual Congress of FRELIMO were workers, peasants, and soldiers. The meetings that Central Committee members held in the countryside before the Congress aroused lively criticism and discussion.

President Samora Machel has been president since independence in 1974, and he is a charismatic leader. He and his administration have been responsive to criticism and to the needs of ordinary people. Government has been flexible in its policies and has been ready to recognize mistakes and change course. The people's stores, taken over by the government when the owners

The fourth Congress of Mozambique's ruling FRELIMO party moved away from large development projects in favor of smaller projects and grass roots socialism.

fled in 1974, were given back to private ownership because they did not operate effectively. The 1983 party congress discussed the failings of the state farms and determined that small local communal farming efforts should be stressed in the future. Members agreed to encourage private agricultural enterprise, which had formerly been banned.

President Machel and the government have also responded quickly to complaints about the brutality of security forces and corruption of bureaucrats. A major "clean up" campaign took place in 1982 and 1983; police officers and civil servants have been brought to trial. In line with Mozambique's "teaching and learning" approach, those accused of brutality and corruption are often sent to isolated "reeducation camps" rather than to prison. There is no evidence of a wealthy elite class.

THE PROBLEMS FACING MOZAMBICANS

"In fact we are not a developing country. We are an underdeveloping coun-

try. . . . We are getting poorer and poorer each year," according to the Minister of Information, Jose Luis Cabaco. Mozambique is very poor, and although the people work together to improve their circumstances, progress is not evident. Mozambique is not naturally wealthy; except for coal, there are no extensive mineral deposits. The predominantly rural population is sparsely distributed. Agriculture is the mainstay of the economy, but at the time of independence less than ten percent of the arable land was cultivated. Foods and cash crops—including cotton, sugar, tea, and, especially, cashew nuts—have been hard hit by recent droughts, and, most recently, by a terrible cyclone and floods. The state farms have lowered, rather than increased, production of crops such as rice. The world recession means that prices for exports have dropped, while the prices of imports rise.

Its heritage also holds Mozambique back. The country was under Portuguese rule for over 400 years, until the revolution of 1974 in Portugal brought freedom to the colonies

		FRELIMO liberation movement officially launched; FRELIMO's leader, Eduardo Mondlane, killed by parcel bomb **1962**		South African commando unit attacks Maputo to search out and destroy ANC leaders; 12 killed **1981**	About 400 Security officers fired for abuses as part of a major clean up campaign by government **1982**
Portuguese explorers land in Mozambique **1497**	Mozambican laborers begin migrating to South African mines **1880-1890**		Liberation struggle successful when Portuguese revolution brings independence **1975**		

• 1984

January 1984: Cyclone "Domoina" destroys crops and trees spared by the drought; flood damage is extensive	March 1984: Nkomati Accords, non-aggression pact between South Africa and Mozambique, is signed	April 1984: Mozambique limits ANC presence to 25 persons; others leave

as well. Despite Portuguese claims that African peoples of its "overseas territories" were given opportunities for advancement, this was not the reality. At the time of independence, only ten percent of the population could read and write Portuguese or other languages. Today, thirty percent of the children under twelve are malnourished, and the per capita income is about $270 yearly. The struggle for independence under FRELIMO during the 1960s and early 1970s encouraged unity, but it could not increase the standard of living. Two hundred and fifty thousand Portuguese residents of the area emigrated after 1974, taking their skills and capital with them. Only ten thousand citizens of Mozambique are of Portuguese origin today, and they have the same rights as other citizens. There are eight Portuguese and two Asian Mozambicans among the twenty-one Cabinet members.

The continuing war against the Mozambican National Resistance (MNR) has been a barrier to progress. The MNR was first organized under white Rhodesian auspices in 1975-1976 during the liberation wars in Zimbabwe. When Zimbabwe became independent, the MNR headquarters was transferred to Transvaal in South Africa. Anywhere from three thousand to ten thousand MNR fighters now operate in a majority of the provinces. Although these fighters have tried to appeal to traditional beliefs and spirit mediums, they do not seem to have a popular following in Mozambique, and they have no plan for improving the life of the people. They attack the new developments such as the health

centers and try to create fear by using torture. Some of those who have been threatened in the isolated areas have fled to Zimbabwe. The MNR has attacked vital transport links and fuel depots, facilities that serve Malawi and Zimbabwe as well as Mozambique. The MNR has also interfered with drought relief.

THE NKOMATI ACCORDS

In March 1984, Mozambique signed a non-aggression pact with South Africa, a state with which it has had hostile relations. Mozambique's present difficulties, as well as the former colonial reliance on South Africa, influenced this seeming turnabout.

In this pact, South Africa agreed to stop support for the MNR, and Mozambique will prohibit ANC bases that would take action against South Africa. The pact has only been in existence for a few months. The MNR seems to have grown stronger since the signing of the accords. The ANC, while maintaining activity in South Africa itself, has been limited in Mozambique. Only twenty-five members have been allowed to stay, despite Mozambique's continuing diplomatic and moral support for the liberation struggle.

Although security was the main reason for the accords, other issues are being mutually addressed. The two nations will run the Cabora Bassa Dam jointly, and there will be opportunities for South African tourism in Mozambique.

Mozambique has other ties with South Africa, which go back in history, and the independent government has readily admitted that it depends on these inherited ties.

Migrant workers go south to work in the South African mines and, although this flow of labor has been cut back to about thirty thousand or forty thousand (from one hundred thousand), the foreign exchange that workers bring back home is much needed by Mozambique. Trade with South Africa remains important, and Mozambique sells power from the Cabora Bassa Dam to its powerful southern neighbor.

The major change in Mozambique's foreign relations—beside the new relationship with South Africa—is its relationship with the United States. The United States government has lifted its ban on direct economic aid to Mozambique and has given a half million dollars in relief. Mozambique is seeking western investment; Exxon has signed an agreement for oil exploration.

CONCLUSION

In the years since 1974, Mozambique has sought to maintain a real independence. Recent events—such as the drought, the attacks of the MNR, and the Nkomati Accords—act to restrain and influence the country's actions. In a different way, the popular expression of the liberation struggle is still applicable: *"A Luta Continua"* ("The Struggle Continues").

DEVELOPMENT

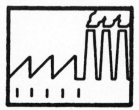

Cashew nuts are Mozambique's chief export. Under the Portuguese, forced labor was used on the plantations. Present state farms for cashew production have not been particularly successful. The work of preparing the nuts for export is hard and even dangerous because of corrosive substances released during shelling.

FREEDOM

The fourth Party Congress of FRELIMO, in June 1983, emphasized local initiative, the decentralization of power and resources, popular assemblies, and people's tribunals. Campaigns against abuses by the security forces and against corruption are a response to popular complaints.

HEALTH/WELFARE

Medical care for everyone is a government priority in Mozambique. The immunization campaign that vaccinated ninety-five percent of Mozambicans against measles, tuberculosis, tetanus, and small pox is beginning to have positive results, and infant mortality figures have improved.

ACHIEVEMENTS

Women have played an increasingly important role in the government and economy of Mozambique. One hundred and five of the 667 members of the fourth Party Congress in June 1983 were women. The Organization of Mozambican Women has had a major influence in bettering women's conditions.

Namibia

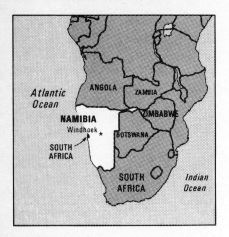

GEOGRAPHY

Area in Square Kilometers (Miles): 824,292 (318,261)
Land Usage: primarily desert
Capital (Population): Windhoek (76,000—1974)
Climate: arid; semi-arid

PEOPLE

Population
Total: 1,086,000 (1982 est.)
Per Square Kilometer (Mile): 13 (3.4)
Annual Growth Rate: 3%

Health
Life Expectancy at Birth: 41 years
Infant Death Rate (Ratio): 120/1,000

Languages
Official: English; Afrikaans
Others Spoken: Ouambo; Kavango; Nama/Damara; Herero; various Khoisan; German

Religion(s)
less than 50% Christian; over 50% indigenous beliefs

Education
Adult Literacy Rate: 45% males; 31% females (white only)

COMMUNICATION

Telephones: 50,300
Newspapers: 3 dailies

TRANSPORTATION

Highways—Kilometers (Miles): 54,500 (33,866)
Railroads—Kilometers (Miles): 2,340 (1,454)
Four international airports

GOVERNMENT

Type: under South African administration
Constitution: none
Former Colonial Status: German; South African
Independence Date: none
Head of State: Willie van Niekerk (administrator-general)
Branches: executive (administrator); judicial (Supreme Court)
Legal System: based on Roman-Dutch law and customary law
Political Parties: approximately 50 political parties; Action Front for the Preservation of the Turnhalle Principles; Federal Party; Democratic Turnhalle Alliance; South West Africa People's Organization (SWAPO)
Suffrage: universal within ethnically-based governments

MILITARY

Number of Armed Forces: 50,000 South African and South African-trained troups
Military Expenditures (% of Central Government Expenditures): $63,100,000,000 (6.7%)
Nuclear Weapons Status: none
Foreign Aid: South Africa
Current Hostilities: internal conflicts between South African-controlled government and African liberation groups such as SWAPO

ECONOMY

Currency ($ US Equivalent): 1 South African rand = $1
Workforce: 68% agriculture; 15% railroads; 13% mining; 4% fishing
Inflation Rate: 10% (1982)
Natural Resources: diamonds; copper; lead; zinc; uranium; silver; cadmium; lithium; coal; possible oil reserves; fish
Agriculture: corn; millet; sorghum; livestock
Industry: canned meat; dairy products; tanned leather; textiles; clothes; mineral concentrates
Energy Production: 540,000 kw capacity
Energy Consumption Per Capita: 1,251 kwh

FOREIGN TRADE

Exports: uranium; diamonds; copper; lead; zinc; silver; cadmium; lithium; fish; cattle; sheep pelts
Imports: construction materials; fertilizer; grain and other foodstuffs; manufactured goods
Major Trading Partners: South Africa; Western Europe
Selected Membership in International Organizations: SWAPO holds UN observer status

| Germany is given rights to colonized Namibia at the Conference of Berlin **1884-1885** | Herero, Nama, and Damara rebellions against German rule **1904-1907** | South Africa assumes League of Nations mandate **1920** | UN General Assembly revokes South African mandate; SWAPO begins war for independence **1966** | Bantustans or "homelands" created by South Africa **1968** | Massive strike paralyzes economy **1971** | Turnhalle process begins **1975** | Western Five contact groups formed to negotiate for South African withdrawal from Namibia **1977** | Internal government formed by South Africa under Turnhalle process **1978** | Reagan links withdrawal of South African troops with withdrawal of Cuban troops in Angola **1981** |

1983

NAMIBIA

This sparsely populated and arid country is the focal point of current political strife in Southern Africa. Its population of one million, half of which belongs to one of the Ovambo ethnic groups, is dominated by a minority of seventy-five thousand whites (mostly Afrikaners and Germans) through policies of *apartheid,* which are implemented by South Africa. Such domination is currently being challenged by SWAPO (South West Africa People's Organization), which is waging a war of independence against the South African occupation of the country.

During its pre-colonial era, Namibia was not the vast wasteland that some have described it as. Early travellers' accounts show regular trade between the various ethnic groups. From the late 1700s on, the country has been strongly influenced by South Africa—first, through market demands and later, by direct South African control. The expanding Cape Colony initially siphoned off many traditional forms of wealth, such as cattle, to the growing economies of Europe. The Cape market also created the demand for new goods such as ostrich feathers and ivory, which found their way into the fashionable circles of Europe.

Namibia was officially a German colony from 1884 to 1919. During this time, land began to be taken from native Namibians for use by white settlers. In response to this, there were a number of local uprisings against colonial authority, and these culminated in the Herero and Nama War of 1904-1907. At first, the response by the German Colonial Office was devastating.

The expeditionary force sent to suppress the rebellion caused the deaths of seventy percent (or 92,258 out of 130 thousand people) of the Herero, Damara, and Namas.

At the end of World War I, the colony was mandated to South Africa by the League of Nations as a trust territory. The history of this mandate has been controversial, with critics claiming that South Africa violated the terms of the mandate by introducing apartheid and by developing the economy for its own benefit. The battle was joined by the United Nations when, at its inception, it took over administration of League of Nations mandates. During the 1950s and early 1960s, three cases regarding UN control over the mandates were brought before the International Court of Justice (IJC) at the Hague. In 1966 the UN revoked South Africa's mandate, making continued South African presence in Namibia illegal. In 1971, the IJC reaffirmed this decision. Since that time, diplomatic efforts have been aimed at ending South African occupation and bringing about independence.

At present, the country is embroiled in an international dispute involving SWAPO, South Africa, the Frontline States (Angola, Botswana, Mozambique, Tanzania, Zambia, and Zimbabwe), the Western Five Contact Group (West Germany, France, Britain, Canada, and the United States), the United Nations, and UNITA (a South African-backed rebel group in Angola). However, the main conflict is between SWAPO and South Africa. Since the late 1950s, SWAPO has sought an end to South African rule of Namibia and to apartheid. At first its tactics were peaceful,

| August: UN Secretary General Perez de Cuellar travels to Southern Africa to begin another diplomatic initiative toward ending the conflict | January 1984: South Africa and Angola announce agreement over process to withdraw South African troops from southern Angola | May 1984: South Africa, SWAPO, and the MPC meet in Lusaka, Zambia, to discuss peace process |

consisting of protests and appeals to local authorities, foreign governments, and the UN. In December of 1959, in what is called Namibia's Sharpeville, police opened fire on members of a peaceful crowd in Windhoek, who had gathered to protest their forced removal to a new ghetto. Thirteen persons died, and fifty-three were wounded. After this, SWAPO made plans for a guerrilla war, which it initiated in August of 1966. Over the years, the stakes—in terms of numbers of troops and sophistication of equipment—in this war have steadily increased on both sides.

Today the conflict is one of two independence struggles in Southern Africa—the other being within South Africa itself. In recent years, in what it calls an attempt to bring stability to the region, the United States has taken the diplomatic lead in attempting to end the war. With the inauguration of President Ronald Reagan in 1981, South African withdrawal from Namibia was linked to the withdrawal of Cuban troops in Angola. While South Africa and the Thatcher government in Britain have welcomed this concept, it has met with little approval from either the Frontline States or other members of the Western Five, thus producing little progress toward a settlement.

DEVELOPMENT

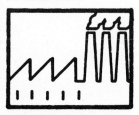

As a result of decades of apartheid and apartheid-like policies, economic wealth is concentrated in the hands of whites, and much of the country's wealth is exported. For example, the mining industry (excluding diamonds) paid only 2.3 million rands in taxes on 534 million rands of sales during 1982.

FREEDOM

Namibia is often called the last colony of Africa. Anywhere from twenty thousand to eighty thousand South African troops occupy the country. During the 1970s, South Africa publicly stated its commitment to Namibian independence. It attempted to create a friendly government that could act as a challenge to SWAPO. This process was known as the *Turnhalle.*

HEALTH/WELFARE

Unemployment among non-whites has always been high. A severe drought in the 1980s has decimated what little agricultural output non-whites could produce. Poverty and malnutrition are extremely widespread. Educational expenditures are racially skewed, with white children receiving four times as much as black children.

ACHIEVEMENTS

As part of the *Turnhalle* process, South Africa has ended the so-called "heartbreak" elements of apartheid: the Mixed Marriages Act, the Pass Laws, and Group Areas Act. It has also given all citizens certain voting rights. SWAPO and the UN have established a training center for Namibians in Zambia for the purpose of educating officials to run the country after independence.

South Africa*

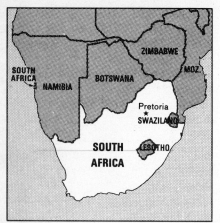

GEOGRAPHY

Area in Square Kilometers (Miles):
1,222,480 (437,872)
Land Usage: 12% arable; 2%
forests; 86% desert, waste, or urban
Capital (Population): Pretoria (administrative); Cape Town
(legislative); Bloemfonteim (judicial)
Climate: temperate; semi-arid; arid

PEOPLE
Population
Total: 31,008,000 (1982 est.)
Per Square Kilometer (Mile): 25 (71)
Annual Growth Rate: 2.9%
Rural/Urban Population Ratio: 50/50
Ethnic Makeup of Population: 69.9%
African; 17.8% white; 9.4% colored; 2.9% Asian

Health
Life Expectancy at Birth: 63 years
Infant Death Rate (Ratio): 96/1,000
Average Caloric Intake: 116% of
FAO minimum
Physicians Available (Ratio): 1/2,010
(1970)

Languages
Official: Afrikaans and English
Others Spoken: Xhosa; Zulu;
Sesotho; Tswana; other Bantu
languages

Religion(s)
81% Christian; 19% Hindu and
Muslim

Education
Adult Literacy Rate: whites 99%;
Africans 50%
School Attendance: primary: 87%
boys, 90% girls; secondary: 87%
boys, 81% girls

*The single set of statistics presented here are
misleading because they do not indicate the
significant differences in standards of living between whites and the majority of non-whites.
For instance, the infant mortality rate recorded
here is 96/1,000. However, the figure among
Africans in the homelands is estimated at
240/1,000. The rate among whites in 1974 was
18.4/1,000. Other indicators can be expected to
diverge widely.—ed.

SOUTH AFRICAN WRITING

Contemporary South African writers of all races have created plays,
novels, and poems that give readers an understanding of and a feeling for
the pains and problems of living in the apartheid state. Their writings tell
of joys as well as sorrows, and the writers are varied and talented. Some,
such as Ezekiel Mphahlele, have lived as exiles in other parts of the
world. His work *The Wanderers* was written from the point of view of the
exile. He has now returned to South Africa. Dennis Brutus is in political
asylum in the United States and his poetry (such as *Letters to Martha*) as
well as his anti-apartheid activities reveal his continuing commitment to
change in South Africa. Alex LaGuma has written of the experiences of
prison life in *The Stone Country.* Nadine Gordimer's novels, such as
July's People, and short stories, such as those in the volume *A Soldiers
Embrace,* are sensitive and beautifully written. Alan Paton's *Cry the
Beloved Country* remains a classic picture of the losses due to the
apartheid system, and Athol Fugard's plays, such as *Harold and the
Boys,* have been presented in many parts of the world.

COMMUNICATION

Telephones: 2,750,000
Radios: 8,225,000
Televisions: 2,050,000
Newspapers: 23 dailies; total circulation 2,000,000

TRANSPORTATION

Highways—Kilometers (Miles):
229,090 (142,356)
Railroads—Kilometers (Miles):
35,434 (22,018)
Three international airports

GOVERNMENT

Type: republic
Constitution: November 3, 1983
Former Colonial Status: British;
Dutch
Independence Date: May 31, 1910
Head of State: Marais Viljoen (state
president); Pieter W. Botha (prime
minister)
Branches: prime minister; state
president; Cabinet; Parliament;
Judiciary—divided into 4 provinces
Legal System: based on Roman-
Dutch law and English Common
Law
Political Parties: National Party;
Progressive Federal Party; New
Republic Party; Conservative Party;
Labour Party
Suffrage: whites, Asians, Coloureds
over age 18

MILITARY

Number of Armed Forces: 92,700
Armed Forces/Population: 1/276
*Military Expenditures (% of Central
Government Expenditures):*
$2,900,000,000 (18.4%)
Nuclear Weapons Status: nuclear
weapons capability suspected;
government denies it has tested
nuclear weapons
Foreign Aid: none
Current Hostilities: conflict with
African nationalists in South Africa
and Namibia; withdrawing from
Angola

ECONOMY

Currency ($ US Equivalent): 1 South
African rand = $1
GDP: $74,330,000,000
Per Capita Income/GNP: $2,670
Workforce: 30% agriculture; 29% industry; 41% services
Inflation Rate: 12.5% (1970-1980)
Natural Resources: gold; diamonds;
mineral ores; uranium; fish
Agriculture: corn; wool; wheat;
sugar cane; tobacco; citrus fruits;
dairy products
Industry: mining; automobile
assembly; metal working; machinery;
textiles; iron and steel; chemicals;
fertilizer; fishing
Energy Production: 20,600,000 kw
capacity
Energy Consumption Per Capita:
3,439 kwh

FOREIGN TRADE

Exports: wool; diamonds; corn;
uranium; sugar; fruit; hides; metals;
metallic ores; asbestos; fish products;
gold
Imports: motor vehicles; machinery;
metals; petroleum products; textiles;
chemicals
Major Trading Partners: United
States; West Germany; Japan; UK
*Selected Membership in International
Organizations:* UN (voting rights in
General Assembly suspended in
1974)

SOUTH AFRICA

South Africa is one country but two worlds. One, the minority white world, is affluent, healthy, well-educated, and in charge. The non-white world is a "third world"—poor, malnourished, poorly-educated, and controlled. The contrast is exaggerated; yet it exists. The minority white government of South Africa, following a policy of *apartheid* (separateness), maintains the division of these two worlds, while exerting control over the non-white world. In the workplace, the marketplace, the street, and other places where people meet, whites can always dominate.

THE SYSTEM OF APARTHEID

The system of *apartheid* in South Africa has a long history. The laws implementing the separation of whites and non-whites began after the Nationalist Party came to power in 1948, but the system of apartheid was built on early twentieth-century events and laws. Some would claim that racial discrimination started as far back as 1652, when the first Dutch settlers came to the Cape. A few of the keystones of the system today include racial classification, the establishment of *Bantustans* (or "homelands"), the restrictions of the Group Areas Act, job classification, a pass system, and a vast array of security legislation, which is backed up by force.

In South Africa, every citizen is classified according to race. The arbitrary divisions set up by the Race Classification Act are: White, Coloured, Asian, and Bantu. Seventeen percent of the population (4.5 million) are whites, the Coloured (2.6 million) are of mixed races. The Asians, the smallest group, number approximately 800 thousand, and are descendants of the Indian people who first came to South Africa in 1860. The majority of South Africans (sixteen to seventeen million) are classified as Bantu-speaking Africans; they belong to many different groups, including the Tswana, Sotho, Zulu, and Xhosa.

Today in South Africa, this classification by race determines every aspect of one's life from birth to death. Thousands of laws determine the limits of achievement and action if one is not white. In 1981-1982, 800 persons were reclassified by race and, thus, found themselves faced with entirely new present circumstances and future prospects.

Apartheid or separate development means more than different laws for different "races." No black is considered a citizen of South Africa, and no black can vote for the South African government. Every Bantu-speaking person is supposed to be a citizen of his or her "nation." Asians and Coloureds who have no homelands in South Africa have limited rights in South Africa. A set of ten Bantustans have been devised for the Bantu-speaking ethnic groups. Supposedly, these homelands are built around some of the areas where different peoples have historically lived. Only thirteen percent of the land of South Africa has been allocated to these homelands, where seventy percent of the people are expected to live. Most of the land is poor, eroded, and far from industry and resources. Many of the residents leave, legally, to work in the mines, farms, and factories of South Africa.

Every Bantu-speaking person is considered a citizen of a homeland, and the South African government intends that all homelands should become independent. Some of the Bantustans have already received supposed independence. Transkei, Ciskei, Venda, and Bophuthatswana, for example, have elected black governments and have developed their own budgets and their own laws. Their independence is a facade covering both continuing South African influence and the continuing dependence of these underdeveloped areas on South Africa. No outside country has recognized their independence.

Meanwhile, almost half of the Africans who are considered citizens of these homelands live in the "white" areas of South Africa. A vast number of South Africans who were classified as members of these

(United Nations photo)

The system of apartheid makes it impossible for most black South Africans to share in South Africa's economic prosperity.

groups were raised in cities far from their so-called "homelands" and may neither speak Bantu languages nor think of themselves as Tswana, Sotho, Zulu, or Xhosa. They are South Africans. Most have little desire to return to the homelands. In recent elections for the government in Bophuthat-swana, for instance, only 135 persons residing outside the area voted.

A large number of Africans (perhaps twenty-five percent) have rights through employment, marriage, and birth to be in urban areas of "white" South Africa. All must have jobs, and they must carry passes that include their work permits. "Illegal" wives and children come to cities to be with the working men, whom they might otherwise see for only a few weeks a year. In 1982, 200 thousand people were apprehended for pass law violations, and most were shipped back to their homelands. Recently, a government-appointed Commission of Inquiry on the legal system recommended that the pass laws be abolished, while rejecting the government's proposal that separate legal systems be established for blacks and whites.

Africans who work in the white areas, as well as Coloured and Asian people who have no homelands, are restricted as to where they can live by the Group Areas Act. "Racial reshuffling" occurs as the increased demands by all groups for housing leads to the reclassification of different sections of cities, and as historically legal black settlements or "black spots" are removed from the countryside. Squatter settlements, which grow up outside cities such as Pretoria and Cape Town, include "legal" residents for whom no "legal" housing is available as well as "illegal" men, women, and children who can be shipped back home. An estimated 3.5 million "illegal" persons have been resettled in camps in or on the borders of the homelands in conditions similar to or worse than those of Least Developed Countries all over the world.

Laws restrict Africans at the workplace. The sophisticated and advanced economy of South Africa—built on the mining of gold (which provides the major product for export), diamonds, and other raw materials—is dependent on black labor. Workers in the vast array of industries and mines are restricted in the jobs that they can hold.

Even with recent advances, the pay that Africans receive is far less than that of white workers. Foreign companies, including many from the United States, have profited from such unequal treatment—even though such treatment may be against the law in their own countries. Employers readily admit that white South Africa cannot maintain its industrial development without the labor force from Transkei and other Bantustans. There is a scarcity of skilled labor in modern South Africa, which authorities try to solve through the encouragement of white immigration rather than through the training of black South Africans.

The apartheid system is maintained by a net of anti-terrorist, anti-Communist legislation, which is wide enough and vague enough to catch anyone suspected of opposition to the system. The legal right of the security forces to detain persons without charging them has been especially effective in crushing opposition to apartheid. The military can rely on a sophisticated weaponry, and all white males are required to put in two years of service and later serve as reserves, who can be used at home as well as abroad.

Naturally, whites and blacks have very different perceptions of their country. According to a survey of the South African

(United Nations photo by Milton Grant)

Resistance groups have gained international recognition in their struggle against the South African regime.

African National
Congress (ANC)
is founded
1912

Nationalist
Party comes to
power on an
apartheid platform
1948

The Sharpeville
Massacre: Police
fire on demon-
stration; over
sixty deaths
result
1961

Soweto Riots
are sparked off
by student
protests
1976

IMF approves
credit line of $1.1
billion; South
Africa's Defense
Force attacks
ANC bases in
Meseru, Lesotho
1982

1984

January 1984:
A wave of
union strikes;
Labour party
accepts new
constitution and
decides against
referendum of
coloured
community

March 1984:
Nkomati Accords,
a non-aggres-
sion pact, is
signed by South
Africa and
Mozambique;
Koeberg nuclear
plants begins
generating
electricity

August 1984:
Date set for
elections to
Indian and
coloured parlia-
ments; UF/UDF
call for boycott
of any elections

Institute of International Affairs, a majority of whites think that blacks are well-treated, that they have no reason to rise against the government, and that contemplated reforms are appropriate. Agitators are thought to be inspired by Communists. Whites feel threatened by the general international hostility against South Africa and consider themselves beleaguered by hostile neighbors. They believe that military action against outsiders is acceptable and will be successful.

Blacks have a different view. The changes that whites call reforms are seen as minute and insignificant. Blacks believe all "progress" has been backwards, and many feel trapped in a prison where whites hold the keys. They are "dying by installments," as one person put it. They see little opportunity to control their own lives, and many believe that violence is the answer.

IS THE SYSTEM CHANGING?

During 1982-1983, there has been much publicity and some optimism expressed about possible changes in the apartheid system. Yet, the moves to liberalize the system are limited and are accompanied by an ever-increasing control and development of power by the government.

A new billed passed in the white Parliament in 1983 and approved in a national referendum in November 1983 brings Asian and Coloured representatives into the South African government. Each group will have its own separate chamber. The bill "tidies up" the original apartheid system by giving a place to Coloured and Asians for whom there are no homelands. It also gives increased powers to the president, who will be the head of state under the revised government. More significant, the proposed government system completely excludes blacks and seems designed to divide non-whites by offering participation to Asians and Coloureds. Although the Coloured Labor Party has accepted the proposed measure, many Coloureds and Asians are deeply opposed to it and have organized with blacks against it. The complexity of South African society is indicated by the fact that many right-wing whites are also deeply opposed to the measure, which they believe would "open the flood gates" for change. A new Conservative Party has been formed by those who have broken with the Nationalists over this issue.

Other recent moves of the government do away with some injustices in South Africa without disturbing the major outlines of apartheid. Some of the "petty" apartheid regulations are no longer enforced. Signs announcing separate facilities for whites and non-whites have been taken down at telephones, park benches, and rest rooms. The Hilton Hotel is open to anyone who can afford it. Unequal income tax regulations have been abolished; blacks no longer pay more than whites. Special committees have been established to review the Mixed Marriages and Immorality acts, though it seems unlikely that restrictions on intimate relations between the races will ever be abolished when schools and other institutions are separated by law.

The changes that have occurred seem designed to implement apartheid policies— rather than to change them. They are reminiscent of the former practice in the United States of creating "separate but equal" facilities. Thus, the courts say people cannot be moved from residences in the "wrong" area unless alternative housing exists, but this alternative housing may be like the new suburb planned for Cape Town workers, which will require a forty-mile commute. The government has allocated more money for the education of non-whites, but schooling remains segregated, and the funds for educating whites are nearly nine times larger than those made available for blacks.

There have been more substantive changes for workers. Job reservation laws have been eliminated for most blue collar workers, and many skilled jobs are now held by blacks in industries other than mining. In 1979 black unions in industries became legal, and now miners are allowed to form unions as well. Moreover, in December 1982, the government declared that such unions need not register with the government. There are now 300 thousand workers in the non-racial independent unions, including eighteen thousand in the mines, and more are eager to join. Strikes are not allowed by law, but 294 strikes occurred in 1982. Union leaders are working to develop unity among the varied union groups. Meanwhile, union leaders have negotiated with the management of individual factories for modest wage increases.

Such trends for the worker must always be viewed in conjunction with the govern-

ment's stepped-up enforcement of influx control (i.e., police check of passes) during the same period. There has been continuing unemployment for blacks, continued forced resettlement of non-whites, and continual build-up of the armed forces, as well as the increased requirements for reserve service by white males. All of these moves increase the control of the white government over non-whites in South Africa.

BLACK INDEPENDENT ACTION AND RESISTANCE

The opportunities for independent action for non-whites in South Africa are limited. Although protests against the system of apartheid have as long a history as the system itself, organizations and avenues of protest against the system have been closed off. During the 1950s, many organizations— including the African National Congress (ANC), founded in 1912—joined in non-violent protests against the system, but their positive achievements, such as the development of the influential Freedom Charter and the widespread acceptance of its goals, did not change apartheid.

The year 1960 was a crucial one for protesters. In 1960 police fired at participants in a peaceful pass demonstration at Sharpeville, and over sixty persons were killed. The government assumed emergency powers, banned the ANC as well as the more recently formed Pan African Congress (PAC), and made even mild protests difficult. The Black Consciousness Movement, which developed during the early 1970s, led by Steve Biko, an activist in the African National Congress, aroused the black youth of South Africa. But after riots in Soweto, a Johannesburg suburb, the government suppressed the movement, and Steve Biko was killed while in jail.

Today, the Azanian People's Organization (AZAPO) has been revitalized by leaders who have been just released from prison or who have just returned from being banned. AZAPO is allowed to exist and has just held its third annual congress, but the organization seems certain to be as closely watched as other possible arenas of African resistance. One such organization is *Inkatha*, a Zulu movement started by Chief Buthelezi, who maintains a vigorous dialogue with the white government. The vigorous and growing trade unions give opportunities for non-white action, and community groups also offer possibilities for local initiatives.

New and lively local newspapers in black communities are providing a focus for community and union publicity. Yet it is impossible to predict if they will survive. The major commercial black newspapers, the *Mail* and the *Sunday Mail*, were banned in January 1981. There are over 100 laws with which newspapers must comply. These laws deal with *how* the news is to be reported and *by whom*. Violating these laws can bring about a newspaper's demise. Police infiltration of black groups is routine, as are raids such as the March 1981 "sweep" of Soweto, when the area was cordoned off and searched house by house.

Churches have been centers of black initiative and independence for many years. These churches have included not only the established Christian churches, which are part of worldwide communions, but also the great variety of independent African Christian churches, which have deep roots in South Africa. The South African Council of Churches (SACC), led by Bishop Desmod Tutu, is a significant organization. Bishop Tutu has spoken out against apartheid, and practical programs have been established by SACC for some of apartheid's victims. The government would like to restrict these activities, and a recent commission study recommended that SACC be designated an "affected organization," which would mean that the foreign funds

from organizations such as the World Council of Churches and other international groups that support its activities would be cut off.

Some groups are trying to unify the forces that oppose the regime. The United Democratic Front (UDF) initiated by Reverend Allan Boesak, a Coloured theologian, among others, has rallied groups against the government proposals for constitutional reform. Another front, the National Forum, has been organized by leaders of AZAPO.

Peaceful protest seems an ineffectual recourse against the apparently immovable forces in power, but the weapons of violence are extraordinarily difficult for non-whites to acquire. Moreover, for decades those who fought the system were determined to do so non-violently. The violence that ensued during the demonstration at Sharpeville and the repression that followed in the early 1960s convinced many people, including ANC leader Nelson Mandela, who has been jailed for over twenty years, that they would have to resort to violence. Yet violence has been used with restraint. For instance, the Spear of the Nation, the striking wing of the ANC, has sought to destroy strategic South African targets, while purposefully avoiding the taking of human lives.

Now violence is escalating. In May, 1983, seventeen persons died, and 188 were injured in a car bomb explosion near the Pretoria headquarters of the South African Air Force. The ANC took responsibility for this action (which resulted in retaliation by the South African armed forces against a supposed ANC headquarters in Maputo, Mozambique). Leaders such as Desmond Tutu and Chief Buthelezi have predicted that such acts will increase.

CONCLUSION

While increased violence is likely in

South Africa, it is also likely that South Africa will be able to keep those forces that would use violence in line. The South African government can marshall all the resources of this advanced industrialized state to maintain military dominance and totalitarian control over resistant peoples, and it has support from outside countries as well. Non-whites cannot possess arms—even black policemen are not allowed to use them—yet few whites are without them. The policies of South Africa within the Southern African region have been described in the regional essay (see p. 179), and these policies operate effectively to cut off secret arms flows from the north.

The world community has condemned apartheid and has taken some actions against the apartheid state. An arms embargo was instituted by the United Nations in 1977 and, in many countries, anti-apartheid work is carried out by independent groups. Recognizing South Africa's dependence on foreign investment, many groups in the United States and Britain have worked on divestment campaigns to persuade foreign investors to get out of South Africa. Cultural and sports boycotts have publicized the evils of the system. Yet many governments continue to meet South Africa's needs. The 1983 loan from the International Monetary Fund will help South Africa survive the world recession. United States bank-lending to South Africa has risen dramatically. Because businesses disregard United States trade restrictions, export regulations to South Africa have been softened under the Reagan administration, and South Africa has been able to secure needed specialized equipment. South Africa has managed, with the help of its friends, to build up a superior arsenal of arms. Thus, the interactions of the entire world help to maintain the two worlds of South Africa.

DEVELOPMENT	FREEDOM	HEALTH/WELFARE	ACHIEVEMENTS
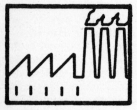			
Weaknesses in the developed economy of South Africa include its lack of oil resources, severe shortages of skilled labor, which exist because the government has not opened up many jobs to black workers, and the country's dependence on foreign investment, seventy percent of which comes from Europe.	The Republic of South Africa Constitution Bill, passed by white voters in a November referendum, adds two chambers—one for Asians and one for Coloureds—to the white legislature. The bill provides for a powerful president and gives no political rights to the black majority. Some groups have called for a boycott of the August 1984 elections to the new chambers.	Higher education for black South Africans, like primary and secondary education for blacks, is inferior to that of whites. Blacks cannot attend white universities except under special circumstances, and only ten thousand have gained entrance to the five major black universities. One report indicates that only 10,700 blacks in South Africa have university degrees.	A 1979 legislation allows for the existence of black unions, and ten percent of the black workforce (300 thousand people) is now unionized. Limits on black employment in blue-collar jobs have been eliminated, except in mining, and blacks now outnumber whites in some skilled labor fields such as construction, carpentry, and bricklaying.

Swaziland

GEOGRAPHY

Area in Square Kilometers (Miles):
17,366 (6,704)
Capital (Population): Mbabane (administrative: 29,875—1981); Lobanta (royal and legislative)
Climate: temperate; subtropical; semi-arid

PEOPLE
Population
Total: 585,000 (1982 est.)
Per Square Kilometer (Mile): 34 (87)
Annual Growth Rate: 2.5%
Rural/Urban Population Ratio: 85/15

Health
Life Expectancy at Birth: 54 years
Infant Death Rate (Ratio): 135/1,000
Average Caloric Intake: 97% of FAO minimum
Physicians Available (Ratio): 1/7,670

Languages
Official: English; Siswati
Others Spoken: Zulu; Sesotho; Nguni

Religion(s)
53% Christian; 47% indigenous beliefs

Education
Adult Literacy Rate: 57% males; 53% females
School Attendance: primary: 100% boys, 100% girls; secondary: 41% boys, 40% girls
Teacher/Student Ratio: 1/30

COMMUNICATION
Telephones: 10,700
Radios: 85,000
Televisions: 1,500
Newspapers: 1 daily; total circulation 8,000

NCWALA

Visitors to Swaziland are frequently impressed with the pageantry associated with many of its state occasions. The most important ceremonies take place annually during the lunar *Ncwala* month in December and January. This is a time when the nation reaffirms its bonds with the royal house. As the month begins, runners are sent to collect water from the ocean and various rivers, thus reestablishing their historic association with the Swazi. The main festival lasts for six days and includes the king's tasting of the first fruits, blessings to the ancestors, and prayers for rain. During the entire period, there is much ritual dancing—the most important of which is performed during the fourth day by the king and other members of royalty. Because only the king can conduct the Ncwala ceremonies, they will not be held until the new king comes of age.

TRANSPORTATION
Highways—Kilometers (Miles): 3,450 (2,193)
Railroads—Kilometers (Miles): 292 (181)
One international airport

GOVERNMENT
Type: monarchy
Constitution: 1978
Former Colonial Status: British
Independence Date: September 6, 1968
Head of State: Princess Ntombi (Queen regent); Prince Makhosetive (heir apparent); Prince Bhekimpi, (Prime Minister)
Branches: king (chief of state); prime minister; Cabinet; bicameral Parliament; High Court
Legal System: based on South African Roman-Dutch law and customary law
Political Parties: Imbokodvo National Movement
Suffrage: universal for adults

MILITARY
Number of Armed Forces: 5,000
Armed Forces/Population: 1/226
Nuclear Weapons Status: none
Current Hostilities: none

ECONOMY
Currency ($ US Equivalent): 1 lilangeni = $1
GDP: $364,400,000
Per Capita Income/GNP: $940
Workforce: 74% agriculture; 9% industry; 17% service
Inflation Rate: 11-16% (1970-1980)
Natural Resources: iron ore; asbestos; coal; timber
Agriculture: corn; livestock; sugar cane; citrus fruits; cotton; rice; pineapples
Industry: milled sugar; cotton; processed meat and wood; tourism; chemicals; machinery; beverages; consumer goods; paper mill; mining
Energy Production: 75,000 kw capacity
Energy Consumption Per Capita: 251 kwh

FOREIGN TRADE
Exports: sugar; wood products; iron ore; asbestos; citrus fruits; canned fruits; meat products
Imports: motor vehicles; fuels and lubricants; foodstuffs; clothing
Major Trading Partners: United States; South Africa; Japan; UK
Foreign Debt: $239,400,000
Selected Membership in International Organizations: UN; OAU; Commonwealth of Nations; African Development Bank; Non-Aligned Movement; Southern Africa Development Coordination Conference (SADCC)

Zulu and South
African whites
encroach on
Swazi territory
1800s

Protectorate
established by
the British
1900

Independence
restored
1968

Parliament
dissolved
1973

Government
forced to stock-
pile diamonds
as demand
plummets
1981

King Sobuza dies
1982

1983

October: Voters
to go the polls to
elect 80 electoral
college mem-
bers; new sedition
and subversive
activities law
is passed

December 1983-
January 1984:
New sedition
laws result in a
number of politi-
cal arrests

April 1984:
The announce-
ment of a Swazi-
South African
non-aggression
pact leads to
violent clashes
between Swazi
security units
and elements of
the ANC

SWAZILAND

Swaziland is a landlocked kingdom about the size of Hawaii, which is sandwiched between the much larger states of Mozambique and South Africa. Many casual observers have tended to look upon the country as a peaceful island of "traditional" Africa that is seemingly immune to the continent's contemporary conflicts. An extended power struggle following the death of the long-reigning King Sobuza II as well as a diplomatic deal involving the possible transfer of territory and citizens from South Africa have, in the past year, shattered such illusions.

EXTERNAL PRESSURES

Since the late eighteenth century, the fortunes of Swaziland have been subject to external pressures. From 1900 until the restoration of independence in 1968, the kingdom existed as a British protectorate, despite sustained pressure for its transfer to South Africa's jurisdiction. Local white settlers, who at the time made up only two percent of the population but who controlled over two-thirds of the protectorate's land, supported this proposed transfer.

Throughout the colonial period, the ruling House of Dlamini, which was led by the energetic Sobuza II after 1921, successfully served as a rallying point for national self-assertion—a factor that no doubt contributed to the overwhelming popularity of the royalist *Imbokodvo* party in the elections of 1964, 1967, and 1972. In 1973, Sobuza dissolved the Parliament and repealed the Westminster-style Constitution, characterizing it as "un-Swazi." In 1979, a new, non-partisan Parliament was chosen, partly through indirect elections and partly through direct appointment by the king. However pre-eminent authority has remained with the king and his advisory council, the *Liqoqo*.

Sobuza's death in late 1982 left many wondering if Swaziland's unique monarchist institutions would survive. A prolonged power struggle has increased tension within the ruling order over the past year. The Liqoqo has appointed both a new prime minister, Prince Bhekimpi, and a new Queen Regent, Ntombi. Ntombi's teenage son, Prince Makhosetive, has been designated as the future king. Indirect elections in October 1983 seem to have consolidated the power of the new leadership, but reports of serious opposition continue.

One of the major challenges facing any Swazi government is the nature of its relations with its powerful neighbor: South Africa. Under Sobuza, Swaziland managed to maintain its political autonomy, while recognizing its economic dependence on South Africa. The delicate relationship has recently been altered as a result of a new non-aggression pact between the two countries and a now-aborted land deal. As a result of the non-aggression pact, whose origins are a matter of dispute, Swazi security forces have moved forcefully against suspected ANC activists in recent months. The land deal would have transferred lands from two South African "homelands" to Swaziland, giving the country access to the sea. The South African government cancelled the agreement after protests from the affected population within South Africa. Despite this setback, cooperation between the two governments continues.

ECONOMY

Swaziland's economy, like its politics, is the product of both internal and external initiatives. Since independence, the nation has enjoyed a high rate of economic growth led by the expansion and diversification of agriculture. Sugar, fruits, cotton, and rice are major cash crops. Wood products and beef are also of growing economic importance. Success in agriculture has in turn promoted the development of secondary industries, such as a sugar refinery and a paper mill. The major iron mine closed in 1977, but the loss of revenues from that facility has been offset by increased exploitation of coal and asbestos. Tourism, which depends on weekend traffic from South Africa, is another source of revenue.

Swazi development has relied on capital-intensive (rather than labor-intensive) projects. These projects have increased the disparities in local wealth and have meant continued dependence on South African investment. Underemployment is a major problem, and each year thousands of Swazi migrate to South Africa in search of job opportunities—a pattern established early in the twentieth century. Swaziland is not an island apart; it is part of the continent, a microcosm of contemporary Africa, illustrating both its problems and its progress.

DEVELOPMENT

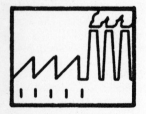

Many of the government's ambitious schemes center on the anticipated access to the sea that would result from the land agreement with South Africa.

FREEDOM

The present political order restricts many forms of opposition. Its defenders claim that local councils, *Tikhudlas,* allow for popular participation in decision making. There have been few reports of serious human rights violations.

HEALTH/WELFARE

Primary school enrollment now approaches 100 percent, although quality has not kept pace with quantity, according to the government's own evaluations. The country's low life expectancy and high child mortality rate are attributed to an overemphasis on curative, rather than preventive, medicine.

ACHIEVEMENTS

Despite some present differences, the Swazi royal family have long been patrons of the African National Congress (ANC), the major South African liberation movement. At Sobuza's funeral, senior officials of both the ANC and the white minority government claimed to be representing South Africa.

Zambia

GEOGRAPHY

Area in Square Kilometers (Miles):
752,972 (290,724)
Land Usage: 10% arable; 10% grazing; 13% forests; 61% scattered-tree grassland; 6% marsh
Capital (Population): Lusaka
(641,000—1980)
Climate: tropical to subtropical

PEOPLE

Population

Total: 6,163,000 (1982 est.)
Per Square Kilometer (Mile): 8 (21)
Annual Growth Rate: 3.1%
Rural/Urban Population Ratio: 57/43

Health

Life Expectancy at Birth: 51 years
Infant Death Rate (Ratio): 106/1,000
Average Caloric Intake: 90% of
FAO minimum
Physicians Available (Ratio): 1/7,670
Access to Safe Water: 42%

Languages

Official: English
Others Spoken: Bemba; Nyanja;
Tonga; Lozi; Cibema; Cinyanja;
Citonga; Silozi; Kilunda; Kikaonde

Religion(s)

12% traditional indigenous beliefs;
7% Christian; 71% Hindu and
Muslim

Education

Adult Literacy Rate: 79% males;
58% females
School Attendance: primary: 100%
boys, 90% girls; secondary: 21%
boys, 11% girls

NONTRADITIONAL CHURCHES

More than 500 thousand persons in Zambia are Christian and many of the churches are independent of Western Christian affiliation. Churches such as the Apostolic Church of John Maranke combine traditional practices of healing and special rituals that honor the ancestors with Christian and Western beliefs and forms. Even the established churches such as the Roman Catholic Church have been influenced by traditional beliefs. The popular Zambian Archbishop Milingo was summoned to Rome in April 1982 because Catholics believed that his healing ceremonies for individuals supposedly possessed by evil spirits went against Church doctrine. He was later replaced in Zambia and has become head of the Pontifical Commission for Migration and Tourism in Rome.

COMMUNICATION

Telephones: 60,500
Radios: 150,000
Televisions: 70,000
Newspapers: 2 dailies; total circulation 110,000

TRANSPORTATION

Highways—Kilometers (Miles):
36,809 (22,872)
Railroads—Kilometers (Miles): 2,014
(1,251)
Two international airports

GOVERNMENT

Type: republic
Constitution: 1973
Former Colonial Status: British
Independence Date: October 24,
1964
Head of State: Kenneth David Kaunda (president)
Branches: president; Cabinet;
unicameral National Assembly; High
Court
Legal System: based on British law
and customary law
Political Parties: United National Independence Party
Suffrage: universal for adults

MILITARY

Number of Armed Forces: 15,500
Armed Forces/Population: 1/401
Nuclear Weapons Status: none
Current Hostilities: none

ECONOMY

Currency ($ US Equivalent): 1.4
Zambian kwacha = $1
GDP: $3,830,000,000
Per Capita Income/GNP: $640
Workforce: 67% agriculture; 11% industry; 22% services
Inflation Rate: 8.1% (1970-1980);
12% (1982)
Natural Resources: copper; zinc;
lead; cobalt; coal
Agriculture: corn; tobacco; cotton;
peanuts; sugar cane
Industry: foodstuffs; beverages;
chemicals; textiles; fertilizer
Energy Production: 1,453,000 kw
capacity; 7,300,000 kwh produced
Energy Consumption Per Capita: 969
kwh

FOREIGN TRADE

Exports: copper; zinc; lead; cobalt;
tobacco
Imports: manufactured goods;
machinery; transport equipment;
foodstuffs
Major Trading Partners: UK; Japan;
West Germany; United States; South
Africa
Foreign Debt: $3,268,900,000
Selected Membership in International Organizations: UN; OAU; Commonwealth of Nations; African
Development Bank; Non-Aligned
Movement; Southern Africa
Development Coordination Conference (SADCC)

		Federation of Northern Rhodesia, Southern Rhodesia, and Nyasaland is			Zambia becomes a one-party state under the United	Kaunda calls for a major emphasis on rural recon-		Kaunda meets with South African prime minister; Zambia
Rhodes' South African Company is chartered by the British government **1889**	Development of the Copperbelt **1924-1934**	formed; still part of British Empire **1953-1963**	Zambia celebrates independence **1963**	Nationalization of 51% of all industries occurs **1969**	National Independence Party (UNIP) **1972**	struction in his "watershed" speech **1975**	Suspected coup leads to a state of emergency **1980**	reopens discussion with IMF over debt and credit terms **1982**

1983

February: At the end of treason trial, 7 Zambians receive death sentences for their role in the 1980 plot	March: Austerity measures are launched, including third devaluation in 7 years and lifting of price controls	October: Kaunda is reelected with ninety-four percent of the voter turnout; Harry Nkumbula, a father of Zambian nationalism, dies and is accorded a state funeral

ZAMBIA

"I always try to see that power is given a human face. It is people who handle power and people who are on the receiving end of it—therefore supreme power must be vested in them."

Kenneth Kaunda,
Letter to My Children

Kenneth Kaunda, the leader of Zambia's independence movement during the 1950s and 1960s and the President of Zambia since 1964, has often expressed his concern to maintain contact with citizens and their problems and to use government power for the people's welfare. External factors and internal changes have increased the challenge of these goals.

URBAN MIGRATION

Approximately forty-seven percent of Zambia's nearly six million people live in towns and cities. Peoples from all of the seventy or more different ethnic groups, speaking as many different languages (and often English as well), come to the cities to visit or to stay with relatives and friends. Migration to the towns is expected to increase in the future. This is not surprising, for, while life in the cities is hard, life in the countryside is harder and continually grows more difficult. Rural farmers make less than one-third of the wages of urban workers. Even if the visitor does not find a job in the city—and jobs are hard to find—there are still reasons for coming. Schools, health facilities, and good water are more readily available in the cities.

The urban population in Zambia is higher than in other countries of Africa because the copper mines stimulated the develop-

ment of such centers during the past century. White settlers came to the present Copperbelt in the late nineteenth century to search for minerals. The British South Africa Company, founded by Cecil Rhodes, and chartered by the British government, received concessions from the chiefs and claimed the lands. Of the thirty-nine thousand ex-patriates in the country today, most are connected with the industry. The copper began to be developed intensively in the years from 1924 to 1934. Copper became the source of Zambia's prosperity and presently accounts for eighty-seven percent of the exports. However, since 1974-1975 the prices of copper and cobalt, the second major mineral, have declined on the world market.

ECONOMIC WOES

Zambians also suffered economic hardship in the 1970s when Zambia supported the liberation struggles of Angolans and Mozambicans against Portugal and of Zimbabweans against the Rhodesian government. Zambia took a leading role in the economic boycott of Rhodesia, reducing its imports from nearly forty percent of Zambia's total imports to almost nothing.

When Zimbabwe became independent in 1980, it was expected that Zambia's economic situation would improve. This did not happen. In addition to the unfavorable conditions of the world market, South Africa's destabilizing tactics continued to affect Zambia—interfering with its rail lines, for instance. Problems of mismanagement on the home front contributed to an economic situation that has been described as "in disarray" or, more grimly, as "chaotic."

"HUMANISM" ESPOUSED

The Zambian government seeks answers to these economic problems. Kenneth Kaunda, the leader of Zambia's independence movement during the 1950s and 1960s and the President of Zambia since 1964, has continued to espouse a moderate Christian "humanism" akin to Western liberalism. However, he has now added a socialist component. In his "watershed" speech of 1975, Kaunda stressed the importance of rural development. Yet, problems of the rural areas worsen. Economic difficulties have led to an international debt, which amounted to $2.3 billion in 1981. Recent renegotiations with the International Monetary Fund have led to the third currency devaluation in seven years, an austerity budget, cuts in food subsidies for urban dwellers, and rising prices.

ZAMBIA AND AFRICAN AFFAIRS

Kaunda has taken a leading role in seeking peace for the Southern African region. He has met with South African leaders, and he has brought together the opposing parties in Angola and Namibia. Kaunda has played a prominent role in SADCC, and he is expected to be a leading figure in OAU affairs in the coming year.

DEVELOPMENT

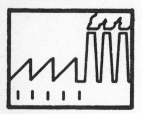

Efforts have been made to give more voice to workers in Zambian industries. Workers now choose their own representatives to boards of directors, and ex-patriates who work in the mines are being phased out.

FREEDOM

President Kaunda has maintained and followed a Christian and Gandhian humanist philosophy through the hard times since independence, and he has been determined to maintain civil rights for all people within the country, whatever their race, creed, color or language.

HEALTH/WELFARE

The recent rise in the price of maize and fertilizers will affect the cost of living. Kaunda has emphasized his continuing "moral obligation to lift the living standards of the people" but has stressed the need to raise prices to acquire foreign exchange that can revive industries now working at only forty percent capacity.

ACHIEVEMENTS

Zambia's educational system was very deficient at the time of independence, and there were fewer than one hundred Zambian college graduates. The University of Zambia, founded through contributions from all over the country had 312 students in 1966 and 4,037 enrolled in 1981.

Zimbabwe

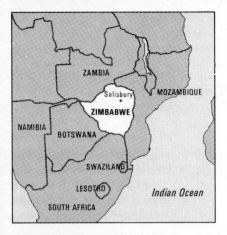

GEOGRAPHY

Area in Square Kilometers (Miles): 390,759 (150,873)
Land Usage: 40% arable; 60% suitable for grazing
Capital (Population): Harare (656,000—1982)
Climate: subtropical

PEOPLE

Population

Total: 7,540,000 (1982 est.)
Per Square Kilometer (Mile): 19 (50)
Annual Growth Rate: 3.5%
Rural/Urban Population Ratio: 77/23

Health

Life Expectancy at Birth: 54 years
Infant Death Rate (Ratio): 74/1,000
Average Caloric Intake: 86% of FAO minimum
Physicians Available (Ratio): 1/6,580

Languages

Official: English
Others Spoken: Shona; Ndebele; others

Religion(s)

Christian; indigenous beliefs; Muslim

Education

Adult Literacy Rate: 78% males; 64% females
School Attendance: primary: 100% boys, 100% girls; secondary: 18% boys, 13% girls

COMMUNICATION

Telephones: 214,000
Radios: 330,000
Televisions: 80,000
Newspapers: 2 dailies; total circulation 111,000

TRANSPORTATION

Highways—Kilometers (Miles): 85,237 (52,964)
Railroads—Kilometers (Miles): 2,743 (1,704)
Two international airports

GOVERNMENT

Type: republic
Constitution: 1980
Former Colonial Status: British (formerly Rhodesia)
Independence Date: April 18, 1980
Head of State: Canaan Banana (president); Robert Mugabe (prime minister)
Branches: president; prime minister; Cabinet; Parliament (bicameral); High Court
Legal System: English Common Law tradition
Political Parties: Zimbabwe African National Union - Patriotic Front; Zimbabwe African People's Union; others
Suffrage: universal over 18 years

MILITARY

Number of Armed Forces: 34,000
Armed Forces/Population: 1/223
Military Expenditures (% of Central Government Expenditures): $464,800,000 (17.2%)
Nuclear Weapons Status: none
Current Hostilities: scattered banditry

ECONOMY

Currency ($ US Equivalent): 1 Zimbabwe dollar = $1
GDP: $5,900,000,000
Per Capita Income/GNP: $850
Workforce: 60% agriculture; 15% industry; 25% services
Inflation Rate: 8.8% (1970-1980); 18% (1982)
Natural Resources: gold; other minerals
Agriculture: tobacco; corn; sugar; cotton; livestock
Industry: mining steel; textiles; chemicals; vehicles

FOREIGN TRADE

Exports: tobacco; asbestos; copper; tin; chrome; gold; nickle; meat; clothing; sugar
Imports: machinery; petroleum products; wheat; transport equipment
Major Trading Partners: South Africa
Foreign Debt: $1,768,500,000
Selected Membership in International Organizations: UN; OAU; Southern Africa Development Coordination Conference (SADCC)

| Heyday of the gold trade and Great Zimbabwe 1400s-1500s | Ndebele state emerges in Zimbabwe 1837 | Pioneer Column; arrival of the white settlers 1890 | *Chimurenga;* rising against the white intruders ending in repression by whites 1896-1897 |

ZIMBABWE

The independent republic of Zimbabwe was "born" on April 7, 1980. Its birth had been prolonged, painful, and difficult. The new country emerged from years of hardship and violence in a cruel war. Before the creation of Zimbabwe, the country was called Rhodesia. Whereas the name of the new state is intended to symbolize the social and political aspirations of an aroused African majority, the name "Rhodesia" had rallied those who believed in the cause of the privileges of a small minority—the white Rhodesians—who defined themselves as the sole representatives of the nation.

White settlers had entered the country from the south with the Pioneer Column (white miners and settlers who migrated from South Africa) in 1890. After thirty-four years of British South Africa Company administration, what was then called Southern Rhodesia became a self-governing British Crown colony. "Self-government" was, however, virtually confined to a white electorate. In 1953, Southern Rhodesia became the focal point of a federation of British colonial territories, the Federation of the Rhodesians and Nyasaland, which the settlers hoped might develop into a dominion such as Canada or South Africa. White immigration was encouraged, and white domination was ensured.

The Federation of the Rhodesians and Nyasaland collapsed when Britain acknowledged the right of two of its members to secede after African nationalist movements there became too strong to contain. These territories are now the independent states of Malawi and Zambia.

WHITE RHODESIANS SEEK INDEPENDENCE

In Rhodesia, the settlers were afraid that the reforms that the federation inspired might go too far. They rallied around the Rhodesia Front Party, which rejected any prospect of change and led the country to a Unilateral Declaration of Independence (UDI) in 1965. At first it appeared that they might achieve their objective. On the south, Rhodesia was bordered by a sympathetic South African government, and it was flanked by two Portuguese colonies, Angola and Mozambique, where the occupying power was committed to war

(United Nations photo)

During the armed struggle of the 1970s the minority Rhodesian government resettled many Africans in controlled villages.

against any African nationalist threat. In this context, a United Nations-sponsored economic and arms boycott proved inadequate to topple the Rhodesia Front under its determined leader, Ian Smith. African nationalists decided to turn to armed struggle in the countryside to achieve their aims.

The tide began to turn as fighting intensified in Mozambique and that colony became independent following the collapse of the Portuguese dictatorship in 1974. Despite taking much punishment from the Rhodesian army, the Mozambique authorities gave effective support to a growing Zimbabwe guerrilla struggle that seriously threatened the Smith regime as it rallied the

rural African population. For the African fighters, the war was a second *Chimurenga* (a Shona expression meaning "fighting in which everyone joins"), inspired by the bloody though unsuccessful risings of the Shona-speaking majority against white settlers in 1896-1897.

INTERNAL SETTLEMENT FAILS

Smith came under intense pressure from the West to come to a settlement. At first an "internal settlement" excluding those nationalists fighting in the bush was instituted in 1978, but, despite the presence of an African prime minister, Bishop Abel Muzorewa, this failed to halt the nationalists' military attacks. Finally, in 1979, all

Southern Rhodesia proclaimed a British Crown colony **1924**	Unilateral Declaration of Independence **1965**	Elections following cease-fire bring victory to ZANU-PF and an end to the war **1980**	Nkomo dismissed from the Cabinet; South Africa-based ex-Rhodesian soldiers are killed in Zimbabwe **1982**

■●■■■■■■■■■■■■■■■■■■■●■■■■■■■■■■■■■■■■■■■■■■■■■●■■■●■■■■■■■■●■ 1984

January-February 1984: Fifth brigade returns to Matabeleland to combat anti-government rebels	April 1984: Mugabe objects to Catholic Church report on Matabeleland human rights violations	August 1984: ZANU Congress will discuss the road to unity and ways of developing the one-party state

the belligerent parties met at Lancaster House in London to agree on a cease-fire and to set up a national election, which resulted in a great victory for African nationalists. A majority of all seats was won by the Zimbabwe African National Union-Patriotic Front (ZANU-PF), and its leader, Robert Mugabe, became the first prime minister of Zimbabwe in 1980.

PROBLEMS FORMIDABLE

The political, economic, and social problems inherited by the Mugabe regime were, and still are, formidable. Until independence, there were really "two nations" in Rhodesia: black and white. Segregation in most areas of life such as housing and the state school system was the norm, and African facilities were generally vastly inferior to white facilities. Approximately half the national territory was reserved for whites only. On "white" land, a prosperous capitalist agriculture, which was based on growing corn and tobacco for export as well as a diversified mix of crops for domestic consumption, flourished.

The workforce for these plantations, together with the large number of domestic servants, constituted a particularly impoverished and oppressed portion of the population. On "black" land, the Tribal Trust Lands, most of the land was poor and dry; there were few roads and communications facilities. Most of the adult population had to work in the "white" part of the country much of the time. While skilled Africans found few job opportunities until the manpower shortage during the 1970s war became overwhelming, everything was done to encourage white immigration. Indeed, the majority of whites resident in 1980 were the products of post-World War II immigration from Britain and South Africa, a large minority coming after UDI.

WHITES CONTROL ECONOMY

The new government could not entirely dismantle the privileged settler world partly because after UDI, whites had created what was by African standards a relatively prosperous and self-sufficient economy, which could not simply be destroyed without great national loss. Rhodesia was the most industrialized nation between Egypt and South Africa. The Mugabe government has been anxious to prevent white disaffection from negatively affecting the economy.

Also, the Lancaster House agreement essentially tied Mugabe's hands. Private property is legally enshrined in Zimbabwe and cannot be confiscated without generous compensation. Socialism certainly remains the government's long-term goal, but it has no overall plan to attain such a transformation. Change has, in fact, been piecemeal, and it has been limited in the social and economic, as opposed to the political, spheres. Thus, Zimbabwe remains a capitalist country with a socialist-inclined government. One-fifth of the seats in Parliament are retained by the small white minority that votes on a separate roll and continues to function as a significant political force.

ZANU-PF/ZAPU SPLIT

Another serious problem has been the split between Mugabe's ZANU-PF and the Zimbabwe African People's Union (ZAPU) led by Joshua Nkomo, an important politician since the 1950s. ZANU broke away from ZAPU in 1963 over personal and tactical disagreements rather than issues of principle. The result was open fighting in the African township of the capital, Salisbury, which has now been renamed Harare. ZAPU had originally been the dominant national movement but the

(Oxfam America photo)

These children may be going to school but they also contribute time and labor to the vital tasks of food production, often in school gardens.

(Oxfam America photo)

In this Zimbabwean farmer's organization, as in many African institutions, decisions are often made by consensus, arrived at after long discussions.

military successes of ZANU under its brilliant commander, the late Josiah Tongogara, won over many people.

During the war, many attempts were made in vain to re-unite ZANU and ZAPU, both by Zimbabweans and sympathetic foreigners. Only briefly after the ceasefire did they agree to form a "Patriotic Front" for negotiating with Smith and international forces.

Although both parties want to function on a national basis, the 1980 election revealed that ZAPU strength had largely become limited to the southwestern portion of the country and to the Ndebele-speaking minority of the population. ZAPU has insistently rejected demands for a merger that could turn Zimbabwe into a one-party state, as Mugabe desires, while ZANU-PF denounces ZAPU as disloyal.

There have been strong tensions. Initially Nkomo and several ZAPU men received ministerial appointments, but discoveries of secret arms caches that the government claimed ZAPU intended to hoard until the right moment for a coup strained relations and led to Nkomo's dismissal in February 1982. Late in 1982 and again in early 1984, the North Korean-trained Fifth Brigade was dispatched to Matabeleland, the ZAPU stronghold, where many incidents of violence against whites and those supporting ZANU-PF, had been reported. In March 1983, after a raid on his home, Nkomo fled across the frontier to Botswana, where many Ndebele refugees have gathered. He remained out of the country until August, when he returned and resumed his seat in parliament. In early 1984, human rights violations by the army were taken up by a closed committee and later detailed by a report of the Catholic Church.

SOUTH AFRICAN RELATIONS

The conflict between ZANU-PF and ZAPU in Zimbabwe makes for a difficult security situation. Zimbabwe and South Africa have poor relations. The South African government, which once backed Ian Smith, supported Muzorewa in the national elections and was stunned by Mugabe's victory. It is difficult for the South African regime to accept a government led by men with socialist ideals, who came to power through an effective guerrilla campaign against an allied neighboring regime.

At the same time, Zimbabwe is in need of good economic relations with South Africa. During the UDI period, trade links with South Africa intensified, and South African investment became very sizable in Zimbabwe. Zimbabwe firmly opposes South African domestic policies and has worked to establish closer economic ties with such neighbors as Mozambique as an alternative to continued dependence on its neighbor to the south. However, Zimbabwe permits only a modest civilian presence of the African National Congress and other South African liberation organizations within its borders.

INITIAL OPTIMISM

During the first year after independence, the economy situation of Zimbabwe was favorable enough to allow for a large measure of optimism in the new state's ability to meet the challenges ahead. With the lifting of sanctions, mineral, corn, and tobacco exports expanded and import restrictions were eased. Worker's incomes rose, and a minimum wage, which covered even farm employees, was introduced for the first time. The rise in purchasing power benefitted industry.

Zimbabwe had hopes that foreign investment and aid would pay for an ambitious scheme to buy out many white farmers and to settle African peasants on their land. There was a rapid expansion in educational and rural health facilities, while Africans began to enter the civil service in large numbers.

CONDITIONS DETERIORATING

Unfortunately, conditions have deteriorated since 1981. The stagnation in world trade has brought down the value of Zimbabwean exports and forced the government to control imports strictly. The most severe drought in a century has reduced agricultural production. In 1983 only a huge reserve prevents Zimbabwe—normally a large exporter—from requiring corn imports. Real growth, estimated at over ten percent in 1980, fell to two percent in 1982 and will actually become negative in 1983, according to some estimates.

Foreign investment has been slow in coming to Zimbabwe because of the nation's security problems. Foreign aid grants have been disappointingly small. The Reagan administration, Zimbabwe's principal source of aid, expressed anger in 1983 at Zimbabwe's refusal to support the American position on the Korean airline incident and at Zimbabwe's co-sponsorship of the UN condemnation of the American invasion of Grenada. Zimbabwe's foreign policy of non-alignment led to a serious cut in aid money.

During its first years in power, the ZANU-PF government was able to promote some significant reforms, but it acted with surprising caution, given its commitment to revolutionary change. The state was slow to invest in the economy directly, and efforts at land reform lagged. At the same time, many ministers and high officials have begun to acquire large farms and other properties while enriching themselves. The country's economic circumstances appeared to block any further attempts to put socialism into practice. Zimbabwe had to devalue its dollar at the end of 1982 and to negotiate with the International Monetary Fund for a substantial loan in 1983. This would require acceptance of cutbacks in public spending and an end to social reforms.

INTERNAL CONFLICTS

Powerful forces continue to regret the defeat of Rhodesia and the African nationalist victory. Thus in June 1982, the army came into conflict with and killed several ex-Rhodesian soldiers who had infiltrated from South Africa. Ian Smith, still a member of Parliament, has had his passport removed while Bishop Muzorewa was detained in October 1983 for allegedly conspiring against the government.

During 1983, there was international controversy over the case of the seven former Rhodesian Air Force men who were detained on suspicion of sabotage, following destruction of much of the air force in the wake of Mugabe's victory. The airmen were tortured during their confinement, and several were re-detained after their trial ended in an acquittal. The attention paid to this and other human rights problem areas—as contrasted with the rather easy handling Ian Smith's people always received in the Western press—has been noted angrily by representatives of the new Zimbabwe. Among other measures, they have banned newsmen from entering the country if they are based in South Africa.

ZIMBABWE'S ACCOMPLISHMENTS

The difficulties Zimbabwe faces should not overshadow its accomplishments. First, the success of the war created an unprecedented sense of public confidence in the possibility of developing a democracy. Second, in a short time, Zimbabwe has succeeded in providing a minimum of welfare benefits—notably in health and education—to the majority of its people. Finally, Zimbabwe has so far been able to offer to its racially-mixed population a peaceful non-racist solution to the bitter conflict between the "two nations."

The majority of white citizens remains in the country, although their numbers are gradually diminishing. A large minority of former Rhodesia Front supporters in Parliament deserted the ranks and reclassified themselves as independents. As a result of by-elections in 1982 and 1983, the independents now constitute a majority of the white representatives. ZANU and Mugabe see the one-party state as the solution for problems of unity and development, and Mugabe has called for a public debate on the idea.

If a definitive solution to the bitter ZANU-ZAPU division could be devised, the new country will have gone far toward healing the wounds of a devastating war. At the same time, in terms of the revolutionary hopes that the struggle raised, Zimbabwean performance (and social transformation) has often seemed disappointing both to sympathetic outsiders and to the mass of poor citizens who believed in the *Chimurenga.*

DEVELOPMENT	FREEDOM	HEALTH/WELFARE	ACHIEVEMENTS

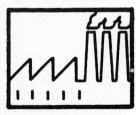

DEVELOPMENT

Much of the land controlled by whites is actually under-utilized and suitable for settlement by African communities. The Zimbabwean government has very gradually been surveying and giving over some of this land to ex-fighters and land-hungry peasants in a campaign to restructure agriculture.

FREEDOM

The new Zimbabwe has often been criticized in the Western media for detaining or harassing former Rhodesia Front leaders and supporters. In turn, the Mugabe government proclaimed the criticism is exaggerated and inspired by those who seek to prove that socialism and African nationalism in Zimbabwe are failures.

HEALTH/WELFARE

Since 1980, the Zimbabwean government has been determined to extend a basic education to all children. In only two years, the number of students in primary and secondary schools has risen from 800 thousand to 2.2 million.

ACHIEVEMENTS

One of the hardest tasks facing Zimbabwe in 1980 was dismantling segregated institutions. A peaceful and systematic desegregation of hospitals, schools, neighborhoods, and trade unions is underway.

Topic Guide to Articles: Southern Africa

TOPIC AREA	TREATED AS AN ISSUE IN	TOPIC AREA	TREATED AS AN ISSUE IN
Current Leaders	1. Under New Management 4. The Father of Namibian Nationalism Stays Firm	**Regional Concerns**	2. Waging a War of Sabotage in South Africa 4. The Father of Namibian Nationalism Stays Firm 5. The Nkomati Accords 7. Pax Pretoriana
Economy	1. Under New Management 2. Waging a War of Sabotage in South Africa 3. Notes from a Cooperante	**Religion**	6. Milingo Defends His Healing Mission 8. Christians and Socialists
Military	2. Waging a War of Sabotage in South Africa 7. Pax Pretoriana	**Resistance Movements**	2. Waging a War of Sabotage in South Africa 4. The Father of Namibian Nationalism Stays Firm
Political Development	1. Under New Management 3. Notes from a Cooperante 4. The Father of Namibian Nationalism Stays Firm 5. The Nkomati Accords 7. Pax Pretoriana		

Southern Africa: Articles Section

Article 1

THE ECONOMIST APRIL 21, 1984

Under new management

Four years ago this week, Zimbabwe became independent. Born from a civil war that had killed 30,000 people and brought the economy to a halt, the new country seemed set for a shaky start. For two years, the sceptics were confounded: under the prime minister, Mr Robert Mugabe, old enemies were reconciled and Zimbabwe's economic growth was the fastest in the world. The past two years could hardly have been more different. The economy has stagnated, political tension increased. Which period reflects the true Zimbabwe? Our economics editor, Rupert Pennant-Rea, went to find out.

"This is the jewel in Africa's crown. Don't tarnish it." Thus President Julius Nyerere of Tanzania, saying goodbye to Mr Robert Mugabe after attending Zimbabwe's independence celebrations in 1980. Despite long years of war and international sanctions, the country that had been called Rhodesia glittered brightly in the sun. Its gnp per person was around US$850, three times Tanzania's average, twice Kenya's, slightly higher than Nigeria's. It grew all its own food, with some to spare. It had a decent sprinkling of minerals and more manufacturing industry than any other African country bar Nigeria and South Africa. It could call on the skills and capital of 220,000 whites in a total population of 7½m. It had 12,000 black graduates; Zambia, when it became independent in 1964, had barely a dozen. No wonder President Nyerere was impressed.

Today the jewel looks tarnished—though nature, not Mr Mugabe, should take most of the blame. Zimbabwe has just had another bad rainy season, the third in a row. Parts of the country are scorched, the rest is parched. Smaller dams have dried up, water has been rationed. The huge maize silos, overflowing only three years ago, are now empty. Zimbabwe will have to import maize this year, though it has little foreign exchange to pay for it. Like many countries in Africa, it will need food aid.

Before dismissing Zimbabwe as just another African cliché, outsiders need to guess what would have happened if nature had been kinder these past three seasons. Are the basic policies and priorities such that, with more rain, Zimbabwe will fulfil its obvious potential? To start

answering that question, go back to 1980, and the reasons why President Nyerere was apprehensive about Africa's jewel.

Eight years of civil war had left Zimbabwe with abandoned farms and villages, thousands of refugees and three armies to integrate. Black politicians may have shelved their differences for a time to unite as the Patriotic Front, but their guerrillas never did and the general election of March, 1980, had revived old frictions. Most whites had been shocked by Mr Mugabe's victory; if he really was the Marxist menace which they had long been branding him, they would take their skills out in a flash. That had happened in Mozambique in the mid-1970s, and its economy had never recovered.

One man who knew Mozambique well was Mr Mugabe. He spent five years there, before the Lancaster House agreement allowed him to return home for the 1980 elections. For him, Mozambique had been more than a springboard for guerrilla war; it had also shown him some of the problems of peace. As soon as he had won the election, he started telling whites that the new Zimbabwe needed them. He kept many on in senior positions in the army, judiciary and civil service. He appointed two white ministers to his cabinet.

There were no reprisals, no trials of the former white masters. Mr Ian Smith, the Rhodesian prime minister for 15 years, is still a member of Zimbabwe's parliament, being paid a salary to grizzle and gripe about how things have changed. One of his party's biggest paymasters in years past, Mr D. C. "Boss" Lilford, still strolls around the paddock at the racecourse in the capital, Harare. Few revolutionaries

have been as magnanimous in victory as Mr Mugabe and his ministers. They had reason enough to hate whites; they chose to hate racialism instead.

The soothing of white nerves was Mr Mugabe's earliest achievement in government, and also the easiest. Many whites expected the worst, so were pleased when it did not happen. But black people had high hopes of their new government, and could be quickly disappointed. Hundreds expected political office, thousands wanted jobs in the public sector, millions looked forward to more land, higher wages, better schools and clinics. Young men who had sacrificed much as guerrillas came home to claim their reward. Those pressures were acute, and still are.

Outsiders also expected much of the new Zimbabwe. Communist countries, which had armed the guerrillas and supported their political leaders through years of exile, wanted the solidarity to remain when the exiles returned. The western world hoped Zimbabwe would open its doors to the trade and investment that, because of sanctions, had formally been denied Rhodesia. But the conflicting hopes of east and west mattered less than the pressure that could come from the south. As it had been a lifeline to white Rhodesia, so South Africa could now choke the new Zimbabwe. It did not want its neighbour to be a haven for guerrillas, nor an economic success that would disprove its white supremacist claims.

In judging which hopes have been fulfilled and which dashed, the most misleading guide of all is the utterances of Zimbabwe's politicians. Something about the country seems to inspire political hyperbole. When he was prime minister, Mr Smith pontificated about preserving western civilisation while defying the western democracies. Today, Mr Mugabe and his ministers use the rhetoric of Marxism, admire Mr Fidel Castro and refer to themselves as comrades. Yet Zimbabwe is light years away from Castro's Cuba, just as Rhodesia was from any post-feudal western society. Harold Macmillan was only half right: his "wind of change" blowing through Africa has been at least as much a change of wind.

The verbiage is not without purpose, of course. The pressures on Mr Mugabe are too great to be satisfied by the concrete achievements of just four years, even if there had been no drought. Slogans are used to keep different groups happy, to make them feel that the government is really on their side. When Mr Mugabe addresses a rally of his party—particularly when he is speaking in his native Shona—he sounds far more radical than when he is talking to a dozen businessmen.

Politicians everywhere play to their audience and nobody minds too much. But Zimbabwe is still so new, its government so unknown, that every ministerial word is studied with a care worthy of Kremlin-watchers. Diplomats do it, local pundits do it (though rarely in print) and so does the outside world. When Zimbabwe joins Nicaragua in sponsoring a UN resolution condemning the American invasion of Grenada, it seems to be as hostile to the United States as the Sandinistas are. But the UN currency is words, and words are little guide to the reality of Zimbabwe.

They count for something, though. By the yardsticks of tourism and foreign investment, Zimbabwe is putting the world off. It has some tourist areas of world class and an incomparable climate. Yet during this past northern-hemisphere winter, its resorts were seldom full. Most

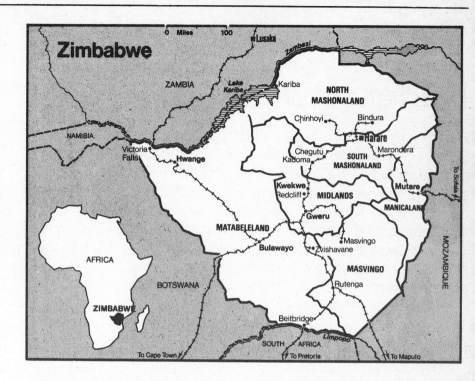

of the tourists were white and brown Zimbabweans prevented by exchange controls from travelling abroad.

The lack of foreign investment is more serious. In four years of independence—and after 15 years when sanctions starved the country of capital—Zimbabwe has attracted only US$25m of private foreign investment. That is the amount that went into developing countries as a group every 15 hours last year, and what a similar-sized country like Ivory Coast got in six months in 1981. Apart from one large investment by Heinz, the American multinational, foreign companies have stayed away in droves.

Zimbabwe's politicians tend to blame these failures on the international press. Certainly it is quick to report the bad news about Zimbabwe, and one white

farmer being killed still gets more column inches than the murder of scores of blacks. Having reported a black-white war for years, journalists (and their editors at home) are stuck in a groove that rarely does justice to the new Zimbabwe. But the politicians and their rantings are also to blame if Zimbabwe sounds to the outside world like Speakers' Corner without the jokes.

On the ground, Zimbabwe is a different sort of place. It is being governed pragmatically, because that is often the only way to keep conflicting pressures at bay. That does not necessarily mean that it is being governed well: in some areas pragmatism has produced paralysis, holding back economic growth and reducing the government's room for manoeuvre elsewhere....

Article 2   THE CHRISTIAN SCIENCE MONITOR   September 16, 1983

Waging a war of sabotage in South Africa

The African National Congress dazed South Africa's white rulers when it hit high-security police and power installations in 1982 and '83. The outlawed movement, which went underground in 1960, claims it is forced to resort to sabotage because all nonviolent channels of protest have been closed by the government.

By David Winder
Staff correspondent of
The Christian Science Monitor

THE atmosphere was electric.

Thousands of blacks were marching on Johannesburg. Tens of thousands were marching on Cape Town. The police and Army roared into action. Roadblocks shot up. Tanks rolled into position. Jet fighters buzzed African crowds at rooftop level.

The time: March 1960. It was the month of mass passive resistance demonstrations against the South African race laws. It was also the time of Sharpeville, when 69 Africans protesting the carrying of passes were shot dead by the South African police.

The South African government was facing its sternest test. There was an alarming flight of capital out of the country. Either the government would regain control through a massive crackdown, or the resistance movement would seize this opportunity to change the existing apartheid order.

Reports of nationwide unrest snowballed on the day of Sharpeville. A prominent professor on the small campus of the University of Natal in Pietermaritzburg then gathered his white students together, and in the hushed tones of one who believes history is in the making, said flatly: "I think the government will fall tonight."

"We thought exactly the same thing at the time," says Mfanafuthi Makatini, who heads the observer mission to the United Nations of the outlawed African National Congress (ANC).

The government didn't fall. It prevailed through batons and banning orders, through sweeping pre-dawn raids on the houses of suspected revolutionaries and through a flurry of legislation that tightened the screws on political dissent. African (black), Indian, and white opponents of the government were scooped up in the detention net.

Organizations such as the ANC and its rival, the Pan African Congress (PAC), were banned shortly after Sharpeville. Hundreds of activists like Mr. Makatini and the ANC's current president, Oliver Tambo, escaped through neighboring African countries and regrouped to fight another day.

The dawning of that day has apparently come. For within the last two years the underground resistance movement, which has become virtually synonymous with the ANC, has carried out over a hundred highly selected acts of sabotage that have put South Africa's security forces on edge and left whites uneasy about what might follow next.

Ruth Mompati, chief executive of the ANC's branch in the United Kingdom, says that what agitates the South African authorities is that the ANC has been able to carry out daring acts of sabotage under the noses of South African security forces. In a recent interview in London, she said:

"We hit Sasol [the oil-from-coal refinery near Johannesburg], which is high security. And then we hit Koeberg [a nuclear power sta-

tion near Cape Town], which is also high security, twice in a month. First they said it was an electrical fault that would take six weeks to correct. We didn't worry. We went back again. We hit it four times at regular intervals with limpet mines. They couldn't say it was an electrical fault after that. They couldn't believe it could happen in the heart of their Afrikanerdom. This is what is making South Africa so angry, and their followers are starting to see their weaknesses."

By all accounts, including reports from South African intelligence, Pretoria has seen the enemy and the enemy is the ANC.

How vulnerable, then, is the South African government? Who belongs to the ANC, and what is its strategy? To what extent will strife in South Africa drag in South Africa's closest black neighbors — Angola, Zambia, Botswana, Lesotho, Zimbabwe, Swaziland, Mozambique, and Tanzania — to which South African political opponents have fled?

These questions are uppermost in the minds of Africa watchers. They have become more pressing since the ANC claimed responsibility for the May 20, 1983, bomb attack outside Air Force Headquarters, Pretoria. As many as 17 people were killed, eight of them black, and more than 200 injured in South Africa's worst incident of sabotage.

The blast was carried out in broad daylight, a departure from the past, and killed civilian bystanders. The attack immediately raised questions as to whether the ANC, in escalating its campaign, was moving away from buildings and installations toward indiscriminate civilian killings.

ANC official Ruth Mompati denies that the ANC is shifting tactics:

"It's been our policy, and still is, to hit hard targets — military and economic targets. Even in Pretoria we chose military targets. One was the South African Air Force; the other, security intelligence headquarters. These were two places we hit. We killed Air Force personnel. They were military men. We didn't hit a supermarket or concert hall where there were lots of civilians."

The latest ANC attack, together with earlier bombings of the Sasol and Koeberg plants and rocket attacks on the center of the South African military establishment, point to an efficient and sophisticated operation.

The sudden resurgence of ANC activity is traced to the 1976 Soweto riots when African schoolchildren resisted learning the Afrikaans language as a compulsory subject in school. Press reports at the time estimated the number of fatalities, including children, at between 172 and 600. Thousands of politicized students fled the country and took up arms in ANC camps. They apparently pushed the leadership to take more drastic action.

Until then, the ANC was belittled in the eyes of other world revolutionaries as too comfortable and too cozy; an organization of largely middle-class coat-and-tie professionals that had little to show for the 70-odd years it had been around.

That image now has changed so dramatically that the whole destabilizing of southern

EVOLUTION OF THE AFRICAN NATIONAL CONGRESS:

1912	ANC founded.
1949	Program of Action, including nonviolent civil disobedience, starts.
1953	Civil disobedience discontinued when South African government passed law providing stiff penalties for those who break even minor laws.
1959	All-black Pan-African Congress (PAC) forms in protest of ANC's multiracial membership.
March 1960:	Nationwide passive resistance demonstrations. 69 killed at Sharpeville. South Africa declares state of emergency.
April 8 1960	ANC, declared illegal, goes underground.
Dec. 1961	ANC leader Nelson Mandela forms military wing of the ANC. The group begins its sabotage campaign.
1963	South African police find underground ANC headquarters in Johannesburg suburb of Rivonia.
1964	Mandela convicted at Rivonia trial and is given a life sentence.
1976	African riot in Soweto against forced use of Afrikaans language in school curriculum. Thousands of school-age children flee South Africa; many link up with ANC forces outside the country.
June 1980	Bombing of Sasol, South Africa's oil-from-coal refinery.
August 1981	Rocket attack on Voortrekkerhoogte, Pretoria, center of country's military establishment.
Dec. 9 1982	South Africa, in retaliation for alleged ANC sabotage staged from bases in Lesotho, attacks ANC residences in Lesotho capital of Maseru. 40 killed.
Dec. 18 1982	Bombing of South Africa's only nuclear power station at Koeberg, outside Cape Town.
May 20 1983	Car bomb explodes outside Air Force Headquarters, Pretoria. 17 killed, more than 200 injured in worst sabotage incident in South African history.
May 23 1983	South Africa retaliates with air strike against suspected ANC targets in Mozambique's capital. 6 killed, more than 20 wounded.
June 9 1983	Three ANC members charged with attacking police stations hanged.

Africa — triggered by sabotage within the white-ruled republic and by retaliatory raids and explosions in neighboring African states carried out by South Africa or sympathetic groups — is directly linked to ANC activity. This is because South African retaliatory attacks are directed at countries that Pretoria suspects are launching pads for guerrilla attacks into South Africa.

While the ANC has several times exposed the vulnerability of the South African security system by penetrating high-security installations like the Koeberg nuclear plant, it still faces a formidable foe.

South Africa enjoys the position of a regional superpower. Its gross national product is 10 times that of its southern African neighbors. Its Army is one of the strongest and best trained on the African continent. Living side by side with white-ruled South Africa are economically and militarily weak black African states that now know that, given a pretext, the giant next door will not hesitate to blast countries it suspects of harboring ANC groups.

On Dec. 9, 1982, South Africa struck in a lightning commando raid against suspected ANC guerrillas in Maseru, the capital, of Lesotho. At least 40 people were killed. On May 23 this year South African jets attacked what turned out to be a jam factory in Maputo, Mozambique's capital. Six people were killed and more than 20 were wounded.

Both attacks, whose severity shocked neighboring African states, were regarded by many Western diplomats as overkill, particularly since South Africa has failed to provide convincing evidence of ANC military bases.

But the political lesson that South Africa intended to deliver was apparently taken to heart for most of its neighbors are showing much greater wariness now about supporting the ANC. And Mozambique, despite the Marxist character of its government, is dependent for its economic survival on South Africa.

A recent diplomatic visitor to South Africa who has closely monitored that government's political strategy suggests the following scenario on how South Africa attacked the Mozambican capital:

Word goes out from approaching South African pilots to the Maputo airport that "We're going after specific targets not Mozambican. We're not engaging Mozambican security forces." After warning Mozambique to stand clear, South African jets move in. Mozambican military installations are left intact and Maputo is signaled that the raid is over. According to the diplomat, the Maputo control tower doesn't exactly come on the air and say "thank you," but that, essentially, is the response.

Despite growing African reluctance to provoke South Africa, Western diplomats doubt whether African states would ever turn their backs completely on fraternal ties with the ANC. The ANC, for instance, has its headquarters in Lusaka, the capital of Zambia. It maintains a school for some 900 students in Morogoro, Tanzania. ANC refugees have been present in all the neighboring states. But South African pressure has been so evident in

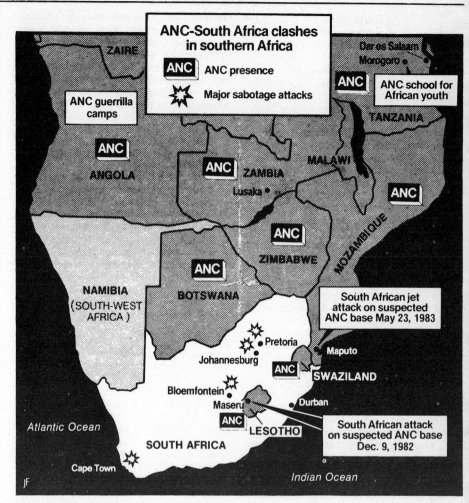

the last few months that it has neutralized the countries of Botswana and Swaziland, which have virtually given the ANC its marching orders to leave. Angola and Mozambique, two Marxist neighbors of South Africa, are also restraining ANC activity. Zambia's position is described as a country that accepts the political presence of the ANC, but for hard-nosed economic reasons discourages any ANC military activity.

Zambia's southern neighbor, Zimbabwe, although a Marxist state, also takes a pragmatic line and tries to keep its hands clean of military involvement with the ANC. There is an ideological reason for Zimbabwe's stand: Prime Minister Robert Mugabe is pro-Peking and until recently shunned Moscow. He has not warmed to the ANC because of its relationship with the Soviets and its close identification with Mugabe's arch rival, Joshua Nkomo, whose faction enjoyed Moscow's backing in the pre-independence struggle.

Only tiny Lesotho, to the amazement of Western diplomats, seems to refuse to get the message that it mustn't mix coexistence with South Africa and shelter for ANC guerrillas — although here, too, there are signs that Lesotho is looking for a way out.

From time to time the ANC has had training camps in many southern African states

and has held mock battles in anticipation of possible encounters with South African forces. The most conspicuous training grounds have been in northern Angola, with small commando units popping up in South Africa from across several national borders.

The South African Embassy also insists there are bases in Zambia and Mozambique, but for security reasons declines to elaborate. An embassy official claims evidence was found in Beirut after the Israeli invasion of Lebanon of ANC officials given PLO military training. The ANC insists that it has no bases in neighboring countries nor does it allow its members to carry guns in these countries. The ANC has conceded that in March 1979 South African jets tried to knock out a military training school in Angola.

The heat that South Africa is applying to its northern neighbors is apparently forcing the ANC to move its camps further north. According to Thomas Karis, a professor at the Graduate School of the City University in New York City and an acknowledged expert on the ANC: "Training goes on continually in a number of countries, but they're not in the front-line states. They're very careful about that."

According to Professor Karis and other ANC experts, much of the training is carried out by East Germans. South African sources agree that East Germans are involved, adding that the Soviet Union, Libya, and the United Nations are prominent among those funding the ANC. The UN, which provides development and support programs, is known to fund several world liberation movements such as the ANC.

Yet preoccupation with the ANC outside the borders of South Africa begs the question of how much the ANC is a direct threat to South Africa from *within* South Africa.

There is some suggestion that South Africa's much publicized attacks north of its borders are calculated not only to cow the neighboring or so-called front-line states, but also to create an illusion to quiet agitated whites that the threat to their lives comes from beyond the country's borders.

The quandary as to how far South African authorities wish to admit either the number of ANC fighters who might have crossed the borders back into South Africa or the groundswell of support within the resident black population is revealed by the conflicting evidence emanating from South Africa.

In February last year the Rabie Commission for Security dismissed the threat of the ANC by saying that only a small minority of Africans belonged to the ANC. An official of the South African Embassy in Washington said the number of ANC within the country is "very, very small indeed." South African military spokesmen, however, have spoken of "guerrillas everywhere."

How well some ANC members have been able to penetrate South Africa, avoiding detection, is provided by Tom Lodge of the University of Witwatersrand in Johannesburg. who has made a thorough study of the ANC.

According to South African press accounts, Professor Lodge cites the example of one insurgent who entered the country in 1979 and was captured only 21 months later after he was involved in attacks on police stations — at Moroka, Orlando, and Wonderboom in the Pretoria-Johannesburg area — and in the limpet mining of a power plant in Pretoria.

According to a purported classified US intelligence document, dated April 15, 1982, which came into the hands of Trans-Africa, a black American lobby group on African affairs, the ANC has 1,000 to 2,000 persons taking military training outside South Africa. The document also says there are perhaps 2,000 to 3,000 persons inside South Africa who secretly belong to the banned organization.

A number of African experts pressed on this point say that nobody is sure about ANC numbers, but a general consensus is that with 1976 riots in Soweto some 4,000 to 6,000 young Africans fled South Africa and enlisted with the military wing of the ANC outside the country's borders. Estimates put the number of ANC guerrillas outside South Africa at upward of 5,000.

Despite these acts of sabotage, Gwendolen M. Carter of Indiana University, a longtime observer of the southern African scene, believes that the ANC is more concerned with "winning the hearts and minds" of the black population than scoring military victories.

Says William J. Foltz, professor of political science at Yale University: "What is of interest is not the number of armed people they have. It is the number of people building networks and building cell structures in South Africa."

What acts of sabotage achieve, these experts day, is to publicize to blacks within South Africa that the ANC is the one organization that is fighting the government.

To Professor Foltz, "The ANC almost certainly represents in an aspirational sense the feeling of a large proportion of the black population."

In 1981, an opinion poll carried out by the Johannesburg Star indicated that 40 percent of urban blacks would vote for ANC candidates in free elections. In that poll, Nelson Mandela — a charismatic ANC leader who has developed into something of a folk hero among many blacks — turns up as easily the most respected black leader.

Mandela, who eluded police for a long time and is now regarded as South Africa's No. 1 political prisoner, received a 76 percent popularity rating. He has spent the last 19 years in a maximum security cell. He receives occasional visits from his activist wife, Winnie Mandela, who has been exiled to a remote area.

Dr. Carter who was in Soweto, the large exclusively black city outside Johannesburg in February, says she saw "ANC slogans and Mandela pictures in back alleys, which I thought was pretty daring."

Thousands have turned out recently for funerals of ANC activists inside South Africa. On such occasions ANC adherents and supporters have blatantly waved the black, yellow, and green ANC flag and sung ANC songs even though the organization is banned.

The ANC has gradually been winning more adherents of the Black Consciousness movement. Among them is Barney Pityana, one of the founders of the consciousness movement.

In the eyes of the South African government, the ANC is denounced as a communist front that kills innocent victims. Professor Karis says he sees the organization as essentially "nondoctrinaire. There is room for Marxists and non-Marxists and there is room for Christians."

Although an overwhelmingly black organization, the ANC nevertheless contains a small group of dedicated white communists. One such communist is Joe Slovo, who operates out of Mozambique. South African authorities believe he has masterminded numerous sabotage attacks. The ANC has an alliance with the banned largely white South African Communist Party and the South African Congress of Trade Unions.

White membership was the issue that led to the 1958 split in the ANC and the formation the following year of the rival and now largely ineffective PAC. The founders of the PAC believed pro-Moscow whites were diluting African nationalism. The role of whites, however, remains a sensitive issue in the organization. When pressed on it, Ruth Mompati of London's ANC office says: "There is no way we can say to the whites, 'Now that we have got rid of the regime you can get out.' Some are fighting in the trenches now."

Mr. Makatini of the ANC's UN office says the black Soweto youths who crossed the borders in 1976 "still had a lot of reactive racism. They were anti-white." It took some time to change this, but it came, he said, when black youths saw there were Indians and whites fighting with them."

So far, many analysts believe that despite obvious gaps in South Africa's security system, South Africa is a long way off from being another Northern Ireland or Lebanon. And thus far South Africa has limited its reprisals to targets outside of South Africa.

But one American analyst of the ANC is concerned about the future if bombings become more frequent and the government is forced to take stronger measures. "What happens if the government decides to seal off half of Soweto and make a thousand arrests every time a bomb goes off."

That, he implied, would present the ANC with a moral dilemma in which retribution could far outweigh the crime.

Article 3

AFRICA NEWS/February 7, 1983

MOZAMBIQUE

NOTES FROM A COOPERANTE

[AN] Eight years after its independence, Mozambique remains one of the world's poorest countries. Its stated goal of hauling itself out of underdevelopment within a decade has fallen victim to the magnitude of the political and economic problems it has experienced.

Still, the Marxist FRELIMO government has made gains, especially in social areas such as health and education. And its bold experiments in participatory decision-making structures have attracted idealistic young workers— *cooperantes* — from many countries.

Today, the economic advances are overshadowed by a widening war against South African-backed insurgents calling themselves the Mozambique National Resistance (MNR). Political ideals such as open debate and rehabilitation of criminals have been compromised by the exigencies of battle.

For example, one of independent Mozambique's first acts was to abolish the death penalty. But in the climate of worsening security, capital punishment was reinstated, and last month crowds watched the public executions of seven confessed MNR guerrillas. Journalists speculate that this unprecedented measure was designed to reassure the population in an area where MNR atrocities have been mounting.

While Mozambican officials remain remarkably frank about problems and failures, whether it be agricultural shortfalls or abuses of authority, a clampdown on news about the war has generated strong, if careful, debate. In a front-page editorial last October, Mia Couto, editor of the government newspaper *Noticias,* criticized the lack of openness, saying, "If silence is our only answer, we cannot bemoan the effects caused by enemy information."

Both sympathetic foreign observers and Mozambican government officials say they hope that FRELIMO's 4th Party Congress, scheduled for April, will provide a forum for dealing with problems and renewing flagging optimism. In thousands of local and regional meetings, people are being encouraged to air their grievances and participate in devising and implementing solutions.

In this report, *AFRICA NEWS* presents excerpts from a speech by Mozambican president Samora Machel to the executive committee planning the Congress. Accompanying it is the final letter from Jean Raisler, the American *cooperante* who has shared her experiences in Mozambique with *AFRICA NEWS* readers for the last two years (see *AN,* May 18, 1981; July 6, 1981; November 16, 1981; March 1, 1982; September 13, 1982).

Nurse-midwife Raisler, her husband Jon Cohn, and their children Joshie and Josina (born in Mozambique) are due home this month. In a note, Raisler says she hopes that "talking about some of the problems gives readers a more realistic picture of how difficult it is to build a new social system in a hostile world, and on the ruins of a distorted colonialism."

Mozambican Asians: their status is the same as that of other citizens. / *Africa News*

Dear friends,

Many changes here in the last months. In August, the "armed bandits" crossed the Zambezi river, driven north by routes in Manica and Sofala provinces. So now the war has come to Zambezia.

Officially, nothing is happening. The newspapers and radio are not reporting MNR activity these days. So information is by word of mouth, the rumors the government denounces. But the situation can't be hidden from the people, and often the rumors are true.

The *bandidos* seem to be moving through our province in groups of 50 to 100 or so. They have mined many roads and burned vehicles to paralyse transport. Some towns have been isolated this way, and people, cars, and trucks have been blown up. Movement of food and supplies has become more difficult than ever. The guerrillas attack strategic industries like tea and cotton, burning factories and warehouses, and firing mortars into the production units.

Workers flee, and production declines or stops. Stores, crops, and army bases are robbed, to supply the guerrillas with arms, food, and goods to use or trade with the population. Even hospitals have been ransacked, and ambulances burned. Citizens are kidnapped to carry stolen goods to forest hideouts, and they are given forced training and compromised in illegal activities.

The people seem to fear and dislike the *bandidos,* and report their whereabouts to the authorities. But it may take a few days for the army to arrive, and by then the enemy has moved on. And when people don't feel that the army can protect them, they sometimes abandon an area.

Quelimane is calm, though people gossip endlessly about the latest troubles in the districts. The climate is hot, humid, and apathetic. It's hard to find folks who feel that their lives are improving. People focus on how difficult it has become to arrange food and goods. They seem to forget or take for granted new opportunities in education, expanded health care, and the chances for Mozambicans to hold leadership positions which were not possible under the Portuguese.

In fact, hardship does abound. Plenty of destabilization from South Africa, and denial of trade and aid from other countries who want to see the black Marxist government fall. Then also the Portuguese exported or wrecked what they could at independence, leaving a tradition of passivity, bureaucracy, and underdevelopment that's hard to break.

Internal factors also weigh heavily. Production is dropping, especially in agriculture. The government has had to make hard decisions about where to put the little foreign currency it has. So far, it has invested heavily in Eastern bloc-style development projects, like large state farms with mechanical harvesters. Too often the equipment breaks down and lies useless, but it's not in the plan for peasants to collect the crops by hand. Peasant agriculture, small-scale production, and small shops receive little help. With the shops almost empty, the peasants return to subsistence farming. Why bother to produce a surplus, when the money just piles up in the house? These days, people often refuse to sell food for money, preferring to trade it for soap or sugar.

For people to accept and understand the sacrifices they are making, their participation in political life must develop. Otherwise, scarcity becomes fertile soil for reaction to grow in. The ideas that come from the government in Maputo often seem good and wise. But the middle-level cadre who link government to the people are spread very thin, so it is easy to continue in the passive mode of colonial times — not to think actively about why the country is hurting, or what you could do to turn the situation around. Better leave it to 'the higher authorities' to resolve.

Many people are hoping that FRELIMO's 4th Party Congress, which will be held this year, will open up some new ways of dealing with Mozambique's problems. The party principles are being discussed throughout the country, in meetings of party members, representatives of mass organizations, and selected workers and peasants. Central Committee members are leading the study sessions in the provinces.

Noticias recently reported a discussion in Sofala Province where people raised the many problems that have plagued the communal villages. If these types of issues can be raised and dealt with openly, it should help greatly in resolving some of the problems that have dogged FRELIMO's plans

More *cooperantes* evacuated from the districts are arriving in Quelimane. Some will transfer to more peaceful areas. some will augment the workforce of this city. others chafe at feeling superfluous here and return quickly to the war zones. Our house has been busy these months with comings and goings; people waiting for transport in and out of the province, conferring with their ministries, organizations, and families about what to do. We acquired three nice roommates in the transfer process: an Australian doctor, a Dutch nutritionist and an 8 month-old baby.

Long talks with friends from the districts about how they could continue to work effectively once they are grounded in a town hospital, unable to travel to the small health posts that are the people's contact point with *Saude* [the Health Ministry]. People plan hide-outs in case of an attack: up the mountain, into the corn field, to a friend's house on the outside of town. Kidnappings of *cooperantes* are up this year. Obviously we are targets, to scare off technical aid.

Recently the minister of health met with our provincial health administrators here in Zambezia. His theme: how to develop our health services in light of the enemy activity. The visit came as a relief to many people; the first official recognition that something really is happening here. Now it becomes possible and necessary to begin to deal with it.

Saude is in a tough position. It's vital to keep health services running in troubled zones . . . abandoning an area demoralizes the people and is a costly admission of the enemy's power. But it's difficult to mobilize health workers, who are acutely aware when a midwife is kidnapped, a nurse is murdered, or a health post is attacked. So people resist their transfers passively and find a hundred reasons to remain in Quelimane.

We are feeling very ambivalent about returning home. If it were not for Jon's father being so ill, I think we would renew our contract. We have grown accustomed to a humane, unhurried way of life here. Despite the *inimigo* [enemy], I never felt so safe in New York or San Francisco. Joshie can roam the neighborhood with his friends, and we are confident that no harm will come to him. Life is hard, but people do everything possible to make it easier for us. We have learned that we can really make do with less and improvise more than we had imagined (granted that our 'less' is more than most people have).

It is nice to feel important because you are providing a service that people clearly want and need. Many people in town know us, and stop me on the street so they can carry Josina a ways.

We worry about finding work in the States, with all the news about high unemployment. Or about being bored in jobs that seem limited in comparison to the scope and responsibility we've grown used to here. The best part will be to be with friends and family again.

People are loosening up with us some. We have end-of-the-contract conversations in which friends and co-workers open up about their lives, marriages, work and the current situation in ways that surprise us greatly. Perhaps as we are leaving, we become a kind of safety-valve for frustrations and discontents that are hard to express.

Josina is a joy, fat and smiling, determined to sit and crawl, and she babbles away with fierce concentration. Josh is busy rehearsing the end-of-the-year school play. As far as I can tell, it's about a group of little soldiers, and it features the hit single: "Resolutely Aiding the Decisions of the 4th Party Congress"! Love from us all.

Article 4

AfriqueAsia, April 1984

The Father of Namibian Nationalism Stays Firm

Sixteen years of prison have failed to break the spirit of one of southern Africa's most outstanding nationalist figures. He emerged from prison on March 1 more committed than ever to the cause of his people's freedom.

By Colm Foy

On March 1st, one of SWAPO's greatest militants, Herman Toivo Ya Toivo—his name means "Hope and Hope"—was released after 16 years of a 20-year prison sentence imposed by the South African regime under its 1967 Terrorism Act.

At his trial in 1968, Toivo had told his South African judges : "We are Namibians and not South Africans. We do not recognize and will never recognize that you have the right to govern us . . ." It was a position he was to stick to throughout his years in prison, most of which he spent on Robben Island in the company of Nelson Mandela and Walter Sisulu, leaders of the South African freedom struggle.

Herman Toivo Ya Toivo (center) meeting with Patrick Lekhota (left) and Mohammed Valley of the United Democratic Front of South Africa at airport en route to Lusaka.

Agence France-Presse

Pretoria's Disappointment

No reasons were given by Pretoria for the release of a man so closely identified with the liberation struggle of Namibia, but they may have been thinking that sixteen years in one of their jails might have broken the spirit of this symbol of Namibian resistance. They may well have

thought that he might be used to force a split in SWAPO's ranks and force a divided liberation movement to come to the negotiating table. Perhaps they imagined that a softened Mr. Toivo might be encouraged to join forces with Andreas Shipanga, leader of the renegade "SWAPO-Democrats," against SWAPO itself, thus confusing the Namibian people and opening the way for South Africa to

install a regime more to its liking in a future independent Namibia.

If these were indeed the hopes of the leaders of South Africa, they will have been sorely disappointed by Toivo Ya Toivo's statements since his release.

Almost from the first moments of his freedom, the co-founder of SWAPO was reassuring Namibians and his own leadership that he supported SWAPO and its policies now as much as ever. Speaking to a welcoming crowd in the black township of Katatura, near the Namibian capital Windhoek, he said, "I went to prison for the freedon of my people, I went to prison for the freedom of my country—I will not be free until they are free." Later, in Lusaka, and in the company of SWAPO President Sam Nujoma, he repeated his opinion that his place was to accept "any capacity SWAPO gives me in the cause of Namibia's independence." On March 17 it was announced that he had been appointed to his movement's politburo.

Rather than diminish the veteran fighter's resolve to continue the fight for Namibia, his 16 years in South African jails seem to have strengthened it and made him pessimistic about the possibilities for an early settlement with Pretoria. Toivo told journalists in Lusaka that statehood for his country had been nearer in 1978 than it was now and that he felt

South Africa would delay independence until it could guarantee a pliable regime in Windhoek. Since everyone knew that SWAPO would win any free elections held in the territory, South Africa was therefore not interested in holding any.

The sixty-year-old freedom fighter went on to say that, for the same reasons, he did not feel the South African ceasefire agreement with Angola represented an advance for SWAPO and Namibia.

Thus, Herman Toivo Ya Toivo, known to his people as "the father of Namibian nationalism," has identified himself firmly with the current SWAPO leadership and its policy.

He sees the freedom struggle of the Namibian people as being linked to that of the South African people. He told the Windhoek Observer : "As far as I am concerned, my mission is to liberate Namibia but . . . we will not be free as long as our brothers and sisters are living in oppression in South Africa."

Futile Negotiations

Similarly, he is not prepared to collaborate with those he identifies as traitors to his cause. Toivo told the same newspaper that Andreas Shipanga had been to see him in prison but "as soon as I saw who it was I turned my back. If he is an enemy of SWAPO, then he is no friend of mine," he said.

On March 12, SWAPO said: "The answer to the independence and freedom of our country does not lie in time-wasting negotiations, but through the barrel of a gun . . . the struggle waged by the oppressed people of Namibia against the ruthless racist regime of Pretoria must be carried on until our country is totally liberated once and for all." It is a statement Herman Toivo Ya Toivo might quite happily have written himself.

Article 5

AFRICA REPORT • May–June 1984

The Nkomati Accords

BY JOSÉ LUIS CABAÇO

José Luis Cabaço is the Mozambican minister of information. The Nkomati Accord, an agreement on nonaggression and good neighborliness, was signed by the governments of Mozambique and South Africa on March 16, 1984.

The Nkomati Accord is a result of Mozambican policies whose origins can be traced back to the founding of the national liberation movement, Frelimo, 22 years ago. These policies, the pursuit of peace and national sovereignty, were adhered to by Frelimo's first president, the late Dr. Eduardo Mondlane, and have remained constant features of Mozambique's political position ever since.

Under Mondlane's leadership, Frelimo explored every avenue for a peaceful solution to the problem of Portuguese colonialism before embarking on an arduous armed struggle that cost the lives of thousands of Mozambicans. And in 10 years of anticolonial war, Frelimo tenaciously defended the principle of national sovereignty, never bowing to the wishes of foreign powers, even friendly powers.

Mondlane's belief in peace and national sovereignty has been consolidated by President Samora Machel, and these principles are enshrined in the constitution that was adopted when independence was finally won in 1975. But it has to be admitted that Mozambique's lead-

ers have not been able to convince all of the world all of the time that we are serious about these matters.

Both before and after independence, we have been depicted in some countries as (1) warlike and (2) elements in the East-West conflict. We are neither. Mozambique's position in the struggle for Zimbabwean independence proves this. Shortly after our own independence, we were active in promoting the Victoria Falls talks between the Zimbabwean nationalists, the Rhodesians, and the South Africans, which were aimed at finding a peaceful solution to the Rhodesian problem. Mozambique's representative was Oscar Monteiro, who is now justice minister, and who has played a prominent part in the recent security negotiations with South Africa.

When all attempts to solve the Zimbabwe problem by peaceful means failed, Mozambique gave its full support to the Zimbabwean liberation movement, composed in 1976 of guerrillas from both ZAPU and ZANU. And it is worth recalling that from the time ZAPU left the alliance later that year, only two countries in the world gave total, unconditional support to ZANU until the end—Mozambique and Tanzania. This was our government's sovereign decision, influenced by no one, and we are proud of it.

Mozambique supported all Zimbabwe peace initiatives, including the Geneva conference at the end of 1976. And when Britain launched its initiative for a settlement in 1979, Mozambique was among the first to see the opportunity for peace and played an active and constructive part at the Lancaster House conference.

The talks Mozambique has held with South Africa are equally a part of this policy of peace and sovereign independence. Mozambique has had contacts with South Africa, aimed at establishing peaceful coexistence, since 1975.

From the time of the first ministerial-level contacts in 1982, Mozambique has proposed the principle of a non-aggression and good-neighborliness pact. Efforts to reach a security agreement with South Africa were not helped by the initial attitude of the Reagan administration, which we felt was one-sided and based on the old idea that Mozambique was a pawn in the East-West cold war.

Perhaps encouraged by Washington's attitude, South Africa became increasingly belligerent towards Mozambique, launching army and air force attacks and recruiting Mozambican malcontents to wage a terror and sabotage campaign against my country.

Over the last few years, however, and after many diplomatic contacts, it appears that the U.S. administration has had the ability to understand the true essence of the conflict in southern Africa and to understand the sovereign nature of the Mozambican state. This has led to agreement on points of view on how to solve the problem of destabilization in southern Africa. Modifications in the U.S. position have been a positive element in the search for peace in the region.

Mozambique will continue to pursue the objectives of defending its national sovereignty and independence, and promoting peace and development. The Nkomati Accord is a part of this policy.

Article 6   The Weekly Review, December 9, 1983

Milingo Defends His Healing Mission

HIS fellow African bishops accused him of witchcraft; Rome detained him at the Vatican for a year, half of it incommunicado, while doctors tested him for insanity and other diseases and the church hierarchy investigated a possible breach of the canons of the Roman Catholic faith. His supposed crime: healing the sick and exorcising evil spirits by the power of prayer. Finally released from his confinement at the Vatican, Archbishop Emmanuel Milingo of Zambia last week ended an eight-day visit to Kenya during which he continued with his faith healing mission - the first on the African continent since he was summoned to Rome in April last year. Although no longer the primate of the archdiocese of Lusaka, it was an emotional moment for Milingo to be back among his own African people for the first time in one and a half years. For his supporters in Kenya, it was a moment of sweet victory. For the archbishop's critics and other detractors, their opposition to his healing mission remained as strong as it was before Milingo left for the Vatican.

It all began on April 13, 1973, when Milingo, then the primate of Lusaka, was confronted by a woman who said she was hearing strange voices that disturbed her. The woman said the voices seemed to come from her young child who she had become convinced was a little beast. During the bouts of hallucination when she imagined she was hearing the voices, the mother was inclined to kill the child. Milingo's only way of solving the problem was through "traditional" Catholic prayer. He took the woman to the chapel and offered mass. There was no improvement. Confession and more traditional prayers were offered; mass was celebrated several times, but nothing happened. The archbishop was helpless and told the woman so; but she would not leave him, as if she had some strange insight that he had the power to help.

One day the woman came to see Milingo in his office. She had nearly killed her baby the night before and was still hysterical with shock. This time, the archbishop decided not to offer traditional prayers but to pray for her right there in the office. He lay his hands on her and made the sign of the cross. Says the archbishop, "Immediately, there came a strange power that controlled her that I could communicate with her soul by a mere blessing". Milingo said, "I could suddenly feel her problem as if it was a tangible thing. She was possessed by an evil power which was causing the hallucinations, producing voices and changing her baby into a little animal that she was inclined to destroy". The archbishop felt an overpowering urge to command the evil power to let go of the woman in the name of Jesus. He did so, and the woman was cured. Afterwards, the archbishop tried to go back to his typing in the office, but the strange power that had gripped him was still in him. He paced up and down as he tried to understand what had happened.

About a week later, another mother brought to him a child who had swellings in the legs caused by blockages in the blood flow. Without hesitation, the archbishop had the courage to say he could deal with the problem. He prayed for the child and normal blood flow was restored. Over the next six months, Milingo had numerous experiences with healing the sick of all kinds of illnesses - weak limbs, chest and stomach problems, skin diseases, tumours, infertility, disorders of the central nervous system and the spinal cord and many others. People travelled from all over Zambia and beyond for his healing.

After his first experience, however, Milingo found himself drawn towards working against evil spirits and he continued to intensify his exorcism, falling afoul of the orthodox clergy and the white missionaries in Zambia. They wrote to Rome protesting against Milingo's practice, accusing him of using "herbs and roots" in his healing sessions. Rome responded promptly in February, 1974, ordering Milingo in writing to stop his healing ministry.

Milingo says the traditional church leaders and the white missionaries were prejudiced against him right from the beginning. The reference to herbs and roots, which he calls "an obvious lie", to him indicated that his critics just could not believe that God could work miracles through an African. He himself did not understand what was happening, but he says he would have been unfair to himself and his faith if he were to pretend he had not experienced healing; he tried to comply with the order from the Vatican, however, by avoiding the sick people who followed him everywhere he went. After months of living like a fugitive in his efforts to avoid the sick, Milingo finally could not control the power in him, Rome or no Rome. He says he had received the gift from God without asking for it and it was not for him to limit its application.

One day when he was about to go into a meeting with priests, a possessed woman was brought to him. She had been sent away by three husbands because of the evil spirits in her and desperately needed help. Even with the ban from Rome still in force, the woman refused to leave him. Milingo decided to pray for her and exorcise the evil spirit right there in the presence of the priests. This was to become one of Milingo's most depressing experiences. After the evil spirit was cast out, the priests fell over with laughter. One of them, an African, said the "illness" was just one of those "hysterical moods of women", of which he had seen many, and an aspirin would have done the trick. "I felt so alone and rejected," says Milingo. For the months afterwards, Milingo was completely isolated. No one in Zambia could help him understand what was happening. In 1976, he travelled to the United States where the charismatic renewal movement was spreading fast within the Roman Catholic Church, with measured acceptance by the Vatican. The movement began in the US in 1967

Milingo: first visit to Africa since his release from the Vatican

when a group of students studying the Acts of Apostles started to question the discrepancies between their modern faith and that of the early Christian communities. They prayed for the "release of the spirit" in their lives, and subsequently began speaking in tongues, uttering prophecies and faithhealing, among other things. While in the US, Milingo took part in the first international leadership course in charismatic renewal. At the end of the course, he was told he had the gift of healing the sick but, as he was an archbishop, the leaders of the movement were reluctant to lay their hands on him so that he could receive the gift of speaking in tongues as this was contrary to church protocol. In response, Milingo argued that even John baptised Christ; in the end, they prayed for him and blessed him and he received the gift of tongues.

The following year, Milingo was in Rome taking studies in the Roman Catholic Christian renewal in an effort to understand better the gift given him by God, when, one night while in bed, he went into a kind of trance during which he heard a voice telling him to "go and preach the gospel". Says the archbishop, "The words were so strong, so living, I knew it was a message from God". He went back to Zambia more confident of himself and continued with his healing ministry, this time totally ignoring his detractors and the ban by the Vatican. He spread his healing missions outside his native country, travelling to other African countries to minister to the sick and to cast out devils. But, in 1978, the African bishops got together at the Episcopal Conference, where a fresh order was issued to stop Milingo from faith healing. Again, Milingo ignored the order. By 1980, his speaking in tongues while praying for the sick was labelled "mere tribal incantations", and two years later the papal pro nuncio in Lusaka, Archbishop George Zar, at the instigation of some of the African bishops, publicly accused Milingo of witchcraft. The Vatican immediately removed the authority of the archdiocese of Lusaka from Milingo and appointed Kenya's Maurice Cardinal Otunga temporary apostolic administrator. A papal commission, made up of Otunga and Bishop Kirima of Mombasa, was also set up to investigate the allegations against Milingo and report to the Vatican.

The accusation of witchcraft was said to arise out of reports that when he prayed for the sick Milingo underwent a transformation into something other than a Roman Catholic bishop, mumbling unintelligible chants (speaking in tongues), making him, at best, an African medium or, at worst, a witchdoctor. There were also accusations that the archbishop was trying to form his own sect of an African Roman Catholic church.

One of Milingo's most fervent goals is to inject more African values into the practice of the Roman Catholic faith on the continent. This objective is based on his strong belief that religion is only meaningful when practiced within the social and cultural realities of the community of the practitioners. He says it took him the usual 16 years ofter entering the seminary, to become a priest - a period he calls a "process of brainwashing and indocrination" with foreign values. The archbishop told *The Weekly Review* that by the time one came out at the other end of the line, African values had almost become equated with sin and things that are evil. "After a lifetime of working and thinking in Latin, the process of rediscovery of self is a difficult one and takes great moral courage," he said. Archbishop Milingo feels it is this lifetime of indocrination in foreign values that has blinded his detractors to the truth. They find it difficult to accept and believe that Africans can heal the sick and cast out demons. Yet he believes there are many more African clergy and laymen who have the gift of faith-healing, but they lack the courage to face up to the challenge posed by the opposition of the orthodox and the traditionalists. "God cannot be so poor that he could only afford to give the gift to Milingo," he says.

Milingo also questions some of the traditional Roman Catholic practices, such as praying through hosts of saints and the Virgin Mary, rather than through Jesus Christ. "All things that came to be were through him (Jesus), and only he can intercede with God the Father on our behalf. Not St. Patrick, nor Peter, nor Paul. Not even the Virgin Mary. That is what the scriptures say." During most of his sermons, Milingo castigates Roman Catholics for having lost track of who was the founder of their religion. Talking about this to *The Weekly Review*, the archbishop said, "The gospel is not just words for putting into the library. It must be alive. Roman Catholics need to be taught to sing Jesus". Concerning the Virgin Mary, the bishop said, "She shares that responsibility of being the mother of Christ, but she is not to be worshipped" "I must, however, add that Mary to me is a mother, the mother of the human race. Her greatness cannot be challenged."

These radical views, his standing up against Rome on the question of faith healing, and the large numbers of supporters he had among the faithful in Africa and as far afield as Europe and the United States, formed part of the basis for the accusation that Milingo was seeking to form his own church. Milingo denies the charge that he wanted to start his own church just as strongly as he refutes the charges of witchcraft. "I am a subject of the Roman Catholic Church and a follower of Jesus Christ. I have never had or intended to have followers, and there are no people who feel that they are Milingo's followers. No one has ever cosidered me a leader"

The investigation team appointed by the pope and headed by Otunga supported the allegations against Milingo and on the basis of their report it was recommended that Milingo be summoned to Rome for a year of "theological studies and quiet reflection" and to "seek medical advice from the doctors". Milingo would not personally discuss what actually happened in Rome. Church sources close to him, however, say he was subjected to exhaustive psychiatric tests. A complete psychological profile was drawn up as Vatican experts investigated his background for any history of insanity or other psychological disorders in the archbishop's lineage, any practitioners of witchcraft among his ancestors, whether or not Milingo in his early years had any inclination towards such things or was ever exposed to their practice in his childhood. A similarly exhaustive medical examination was carried out - blood and urine tests, Xrays, bone scans, and examination of other body organs and fluids - to see if he suffered from any diseases that could lead to occasional emotional or psychological disturbances. All results were negative. During the same period, Milingo was kept busy with numerous theological papers and other works on the philosophy of the Roman Catholic faith as part of his re-indoctrination, while Vatican theologians and other experts reviewed and studied the archbishop's books and published papers for possible breaches of the faith and oaths of office. (Milingo has written four books, among other published works, *Demarcations, My God Is A*

Milingo and assistants pray over sick person in a car

Living God, The Healing Ministry and *If I Tell You, You Will Not Believe Me*).

Finally, the authorities at the Vatican handed over their report, together with the Otunga report, to Pope John Paul II in June this year and, on July 5, the pope finally granted Milingo an audience - one year and two months after the archbishop had arrived at the Vatican. Milingo says the pope neither condemned him, nor tried to correct him. "You have brought the gift of healing to the Vatican," the pope is reported to have said. He is also reported to have consoled Milingo by equating the examinations the bishop had undergone with the humiliation of Padre Pio, the Francescan friar who had stigmata in his hands and was shunned by the church for healing the sick and exorcising demons. But while the pope assured Milingo that the Holy See would safeguard the archbishop's healing ministry, there was a problem concerning Milingo's return to Lusaka. Milingo simply puts it that the Vatican wanted him to concentrate on faith healing without the extra responsibilities of running a diocese, and therefore prevailed on him to resign as primate of Lusaka and offered him a number of options, of which the pope accepted the archbishop's appointment as a special delegate to the Pontifical Commission on Immigration and Tourism, which deals with the spiritual welfare of refugees and migrants the world over.

Other sources, however, say, the Vatican saw Milingo's return to Zambia as source of great embarrassment, and therefore undesirable. Had he gone back as primate of Lusaka, it would have been to a hero's welcome among the faithful. With most of the Zambian and other African bishops still opposed to his faith-healing practice, this would have led to a possible split in the Roman Catholic Church, a development the Vatican was anxious to avert. And at 53, Milingo is far from the retiring age of 75, unless it was to be on health grounds which the doctors had already ruled out in their earlier examinations which proved the archbishop fit and sound. Milingo's closest friends still believe the Vatican will not allow the archbishop even to travel to Lusaka under his new assignment until a new primate has been appointed there. Since his "release" from the Vatican in July, Milingo has travelled widely on faithhealing missions in Europe, Australia, Canada, the United States, and the Caribbean.

The extent of Milingo's isolation among the clergy in Africa was well demonstrated by the coordination of his visit to Kenya from Novemberr 26 to December 4. Although the archbishop was accomodated at the premises of the Association of the Episcopal Conference of Eastern Africa (Amecea) on Gitanga Road, no senior officials of the Roman Catholic Church in Kenya were involved in his visit - except the secretary general of the Kenya Catholic Secretariat, Father Morris Luanga, who did his best to see the archbishop was as comfortable as possible in between his various functions. The archbishop was a guest of the Guadalope Parish Church at Woodley and all the arrangements for his healing sessions (conducted at Joseph Kang'ethe Social Hall near the church) were made by the laity of Guadalope Parish. He had no official church transport and was driven from place to place in private cars of a group of parishioners who accompanied him everywhere, together with a group of nuns from the Assumption Sisters Convent on Riverside Drive.

Messages were passed by word of mouth as to where the sick should come for healing; the organisers shunned the press for fear of being identified in the subsequent publicity, with some claiming they would be excommunicated if discovered. Others feared that the publicity might open a new controversy, resulting in Milingo's being detained again by the Vatican, or his visit being cut short by church officials in Nairobi. It was not until he had been in Nairobi for three days that the press got wind of his presence. On one occasion, newsmen had to shadow a car carrying a group of unsuspecting nuns to get to where the archbishop was.

Contrary to what most people would expect, there is nothing dramatic at Milingo's faith-healing sessions. Long prayers are offered by the archbishop assisted by three aides - a Milan businessman, a nun and a Kenyan medical student who is also studying faith and psychic healing. First the prayers are offered for inner healing of the soul, then the physical healing of all kinds of diseases. Milingo reels off the various diseases like a medical encyclopaedia. During the prayers, Milingo goes into a mild trance and begins speaking in tongues. At the conclusion of the prayers, the congregation bursts into song as the sick line up and walk forward to be anointed with oil and individually prayed for by the archbishop who is still speaking in tongues. Those who are not sick but want to be blessed are also welcome to be anointed and prayed for.

There are no cripples throwing away their crutches and walking on the spot. The healing is gradual. People who had been crippled for years, however, have been known to be walking within a matter of weeks of being blessed and prayed for by Milingo. Evil spirits, however, are another matter, as they have to be exorcised on the spot. As the archbishop touches the forehead of most possessed people, the victims seem to go into some kind of sleep or coma. When they wake up minutes later, they are practically cured. There are, however, some cases when the demons resist and Milingo has explicitly to command them as his aides hold the struggling victim. "In the name of Jesus we send you away. In the name of Jesus we command you not to touch anyone else. The power of Jesus sends you to hell where you belong." Says Milingo, "We have not yet come across a really difficult case." In between the healing sessions at the social hall and the mass that he celebrated daily at the Guadalope Church, Milingo found time to visit in their homes people who were too sick to come to the hall.

Milingo says he chose Kenya for his first African visit since his release because Kenyans have a special place in his heart - a strong contrast, given the fact that it was Kenyan church officials who drew up the report that formed the basis of his detention in Rome. He says Kenyans were among those who kept trust in him when he was in confinement and never lost touch, many of them telephoning him whenever the opportunity arose. He was also grateful for the way the Kenya press "systematically and not emotionally" defended him throughout his trials and consistently corrected the "misconceptions perpetuated by the western press" about his healing practice. Coming to Kenya was also another opportunity for the archbishop to be reminded of his continuing isolation in his pioneering calling among the hierarchy of the church on the continent. It is understood that when Otunga gave the archbishop an audience last Friday, two days before the archbishop left Nairobi for the Vatican, he (Otunga) would only meet Milingo in Milingo's capacity as a bishop, not as a faith-healer. It is understood the subject of healing was not even broached during the short audience. Asked for his reaction to this continuing isolation and apparent rejection, Milingo said, "It is not charity to discuss the negative. I have the freedom to go and heal anywhere. That is worth the suffering I have been through,"

Article 7   THE NEW REPUBLIC   APRIL 2, 1984

Stability in southern Africa?

PAX PRETORIANA

BY JOHN DE ST. JORRE

John de St. Jorre, author of *A House Divided: South Africa's Uncertain Future*, is a senior associate at the Carnegie Endowment for International Peace in Washington. He has just returned from a five-week trip to southern Africa.

Cape Town

SOMETHING CURIOUS is going on in southern Africa. Black Marxists are drinking cocktails with Afrikaner officials. United States diplomats are basking in praise on both sides of the color divide. Peace rather than brimstone is in the antipodean summer air. For the last month or so, American diplomacy has been engaged in a high-wire act aimed at simultaneously easing the Cubans out of Angola and the South Africans out of Namibia, improving U.S. ties with Marxist Mozambique and Angola, and whittling down Soviet influence in the region. Africa, traditionally the poor relation of U.S. diplomacy, now ironically offers the Reagan Administration its one realistic chance of a foreign policy success before the election.

It is an enormously ambitious enterprise. If it succeeds, it will give the Administration a significant diplomatic victory and will be a personal triumph for its architect, Chester Crocker, the Assistant Secretary of State for African Affairs. If it fails, the fragile peace that has settled on the region will be shattered, Soviet and Cuban influence will wax instead of wane, the United States—always on the margin—will become virtually irrelevant, and President Reagan's scoreboard of foreign successes will continue to register a resounding zero.

The fragility of the diplomacy is underscored by the United States' lack of real power in the process. Apart from the offer of closer diplomatic ties and economic aid, U.S. leverage is limited. Its role is that of broker rather than mover-and-shaker. That title sits firmly on the shoulders of South Africa, whose ruthless military, political, and economic pressures on its black neighbors brought them first to their knees and then to the negotiating table. If peace descends on the region it will not be an American peace, it will be a Pax Pretoriana.

There are three acts in the drama, and the curtain has just risen on the first. Act One envisages a successful military disengagement in southern Angola in which South African forces will withdraw to the Namibian side of the border. Angola will ensure that the vacuum is not filled either by its Cuban allies or by SWAPO guerrillas who have been fighting for Namibia's independence for almost two decades. A joint monitoring commission of Angolan and South African officials has been created to observe the pact, and a small delegation of U.S. diplomats has set up shop in Windhoek, the Namibian capital, to provide backup support if needed.

SWAPO's president, Sam Nujoma, has promised to respect the pact. The other major actor, Jonas Savimbi, leader of UNITA, the dissident Angolan group that has been locked in a struggle with the Angolan government since the country's independence from Portugal in 1975, has also agreed not to move into the cease-fire zone.

Act Two, assuming that all goes according to plan, has a more complex story line. The Reagan Administration has linked the decolonization of Namibia by South Africa with the removal of the twenty-five thousand Cuban troops from Angola. Act Two will be the time for some hard decision making by President José dos Santos's M.P.L.A. government in Luanda and Prime Minister P. W. Botha's government in Pretoria. The Angolans will have to commit themselves to saying goodbye to the Cuban combat forces, which have helped them to maintain power for the last nine years; and South Africa will have to decide whether or not to hand over the huge but sparsely populated buffer state which it seized from the Germans in the First World War and has held ever since.

If both sides take the plunge, the Angolan government will face the formidable Savimbi alone, and the South Africans will have to accept United Nations-supervised elections in Namibia, which will almost certainly lead to a SWAPO victory in Windhoek and another black radical state on their borders.

Act Three will inevitably be something of an anticlimax, assuming the players do not walk off the stage in Act Two. It will see an end to the hostilities within Namibia, the arrival of a multinational U.N. military group, a gradual pullback of South African forces, and, after seven months of open politicking, the holding of elections for a constituent assembly, the writing of a constitution, and the hoisting of a new flag over Windhoek. At the same time most, if not all, the Cuban troops in Angola will sail off into the sunset, and the United States will ring down the curtain by recognizing the Angolan government, thus opening the door to U.S. economic aid to help rebuild Angola's shattered economy.

The breathing of new life into this scenario has caught many people by surprise, not least the conservative and liberal opponents of Crocker's strategy of "constructive engagement." Senator Jesse Helms, the Heritage Foundation, and others on the right see a sellout of Savimbi's UNITA and Holden Roberto's F.N.L.A., the other, much smaller pro-Western Angolan dissident movement; and they bitterly oppose the prospect of U.S. diplomatic recognition of the Marxist M.P.L.A. government in Luanda.

Liberals are more confused than angry. They have roundly condemned Crocker's policy as morally wrong for having produced a "tilt" toward Pretoria. Yet Namibia's independence has always been high on their agenda, so they are a little shaken to see Crocker's strategy of cozying up to the South African government beginning to produce diplomatic results. Their genuine desire for Namibia's independence now sits uncomfortably with the possibility that it could be brought about by their Republican opponents using a strategy they have universally condemned as immoral and unworkable. Left-wing criticism has also been muted by the vision of southern Africa's black Marxist leaders striking deals with the detested apartheid regime in Pretoria. The old racial and ideological lines, so clear in the past, have suddenly started to wobble. It is all very puzzling.

There is an important prologue to the events now taking shape. For the last three years South Africa has been exerting pressure on its black neighbors in a systematic and relentless process of destabilization. The fact that Pretoria went about this self-appointed task without any serious impediment from the United States, if without any encouragement either, suggests that Crocker's policy might

have been engaged but was not very constructive during that period. On the other hand, there is no way of knowing if the South Africans would have curbed their aggressive tendencies had there been a sterner and more hostile government in Washington. They might have gone ahead anyway.

The aim of South Africa's strategy was to destroy the capability of its black revolutionary opponents, SWAPO in Namibia and Angola, and the African National Congress (A.N.C.) elsewhere in the region. Cross-border raids, military support for dissident movements, dirty tricks (such as letter bombs and assassinations), and throttling its neighbors' vital economic lifelines had, in sum, a devastating effect. One by one, Lesotho, Zimbabwe, Mozambique, and finally Angola, have swallowed their pride if not their principles and genuflected before the regional superpower.

Some of the deals now being struck are similar to previous, more tacit arrangements. Zimbabwe, for instance, has closer economic ties and security connections with South Africa than ever, although the political gap appears unbridgeable. Business with the South

MAP OF SOUTHERN AFRICA BY KENNY GRADY

Africans is always handled by civil servants. Prime Minister Robert Mugabe refuses to allow government ministers to take part despite constant South African invitations and blandishments.

Mugabe also maintains a high level of anti-South African rhetoric in his speeches and in the state-run media. The smaller states—Lesotho, Swaziland, and Botswana—all have official links with South Africa, but sustain a public anti-apartheid stance and have withheld diplomatic recognition of the white-ruled Republic.

But there has been a major change in Mozambique,

formerly South Africa's most radical and implacable neighbor. President Samora Machel's FRELIMO government is not only talking to the South Africans at the highest level but is also mapping out a long-term relationship with an eagerness verging on enthusiasm.

The key element in the package currently is security. In return for South Africa cutting off aid to the dissident Mozambique National Resistance movement (M.N.R.), which has been ravaging large areas of the country, the Mozambique government has contracted to curb the activities of the A.N.C. inside Mozambique. Other issues include South African technical and economic assistance, the expanded use of hydroelectric power from Mozambique's Cabora Bassa dam, and the revival, improbable though it may seem, of South African tourism in Mozambique. Diplomatic relations appear unlikely, but Mozambique is ready to sign some form of nonaggression pact with South Africa. It is not exactly a southern African "Camp David," but it is still a remarkable turn of events.

WHAT HAPPENED? The short answer is that Machel had no alternative. Virtually every known natural and man-made disaster has struck Mozambique: droughts, cyclones, floods; botched social and economic policies; a chronic shortage of skilled manpower (ever since the Portuguese left en masse at independence); a drop in world prices for the country's agricultural exports; and the cancerous armed rebellion, backed by South Africa, that threatened the survival of the government. Machel first tried to get help from everyone but the South Africans. He went to Moscow to solicit his Soviet friends. They replied that they could afford no more than they were already giving him (arms, heavy machinery, food, and fuel). A tour of Western Europe produced little of substance. Portugal, the former colonial power, was ready to provide technical assistance, but had no cash to spare. The Cubans were a possibility—both as soldiers and as technicians—but South Africa made it very clear it would not permit a Cuban presence on terrain so close to its own.

That left the Americans. Relations had risen from rock bottom early in the Reagan period, when four members of the U.S. Embassy in Maputo were thrown out as alleged spies, and the Mozambicans credit Frank Wisner, Crocker's deputy and point man with the Africans, with much of the improvement. But the United States had a price: Mozambique would have to mend its fences with South Africa first and then American aid could follow. (There is speculation that a $200 million aid package, plus food aid, over a four-year period was dangled in front of the Mozambican government.) Machel's revolutionary party, FRELIMO, debated and agonized over its limited choices. Finally Machel agreed to do what the Americans and the South Africans asked of him.

If the Mozambican-South African relationship can now be characterized as friendly, the feeling in Maputo toward the United States has the overtones of a love affair. Two senior officials there told me recently they were praying for a Reagan victory in the U.S. election in November. One wonders what the two Jesses—Helms and Jackson—will make of that.

THERE IS a psychological, though not a physical, connection between the Mozambican-South African détente on the eastern flank of the region with the infinitely more complicated negotiations going on in the west. The genesis is identical. First, the South African hammer (the most recent punitive incursion into Angola only ended in January); then the American sweet talk behind the scenes; and, finally, face-to-face talks between the main parties, hosted by President Kaunda of Zambia in Lusaka.

But in Angola the mutual mistrust is palpable and the whole exercise immensely fragile. There seems little doubt, however, that both Angola and South Africa are ready for a military disengagement in the south of the country, Act One of Crocker's script. In Angola the growing power of Savimbi's UNITA movement, which is striking boldly beyond its traditional home base in the southeast, and the country's parlous economic condition have convinced the government it is time to talk.

On the South African side, P. W. Botha, in a key speech to parliament on January 31, made it clear that if there were a choice between the interests of South Africa and those of Namibia, he would put South Africa first. He also stressed that there was no long-term military solution to the problem, that Namibia imposed a heavy financial burden on the Republic, which is passing through its worst economic crisis since the 1930s depression, and that it was time the internal parties in Namibia got their act together. Although there is nothing intrinsically new in all this, the tone and urgency of the prime minister's remarks have impressed observers in South Africa that the government is gearing itself, as well as educating the public, for an eventual Namibian withdrawal.

There are some other straws in the wind indicating a shift of attitude. Botha's own political fortunes, after his impressive victory in the constitutional referendum last November, have brightened while the threat from the right wing of Afrikanerdom has correspondingly diminished. The number of Afrikaners in Namibia, a potentially dangerous right-wing fifth column, has declined considerably in recent years. Moreover, Botha himself appears to have lost patience with the place; and he is obsessed, according to some of his close advisers, with his new constitution, which will extend some limited political power to the Coloured and Indian communities and will be inaugurated later this year.

Another development has been the realization that the South African Army, for all its bravado and upbeat campaign assessments, cannot eradicate SWAPO. The last incursion into Angola, Operation Askari, was less than a total success. SWAPO's rainy season offensive was certainly blunted and many of the guerrillas driven farther north, but most lived to fight another day. Meanwhile, the South

Africans suffered their highest casualties ever (over 10 percent of their force, if the conventional military tally for ten injured for every person killed is used) in unprecedented clashes with the Angolan Army and Cuban forces. There was also a questioning of the war in the Afrikaans press, especially by mothers asking why their sons were fighting and dying so far away from home.

That is not to say the government had made a final decision. The army appears unhappy at the idea of giving up so much military real estate where it has built up an elaborate infrastructure and whence it can launch attacks against its enemies at a safe distance from South Africa's own borders. General Magnus Malan, the minister of defense, accompanied by five generals, had to visit troops in the border areas to explain the political directives of the government and ensure that they were obeyed.

Of course, Pretoria does not have to make an irreversible decision until Act Two is reached, and the Angolans have produced their calendar for the Cuban withdrawal. Both Washington and Pretoria have reiterated many times that South Africa cannot be expected to hand over Namibia to U.N.-supervised elections until the Angolans have agreed to dispense with the Cubans.

What are the chances of the curtain ringing down on Act One and rising again on Act Two? The good news is that the South Africans and Angolans are now on the ground in southern Angola monitoring the South African withdrawal. Reports of SWAPO guerrillas moving south through the area are being investigated. The small U.S. team of mediators is established in Windhoek. South Africa has also recently released a longtime Namibian nationalist leader, Herman Toivo ja Toivo, one of the founders of SWAPO, after sixteen years in jail.

BUT THERE is a long way to go. There are other parties, the most important and potentially disruptive being Savimbi's UNITA movement, which has not yet been offered anything. Though Savimbi has promised not to move into the area vacated by South African troops in southern Angola, he has continued his operations elsewhere. And, as if to underline Savimbi's pivotal position, UNITA kidnapped seventy-seven foreigners in a diamond mining town in the northeast shortly after the Angolans and South Africans met in Lusaka.

UNITA is a much more formidable outfit than the dissident M.N.R. group in Mozambique. Even if the South Africans cut off all support, Savimbi, who has spent almost two decades in the bush fighting first the Portuguese and later the M.P.L.A. government, could survive. With strong Ovimbundu support (about 40 percent of the country's population), some help from other foreign friends (Morocco and Zaire, for example), and an effective and loyal movement behind him, he could continue to pose a serious threat to the Angolan government. Further, the disadvantage of losing South African support would be more than offset, assuming Act Two has run its course, by the Angolan government's loss of its Cuban allies.

The obvious solution would be for a rapprochement between the M.P.L.A. and UNITA, resulting in some form of coalition government in Luanda. This is clearly what the South Africans would like. Their man in Luanda would be the best insurance that the Cubans would not be invited back. The Americans would also welcome a coalition. It would blunt the attack of their right-wing domestic critics because the Angolan government would no longer be wholly Marxist. But the animosity toward Savimbi runs deep in Luanda, and the M.P.L.A. government has neither the strong leadership nor the same unity that is found on the other side of the continent in Maputo. A coalition therefore seems unlikely, and that means UNITA remains a loose gun on the stage.

THERE ARE others who are not happy about what is going on, notably the Soviets and the Cubans, neither of whom wants to hand the United States a diplomatic victory or lose influence with long-established African friends. However, they cannot compete with American offers of aid (a package is almost certainly in the pipeline for Angola, as well as Mozambique, if all goes well), and they are aware that their influence is limited by African sensitivities about their sovereignty. The Soviet relationship with Mozambique seems more balanced than with Angola where, after boosting the government's feeble military capability last fall, and bluntly warning the South Africans to curb their military activities, Moscow now appears upset at not being properly briefed on Angola's role in the sudden burst of diplomacy.

Unlike its displays of unwarranted optimism for a Namibian settlement in the past, the Administration is stressing the delicacy of the negotiations and the many obstacles yet to be overcome. The whole thing could unravel at any moment, threatening the Mozambican-South African dialogue as well.

Three developments are already causing concern. First, South Africa's withdrawal from southern Angola is behind schedule and is proceeding at a snail's pace. Second, SWAPO insurgent activity inside Namibia has markedly increased. Finally, Pretoria has recently proposed a roundtable conference of *all* the parties in Namibia and Angola, a move that took the United States by surprise, and appears to be aimed at eliminating the U.N.'s role, which would drastically alter Acts Two and Three. Crocker, it seems, is not the only scriptwriter in town.

And even if Crocker pulls it off, there is the question of longer-term stability in southern Africa. An independent Namibia will end SWAPO's long struggle, but the A.N.C. of South Africa is not going to give up simply because it has been deprived of some of its forward support. There is also another danger. People who are forced to go down on their knees to sue for peace tend neither to forget nor to forgive the humiliation. Morover, apartheid within South Africa is still alive and well despite some reformist modifications. Pax Pretoriana may look logical on the surface, but it is riddled with internal contradictions. Although it may produce a temporary rapprochement in the region, it is unlikely to usher in an era of permanent peace.

Article 8   **WEST AFRICA**   21 May 1984

Christians and Socialists

By Mark Doyle

ANYONE who has read *Das Kapital* will recall the enthusiasm, the relish even, with which Karl Marx attacks establishment Christianity. The MPLA government in Angola, although Marxist-Leninist, takes a softer line. In its constitution (Article 25), the MPLA "recognises the equality and guarantees the practice of all forms of worship compatible with public order and the national interest".

However, there is still tension between churches and the state. "Quite clearly," a source close to the government said, "a practising Christian cannot also be a member of the Party."

Since, under a democratic centralist system, being a member of the Party is the principal route to influence, the Christian dilemma is real. The fact that most of Angola's present-day leaders were educated at mission schools — Catholic, Baptist or Congregational — complicates matters considerably, "and some of them may pray in private", an Angolan Christian said.

Delegation

The position of Christians in Angola was aired recently when a delegation from the Angolan Council of Evangelical Churches (CAIE) went on a tour of West Germany, Britain, Canada and the US. Led by the Reverend Daniel Ntoni Nzinga, the Baptist Secretary-General of the CAIE, the delegation also comprised the Reverend Julio Francisco, Mrs. Eva Chipenda and Nsona Velado Nascimento.

Evangelical churches in Angola are estimated to represent a third of all professed Christians, who may themselves only total a third of the population. The Catholic church — which under the Portuguese was effectively an arm of the state — claims most of the converts in the country, and

the majority of towns still have a functioning Catholic church, mission or school.

But if the Protestant churches can distance themselves from the Portuguese, they still have a history to live down, a consequence of the various missionaries' scramble for Angola. Baptists from the US, for example, went to the northern Kikongo part of the country, the Methodists to the Kimbundu areas and the Congregationalists to the Ovibundu region.

In dividing up the country in this way, explained the Reverend Nzinga, ethnic divisions were emphasised, implicitly encouraging a variety of "cultural confrontations". In the socio-economic sphere, too, the churches were implicated, in the forced-labour migrations which the Portuguese organised.

The churches' role in certain oppressive practices highlights the problem of Christians and Socialists in the Third World. Historically, European churches — Protestant, Catholic or nonconformist — have adapted **in response to the demands of the capitalist** framework in which they operate.

The colonialist export of that framework, first by missionaries and later by political and economic operators, meant that the church was often the front line of an imperialist onslaught. Yet paradoxically, Christianity has in some cases been turned into a weapon of the poor, particularly in some South American countries, and notably in Namibia.

In Angola, although the church has no formal place in the Marxist state, many Christians — if not their leaders — have been active members of the movement which ushered the government in.

With the consolidation of the MPLA's power in Angola, Christians began to fear what Ntoni Nzinga called the "new ideology". But their fears of the MPLA were to some extent dissipated during a State-Church consultation in Luanda in March 1983, addressed by planning minister Lopo do Nascimento, when a continuing dialogue between the two was recommended.

There are obvious advantages for both in such a dialogue: access to party and government machinery (the press, foreign connections, the banking system or even military protection), could bring the churches in from the cold; and access to established church infrastructure (schools, hospitals and mission clinics) could — and to some extent already does — provide practical help to a severely stretched state.

However, the ideological clash is almost bound to continue resurfacing. Early last month, for example, a meeting of Catholic bishops recommended "national reconciliation", a thinly-veiled call for talks with South African-backed rebel Jonas Savimbi. The authorities, the Catholics said, should "try their hardest to end the war". The official MPLA position is that talks with "Judas" Savimbi, South African "puppet", are out of the question.

The Evangelical churches did not have an official position on talks with Savimbi, Ntoni Nzinga said, and when asked if his organisation would prefer a non-Marxist government, he replied that "Christians can be Christians in any society".

Call for 'true pacifists'

A communiqué from the CAIE delegation nevertheless called for unity from among "the different political positions assumed by some of Angola's sons". It further appealed to Angolan Christians to become "true pacifists" and, tip-toeing through the dilemma, said, "a church must live within the reality of the nation, which means having an apostolic consciousness and a spirit of unity. This means that it should present a gospel which may be able to help men feel the real consequences of this life, both in the political and the social sense. In this way it will contribute to the national unity and will fulfil the strong desire to help one's neighbour".

A recent editorial from the (presumably atheist) official news agency praised "people who feel fulfilled because they know that they are being useful by helping others to build a better life, contributing to the building of something more just and making the aspirations of other people's become a reality". The news agency was not referring to Christians, but to the Cubans.

Clearly, there is room for practical compromise between the churches and the state in Angola, as the wide freedoms afforded to Christians demonstrate. The MPLA's concern, however, is that the divisions nurtured by the Portuguese and the European missionaries, which certain tribalists now encourage, could negate efforts to foster national unity.

Credits

Glossary of Terms and Abbreviations

African Development Bank Founded in 1963 under the auspices of the United Nations Economic Commission on Africa. All loans are made to African countries, although other nations can subscribe. In 1982, the bank (which is centered in Abidjan, Ivory Coast) loaned out $362 million.

African Socialism A term applied to a variety of ideas (including those of Nkrumah and Senghor) about communal and shared production in Africa's past and present. The concept of African socialism was especially popular in the early 1960s. Adherence to it has not meant the governments have excluded private capitalistic ventures.

Afrikaner A South African of Dutch descent who speaks Afrikaans and is often referred to as a Boer (Afrikaans for farmer).

Amnesty International A London-based human rights organization whose members "adopt" political prisoners or "prisoners of conscience" in many nations of the world. The organization generates political pressure and puts out a well-publicized annual report of human rights conditions in each country of the world.

ANC (African National Congress) Founded in 1912, and now banned, the ANC's goal was to work for equal rights for blacks in South Africa through non-violent action. "Spear of the Nation," the ANC wing dedicated to armed struggle, was organized after the Sharpeville massacre in 1960.

Apartheid Literally "separateness." The South African policy of segregating the races socially, legally, and politically.

Assimilado The Portuguese term for those native Africans who became "assimilated" to Western ways. Assimilados enjoyed equal rights under Portuguese law.

AZAPO (The Azanian People's Organization) Founded in 1978 at the time of the Black Consciousness Movement and recently revitalized, the movement worked to develop chapters and bring black organizations together in a national forum.

Bantustans Areas, or "homelands," to which black South Africans are assigned "citizenship" as part of the policy of apartheid.

Berber The collective term for the indigenous languages and people of North Africa.

Bicameral A government made up of two legislative branches.

Caisse de Stabilization A marketing board which stabilizes the uncertain returns to producers of cash crops by offering them less than market prices in good years while assuring them of a steady income in bad years. Funds from these boards are used to develop the infrastructure, to promote social welfare, or to maintain a particular regime in power.

Caliphate The office or dominion of a caliph, the spiritual head of Islam.

Cassava A tropic plant with a fleshy, edible rootstock; one of the staples of the African diet.

CEEAC (Economic Community of Central African States An organization of all the Central African states, as well as Rwanda and Burundi, whose goal is to promote economic and industrial cooperation among its members.

Chimurenga A Shona term meaning "fighting in which everyone joins," used to refer to Zimbabwe's fight for independence.

Coloured The South African classification for a person of mixed racial descent.

Commonwealth of Nations An association of nations and dependencies loosely joined by the common tie of having been part of the British Empire.

Creole A person or language of mixed African and European descent.

Dergue From the Amharic word for "committee," the ruling body of Ethiopia.

EAC (East African Community) Established in 1967, the EAC grew out of the East African Common Services Organization begun under British rule. EAC included Kenya, Tanzania, and Uganda in a customs union and involved a common currency and development of infrastructure. It was disbanded in 1977, and the final division of assets was completed in late 1983.

EC (European Communities) The umbrella organization encompassing the European Economic Community, the European Coal and Steel Community, and the European Atomic Energy Community.

ECA (Economic Commission for Africa) Founded in 1958 by the Economic and Social Committee of the United Nations to aid African development through regional centers, "field agents," and the encouragement of regional efforts, food self-sufficiency, transport and communications development, and other areas.

ECOWAS (Economic Community of West African States) Established in 1975 by the Treaty of Lagos, the organization includes all the West African states, except the Western Sahara. The organization's goals are to promote trade, cooperation, and self-reliance among its members.

EEC (The European Common Market) Established January 1, 1958, the EEC seeks to establish a common agricultural policy between its members as well as uniform trade and travel restrictions among member countries.

Enclave Industry   An industry run by a foreign company that uses imported technology and machinery and exports the product to industrialized countries; often described as a "state within a state."

FAO (Food and Agricultural Organization of the United Nations)   Established October 16, 1945 to oversee good nutrition and agricultural development.

FEA (French Equatorial Africa)   The French colonial federation that included the present-day People's Republic of the Congo, the Central African Republic, Chad, and Gabon. The administrative headquarters was Brazzaville, People's Republic of the Congo.

Franc Zone   The organization includes members of the West African Monetary Union and the monetary organization of Central Africa that have currencies linked to the French franc. Reserves are managed by the French Treasury and guaranteed by the French franc.

Freedom Charter   Established in 1955, it proclaimed equal rights for all South Africans and has been a foundation for almost all groups in the resistance against apartheid during the last twenty-eight years.

Free French Conference   A 1944 conference of French-speaking territories, which proposed a union of all the territories in which native Africans would be represented and their development furthered.

French West Africa   The administrative division of the former French colonial empire that included the present independent countries of Senegal, Ivory Coast, Guinea, Mali, Niger, Upper Volta, Benin, and Mauritania. The headquarters was Dakar, Senegal.

Frontline States   A caucus supported by the Organization of African Unity (consisting of Tanzania, Zambia, Mozambique, Botswana, and Angola) whose goal is to achieve black majority rule in all of Southern Africa.

GDP (Gross Domestic Product)   The value of production attributable to the factors of production in a given country, regardless of their ownership. GDP equals GNP minus the product of a country's residents originating in the rest of the world.

GNP (Gross National Product)   The sum of the values of all goods and services produced by a country's residents at home and abroad in any given year, less income earned by foreign residents and remitted abroad.

Griots   Professional bards of the Western Sudan, some of whom tell history and are accompanied by the playing of the Kora or harp-lute.

Guerrilla   Any member of a small force of "irregular" soldiers. Generally, guerrilla forces are made up of volunteers who make surprise raids against the incumbent military or political force.

Harmattan   In West Africa, the dry wind that blows from the Sahara Desert in January and February.

Homelands   See Bantustans

Hut Tax   Instituted by the colonial governments in Africa, this measure required families to pay taxes on each building in the village.

IMF (International Monetary Fund)   Established December 27, 1945 to promote international monetary cooperation.

Islam   A religious faith started in Arabia during the seventh century by the Prophet Muhammad and spread in Africa through African Muslim leaders, migrations, and holy wars.

Kgotla   A public forum of the Tswana people in which all the political and judicial affairs of a community are decided.

KWH (kilowatt hour)   The energy equal to that expended by one kilowatt (one thousand watts) in one hour.

League of Nations   Established at the Paris Peace Conference in 1919, this forerunner of the modern-day United Nations had 52 member nations at its peak (the United States never joined the organization) and mediated in international affairs. The league was dissolved in 1945 after the creation of the United Nations.

Maghrib   An Arabic term, meaning "land of the setting sun," that is often used to refer to the former French colonies of Morocco, Algeria, and Tunisia.

Malinkē (Mandinka, or Mandinga)   One of the major groups of people speaking Mande languages. The original homeland of the Malinke was Mali, but the people are now found in Mali, Guinea-Bissau, Gambia, and other areas where they are sometimes called Mandingoes. Some trading groups are called Dyula.

Marxist-Leninism   Sometimes called "scientific socialism," this doctrine derived from the ideas of Karl Marx as modified by Lenin; it is the ideology of the Communist Party in the USSR and has been modified in many ways by other persons and groups who still use the term. In Africa, some political parties or movements have claimed to be Marxist-Leninist but have often followed policies that conflict in practice with the ideology; these governments have usually not stressed Marx's philosophy of class struggle.

Mfecane   The movement of people in the eastern areas of present-day South Africa to the west and north as the result of wars led by the Zulus.

Muslim   A follower of the Islamic faith.

NAM (Non-Aligned Movement) A group of nations that have chosen not to be politically or militarily associated with either the West or the Communist bloc. At the 1979 meeting in Havana, Cuba, there were ninety-five member nations.

OAU (Organization of African Unity) An association of all the independent states of Africa (except South Africa) whose goal is to promote unity and solidarity among African nations.

OPEC (Organization of Petroleum Exporting Countries) Established in 1960, this association of the world's oil producing countries seeks to coordinate the petroleum policies of its members.

PAIGC (African Party for the Independence of Guinea-Bissau and Cape Verde) An independence movement that fought during the 1960s and 1970s for the liberation of present-day Guinea-Bissau and Cape Verde from Portuguese rule. The two territories were ruled separately by a united PAIGC until a 1981 coup in Guinea-Bissau caused the party to split along national lines. In 1981, the Cape Verdean PAIGC formally renounced its Guinea links and became the PAICV.

Parastatals Agencies for production or public service that are established by law and, in some measure, government organized and controlled. Private enterprise may be involved, and the management of the parastatal may be in private hands.

Pastoralist A person, usually a nomad, who raises livestock for a living.

Pidgin English A language that is based on English, but that has been adopted to the indigenous language and grammar. See Creole.

Polisario Front Originally a liberation group in Western Sahara seeking independence from Spanish rule. Today it is battling Morocco (and, until recently, Mauritania), which claims control over the Western Sahara.

Rhodes, Cecil Late 19th century imperialist mining magnate, Prime Minister of Cape Colony. He encouraged British expansion into areas north of present South Africa and exploitation of resources.

SADCC (Southern African Development Coordination Conference) An organization of nine African states (Angola, Zambia, Malawi, Mozambique, Zimbabwe, Lesotho, Botswana, Swaziland, and Tanzania) whose goal is to free themselves from dependence on South Africa and to cooperate on projects of economic development.

Sahel In West Africa, the borderlands between savanna and desert.

Selassie, Haile Ethiopia's last emperor, who claimed to be descended from Solomon and the Queen of Sheba.

Senegambia A confederation of Senegal and Gambia signed into agreement in December 1981 and inaugurated February 1, 1982. The confederation will be ruled by a Cabinet of five Senegalese and four Gambians.

Sharia The Islamic code of law.

Sharpeville Massacre The 1960 pass demonstration in South Africa in which sixty people were killed when police fired into the crowd; it became a rallying point for many anti-apartheid forces.

SWAPO (Southwest African People's Organization) Angola-based freedom fighters who have been waging guerrilla warfare against the presence of South Africa in Namibia since the 1960s. The United Nations and the Organization of African Unity have recognized SWAPO as the only authentic representative of the Namibian people.

Tsetse Fly An insect which transmits sleeping sickness to cattle and humans. It is usually found in the scrub tree and forest regions of Central Africa.

UDF (United Democratic Front) A recently founded, multi-racial, black-led group in South Africa that gained prominence during the 1983 campaign to defeat the government's Constitution, which would have given limited political rights to Asians and Coloureds only.

UNESCO (United Nations Educational, Scientific, and Cultural Organization) Established November 4, 1946 to promote international collaboration in education, science, and culture. Headquarters: Paris, France.

Unicameral A political structure with a single legislative branch.

Ujamaa In Swahili "familyhood." Government-sponsored cooperative villages in Tanzania.

UN (United Nations) Established June 26, 1945, through official approval of the charter by delegates of fifty nations at an international conference in San Francisco. The charter went into effect on October 24, 1945.

Wabenzi In Kenya, the popular name for the wealthy middle class members who drive Mercedes Benz cars.

World Bank A closely integrated group of international institutions providing financial and technical assistance to developing countries.

Bibliography

RESOURCE CENTERS

Ten federally funded Title VI African Studies Centers provide special services for schools, libraries and community groups. Contact the center nearest you for further information about resources available:

African Studies Center
Boston University
270 Bay State Road
Boston, MA 02215

African Studies and Research Programs
Howard University
Washington, DC 20059

African Studies Program
Indiana University
Woodburn Hall 221
Bloomington, IN 47405

African Studies Educational Resource Center
100 International Center
Michigan State University
East Lansing, MI 49923-1035

African Studies Program
630 Dartmouth
Northwestern University
Evanston, IL 60201

Africa Project
Lou Henry Hoover Room 223
Stanford University
Stanford, CA 94305

African Studies Center
University of California
Los Angeles, CA 90024

Center for African Studies
470 Grinter Hall
University of Florida
Gainesville, FL 32611

African Studies Program
University of Illinois
1208 W. California, Room 101
Urbana, IL 61801

African Studies Program
1450 Van Hise Hall
University of Wisconsin
Madison, WI 53706

REFERENCE WORKS, BIBLIOGRAPHIES, AND OTHER SOURCES

Africa South of the Sahara 1983-1984 (updated yearly), London: Europa Publications, Ltd., 1982.

Africa on Film and Videotape 1960-1961, A Compendium of Reviews, East Lansing, MI: Michigan State University, 1982.

Africa Today, An Atlas of Reproductible Pages, Wellesley, MA: World Eagle, 1983.

Scarecrow Press, Metuchen, New Jersey, publishes The African Historical Dictionaries, a series edited by Jon Woronoff. There are now 37 dictionaries, each under a specialist editor, and more are forthcoming. They are short works with introductory essays and are useful guides for the beginner, especially for countries on which little has been published in English.

MAGAZINES AND PERIODICALS

African Arts
University of California
Los Angeles California
Beautifully illustrated articles review Africa's artistic heritage and present creative efforts.

Africa News
P.O. Box 3851
Durham, NC 27702
A weekly with short articles that are impartially written and full of information.

Africa Now
212 Fifth Ave, Suite 1409
New York, NY 10010
A monthly publication that gives current coverage and includes sections on art, culture, and business, as well as a special series of interviews.

Africa Report
African American Institute
833 UN Plaza
New York, NY 10017
This bi-monthly periodical has an update section, but most of each issue is devoted to broad-based articles by authorities giving background on key issues, developments in particular countries, and United States policy.

The Economist
P.O. Box 2700
Woburn, MA
A weekly that gives attention to African issues.

UNESCO Courier
UNESCO, Place de Fontenox
75700 Paris, France
This periodical has frequent short and clear articles on Africa, often by African authors, within the framework of the topic to which the monthly issues are devoted.

West Africa
Holborn Viaduct
London EC1A Z FD, England
This weekly is the best source for West Africa including

countries as far south as Angola and Namibia. Continent-wide issues are also discussed.

NOVELS AND AUTOBIOGRAPHICAL WRITINGS

Chinua Achebe, *Things Fall Apart* (Exeter, NH: Heinemann, 1965).
This is the story of the life and values of residents of a traditional Igbo village in the nineteenth century and of its first contacts with the West.

_____, *No Longer at Ease* (Exeter, NH: Heinemann, 1963).
The grandson of the major character of *Things Fall Apart* lives an entirely different life in the modern city of Lagos and faces new problems, while remaining committed to some of the traditional ways.

Okot p'Bitek, *Song of Lawino* (Exeter, NH: Heinemann, 1983).
A traditional Ugandan wife comments on the practices of her Western-educated husband and reveals her own life-style and values.

Nadine Gordimer, *July's People* (New York: Viking, 1981).
This is a troubling and believable scenario of future revolutionary times in South Africa.

_____, *A Soldier's Embrace* (New York: Viking, 1982).
These short stories cover a range of situations where apartheid affects peoples' relations with each other. Films made from some of these stories are available at the University of Illinois Film Library, Urbana-Champaign, IL.

Cheik Amadou Kane, *Ambiguous Adventure* (Exeter, NH: Heinemann, 1972).
This autobiographical novel of a young man coming of age in Senegal, in a Muslim society, and, later, in a French school illuminates changes that have taken place in Africa and raises many questions.

Alex LaGuma, *Time of the Butcherbird* (Exeter, NH: Heinemann, 1979).
The people of a long-standing black community in South Africa's countryside are to be removed to a Bantustan.

Camara Laye, *The Dark Child* (Farrar Straus and Giroux, 1954).
This autobiographical novel gives a loving and nostalgic picture of a Malinke family of Guinea.

Ousmane Sembene, *God's Bits of Wood* (Exeter, NH: Heinemann, 1970).
The railroad workers' strike of 1947 provides the setting for a novel about the changing consciousness and life of African men and women in Senegal.

Wole Soyinka, *Ake: The Years of Childhood* (New York: Random House, 1983).
Soyinka's account of his first eleven years is full of the sights, tastes, smells, sounds, and personal encounters of a headmaster's home and a busy Yoruba town.

Ngugi wa Thiong'o, *A Grain of Wheat* (Exeter, NH: Heinemann, 1968).
A story of how the Mau-Mau Movement and the coming of independence affected several individuals after independence as well as during the struggle that preceded it.

INTRODUCTORY BOOKS

Peter Adamson, "The Rains: A Report from a Village in Upper Volta," *New Internationalist* (February, 1983).
This story-report of a family and village in Upper Volta takes up the entire issue.

S.A. Akintoye, *Emergent African States: Topics in Twentieth Century African History* (London: Longman, 1976).
Individual case studies are dated, but the background within them, as well as in the larger studies remains valuable.

Gerald Moore and Ulli Beier, eds., *Modern Poetry from Africa* (Baltimore: Penguin, 1963).

Philip Curtin and Paul Bohannan, *Africa and Africans* (Garden City, NY: Anchor, 1971).
This is a readable and useful introduction to African culture and history.

Philip Curtin, Steven Feierman, Leonard Thompson, and Jan Vansina, *African History* (Boston: Little Brown, 1978).
This rich text is well-written, thought-provoking, and emphasizes social, economic, and intellectual developments as well as the anthropologist's and the historian's perspective.

Basil Davidson, *The African Genius* (Boston: Little Brown, 1979). Also published as *The Africans*.
Davidson discusses the complex political, social, and economic systems of traditional African societies, translating scholarly works into a popular mode without distorting complex material.

_____, *Let Freedom Come* (Boston: Little Brown, 1978).
A lively and interesting history of Africa in the twentieth century.

Adrian Hastings, *A History of African Christianity, 1950-1975* (Cambridge, England: Cambridge University Press, 1979).
This is a good introduction to the recent impact of Christianity in Africa.

Charlotte and Wolf Leslau, comp., *African Proverbs* (Mt. Vernon, NY: Peter Pauper Press, 1962).

John Mbiti, *African Religions and Philosophy* (New York: Praeger, 1969).
This work by a Ugandan scholar is the standard introduction to the rich variety of religious beliefs and rituals of African peoples.

D.T. Niane, *Sundiata: An Epic of Old Mali* (Atlantic Highlands, NJ: Humanities Press, 1965).
This oral tradition about the founder of the Mali Empire was told to D.T. Niane by the griot Mamadou Kouyate and is famous in many parts of West Africa.

J.H. Kwabena Nketia, *The Music of Africa* (New York: Norton, 1974).
The author, a Ghanaian by birth, is Africa's best known ethnomusicologist.

Evelyn Jones Rich and Immanuel Wallerstein, *Africa Tradition and Change* (New York: Random House, 1972).
Each of the selections in this excellent collection of source readings is accompanied by an introduction and questions. This work is especially good for senior high school students, but will be enjoyed by every age group.

Chris Searle, *We're Building the New School: Diary of a Teacher in Mozambique* (London: Zed Press, 1981; distributed in the United States by Laurence Hill & Co., Westport, CT).
A lively book, which shows that the lives of students and teachers in this new nation are both exciting and difficult.

J.B. Webster, A.A. Boahen, and M. Tidy, *The Revolutionary Years: West Africa Since 1800* (London: Longman, 1980).
An interesting, enjoyable, and competent introductory history to the West African Region.

Frank Willett, *African Art* (New York: Oxford University Press, 1971).
A work to use for reference or to read for pleasure by one of the authorities on Nigeria's early art.

Crawford Young, *Ideology and Development in Africa* (New Haven, 1982).
This book will give readers a deeper discussion of the theories and practices of governments than is found in *Africa 1984.*

COUNTRY AND REGIONAL STUDIES

Guy Arnold, *Modern Kenya* (New York: Longman, 1981).

Tony Avirgan and Martha Honey, *War in Uganda: The Legacy of Idi Amin* (Westport, CT: Lawrence Hill and Co., 1982).

Billy Dudley, *An Introduction to Nigerian Government and Politics* (Bloomington, Indiana University Press, 1982).

John Ballard, "Four Equatorial States," in *National Unity and Regionalism in Eight African States,* ed., Gwendolyn Carter (Ithaca, New York: Cornell University Press, 1966).

Sheldon Gellar, *Senegal: An African Nation Between Islam and the West* (Boulder, CO: Westview Press, 1981).

Tony Hodges, *Western Sahara: The Roots of a Desert War* (Westport, CT: Lawrence Hill and Co., 1983).

Allan and Barbara Isaacman, *Mozambique from Colonialism to Revolution, 1900-1982* (Boulder, CO: Westview Press, 1983).

Victor T. LeVine, *The Cameroon Federal Republic* (Ithaca, NY: Cornell University Press, 1971).

Bereket Habte Selassie, *Conflict and Intervention in the Horn of Africa* (New York: Monthly Review Press, 1980).

Adele Smith Simmons, *Modern Mauritius: The Politics of Decolonization* (Bloomington: Indiana University Press, 1982).

Study Commission on US Policy Toward Southern Africa, *South Africa: Time Running Out* (Berkeley and Los Angeles, University of California Press, 1981).

Sources for Statistical Reports

U.S. State Department, *Background Notes* (1981 and 1982).

C.I.A. *Factbook* (1982).

Africa South of the Sahara 12th Edition (Europa Publications, Ltd.).

World Bank, *World Development Report* (1983).

UN *Population and Vital Statistics Report* (January 1983).

UN *World Health Statistics* (1982).

The Statesman's Yearbook 119th Edition (St. Martin's Press).

Population Reference Bureau, *World Population Data Sheet* (1982).

UNESCO Statistical Yearbook (1983).

Index

Achebe, Chinua, 56
Addis, Ababa, 137
adma, 52
Affar, 128, 135
Aflatoxine, 61
Africa: 1-17; *see also* Central Africa; East
   Africa; North Africa; Southern Africa; West
   Africa
Africanization, and Kenya, 141
African National Congress (ANC): 185, 217;
   vs. South Africa, 181, 182, 203, 204,
   216-219
African Party for the Independence of Guinea-
   Bissau and Cape Verde (PAIGC), 35, 43
Afro-Shirazi Party, 157
agriculture: 16, 17; in Nigeria, 59-60; in North
   Africa, 20; in Tanzania, 158; *see also*
   cassava; cocoa; coffee; cotton; food produc-
   tion; maize; millet; peanuts; rice; slash and
   burn agriculture; sorghum; sugar; tobacco
ahma, 52
Ahidjo, Ahmadou, 93, 113, 117, 118
Algeria, 19, 20, 21, 23, 24
Alliance of the Ba-Kongo (ABAKO), 108
All People's Congress (APC), 63
almamis, 40
Almoravids, 52
American Colonization Society, 48
Amharic peoples, 139
Amin, Idi, 128, 160, 161, 169
Amnesty International, 41, 120
ancient kingdoms, 1, 28, 32, 99, 107
Angola: 9, 13, 87, 112, 179-181, 185, 186;
   and Cabinda, 186; Catholic Church in, 232,
   233; and South Africa, 187, 188, 228, 229,
   231
angolares, 104
Annobon, 100, 101
apartheid, 180, 181, 199, 200-204, 216, 217
Aptidon, Hassan Gouled, 134
art, African, 87, 107
Arusha Declaration, and Tanzania, 157, 158
Axum Kingdom, 137
Azande peoples, 107
Azanian People's Organization (AZAPO), 203,
   204
Azuike, M.C., 76

Bagaza, Jean-Baptiste, 131
balance-of-trade, 17
Bamana people, 51
Banda, Ngwazi Hastings Kamazu, 4, 194
Bantu-speaking people: 125; and apartheid,
   201, 202
Bantustans, 201, 202
Barre, Siad, 127, 128, 152, 153, 164-166
Bassa people, 49
Bateke people, 89
Batepa Massacre (1953), 105
bauxite, 17, 40, 43
Beavogui, Lansana, 79
Belgium, and Zaire, 106, 108
Benin, 27, 32, 33
Berber, 21
Biafra, 58
Biafran Civil War, 4
Biya, Paul, 93, 113, 117, 118
Black Consciousness Movement, 203
"black spots," 202
Boers, 179
Boganda, Barthelemy, 90, 94, 95, 113
Bokassa, Jean-Bedel, 95, 113, 120-121
Bongo, Albert Bernard (Omar), 103, 111, 113
Book of African Verse, A (Reed), 143

Bophuthatswana, 201
Botha, Pieter, 181, 198, 230
Botswana: 179, 180, 185, 189-190, 229; and
   South Africa, 182, 190, 218
boundaries, colonial origin of African states',
   3, 27
Bourguiba, Habib, 23
Bourkina Fasso, *see* Upper Volta
Brazzaville, 14, 99
Brotherhood of the Cross and Star, 1
Brutus, Dennis, 200
Buadu, Charles, 75
Bugandans, 125
Buhari, Muhammed, 58, 59, 71, 72
Burundi, 112, 125, 126, 128-131, 148

Cabinda, 186
Cabora Bassa Dam, 197
Cabral, Amilcar, 35, 42, 43, 78
Cabral, Luis, 43
caisse de stabilization, 45
Cameroon: 17, 87, 88, 90, 92-93, 113; north-
   south tension in, 117-118
Cape Colony, 199
Cape Verde: 34, 35; drought and food aid to,
   77-79
Cape Verdeans, in United States, 34
capitalism, in Africa, 4, 9, 45
cash crops: African, 3, 61; of Benin, 32; of
   Gambia, 37; of Ivory Coast, 45; of West
   Africa, 27
cassava, 15, 16, 27, 49
Catholic Church, *see* Roman Catholic Church
cattle-herding: in East Africa, 125; in the
   Sahel, 76-77
Central Africa, 87-123
Central African Republic, 87, 88, 90, 94-95,
   113
Central Intelligence Agency (US), 108
cereal imports, into Africa, 15-16
Chad: 96-97, 113; civil war in, 87, 88, 96, 97,
   116-117
Chama Cha Mapinduzi, 157
children, importance of, 1
Chilembwe, John, 193
cholera, 2, 101
Christianity: in Ethiopia, 136, 139; in Rwanda,
   148; in Sudan, 155; in Zambia, 207
Christina, Orlando, 6
Chokwe peoples, 107
Chwezi, 128
CIA, 108
Ciskei, 201
civil war, 138
cloves, 144
cobalt, 130
cocoa, 3, 17, 27, 32, 39, 45, 65, 88, 105
coffee, 3, 17, 27, 32, 45, 88, 105, 131, 148
colonialism: 3, 4, 9, 11, 30; in Central Africa,
   89, 91, 93, 95, 99, 101, 103-105, 107,
   108; in North Africa, 21; in West Africa,
   29, 41, 43, 45, 51, 57, 63, 69; *see also*
   Belgium; France; Great Britain; Portugal;
   Spain
Coloured Labor Party, 203
Commission for Organizing the Party of the
   Working People of Ethiopia (COPWE),
   138, 163
Commission on Refugee Relief, UN (UNHCR),
   2, 135, 172
Committee for Struggle Against Drought in the
   Sahel (CILSS), 28
Comoros island, 126, 129, 130, 132, 133
Congo: 87, 88, 90, 98-99, 113; oil in,
   114-116, 122

Congo-Ocean Railroad, 99
Convention People's Party (CCP), 38
cooperants, 219, 220, 221
copper, 3, 17, 107
Costa, Manuel Pinto da, 105, 114
cotton, 17, 88, 105
coup d'état: in Ethiopia, 137, 138, 163, 164; in
   Kenya, 142; in Nigeria, 71, 72; in Republic
   of Seychelles, 150; in Somalia, 152
coup of sixty rifles, 150
Creoles, 63
Crocker, Chester, 228, 229, 231
Cry the Beloved Country, 200
Cuba, and Angola, 228, 231
Customs and Economic Union of the Central
   African states (UDEAC), 90, 111

Dacko, David, 95, 113, 121
Dahomey Kingdom, 28, 32
Dakar, 61
Dan mask, 46
Dar es Salaam, 126
dark continent, image of Africa as, 8-11
debt, African, 2, 9, 46, 59
Democratic Front for the Liberation of Somalia,
   164
Denard, Bob, 133
Dergue, and military coup in Ethiopia, 137,
   138
d'Estaing, Giscard, 41, 121
Development Bank, 128
Diego Garcia, 129, 144, 145
Dikko, Umar, 59
Diori, Hamani, 55
Diouf, Abdou, 61, 81
discrimination, and apartheid in South Africa,
   180, 181, 199
Djibouti, 126, 127, 128, 134-135, 163, 166
Doe, Samuel Kanyon, 48, 49
drought: 1, 11, 27, 28, 35, 37, 43, 51, 53, 55,
   61, 67, 139, 153, 190, 213; and Cape
   Verde, 77-79; in East Africa, 127, 128; in
   Southern Africa, 183, 184
Dyoula, 29

East Africa, 124-129, 163-168
East Africa Common Services Organization
   (EACSO), 128
East African Community (EAC), 128, 175-177
East African Railways, 176
Economic Commission on Africa (ECA), 91,
   111
Economic Community of Central African States
   (ECCA) or (CEEAC), 91, 111
Economic Community of the Great Lakes States
   (CEPGL), 111
Economic Community of West Africa (CEAO),
   31
Economic Community of West African States
   (ECOWAS), 5, 30, 31, 57, 80, 82, 83,
   111, 112
economic growth: African, 3, 9, 10; in West
   Africa, 49
education, 4
Egypt, 19, 20, 21-22, 23, 126, 165
Elar-ayong, 101
elders: role of, in African family, 1; Poro, 47
Emecheta, Buchi, 56
England, *see* Great Britain
Equatorial Guinea, 87, 90, 100-101, 113
Eritrea, 163, 167
Eritrean movement, in Ethiopia, 139, 163, 164,
   166, 167
Ethiopia, 125-127, 135-139, 153, 163-164
eucalyptus plantation, in Congo, 114